Our Catholic **Faith**
Living What We Believe

Michael Pennock

ave maria press   notre dame, indiana

Online Resources

There are many resources for this text, including Chapter Tests and Handouts, available online. Go to www.avemariapress.com and follow these steps:

1. Click on the "High School Textbooks" link at the top of the page.
2. Choose "Classroom Resources" from the pull-down window.
3. Click on *Our Catholic Faith: Living What We Believe.*

Scripture texts in this work are taken from the *New American Bible with Revised New Testament and Revised Psalms* © 1991, 1986, 1970 Confraternity of Christian Doctrine, Washington, D.C. and are used by permission of the copyright owner. All Rights Reserved. No part of the *New American Bible* may be reproduced without permission in writing from the copyright owner.

English translation of the *Catechism of the Catholic Church* for the United States of America copyright © 1994, United States Catholic Conference, Inc.— Libreria Editrice Vaticana. Used with permission.

Theological Consultant:
Edward P. Hahnenberg, PhD
Chair in Catholic Systematic Theology
John Carroll University
University Heights, Ohio

Religious Education Consultant:
Michael Horan, PhD
Professor of Theological Studies
Loyola Marymount University
Los Angeles, California

Founded in 1865, Ave Maria Press is a ministry of the United States Province of Holy Cross.

Engaging Minds, Hearts, and Hands for Faith® is a trademark of Ave Maria Press, Inc.

www.avemariapress.com

ISBN-10 1-59471-267-0 ISBN-13 978-1-59471-267-8

Project Editor: Jared Dees.

Cover design by Kristen Hornyak Bonelli.

Text design by Brian C. Conley.

Printed and bound in the United States of America.

Contents

Introduction to the **Teacher's Wraparound Edition**

Overview

This Introduction to the Teacher's Wraparound Edition will provide information on the following:
- Catechetical dimensions for an introductory course on the Catholic faith;
- An overview of the key features of each chapter of the Student Text;
- The curriculum model used in both the Student Text and this Teacher's Wraparound Edition (TWE);
- The format of this TWE;
- Mailing addresses for films and videos;
- A weekly planning chart.

Catechetical Dimensions of This Course

The United States Catholic Bishops' document *In Support of Catechetical Ministry* makes several observations about the state of catechesis and the challenges facing both catechists and those being catechized, including:

> We live in an increasingly secular and materialistic society, which is often at odds with our Christian messages and values. The emphasis on individual rights has eroded the concept of the common good and our ability to call people to accept revealed teaching that cannot be changed by democratic process. The disintegration of the community and social structures that once supported religious faith and encouraged family life has been replaced by a media- and technology-driven culture that makes catechesis especially difficult. Religious instruction and catechesis compete against entertainment and sports for time in people's busy lives.
>
> Catechists today face the difficult task of proclaiming the good news of Christ Jesus in such a way that it will be heard, accepted, and authentically understood in this culture. They must reach out to those who are unevangelized and uncatechized, as well as work with the large numbers of people today who have not been fully catechized.[1]

High school religion teachers know only too well how difficult it is to catechize teenagers in a culture that is driven strongly by the popular media and developing technology. We also know how many students come to us with an uneven background in their knowledge of the basics of the faith. Some students enroll in Catholic high schools unevangelized, having never really heard the Good News of Jesus.

Today's high school students have grown up in a secularized world that bans public displays of religion, permits abortion on demand, winks at marital infidelity while redefining the nature of marriage, and lionizes media figures who present a false image of the ideal human person. Sadly, too many students have not experienced the witness and practice of the faith that should be provided in the family, the domestic church.

The task for the high school religion teacher is formidable. As catechists, we must reach out to teenagers coming to this course with each of these varied backgrounds. Pope John Paul II explained how in the apostolic exhortation *Catechesi Tradendae*:

> Catechesis should help Christians to be, for their own joy and the service of all, "light" and "salt." Undoubtedly this demands that catechesis should strengthen them in their identity and that it should continually separate itself from the surrounding atmosphere of hesitation, uncertainty and insipidity. (56)

Thus, as religion teachers, we must help students to be light and salt by strengthening them in their identity. And what is this Christ-revealed identity? Contrary to the many views of the human person that society offers to our young people, Jesus reveals the Good News that each person is a unique, unrepeatable creation of a loving God with many gifts to develop and then use in service for others. Also, each person is destined for an abundantly happy, eternal life of fulfillment in union with our loving, Triune God. Our students must repeatedly hear this gospel truth about who they really are. They need to hear and experience God's unconditional love.

And where can they hear this message as we separate them from an "atmosphere of hesitation, uncertainty and insipidity"—the second part of our task? We believe they can hear this message in the Catholic Church where Christ and his Holy Spirit dwell. In the Church, all people can uncover the Good News of salvation, truths that will set us free and keep us on the path to eternal life. The Church offers the holy signs and rituals that will unite us to Christ and enable us to live grace-filled lives, as well as a rich tradition of prayer that will help us on our spiritual journey to the Father.

For many of our students, we are the main window to what the Church teaches and who the Church is. They must hear and experience Christ's love from us. But as representatives of the Church entrusted with Christ's truth, we also have the task of helping our students learn and then articulate the foundational teachings of the Church. We hope they can do this with joy, confidence, and enthusiasm because they are indeed *light* to help others discover the Way, the Truth, and the Life. And they are *salt* that will flavor the world with the love of Jesus Christ and help preserve it from the despair caused by terrorism, abject poverty, and the dehumanizing effects of treating God's beautiful creatures as objects to use rather than as people to be loved and cherished.

The Student Text was written in conformity with the *Catechism of the Catholic Church* (*CCC*), a sure guide in teaching the Catholic faith. In truth, it is an adaptation for beginning high school students of this "organic presentation of the Catholic faith" (*CCC*, 18). It presents in a simple, straightforward way the four pillars covered in the *Catechism of the Catholic Church*: the baptismal profession of faith (the Creed), the sacraments of faith, the life of faith (the Commandments), and prayer (especially the Lord's Prayer).

Through the reading and study of *Our Catholic Faith: Living What We Believe,* your students will be given a systematic catechesis and have a common starting point for subsequent catechetical efforts throughout their high school careers. Furthermore, they will develop a common religious literacy of fundamental terms. And throughout their study, they will be asked to apply the truths of the faith to their own lives so they may come to see that the riches of our Catholic faith can help them in a practical way to live meaningful, happy, and productive lives for others.

Background for the Religion Teacher

A teacher of an introductory faith course in a Catholic high school should be versed in the *Catechism of the Catholic Church* (*CCC*), the point of organizational reference for the Student Text. The various topics discussed in each chapter of the Student Text always include references to the appropriate paragraphs of the *Catechism*. The function of this aid is to give an organic synthesis of the fundamental content of Catholic doctrine in light of the Second Vatican Council and the whole of the Church's Tradition. It is a sure norm of teaching the faith that lies behind the fourfold structure of the Student Text: believing in the Triune God and his saving plan, celebrating the sacramental life, living a life of love of God and neighbor, and praying.

Second, as one fulfilling the role of catechist, a high school religion teacher should review some of the basic principles of how we should conduct our catechetical ministry in light of the *General Directory for Catechesis (GDC)*.[2] Some relevant points of this document are reviewed in the TWE, but you should conduct a more focused study of the *General Directory for Catechesis*, perhaps as a departmental discussion and sharing project for the coming academic year. Here are five essential points from the *GDC*:

1. The Church exists in order to evangelize. Jesus instructed his followers to proclaim (Mk 16:15), make disciples and teach (Mt 28:19–20), be witnesses (Acts 1:8), baptize (Mt 28:19), "do this in memory of me" (Lk 22:19), and "love one another" (Jn 15:12). Thus, proclamation, witness, teaching, sacraments, and love of neighbor are all ways to transmit the Good News, which calls on people to conversion and faith in Jesus (46).

This reminds us to not lose sight of an essential role of our job as catechists: "conversion to Jesus Christ, full and sincere adherence to his person and the decision to walk in his footsteps. Faith is a personal encounter with Jesus Christ, making of oneself a disciple of him" (53).

We must never forget that this is why ours is essentially a joyful task, to preach the Good News of Jesus Christ. Faith is God's gift to our students; it is not something that we dispense. Our job is to proclaim, witness, and so forth. With the gift of faith, our students begin the process of lifelong conversion that leads to the profession of faith and a journey to perfection (56).

2. Catechesis, part of the ministry of the word, promotes and matures initial conversion, educates in the faith, and incorporates people into the Christian community. Its aim is "to encourage a living, explicit and fruitful profession of the faith" (61, 66). The *GDC* explains that when catechesis takes place in our schools, religious instruction should rank as a scholastic discipline with the "same systematic demands and the same rigor as other disciplines." The Christian message should be presented with the same seriousness and depth that other scholastic subjects do (73).

More explicitly, the aim of all catechesis "is to put people not only in touch, but also in communion and intimacy, with Jesus Christ" (*GDC, 80,* quoting *Catechesi Tradendae,* 5). This involves the following tasks: promoting knowledge of the faith, liturgical education, moral formation, teaching to pray, educating for community life, and equipping disciples with a missionary spirit (85–87).

3. At the heart of catechesis is the person of Jesus Christ. Jesus came to transmit the Word of God, but let us not forget that he is the Word of God. Therefore, catechesis must be Christ-centered, whereby we present Christ and everything in relation to him. He is the center of salvation history. "The Church, and in her name, every catechist, can say with truth: 'my teaching is not from myself: it comes from the one who sent me' (Jn 7:16). Thus, all that is transmitted by catechesis is "the teaching of Jesus Christ, the truth that he communicates, or more precisely, the Truth that he is . . . ." "The Gospels, which narrate the life of Jesus, are central to the catechetical message . . . ." Furthermore, "every mode of presentation must always be christocentric-trinitarian: Through Christ to the Father in the Holy Spirit" (98–99).

Thus, in an introductory course on the faith, a teacher must always remember that the content we teach is ultimately centered on Jesus. It is Jesus who reveals the Triune God and who calls us into community in Christ's Church. We profess our belief in the Creed. We celebrate our life in Christ through the liturgy. We live Christlike lives by being Beatitude people and following his Commandments. We enter into a personal dialog with the Father, Son, and Holy Spirit through prayer.

This course must include *cognitive* content so that the students are exposed to and can articulate the basics of the faith. But it must not stop there. The affective and behavioral domains are also important in catechesis, because the Gospel requires *metanoia*, repentance. Therefore, the Student Text includes various exercises, prayer reflections, activities, and discussions to involve the whole learner, to encourage conversion not just of the mind but of the heart and in one's behavior, too. Students need *to know* but also to discover, develop, respond, compare and contrast, pursue, identify, celebrate, feel, pray, live, proclaim, show concern, and discuss what they learn.

Although this course focuses on the Catholic faith in the Triune God, it does not neglect the beliefs of other religions. The teachings of the Church in the area of ecumenism are covered in Chapter 4, teachings that explain how God wills the salvation of all and how some means of sanctification can be found outside Christ's Church. As Catholic teachers working in Catholic institutions, we need not apologize for presenting our belief that Jesus founded his Church, lives in it, and works and teaches in it through the Holy Spirit.

4. The catechist is a mediator. Method does not make the catechist. A catechist is a mediator for the Holy Spirit. That said, as catechists, we need a solid spirituality, a transparent witness of our lives, and solid human and Christian virtues to allow the Lord to work through us. It is a task of the catechist to facilitate communication between people and the mystery of God and between the subjects themselves, as well as the Catholic faith community (156).

The text is not a panacea. It is a tool. We must remember that the faith of our student is God's gift to them; it cannot be coerced. Our own faith, enriched by prayer and a close personal relationship with Christ Jesus and his Church, will be the textbook students will read more carefully than any other. Our love of our students and our genuine concern for their welfare make the Gospel of Jesus Christ and his Church more credible than a heap of words.

Finally, our ongoing formation as catechists requires us to have sufficient knowledge of the message we teach, of the students to whom we teach it, and the social context in which they live (238).

5. Catechesis invites youth to maturity in the Catholic faith. The *General Directory of Catechesis* accurately notes that our youth all too often live in "a world of disenchantment, of boredom, of angst, and of marginalization." Some are even alienated from or are indifferent to the Church, often because of a lack of spiritual and moral support in the family or poor catechesis in their past (182).

What we can offer them is the explicit proposal of Christ to the young man in the Gospel (Mt 19:16–22), a loving invitation to follow him more intimately. Like Jesus, we must reveal to them their "singular richness" and invite and challenge them in love to grow personally for the benefit of our larger society and the Church itself. Christ needs these teens; his Church needs them as well. We must help them see that they are apostles on the move who have much to contribute (183).

The three goals of the Church's ministry to adolescents outlined in the recent document Renewing the Vision of Youth Ministry *help to remind catechists of key tasks associated with their vocation:*[3]

> **Goal 1:** To empower young people to live as disciples of Jesus Christ in our world today.
> **Goal 2:** To draw young people to responsible participation in the life, mission, and work of the Catholic Church.
> **Goal 3:** To foster the total personal and spiritual growth of each young person.

Essential Features of Catechesis

The teaching of an introductory course in the Catholic faith brings several critical elements in adolescent catechesis into focus. *Catechesi Tradendae* (21) stresses four essential features of catechesis:

1. It must be *systematic*; that is, not improvised but programmed to a precise goal.

2. It must deal with *essential knowledge*, not claiming to tackle all the disputed questions or make itself into theological research or scientific exegesis.

3. It must be *sufficiently complete*, not stopping short of initial proclamation.

4. It must be *open* to other factors of Christian life.

Systematic

The Student Text borrows its time-tested outline from the *Catechism of the Catholic Church*, the "four pillars" of catechesis: the creed, the sacraments, Christian life (morality), and prayer. The comprehensive approach of the text uses the theological virtues to unify the four pillars: faith finds expression in the creed; hope is celebrated in the Christian mysteries; love is lived out in Christian morality; and all the virtues are expressed in an active prayer life exemplified beautifully in the Lord's Prayer.

Essential Knowledge

Nothing in catechesis is more essential than a discussion of the creed, sacraments, morality, and prayer. These are the basics of the Catholic faith. Pope John Paul II observed:

> In the course of the centuries an important element of catechesis was constituted by *the traditio Symboli* (transmission of the summary of the faith), followed by the transmission of the Lord's Prayer. (*CT*, 28)

As noted earlier, the entire book is referenced to the *Catechism of the Catholic Church*. As you page through the Student Text, you will quickly discover ample evidence that all the key sections of the *Catechism* are covered, however briefly.

In an introductory course of this kind, there is scant space and time to cover the essentials. Also, given the nature of the younger high school student, you will not find contemporary theological speculation that, in any case, might confuse students as to what is magisterial teaching and what is not.

Teachers do, as a matter of course, go beyond the *Catechism* and do some "theologizing" in our presentations. To help students understand particular doctrines and other Church teachings, we will typically

- instruct,
- share personal experiences and examples,
- ask questions,
- relate real-life experiences,
- witness,
- point to the example of holy people.

By teaching in this way, our own faith journey shines through the instructional act. Open-minded, warm, loving, empathetic teachers who are proud of their Catholic faith are wonderful complements to this introductory course. *Catechesi Tradendae* again offers some guidance:

> Catechists for their part must have the wisdom to pick from the field of theological research those points that can provide light for their own reflection and their teaching, drawing like the theologians, from the true sources, in the light of the Magisterium. They must refuse to trouble the minds of the children and young people, at this stage of their catechesis, with outlandish theories, useless questions, and unproductive discussions, things that Saint Paul often condemned in his pastoral letters. (61)

Sufficiently Complete

In their *Guidelines on Doctrine for Catechetical Materials,* the bishops of the United States highlight themes of *Catechesi Tradendae* and the National Catechetical Directory entitled *Sharing the Light of Faith,*[4] now revised as the *National Directory for Catechesis.* This document explains that "doctrinal soundness implies, first of all, a complete and correct presentation of Church teaching with proper attention to its organic unity." This, of course, is what the *Catechism of the Catholic Church* strives to do. Second, doctrinal soundness requires teaching to "be presented clearly and in a manner that can be readily understood."[5] These two foundational points lead to the four essential dimensions of catechesis, all of which appear in the Student Text:

1. Catechesis must proclaim Christ's message, a task that takes place within the Church, which is a believing community of faith.

2. Catechesis must help develop the Church by keeping traditions alive and recommending activities that build up the Church.

3. Catechesis should lead people to worship and prayer.

4. Catechesis should clearly explain the Church's moral teaching to help students strive for holiness and witness to Christian virtues, that is, to motivate them to Christian living and service, especially respect for life, service to others, and working to bring about peace and justice.

The Student Text recognizes that catechesis is not sufficiently complete unless all these elements are woven together. The Student Text, assisted by this Teacher's Wraparound Edition, attempts to cover all four elements. For example:

- It reiterates the Good News of Jesus' message (especially in the Introduction and Chapters 2 and 9).
- It fosters community through various exercises, for example, reflections that ask students to discuss with others or work together on common projects (see the small service project in Chapter 4).
- It includes catechesis on worship in Chapters 6 and 7, catechesis on prayer in Chapter 10, and prayer experiences in each chapter of the text. The text also highlights the scriptural Word of God, particularly in the Knowing Christ through Scripture features found in each chapter.
- The Student Text includes two chapters on the Christian moral life (Chapters 8 and 9). Chapter 8 reviews the basics of Catholic morality, including key moral principles to guide one's life and a discussion of conscience. Chapter 9 discusses the Beatitudes and the Ten Commandments and what each has to do with loving God above all and one's neighbor as oneself. In addition, students are invited several times throughout the text to translate Christian moral living into action by way of various service projects.

Open

Through reflection exercises, discussion questions, prayer experiences, ideas for service, and so forth, the Student Text and this Teacher's Wraparound Edition continually relate the doctrinal themes to the real lives of students. As stated in the Preface to the Student Text, the reader will find that the text's content appeals to the head, the heart, and the hands with

- intellectually challenging exercises and projects designed to stimulate you to learn more about the Catholic faith;
- presentations and activities that promote a prayerful study of the Scripture and connect you to the Church's liturgy;
- stimulating applications that encourage you in service learning and ministry.

Doctrinal Elements of a Curriculum Framework

As an overview of the Catholic faith, *Our Catholic Faith: Living What We Believe* includes many elements presented in the Doctrinal Elements of a Curriculum Framework for the Development of Catechetical Materials for Young People of High School Age (2008). Although this book is designed as an overview course and not for any specific course outlined in the Framework, the author made many efforts to ensure that the revision of the text would present the same scope of theological doctrine. For instance, the new Profile of Faith, Explaining Your Faith, and Knowing Christ through Scripture features were added and supplemented to connect with the Framework. In addition, take the following connections to the six core courses of the Framework into consideration:

I. Revelation of Jesus Christ in Scripture

Chapter 1 specifically addresses the topics in the first course of the core curriculum of the Framework. Like the course, Chapter 1 introduces the proofs of God's existence and then provides a basic overview of Divine Revelation, including both the Old and the New Testaments.

II. Who Is Jesus Christ?

Chapter 2, "Jesus Christ: Lord and Savior," is densely packed with information about Jesus Christ that addresses the Framework course on the Second Person of the Blessed Trinity, including the mystery of the Incarnation and his public life. In addition, Chapter 3, which focuses on the Holy Spirit and the Trinity, also has important connections to the second course of the Framework.

III. The Mission of Jesus Christ (The Paschal Mystery)

Chapter 2 also has a specific section dedicated to Christ's Paschal Mystery that introduces many of the topics that this third course covers in detail. Chapter 5 focuses on the Redemption and the Communion of Saints, which have important connections to Christ's Paschal Mystery. Chapters 8 and 9 focus on Catholic morality, and Chapter 10 focuses on prayer, all of which can be found at the end of the third course.

IV. Jesus Christ's Mission Continues in the Church

Chapter 4, "The Church: The Body of Christ," is directly related to the fourth course in the Framework. Like the course, Chapter 4 focuses on the images of the Church in Scripture, the marks of the Church, and the role of the Church in the world today.

V. Sacraments as Privileged Encounters with Jesus

Chapters 6 and 7 present the Seven Sacraments, which, like the fifth course of the Framework, are connected with the life of Christ. The essential elements of each sacrament are included, as well as the effects and implications for each one.

VI. Life in Jesus Christ

Chapters 8 and 9 deal specifically with Catholic morality, the subject of the sixth course in the Framework. Chapter 9 shares the special focus of the Ten Commandments and the Beatitudes. Chapter 8 develops the idea of sin and conscience formation that can also be found in this course.

Elements Common to the Student Text

The Student Text is organized around a format that includes several common elements in each chapter. Some of these main elements are detailed in the subsections that follow.

Chapter Openers

Each chapter opens with a quotation from the Bible that is related to the major topic of the chapter. This is appropriate because, as the *General Directory for Catechesis* teaches:

> [T]he Church desires that in the ministry of the word, Sacred Scripture should have a pre-eminent position. In concrete terms, catechesis should be "an authentic introduction to *lectio divina*." . . . (127)

A brief topic outline lists the main sections of the chapter with a sentence explaining what each chapter entails.

Next there is a story or short anecdote that introduces one of the main topics of the chapter. These short stories or anecdotes serve to engage the students and to relate some aspect of the chapter to everyday life.

Most chapters have at least one exercise that requires self-reflection on spiritual gifts or virtues, or a pre-test to pique student interest in what is to follow. These are typically followed by reflection questions to encourage student sharing.

For Review and For Reflection Questions

At the end of each section of the Student Text there are For Review questions related to the topic of the texts. These questions reflect the objectives of the text and each lesson in the Teacher's Wraparound Edition.

You may decide early on in the course to have students keep all of their answers to the For Reflection questions in a journal. These questions work well either as homework or as in-class exercises and are typically suitable for sharing with partners or in small groups.

Knowing Christ through Scripture

Research and reading exercises from either the Old or New Testament are included within each chapter. Students are provided with specific Scripture passages and are asked questions about the events in the passages. Typically, students are asked to write out their findings individually or in small groups.

Church Documents

Many chapters include key passages from Church documents, typically from the Second Vatican Council, especially *The Dogmatic Constitution on the Church*. Several end-of-the-chapter activities also direct students to read designated chapters from the documents, most of which can be found online.

Profiles of Faith

The biographies of Christian saints and heroes are profiled in the text: the Blessed Mother (Introduction), St. Thomas Aquinas (Chapter 1), the early followers of Jesus (Chapter 2), Blessed Pope John XXIII (Chapter 3), St. Teresa of Avila (Chapter 4), St. John Bosco (Chapter 5), Bl. Kateri Tekawitha (Chapter 6), the students themselves (Chapter 7), Sr. Josephine Bakhita (Chapter 8), St. Thomas More (Chapter 9), and Fr. Patrick Peyton, C.S.C. (Chapter 10). Quotations and Internet links are also provided to supplement the biographies.

Explaining Your Faith

The Explaining Your Faith feature offers an apologetic dimension in which "tough issues" non-Catholics typically raise are posed in a simple question-and-answer format. The answers provided are ones students can easily share in their own discussions with those who question a particular point of Catholic or Christian teaching. Two brief examples: In Chapter 1, the question of a good God who permits evil is posed. In Chapter 7, the issue of why Catholics have to confess their sins to a priest is raised. You may want to develop these questions into simple debates or role-playing skits in your classes to help students develop skills at evangelizing or defending their faith.

Vocabulary Words

In an attempt to develop religious literacy, the Student Text clearly defines some important terms that every student is expected to know. These terms are boldfaced within the text and defined in the accompanying margin. Also, these terms and definitions appear on most of the Chapter Tests. Students can also find each of these important terms in the Glossary at the end of the book. The terms defined in *Our Catholic Faith: Living What We Believe* are:

Abba	Blessing	Contrition	Evangelization
Abortion	Calumny	Covenant	Fruits of the Holy Spirit
Absolution	Canon law	Deism	Gifts of the Holy Spirit
Adoration	Capital sins	Despair	Gospel
Adultery	Cardinal virtues	Detraction	Grace
Advent	Catechesis	Diaconate	Great Schism
Agnostics	*Catechism of the Catholic Church*	Divine missions of the Blessed	Heaven
Amen	Catechumen	Trinity	Hell
Annulment	Catholic	Divine providence	Heresy
Apostasy	Celibacy	Doctor of the Church	Hierarchy
Apostle	Charism	Dogma	Icons
Assumption	Chastity	Ecumenical council	Idolatry
Atheist	Chrism	Ecumenism	Immaculate Conception
Avarice	Christ	Epiclesis	Immanence
Beatific Vision	Christian morality	Epiphany	Incarnation
Beatitudes	Church	Eschatology	Infallibility
Bible	Common good	Essential rite	Intercession
Bishop	Communion of Saints	Euthanasia	Justification
Blasphemy	Concupiscence	Evangelical counsels	Kingdom of God
Blessed Trinity	Contemplation	Evangelists	Laity

Last (general) judgment	Paraclete	Resurrection of the body	Solidarity
Latin Rite	Parousia	Revelation	Sorcery
Lectio Divina	Particular judgment	Rite	Sources of morality
Lent	Paschal Mystery	Sacrament	Subsidiarity
Liturgy	Passions	Sacrament of Anointing of the	Theological virtues
Magisterium	Perjury	Sick	Theophany
Marks of the Church	Petition	Sacrament of Holy Orders	Transcendence
Meditation	Polygamy	Sacrament of Matrimony	Transubstantiation
Modesty	Polytheistic	Sacrament of Penance	Triduum
Monotheistic	Praise	Sacramental character	Venial sin
Mortal sin	Prayer	Sacramentals	Viaticum
Mystery	Precepts of the Church	Sacred Tradition	Vices
Natural law	Presbyters	Saint	Virgin birth
Neophytes	Presumption	Salvation	Virtues
Oath	Protestant	Sanctifying grace	Yahweh
Original Holiness and Justice	Purgatory	Sin	
Original Sin	RCIA	Social justice doctrine	
Parable	Religion	Society	

Chapter Quick View and Learning the Language of Faith

Each chapter concludes with a bulleted list of summary points called the Chapter Quick View. These points are helpful for reviewing the chapter and assisting the students in studying for the Chapter Test. Also, additional review questions about vocabulary appear in the Learning the Language of Faith feature.

Ongoing Assignments

This section includes several ideas for students to extend the chapter lessons, usually through long-term assignments. Examples include doing further research from the Bible or Church documents, listening to music, creating art works, interviewing parents and grandparents, researching Internet sites, putting together PowerPoint presentations, composing prayers, reading about and reporting on Christian saints, evaluating television programs and other media that touch on human dignity, and a variety of other projects and activities.

Christian service is an underlying theme that recurs throughout the book. A common thread in these application projects is for service involving a corporal work of mercy. For example, Jesus is presented as a model of service. His Church continues his role as Prophet, Priest, and King. Students are asked to examine their own gifts and commit themselves to use them in the service of others. *Suggestion*: Plan soon to incorporate at least one service project assignment in the course. Begin by reviewing the suggestions offered throughout the text in the Ongoing Assignment sections. It is vital for students, as individuals or in small groups, to do some type of Christian service in conjunction with the core work in this introductory course on the Catholic faith.

Prayer Reflection

Each chapter includes a prayer reflection, most tied in with a traditional or well-known prayer. Many important Catholic prayers are also included in the Catholic Handbook for Faith in the Appendix of the Student Text.

Students also have ample opportunities to compose their own prayers in several exercises recommended throughout the text. Typically, students are instructed to be creative in prayer composition, for example, by employing visuals to illustrate a theme of their prayer.

A major catechesis on prayer is given in Chapter 10. The Lord's Prayer is discussed in some depth there.

Catholic Handbook for Faith

The Catholic Handbook for Faith, included in the Appendix of the Student Text, contains prayers, teachings, creeds, Church history, sacraments, and practices that will help students review and remember several important prayers and practices that will be necessary throughout a Catholic high school curriculum and beyond.

Curriculum Plan of the Student Text

A major source of a course's curriculum is the objectives of a school's religious education program. Ideally each religious education department develops and publishes its objectives for the four-year program, incorporating the following elements of a systematic catechesis:
- the teaching of the Christian *message* as it is handed down in the Catholic Tradition;
- the fostering of *Christian community*;
- the development of student skills in *serving* others;
- the celebration of Catholic identity through *liturgy*.

High school catechists draw on a variety of sources to develop the objectives of a four-year theology curriculum, including the *Catechism of the Catholic Church*, the *General Directory for Catechesis*, the National Catechetical Directory *(Sharing the Light of Faith)*, the *National Directory for Catechesis*, *Catechesi Tradendae*, *To Teach as Jesus Did*, directives from the local bishop and diocesan religious education office, national catechetical guidelines, and other pertinent documents.

In addition, research findings on adolescent growth and development, needs analyses of students, practical classroom experience, the charism and spirituality of the religious orders that staff the schools, and parent surveys all help religious educators put together a solid, relevant, integral, and interesting program for students.

A key to improving the curriculum is the periodic evaluation of program and course objectives. Objectives adopted for certain courses dictate the specific content to be taught, its scope, sequence, and organization. They guide us in selecting the specific day-to-day methods and media we employ to teach our classes. They help us resist fads and control the overall direction of our course and programs.

The curriculum model suggested for this course encourages periodic evaluation to help verify how effectively goals are being met. Evaluation can help religion departments to judge the suitability of the scope of coverage of key concepts, to adjust sequencing of the material, and to check the reliability of methods and choice of media to accomplish goals. Another benefit of evaluation might be to reveal that some goals are unrealistic and not worth the time and energy expended on them.

Evaluation can take many forms. For example, quizzes and tests can help in determining the effectiveness of both teaching and learning. Also provided in this Teacher's Wraparound Edition are various means of assessing student learning prior to quizzes and tests. Parent and student surveys can suggest ways needs are being met or not being met.

The text subscribes to a "closed-loop" model of curriculum. In schematic form it looks like this:

O B J E C T I V E S		Content
		Scope
		Sequence and Content Organization
		Method
		Media
		Evaluation

A description of how this model works in planning and implementing a curriculum follows.

Objectives

Each chapter in the TWE lists several student objectives for the main sections of the Student Text. (Objectives gleaned from *Guidelines for Doctrinally Sound Catechetic Materials* were discussed under "Sufficiently Complete" catechesis on page viii.) Among the major objectives for the students are to:

- reflect on the meaning of Christian faith and their own faith journey in the Catholic Tradition;
- appreciate the goodness to be found in the Catholic faith;
- be able to explain the articles of the Nicene Creed;
- characterize the Revelation of our loving Father, revealed most fully in his Son, Jesus Christ;
- offer a demonstration for God's existence;
- explain the reality of sin in the world, the concept of salvation, and the invitation of God's forgiveness;
- reflect on the meaning of the Good News of Jesus for human destiny and for their own lives;
- discuss the meaning of major Church doctrines that define Christ's identity;
- summarize the message of Jesus;
- explain the role of the Holy Spirit in salvation history;
- identify the gifts and fruits of the Holy Spirit and how these are evident in their own lives;
- demonstrate a basic understanding of the relationship among the three Divine Persons of the Blessed Trinity;
- characterize the Church as mystery, People of God, Body of Christ, sacrament, Temple of the Holy Spirit, and servant;
- understand what it means to be a member of Christ's body and consider their valuable function in the Church;
- discuss the role of the Magisterium in Christ's Church;

- explain each mark of the Church: one, holy, catholic, and apostolic;
- recognize their role in the Communion of Saints;
- gain inspiration from the lives of the saints;
- identify Church teaching about the eschaton ("last things");
- define the meaning of the term *sacrament*;
- articulate an understanding of the Sacraments of Initiation, Sacraments of Healing, and the Sacraments at the Service of Communion by identifying their unique signs, explaining their rituals, and explaining how they are moments of grace for the individual and the community;
- explain the sacramental nature of the Church and grow in appreciation of the seven ritual sacraments, especially the Eucharist;
- identify the liturgical year;
- demonstrate an understanding of sin by identifying its different types and how it affects one's relationship with God, others, and self;
- define conscience and discuss the steps for making moral decisions;
- know the meaning of the Beatitudes;
- recite the Ten Commandments and discuss what each requires and what each outlaws;
- distinguish between and among the theological and cardinal virtues;
- explain key principles of Catholic morality and apply them to several moral problems;
- recognize the sources of Catholic social justice teaching and illustrate several themes of this teaching;
- explain terms like grace, justification, merit, redemption, and salvation;
- define prayer and discuss its types;
- experience a number of prayer forms;
- appreciate the special role of Mary in the lives of Christians and the value of special devotion to the saints;
- identify and explain key Marian doctrines;
- engage in a meaningful service project;
- contrast the beliefs of certain non-Catholic religions to those of the Catholic faith;
- explain what the Church teaches about other religions in God's plan of salvation;
- develop "religious literacy" by identifying and defining key terms.

Content and Scope

The content of the text includes an overview of essential Church teachings as they appear in the various articles of the Apostles' Creed; a review of each sacrament; a discussion of the theological and cardinal virtues; the essential Catholic teachings about moral principles; a discussion of the requirements of the Beatitudes, Ten Commandments, and other demands of Catholic social justice teaching; and a primer on prayer, with special emphasis on the meaning of the Lord's Prayer. Student mastery of key terminology is an important aim of the book. Because of the breadth of coverage, the book deals solely with magisterial teaching on the topics.

As with most textbooks, *Our Catholic Faith: Living What We Believe* stresses the cognitive domain of learning. After completing the course, students should have a basic knowledge of Church teachings in the main subject areas outlined in the contents of this text as well as mastery of religious vocabulary, especially as highlighted in the glossary. The cognitive nature of the text and course will help students to recall, recognize, and comprehend these main topics. However, other exercises and Reflection and Discussion Questions also move students to the higher levels of cognitive learning: the skills of application, analysis, synthesis, and evaluation.

Also, the text includes exercises and activities that appeal to the affective or behavioral domains of learning. Many of the Discussion Questions, Writing Assignments, and some values exercises encourage students to acquire "heart knowledge." Questioning, reflecting, imagining, internalizing, appreciating, responding to, examining, deciding—these are the outcomes that help students apply the meaning of Church doctrines for their own lives.

As noted previously, an Ongoing Assignments section is part of the conclusion of each chapter. These exercises pertain especially to "hand knowledge," that is, to the behavioral domain.

Because of the nature of an introductory course, the scope of *Our Catholic Faith: Living What We Believe* is broad. Though the text presents a survey of faith, the many interactive assignments and reflection activities help to make the text much more than an encyclopedic reference.

Sequence

The Student Text begins with a short introduction that discusses the importance of faith and provides a brief summary of key Catholic beliefs.

The Student Text then follows the outline of the *Catechism of the Catholic Church* with chapters and part openers. The part opener to the Creed outlines the meaning of the term *creed* and discusses the Nicene and Apostles' Creeds. The part opener to the sacraments defines terms like *liturgy* and *sacraments* and discusses their relationship to the Blessed Trinity. The part opener to the chapters on morality briefly summarizes Catholic morality as the response to Christ in love. The sequence is as follows:

- The Profession of Faith (We Believe: The Apostles' Creed—Chapters 1–5)
- The Celebration of the Christian Mystery (We Hope: Celebrating the Christian Mystery—Chapters 6–7)
- Life in Christ (We Love: Our Life in Christ—Chapters 8–9)
- Christian Prayer (Chapter 10—Prayer)

The recommendation is to follow the outline of the Student Text in teaching the course. However, teachers may consider reversing the order of the parts on sacraments and morality. Students might be ready for the more practical issues of morality immediately after being introduced to the tenets of the Creed. Also, Chapter 10, on prayer, can be introduced at almost any point in teaching the course, although it is best to have concluded teaching the material on Jesus and the Blessed Trinity beforehand.

Chapter outlines for *Our Catholic Faith: Living What We Believe* follow:

Introduction: Our Catholic Faith
Importance of faith as one of the theological virtues
What faith enables us to do
Brief summary of key Catholic beliefs

Part I: We Believe: The Apostles' Creed
Meaning of "creed"
The Nicene Creed and the Apostles' Creed

Chapter 1: Our Loving God: Father and Creator
One, true God (monotheism, polytheism, deism, atheism, agnosticism)
Intellectual proofs for God's existence
Heartfelt proofs for God's existence
Understanding God: both transcendent and immanent
Divine Revelation and Sacred Tradition
God's name (Yahweh) and his divine attributes
God the Father, First Person of the Blessed Trinity, Abba
God the Creator of all that is seen and unseen
The Fall and Original Sin
Perennial questions: the problem of evil and an all-good God; God's knowledge and human freedom

Chapter 2: Jesus Christ: Lord and Savior
Beliefs about Jesus Christ: the Incarnation and its meaning; meaning of the name *Jesus* and titles *Christ, Son of God, Lord, Suffering Servant, Son of Man*
Evidence for Jesus and his life: Roman and Jewish sources, the Gospels themselves
Contents of the New Testament and the formation of the Gospels
Mysteries of Christ's life:
- Infancy narratives, doctrine of virgin birth, his relatives
- Baptism of Jesus
- Temptations in the wilderness
- Jesus' preaching ministry
- Miracles of Jesus
- Transfiguration

The Paschal Mystery: suffering, Death, Resurrection, and Glorification of Jesus
- Jesus died for our sins.
- He suffered under Pontius Pilate (Jews as a people not to blame for his death).
- He rose from the dead.
- He ascended into Heaven and will come again to judge the living and the dead.

Key doctrinal beliefs about Jesus: early heresies and the teachings of the early councils about Jesus

Chapter 3: The Holy Spirit and Blessed Trinity
Gifts of the Holy Spirit
The Holy Spirit in the Bible
Jesus and the Holy Spirit
Name, title, and symbols (fire; tongues of fire; anointing with oil, water, hand; dove; finger of God; cloud and light) of the Holy Spirit
The Holy Spirit in the life of Christians
Where the Holy Spirit is present today

Mystery of the Trinity—Jesus reveals the Trinity

The Spirit reveals the Father and the Son

The Immanent Trinity

The Salvific Trinity

The divine missions

Chapter 4: The Church: The Body of Christ

Definition of *Church*

The Church as mystery of God's love

Church as sacrament

Church as People of God with mission of message, community, service, and worship

Church as Body of Christ

Church as Temple of the Holy Spirit

Membership (hierarchy and laity) and ministries in the Church

Church as prophet and the special role of the Magisterium

Church as priest and the various vocations in the Church

Church as king

Non-Catholics and salvation

Marks of the Church: one, holy, catholic, and apostolic

Ecumenism: the Church and other religions

The Catholic Church and non-Christians

The Catholic Church and non-Catholic Christians

Baptists in America contrasted with Catholic beliefs

Chapter 5: Communion of Saints, Forgiveness of Sins, Eternal Life

Communion of Saints

Devotion to the saints

Mary, the greatest saint, and teachings about her: Immaculate Conception, Ever -Virgin, Mother of God, Mother of the Church, Assumption of Mary

Veneration of Mary

One Baptism for the forgiveness of sins

Types of sin: original and actual; venial and mortal; vices

Forgiveness of post-baptismal actual sins

The last things: eschatology and death

Resurrection of the body

Particular judgment

Heaven, Purgatory, Hell

General judgment

Meaning of the word *Amen*

Part II: We Hope: Celebrating the Christian Mystery

The liturgy

The liturgy and the Blessed Trinity

Sacraments

Chapter 6: The Sacraments of Initiation

Our need for signs and symbols

Sacraments of Initiation; historical overview and the Rite of Christian Initiation of Adults (RCIA)

Baptism

Infant baptism

Baptismal symbols: water, oil, white garment, candle

Effects of baptism

Salvation and unbaptized babies

Confirmation—biblical roots and historical dimensions

Confirmation and the Holy Spirit

The Rite of Confirmation

Eastern Rite Christians

The various names for Eucharist: Eucharist, Lord's Supper, breaking of the bread, Eucharistic assembly, Holy and Divine Liturgy, Most Blessed Sacrament, Holy Sacrifice, Holy Communion, Holy Mass

The Celebration of the Mass

The liturgical year

Sacramentals

Chapter 7: Sacraments of Healing and Ministry

Sacrament of Penance and its names: Reconciliation, conversion, confession, forgiveness
Rite of Penance: acts of penitent (contrition, confession, satisfaction); God's action
Why confession to a priest?
Sacrament of Anointing of the Sick
Rite of the Sacrament of Anointing
Effects of the Sacrament of Anointing
Sacrament of Holy Orders
Roles of ordained ministers: episcopacy, presbyterate, diaconate
Ministries and graces of the sacrament
Rite of Holy Orders
Clerical celibacy
The Eastern Orthodox Church
The Sacrament of Matrimony
Preparation for marriage
Effects of the Sacrament of Matrimony
Rules for a successful marriage
Divorce and annulment

Part III: We Love: Our Life in Christ

Chapter 8: The Basics of Catholic Morality

Practicing the cardinal virtues
Humans made in God's image: dignity and worth, thinkers with freedom, responsible, wounded by sin, children of God, friends of the Lord
Humans and society: social beings and the Church's social justice doctrine
Conscience and moral decisions
Forming your conscience
Following your conscience
Virtues and other helps to live a moral life
Theological virtues
Moral law (natural law, civil law, Old Law, New Law, precepts of the Church)
Sin, justification, and grace
Merit and the vocation to holiness

Chapter 9: Christian Moral Life: The Beatitudes and Ten Commandments

Call to Happiness and the Beatitudes
First Commandment: virtue of religion, sins against
Catholics and religious pictures and statues
Second Commandment: God's and our names are holy; sins against
Third Commandment: how to keep the Lord's Day holy
Fourth Commandment: honor one's parents, respect one's children, obedience to proper authority
Fifth Commandment: respect life and outlaw murder, terrorism, abortion, euthanasia, suicide; capital punishment; Church teaching on war
Sixth and Ninth Commandments: respect one's own sexuality and that of others; chastity, modesty, purity; sins against these values
Marriage: open to life and love
Sins against marital love
Seventh and Tenth Commandments: beware of greed, avarice, envy
The virtue of justice: commutative, legal, distributive, social
Good stewardship
Economic justice
Solidarity and preferential option for the poor
Corporal and spiritual works of mercy
Eighth Commandment: Be truthful; sins that violate this commandment

Chapter 10: Prayer

Definition of prayer
Types of prayer: blessing, adoration, praise; petition, contrition, intercession; thanksgiving
The Bible and prayer: Jesus and Mary at prayer
How to pray
Place, time, relax, good attitude, persistence
Addressing God in prayer

Prayer expressions: vocal, meditation, mental
Meditating on a scriptural passage
The Lord's Prayer
Context and background
Meaning of each phrase

Length of Course

Assuming *Our Catholic Faith: Living What We Believe* will provide the basic text for a semester course, here is a possible breakdown of the chapters and topics from the Student Text:

Chapter	Weeks
Introduction	.5
Chapter 1 (God the Father)	2
Chapter 2 (Jesus)	2
Chapter 3 (Holy Spirit and Trinity)	1.5
Chapter 4 (Church)	1.5
Chapter 5 (Communion of Saints/eschatology)	1
Chapter 6 (Sacraments of Initiation)	1.5
Chapter 7 (Sacraments of Healing and Vocation)	1.5
Chapter 8 (Basics of Catholic Morality)	1.5
Chapter 9 (Beatitudes & Ten Commandments)	2
Chapter 10 (Prayer)	1
Feature film	1
Student project	1
Total:	**18 wks**

Of course, this is just a suggestion. You may wish to have several student projects. (In the sample Weekly Planning Chart on page xviii, for example, students will engage in a research project on the saints and will view a film on Mother Teresa. Together, these activities will extend by three days the time allotted for Chapter 5.) You may well show more than one feature film as well. You will have to budget your time accordingly. In addition, be sure to factor in time for review, quizzes, and tests.

You will note that more time is devoted to the Creed than to the sacraments and morality because of the likelihood that these other areas will be studied in greater depth later in the high school curriculum.

If you have time, it would be appropriate to involve the students in a class service project along the lines of one of the corporal works of mercy as suggested in the text. If it is to be a class project, factor in time to plan, execute, and evaluate.

A blank Weekly Planning Chart is included in the Resource Section, starting on page 285. It can also be accessed online at www.avemaria press.com.

Weekly Planning Chart: Unit on Communion of Saints

Day/Pp.	Objectives	Activities	Follow-up work
Mon. 10/10 **pp.** xx–xx	Introduce chapter Get students thinking about "eschatological" questions Introduce term: *Communion of Saints*	Warmup: Introduce Chapter 5 by reading introductory pages. Use 1 Cor. reading for prayer. 1. Have students do "Thinking about End Exercise" and write responses to Heaven, Hell, and funeral questions. Share and discuss. May take whole period. 2. Give overview of Communion on Saints.	Hmwk: Read section on Communion of Saints in chapter. Promise short quiz on HW reading. Assign relevant For Review questions at end of chapter to be worked on during the week. Write in journal.
Tues. 10/11 **pp.** xx–xx	Discuss meaning of devotion to saints Introduce idea of patron saints Assign saints project	Warmup: Recite Hail Mary for opening prayer. Give 5-point quiz on HW reading: emphasis on Church pilgrim, suffering, and triumphant. Correct in class. Read together "Devotion to Saints." Do exercise on patron saints. Introduce resources (books, websites on saints) Assign 1–minute talk to be given Friday on chosen saint.	Hmwk: Read short biography of chosen saint or check website for a bio. Prepare 1-minute talk for Friday.
Wed. 10/12	Illustrate modern saint—Mother Teresa Discuss qualities of what makes for holiness	Warmup: Recite a Memorare for Opening Prayer. Offer petitions to Mary. Invite students to do the same. Begin video on Mother Teresa. Have students note three of her greatest qualities	Hmwk: Continue research on saint. Instruct that there will be 5 extra points given if they can find a picture of their saint to post on bulletin board after their talks.
Thurs. 10/13	Discuss film Explain process of canonization Create and discuss list of qualities of a holy person	Warmup: For prayer, create a litany. Do a whip around room. Each student mentions favorite saint: e.g.: "St. Teresa, R: Pray for us Finish film. Discuss qualities of sainthood. List ten. Apply to how teens might acquire these. Take questions on process of canonization.	Hmwk: Be prepared to give oral report tomorrow. List reference. Type out outline of presentation on one page.
Fri. 10/14	Students present research findings	Warmup: Pray a favorite saint's prayer: Prayer for Peace of St. Francis Assisi. Give directions for talks: short, snappy. Begin talks.	Hmwk: Listen to Sunday readings for one point of how we should live our lives to become holier, more God-like people. Sharing on Monday.

Evaluation of Week:

Mon.: Students a little uncomfortable talking about death, but liked the exercise about what they would do if they only had one week to live.

Tues.: They did well on short quiz. Liked the patron saint exercise. Did not seem overjoyed about the saints project until they learned that it could be easily researched on the Internet.

Wed.: Prayer petitions to Mary did not work. Initial interest in video, but afraid it might be too long.

Thurs.: Film dragged at end, though kids did come up with a good list of qualities for saints. They were fascinated about how one gets canonized.

Fri.: Uneven presentations. Some good, some bad. Did not finish all. One minute not realistic. Must allot more time in the future.

Using Media

Each chapter of the Teacher's Wraparound Edition annotates a sampling of videos that may be used to enhance the content of that particular chapter. There are many options to choose from to help add variety to your courses.

Most of the feature-length productions annotated in the TWE should be relatively easy to find in video stores or in diocesan offices. Over time, some of the shorter videos might be a bit more difficult to obtain or even be withdrawn from use. The works annotated in the TWE were checked against recent catalogues posted on the websites of their providers. Some dioceses have excellent religious educational video libraries from which to borrow. Be sure to check if this resource is available in your diocese.

Some rules for using audiovisuals:

1. *Always preview with an eye toward their suitability for your own students.* In the case of feature films, although we recognize that students can sometimes benefit from some excellent R-rated films, it is prudent not to use anything but G-, PG-, and PG-13-rated films with high school students. Parents are the prime religious educators, and we should not presume to use materials some parents would find objectionable. As far as can be determined, none of the films recommended in the TWE are R-rated.

2. *Order materials early to avoid disappointment.* Consider purchasing DVDs of feature films for your departmental library. You can find many of them at extremely reasonable costs from a source like Amazon.com or Critics' Choice.

3. *Follow up your use of an audiovisual with a discussion and some meaningful assignments.* We should not give our students the impression that viewing a film is an excuse to stop thinking. Provide study sheets on the film so they will be prepared for discussion. You might have selected questions (for example, incomplete quotations) for them to complete while watching the film. A short quiz to check their attention might be in order at the end of a particular day's segment.

Here are some primary sources for purchasing videos and DVDs:

Amazon.com
www.amazon.com

Center for Learning
P.O. Box 910, Evergreen Road
Villa Maria, PA 16155
Toll-Free Tel. 1-800-767-9090
Toll-Free Fax 1-888-767-8080
www.centerforlearning.org

Critics' Choice Video
www.ccvideo.com

Ignatius Press
P.O. Box 1339
Ft. Collins, CO 80522
1-800-651-1531
www.ignatius.com

Insight Media
2162 Broadway
New York, NY 10024-0621
1-800-233-9910
www.insight-media.com

Oblate Media and Communication Videos with Values
1509 Washington Ave., Suite 550
Saint Louis, MO 63103
1-800-233-4629
www.videoswithvalues.org

Our Sunday Visitor
200 Noll Plaza
Huntington, IN 46750
1-800-348-2440
www.osv.com

Paraclete Video Productions Paraclete Press, Inc.
P.O. Box 1568
Orleans, MA 02653
1-800-451-5006
www.paracletepress.com

Paulist Press
997 Macarthur Blvd.
Mahwah, NJ 07430
1-800-218-1903
www.paulistpress.com

Questar, Inc.
P.O. Box 11345
Chicago, IL 60611-0345
1-800-544-8422
www.questar1.com

St. Anthony Messenger Press
28 W. Liberty St.
Cincinnati, OH 45202
1-800-488-0488
www.americancatholic.org

Twenty-Third Publications
P.O. Box 180
Mystic, CT 06355
1-800-321-0411
www.pastoralplanning.com

Vision Video/Gateway Films
P.O. Box 540
Worcester, PA 19490
1-800-523-0226
www.visionvideo.com

Alternate Teaching Methods

There are many different kinds of assignments and teaching approaches that can help you bring variety to the course. Some suggestions are listed here:

Article reading. Consider assigning an article or two from a popular Catholic magazine or a more scholarly journal, depending on the ability of your group. Magazines like *Catholic Digest, St. Anthony Messenger, Liguorian, America, Bible Today*, and *U.S. Catholic* always have interesting articles that younger students can read with both benefit and pleasure. Provide your students with a list of Catholic periodicals available in your school and departmental libraries. As part of the reading assignment, have your students write a summary and evaluation on a large index card, and then report on the article to the class.

Creative parable assignment. Have the students enact, rewrite, update, or present in some other creative way one of the Gospel parables in connection with the students' study of Jesus. This assignment lends itself to a small group project, for example, the videotaping of a student-written drama on one of the parables.

Small- and large-group discussions. Discussion builds Christian community in the classroom and often leads to faith sharing among students. For example, the text sometimes asks students to discuss and do short written reflections on the subject matter of a particular section of the chapter. After small groups have discussed a topic for a time, call on one person from each group to summarize the major points of its discussion to the entire class.

Faith sharing. Throughout the course you'll find several opportunities to give personal Christian witness. For example, you might witness how prayer has helped you in your professional and personal lives. Or you might share with your students your favorite way to pray and explain why you find it particularly meaningful.

Guest speakers. A host of topics lend themselves to guest speakers in this course. For starters, consider inviting a representative of another religion to share what his or her faith teaches on particular issues. Follow up the presentation to compare and contrast those teachings with what the Church teaches and believes. Other topics that lend themselves to dynamic speakers include pro-life issues like abortion, euthanasia, and capital punishment; chastity issues; vocations; drugs and alcohol; and so forth. Be sure the speakers are orthodox in their Catholic faith and are able to talk intelligently to high school students.

Internet. Many links to relevant websites are annotated in the "Resources" section for each chapter starting on page 2 and also online at www .avemariapress.com. It is highly recommended that you assign several short projects that familiarize your students with the wealth of excellent Catholic websites on the Internet. Your more tech-savvy students could also construct web-based pages of essential information on some aspect of the Catholic faith under consideration.

Interviewing. Several assignments throughout the Student Text direct students to interview their parents or other adults. This can open up dialog and help parents exercise their own ministry of religious education. At times, it is appropriate for students to give feedback to the entire class on the results of their interviews.

Journal-keeping. Students can collect many of their written reflections in a journal. This would include the short Scripture-reading assignments given, as well as the self-reflection exercises. Journal writing can also be a helpful way to pray. Explain its value to your students. Consider making the journal a significant part of the student's grade for the course.

Lecture and note-taking. A great lecture on your part can stimulate student interest, introduce difficult material, organize units logically, and summarize key ideas. Requiring students to take notes on key points teaches an essential skill that will help them in all their courses. Perhaps you can spend a short session on how to take good notes in your class. You may wish to duplicate a sketchy outline of your lecture, leaving enough space for students to fill in the missing material that you put on the board or use as part of a PowerPoint presentation. Students can keep these handouts in a separate section of a three-ring binder journal/notebook, and you can award points for completeness and neatness.

Prayer. Each chapter contains a prayer reflection. You can add to these by using the Scripture quotations that begin each chapter as well as other prayers provided. Also, consider celebrating the Sacrament of Penance and at least one Eucharist during your semester together. Have students plan the readings for the Eucharist. If teaching the course during second semester, you might tie the Eucharist into the Triduum or the Holy Thursday celebration of the first Eucharist.

Text reading and summary. Throughout this Teacher's Manual, students will be instructed to read the text. Perhaps you will teach them how to highlight key material and then note it for later study. Also, you may direct students to write out all the answers to the For Review questions and include them in a separate section of their journal. Most test items provided for in this Teacher's Manual come from these For Review questions. Students are sure to do well on the Chapter Tests if they can master the answers to these questions. These skills will translate to many courses the students will take in other subject areas throughout high school.

Service project. As mentioned before, it is recommended that students engage in some short service projects as individuals or as a class sometime during their time in your class.

Values exercises. Most chapters in the Student Text have at least one key exercise designed to get them to think in personal terms about some aspect of their Catholic faith, their relationship to Jesus, their life in the Christian community, or their current beliefs about and practice of Catholicism. Be sure to allot time to discuss these.

Various creative assessments. A long-range assignment is a valuable part of the learning experience. There are many possibilities. For example, students might:

- Read and report on the life of a saint.
- Create a video of interviews of practicing Catholics and their beliefs about any number of issues.
- Produce a video, art project, or musical work that celebrates the beauty of God's creation.
- Write a short question-and-answer catechism of Catholic beliefs for students preparing for Confirmation.
- Create a personal prayer book.
- Attend the baptism of an infant and report on the ritual.
- Research what other religions believe about the afterlife.
- Create a PowerPoint presentation on some aspect of Catholic belief or practice, using visuals downloaded from the Internet.
- Draw or create symbols for various images of the Church or each of the sacraments. Decorate the classroom with their productions.
- Write letters to Catholic political figures asking them to vote pro-life or inquiring what their positions are on various social justice issues.
- Assign passages from various books of the Bible for students to read, summarize, and report on.
- Take a field trip. Perhaps there is a Marian shrine nearby or a church or cathedral with interesting religious art or architecture. A tour of the diocesan offices or an agency sponsored by Catholic Charities might be arranged. Students are often unaware of the many services provided by the local church.
- Groups of three to six could research and debate controversial topics troubling the Church today, for example, the decline in religious vocations and what can be done about it.
- Design a board game to quiz knowledge about the Catholic faith.
- Create a webpage for Catholic youth.
- Research religious artwork and music. Make a presentation on the findings.
- Read and report on topics in the *New Catholic Encyclopedia*.
- Create word puzzles on key terms used in the course.

Also, note the multiple intelligences learning styles and their relationship to other long-term projects detailed in the section that follows. The Teacher's Wraparound Edition contains a variety of different activities, based on multiple intelligence learning. Among these activities are:

Intelligence	Type Activities
Bodily/Kinesthetic	dance, gesture, movement, drama, clowning, mime, puppetry
Interpersonal/Relational	games, competitions, discussions
Intrapersonal/Introspective	reflection questions, prayer, journal writing
Logical/Mathematical	games, research, constructing scale models
Musical/Rhythmic	singing, music, raps, poetry
Naturalist	architecture, photography
Verbal/Linguistic	oral presentations
Visual/Spatial	art projects, working with textiles

Projects and Assignments Using Multiple Intelligences Learning Styles

Multiple Intelligences is a term used to describe the ways people learn. Developed by Howard Gardner, a professor at the Harvard Graduate School of Education, the multiple intelligences allow for eight ways for a student to learn in ways that fit his or her preferred "learning style." Though people learn using all eight learning styles, each person has preferred ways of acquiring and processing information. The best learning takes place when teaching methods offer processes, assignments, and projects for all eight learning styles with opportunities for students to access their preferred learning styles and proceed from their chosen strengths.

This section offers (1) a brief description of Gardner's eight multiple intelligences, (2) information about which methods students who learn in each of these styles prefer, and (3) two semester-long assignments for each learning style.

It is suggested that you allow the students to choose and complete one or two of these assignments over the course of the semester. (You may also wish to allow the students to substitute their own projects or ones listed in the Student Text as substitutes for one or both of the choices listed here.) The assignments are intended to provide a broad scope of their study of the topics introduced in *Our Catholic Faith: Living What We Believe*.

Bodily/Kinesthetic Intelligence

The Bodily/Kinesthetic Intelligence involves the capacity to use one's whole body to express ideas and feelings. It specifically involves using one's hands to create things or to skillfully manipulate objects. A concrete way to think of people who learn in this style is that they must be active and engaged in a "learning by doing" assignment or project. Methods include:

- developing and performing role plays;
- participating in a theater performance;
- creating and/or demonstrating a use of a relevant tool, instrument, or utensil;
- exercising or competing in athletics.

Student Assignments

- In a group of at least three students, prepare a dramatic reading of the Magnificat (Lk 1:46–55), the canticle of Mary. The group can either divide the Magnificat by verses or each person can prepare his or her own interpretative reading. Share the reading with a drama teacher. Record the teacher's comments on the performance. Incorporate any positive suggestions. Then perform the reading before the class.
- "There is a beauty, immensity, symmetry, and power in our world that forces us to conclude that a Grand Designer made it all" (see page 19 of the Student Text). Use a digital camera to create a photo essay with scenes that help to depict God as the Grand Designer of all of creation. Put the photos on a school website (e.g., campus ministry link) for all to enjoy. *Option:* Create your own artwork with scenes of God's creation.

Interpersonal/Relational Intelligence

This intelligence involves the ability to perceive and appreciate the feelings, moods, intentions, and motivations of other people. These types of learners flourish well working in groups, teams, or with a partner. Learning methods include:

- brainstorming ideas;
- playing cooperative games;
- dialoguing with others;
- working on a group project.

Student Assignments

- Work with a group of teens to develop a "sister program" between the youth of two parishes of different ethnic, economic, or social makeups. This might involve joint projects between the parish youth groups, co-sponsoring a dance, participating in a social justice project together, or organizing a core team of youth from both parishes to discuss common problems and possible solutions.
- Work with peers to help plan and participate in a retreat for children preparing for First Communion. Arrange with a parish director of religious education to have a role in executing the day. For example, your group can help to prepare the retreat space (e.g., set up chairs, prayer corners, space for liturgy), give witness talks (e.g., remembrances of your own First Communion), facilitate small groups, help prepare lunch, provide music, and lead prayer.

Intrapersonal/Introspective Intelligence

Intrapersonal/Introspective Intelligence is the ability to base one's actions on self-understanding. Being in touch with one's dreams, feelings, moods, intentions, motivations, and spirituality is a key aspect of this intelligence. People who learn best in this intelligence usually prefer to work alone on self-directed assignments. Examples of learning methods are:

- writing reports or research papers;
- keeping a journal;
- explaining the personal connection of some given information;
- identifying with characters in a story.

Student Assignments

- Study the life of Karol Wojtyla before he became Pope John Paul II. Write about one or more significant experiences from his early life that influenced him as pope. For example, how did his experience growing up in Communist-controlled Poland lead to his role in assisting in the overthrow of the Soviet regime once he became pope?
- Read about major beliefs and practices of Islam. Write a report comparing these beliefs and practices to counterparts in Christianity. Also, research and report on the origins of these Islamic beliefs and practices.

Logical/Mathematical Intelligence

Logical/Mathematical Intelligence includes the skill to work well with numbers and to use reason to solve problems. Persons who learn well in this style are adept at categorizing and exploring relationships within a set of data. They tend to find it difficult to function in an environment that is chaotic or one in which the goals are not clearly defined. Methods that work well in this learning style are:

- categorizing names, places, and events;
- outlining bodies of material;
- exploring patterns and relationships;
- problem solving.

Student Assignments

- Draw a floor plan of a local church or famous worldwide church or cathedral to scale. Using geometric theorems, estimate the height dimensions, window and door dimensions, and the like. Use graph paper for the floor plan. *Optional*: Build an interior model of the church you have selected. See www.silk.net/RelEd/architect.htm for more information on church architecture, including information on famous churches and cathedrals worldwide.
- Research the origins of Christianity in at least ten major nations of the world. In your report, include information about the date and place of the first missionary efforts, the names and biography sketches of the first missionary efforts, special challenges faced by the missionaries, distinct applications to Christianity in the nation, and the state of Christianity in the nation today.

Musical/Rhythmic Intelligence

The ability to distinguish rhythm, pitch, and melody is a characteristic of this intelligence. People who prefer to learn in this style often express themselves in musical forms. They enjoy being surrounded by sound and rhythm and understand these as learning tools. Some methods preferred by learners in this style are:

- making and playing instruments;
- setting stories to music;
- creating and/or performing in a musical;
- writing new lyrics for familiar tunes.

Student Assignments

- Write a song with rap lyrics that teaches one of the truths of the Catholic faith (e.g., the Ten Commandments, the Beatitudes, the Apostles' Creed). Incorporate in the lyrics a tool for helping the listener remember the list you are focusing on. Perform your rap for others.
- Listen to at least four different types of Catholic music (e.g., traditional classics, folk liturgical music, contemporary pop) and write a music review of each. *Optional*: Attend and review a concert of liturgical music.

Naturalist Intelligence

A person with preference for Naturalist Intelligence is at home in the natural environment. He or she appreciates the joys of nature, and is comfortable raising and caring for plants and animals. This person would also enjoy events in the lines of camping, hiking, and many other outdoor activities. A person with a preference for learning in the Naturalist Intelligence learning style appreciates methods like:

- experimenting in a lab setting;
- classifying elements in the natural world;
- "digging" or any simulation of an archaeological experience;
- demonstrating proper procedure and care for gardens or animals.

Student Assignments

- Read about the life of Gregor Mendel, an Austrian monk who, in experimenting with the cross-pollination of plants, discovered the principles that make up the inheritance of physical characteristics. Read and support Mendel's theories using his text *Experiments on Plant Hybridization* and by developing some cross-pollination experiments of your own.
- Craft a private prayer space in the middle of a nearby forest, along a lakeshore or seashore, in the mountains, in a city park, or in some other out-of-the-way exquisite natural scene. Mark the place with a cross made from stones and placed on the ground. Spend some time in prayer. Return at a later date to see how your prayer space has been changed. Take a group of friends with you. Pray a decade of the Rosary or share personal reflections and petitions.

Verbal/Linguistic Intelligence

A Verbal/Linguistic Intelligence involves aptitude with both the spoken and written word. A person who learns best with this intelligence appreciates being able to see things in print, hear spoken words, and say things aloud. Memorization is also a key learning method. Other methods preferred by this type of learner are:

- debating;
- reading and summarizing the material;
- memorizing and repeating aloud many facts;
- writing essays.

Student Assignments

- Make a list of *Jeopardy*-type answers for categories like the Ten Commandments, Scripture, beliefs about Jesus, sacraments, saints, and other subject areas found in the text. Make a question sheet to correspond for each of the answers. Then host a *Jeopardy* game pitting three classmates against each other using the answers and questions you have developed. As in the game show, as the questions accelerate from easier to harder, award more points.
- Take a survey of your peers, asking them why they are Catholic. Record anecdotal evidence. Then write a 500-word essay, "Why Teenagers Say They Are Catholic."

Visual/Spatial Intelligence

This intelligence style caters to people who learn by visualizing and dreaming about concepts and ideas. Learners in this style incorporate both sight as well as mental images. Whereas printed materials may frustrate these learners, visuals in the forms of charts, pictures, graphs, and maps help them to grasp a topic. Other methods that work well for learners in this style include:

- drawing, painting, and sculpting;
- creating collages, posters, and murals;
- designing maps and graphs;
- producing video.

Student Assignments

- Volunteer to design a trademark or logo for your school's campus ministry department and/or the posters and advertisements used to promote upcoming events throughout the year.
- Redesign old dolls to dress like famous Catholic saints, wearing either their traditional religious habit or the typical clothing of the day. Develop a short biography for the saint(s) you have chosen. Then share the story of the saint along with the doll you made with a group of younger students.

Evaluation

Theology courses in Catholic high schools are part of a rigorous curriculum that is mostly part of a college preparatory track. Evaluation and grades are important to students and teachers alike. They help communicate to students the seriousness of the course. Without testing and other means of evaluation to hold both students and teachers accountable, students especially will take the message that the four-year theology curriculum is less important than curriculums for other fields of study.

A major benefit of evaluation is to determine whether objectives are being met. If good teaching happens, then learning is taking place, too.

The Chapter Tests included in this manual, as well as ones that you will devise yourself, offer one means of evaluation. (The Chapter Tests are available online at www.avemariapress.com and may be redesigned and adapted to fit material you have added or deleted from the study of each chapter.) Besides testing, other ways to judge the effectiveness of your teaching and student learning include observing student attention in class; participation in class discussions; the quality of student questions and responses; journal entries; fidelity to homework assignments; the gathering, reporting, and oral presentation of research; participation in service projects; cooperation with you and fellow students; participation in prayer; personal interviews with each student; and informal interaction.

Theology courses teach to the cognitive ("head" knowledge), affective ("heart" knowledge), and the behavioral ("hands" or action knowledge) domains. Student performance in all these areas should be reflected in the grade you assign for the course.

Assigning grades is a key way to emphasize the importance of this course. However, grades should never be used to manipulate, control, or intimidate students. In Christian charity and justice, many opportunities should be given for students to do well. Grasp of cognitive content should not be the exclusive criterion for grades. Rewarding students for effort, participation, and cooperation helps create a loving and just classroom.

Pretest

You may wish to give a pretest of basic knowledge of the Catholic faith at the beginning of the course. Do an item analysis of the percentage missed for each question. This knowledge can help you tailor the course to teach more carefully those areas in which students have displayed a poor background or a weak grasp of the matter.

Format of the Teacher's Manual

Each chapter of this Teacher's Wraparound Edition includes the following regular elements:

- **Overview of the Chapter** is an overview of the content, approach, and rationale of the chapter.
- **Printed Materials** lists ten to fifteen books that provide further background reading for teachers.
- **Audiovisual Materials** includes suggestions for feature-length motion films as well as shorter productions you can use with your students.
- **Internet Links** list some good websites that you and your students can research.
- **Chapter Outline** describes the section titles within each chapter.
- **Advance Preparations** provides a brief overview of the activities that will need preparation ahead of time. Review these bullet points before beginning instruction on the chapter to gather the necessary materials for class or to invite certain guest speakers.
- **Handouts** are enrichment or extra exercises not included in the Student Text. They are reprinted in the "Resource Section" of the TWE (starting on page 285 and also online at www.avemariapress.com).

The teaching approaches offered in the TWE divide chapters into several teachable sections, usually connected to the main headings in the Student Text. Generally, they are arranged to cover the text under one or two main headings in the Student Text. For each of these sections, the Teacher's Wraparound Edition follows this format:

- **Objectives** of the particular section.
- **Preview** of the section being taught.
- **Bell Ringers** to help students get started in the class.
- **Teaching Approaches** provide descriptions of lesson activities to help students master each learning objective.
- **Background Information** for teachers to help contextualize the particular section of the chapter.
- **Homework Assignment** offers a series of assignments to review the previous lesson and prepare for the next lesson.
- **Extending the Lesson** includes project ideas, research topics, journal entries, and the like.
- **For Enrichment** activities are offered for some of the sections of each chapter. These optional ideas provide suggestions for long-term projects and opportunities to extend knowledge and appreciate certain topics covered in the text.
- **For Review and Knowing Christ through Scripture Answers** are provided for the questions included within the Student Text.
- **Chapter Tests** usually contain a sample test of twenty-five items. (The tests are included in the "Resource Section" and also online.) These tests use a variety of question types (true/false, matching, fill-ins, multiple choice, short answers, essay, etc.). It is highly recommended that teachers also construct their own quizzes and tests to evaluate the specific learning outcomes of their courses.

A helpful new feature of the revised version of *Our Catholic Faith: Living What We Believe* is the addition of the activity categories for each Bell Ringers, Teaching Approaches, Extending the Lesson activity, and For Enrichment activity. These categories include:

- **Direct Instruction** indicates that a teacher will describe certain information or summarize material in the Student Text using lecture, PowerPoint presentations, instruction at the board, and other means of teaching students directly.
- **Class Discussion** suggests topics and questions for the class to discuss in response to the Student Text.
- **Class Activity** offers creative activities that involve the entire class.
- **Group Discussion** suggests topics for pairs or groups to discuss and share with the class.
- **Group Activity** offers directions for groups to gather and work together to accomplish certain tasks.
- **Group Presentation** suggests opportunities for groups to share their work with the rest of the class.
- **Writing Assignment** offers students the opportunity to respond to questions in writing.
- **Journal Assignment** provides students with prompts to reflect and respond in their journals.
- **Individual Activity** suggests creative assignments for students to complete on their own.
- **Student Presentations** are opportunities for students to share their work on in-class projects or Ongoing Assignments.
- **Video Presentations** suggest films and clips to show students as well as suggested topics for discussion.
- **Guest Speaker** provides suggestions for invited guests to speak on certain topics.
- **Chapter Test** suggests times to provide students with the opportunity to complete the Chapter Test.
- **Prayer Experience** presents various opportunities and instruction for prayer for individuals, groups, and the entire class.

Online Access

Ave Maria Press offers a variety of online resources for every textbook. Go to the "Classroom Resources" page at www.avemariapress.com to see crossword puzzles, chapter reading guides, PowerPoint presentations, handouts, and other resources. Access to specific material from the Student Text and Teacher's Wraparound Edition of *Our Catholic Faith: Living What We Believe* is available online as well. Send an e-mail to reled@nd.edu to request the teacher-only material. You will receive an e-mail response with links to files saved in both PDF and Word formats.

Notes

1. *In Support of Catechetical Ministry* (Washington, DC: United States Conference of Catholic Bishops, 2000).

2. *General Directory for Catechesis* (Washington, DC: United States Conference of Catholic Bishops, 1997).

3. Secretariat for Family, Laity, Women & Youth, *Renewing the Vision of Youth Ministry* (Washington, DC: United States Conference of Catholic Bishops, 1993).

4. *Sharing the Light of Faith*. The National Catechetical Directory for Catholics of the United States (Washington, DC: United States Conference of Catholic Bishops, 1979).

5. *Guidelines for Doctrinally Sound Catechetical Materials* (Washington, DC: United States Conference of Catholic Bishops, 1990), 4.

Introduction:
Our Catholic Faith

Our Catholic Faith

Overview of the Introduction

The Introduction to *Our Catholic Faith: Living What We Believe* presents faith as one of the theological virtues that enables us to respond to God's Revelation. More specifically, as the *Catechism of the Catholic Church* teaches, it is a personal adherence to God that involves "an assent of the intellect and will to the self-revelation of God [that he] has made through his deeds and words" (176). This type of faith leads to personal friendship with the Lord Jesus, the most important goal of our catechesis with youth—to lead them to Jesus Christ, our Lord and Savior.

Among the truths God has revealed is that each person, including in a special way the students who are readers of the text, is a precious, unique child of God worth dying for. This is the Good News Jesus came to proclaim in word and deed and what his Church continues to teach today. It is a recurring, important theme found throughout the Student Text.

In this chapter, the students read that faith is a theological virtue that empowers us to respond to God's free self-communication (Revelation) and that faith makes it possible for us to accept Jesus Christ and to partake of the life of the Holy Spirit. Our faith response must be free. Also, faith is not just an individual act, but also an act of the Church. It is through the Church's Sacrament of Baptism that we are united to this family of faith who believes in Jesus as Lord.

The Introduction to the Student Text also reviews some of the major beliefs of the Catholic faith, teachings that are rooted in Scripture and Tradition and guided by the

Resources

 ### Audiovisual Materials

Chariots of Fire

A true story of two world-class runners. Of particular note is the person of Eric Liddell, who ran for God's glory, not his own. Strong statement of the role faith plays in a person's life. (124-minute feature film, DVD/VHS, Amazon.com, Gospel Films)

Mary of Nazareth

From acclaimed French film director Jean Delannoy. A perspective on the life of Jesus from the eyes of the Blessed Mother. (115-minute video, Questar, Ignatius Press)

October Sky

Based on the true story of Homer Hickman from a coal-mining town in West Virginia. After he saw the *Sputnik* in the night sky in 1957, he built his own rocket with the help of his friends. His dogged determination helped make his dream come true. Can be used to show the power of faith. (108-minute feature film, DVD, Amazon.com, Critics' Choice)

Rudy

A crowd-pleasing, inspiring film based on the true story of a young man who dreamed of playing football for the Notre Dame Fighting Irish. Shows the power of faith. (112-minute feature film, Critics' Choice, Amazon.com)

Together in Faith

The Catholic faith calls each person to know, love, and serve God in our daily lives. This video gives a brief overview of Catholicism. (20-minute video, Harcourt)

Ultimately faith is the only key to the universe. The final meaning of human existence, and the answers to the questions on which all our happiness depends, cannot be found in any other way.

—Thomas Merton in *Seeds of Contemplation*[1]

Introduction

Magisterium, the Church's official teachers. The *Catechism of the Catholic Church* is introduced as an authoritative, systematic, and comprehensive source of essential beliefs and teachings of the Catholic faith and the main reference for the Student Text.

The chapter includes a profile of two models of faith: Abraham, the father of our faith (Rom 4:16), and Mary, the Mother of God. Both Abraham and Mary are models of faith for their "yes" to God's will. Abraham was called by God to leave his home and have faith that he would be the father of many descendants, despite his old age and childlessness. The major events of Mary's life point to a person who faithfully walked with her son though she did not comprehend perfectly at the time all that was taking place. She prayed, and she served. Abraham and Mary's fiat—their "yes" to God's will—can serve as an example to all of us to be open to God's work in our lives, even though we may not fully understand what is going on. This is true faith.

Chapter Outline

- A Faith Test
- The Importance of Faith
- Knowing Christ through Scripture: Abraham, Model of Faith
- Profile of Faith: Mary, the Model Christian

Advance Preparations

- Have note cards distributed to the students in the first section of this chapter.
- Plan to play a recording of instrumental music during the Prayer Service during the Review Lesson.

Resources

Printed Materials

Bezancon, Jean-Noel, Philippe Ferlay, and Jean-Marie Onfray. *How to Understand the Creed*. New York: Crossroad, 1988.
    A treatment of the Nicene Creed in the Crossroad adult education series produced by leading French catechists. Excellent teacher background.
Bishops of Belgium. *Belief and Belonging: Living and Celebrating the Faith*. Collegeville, MN: Liturgical Press, 1990.
    A compact, highly readable, and attractively presented overview of the Catholic faith that strives to link faith, celebration, and living the Gospel.
Chaput, Archbishop Charles, OFM, Cap. *Living the Catholic Faith: Rediscovering the Basics*. Ann Arbor, MI: Servant Publications, 2001.
    Excellent and thought-provoking.
Coleman, Bill, Patty, and Lisa. *Basics of the Catholic Faith*. Mystic, CT: Twenty-Third Publications/Bayard, 2000.
    An excellent classroom resource.
Foley, Leonard, O.F.M. *Believing in Jesus*. Fourth Revised Edition. Cincinnati, OH: St. Anthony Messenger Press, 2001.
    A concise overview of the Catholic faith.
Hardon, John A., S.J. *Pocket Catholic Dictionary*. New York: Doubleday, Image Books, 1985.
    Another handy reference for both students and teachers.
Johnson, Kevin Orlin. *Why Do Catholics Do That?* New York: Ballantine Books, 1995.
Johnson, Luke Timothy. *The Creed: What Christians Believe and Why It Matters*. New York: Doubleday, 2003.
    A very good contemporary introduction to the ancient Christian creed with an attempt to relate it to today's adult living in a secular world.
Marthaler, Berard L. O.F.M. Conv. *The Creed*, rev. ed. Mystic, CT: Twenty-Third Publications, 1993.
    Highly recommended. This source will enrich your teaching of the entire book.
McBride, Alfred. *Father McBride's Teen Catechism*. Huntington, IN: Our Sunday Visitor Press, 1996.
O'Donnell, John, S.J. *A Faith You Can Live With: Understanding the Basics*. Kansas City: Sheed & Ward, 1999.
Pilarczyk, Archbishop Daniel E. *Believing Catholic*. Cincinnati, OH: St. Anthony Messenger Press, 1999.
Rohr, Richard, and Joseph Martos. *Why Be Catholic?* Cincinnati, OH: St. Anthony Messenger Press, 1989.
    A readable, honest, and interesting attempt is made to answer the question of the book's title. Addresses the positive as well as the shadow side of Catholicism. Discusses how we can be Catholic in our contemporary world.

A Faith Test

Objectives

In this lesson, students will:

- know that they are born with great worth and value in God's love.
- understand that God has destined us for an eternal life of happiness with the Blessed Trinity and our loved ones in Heaven.

Preview

St. Augustine's famous quotation—"You have created us for yourself, O God, and our hearts are restless until they rest in you"—reminds us that each person is "wonderful" in God's eyes and that our destiny is with him. This introductory text with a short story asks the students to consider why they are wonderful and how God's unconditional love differs from the conditional acceptance promoted by secular society.

Bell Ringers

- Write "Who am I?" on the board. Distribute note cards to the students. On the blank side, have them write their first and last names. On the lined side, ask them to describe themselves. Give them some suggestions, such as name, nicknames, hometown/neighborhood, birthplace, clubs/sports, hobbies, church, or favorite school subject. Have each student stand and introduce themselves to the class, and then collect the note cards. These can be used throughout the year to randomly call on students during class discussions.

Teaching Approaches

- Have the students write down a list of expectations that society, particularly in the media, has for them. For example, students might include being wealthy, powerful, thin, muscular, or a drinker. Then, have them share their lists with the class.
- Read or paraphrase the opening story in the first two paragraphs of "A Faith Test" (page 2). Ask the students to share what they think they would have done in that situation and why. Then, assign the rest of the text, "A Faith Test" (pages 2–3) for private reading.
- **Video Presentation:** Play the part of the movie *Rudy* when the priest refuses to allow Rudy on the bus to tour Notre Dame because he isn't a good enough student. (This scene is from the early part of the movie.) Then call on volunteers to share how they felt when someone doubted them and what they did about it.
- Reread the second-to-last paragraph of the text section to the students, including the quotation of St.

A Faith Test

A missionary who entered Russia soon after the collapse of the Berlin Wall recalled that before the fall of the Soviet Union, Christians had to meet in secret to pray and worship because of the totalitarian, communist government that forbid the practice of religion. On one occasion, a group of Christians had gathered in a small house to study the Bible together. Suddenly, three Soviet soldiers brandishing rifles broke down the door and forcefully entered the house. One of the soldiers announced that anyone who was not a Christian was free to leave but the others who called themselves Christians should remain in the house.

All the worshippers were terrified. After a few nerve-wracking moments, most of the people fled the house. Only a few brave souls remained. Then one of the soldiers silently closed the door and locked it. All three of the soldiers put down their rifles and sat down with the remaining believers. They explained to those who were faithful enough to testify to their belief in our Lord that they, too, were Christians and only wanted to worship with true believers.[2]

This story asks us to consider whether we would have the strength of character to pass a test of faith. Would you stay true to Jesus in the face of a threat to your life? How do you profess your faith in much safer conditions? Do you try to live it? Do you let Jesus our

Savior shine through you? Do you bring him and his Gospel to others?

One thing is for sure: our Lord Jesus remains faithful to each of us. He has given us all that we have—life, health, talents to develop, our friends, the privilege of living in a time and place where we can worship freely, and so many other gifts. Moreover, Jesus has given us the promise of eternal life. He loves us beyond what we can imagine, revealing the truth of how valuable we are to him. Consider Jesus' sacrifice on the Cross. Picture him hanging there, looking into your eyes, and proclaiming with his last breath, "You are precious to me and to my Father. I am giving my life for you. I love you!" What a powerful, life-changing message. The question remains, however: do you really believe it?

Faith is a great gift that the Holy Spirit bestows on us at Baptism. This gift enables us to enter into a loving, personal, and intimate relationship with the Blessed Trinity. The gift of faith enables us to trust in Jesus Christ and the Good News of Salvation he has won for us and communicates to us. The gift of faith allows us to believe with all our hearts the truth of the Lord's proclamation that each one of us is precious and wonderful in his eyes.

The compelling, life-affirming Gospel message goes against what so many elements in our contemporary society teach us. Advertisements, pundits, and "the beautiful people" whom the media hold up to us to admire often preach an anti-Gospel message. It goes something

Background Information

St. Augustine

Considered one of the greatest theologians in the Church, Augustine was born in northern Africa, not far from the town of Hippo, in 354. Raised by a violent and idolater father, Patricius, and his Christian and holy mother, St. Monica, Augustine had a checkered youth, studying rhetoric and entering into relations with a woman outside of marriage. After years of praying for her son, Monica was alive to witness Augustine's conversion and baptism in 387. He was later consecrated bishop of Hippo. Augustine died on August 28, 430 (his feast day). He is one of the Latin Fathers of the Church.

For Enrichment

Assign the students to find out what happened to Daniel Ruettiger (the real-life "Rudy") following his days after he attended Notre Dame up to the present. Ask them to answer the following questions: Do you think Rudy's heart remains restless? What has he done to settle his restless heart that you would do differently?

like this: "You are only worthwhile if you are good-looking, rich, live in a certain neighborhood, achieve high grades in school, are athletically superior, have a great sense of humor, or you fill-in-the-blank." All too often, your God-given worth and value are only acknowledged if you fulfill certain conditions or live up to others' expectations. Rarely will you hear the message that you are wonderful, precious, and valuable simply because you are you—a child of God with inner value and worth.

The message Christ proclaims is that we have value, dignity, and worth simply because God has made us in his image and likeness. God has destined us for an eternal life of happiness with the Blessed Trinity and our loved ones in Heaven. In the words of the great St. Augustine (AD 354–430) in his *Confessions*, "You have created us for yourself, O God, and our hearts are restless until they rest in you."

Life is filled with many deep questions that humans living before Christ had trouble answering: Why am I here? What is my destiny? What is the meaning of life and of death? Does God exist? If so, what is God like? How should I act? The Life, Death, and Resurrection of Christ answer these and other difficult questions. With Christ, human life has great and eternal meaning and dignity.

For Reflection

Imagine Jesus talking to you as a friend. What three things could he say about you that show you are valuable to him?

The Importance of Faith

Which vision of life is correct? The Christian view that holds you are a precious, unique child of God worth dying for? Or society's view that your worth is tied only to your appearance, what you can do, or how much you own?

How you answer these questions will make all the difference in your life. This textbook will make the point that Christ and his Church make, that you have great worth. Faith in Jesus Christ will help you counteract the false message that you only have value and worth if you meet certain conditions. Faith will help give you a true perspective on life and human destiny.

What is faith? Faith is a virtue. The *Catechism of the Catholic Church* defines virtue as:

An habitual and firm disposition to do the good. . . . Human virtues are firm attitudes, stable dispositions, habitual perfections of intellect and will that govern our actions, order our passions, and guide our conduct according to reason and faith. They make possible ease, self-mastery, and joy in leading a morally good life. (*CCC*, 1803–1804)

Traditionally, there are two categories of virtues: the cardinal virtues and the theological virtues. The cardinal virtues include prudence, justice, fortitude, and temperance. They get their name from the Latin word *cardo*, which means "hinge."

virtues
"Firm attitudes, stable dispositions, habitual perfections of intellect and will that govern our actions, order our passions, and guide our conduct according to reason and faith" (*CCC*, 1804).

theological virtues
Three important virtues bestowed on us at Baptism that relate us to God: *faith* (belief in and personal knowledge of God); *hope* (trust in God's Salvation and his bestowal of the graces needed to attain it); and *charity* (love of God and love of neighbor).

Homework Assignment

1. Read the text section "The Importance of Faith" (pages 3–4) through to the subsection "What Catholics Believe" (pages 6–7).

2. Search the Internet, magazines, and newspaper for advertisements depicting common expectations of society. Print or cut out one of these to bring to class.

3. Choose three of the listed Ongoing Assignments on page 10 to complete prior to the conclusion of this chapter.

Augustine. Talk about the restlessness experienced by Rudy and how he went about satisfying it. Cue the video toward the end and play the scene where Rudy enters Notre Dame Stadium and plays in his one and only game for the Fighting Irish.

-   **Journal Assignment:** Throughout this course, students will be prompted with For Reflection questions and Journal Assignments. Have them take out their journals and remind them to either put their names inside of them or decorate them in a way that they will know it is theirs. For this assignment, give the following questions: *What part of you do you feel is "not good enough?" Where did this feeling come from? Make a list of things that you like about yourself.*

-   When the students have finished journaling, read the following passages from the Bible: John 3:16 and Genesis 1:26–31. Refer to the creation account in the book of Genesis. Point out that at the end of each day, we read that "God saw that it was good." But on the sixth day—the day God created people— God saw that it was *very* good. Note that God made people in his divine image, thus giving them dignity and worth in his eyes. Challenge students to step out of their comfort zone, stand up in front of the class, and say out loud, "I am very good!"

-   **Journal Assignment:** Invite students to write a response to the For Reflection question on page 3.

-   **Class Discussion:** Invite the students to reread the final paragraph of this section. Invite students, one by one, to come to the board and write other examples of "life's most difficult questions." Call on five students to form a panel in front of the class to discuss the questions listed in the final paragraph of the section. Allow at least two panelists to share a response to each question. After some time, invite other students to take the place of one of the panelists or have them pose questions to the panelists while sitting at their desks.

-   Close by referring to the quotation by Thomas Merton at the beginning of this section. Note the importance of faith in seeking the answers to these difficult questions.

The Importance of Faith

(pages 3–5)

Objectives

In this lesson, students will:

-   know there are two categories of virtues—the cardinal virtues and the theological virtues (faith, hope, and charity, or love).

- explore the virtue of faith more closely, understanding it as the human response to God's Revelation and a gift from God that is freely accepted.

Preview

This lesson defines the virtue of faith, placing it in the category of the theological virtues. Looking at the meaning of faith more closely, it is understood as the human response to God's Revelation. Faith helps us to commit ourselves to God, both our intellects and our wills. Faith is not just an individual act; it is an act of the Church. It is faith that results in religion.

Bell Ringers

- **Small-Group Activity:** Invite students to take part in the "Reach Out" exercise on page 4. Afterward, invite each student to share what they learned about the person they met.
- Have students share the advertisements they found on the Internet, in a magazine, or in the newspaper. Post them on the wall in the classroom or on a poster board that can be hung on the wall.

Teaching Approaches

- **Writing Assignment:** Have the students write and circle the words "Faith," "Hope," and "Charity" in the middle of three separate sheets of paper. Model the creation of a mind-map (concept map) using the word Faith. Have the students offer words, phrases, and definitions they associate with faith or that they learned in their reading, and organize them in a mind-map on the board. After students understand the mind-mapping technique, have them mind-map Hope and Charity on their own.
- Review each of the teachings on faith covered on pages 4–5. Write the following on the board and then have students explain each in more depth:
  - Faith makes it possible for us to accept Jesus as Lord.
  - Faith makes it possible to partake in the life of the Holy Spirit.
  - Faith is a gift from God, but our response to faith must be freely given.

Revelation
The way God communicates knowledge of himself to humankind, a self-communication realized by his actions and words over time, most fully by his sending us his divine Son, Jesus Christ.

Many other virtues derive from these four, which we will discuss later in this book.

Faith belongs to the set of virtues known as the theological virtues (*CCC*, 1812–1828). The theological virtues are gifts from God infused into our souls. They enable us to live in relationship to the Blessed Trinity. Their origin, motive, and object is the one Triune God. The theological virtues are:

1. *Faith.* Faith enables us to believe in God and all that he has said and revealed to us. It also helps us to accept what the Church proposes for our belief, because God is truth himself. Catholics are called not only to cultivate their faith, but also to proclaim, bear witness to, and spread it to others.
2. *Hope.* The virtue of hope leads to a desire for Heaven and eternal life. It helps us trust in Christ's promises and rely on the help of the Holy Spirit and his graces, not our own strength and abilities. Hope keeps us from getting discouraged as we live the Christian life. Hope makes it possible for us to strive for true happiness and live in imitation of Christ.
3. *Charity* (love). Charity, or love, is the greatest of the virtues. Charity empowers us to love God above all things for his own sake and our neighbor as ourselves for the love of God (*CCC*,

1822). This key virtue helps us practice all the other virtues. It uplifts our human ability to love, raising it to the perfection of divine love.

More about Faith (CCC, 26; 91–100; 142–165; 176–197)

Let's explore the virtue of faith more closely. As noted, faith is a God-given virtue that helps a person firmly embrace the truly Good News of our essential goodness and wonderfulness. Faith, in fact, can be thought of as our "lifeline" to God.

Faith is the human response to God's Revelation, that is, God's free gift of self-communication. Faith, a gift of the Holy Spirit, enables us to commit ourselves to God totally, both our intellects and our wills. In addition,

1. Faith makes it possible for us to accept Jesus as Lord. It endows us with the ability to imitate his life of loving service. Because of faith we can believe God's revealed truths because he is the one who has revealed them to us.
2. Faith in Jesus makes it possible for us to partake of the life of the Holy Spirit, who testifies to us who Jesus is. Thus Christian faith proclaims belief in one God who is a Trinity of Persons: Father, Son, and Holy Spirit.
3. Faith is a gift, but our response must be free. No one can be forced to embrace faith against his or her will.

 Reach Out

Be a model of Catholic faith and hospitality. Introduce yourself to a classmate you don't know or don't know well. Find out one thing about this person that makes him or her special. Then promise yourself that during the coming school year, you will be friendly to this person and other people you may have ignored in the past.

Background Information

Abraham

According to Genesis 11:27–32, Abraham and his family had their origins in Ur, a city in the southern Euphrates Valley. From there they migrated north to Haran, the traditional home of Abraham according to the Bible. Abraham's call to move his family to Canaan is usually dated around 1800 BC. At Canaan, Abraham made a covenant with God. He would be the father of a great nation of people.

Resources

 Internet Links see www.avemariapress.com

Thus, faith is also a free human act in which our hearts and minds cooperate with God's free gift of grace.

4. Abraham and Mary are two models of faith. Abraham, the Father of Faith, obeyed God by leaving his homeland to become a pilgrim to the Promised Land. Because of his faith, God created a people through Abraham and prepared the way for the Messiah. Mary, the Mother of Christ, approached her entire life as a resounding yes to God's work. Her fidelity helped fulfill God's plan of Salvation through her Son, Jesus Christ.

Faith is an act of the Church. Faith results in religion (Latin for "binding into a relationship"). Religion binds us into a relationship with God. Our Catholic religion extends God's invitation to believe in, accept, and dedicate our lives to Christ. Because of God's love for us, at Baptism Catholics become members of the Church, which is a family of faith who believes that Jesus is Lord.

The faith of the Church comes before the faith of the individual. The faith of the Church gives life to and supports and nourishes the individual Christian. If we cooperate with faith, we are on the path to eternal life. If we ignore faith, we are subject to God's disapproval:

> Whoever believes in the Son has eternal life, but whoever disobeys the Son will not see life, but the wrath of God remains upon him. (Jn 3:36)

religion
The relationship between God and humans that results in a body of beliefs and a set of practices: creed, cult, and code. Religion expresses itself in worship of and service to God and by extension service to all people and all creation.

ecumenical council
A worldwide, official assembly of the bishops under the direction of the Pope. There have been twenty-one ecumenical councils, the most recent being the Second Vatican Council (1962–1965).

From the Documents

"The obedience of faith . . . is to be given to God who reveals, an obedience by which man commits his whole self freely to God, offering "the full submission of intellect and will to God who reveals," and freely assenting to the truth revealed by Him. To make this act of faith, the grace of God and the interior help of the Holy Spirit must precede and assist. (*The Dogmatic Constitution on Divine Revelation*, No. 5)

This passage on faith comes from the Second Vatican Council, the twenty-first **ecumenical council** of the Church, held from 1962 to1965. This council reformed the Church's liturgy. It also taught on important topics like the Church in today's world, the Church's relationship to other religions, and the role of the laity.

The Dogmatic Constitution on Divine Revelation is one of four constitutions produced at the Second Vatican Council. The document emphasizes how the Holy Spirit guides the Church by means of Sacred Tradition, Sacred Scripture, and the teaching authority of the Church. The document teaches Revelation primarily as God's self-disclosure and secondarily as God's will and intentions. The document also encourages Catholics to read the scriptural Word of God.

Type in *The Dogmatic Constitution on Divine Revelation* in an Internet search engine. Locate the document online at the Vatican website. Read chapter one of the document, and then answer these questions:

1. How does God speak to us through Jesus Christ?
2. Who is the fullness of Revelation?
3. Why did God choose to reveal himself?

- **Writing Assignment:** Direct students to the feature "Knowing Christ through Scripture: Abraham, Model of Faith" on page 6. Have the students read and complete the Scripture assignment.
- **Small-Group Activity:** Have students get into groups of three or four. Have them check their answers to the Knowing Christ through Scripture assignment. Then ask them to list one specific way Abraham's faith was a response to God's Revelation and how Abraham freely accepted the gift of faith.
- Summarize the material in the "From the Documents" feature (page 5). Point out that, indeed, a person needs God to obtain the gift of faith. Faith is a gift from God that God reveals to a person through the Church (e.g., in its Tradition and through Scripture). Encourage the students to read Chapter 1 of *The Constitution on Divine Revelation*, noting how God reveals himself to man (most especially in the person of Jesus Christ).

For Enrichment

Read "The Testing of Abraham" in Genesis 22:1–19. Rewrite the story in a modern context depicting how someone shows his or her love of God before all else.

Homework Assignment

1. Read the text subsection "What Catholics Believe," including the separate feature "Profile of Faith: Mary, the Model Christian" (pages 6–8).

2. Answer the first four For Review questions on page 7.

What Catholics Believe

(pages 6–8)

Objectives

In this lesson, students will:

- identify the essential Catholic beliefs.
- understand that Catholic beliefs and teachings are rooted in two sources of God's Revelation: Sacred Scripture and Sacred Tradition.
- know that through her "yes" to following God's will, Mary is the model of Christian faith.

Preview

The material covered in the subsections "What Catholics Believe (pages 6–7) offers a short overview of the entire course, a survey of the Catholic faith. Also, the students are reminded that Catholic beliefs and teachings are rooted in both Sacred Scripture and Sacred Tradition, which give us God's Revelation. A feature on Mary, the Mother of God, portrays her as the model Christian, the model of faith. It traces Mary's life as depicted in Scripture.

 Bell Ringers

- **Writing Assignment:** Have the students rank the top five most essential Catholic beliefs from pages 6–7 on a sheet of notebook paper.
- Read each belief on pages 6–7. Instruct the students to stand when their top Catholic belief is read and be able to explain why they chose that belief. Afterward, ask the students to share which beliefs they find most challenging and why.

KNOWING CHRIST THROUGH SCRIPTURE

Abraham, Model of Faith

The authors of the New Testament looked to the Old Testament patriarch Abraham as the great model of faith, mentioning him seventy times. Jesus himself referred to Abraham in his teachings and even made Abraham a central figure in one of his parables—the Rich Man and Lazarus (Lk 16:19–31). What was it about this Old Testament patriarch that evoked such comment and admiration?

Abram is first mentioned in Genesis 12. There we learn that God called him to leave his home in Haran in northern Mesopotamia with his wife Sarai. God made a covenant with them, promising that they would be the parents of "a host of nations" (Gn 17:5). God also changed their names to Abraham and Sarah and pledged that he would give to Abraham and his descendants the land of Canaan and that he would be their God, watching over and protecting them forever.

Abraham's faith was tested when God asked Abraham to sacrifice his beloved son, Isaac. Despite the personal sacrifice this request required, Abraham gave himself totally to God and was willing to give up his beloved son. God, however, stopped Abraham from committing the deed.

Abraham's total devotion to God became for all the Israelites and later Christians a sign of unswerving faith. Just as the Virgin Mary did not

fully understand what the angel meant when she was to conceive the Son of God, so Abraham did not fully understand what God was promising to him. Yet he believed God's Word and obeyed him.

Read the following references to Abraham. Write your answers to the corresponding questions.

Genesis 12
- What land did Abraham leave at God's command?
- What land did God promise to Abraham and his descendants?

Genesis 17
- How old was Abraham when God made the covenant with him?
- What promise did God make with Abraham?
- What was the sign of the covenant?
- Why did Abraham laugh?

Genesis 21–22
- Who was Ishmael? Through whom would God bless the descendants of Abraham?
- Name evidence that Abraham was willing to sacrifice his son.
- What did God praise about Abraham's willingness to sacrifice his son?

What Catholics Believe

The following are short summaries of Catholic beliefs. These are some of the main beliefs that make us Catholic:

- Jesus Christ is God's Son, the Savior, and the Lord.
- God is a Blessed Trinity, a communion of love, a God worthy of worship and praise.

- The Church is the Body of Christ. Catholics belong to the Communion of Saints and look to saints for inspiration and help. After Jesus himself, Mary, the Mother of God, is the exemplary model of faith.
- The Bible is God's inspired Word.
- Faith is conveyed by a living Tradition, which is guided by the Holy Spirit and authentically interpreted by the Magisterium.

For Enrichment

Use one or more of the Marian websites from www.avemariapress .com to provide more information on devotions to Mary, beliefs about Mary, and titles for Mary. Provide students the opportunity to practice praying one of the devotions they find.

- Read Mary's Magnificat in Luke 1:46–55. Make note of verses that would give hope to the poor. Explain why you chose the verses that you did.
- Complete "The Wedding at Cana" exercise on page 7.

- God can be found in everything. We experience him in a unique and powerful way through the Seven Sacraments, for example, by experiencing Christ's forgiveness in the Sacrament of Penance and by receiving the Risen Lord himself in the Sacrament of the Eucharist.
- We are open to truth wherever it is found. We invite all people to grow with the Church in holiness.
- Love and service are hallmarks of our Christian faith. We are fiercely committed to working for peace and justice.
- We are people of hope who see that we have an eternal destiny of union with our God of love.
- We are open to, and strongly defend, the gift of life in all its richness.

Our Catholic Faith: Living What We Believe is a survey of the Catholic religion. It is divided into three sections:

what we believe (the Apostles' Creed); what we hope (celebrating the liturgy and sacraments); and how we live and pray according to Christ's law of love.

Catholic beliefs and teachings are rooted in Sacred Scripture and Sacred Tradition, which together give us God's Revelation. The Magisterium, the Church's official teaching authority comprised of the Pope and bishops teaching with him, is responsible for authentically interpreting and passing on Divine Revelation to us.

In 1992, an official compendium of Catholic Church teaching was published, the *Catechism of the Catholic Church* (referenced in this text as *CCC* with the appropriate paragraph cited by number). It is an authoritative, systematic, and comprehensive source of essential beliefs and teachings of the Catholic faith. It is the primary source of reference for this text.

Magisterium
The official teaching authority of the Church. The Lord bestowed the right and power to teach in his name on Peter and the Apostles and their successors. The Magisterium is the bishops in communion with the successor of Peter, the Bishop of Rome (Pope).

Catechism of the Catholic Church
A compendium of Catholic doctrine on faith and morals published in 1992 that serves Catholics as "a sure norm for teaching the faith" and "an authentic reference text."

For Review

1. Discuss three qualities of the virtue of faith.
2. Identify *The Dogmatic Constitution on Divine Revelation.*
3. Why do both the Old and New Testaments regard Abraham as a model of faith?
4. Fill in the missing word: Abraham's example teaches us that faith in God requires that we __?__ God.
5. Define *Magisterium*.
6. Identify the *Catechism of the Catholic Church.*
7. How is Mary a model of faith, service, and prayer?
8. Define *saint*.

The Wedding at Cana

Read John 2:1–12.

Think quietly about the scene. How do you imagine Mary's demeanor as a wedding guest? What lesson does this incident teach about prayer? About service?

Background Information

Catechism of the Catholic Church

An ad hoc commission was appointed by Pope John Paul II in 1986 to prepare a catechism of the Church. On June 25, 1992, the Pope approved the work of the commission and said it would be titled the *Catechism of the Catholic Church*. Local catechisms, like the United States' *Baltimore Catechism*, have a long history in the Church. However, the *Catechism of the Catholic Church* was only the second universal, or Church-wide, catechism since the Council of Trent commissioned one in the sixteenth century in response to the Protestant Reformation. Nearly 430 years later, the publication of the *Catechism of the Catholic Church* was truly a landmark occasion. As a universal catechism, the *Catechism of the Catholic Church* is to be used as a point of reference for other local Catechisms. In general, a catechism is a text "which contains the fundamental Christian truths, formulated in a clear way so that their understanding, apprehension and lively reception are made easier."

Teaching Approaches

- Bring one or more copies of the *Catechism of the Catholic Church* to class. Provide some background on the creation and purpose of the *Catechism*. See Background Information on page 9, and the Office for the Catechism website: www.usccb.org/catechism.
- Direct students to turn to the table of contents on page v. Point out that this text is divided into three sections based, in part, on the *Catechism*: what we believe, what we hope, and how we love, and each of the beliefs on pages 6–7 will be covered in detail within the text.
- **Class Activity:** Quiz the students on their knowledge of Mary and Marian devotions. Ask the following questions. Divide the class into teams and use the questions as part of a "quiz bowl" challenge, with one representative of each team getting the chance to answer a question first for points.
  - Who are Mary's parents? (*Anne and Joachim*)
  - What ethnic origin was Mary? (*Jewish*)
  - Where did Mary appear to St. Bernadette? (*Lourdes, France*)
  - What is the date of the feast of the Assumption of Mary into Heaven? (*August 15*)
  - Recite the Memorare. (*see page 305 of the Student Text*)
  - Under which of her titles is Mary the patron saint of the United States? (*Immaculate Conception*)
  - What is the meaning of the Immaculate Conception? (*Mary was conceived and preserved from sin from the moment of her conception.*)
  - When is Mary's birthday celebrated? (*September 8*)
  - Who first said the words "Hail Mary, full of grace" to Mary? (*Elizabeth*)
  - What was the name of the angel who appeared to Mary at the Annunciation? (*Gabriel*)
- Fill in the details of Mary's life from the feature "Profile of Faith: Mary, the Model Christian" (page 8). Point out Mary's "yes" to God in agreeing to be the Mother of God. Ask: "What if God asked you to give up your current life to follow him? What might that mean? How would you respond?"

For Review Answers (page 7)

1. Faith makes it possible for us to accept Jesus as Lord; it makes it possible for us to partake in the life of the Holy Spirit; it is a gift from God that must be freely accepted; and it results in religion.

2. *The Constitution on Divine Revelation* is one of the two basic documents produced at the Second Vatican Council. It emphasizes how the Holy Spirit guides the Church by means of Sacred Tradition, Sacred Scripture, and the teaching authority of the Church.

3. Abraham was regarded as a model of faith in both the Old and New Testament because, like Mary, he believed in God's Word and obeyed him even though he did not fully understand what God was promising to him.

4. "love" or "obey"

5. The Magisterium is the Church's official teaching authority composed of the pope and bishops teaching with him. It is responsible for authentically interpreting and passing on Divine Revelation to us.

6. The *Catechism of the Catholic Church* is an official compendium of Catholic Church teaching, published in 1992. It is the primary source of reference used in this text.

7. Mary was a model of faith when she said "yes" to God's request to be the Mother of Christ. She served God by being faithful to Christ to the end of his life, no matter the hardship. Mary listened to her heart when she made these dramatic decisions in her life. She is a model of prayer.

8. A saint is a holy person who lives in union with God through the grace of Jesus Christ.

PROFILE OF FAITH: MARY, THE MODEL CHRISTIAN

Mary, the Mother of God, is the Queen of the Saints. A **saint** is a holy person who lives in union with God through the grace of Jesus Christ. Mary is the model of faith.

The biblical account of Mary's life begins in Nazareth, a small town in Galilee of Palestine. Mary was engaged to marry Joseph, a carpenter. While at prayer, the angel Gabriel appeared to her and announced that she would have a child, even though she had not had sexual relations. The angel explained:

The holy Spirit will come upon you, and the power of the Most High will overshadow you. Therefore the child to be born will be called holy, the Son of God. And behold, Elizabeth, your relative, has also conceived a son in her old age, and this is the sixth month for her who was called barren; for nothing will be impossible for God. (Lk 1:35–37)

Mary listened carefully to what the angel revealed to her. What the angel said seemed truly impossible—to have a child without having sexual relations with a man. Mary must have been afraid. Still, she trusted and loved God and believed in his power to do anything. Without hesitating, Mary responded, "Behold, I am the handmaid of the Lord. May it be done to me according to your word" (Lk 1:38). Then the angel left her.

Mary's "may it be done to me according to your word" is a powerful symbol of Christian faith. Though she certainly did not fully understand what God had in store for her, Mary said yes to God. Many times we don't fully know every detail of how God is working in our lives. But what God wants from us is not our full understanding. He wants our faith. He leads the way once we surrender to him and allow him into our life.

Luke's Gospel reports that the angel left Mary. But God never left her. She instantly conceived God's Son, physically bearing within her womb the Lord who calls each of us his friend. Mary lived the rest of her life in the very presence of God—raising Jesus, teaching him, looking out for his needs, being a good mother.

Mary's original yes to God was a demonstration of her faith. She was faithful throughout the rest of her life. She didn't give up when things got tough. She stayed with Jesus to the end, standing beneath the Cross at his horrible death. She cried the same tears any loving mother would cry at the death of a son.

Mary was faithful to Jesus in many ways. An incident described in the Gospel of Luke reveals one of these ways. When Jesus was twelve years old, he became lost from his parents while returning home from a pilgrimage to Jerusalem for the feast of Passover. He had remained in the Temple, asking and answering questions of the eminent teachers of the day.

Read Luke 2:41–52

Imagine Mary's fear and apprehension when she thought she had lost her son. Mary and Joseph did find Jesus. He then returned with them to Nazareth, where he lived under their authority. Note Mary's reaction to this incident in Luke 2:51: "His mother kept all these things in her heart." This is the Gospel's way of telling us that Mary prayed. She did not fully comprehend everything about her son. But she meditated on the events in his life and the words that he spoke.

Mary teaches us how to be faithful to Jesus Christ, simply to pray and serve. Meditate on how God speaks to you in your life. Keep his words close to your heart. And then, like Mary, take the Lord who has been given to you and serve others in his name.

Homework Assignment

1. Answer the final four For Review questions on page 7.

2. Review the highlighted vocabulary terms and definitions from throughout the chapter.

For Reflection

- Write about a time when your faith was put to the test. What did you do? How did you feel at the time?
- Locate Mary's Magnificat in Luke 1:46–55. Mary prayed this heartfelt prayer after hearing that she was to be the Mother of God. Reflect on Mary's humility. Write in your journal what it means for *you* to be humble. How can you practice the gift of humility as represented by Mary?

saint
A "holy one" of God who lives in union with God through the grace of Jesus Christ and the power of the Holy Spirit and whom God rewards with eternal life in Heaven.

CHAPTER QUICK VIEW

- We possess dignity as children of God, made in his image and likeness. (page 3)
- Faith is one of the theological virtues that relate us to the Blessed Trinity. It enables us to believe in God and all that God has revealed to us. (page 4)
- A virtue is "an habitual and firm disposition to do the good." (page 3)
- Faith results in religion, which binds us into a relationship with God. Christian faith results in the Christian religion where we believe in, accept, and dedicate our lives to Jesus Christ. (page 5)
- Faith is a response to God's Revelation, that is, his free gift of self-communication. It is a gift and requires free acceptance. (page 4)
- Abraham, from the Old Testament, is known as the Father of Faith. The best model of Christian faith is Mary, the Mother of God, who lived a faithful life of service and prayer. (page 5)
- Faith requires obedience, that is, submission of one's intellect and will to our loving God who has freely given himself to us. (page 5)
- The Magisterium of the Church is responsible for interpreting and transmitting Catholic beliefs and teachings that are found in Sacred Scripture and Sacred Tradition. (page 7)

Learning the Language of Faith

Write two sentences. Each sentence should include the glossary terms from the Introduction listed below:

- Sentence 1: ecumenical council, Magisterium, religion
- Sentence 2: saint, theological virtues

Review Lesson

Objectives

In this lesson, students will:

- review the definitions of the highlighted vocabulary terms in this chapter.
- be able to synthesize the material using the bulleted summary points.
- share a prayer reflection based on Mary's Magnificat.

 ## Preview

This lesson is designed to review the material covered in the chapter, help the students prepare for the Chapter Test, and allow time for shared and personal prayer.

 ## Bell Ringers

- Review the previous lesson by inviting the students to share responses to the final four For Review questions on page 7.
- Collect the students' Ongoing Assignments on page 10 for the Introduction.

Teaching Approaches

- **Vocabulary Review:** Use one of the following ideas to review the vocabulary words for this chapter:

  - **Small-Group Activity:** Divide the students into pairs. Have them make flash cards and challenge each other to provide correct spelling and definitions of each word.

  - **Writing Assignment:** Have the students write each word in a sentence that reflects its meaning. *Optional*: Collect and grade.

  - **Class Assignment:** Have students turn to the Learning the Language of Faith feature on page 35 and complete the crossword puzzle.

- Review the Chapter Quick View on page 9. Note and explain each of the points.

- **Guest Speaker:** Allow time for a person of faith to share with the class "what it means to be Catholic." Possible speakers: a religious sister or brother, parish priest, Catholic parent, older Catholic, teenage Catholic who is not in your class. If no speaker is available, share your personal story.

- **Prayer Service:** Have the students sit in a circle. Choose three or four students to prepare a dramatic reading of the Magnificat (Lk 1:46–55). Allow time for private reflection on the gift of humility as called for in the questions. During the time of reflection, play a recording of instrumental music. Pass a lighted candle around the circle. When a person is holding the candle, ask them to share a prayer intention for someone besides themselves. Pass the candle all the way around the circle so that everyone can share.

Ongoing Assignments

As you cover the material in this chapter, choose and complete at least three of these assignments.

1. Prepare a short report on one of the following:
   - one of the popular Catholic devotions to Mary (for example, the Rosary or a novena)
   - the meaning of three of the titles of Mary (for example, Immaculate Mother, Our Lady of Perpetual Help, Queen of Peace)
   - one of the apparitions of Mary (for example, at Lourdes or Fatima)

2. Write a letter to a person who has been a model of faith to you. Tell the person in the letter why he or she has been an inspiration. Mail your letter or deliver it in person.

3. Research the Magisterium of the Church by creating a list of the following:
   - The Popes of the twentieth and twenty-first centuries
   - The current bishop of your diocese and his last two predecessors
   - The name of your pastor and his last two predecessors

   Write a short biographical sketch of one of the above.

4. Interview one of your parents to find out answers to the following questions:
   - How has your faith helped you as a parent?
   - Who serves as a model of faith for you?
   - How has the Catholic Church nurtured your faith?

5. Create a PowerPoint presentation on key events in the life of Abraham as depicted in works of art. Research under "Genesis: Patriarchal History."

Prayer Reflection

> But without faith it is impossible to please him, for anyone who approaches God must believe that he exists and that he rewards those who seek him. (Heb 11:6)

Dear Lord,
Help strengthen my faith in you, your loving Father,
   and the Holy Spirit who guides me.
Help me believe that all that I have
   and all that I am is a gift from you.
Help me be true to my beliefs
   and to have the courage to share them with others.
Lord, I do believe.
Thank you for the gift of faith. Amen.

- *Reflection*: In what area of your life is your faith especially strong?
- *Resolution*: Those who are good witnesses to their Catholic faith have a personal relationship with Jesus Christ and a good knowledge of Catholic teachings. Resolve now to grow closer to Jesus in the coming months and to study diligently to learn more about your Catholic religion so you, too, can be a strong witness to Christ and his Church.

Homework Assignment

1. Study for the test on the Introduction.

2. Read Part I: We Believe: The Apostles' Creed (pages 11–13).

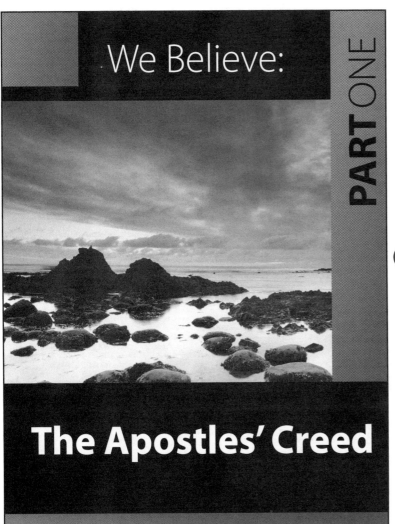

We Believe:

The Apostles' Creed

 PART ONE

Part I: **We Believe: The Apostles' Creed** (pages 11–13) **Lesson**

Objectives

In this lesson, students will:

- take a test on the material from the Introduction (pages 1–10).
- recite the Apostles' Creed and understand its importance as a summary of the Catholic faith.

Preview

After the students complete the Introduction Test, allow time for a quick preview of Part I: We Believe: The Apostles' Creed. The Student Text lists the entire Apostles' Creed on page 13. Page 13 explains how the essential Christian doctrine—the Blessed Trinity—is highlighted in the Apostles' Creed. The beliefs of the entire community are expressed and strengthened when this Creed is prayed in a group setting. Plans should be made for the students to experience the Creed as a group prayer as a conclusion to the activities and discussions that follow.

Teaching Approaches

- **Chapter Test:** Distribute the Introduction Test (starting on page 285 and also online at www.avemariapress.com). Allow enough time for completion (at least 25 minutes). Collect the tests when students are finished.

- **Writing Assignment:** When students are finished with the test, ask students to try to write their own creed by listing at least five important things they believe about God. Each statement should begin with the words "I believe . . ." Encourage them to work on expressing each belief clearly and simply and to order the beliefs by importance, by related topic, or in whatever way makes most sense to them.

- Give a brief explanation of the history of the Apostles' Creed, emphasizing its origins in the earliest days of the Church. Present evidence of its continued importance in the Church today; for example:
  - ◆ it provides the framework for Part One of the *Catechism of the Catholic Church*
  - ◆ it is an integral part of the Rite of Christian Initiation of Adults (RCIA) presented to the elect during the period of immediate preparation to receive the sacraments

- Take this opportunity to introduce students to the format of the *Catechism*. You should have copies in your classroom that are available to the students for use as reference books throughout the year. If possible, give one to each student or have them share in groups of two or more. Explain the paragraph numbering system used in the *Catechism* and ask them to find and read paragraph 194 about the Apostles' Creed (also see Background Information, on page 15). Then, point out the organization of the following chapters, which take phrases of the Creed as their titles and subjects.

- Ask the students to turn to page 13 in their textbooks and read the Creed silently for a moment. Prepare them for the lessons to come by explaining which portions of the Creed will be addressed in each of the first five chapters of this textbook:

Creed: An Expression of Faith (CCC, 166–197)

Faith results in a relationship with Jesus Christ and the Church. Faith brings about the Catholic religion, which has three aspects to it:

- what we believe,
- how we worship and pray,
- and how we live in response to our beliefs.

The *what* of Catholic faith is summarized in its various creeds, including the Church's two most popular creeds—the Nicene Creed, which is recited publicly during Sunday Mass; and the Apostles' Creed, which each believer professes personally at Baptism and at the beginning of each Rosary.

A *creed*—from the Latin word *credo* ("I believe")—is a statement of belief. A person who recites a creed makes a personal act of faith. Yet a Christian profession of faith is always made as part of the Church. Our faith comes from God through the Church; it is not something we invent. We believe as a community of believers. Professing our faith in a creed helps unite us to fellow believers. It is similar to the sense of unity and patriotism that results when citizens pledge their allegiance to the flag.

You are probably familiar with the Nicene Creed professed at Mass. It formulates essential Christian doctrines about God the Father, God the Son, God the Holy Spirit, the Church, Salvation, and human destiny. It resulted after decades of controversy begun by Arius, an Egyptian priest. Arius denied that Jesus, the Son, always existed with the Father. Therefore, he rejected the divinity of Christ.

The raging Arian controversy caused extreme dissension in the Church. Due to this, the Emperor Constantine convoked the first general (or ecumenical) council at Nicea in 325. One of its major achievements was to reaffirm clearly the divinity of Jesus by issuing the Nicene Creed. The second ecumenical council, the Council of Constantinople (381), endorsed and expanded this creed. The Nicene Creed has served as an excellent summary of Catholic faith ever since.

Based on Part I of the *Catechism of the Catholic Church*, Chapters 1 to 5 of this text are organized around another faith summary, the Apostles' Creed, which was developed between the second and ninth centuries. The Apostles' Creed is firmly rooted in an early baptismal creed used in Rome in the second century. This is significant because Peter, the first of the Apostles and the Christ-appointed leader of the Church, came to Rome to establish the Church there. Thus, the great authority of the Apostles' Creed goes all the way back to the theological formulas that arose during the time of Peter (the first Pope) and the Apostles.

The Apostles' Creed is simple, short, logically ordered, and prayerful. It highlights the essential Christian doctrine of the Blessed Trinity by proclaiming faith in:

I believe in God, the Father almighty, creator of Heaven and earth.	**Chapter 1**
I believe in Jesus Christ, his only Son, our Lord. He was conceived by the power of the Holy Spirit, and born of the Virgin Mary. He suffered under Pontius Pilate, was crucified, died, and was buried. He descended to the dead. On the third day he rose again. He ascended into Heaven, and is seated at the right hand of the Father. He will come again to judge the living and the dead.	**Chapter 2**
I believe in the Holy Spirit,	**Chapter 3**
the holy catholic Church,	**Chapter 4**
the communion of saints, the forgiveness of sins, the resurrection of the body, and the life everlasting. Amen.	**Chapter 5**

- the first Divine Person (the almighty and eternal God the Father) and the work of creation;
- the second Divine Person (Jesus Christ, God-made-man) and his work of Redemption;
- and the third Divine Person (the Holy Spirit), who is the origin and source of sanctification that comes to us through Christ's one, holy, catholic, and apostolic Church (*CCC*, 190).

The Apostles' Creed

I believe in God, the Father almighty,
Creator of heaven and earth,
and in Jesus Christ, his only Son,
our Lord,
who was conceived
by the Holy Spirit,
born of the Virgin Mary,
suffered under Pontius Pilate,
was crucified, died and was buried;
he descended into hell;
on the third day he rose again
from the dead;
he ascended into heaven,
and is seated at the right hand
of God the Father almighty;
from there he will come to judge
the living and the dead.
I believe in the Holy Spirit,
the holy catholic Church,
the communion of saints,
the forgiveness of sins,
the resurrection of the body,
and life everlasting. Amen.

Comparing the Creeds

Refer to the Nicene Creed on page 285. In your journal, note five ways the Nicene Creed expands the Apostles' Creed.

Homework Assignment

Read the text section "One, True God" (pages 16–17).

Background Information

The *Catechism of the Catholic Church* teaches about the Apostles' Creed:

> *The Apostles' Creed* is so called because it is rightly considered a faithful summary of the Apostles' faith. It is the ancient baptismal symbol of the Church of Rome. Its great authority arises from the fact that it is "the Creed of the Roman Church, the See of Peter, the first of the apostles, to which he brought the common faith." (*CCC*, 194)

Extending the Lesson

Small-Group Activity: Have the students memorize the Apostles' Creed on page 13 and take turns reciting it with a partner. *Option:* Divide the class into groups of six. Have the students take turns going around the group reciting the tenets of the Creed.

Video Presentation: The video *The Apostles' Creed: Knowing What We Believe* (95 minutes, Paraclete Press, 2003) provides an ecumenical look at what living the Creed entails. Consider showing some or all of the presentation to the students.

Introduction Test Answers

All questions are worth 4 points each.

Part 1: True or False

1. F
2. T
3. F
4. F
5. T
6. F
7. T
8. F
9. T
10. T

Part 2: Multiple Choice

11. B
12. B
13. C
14. C
15. A

Part 3: Short Fill-ins

16. virtue
17. Revelation
18. Magisterium
19. saint
20. Blessed Mother Mary

Part 4: Short Answers

21–22. There are many acceptable answers. The students should acknowledge belief in Jesus as God's Son, the central dogma of the Blessed Trinity, Mary as the exemplar of Christian faith, the Church as the Body of Christ, the inspiration of the Bible, the need for love and service. Possible answers are found in the Student Text in the subsection on "What Catholics Believe" (pages 6–7).

23–25. Answers may include:
- Faith makes it possible for us to accept Jesus as Lord.
- Faith makes it possible to partake in the life of the Holy Spirit.
- Faith is a gift from God, but our response to faith must be freely given.
- Faith results in religion.
- Mary and Abraham are two models of faith.

1 Our Loving God: Father and Creator

Overview of the Chapter

The focus of Chapter 1 is God the Father. The chapter begins by treating various beliefs about God, some from the viewpoint of atheists, agnostics, deists, and so forth. In today's increasingly secular society, Christians are faced with the challenge of proving to others that God exists. Pope Benedict XVI addressed this issue in his encyclical *Spe Salvi* by arguing that without home in God, atheism turns to humanity as the source of morality, thus establishing today's moral relativism. This is the challenge before this and the next generation of believers.

Faith in God is presented as reasonable, the conclusion drawn by the vast majority of people. A story is told about Mahatma Gandhi. An atheist approached him to enlist Gandhi's aid in organizing and promoting an anti-God society. Gandhi replied, "It amazes me to find an intelligent person who fights against something which he does not at all believe exists."

It is intelligent to believe in God, and the so-called proofs for God's existence show this. The chapter presents all five "proofs" for God's existence, so carefully presented by one of the Church's great theologians, St. Thomas Aquinas. (His remarkable life is also chronicled in this chapter.) "Heart proofs" for God's existence are discussed because "the desire for God is written in the human heart, because man is created by God for God" (*CCC*, 27).

Our Loving God: Father and Creator

Questions of God's existence are a prelude to the belief that God, who is both transcendent and immanent, has revealed himself to humans. The heart of the chapter treats God's Divine Revelation through salvation history. The chapter discusses how God revealed himself through covenants in the history of the Chosen People and how he promised to send a messiah. It discusses how Sacred Scripture and Sacred Tradition, important terms that are defined in the chapter, are two fonts of the single "Deposit of Faith." They reveal that God is a God of love and of truth. More specifically, the Old Testament shows that God revealed himself as Yahweh, a merciful, creative, loyal, passionate, and loving God who chose for him a people to draw all of humanity to himself.

The Apostles' Creed reveals only one of God's divine attributes: omnipotence. The chapter adds to this by providing Aquinas's famous list of God's qualities: unique, infinite and omnipotent, eternal, immense, embracing all, immutable, utterly simple, personal, and holy.

Scripture also reveals God as a Trinity of Persons, a topic to be treated in more detail in Chapter 3 of the Student Text. The present chapter focuses on the First Person, God the Father, whom Jesus said we can address as *Abba*. Jesus is the unique Son, but we are privileged to be invited by him into the intimacy of the divine family. Although we should address God as Father, students learn that God is pure Spirit beyond the human distinction of male and female. Images of motherhood also appear in Scripture to help us understand the nature of God's self-sacrificing love for his children (see *CCC*, 239).

An activity part of the chapter requires students to read Genesis's first and second creation accounts. In these biblical passages, students will learn some important truths about the loving Creator of Heaven and earth, of all that is seen (our beautiful world) and the unseen (the world of angels and demons). He is an awesome God who created out of nothing. He both transcends his creation and intimately sustains it. He guides it through divine providence. He creates humans in his image and likeness, creatures of incomparable worth, males and females who come into existence out of love and who are destined for love.

Salvation history reveals that humans are fundamentally good; however, we have a fallen human nature. Original Sin and its effects are discussed. Happily, the Good News of God's promise to send a savior to rescue us and restore humanity's proper relationship to God is the high point of Divine Revelation in the Old Testament. This promise, of course, is fulfilled in the coming of Jesus Christ, the subject of Chapter 2 of the Student Text.

Chapter 1 concludes with the answers to two questions that can help students explain their faith to others: "Why is there evil in the world if the creator God is all-good? Does God's omniscience impinge on human freedom?"

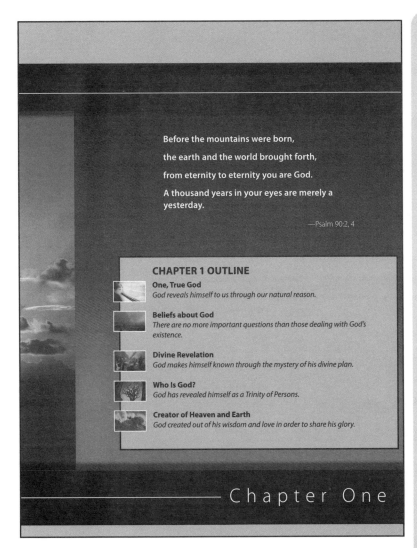

Before the mountains were born,

the earth and the world brought forth,

from eternity to eternity you are God.

A thousand years in your eyes are merely a yesterday.

—Psalm 90:2, 4

CHAPTER 1 OUTLINE

One, True God
God reveals himself to us through our natural reason.

Beliefs about God
There are no more important questions than those dealing with God's existence.

Divine Revelation
God makes himself known through the mystery of his divine plan.

Who Is God?
God has revealed himself as a Trinity of Persons.

Creator of Heaven and Earth
God created out of his wisdom and love in order to share his glory.

Chapter One

Resources

 ### Audiovisual Materials

Bruce Almighty
   This fictional and funny film tells the tale of Bruce Nolan (Jim Carrey), who learns valuable lessons about life, love, and dependence on God. Bruce struggles with the effects of being God for a few days and realizes he is not up to the challenge (102-minute feature film, DVD, Universal Studios, Amazon.com).

Cloud of Witnesses: Thomas Aquinas/Early Reformers
   Part 1 of this video was produced in Roccasecca, Italy, the birthplace of Thomas Aquinas. It presents the world of the Middle Ages when Aquinas struggled with his faith versus scientific reason (40-minute video, Cokesbury).

Finding God in All Things
   Produced in association with Loyola Productions, this video reveals how God can be found at all times and in all things—in times of joy and pain, in Mass and the sacraments, and in everyday life. Study guide included (22-minute video, Videos with Values).

Inherit the Wind
   The classic story of the Scopes Monkey Trial where the infallibility of the biblical text is debated. Provides an excellent context for a discussion of the Catholic approach to biblical inspiration (128-minute feature film, DVD, Critic's Choice Video and DVD; Amazon.com).

Nature's Serenade: The Four Seasons
   A spectacularly filmed video of many beautiful nature scenes set to Antonio Vivaldi's "The Four Seasons." A wonderful meditation on the marvels of God's creation (46-minute videocassette, Questar, Inc., Reader's Digest, Amazon.com).

continued on page 19

Chapter Outline
- One, True God
- Beliefs about God
- Divine Revelation
- Who Is God?
- Creator of Heaven and Earth

Advance Preparations
Note the Ongoing Assignments on page 36. Decide how you will assign one or more of these projects and what the due date will be. You may also consider weighing the grade on each of the assignments based on degree of difficulty. Encourage the students to begin the assignment early in the coverage of Chapter 1.

One, True God (ST pages 16–17)
- Invite an adult who has converted to the Catholic faith to speak to the students about his or her faith in God for the Guest Speaker on page 18.
- A clip of the movie *Bruce Almighty* for the Video Presentation on page 18.

Beliefs about God (ST pages 17–22)
- Bring blank index cards for the Individual Assignment on page 20.
- Have the video *Cloud of Witness: Thomas Aquinas/Early Reformers* available for the optional Extending the Lesson Video Presentation on page 22.

Divine Revelation (ST pages 22–25)
- Blank index cards for the Individual Activity on page 26.

Who Is God? (ST pages 26–28)
- A collection of images of Jesus from the Internet for the Direct Instruction on page 28.
- Clips of God's appearance to Moses in the burning bush for the Video Presentation on page 29.
- Small bags or bowls for the Class Activity on page 29.
- Sheets of poster board for the Class Activity on page 28.
- Copies of Chapter 1, Handout 1 "My Father Is a Good Man" (starting on page 285 and also online at www.avemariapress.com) for the Writing Assignment on page 29.

Creator of Heaven and Earth (ST pages 28–32)
- Copies of Chapter 1, Handout 2 "Creation Quiz" (starting on page 285 and also online at www.avemariapress.com) for the Individual Activity on pages 30–31.
- A large handheld mirror, a small container of mud or wet clay, a bottle of water, a large bowl, and a few paper towels available for the Class Activity on page 33.
- Blank index cards or copies of Chapter 1, Handout 3 "Sample Memory Cards" (starting on page 285 and also online at www.avemariapress.com) for the Class Activity on page 36.

Chapter 1 Test Lesson
- Copies of the Chapter 1 Test (starting on page 285 and also online at www.avemariapress.com).

One, True God (pages 16–17)

Objectives

In this lesson, the students will:
- review the main tenets of the Apostles' Creed.
- analyze personal beliefs about God.

Preview

This introductory chapter focuses on God the Father. Although we may not be able to see him, God is real and he is with us. The students will also complete an activity to help gauge their own beliefs about God and to continue to understand essential Catholic beliefs about God.

Bell Ringers

- **Writing Assignment:** Have students make a list of evidence that God is real and a second list of arguments and evidence that God is not real.
- **Class Discussion:** When students are finished, ask them to share their most convincing arguments and copy them on the board. Discuss why certain arguments on both sides seem reasonable.

Teaching Approaches

- **Guest Speaker:** Invite an adult convert to Catholicism to speak with your class about his or her experience. Ask them to focus on their journey to belief in God and to share their memories of the Presentation of the Creed. You can help them to prepare their talk by giving them a list of questions you would like them to answer, such as the following:
  - How old were you when you became a Catholic?
  - When did you first begin to believe in God?
  - What does the Apostles' Creed mean to you?
  - How were you presented with the Creed? What do you remember of the ceremony?
  - Do you still have your copy? Where do you keep it?
- **Video Presentation:** Review the opening story about the boy on the train on page 16. Ask a student to describe the meaning of the story. Play the part of the movie *Bruce Almighty* where the main character, Bruce Nolan (Jim Carrey), is driving, frantically cursing God for not answering his prayers. In this scene, God reveals himself in many ways, but Bruce is unable to notice.
- **Journal Assignment:** Have the students turn to the For Reflection feature on page 17. Invite them to write a response in their journals. If they have trouble, remind them of the opening story or the movie clip that you showed.
- **Class Activity:** Post large papers or signs in the four corners of the classroom labeled "Strongly Agree," "Agree," "Disagree," and "Strongly Disagree."

One, True God

Once there was a young boy traveling in a train car unattended by an adult. An elderly gentleman noticed that the child was all alone and began to chat with him.

"Are you traveling by yourself?"

The youngster replied, "Yes, sir."

"How far are you going?"

"To the end of the line."

"Aren't you afraid to take such a long trip all alone?"

"Not at all."

"Why not?"

"Because my daddy is the engineer."³

What the elderly gentleman could not see with his naked eye was that even though the boy seemed to be isolated and alone, he really was not. Humans are never alone, even in the darkest of circumstances. God is always present to us, from the very first moment of our existence until our last breath. Just as the elderly man did not recognize that the boy's father was really nearby and leading the journey, some people today do not see how God is present and active in our lives.

atheist
A person who denies the existence of God.

We need never fear the journey if we realize that God is our Father, a loving Father, and that he is in charge, directing us to our destination. Just as the engineer is invisible to the passengers, we cannot directly see how God is leading us on. But he is. The boy in our story seemed alone. However, he was not lonely because he knew his father was with him. So it is with God and us. We will never be lonely and fearful because we believe that God is everywhere and that he is in charge and leading us, if we but let him. We need to have faith, put our lives in his hands, and enjoy the life journey by frequently recalling God's presence and guidance and then by noticing and helping the people around us on our journey together.

Not everyone, of course, agrees that there is a Creator of the universe who guides it and is constantly present to it. For example, in the recent decades, several prominent atheists have published popular books that ridicule religion and believers. Atheists deny the existence of God.

In contrast to this view, this chapter will show that to believe in God is

Homework Assignment

Read the section "Beliefs about God" (pages 17–22).

Extending the Lesson

Read 1 Kings 19:9–13. In this story, Elijah retreats to a cave in Mount Horeb where he witnesses God pass by, not in the wind, or an earthquake, or in a fire, but in a whisper. Have students suggest what they think this Scripture passage is trying to say about God.

eminently reasonable. As Psalm 19:2 puts it, "The heavens declare the glory of God; the sky proclaims its builder's craft." This chapter will also discuss how God revealed himself not only as the Creator of all that exists, but also as a loving Father who entered into a relationship with the magnificent creatures he made. Belief in the one true God is central to all other aspects of our Catholic faith. He is the God we profess in the Apostles' Creed.

For Reflection

Think of and share an appropriate symbol for your own life journey.

Beliefs about God

Few questions are more important than the question of God's existence. Through history, the vast majority of people have worshiped some kind of deity. For example, the ancient Egyptians, Greeks, Romans, Aztecs, and many other civilizations all had involved systems revolving around belief in gods.

Today, reasonable estimates conclude that over 90 percent of people around the world believe in some type of God.

The number of people who belong to the world's great religions attests to this. Christianity, Judaism, and Islam together claim over 50 percent of the world's population. They are all **monotheistic** religions, that is, they believe in one (*mono*) God (*theos*). On the other hand, popular Hinduism is **polytheistic**, that is, holding belief in many gods and goddesses. Buddhism, though not believing in a personal god, does hold that there is a sole Ultimate Reality in the universe.

monotheistic
Religions that believe that there is only one God. Christianity, Judaism, and Islam are the three great monotheistic world religions.

polytheistic
Religions that believe in multiple gods and goddesses. The ancient Greeks and Romans were polytheistic, as is the Hindu faith.

God Statements

Here are different statements that reflect various ideas people hold about God and his existence. Analyze each one. Why do you accept or reject any of the statements? Which of the statements must a Catholic believe? Which of the statements are, in your judgment, clearly false?

1. God exists and makes a difference in my life. He is interested in me and concerned about my welfare.
2. Although God exists, I cannot imagine how he could be interested in me. I am like a grain of sand in an infinite universe. How could an infinite, all-powerful Being care about me?
3. How can you say there is a God when there is so much innocent suffering, like victims of terrorist attacks, natural disasters, or ravaging diseases? In the words of the ancient philosopher Epicurus, *"Is God willing to prevent evil, but not able? Then he is not omnipotent. Is he able, but not willing? Then he is malevolent. Is he both able and willing? Then whence cometh evil? Is he neither able nor willing? Then why call him God?"*
4. Science will one day explain the "mysteries" of the universe. There is no need to invent a God to explain what we don't know today.
5. "God is not what you imagine or what you think you understand. If you understand, you have failed" (St. Augustine, *De Trinitate*).
6. Since no one can definitely show there is a God, why not simply say, "I don't know if God exists or not"?
7. "A baby is God's opinion that the world should go on" (Carl Sandburg, 1878–1967).
8. Jesus is God speaking in a language that humans can understand. He is God, my Lord and Savior!

Read the first statement from the "God Statements" feature on page 17. Direct the students to move to the part of the room that shows whether they agree or disagree with the statement. Call on students in each part of the room to explain why they agree or disagree. Repeat for all of the statements and add some statements to continue the discussion.

Beliefs about God (pages 17–22)

Objectives

In this lesson, students will be able to:

- distinguish between theists (monotheists, polytheists, and deists), atheists, and agnostics.
- explain Aquinas's five "proofs" for the existence of God and evaluate how compelling they find those proofs.
- apply the four proofs offered in this section to their own lives.

Preview

This lesson examines the logical proofs for God's existence. Atheists and agnostics make intellectual arguments against the existence of God. This lesson will equip students with the knowledge and ability to logically support the existence of God with reasonable arguments.

Bell Ringers

- **Journal Assignment:** Write the following two questions on the board before students arrive:

Audiovisual Materials continued from page 17

Nature's Symphony
Outstanding nature scenes from many famous national parks set to the music of Tchaikovsky, Strauss, Mozart, Puccini, Grieg, and Mussorgsky. Excellent meditation on God's wondrous creation (60-minute videocassette, Questar, Inc., Reader's Digest video, Amazon.com).

Oh God
A humorous and at times insightful parallel to the story of Moses. A grocery clerk is chosen by God to speak his word to the people. More reverent treatment of God than Jim Carrey's 2003 movie, *Bruce Almighty* (104-minute DVD, Critics Choice Video & DVD, Amazon.com).

The Prince of Egypt
Dreamworks's 1998 animated retelling of Moses, the Exodus, and the giving of the Law is appropriate for re-creating this dramatic biblical story.

Surprised by God: Classic Insight Dramas: God in the Dock, The Long Road Home, Missing Person's Bureau
God in the Dock: "In a class action suit, God is placed on trial for all the pain, injustice, and misery suffered by mankind. The results are surprising" (video, Paulist Press).

The Ten Commandments
Cecile B. DeMille's 1950s classic starring Charlton Heston with Yul Brenner and an all-star cast.

Wonders of God's Creation
A condensed version of a three-video set that presents the beauty, wonder, and miracle of God's creation in an unforgettable way (100-minute video, Questar, Inc., Ignatius Press).

Resources

Internet Links see www.avemariapress.com

"What makes you happy? For how long does your happiness last?" Have students spend a few minutes answering the questions in their journals. If you have time, you can encourage students to share some of their answers. This will help you get to know your students better.

- **Class Discussion:** Ask the students to follow up on the discussion by writing or sharing how their ideas about happiness would change if they did not believe in an eternal life. For example, ask: "How does a belief in God and eternal life affect your ideas about happiness?"

Teaching Approaches

- **Individual Assignment:** Briefly introduce the key terms from this section of the text. Have students create "picture cue" flash cards to help them study and recall the meaning of the terms. On one side, have them write the definition of the term. On the other side, have them write the word and draw a picture to help them recall the definition of the term. For example, for the term polytheistic a student might draw many stick-figure gods and goddesses, and for monotheistic they might draw the same picture with all of the gods and goddesses crossed out except one.

- **Class Discussion:** Return to the list of beliefs about God found on page 17. Ask students to identify which statements correspond to terms they have just defined. (Statements 1, 2, and 5 come from a theist's perspective; statements 3 and 4 from an atheist's; and statement 6 from an agnostic's.)

- **Class Activity:** Continue the lesson by referring to the text subsection "Intellectual Proofs for God's Existence" (page 19). Scatter five or six different statements like the following across the board:

  - I believe the sun is shining today.
  - I believe that the square root of 529 is 23.
  - I believe that Republicans (or Democrats) do a better job running this country.
  - I believe my mother loves me.
  - I believe I am a good listener.
  - I believe that honesty is the best policy.
  - I believe scientists will find a cure for cancer.

Ask the students to share some of the things they believe and add them to the list. Then ask them to look at all the different beliefs they have shared and consider how they would go about proving each of them. For example, beliefs about the weather can often be confirmed by looking out of the window. Mathematical truths can be proven or disproven by "doing the math." However, many other beliefs are not so easy to justify. Ask the students how they would go about proving some of the beliefs written on the board. What is the evidence that

Deism
The belief that God did create the universe but that he takes no further interest in it.

agnostics
People who claim that God's existence cannot be known.

Some who label themselves as believers take a more philosophical approach to religion. An example is Deism (illustrated in the second statement in the exercise "God Statements"). Many of the founding fathers of the United States of America (including George Washington, Benjamin Franklin, and Thomas Jefferson) were Deists who thought of God as a watchmaker or absentee landlord. In other words, the Deists believed that God created the universe by "winding it up" and then staying outside his creation while it "worked" on its own. Most Deists do not think God destined a special people to know him, nor do they believe that God performs miracles by becoming involved in his creation.

A recent study found that 1.6 percent of Americans claim to be atheists, while 2.4 percent describe themselves as agnostics.[4]

Atheists are people who do not believe in the existence of God, supernatural beings, or in Heaven or Hell. (The third and fourth statements in the exercise on page 17 illustrate some of their reasons.) Many atheists are also *secular humanists*. Secular humanists claim that the world can operate without any recourse to God. Humanism makes the human person and human achievement the center of the universe.

Related to atheists are agnostics (from a Greek word that translates to "don't know"). Agnostics hold that God's existence cannot be proved or disproved. (The sixth statement in the exercise reflects this view.) Agnostics answer "I don't know" when asked if they believe in God and usually act as though God does not exist. Divorced from religion, some atheists and agnostics live a hedonistic life in which the pursuit of pleasure acts as their god.

In contrast to the claims of atheists and agnostics, to believe in God is eminently reasonable. The fact that so many people through the ages have believed in God and have practiced some kind of religion that involves prayer, ritual, sacrifice, and an ethical code is a strong indicator that humans have a religious nature. Humans intuit that there is some Power in the universe much greater and more awesome than themselves.

But what about the great variety of religions? Does the fact that there are so many varying beliefs about God and differences in worship and doctrine disprove God's existence? Not really. Rather, these differences point out that the human intellect can discover a Supreme Being, but that God's complete identity remains a mystery, only to be discovered with God's direct help or revelation. In fact, the Church teaches "by natural reason man can know God with certainty, on the basis of his works" (*CCC*, 50). St. Paul also understood this to be true:

> For what can be known about God is evident . . . because God made it evident. . . . Ever since the creation of the world, his invisible attributes of eternal power and divinity have been able to be understood and perceived in what he has made. (Rom 1:19–20)

There is no ironclad way of proving God's existence. But there *are* signs all around us that point to God. Intelligent people can discover these signs, reflect on them, and reasonably conclude that they point to a Supreme Being. Some of these signs appeal to the intellect, others appeal to the heart or feelings.

Intellectual Proofs for God's Existence

Throughout human history many excellent arguments have been advanced that demonstrate God's existence. St. Thomas Aquinas's (1225–1274) ideas (based on the Greek philosopher Aristotle) provide us with five "proofs" for the existence of God:

1. *The Unmoved Mover.* There is motion in the world (for example, neutrons, electrons, protons, atoms, etc.). Whatever is in motion had to be moved by something else. This "something else" also must have been moved by Something or Someone. Continue imagining back to the beginning of time, and we must conclude there was a First Mover, an Unmoved Mover, which is God.

2. *First Cause.* Nothing causes itself. For example, a painting comes about from an artist who was brought into existence by her parents. Who caused these parents? Keep going back to the beginning, and you must conclude there was a First Cause or Uncaused Cause that was eternal. This Being we call God. Today, even those who accept the Big Bang theory of the origin of the universe are forced to ask questions about where the primeval matter that started everything came from. The only logical answer is a Divine Being, who made it.

3. *Everything Comes from Something* (i.e., "the cosmological argument"). "Nothing" cannot create "something." Therefore, we are forced to conclude there must be one necessary, eternal Being (God) who always was and brought other beings into existence.

4. *Supreme Model.* Persons and things in this world have different *degrees* of qualities like goodness, truth, beauty, justice, and so forth. But we can only speak of different degrees of these qualities by comparing them to a Supreme Model or reference point. This perfect model of goodness, truth, and beauty is the perfect Being we call God.

5. *Grand Designer.* There is a beauty, immensity, symmetry, and power in our world that forces us to conclude that a Grand Designer made it all. A simple spider spinning its web, a beaver building its dam, the earth rotating around the sun, the chemical mix that produces life, the awesome process of human reproduction—all these and countless other realities suggest a God who implanted laws in the universe to make it work right. G. K. Chesterton once said, "Show me a watch without a watchmaker, then I'll take a universe without a Universe-Maker."

A good application of St. Thomas's five proofs is to ask the simple question, "How did we humans get here?" First, scientists have yet to explain how life could have evolved from matter. Second, statisticians say it is virtually impossible for intelligent, human life to appear by mere chance. Third, when we look at the course of human development, we can detect a hidden but powerfully present Intelligence that is leading and guiding us. The mystery of human life and history *has* to be rooted in the Mystery at the heart of the universe.

Heartfelt Proofs for God's Existence

"The desire for God is written in the human heart, because man is created by God and for God" (*CCC*, 27). We see this deep yearning for God reveal itself in many ways, including:

1. *An unquenchable thirst for joy and happiness.* We all want to be happy. We spend a lot of our time and energy doing and getting things that we think will make us happy. Yet our happiness fades, and we soon find ourselves

their mother loves them? How do they know someone is a good listener? Is it possible to "prove" that a particular event will happen in the future? End with a short discussion on which beliefs are reasonable, even though they cannot be "proved," through the use of our senses or our intellect.

- **Direct Instruction:** Next, erase the board and write, "I believe that God exists." When you begin your explanation of Aquinas's five logical proofs, list each beneath the statement you have already written. Point out that these are all proofs that appeal to a person's intellect or reason. They try to show that it is reasonable to believe in God.

- **Writing Assignment:** Direct the students to re-read the text section "Intellectual Proofs for God's Existence" (page 19) and write one paragraph explaining which of the proofs they find most compelling and why. Consider having students add to their "picture cue" flash cards.

- **Class Discussion:** Use the experience from the class assignment to lead a discussion of the four heartfelt proofs of God's existence listed on pages 19–21. Include the following idea in your lecture:

  The uniting principle behind each of these four "proofs" is that God uses our very human experiences to prepare us to know and understand him. The happiness we feel when spending time with our friends is a hint of the happiness we can know spending time with God. The beauty we find in nature is a dim reflection of the beauty of Heaven. The love we feel in our families and from our friends is like the love God wants to share with us.

Resources

 ## Printed Materials

Boadt, Lawrence. *Reading the Old Testament: An Introduction*. New York: Paulist Press, 1984.

A time-tested introduction to the Old Testament. Detailed bibliographies provided.

Brown, Raymond E., S.S., Joseph Fitzmyer, S.J. and Roland E. Murphy, O. Carm. *The New Jerome Biblical Commentary*. Englewood Cliffs, NJ: Prentice Hall, 1990.

An essential one-volume biblical commentary. The background articles are exceptional.

The Catholic Study Bible. New York: Oxford University Press, 1990.

Includes the text of the *New American Bible* with excellent notes. This resource is suitable for high school students and would be an excellent companion to the course.

Daley, Michael J., ed. *Catholic Questions, Wise Answers*. Cincinnati: St. Anthony Messenger Press, 2002.

Written in a question-and-answer format with balanced answers and many references to the *Catechism of the Catholic Church*.

The Essential Catholic Handbook: A Summary of Beliefs, Practices, and Prayers. A Redemptorist Pastoral Publication. Liguori, MO: Liguori Publications, 1997.

This would be another helpful student resource.

Kreeft, Peter J. *Catholic Christianity*. San Francisco: Ignatius Press, 2001.

The text is clear, convincing, orthodox, and organized. An excellent teacher resource.

O'Grady, Rev. John F. *Catholic Beliefs and Traditions*. New York: Paulist Press, 2001.

This is a recently written overview of the Catholic faith.

Poole, Gary, and Judson Poling. *How Does Anyone Know God Exists?* Revised edition. Grand Rapids, MI: Zondervan: 2003.

This short book offers many good discussion starters and is a simple survey of responses to some of the perennial challenges to belief in God.

Rohr, Richard, and Joseph Martos. *The Great Themes of Scripture: Old Testament*. Cincinnati: St. Anthony Messenger Press, 1987.

Chapter 5 of this text offers some good applications of the first eleven chapters of Genesis.

continued on page 25

Extending the Lesson

Video Presentation: Play the first part of the video *Cloud of Witness: Thomas Aquinas/Early Reformers*. Point out the feature on Thomas Aquinas in the text (page 21). For extra credit, have the students research and write a brief report on Aquinas's life.

Class Activity: Try to give the students a heartfelt experience of God. Take them on an "on-campus field trip" to the most beautiful place at your school, like a special garden, or a mural, or perhaps there is a wonderful view from the highest point of the school building. There might be a lovely stained glass window in your school chapel or in the parish church. If nothing occurs to you, poll your students. Ask them to name the most beautiful spot on campus and then take them to it. While you are at this place, ask the students to try to describe the beauty that they see. What makes it beautiful? What is important about beauty? Why do people like beautiful things? Do they think God is beautiful? How?

Class Activity: Hold a series of class debates to determine which proof of God's existence is most compelling. Divide the class into teams of three to four students. Half of the teams will argue that the intellectual proofs are most persuasive. The other teams will argue for the more emotional proofs. Each team will need to choose a spokesperson and work together to develop their case.

For the debates themselves, pair up opposing teams to debate each other. As each pair debates, the remaining teams will form the audience. Allow each spokesperson two minutes to lay out his or her team's position. Following the opening comments, each team will have one minute to respond to the other's position. To keep the debates positive, remind the students that their job is to present their own case, not to tear down their opponents. You can invite classmates to ask questions of each team after their initial comments. These questions may challenge the teams' positions or ask for clarification.

For a more complicated series of debates, assign teams to argue in favor of just one particular proof. When you pair up debaters you can match some "intellectual" proofs against others, some "heartfelt" proofs against others, and some "intellectual" and "heartfelt" proofs against each other.

desiring something else. Are we creatures doomed to be ultimately frustrated? We want happiness, but the more we pursue it, the more it slips away. A possible explanation for this reality is that our Creator God implanted in us a kind of homing device that causes us to be restless until we find him. This restlessness for total happiness points to a God who made us this way. Consider the opposite: if there is no God, then there is no meaning to life. Our deep yearning for everlasting happiness and joy becomes a meaningless joke.

2. *An experience of beauty and truth.* So much of the beauty and truth of Heaven is found on earth: a starlit sky, a breathtaking sunset, or a beautiful piece of music. When we experience profound joy in the presence of some awesome experience, when we

encounter truth and it seems so perfectly right, we are getting a taste of God's beauty and truth. God made us, understands us, loves us, and gives us a taste of Heaven on earth.

3. *A sense of personal conscience, moral goodness, and justice.* In the depths of our souls, we sense God's voice teaching us that we must always do good (for example, treat others fairly) and always avoid evil (for example, "Do not murder"). We sense that there is an absolute moral authority—God—that teaches the standard of human behavior. We also imagine a God of justice. It seems unfair to us that cheaters, liars, and killers often prosper in this life while some good people suffer and are taken advantage of. We have a fundamental feeling that things will be reversed someday, that there is a Power

transcendence
A trait of God that refers to God's total otherness and being infinitely beyond and independent of creation.

immanence
A trait of God that refers to God's intimate union with and total presence to his creation.

Understanding God

The Scriptures stress both God's **transcendence** and **immanence**. These terms can help us to understand more about God.

- Transcendence is the quality of God's total uniqueness and infinite greatness compared to his creatures. Psalm 102 puts it this way: "They shall perish, but you remain though all of them grow old like a garment; . . . but you are the same, and your years have no end" (verses 27–28).
- God's immanence, on the other hand, refers to God's being in the world, his closeness to and intimacy with us. In preaching to the Athenians, St. Paul emphasized this quality when he said, "In him we live and move and have our being" (Acts 17:28). A wonderful example of God's immanence is when he allows us mere creatures to receive his very Son, Jesus Christ, in Holy Communion.

1. What kind of God (immanent or transcendent) do you experience when you are happy? Worried? Guilty? Peaceful?
2. Interview two adults and two peers. Ask them for two reasons for believing or not believing in God. Share and compare responses.
3. Choose a piece of *instrumental* music (classical or otherwise) that speaks to you of beauty, truth, or goodness. Listen to the music. Write two or three paragraphs explaining how this music speaks to you of God or other spiritual realities.
4. Read Psalm 33. In your journal, write a verse or verses that express God's transcendence. Then read Psalm 103. Write a verse or verses that express God's immanence.

Homework Assignment

1. Read the feature "Understanding God" (page 20). Choose and complete one of the activities that accompany it. If you choose the third activity related to music, bring a recording of the music to the next class.

2. Answer the five For Review questions on page 22.

3. Read the text section "Divine Revelation" (pages 22–25).

For Enrichment

Class Activity: Have students examine the *Summa theological* online at www.newadvent.org/summa. Have them search for the place where Aquinas writes about the intellectual proofs of God (*prima pars, question 2, article 3*). Next, distribute copies of the *Catechism of the Catholic Church*. Have students explain how the Table of Contents of the two works compare. Are they set up differently? Do they address the same issues?

PROFILE OF FAITH: ST. THOMAS AQUINAS, GREAT THEOLOGIAN

Thomas Aquinas was born in approximately 1225 to a noble family. As a child, his brilliant mind was already asking his Benedictine teachers about God's nature. Against the fierce opposition of his family, at eighteen he joined the relatively new Dominican Order, which had become known for its quality of preachers and teachers.

Thomas studied under the brilliant St. Albert the Great at the University of Cologne. Tradition holds that Thomas merited the nickname "Dumb Ox" for his quiet manner and huge size, but he proved himself to be the most brilliant of all students. Albert reportedly said of him, "This ox will one day fill the world with his bellowing."

After ordination, Thomas received his doctoral degree at the University of Paris. He then embarked on an untiring life of teaching and preaching. But it was his writing that made him a marvel in his own day and the genius theologian of the Catholic Church for all time. A prolific writer of over sixty works, Thomas's masterpiece is the *Summa Theologica* (*Summary Treatise of Theology*, 1265–1273). It marks the summit of *scholastic philosophy*, which reconciled Christian faith with human reason and the works of Aristotle with Scripture.

Thomas's contributions to human thought are immeasurable. Besides his arguments for the existence of God, Thomas explained how human intellect is necessary to understand the knowledge that humans receive through the five senses and to grasp immaterial realities like God and the human soul. Many truths can be known through human reason—like the nature of the material world and the existence of God—but others can only be grasped through Divine Revelation (God revealing it to man)—like God taking human form in the person of Christ. Reason and Revelation work hand in hand and are not opposed to each other. On the one hand, Christian faith can preserve human reason from error. On the other hand, reason can serve the faith, for example, by clearly explaining and defending the truths that God has revealed to us.

Toward the end of his life (December 6, 1273), Thomas had such an ecstatic experience of God that it caused him to stop writing altogether. He said, "I can do no more. Such secrets have been revealed to me that all I have written now appears to be of little value." Thus, he never finished the *Summa*; he died a few months later (March 7, 1274).

Thomas was declared a saint in 1323 and named a **Doctor of the Church**, that is, a person of great learning and knowledge whose works the Church has highly recommended for studying and living the faith.

that will right all wrongs, if not in this life, then in the next.

4. *Love.* Love is a spiritual reality with origins that the material universe cannot explain. In fact, love comes from love itself, the being we call God. (The same argument holds for intelligence; it must ultimately come from intelligence itself, that is, God.)

Given the many signs of head and heart that point to the existence of God, it's easy to see that the French philosopher Blaise Pascal (1623–1662) is right on. He said it is a good bet to believe in God. "If you win, you win everything." With faith in God comes a big payoff—eternal life. With atheism, you only have everything to lose.

Doctor of the Church
A Church writer of great learning and holiness whose works the Church has highly recommended for studying and living the faith.

For Reflection

• With a digital camera, take a picture of something in nature that speaks to you of God, the Masterful Designer of the universe. Print the picture with a caption of several verses from Psalm 104 that express for you the praise that God the Creator deserves.

• Why do you believe in God?

---

1. Definitions should include:
   • *Monotheism*: belief that there is only one God (page 17)
   • *Polytheism*: belief in multiple gods and goddesses (page 17)
   • *Atheist*: a person who denies the existence of God (page 16)
   • *Agnostic*: a person who claims that God's existence cannot be known (page 18)
   • *Secular humanism*: the belief that the world can operate without any recourse to God (page 18)
   • *Deism*: the belief that God did create the universe but that he takes no further interest in it (page 18)

2. The existence of so many religions tells us that human beings have a religious nature, searching for a Supreme Being. (page 18)

3. Answers may vary; see pages 19–21 for descriptions of each proof.

4. Examples will vary; see pages 19–21 for descriptions of heartfelt proofs for God's existence.

5. Examples will vary; see page 20 for the definitions of transcendence and immanence.

6. St. Thomas Aquinas was a great theologian. A Doctor of the Church is a person of great knowledge and holiness.

Background Information

Two Opposing Views of God in Science

In 2006 Richard Dawkins, evolutionary biologist, secular humanist, and enthusiastic atheist, wrote a book titled the *God Delusion*. In it he argues that the Creator certainly does not exist; belief in a personal god is a delusion; and atheists can live happy, moral lives. He discredits the Grand Designer argument, suggesting that there is no solution to the question of who designed the designer other than evolution by natural selection. In the same year, however, another prominent scientist, Francis Collins, wrote a book titled *The Language of God*, in which he argued that belief in God can be proven through biology. In it he describes his conversion to Christianity during his leadership of the Human Genome Project. In the book, Collins shares how his study of the human genome suggests the existence of a Grand Designer and he explains how this concept fits into a framework of evolution by natural selection. For more information about Dr. Francis Collins and his concept of "BioLogos" visit www.biologos.org.

For Enrichment

Class Activity: Divide the class into small working groups of no more than three or four. Randomly assign each group one of the "proofs" and ask them to develop an advertisement or "public service announcement," based on their "proof," designed to convince people of God's existence. They might design a billboard, which would need to have large simple pictures and a short, easily read, and memorable "slogan"; or they might design a magazine or newspaper ad that could include more writing; they might develop a script for a radio spot, which would be nearly all dialog; or they might write a television skit that relied on visual images and dialogue to make their point. Radio and television spots should be kept to thirty seconds.

If possible, share the students' work with the larger school community: post "billboards" in the hallways; run newspaper/magazine ads in the school newspaper; get permission for the students to perform the radio spots over the school intercom during morning or end-of-the-day announcements.

Divine Revelation (pages 22–25)

Objectives

In this lesson the students will:

- trace salvation history through the familiar covenants of the Old Testament.
- compare and contrast Moses of the Old Testament and Jesus of the New Testament.
- understand Jesus Christ's role as the final covenant and last Revelation.
- explain how Sacred Tradition and Sacred Scripture work together to pass on the Gospel message from generation to generation.

Preview

God reveals himself in many ways. Revelation means "unveiling." Divine Revelation refers to this free gift of God's self-communication by which he makes known the mystery of his divine plan. Scripture and Tradition are two ways that God's Revelation is shared. It is important that your students understand that Sacred Scripture as we know it is, in fact, a written record of the Church's earliest Traditions. You will need to use class time to explain the process by which the current canon of Scripture came to be written and accepted as sacred.

Bell Ringers

- **Class Discussion:** Allow some discussion on the "Understanding God" assignment. For example, call on students to share the "kind of God" they experience at different times, various people's reasons for believing or not believing in God, any examples of instrumental music that speaks to them about God, and the verses that express God's transcendence and immanence.

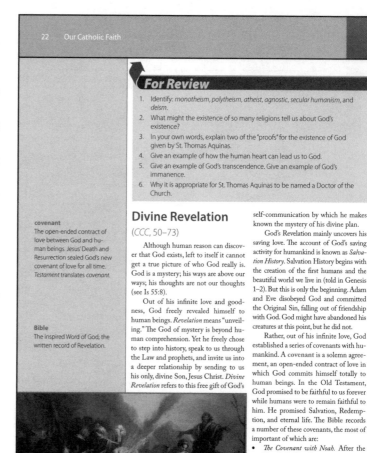

22   Our Catholic Faith

For Review

1. Identify: *monotheism, polytheism, atheist, agnostic, secular humanism,* and *deism.*
2. What might the existence of so many religions tell us about God's existence?
3. In your own words, explain two of the "proofs" for the existence of God given by St. Thomas Aquinas.
4. Give an example of how the human heart can lead us to God.
5. Give an example of God's transcendence. Give an example of God's immanence.
6. Why it is appropriate for St. Thomas Aquinas to be named a Doctor of the Church.

covenant
The open-ended contract of love between God and human beings. Jesus' Death and Resurrection sealed God's new covenant of love for all time. *Testament* translates *covenant.*

Bible
The inspired Word of God; the written record of Revelation.

Divine Revelation

(CCC, 50–73)

Although human reason can discover that God exists, left to itself it cannot get a true picture of who God really is. God is a mystery; his ways are above our ways; his thoughts are not our thoughts (see Is 55:8).

Out of his infinite love and goodness, God freely revealed himself to human beings. *Revelation* means "unveiling." The God of mystery is beyond human comprehension. Yet he freely chose to step into history, speak to us through the Law and prophets, and invite us into a deeper relationship by sending to us his only, divine Son, Jesus Christ. *Divine Revelation* refers to this free gift of God's

self-communication by which he makes known the mystery of his divine plan.

God's Revelation mainly uncovers his saving love. The account of God's saving activity for humankind is known as *Salvation History.* Salvation History begins with the creation of the first humans and the beautiful world we live in (told in Genesis 1–2). But this is only the beginning. Adam and Eve disobeyed God and committed the Original Sin, falling out of friendship with God. God might have abandoned his creatures at this point, but he did not.

Rather, out of his infinite love, God established a series of covenants with humankind. A covenant is a solemn agreement, an open-ended contract of love in which God commits himself totally to human beings. In the Old Testament, God promised to be faithful to us forever while humans were to remain faithful to him. He promised Salvation, Redemption, and eternal life. The Bible records a number of these covenants, the most of important of which are:

- *The Covenant with Noah.* After the Flood, God made a covenant with Noah and his descendants and with "every living creature" (Gn 9:10) that was with Noah on the ark. God promised that never again would a flood destroy the earth.

Background Information

Oral Tradition

Use the following notes to assist you in explaining the process by which the oral traditions of the early Church became the Scriptures that have been passed down to us today:

- Immediately after Christ's Death and Resurrection, the Apostles began to share with each other and with others the stories they remembered about Jesus' life and teachings.
- The Apostles began to spread Jesus' message to others in Jerusalem and in the Gentile communities in neighboring regions.
- Letters containing teachings about Jesus and his message were written from the Apostles and other leaders of the early Church and sent to different communities of Christians.
- Nearly one hundred years after Jesus' Death and Resurrection, the Gospels began to be written, based on the stories that had been handed down orally. There were many different Gospels, written by many different followers of Jesus.
- Gradually, over the next two hundred years, some of the letters and Gospels began to fall into disuse and were understood to contain errors or misunderstandings of the faith, while others became more and more accepted by Christians throughout the world.
- The accepted letters and four of the Gospels became known as the books of the New Testament and remain important and valuable to Christians today. They are accepted as the inspired Word of God.

KNOWING CHRIST THROUGH SCRIPTURE

The Prophet Moses

One of the towering figures in the Old Testament is the prophet Moses. His name is found 750 times in the Old Testament and approximately 80 times in the New Testament. He is the dominant human figure in the Pentateuch, the first five books of the Old Testament, where he is held in the highest regard: "Since then no prophet has arisen in Israel like Moses, whom the LORD knew face to face" (Dt 34:10).

Scripture reports that Moses was born of a Levite couple (Ex 2:1–10) in Egypt. Because of Pharaoh's decree to kill all newborn Hebrew males, Moses was hidden by his mother and then placed in a watertight basket to drift down the Nile River. Pharaoh's daughter rescued Moses, an event witnessed by Moses' sister. She then appointed Moses' own mother as his nurse and later adopted Moses.

As an adult, Moses learned of his identity as a Hebrew and killed an Egyptian who had beaten a fellow Hebrew. He fled to Midian, married, had some children, and made a living as a shepherd until the age of eighty. God then appeared to him in a burning bush (Ex 3:1–6) and commissioned Moses to lead the Israelites out of slavery in Egypt. Moses made a number of excuses why he was not up to the task, for example, that he lacked the gift to speak. But God's will prevailed. God revealed to Moses his name—*Yahweh* ("I am who I am")—and showed him the signs he would perform to help lead the Israelites to freedom.

The Book of Exodus recounts how Yahweh empowered Moses to lead the enslaved Israelites out of Egypt, defying the armies of the pharaoh. Moses led his people to the Sinai Peninsula where he ascended Mount Sinai to speak with God. After spending forty days and nights with Yahweh, Moses received the Ten Commandments on two stone tablets. These represented the Law that the people were to keep as their part of the covenant that God made with them. But when he descended from the mountain, Moses learned that the people were worshiping a golden calf. He broke the tablets in anger for their lack of faith in the one true God. Moses then inscribed a new set of tablets at God's command and placed them in the Ark of the Covenant.

Serving as God's spokesman and interceding for his people, the prophet Moses led the Israelites through the desert and, with God's assistance, helped the people survive various hardships including plagues, earthquakes, and wars with the native peoples. Moses died before entering Canaan, the Promised Land, but he was allowed to see it from a mountaintop. He turned leadership of the Israelites over to Joshua, who then led the people into Canaan.

Moses is known as a great prophet, intercessor, miracle worker, lawgiver, and rescuer. The life and ministry of our Savior, Jesus Christ, the Second Person of the Blessed Trinity, was prefigured in many ways in the life of Moses. For example:

- As a prophet, Moses was God's spokesman. Jesus is the only Son of the Father, who spoke for his Father. "The words that I speak to you I do not speak on my own. The Father who dwells in me is doing his works. Believe me that I am in the Father and the Father is in me, or else, believe because of the works themselves" (Jn 14:10–11).
- Moses prayed to God many times on behalf of the people. Jesus intercedes for us continually before the Father. "It is Christ (Jesus) who died, rather, was raised, who also is at the right hand of God, who indeed intercedes for us" (Rom 8:34).
- Moses performed miracles at God's command to help the people. Jesus performed miracles by his own authority to show God's compassion and mercy and to reveal his identity.

- **Class Activity:** Write the following Scripture passages on the board:
  - Genesis 8:20–22; 9:1, 7–17
  - Genesis 17:1–22
  - Exodus 19:3–8

Ask the students to look up each passage and read the sections silently. Have them answer the following questions:

1. Between whom was this covenant made?
   - God and Noah, his family, and all of earth's creatures;
   - God and Abraham and his descendants;
   - God and the people of Israel whom he rescued from the Egyptians.

2. What did God promise?
   - Never again to destroy his creation;
   - To give Abraham a son and descendants who would become "a multitude of nations";
   - To make Israel the Lord's special nation, "a priestly kingdom and a holy nation."

3. What did God require?
   - That Noah and his sons "be fruitful and multiply";
   - That Abraham and his descendants be circumcised as a sign of their relationship with God;
   - That the people obey God.

4. What quality of God is revealed in each passage?
   - For all three—God's love and compassion for his people are the most prevalent characteristics.

Background Information

What Is Tradition?

Derived from the Latin word for "to hand on," Tradition refers to the content of Revelation (teachings and practices of the faith) and the process of handing on the faith through oral tradition and written scriptures. Tradition is the living communication of the word, brought about by the Holy Spirit.

Printed Materials continued from page 22

Schreck, Alan. *The Essential Catholic Catechism.* Ann Arbor, MI: Servant Books, 2000.
   A reliable recent catechism on Church teaching. The first three chapters would be especially helpful background to the teaching of this chapter.

Welborn, Amy. *Prove It! God.* Huntington, IN: Our Sunday Visitor, 2000.
   Answers to many questions about the existence of God written in language that teens can understand. This is a great resource for crafting responses to tough questions about God.

Teaching Approaches

- **Individual Activity:** Write the following terms and definitions on the board. As you discuss each one, consider allowing students to create "picture cue" flash cards to help remember the terms:
  - ◆ Divine Revelation—the way in which God reveals himself to us, allowing us to know him and to understand his divine plan
  - ◆ Salvation history—the account of God's saving activities that lead us to him
  - ◆ Covenant—a special agreement between God and his people in which God promises to love his people always and asks for their love in return

- **Individual Activity:** Have the students create illustrated timelines of *salvation history* based on the four covenants presented in the Student Text on pages 22–24. Allow them to use blank sheets of copy paper, or consider giving them the option of creating free online timelines at www.readwritethink.org/files/resources/interactives/timeline or www.xtimeline.com. Assign anything they do not finish for homework.

- **Writing Assignment:** Refer students to the feature Knowing Christ through Scripture: The Prophet Moses. Remind students that Moses prefigured Jesus in many ways. Ask them to reread the feature and complete the following in their notes:

  1. Moses _____. Jesus spoke for his Father.
  2. Moses prayed to God many times on behalf of people. Jesus _____.
  3. Moses _____. Jesus performed miracles by his own authority.
  4. Moses gave the Law to the Israelites. Jesus _____.
  5. Moses _____. Jesus' Death, Resurrection, and Glorification have led all of humanity out of slavery to sin.

  Then, assign the Scripture passages and questions to be completed in class or as homework (answers are found on page 27 of this TWE).

- Continue by summarizing the material covered in the subsection "Sacred Scripture and Sacred Tradition" (pages 24–25). Review the material in the section to be sure the students understand the following terms:
  Scripture—The books of the Bible, both Old and New Testaments
  Tradition—The living transmission of the Gospel message through the actions of the Church
  Magisterium—The teaching authority of the pope and bishops, which, with the help of the Holy Spirit, ensures the correct understanding of the Gospel message

- **Direct Instruction:** Use the Background Information (on page 24) to assist you in explaining the process by

---

KNOWING CHRIST THROUGH SCRIPTURE (continued)

- Moses gave the Law to the Israelites. Jesus is the New Lawgiver. His Sermon on the Mount and his command to love are requirements for his followers. "This is my commandment: love one another as I love you" (Jn 15:12).
- Moses led his people out of slavery into freedom. Jesus' Death, Resurrection, and Glorification have led all of humanity out of slavery to sin and brought us the freedom of eternal life with our loving God. "For the wages of sin is death, but the gift of God is eternal life in Christ Jesus our Lord" (Rom 6:23).

Read the following important passages about Moses and the Sinai Covenant. Then answer the following questions:

Exodus 2–4: Moses' Early Life and Commission

- Who gave Moses his name, and what was the basis for the name?

- What was the name of Moses' son?
- Why did Moses remove his sandals?
- Who was to be Moses' assistant?

Exodus 11–14: The Tenth Plague and Exodus

- What was the tenth plague?
- Why were the Israelites to perform the Passover ritual?
- How long did the Israelites spend in Egypt?
- List two Passover regulations.
- What did Moses take out of Egypt? Why?
- How did the Lord lead the Israelites?
- How did the Israelites escape?

Exodus 19–20: Giving of the Ten Commandments

- How did the Lord appear to Moses?
- What is the most important command the Lord gave to the people?

- *The Covenant with Abraham.* Recall that a major chapter in Salvation History is God's covenant with Abraham, the Father of Faith for the Jewish people and our spiritual father because of our shared ancestry with the Jews. Part of this covenant involved circumcision for Jewish males as a way to set apart the people God would form from Abraham's descendants.
- *The Sinai Covenant.* God formed Israel as his people when he freed them from slavery in Egypt at the time of the Exodus. He gave the Chosen People his law through Moses on Mount Sinai. The Law taught Israel to acknowledge Yahweh as the one, living, and true God. But it did not offer a means of Redemption. Through the prophets who came after Moses, God gave Israel hope for Salvation. They proclaimed a new covenant to be written on human hearts. They gave hope for a future Messiah who would bring Salvation.
- *Jesus Christ, the New Covenant.* The climax of Salvation History was the coming of Jesus Christ, God's

Son, the fullness of God's Revelation. Jesus is God's total Word made flesh, the Son who lived among us. He taught us in word and deed about God and completed the Father's work of Salvation. Since Jesus Christ is God's final word, there will be no further Revelation after him. To see Jesus is to see the Father.

Sacred Scripture and Sacred Tradition (CCC, 74–141).

God reveals himself through a single "deposit" of faith. Christ entrusted this deposit to the Apostles. Inspired by the Holy Spirit, they handed it on through their preaching and their writing to the Church, until Christ will come again. This single deposit is found in Sacred Scripture (the Bible) and in the Sacred Tradition of the Church.

Sacred Scripture is like a library of divinely inspired writings (*Bible* means "books"). God used human authors and their unique talents to put into writing what he wanted written, and nothing more. "The books of Scripture

---

Background Information

The Marriage Covenant
According to the *Catechism of the Catholic Church:*

> Christian marriage in its turn becomes an efficacious sign, the sacrament of the covenant of Christ and the Church. Since it signifies and communicates grace, marriage between baptized persons is a true sacrament of the New Covenant (1617).

Extending the Lesson

Have the students take out scrap paper. Read the following items and have them write answers as part of a short quiz on the material covered so far in this chapter.

1. The term that describes the official list of biblical books. (*canon*)
2. The term that refers to God's loving participation in the lives of humans. (*salvation history*)
3. God's self-communication to humans is known as? (*Divine Revelation*)
4. The process and content of handing on God's Word both orally and in writing is known as? (*Tradition*)
5. The written record of God's self-communication is known as? (*Scripture, Bible*)

---

firmly, faithfully, and without error teach that truth which God, for the sake of our Salvation, wished to see confided to the Sacred Scriptures" (*Dogmatic Constitution on Divine Revelation*, No. 11, quoted in *CCC*, 107). This means that the Bible is inerrant; that is, it contains no errors. (See pages 288–290 of the *Catholic Handbook for Faith* for more information about the Bible.)

Sacred Tradition is the living transmission or "handing on" of the Church's Gospel message. We find this Tradition in the Church's teaching, life, and worship. The Apostles, inspired by the Spirit, were the first to receive the gift of faith. They in turn gave it to the care of their successors—the Pope and bishops—to "faithfully preserve, expound, and spread . . . by their preaching" (*Dogmatic Constitution on Divine Revelation*, No. 9, quoted in *CCC*, 81).

Christ commissioned the Apostles to interpret authentically God's Word—both Scripture and Tradition.

This Christ-appointed teaching authority, which extended to the Pope and the bishops in communion with him, is known as the *Magisterium* (from the Latin word for "teacher"). With the help of the Holy Spirit, the Magisterium teaches with Christ's own authority. This is especially so when the Magisterium defines a dogma, that is, a central truth of Revelation that Catholics are obliged to believe.

Recall that faith (*CCC*, 26, 91–100; 142–171) is the theological virtue that enables us to believe in God and all that he has revealed to us and all that the Church teaches regarding our faith. Through faith we can commit our whole lives to God and say yes to the gift of Revelation given to us in Christ our Lord. In summary, the free response of faith makes us part of the Church and enables us to accept Jesus as Lord, partake in the life of the Blessed Trinity, and commit ourselves totally to God, both with our intellects and wills.

Sacred Tradition
The living transmission of the Church's Gospel message found in the Church's teaching, life, and worship. It is faithfully preserved, handed on, and interpreted by the Church's Magisterium.

dogma
A central truth of Revelation that Catholics are obliged to believe.

For Review

1. Define: *Divine Revelation, Salvation History, covenant,* and *faith.*
2. List four covenants that God made with humankind.
3. Where is the single deposit of faith found?
4. Discuss three ways Moses prefigured Jesus Christ.

For Reflection

- The Old Testament offers a variety of images for God. Read the following passages: Deuteronomy 32:11; Psalm 24:8, 10; Isaiah 49:15; Hosea 11. Note the image of God highlighted in the passages.
- Compose your own prayer of praise using a personally meaningful image for God.

Homework Assignment

1. Write answers to the For Review questions on page 25.
2. Write answers to the For Reflection questions on page 25 in their journals.
3. Read the text section "Who Is God?" (pages 26–28).

Background Information

The Development of the Canon

The biblical canon—the list of official books of the Bible—was not officially approved by the Church Magisterium until 1546 during the Council of Trent. Prior to the official recognition, the canon was already well established in its present form. In the fourth century, St. Athanasius cited the current twenty-seven books as the official canon that would later be translated into Latin by St. Jerome in the Latin Vulgate version of the Bible.

which the oral traditions of the early Church became the Scriptures that have been passed down to us today. Stress to the students that God was active at each step of the process, inspiring not just the authors who wrote the letters and Gospels, but also the storytellers, who passed on the stories before they were written down, as well as the communities of Christians and their leaders, the bishops who followed the Apostles, who approved or rejected the different writings that were circulated around the Church, giving to those that were approved the authority of Scripture. Thus, Scripture itself comes out of Tradition—the actions of the Church, the community of faith, that work to pass on the message of Jesus. Understanding this process now will help your students in later studies of the Scriptures.

- **Class Discussion:** Choose a tough passage from the New Testament, such as Jesus' forbiddance of divorce (Mt 19:1–12). Have each student read it silently; then invite each student to share what they think it means with the class. Note some of the differences in interpretation. Based on the differences in interpretation, ask the students why they think it is important for the Magisterium to be in place. Explain that Sacred Tradition is essential; otherwise, the Gospel message could easily be distorted by false teachers.

Knowing Christ through Scripture
Answers (page 24)

Exodus 2–4: Moses' early life and commission
- The Pharaoh's daughter named him Moses, from the Hebrew word for "draw out."
- Gershom
- God told him to remove his sandals because he was on holy ground.
- Aaron

Exodus 11–14: The Tenth Plague and Exodus
- Death of the first-born
- To recall how the Lord passed over them and freed them from Egypt
- Four hundred and thirty years
- No foreigner may partake in it. It must be eaten in a house. No bones can be broken. Circumcision is necessary to participate.
- Joseph's bones; he made the Israelites swear that they would carry his bones away with them when the Lord comes.
- As a cloud
- The Israelites escaped by crossing the Red Sea.

Exodus 19–20: Giving of the Ten Commandments
- The Lord appeared in fire and the cloud.
- You shall not have other gods besides me.

1. Definitions should resemble the following:
* *Divine Revelation*: free gift of God's self-communication by which he makes known the mystery of his divine plan (page 22)

* *Salvation History*: God's saving activity for humankind (page 22)

* *Covenant*: open-ended contract of love between God and human beings (page 22)

* *Faith*: belief in and personal knowledge of God (page 25)

2. The covenant with Noah, the covenant with Abraham, the Sinai covenant, and the New Covenant, Jesus Christ

3. Sacred Scripture and Sacred Tradition

4. Moses prefigured Christ as God's voice to his people in the way he interceded on behalf of God's people, through the miracles he performed, by giving the Israelites the Law, and by freeing them from Egypt.

Who Is God? (pages 26–28)

Objectives

In this lesson, the students will:
* explain the significance of the name Yahweh.
* describe many of the characteristics of God.
* explain the importance of addressing God as Father.

 Preview

This might be a good lesson in which to make use of multimedia resources. The story of God's appearance to Moses in the burning bush has been brought to life vividly in many different movie versions. Watch as many as you can find before choosing the two or three you think will make the best impression on your students. See the list of suggested videos for this chapter for some suggestions. Also, the students will examine God's place as Father, as first described by Jesus. The students will also look at some different images in the Scripture exercises found in this section.

Bell Ringers

* **Individual Activity:** Write the following question on the board: "Who is God?" Have the students answer the question by drawing God. When the students have finished their drawings, ask them to share their images.

* **Direct Instruction:** Perform an Internet search for images of God and show them to the students. Focus on the most common images of God, which depict him as an old man with a beard. Ask the students to discuss where they think the images had their roots.

Who Is God? (CCC, 205–237; 268–271)

A name expresses a person's inner identity. When Moses encountered God in the burning bush, God revealed his name to Moses—Yahweh, "I Am" (see Ex 3:4–14). This holiest of all names can also mean "I am he who is," "I am who I am," or "I am who am." The name Yahweh shows that God is not some impersonal force but one who creates everything out of nothing and keeps it in existence. God is *omnipresent*; he is everywhere.

The name Yahweh also acknowledges God's mystery. Moses knew this when he took off his shoes and bowed in reverence. God's omnipotent and eternal nature is beyond human understanding. Yahweh reveals himself to be the Holy One in our midst, a God of truth and love. "God's truth is his wisdom, which commands the whole created order and governs the world" (*CCC*, 216).

In fact, God's only motive for revealing himself, for choosing the Jews from among all people, is his totally free gift of love. This love is constant. Despite human sinfulness, the Lord is "a merciful and gracious God, slow to anger and rich in kindness and fidelity, continuing his kindness for a thousand generations, and forgiving wickedness and crime and sin" (Ex 34:6–7).

Attributes of Almighty God

God has revealed for us several of his attributes. The Apostles' Creed identifies only one of God's attributes: *omnipotence*. This means that God is almighty. God's power is unlimited, but it is loving, merciful, and gracious power.

The almighty God possesses many other qualities that are part of his mysterious nature. These attributes are beyond our comprehension and can only be understood by analogy, that is, by comparing something familiar to something unfamiliar. For example, we examine God's perfection by looking first at a human quality like intelligence. Second, we understand that God's intelligence is not like human intelligence since human intelligence is limited. Third, we state that God transcends, that is, goes infinitely beyond anything humans can understand. God is a perfect being. God is intelligence itself. God is, thus, all-knowing.

St. Thomas Aquinas listed the following nine attributes of God that are evidenced through history and in Scripture:

1. *God is unique.* There is no God like Yahweh (see Is 45:18).

Extending the Lesson

Class Activity: Encourage the students to come up with as many adjectives as they can think of that describe God. This can be done individually, in small groups, or as a class, whichever works best for your students. They can list them in their journals, on large sheets of poster board, or on the chalkboard, but be sure they write them down so that they can check their list later against the list in the Student Text (see pages 26–27). This activity can be done as a team challenge activity. Divide the class into teams. Set a timer for five minutes and have each team make as long a list of adjectives as they can that describe God. The winning team will be the team that comes up with the longest list of adjectives that *no other team* includes.

2. *God is infinite and omnipotent.* God is everywhere, unlimited, and all-powerful. God can do everything (see Ps 135:5–6).

3. *God is eternal.* God always was and always will be. God is the one being who cannot not be (see Is 40:28).

4. *God is immense.* God is not limited to space (see 1 Kgs 8:27).

5. *God contains all things* (see Ws 8:1).

6. *God is immutable.* God does not change—ever (see Ps 102:25–28).

7. *God is utterly simple—a pure Spirit.* The opposite of simple is complex, which means divisible into parts. In God there are no parts, no divisions. God is not material. God's image cannot be made (see Ex 20:4).

8. *God is personal.* God is alive (the source of all life), knows all things, and loves and cares beyond limit. The saving God manifested personal love through the compassionate acts in the history of the Israelites and most supremely by sending his Son, Jesus Christ, to all people (see Jer 31:3).

9. *God is holy.* Holiness is a quality of being absolutely other than creation (see Is 55:8). God's goodness and love are unlimited. We cannot praise the holy God enough.

God the Father (CCC, 232–242; 261–262).

God the Father is the first Person of the Blessed Trinity. God has revealed himself as a Trinity of Persons. Jesus addressed God as Father (for example, John 17:1) and taught others to do so. God the Father named Jesus as his Son (for example, Luke 3:22). God the Son revealed that the Father would send the Holy Spirit in his name, a Spirit of truth and love (for example, John 14:16–17).

The Blessed Trinity is the central mystery of faith and the source of all other mysteries. This mystery reveals that

Jesus is the visible image of God the Father and that the Holy Spirit is sent by the Father in the name of the Son. The activity of the one true God—who is Father, Son, and Holy Spirit—reveals, reconciles, and unites himself to us. This is the story of Salvation History. (The dogma of the Blessed Trinity is presented in more detail in Chapter 3.)

Jesus taught us to pray to Abba, our Father. *Abba* is a child's word in Aramaic for "father," something like "daddy." It is a word of endearment and love. By addressing God as Abba, Jesus showed that God is a loving Father, one whose children should approach him with love and confidence and treat each other as brothers and sisters.

Jesus' relationship to the Father is unique. God the Father is in eternal relationship with his only Son, who in turn is eternally in relationship to his Father. Jesus is the Word of God who is with the Father from all time; the Word of God is God. Jesus also taught:

Yahweh
The sacred Hebrew name for God that means "I am who am," "I am," or "I am who I am."

Blessed Trinity
The *central* dogma of the Christian faith that there are three Divine Persons—Father, Son, and Holy Spirit—in one God.

Abba
An Aramaic term of endearment meaning "daddy." Jesus used this word to teach that God is a loving Father.

For Enrichment

Writing Assignment: After reading the material in the text subsection "God the Father," ask the students to complete Chapter 1, Handout 1 "My Father Is a Good Man" (starting on page 285 and also online at www.avemariapress.com). (Some students in your class may have very limited or no contact with their fathers. They may cross out "father" and substitute a grandfather, uncle, older brother, or even a close family friend whom they consider a "father figure" if they choose.) Collect the handouts.

Homework Assignment

1. Write responses to any For Review questions on page 28.

2. Read "Creator of Heaven and Earth" (pages 28–32) including the separate feature "Genesis Creation Accounts" (page 29).

Teaching Approaches

- **Video Presentation:** Read Exodus 3:1–15, God's appearance to Moses in the burning bush, to your class. Then show two or three movie clips depicting this scene. Ask your students to compare the different movie clips—which are most impressive? Which adhere most closely to the Bible account? What significance do they give to the name of God? How is God depicted in the scene? What qualities does he have?

- **Journal Assignment:** This is the first time in the Bible that God's name is asked for or given. Ask your students to imagine that this was their first introduction to God. What do they believe is true about God because of this introduction? Invite them to journal about this reflection.

- **Class Activity:** Focus on the text subsection "Attributes of Almighty God" (pages 26–27). Prepare a small bag or bowl for each group of four or five students containing small scraps of paper on which have been written the Scripture chapters and verses given in support of the nine qualities of God first suggested by Thomas Aquinas (see pages 26–27). Introduce Aquinas's list of qualities to the students but do not have them read the section from the book yet. Instead, list the qualities on the board and describe each one briefly in your own words. Then challenge them to match the qualities you have described with the Scripture passages they look up as they draw the papers from their bag or bowl. With each group drawing randomly, they will not be able to overhear answers from the groups around them.

- **Individual Activity:** Ask the students to look back at the drawing they worked on in the Bell Ringer activity. Ask them which, if any, of the attributes did they initially depict? Have them create a new drawing that depicts the attributes of God in some way, or have them add to their initial drawings.

- **Class Discussion:** Note the text subsection "God the Father" (pages 27–28). Ask the students to describe their "ideal" dad. Also have them offer words that describe the "ideal" dad as portrayed on television, either past or present. Write these qualities down on the board as well in a different place. Compare the two lists. Ask your students whether they think the media does a good job or a poor job portraying dads. Then write this question on the board, above the two lists: **If God is like a father, what kind of father is he?**

- **Journal Assignment:** God is unique, omnipotent, eternal, immutable, holy, yet personable. We call him Father. Even though God is so great, he is quite personal as well. What does this say about God's love for us? If God were to show off a home video of you, his child, what do you think he would show?

For Review Answers (page 28)

1. *Yahweh* means "I am," "I am he who is," "I am who I am," or "I am who am." (page 26)

2. Answers may include: omnipresent, omnipotence, all knowing, unique, eternal, immense, contains all things, immutable, simple, a pure Spirit, personal, or holy (pages 26–27)

3. The Blessed Trinity

4. Jesus addressed God as Father and taught others to do so.

5. *Abba* is a child's word in Aramaic for "father" used by Jesus to address God as a loving Father.

Creator of Heaven and Earth

(pages 28–32)

Objectives

In this lessons, the students will:
*   recognize what Divine Revelation in the Book of Genesis teaches about God and creation.
*   discover God's role and intent in the creation of the earth and of mankind.
*   explain the reality and consequences of Original Sin.

Preview

The most important skill your students need to master in this section is their ability to see the religious truths conveyed in the literal details of the stories of creation. It is essential that they understand that while the creation stories are not to be read scientifically, they are to be taken seriously as providing an accurate assessment of our relationship with God our Creator. Prepare for this lesson by reading and meditating on the first three chapters of Genesis until you are intimately familiar with them and feel comfortable answering any questions your students might have.

Bell Ringers

*   **Individual Activity:** Review the previous lesson by having students re-create their drawings of God that represent the attributes of God. Have them list as many attributes of God that they can recall based on their pictures. Then have them compare their new drawings with their old drawings to see what they missed.
*   **Direct Instruction:** Note the feature on page 29, "Genesis Creation Accounts." Ask the students to prepare for the day's lesson by reading silently this text and the first three chapters of the book of Genesis.
*   **Individual Activity:** After allowing time for the reading, give a "pop quiz" to test their passing knowledge of the details of Genesis 1–3, using Chapter

All things have been handed over to me by my Father. No one knows the Son except the Father, and no one knows the Father except the Son and anyone to whom the Son wishes to reveal him. (Mt 11:27)

It is right and proper to call God "Father." Today, however, some have difficulties with the address of God as Father, claiming that it creates the impression that God is male. This is not true. God is beyond the biological distinction of male and female. Both men and women are made "in the image and likeness of God." Therefore, it is also proper to use images of motherhood to emphasize God's closeness to us and care for us. For example, the book of Isaiah describes God in this way: "As a mother comforts her son, so will I comfort you" (Is 66:13). Images of parental love can be helpful in understanding God. However, human parents are weak and imperfect. God goes infinitely beyond any human standard of parenthood. "No one is father as God is Father" (*CCC*, 239).

Catholics continue to address God as Father because this is the language of Jesus, the language of Revelation, the language of our faith. We call God "Father" because Jesus teaches us to do just that.

For Review

1. What is the meaning of *Yahweh*?
2. List three qualities of Yahweh.
3. What is the central doctrine of Christianity?
4. Why is "Father" an appropriate form of address for God?
5. What is the meaning and significance of *Abba*?

For Reflection
What three qualities do you associate with a good mother? Describe how these qualities can also be applied to God or to Jesus Christ.

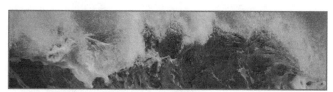

Creator of Heaven and Earth

(*CCC*, 279–308; 315–323; 337–349; 353–384)

Both Scripture and Tradition firmly teach that the Triune God created out of his wisdom and love to show forth and communicate his glory. Creation is not the result of blind chance or fate. God created out of his love, wisdom, and great desire to share his beauty, truth, goodness, and life, especially by making us his adopted children through Jesus Christ by power of the Holy Spirit.

The opening verse in the Bible proclaims that God alone is the Creator of all that exists outside himself; he alone keeps everything that is in existence. Therefore, everything in the world, including human beings, is entirely dependent on God.

Extending the Lesson

Class Discussion: Summarize the answer to the Explaining Your Faith feature about why God allows evil in the world on pages 32–33. Then, discuss students' memories of some major catastrophic events: the terrorist attack on 9/11/2001, Hurricane Katrina in 2005, and the earthquake in Haiti in 2010. Specifically, ask them to recall how people came together in unity to assist those in need.

Genesis Creation Accounts

The book of Genesis includes two stories of creation. These stories are interested in the *why* of creation; they do not describe *how* the world began. The Bible is not a scientific textbook. Rather, it is a record of Revelation about God's love for human beings. What the biblical authors were interested in was religious truth. For example, regardless of how the created world came to be, God is the source of all that is. They also teach the basic reason for human existence and destiny, the meaning and source of evil, God's saving action in human history, and so forth. Thus, when reading these stories, be on the alert for *religious* truth, not scientific fact.

- Read the first creation story (Gn 1:1–2:4a). Name something God created each day. What did God do on the seventh day?
- Read the second creation story (Gn 2:4b–25). Why did God create Eve? What did God forbid?

Divine Revelation teaches other truths about God's creation:

- *God freely created an orderly and good world out of nothing.* No one helped God create. No preexisting matter was present at creation. All that God makes is good. Created through the Word of God, the universe is made for human beings, who are in God's image and likeness.
- *God is totally beyond us. At the same time, God is present to us, upholding and sustaining creation.* God is infinitely greater than his creation, infinitely beyond that which he has made. But because of the love he freely bestows on us, God is present to our inmost being. God is more present to us than we are to ourselves. He does not abandon his creatures but sustains every moment of their existence. If he would forget us for an instant, we would cease to exist. We show great wisdom when we recognize through grateful hearts that we are totally dependent on God for all that we have and all that we are.

- *God guides creation through divine providence.* God guides us on our journey to our final goal of eternal life with the Blessed Trinity. Knowing his Father so well, Jesus taught that we should trust in God's providence with childlike faith. He instructed us to seek God's Kingdom first, trusting that our loving Father will take care of our needs (cf. Mt 6:31–33).
- *God created humans in his image and likeness.* Each person possesses profound dignity. Despite our differences of gender, national or ethnic origins, religion, race, and the like, God calls us into one family. Every person is lovable and worthy of respect—from the first moment of conception to natural death. Humans are the crown of God's creation, possessing both body and soul. God creates immediately our spiritual souls in his image and likeness. The soul empowers us with a spiritual nature that enables us to think, to know the difference between right and wrong, and to love God above all and our neighbors as ourselves. There was a time when we did not exist, but now we are immortal; God will always keep us in existence. We have an eternal destiny

Sharing God's Beauty

God made you a unique and beautiful creation. He expects that you will share your God-given goodness with others. Write a short essay describing the beauty of creation and what you perceive to be your own goodness. Develop in the essay concrete ways for sharing your and God's goodness with others.

Background Information

Some Examples of Angels in the Bible
Angels:

- protect Lot and his family when God destroyed Sodom.
- save Hagar and her son, Ishmael in the desert.
- stop Abraham from sacrificing Isaac.
- announce numerous births and callings.
- assist the prophets.
- announce John the Baptist's birth.
- gain Mary's assent to the birth of Jesus.
- proclaim Christ's birth to the shepherds.
- lead the Holy Family to Egypt.
- serve Jesus in the desert after his forty-day fast.

1, Handout 2 "Creation Quiz" (starting on page 285 and also online at www.avemariapress.com). Answers are on page 31 of this text.

Also have the students answer either orally or in writing the questions at the end of the feature "Genesis Creation Accounts" (page 29).

- Collect the For Review questions and answer any questions students might have about their homework.

Chapter 1, Handout 2 "Creation Quiz" Answers

1. the first

2. the sixth

3. he saw that they were good

4. it was the day on which he rested

5. after—this is the second creation account. The first makes no mention of Adam and Eve.

6. to till and keep it

7. to be helpers to each other, because it is not good to be alone

8. her eyes will be opened, she will be like God, knowing both good and evil

9. they both try to blame another: Adam blames Eve, and Eve blames the serpent

10. God makes them garments from the skins of animals to replace the fig leaves

Teaching Approaches

- **Direct Instruction:** Help your students make connections between the list of truths about God's creation found in their text on pages 29–30 and the two stories of creation they just read. Connect God's actions in these stories with the qualities of God they learned in previous lessons.
- **Writing Assignment:** As either a short essay or a journal entry, complete the description asked for in the feature "Sharing God's Beauty" (page 29).
- **Class Discussion:** Continue with the text subsection "The Fall and Original Sin" (pages 30–31). Draw a line down the middle of the board. On the left side label the column "Before the Fall" and on the right side write "After the Fall." Have students identify terms and share descriptions about what life was like before and after the Fall based on the Student Text and Genesis 1–3. Write their responses on the board and have the students copy them in their notes. For "Before the Fall," make sure they mention Original Holiness and Justice. For "After the Fall,"

make sure they mention the following: loss of God's friendship, loss of grace, loss of Original Holiness and Justice, disunity between God and humanity, disharmony between nature and humans, alienation between people, a fallen human nature, ignorance, suffering, **concupiscence**, and death. Then, add a third column labeled "After Baptism," and make sure students can identify the gift of Christ's life, the erasing of Original Sin, restoration of our relationship with God, and a weakened human nature that remains.

Extending the Lesson

Direct Instruction: Use the following points to expand upon the section "Creator of Heaven and Earth":

- *God freely created a good world out of nothing.* Refer students to Genesis 1:1–5. Ask them to close their eyes and try to imagine a formless void or a mix of dark and light. God brings order when he separates light and darkness so that the benefits of each are available to the earth. This is evidence of his omnipotence, his power.

- *God is totally beyond us, yet he is also present to us.* It is easy to see God's power and transcendence in the stories of creation. We can imagine a powerful force, shaping stars and planets, designing the myriad creatures, large and small that inhabit our world. But ask the students to find a hint of God's immanence in the passages they just read. At the very beginning of the creation story, when the world was still in chaos, God moved like a wind across the waters. In the second story, God forms the first human being out of the earth—now we see God up close and personal. We imagine his hands giving shape to our bodies. His breath fills our lungs for the first time. These are very intimate images.

- *God guides creation through divine providence.* Point out the effort God put into taking care of Adam and Eve: First, he provides everything Adam needs to eat or drink and gives him responsibilities so that he has something meaningful to do with his life. He recognizes that Adam is lonely and creates many more creatures to befriend Adam. When Adam is still lonely, he creates Eve. Even after they have sinned, God continues to care for them. Yes, he punishes them—or rather, allows them to suffer the consequences of their free act—but still he helps them to fashion sturdier clothing than the leaves they come up with on their own. The message behind these details is that God cares for his creation. He acts on our behalf out of that love and care; we can trust him to take care of our needs.

- *God created us in his image and likeness.* Read aloud Genesis 1:26–27. Ask the students to reflect on which of God's qualities we humans have in some degree. We are unique because God has made each of us individually. We are eternal because God made us to live forever with him. We are intelligent, although not omniscient. We are capable of great love, though we sometimes do not act lovingly. We are holy when we strive to imitate Christ. Use the lists of adjectives your class generated to continue the comparison.

- *God made us male and female out of love and for love.* In the original language of the book of Genesis, it is interesting to note that the word we translate as "man" is not a gendered word. That is, it does not indicate a male person or a female person; it is closer to "human being." It is only after the creation of Eve that the language of the story uses the equivalent of "he" and "she." This helps us to understand that men and women were created for each other, to help each other, to love each other, to be equal partners for each other.

- *God is the creator of all things, seen and unseen.* Challenge your students to find a reference to angels in the stories of the creation and the Fall that they read. It occurs at the very end of Genesis 3: "at the east of the garden of Eden he placed the cherubim . . . to guard the way to the tree of life" (Gen 3:24). Challenge your students to think of other references to angels in the Bible (see Background Information on page 31).

- *Though essentially good because God made us, we are tainted by sin.* Remind the students that, according to the story, at the end of every day God looks at what he has created and sees "that it was good." This is especially true of the sixth day when he sees that "indeed, it was very good." (Let the students know that they will be learning more about the effects of Original Sin in the next section.)

---

divine providence
God's loving and watchful guidance over his creatures on their way to their final goal and perfection.

Original Sin
The fallen state of human nature into which all generations of people are born. Christ Jesus came to save us from Original Sin.

and an eternal life in store. Our earthly vocation is to be like Christ, that is, to reproduce in our own lives the image of God's Son.

- *God created us male and female out of love and for love.* God made us with the same dignity—male and female, both equally good. Our sexuality encourages us to seek companionship, to depend on each other, and to love each other.

- *God is the creator of all that is seen and unseen.* This includes belief in angels and devils (*CCC*, 325–336; 350–352; 391–395; 414). Attested to in both Scripture and Tradition, angels are spiritual created beings, "surpassing in perfection all visible creatures" (*CCC*, 330). Personal and immortal, angels possess intelligence and free will. Like humans, they had an opportunity to love and accept their loving Creator or reject him out of prideful self-interest. Angels are those invisible spiritual beings who lovingly worshiped God from the beginning. Jesus Christ is the Lord of the angels who were created *through* and *for* him, serving as messengers (*angel* means "messenger") of his saving plan. Examples include the angel Gabriel at the Annunciation and angels who

were present at Jesus' birth, temptation in the desert, in the Garden of Gethsemane, and at his Resurrection and Ascension. Traditionally, Catholics believe that each of us has a guardian angel to watch over us.

Created good by God, Satan and the other demons became evil by their own doing. Their fall consisted of a free, radical, and irrevocable rejection of God and God's reign. Devils are part of the mystery of evil the human mind can never fully grasp. Satan and his demons are creatures, so they cannot prevent God's reign from growing. For example, though God permits devils to tempt us, he will not permit them to harm us. We need not fear their influence in our lives if we stay close to Jesus through prayer and the sacraments. Jesus Christ is victorious over sin, evil, the fallen angels, and death itself.

- *Though essentially good because God made us, humans are tainted with sin.* Because of Original Sin, the human spirit is often willing, but the flesh is weak (see pages 30–31).

- *Through Jesus Christ and by the power of the Holy Spirit, God invites us into a personal relationship with him* (see Chapter 2).

The Fall and Original Sin
(*CCC*, 385–421)

While the book of Genesis tells how God created people in his image and likeness, it also uses symbolic language to tell how Adam and Eve rejected God's love, resulting in humankind's loss of his friendship. Adam and Eve's Original Sin was their misuse of their God-given freedom and their disobedience in not relying on his goodness. Their decision had serious consequences: the immediate loss of the grace of Original Holiness and

---

Justice received from God. Their Original Sin resulted in disunity between God and all their descendants, caused disharmony between nature and humans, and alienated people from each other.

After the Fall, sin affected all humans. Old Testament stories like Cain's murder of Abel and the many accounts of the Chosen People's failure to keep God's Law attest to this reality. Through Original Sin we have inherited a fallen human nature and are deprived of Original Holiness and Justice. Our human nature is also weakened and is subject to ignorance, suffering, the inclination to sin (known as concupiscence), and death (*CCC*, 404–405).

Though Original Sin is inherited by all, it is not an *actual* sin we personally commit. Rather, we are born into a condition where we are inclined to surrender to the powers of evil in the world. Our own efforts cannot liberate us from this condition. Only Jesus Christ has the power to free us from sin. Baptism gives us Christ's life, erases Original Sin, and restores our relationship with God. However, human nature remains weak, so we need the constant help of the Holy Spirit to fight temptation and choose God's will.

Through Salvation History, God never abandoned his sinful creatures. He created a Chosen People and was passionately faithful to them through their history. The high point of God's loving concern was his promise to send a Messiah who would restore humankind's proper relationship with God:

But you, Bethlehem-Ephrathah too small to be among the clans of Judah, From you shall come forth for me one who is to be ruler in Israel; Whose origin is from of old, from ancient times. (Mi 5:1)

In God's own time, he was true to his word and sent his only Son, Jesus Christ. Jesus' Passion, Death, Resurrection, and Ascension overcame the effects of Original Sin.

The victory that Christ won over sin has given us greater blessings than those which sin had taken away from us: "where sin increased, grace overflowed all the more" (Rom 5:20). (*CCC*, 420)

There is a tremendous reward for those who believe in the one, true God. The reward is manifested in several ways. Here are three:

1. *We come to knowledge of God's greatness and his love for us.* God loves us unconditionally. He created us out of nothing, gave each of us many gifts and talents, and loves us to the point of sending his Son to redeem us and give us everlasting life.
2. *Our life has meaning.* Belief in God reveals our true identity as brothers and sisters of one another. It reveals our dignity and gives us a mission to care for each other and for the precious world God entrusted to us.
3. *God will always care for us.* Salvation History reveals that God will not abandon us when we sin. He will forgive us if we turn back to him. We should always trust him and his love.

For Reflection
- Read the biblical account of Cain and Abel as found in Genesis 4:1–8. In your judgment, what was the true motivation for Cain's action? Write of a time this same motivation was at work in one of your own actions or one you witnessed in some other person.
- Tell two ways that you recognize God in creation.

Original Holiness and Justice
The state of man and woman before sin. "From their friendship with God flowed the happiness of their existence in paradise" (CCC, 384).

concupiscence
An inclination to commit sin that can be found in human desires and appetites as a result of Original Sin.

Homework Assignment

1. Complete the For Review questions on page 32.
2. Complete all Ongoing Assignments from page 36.

- **Class Activity:** Bring a large handheld mirror, a small container of mud or wet clay, a bottle of water, a large bowl, and a few paper towels with you to class. Begin by reminding your students that they are made in the image of God. They might think of their soul as being like a mirror. When God looks at them, he expects to see a reflection of his own goodness.
  - Open the container of mud and scoop out a good amount. Explain to the students that the mud is like the effects of sin: when it is smeared across the mirror, the image in the mirror is blocked or distorted.
  - Hand the muddy mirror to a student and ask them to pass it around the room. Explain Original Sin using the model of the muddy mirror. When Adam and Eve sinned, the stain of that sin marked human nature and was passed on through the generations, just as the mirror is passed from student to student.
  - Ask the students to return the mirror to you. Pour water from your bottle over the mirror until the mud is washed away. Dry it carefully and show it again to your students. As you do so, remind them that the actions of Jesus made it possible for the stain of Original Sin to be washed away in the waters of baptism.
- **Class Discussion:** Make sure to save time to read and discuss the three rewards of faith on page 31 and how they are manifested. Note also the quotation from the *Catechism* on the effects of faith in the Background Information on page 33.
- **Journal Assignment:** Close this lesson by inviting students to respond to the For Reflection question on page 31 in their journals.

Background Information

Effects of Faith
The *Catechism of the Catholic Church* teaches that:

The Symbol of faith confesses the greatness of God's gifts to his work of creation, and even more in redemption and sanctification. What faith confesses, the sacraments communicate: by the sacraments of rebirth, Christians have become "children of God," "partakers of the divine nature." (1692)

For Review Answers (page 32)

1. See pages 29–30 for possible responses.

2. *Original Sin* is the fallen state of human nature into which all generations of people are born. (page 30)

3. The effects of Original Sin include the following: loss of God's friendship, loss of grace, loss of Original Holiness and Justice, disunity between God and humanity, disharmony between nature and humans, alienation between people, a fallen human nature, ignorance, suffering, concupiscence, and death. (pages 30–31)

4. Angels are messengers of God who watch over us. (page 30)

5. Satan and demons are fallen angels created by God who have rejected his will and reign. (page 30)

6. Through belief in God we come to knowledge of God's greatness and love for us, our life has meaning, and God will always care for us. (page 31)

For Review

1. Name five things Catholics believe about God as Creator.
2. Define *Original Sin*.
3. Name two effects of Original Sin.
4. What is the main function of angels in relation to humans?
5. What is the Catholic belief concerning the existence of Satan and demons?
6. What difference can believing in God make for your life?

Explaining Your Faith

How can Christians say God is good and loving when there is so much suffering and evil in the world (CCC, 309–314; 324)?

We should make it very clear first of all that God is supremely good and loving, even in the midst of suffering. God has proven his love in so many ways. For example, he did not have to create the world, but he did—out of love. And he created us humans in his image and likeness and gave us the ability to love and be loved.

Sacred Scripture, the living Word of God, tells the story of God's love through human history, which reaches its climax in the sending of his Son, Jesus Christ. Our Lord's own suffering and Death prove beyond any doubt God's immense love for human beings. Christ has redeemed us from our sins and won for us a share in God's own life for eternity. He has given us the gift of the Holy Spirit and invites each of us into friendship with him. He continues to be present to us in the Catholic Church, the Body of Christ, and comes to us in the sacred liturgy, especially the Seven Sacraments. In the Eucharist, a sacrament of love and union, we can receive the Risen Lord in our own hearts and allow him to live in us.

In short, Salvation History is the story of God's immense love for humanity in general and for each of us as individuals.

Suffering and evil are an unfortunate part of the human story. God, however, does not cause or send suffering. He is all-good and only brings about goodness. Then how do we explain the existence of suffering and evil, a question that has challenged all religions, including Christianity, in all ages? The *Catechism of the Catholic Church* summarizes the dilemma this way: "Faith gives us the certainty that God would not permit an evil if he did not cause a good to come from that very evil, by ways that we shall fully know only in eternal life" (CCC, 324).

By looking at Divine Revelation in Sacred Scripture, we can gain some insight on this last point. For example, the Old Testament book of Job confronts the very question of why bad things happen to good people. Job was a good man who lost all his children and property and contracted a horrible disease. Always trusting God despite his setbacks, Job's sufferings revealed one partial answer to why there is suffering: good can come from it. As the proverb goes, "God writes straight with crooked lines." Job became a more holy man, a better friend, and more trusting of God because of his sufferings. The story of Joseph in Genesis 37–50 also points this out. Joseph was shoved into a ditch and left for dead there by his jealous brothers. Yet from suffering he emerged as the pharaoh's assistant in Egypt, in charge of dispensing food during a worldwide famine. In this position he was able to save his own family from starvation.

A key insight came to Job toward the end of his trials. Job says to God:

> I have dealt with great things that I do not understand; things too wonderful for me, which I cannot know. I had heard of you by word of mouth, but now my eye has seen you. Therefore I disown what I have said, and repent in dust and ashes. (Job 42:3, 5–6)

Job admits that God's ways are mysterious and that ultimately we cannot fully understand them. It takes humility and trust to admit that we can never understand the mystery of innocent suffering and evil in the world. We are not God, and we don't see things from his perspective. We need to know that we are totally dependent on him and not in control of everything. Therefore, we can never adequately explain all the evil that befalls us.

But we can explain some of it. Consider these points:

- *God's created world is on a journey to perfection.* God could have created a "perfect" world where there would be no physical evil. But in God's goodness and wisdom, he decided to create a world that is in a process of becoming. It is not yet perfect. Nature's constructive and destructive forces exist side by side. The more perfect exists alongside the less perfect. "With physical good there also exists physical evil as long as creation has not reached perfection" (*CCC*, 310).

    Just as a renowned concert pianist must toil to perfect his or her skills, so the world undergoes pain to achieve the perfection God has in store. We cannot now appreciate the pain involved in this growth process because innocent people suffer at the hands of nature. But we believe that in God's wisdom this growth is good both for individuals and humanity as a whole as we journey to perfection.

- *The misuse of freedom is the cause of much moral evil.* Out of divine goodness, God created humans and angels as *intelligent* and *free* creatures, not mindless robots or unthinking puppets. The gifts of intellect and free will are what make us beings of tremendous dignity and not mere automatons. But these two gifts require responsibility. We must freely choose to love God and others on our journey toward eternity. When we refuse to love, we sin. And sin brings about incredible evil and suffering.

    Revelation tells us that when some angels chose to sin, they (the fallen angels, or devils) unleashed evil in the world in opposition to God. Satan is known as the father of lies, a deceiver of the whole world. He and the other devils try to get humans to revolt against God through disobedience, that is, to sin. Satan

acts in the world out of hatred for God; and "although his action may cause grave injuries—of a spiritual nature and, indirectly, even of a physical nature" (*CCC*, 395)—his power is limited because he and the other devils are only creatures. He cannot do anything to prevent the building up of God's reign.

Unlike Jesus, who resisted the lies of Satan in the desert, humans from the time of Adam and Eve have given in to his deceptions, which have led to sin. And human sin has resulted in terrible moral evils like war, rape, abortion, drug abuse, prejudice, and greed. God does not *cause* this moral evil. Humans, by misusing their freedom, are the cause. God *permits* moral evil, however, because God loves and respects the free creatures he has made. And in a way known only to God (a truth that Job eventually admitted), God knows how to derive good out of all evil. As St. Paul wrote, "We know that all things work for good for those who love God" (Rom 8:28).

- *Christian faith announces the Good News of Jesus Christ, who conquered the forces of evil.* Certainly, the worst moral evil in the world was for humans to put to death the innocent God-man. Like any normal person, Jesus abhorred suffering and even asked his Father to remove it. But Jesus freely embraced the sufferings that unjustly came his way by submitting to his Father: "May your will be done."

    God heard Jesus' prayer, not by saving Jesus from death, but by saving him *out* of death. Jesus' suffering, Death, and Resurrection have conquered the worst evil: death and separation from God. If we love as Jesus teaches us to do and join our sufferings to him, we will share forever in the Lord's blissful, superabundant, joy-filled life. This is Good News, actually great news, that can help us cope with the mystery of evil and suffering.

Write of a time in your own life when something good came after a period of trial, suffering, or a setback.

Extending the Lesson

Class Activity: You can play a modified team game of *Jeopardy* following these rules:

1. Divide the class into three teams. Each student will represent his or her team to answer one question. Once they have answered one question correctly, another team member will take over.

2. Rather than trying to determine which teams buzzes first, address questions to each team in order. If the first student answers incorrectly, the next team's representative gets a chance to answer.

3. Each question answered correctly the first time earns three points for the team. Each team that answers a question missed by another team scores one point.

4. Following a missed question, play resumes with the team after the team who first missed the question. (For example, Team A misses a question. Team B also misses the answer, but Team C is able to answer correctly. When play resumes, the next question is addressed to Team B.)

5. As in *Jeopardy*, the question is read as a statement and the answer must be given in question format.

Chapter 1 Review Lesson
Objectives

In this lesson, the students will be able to:
- review the highlighted vocabulary terms in Chapter 1.
- check answers to the For Review questions.
- prepare for the Chapter 1 Test.

Preview

This lesson is intended to provide the opportunity to wrap up the material in this chapter and to perhaps cover any lessons that were left undone. It is also intended to serve as a review for the Chapter 1 Test. Plan to allow for opportunities for both individual study and study for students in small or large groups.

Bell Ringers

- **Class Activity:** Have each student rank the top five most important lessons about God the Father from Chapter 1. Suggest that they use the Chapter Quick View for ideas. Then, have them get into groups of four or five and create one master list of the top five most important lessons. Have each group write their lists on the board. Create a master top five list based on these results and discuss why these lessons were so important.

- **Class Discussion:** Discuss the answers to the For Review questions on page 32.

- **Direct Instruction:** Collect all Ongoing Assignments for Chapter 1.

Teaching Approaches

- **Class Activity:** The material from this summary list can be used as the basis for a variety of familiar games such as *Jeopardy*, *Wheel of Fortune*, or even "Hangman." For example, the material in the first Chapter Quick View point can be reformatted as *Jeopardy*-style answers and questions:

    - Who the vast majority of people believe in on the basis of both intellectual proofs and workings of the human heart. *Answer: Who is God?*

    - Persons who do not believe in God. *Answer: Who are atheists?*

    - Persons who do not believe it is possible to prove or disprove God's existence. *Answer: Who are agnostics?*

- **Individual Assignment:** Have the students complete the crossword puzzle on page 35. Point out that the instructions say "If the answer requires more than one word, separate the words with a blank box." Check their answers as a class, and invite them to use the responses to study for the Chapter Test. Answers are on page 37 of this text.

Chapter 1 Test Lesson

Objectives

In this lesson, the students will:
- be tested on the material in Chapter 1.
- report on their Ongoing Assignments from Chapter 1.
- be introduced to the main subject matter of Chapter 2.

 Preview

This lesson is primarily intended for the students to take the Chapter 1 Test (starting on page 285 and also online at www.avemariapress.com). After the test, have the students report on their Ongoing Assignments and then introduce them to Chapter 2.

CHAPTER QUICK VIEW

- The vast majority of people believe in God. St. Thomas Aquinas offered intellectual proofs. The human heart is also able to discover God. Atheists do not believe God exists. Agnostics claim ignorance on the question. Deists picture God as a watchmaker who does not get involved in the world he made. (pages 16–21)
- *Transcendence* is a quality of God's total otherness; *immanence* is a quality of God's closeness to us. (page 20)
- God is an absolute mystery, totally other than humans. (page 22)
- *Divine Revelation* is God's free self-communication of himself by which he makes known the mysteries of his divine plan. (page 22)
- God entered into *covenant* with humankind. A covenant is a solemn, open-ended agreement of love. God promised to care for humans always while humans were to remain faithful to the one true God. God's greatest and final covenant was the sending of his only Son, Jesus Christ, to save humanity from its sins and rescue it from death and the evil one. (pages 22–24)
- *Faith* is the human response to Divine Revelation. (page 25)
- The deposit of Divine Revelation is found in Sacred Scripture and the Sacred Tradition of the Church. (pages 24–25)
- The God of mystery revealed his name to be Yahweh ("I am"). This shows that God is the source of all being, the Holy One in our midst who is pure Spirit, unchangeable, unique, infinite, all-powerful, eternal, immense, merciful, gracious, living, faithful, and true. (pages 26–27)
- The central dogma about the one true God is that he is a Trinity of Persons—Father, Son, and Holy Spirit. (page 27)
- Jesus tells us that we can address God as *Abba*—"Father." However, Jesus has a unique relationship to the Father as his eternal Son. (page 27)
- God made humans in his image and likeness; thus we have incomparable dignity. (page 29)
- God created an orderly and beautiful world out of nothing. This world includes both visible realities and invisible realities like angels and devils. Humans are the summit of God's creation, are in solidarity with it, and must respect and develop it. (pages 29–30)
- Adam and Eve, created in God's image with the ability to think and to love, rejected God through an act of disobedience. This is known as *Original Sin*. All humans have inherited the effects of Original Sin, including an inclination to sin and a fallen human nature that leads to death. (pages 30–31)
- Belief in the one true God gives life tremendous meaning by showing that our Creator loves us beyond what we can imagine and revealing our true identity as his children and brothers and sisters in Christ with an eternal destination of happiness in union with the Blessed Trinity. (page 31)

Extending the Lesson

Class Activity: Using index cards, or by copying onto card stock and cutting out the cards from Chapter 1, Handout 3 "Sample Memory Cards" (starting on page 285 and also online at www.avemariapress.com), create a deck of cards that can be used to play a variety of memory games. On one set of cards write each vocabulary word. On another set, write each definition. Shuffle the two sets together to make one deck for the following games. It will be helpful to have one deck for every four students. This deck can be added to with words and definitions from later chapters as the course progresses. This is an excellent means of reviewing information over the length of the course. If the students have been creating "picture cue" flash cards, invite them to use these cards to review for the test.

Play "Memory" by mixing the cards together and laying them out face down in a grid. Students take turns turning over two cards at a time. If they turn over a word and its matching definition and know that they match, they pick up and keep the pair. If not, the two cards are returned to their face-down position and play resumes with the next player taking a turn. If a player attempts to pick up two cards that do not match, he or she must return the cards and forfeit the next turn. If a player fails to pick up a matched pair, he or she will lose the next turn if any of the other players matches the pair in the next round. Continue until all the words have been successfully matched. This game works best when games are limited to no more than four players.

Homework Assignment

1. Complete any unfinished assignments from Chapter 1.
2. Study for the Chapter 1 Test.

Learning the Language of Faith

Test your knowledge of important terms that you have learned in this chapter and the Introduction. If the answer requires more than one word, separate the words with a blank box.

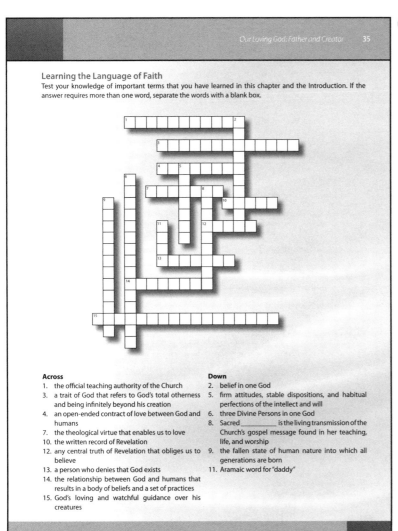

Across

1. the official teaching authority of the Church
3. a trait of God that refers to God's total otherness and being infinitely beyond his creation
4. an open-ended contract of love between God and humans
7. the theological virtue that enables us to love
10. the written record of Revelation
12. any central truth of Revelation that obliges us to believe
13. a person who denies that God exists
14. the relationship between God and humans that results in a body of beliefs and a set of practices
15. God's loving and watchful guidance over his creatures

Down

2. belief in one God
5. firm attitudes, stable dispositions, and habitual perfections of the intellect and will
6. three Divine Persons in one God
8. Sacred _____ is the living transmission of the Church's gospel message found in her teaching, life, and worship
9. the fallen state of human nature into which all generations are born
11. Aramaic word for "daddy"

 Teaching Approaches

- **Chapter Test:** Distribute a copy of the Chapter 1 Test (starting on page 285 and also online at www.avemariapress.com) to every student. Allow approximately 35 to 45 minutes for the students to complete the exam.
- **Class Activity:** Determine a way to check on several of the Ongoing Assignments (page 36). For example, encourage students who did Assignment 1 to choose two students to enact the dialog between an atheist and a believer. Allow students who did Assignment 2 to display their visual presentation on a psalm for the class. For Assignment 5, allow for a short presentation on the findings about the teaching of evolution in the public schools. Collect written reports for each of the assignments as they apply.
- **Prayer Experience**
  - Have the students turn to the Book of Psalms in the Old Testament. Read pages 36–37 about the psalms.
  - Have each student read Psalm 23 silently to themselves. Then, have them read it again, this time inviting them to focus on a word or phrase that jumps out at them.
  - Invite them to write a response to the *Reflection* in their journals.

Learning the Language of Faith Answers (page 35)

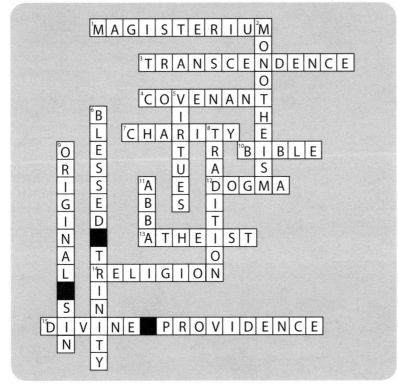

Homework Assignment

Read the Chapter 2 outline and opening section of Chapter 2, "Encouraging Words" (pages 40–41).

Chapter 1 Test Answers

All questions are worth 4 points each.

Part 1: Matching

1. K
2. D
3. H
4. O
5. L
6. G
7. M
8. E
9. B
10. A

Part 2: True or False

11. T
12. F
13. F
14. F
15. F
16. F

Part 3: Short Fill-ins

17. Divine Providence
18. Abba

Part 4: The Apostles' Creed

19. creator of Heaven and earth
20. by the power of the Holy Spirit
21. the resurrection of the body

Part 5: Short Answers

22. Answers may include the following: omnipresent, omnipotence, all knowing, unique, eternal, immense, contains all things, immutable, simple, a pure Spirit, personal, or holy (pages 26–27)

23. The covenant with Noah, the covenant with Abraham, the Sinai covenant, and the New Covenant, Jesus Christ (pages 22–24)

24. The effects of Original Sin include the following: loss of God's friendship, loss of grace, loss of Original Holiness and Justice, disunity between God and humanity, disharmony between nature and humans, alienation between people, a fallen human nature, ignorance, suffering, concupiscence, and death. (pages 30–31)

Ongoing Assignments

As you cover the material in this chapter, choose and complete at least three of these assignments.

1. Write a dialogue between an atheist and a believer who is trying to convince the person that God exists.
2. Read a psalm of praise (for example, Ps 19, 29, 65, or 104). Create a visual presentation to illustrate the object of the praise.
3. Copy into a notebook or journal ten important quotes from the *Dogmatic Constitution on Divine Revelation*. This document is online at the official Vatican website.
4. Decide which attribute of God is being named or described in the following Scripture passages:

   - Lamentations 5:17–20
   - Jeremiah 10:10–12
   - Psalm 139:1–6
   - Isaiah 55
   - Job 37:16
   - Jeremiah 32:17, 27
   - Psalm 139:7–12
   - Isaiah 48:3–5

5. Research current debates on the teaching of evolution in the public schools. Prepare a short written or oral report.
6. Write a report on some of the new information you have discovered in this chapter on either the existence of God or the existence of angels.
7. Read and report on Greg Friedman, O.F.M.'s, "Facing Questions of Faith" *Youth Update* (St. Anthony Messenger Press).
8. Search the Old Testament and New Testament for passages that describe God. Transcribe several favorite Scripture passages into your journal.
9. At a parish function, interview at least five people on why they believe God exists. Prepare a report on your findings.
10. Prepare a PowerPoint presentation on how angels have been depicted in art through the ages.

Prayer Reflection

Inspired by the Holy Spirit, the Psalms proclaim God's steadfast love and fidelity to Israel as God's special possession. The three major types of Psalms are hymns of praise; petitions, which typically end on a note of confidence; and Psalms of thanksgiving. Today, the Church uses the Psalms in her own prayer life, especially at liturgies, for example, the Responsorial Psalm featured during the Mass. Reading and praying the Psalms put us in touch with spiritual feelings that run the gamut of human emotions and desires. They help us lift our minds and hearts to God and cry, "Alleluia!" (which means "Praise Yahweh!")

Psalm 23
The LORD is my shepherd; there is nothing I lack.
   In green pastures you let me graze;
   to safe waters you lead me;
   you restore my strength.
You guide me along the right path
   for the sake of your name.
Even when I walk through a dark valley,
   I fear no harm for you are at my side;
   your rod and staff give me courage.

You set a table before me
   as my enemies watch;
You anoint my head with oil;
   my cup overflows.

Only goodness and love will pursue me
    all the days of my life;
I will dwell in the house of the LORD
    for years to come.

- *Reflection*: How is God guiding and leading you in your life right now? Are you listening to his voice?
- *Resolution*: Resolve to go to Mass one time on your own in the following weeks to thank God in a special way for all the gifts he has given you. Receive the Lord in Holy Communion.

Part 6: Brief Essay

25. Almost anything can be a "proof" for God's existence depending on the individual. So be generous in accepting your students' answers. For full credit, their rationale should match their "proof."

2 Jesus Christ: Lord and Savior

Overview of the Chapter

Brace yourself; this chapter is full of the essentials of the Catholic faith. It begins with a reflection on the person of Jesus; then delves into his life, mission, and ministry; and concludes with a treatment of the nature of Christ. In other words, this chapter provides a brief overview of courses in New Testament Scriptures, Christology, and the Paschal Mystery.

Some suggestions for covering the material in this chapter in an effective way are to use multimedia presentations of the life of Christ and to have students work on a chapter project to summarize the material of each lesson. There are a number of movies in the Resources section of this manual that you should consider showing in parts or in their entirety. Another suggestion would be to assign a project that depicts the life of Christ and his significance on poster board, an illustrated book, or a movie.

The chapter highlights the doctrine of the Incarnation, underscoring the reasons for God becoming man in Jesus Christ: to save humankind so we might know God's love, to be our model of holiness, and so we can become children of God (*CCC*, 456–460). It then examines the truths that lie behind the personal name *Jesus* and his titles of Christ, Son of God, Lord, Suffering Servant, and Son of Man. Students also learn some popular Christian symbols for Christ: the Alpha and Omega, INRI, and the Chi-Rho.

Next the chapter focuses on both the non-Christian sources for Jesus as a historical person and the New Testament sources. The books of the New Testament are listed and a description of the three-stage process of their formation is given: the period of the historical Jesus (6 BC–AD 30/33), the time of oral tradition (AD 30/33–50), and the writing of the New Testament books themselves (AD 50–ca. 120).

Next, the chapter follows the lead of the *Catechism of the Catholic Church* by reviewing the "mysteries" of Christ's life:

- The infancy narratives, which reveal the nature of Christ's entry into the world; his incorporation into the Chosen People; his manifestation to the world; how evil warred against him from the beginning; and how he lived an obedient, humble life in Nazareth (the question of Jesus' so-called brothers and sisters and a definition of the dogma of the virgin birth are also taken up here).
- His public life: his baptism by John the Baptist and its meaning; a summary of his public preaching (truly good news); a discussion of his miracles (powerful signs of a compassionate Savior); and the meaning of his Transfiguration.
- The Paschal Mystery of Jesus' Passion, Death, Resurrection, and Glorification is emphasized as the heart of the Good News of Jesus Christ.

Throughout this lengthy section of the chapter, students are asked to read sections of the Gospels to see how these events play out in salvation history. They are also asked to apply certain lessons from the life of Jesus to their own lives. You may want to read together one of the Passion narratives or view one of the feature films on Jesus at this juncture.

The chapter then moves on to the classic faith formulations of Catholic belief about Jesus. Heresies like docetism, Arianism, Nestorianism, and monophysitism are introduced as the catalysts for the teaching of various early ecumenical councils and the dogmas they proclaimed: Jesus is the only Son of God, true God, begotten not made, one in being with the Father. All was made through the Son. Jesus is one Divine Person with two distinct natures, human and divine. Mary is truly the Mother of God. Jesus possessed a human intellect and a human will. Jesus truly shared our humanity.

The *Catechism of the Catholic Church* reminds us that at the heart of our catechesis is the person of Jesus Christ (426). As *Catechesi Tradendae* affirms:

> Whatever be the level of his responsibility in the Church, every catechist must constantly endeavor to transmit by his teaching and behavior the teaching and life of Jesus. (6)

As religion teachers, we should remind ourselves that our own love for Jesus will supplement greatly the content of this chapter. We must witness to our Lord, sharing with our young people the central role he plays in our lives. Why else would we become religion teachers in the first place?

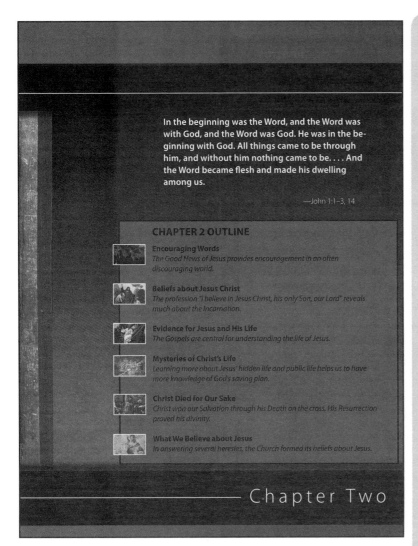

In the beginning was the Word, and the Word was with God, and the Word was God. He was in the beginning with God. All things came to be through him, and without him nothing came to be.... And the Word became flesh and made his dwelling among us.

—John 1:1–3, 14

CHAPTER 2 OUTLINE

Encouraging Words
The Good News of Jesus provides encouragement in an often discouraging world.

Beliefs about Jesus Christ
The profession "I believe in Jesus Christ, his only Son, our Lord" reveals much about the Incarnation.

Evidence for Jesus and His Life
The Gospels are central for understanding the life of Jesus.

Mysteries of Christ's Life
Learning more about Jesus' hidden life and public life helps us to have more knowledge of God's saving plan.

Christ Died for Our Sake
Christ won our Salvation through his Death on the cross. His Resurrection proved his divinity.

What We Believe about Jesus
In answering several heresies, the Church formed its beliefs about Jesus.

Chapter Two

Resources

 Audiovisual Materials

The Bridge
An allegory on God's love for us in Christ. A father must decide to save train passengers or his son who is running on the railway tracks. Powerful (11-minute video, Ignatius Press).

Face of Jesus in Art
A stunning documentary on how Jesus has been portrayed in art through the ages. Very well done (2-hour video or DVD, Vision Video).

Gospel of John
A word-for-word, well-acted, and powerful movie of Jesus based solely on the Gospel of John. Its theatrical release in 2004 garnered very good reviews. The narrator is the distinguished actor Christopher Plummer. Jesus is played very well by the acclaimed actor Henry Ian Cusick. The movie is long and may not appeal to younger students as much as other Jesus movies (180-minute feature film on DVD, available from www.visualbible.com).

continued on page 48

Resources

 Internet Links see www.avemariapress.com

Chapter Outline

- Encouraging Words
- Beliefs about Jesus Christ
- Evidence for Jesus and His Life
- Mysteries of Christ's Life
- Christ Died for Our Sake
- What We Believe about Jesus

Advance Preparations

Assign one or more of the Ongoing Assignments (pages 65–66) projects early in the chapter.

Encouraging Words (ST pages 40–41)
- The song "This Is Your Time" by Michael W. Smith for the Journal Assignment on page 42.
- A bible for each student for the Class Activity on page 43.

Beliefs about Jesus Christ (ST pages 42–45)
- An image of Jesus and a basket or box for the Class Activity on page 44.
- Index cards or sheets of paper and tape for the Class Activity on page 45.
- A biblical concordance or connection to a biblical search engine for the Individual Assignment on page 45.
- Images of early Church symbols for the Individual Assignment on page 45.

Evidence for Jesus and His Life (ST pages 45–49)
- Images of Jesus for the Prayer Experience on page 48.

Mysteries of Christ's Life (ST pages 50–57)
- Copies of Chapter 2, Handout 1 "Questions about Jesus" (starting on page 285 and also online at www.avemariapress.com) for the Group activity on page 53.
- Copies of Chapter 2, Handout 2 "The Infancy Narratives" (starting on page 285 and also online at www.avemariapress.com) for the Direct Instruction on page 53.
- Copies of Chapter 2, Handout 3 "The Kingdom of God" (starting on page 285 and also online at www.avemariapress.com) for the Individual Assignment on page 55.
- Copies of Chapter 2, Handout 4 "Intercessory Prayer Service" (starting on page 285 and also online at www.avemariapress.com) for the Prayer Experience on page 58.

Christ Died for Our Sake (ST pages 57–61)
- Copies of Chapter 2, Handout 5 "Scriptural Way of the Cross" (starting on page 285 and also online at www.avemariapress.com) for the Prayer Experience on page 60.

What We Believe about Jesus (ST pages 61–64)
- A small balance scale and objects of different sizes and weights for the Class Activity on page 64.

Encouraging Words (pages 40–41)

Objectives

In this lesson, the students will:

• recognize how the Gospel offers encouragement versus the often gloomy disposition of humankind.

• take a pre-assessment on some basic facts about Jesus and beliefs in him.

• decide what they want to know about Jesus Christ in this chapter.

• view a motion picture presentation on Jesus that sets the tone for the rest of the chapter.

Preview

Plan to show all or part of one of the films on Jesus suggested in the Resources section on page 41. Consider assigning a project due at the end of this section that summarizes the many parts of the events and meaning of Jesus' life. Also, have them select one or more of the Ongoing Assignments on pages 65–66.

Bell Ringers

• **Class Discussion:** Ask a student to summarize the opening story of the chapter. Discuss how this story made them feel. Ask if the students think they would have done the same.

• **Journal Assignment:** Play the song "This Is Your Time" by Michael W. Smith on CD, MP3, or online video. Explain that this song was written about Cassie Bernall, a high school girl killed during the Columbine high school shootings of 1999. She was killed for answering "yes" to the question, "Do you believe in God?" Like Thomas Vander Woude, she gave up her life for others. Write the following lyrics to the song on the board and ask students to journal about their response: **"Faced with the question [to deny God and live], what would you say?"**

Teaching Approaches

Encouraging Words

The life of Jesus Christ has often been described as "the greatest story ever told." It is a true story that tells of God's immense love for us shown in the Life, Death, and Resurrection of his beloved Son. Jesus has given his all so that we might have eternal life. Christ has also inspired countless of his followers throughout the ages to love in imitation of him. One such follower was Thomas S. Vander Woude.

Thomas was a remarkable man. Known by friends, family, and acquaintances as selfless and humble, he served his country for seventeen years in the navy, then as a commercial airline pilot, and finally as the athletic director at Christendom College in Virginia. He was also a volunteer coach at a Catholic high school, where he was known as a person who always cared for others. A daily communicant with a special devotion to Our Lady of the Rosary, Thomas and his wife raised seven sons, one of whom is a Catholic priest.

At the age of sixty-six, Mr. Thomas Vander Woude made the ultimate sacrifice when he died while helping his youngest son, Joseph, who has Down syndrome. Joseph fell into a septic tank on the family property. Thomas immediately jumped into the tank and positioned himself underneath his son to hold him up. He pushed his son up while a worker helped pull him to safety. The effort, however, sorely taxed Thomas's heart. He collapsed and could not be revived by the paramedics who arrived on the scene.

More than two thousand people, seventy priests, and one bishop attended his funeral Mass. All paid tribute to this great man of faith whose life—and sacrificing death—inspired and continues to inspire them all. His devotion to his

Extending the Lesson

Guest Speaker: Invite an adult and a teenager who each model Christ in their lives to give brief witness talks on the importance of their faith.

Background Information

Suicide Prevention

Issues of discouragement and despair are profound for many adolescents. Teen suicide is one of the leading causes of death for this age group. According to the *Catechism*, although "suicide is contrary to love for the living God . . . grave psychological disturbances . . . can diminish the responsibility of the one committing suicide. We should not despair of the eternal salvation of persons who have taken their own lives" (*CCC*, 2281–2283).

There are many Internet sources for good information on suicide prevention including www.save.org and www.yellowribbon.org. You may want to spend some time reviewing warning signs of depression (the leading cause of teen suicide) and suicide with your class. Make sure to include local suicide prevention hotline numbers in your discussion. Many local numbers can be found at www.suicidehotlines.com.

Life-Giving Words

Jesus preached many words of encouragement in his public ministry. His life-giving words are a good antidote to those times when we get discouraged. Considering Christ's words can comfort us when we get down in situations like the following. Note in your journal three times when you were discouraged. Explain how the Lord can be a source of strength for you in similar situations in the future.

You say . . .	Scripture says . . .
"It's impossible."	"What is impossible for human beings is possible for God" (Lk 18:27).
"No one loves me."	"For God so loved the world that he gave his only Son, so that everyone who believes in him might not perish but might have eternal life" (Jn 3:16).
"I can't forgive myself."	"If we acknowledge our sins, he is faithful and just and will forgive our sins and cleanse us from every wrongdoing" (1 Jn 1:9).
"I am burned out."	"Come to me, all you who labor and are burdened, and I will give you rest" (Mt 11:28).
"I can't do it."	"I have the strength for everything through him who empowers me" (Phil 4:13).
"I feel so alone."	"I will never forsake you or abandon you" (Heb 13:5).

God, to the Blessed Mother, and to his sons led him to make the greatest sacrifice of all. Jesus, for him, was his model and his guide. He lived the Gospel of Jesus Christ.[5]

This chapter focuses on the encouraging Gospel, or "Good News," of Jesus Christ. It examines in more detail the statements that Catholics profess about Jesus Christ in the Apostles' Creed. Other areas of study include the sources for how the Church has collected knowledge about Jesus and the mysteries surrounding Jesus' public life.

For Reflection

- Tell three things you believe about Jesus Christ.
- Who is the person you know who is most like Jesus? Why is this so?
- How would you like your personal relationship with Jesus to develop?

Gospel
A term meaning "Good News." The term refers to (1) Jesus' own preaching, (2) the preaching about Jesus the Savior (Jesus Christ is the Good News proclaimed by the Church), and (3) the four Spirit-inspired written versions of the Good News—the Gospels of Matthew, Mark, Luke, and John.

Homework Assignment

1. Complete the For Reflection questions, in writing, from page 41.

2. Read the text section, "Beliefs about Jesus Christ" (pages 42–44).

3. Read the list of Ongoing Assignment projects on pages 65–66. Plan to make a decision on which project you will do by the next class session.

- **Class Discussion:** Continue the discussion noted in the last section. Ask the students to share which of the "You say . . ." statements from page 41 they feel the most. How do the words of encouragement from Scripture make them feel? Brainstorm ways they can keep these encouraging words in mind in the future.

- **Class Activity:** Pass out bibles to each student. Allow each student to choose one book of the New Testament and skim through it for words of encouragement similar to the four examples found in the Student Text on page 41. If you have more than twenty-seven students in your class, divide some of the longer books in half. Students should also suggest times that the phrases they identify might be most encouraging.

- **Class Discussion:** Share with the class your own brief answer to the second For Reflection question, "Who is the person you know who is most like Jesus?" Ask them to brainstorm qualities that a person who was "like Christ" might have. Keep the list running on the board and ask them to record the list in their notebooks or journals. They can mark the list with stars next to those qualities they think are most important.

- **Individual Assignment:** Have the students write answers on a sheet of paper to the "What Do You Know about Jesus?" quiz on page 42. Then have them turn to page 66 to check the answers (also listed on page 43 of this TWE). Collect their responses and review them to see what areas the students will need the most instruction in this chapter.

- **Class Activity:** Have the students make a list of questions about Jesus that they would like to find answers to during the course of this chapter. Write these questions on a poster board titled "What we want to know about Jesus" and post it in the room to reference throughout the Chapter 2 lessons.

What Do You Know about Jesus?
Answers (page 42)

1.	T	6.	F
2.	A	7.	T
3.	T	8.	B
4.	F	9.	C
5.	C	10.	F

Beliefs about Jesus Christ

(pages 42–44)

Objectives

In this lesson, the students will:

- explain the significance of the Incarnation;
- identify and explain the many titles and symbols for Christ that come from Scripture and the traditions of the early Church.
- explain how Jesus fulfilled the three roles of the Messiah: *priest, prophet,* and *king*.

Preview

There are many famous paintings of Jesus of which inexpensive replications are readily available. Try to find at least five or six in your school library or resource center that reveal different aspects of Jesus: Jesus the teacher with his disciples gathered around; Jesus in the garden or on the cross, the Suffering Servant; the kingly Jesus with scepter and throne perhaps; the Good Shepherd, etc. An Internet search using the words "Catholic art" will bring up many sources if you are unable to find enough variety around your school. Save these images to use as a part of a Prayer Experience in the next lesson.

Bell Ringers

- **Class Activity:** On the board, write the following phrase: "Who do you say that I am?" Underneath it, hang an easily recognizable picture of Jesus. As students arrive, ask them to answer the question on a small piece of scratch paper and put it in a basket or box at the front of the room.

  Begin pulling papers out of the box and reading aloud some of the answers. Most will say "Jesus" or "Jesus Christ" but you should also get some of his other titles or more complete answers. Explain that you will explore many of the titles and symbols for Jesus in the upcoming lesson and will consider their meaning and significance for the faith.

- Have the students sign up for one or more of the Ongoing Assignments on pages 65–66. Tell them that the assignments will be due during the Review Lesson for Chapter 2.

 Teaching Approaches

- **Direct Instruction:** Remind students that the Apostles' Creed forms the foundation for this portion of the textbook. Look back at the section of the Creed that expresses belief in Jesus Christ: "I believe in Jesus Christ, his only Son, our Lord." These words are intended to express believe in the doctrine of the Incarnation.

Incarnation
The dogma that God's eternal Son assumed a human nature and became man in Jesus Christ to save us from our sins. (The term literally means "taking on human flesh.")

Beliefs about Jesus Christ (CCC, 422–463)

The letter to the Hebrews begins this way:

In times past, God spoke in partial and various ways to our ancestors through the prophets; in these last days, he spoke to us through a son, whom he made heir of all things and through whom he created the universe. (Heb 1:1–2)

Yahweh had gradually revealed himself throughout history, but in Christ, God himself came to the world in the person of his Son. Out of love, God wished to speak his final Word, a word that taught us that he is "the way and the truth and the life" (Jn 14:6).

God's Son, the second Person of the Blessed Trinity, took on human flesh in the person of Jesus Christ. The prologue to the Gospel of John (see page 39) is a statement of this belief. God took on our human nature, body and soul. This is known as the doctrine of the Incarnation. God became man in Jesus Christ who is God incarnate. "Belief in the true Incarnation of the Son of God is the distinctive sign of Christian faith" (CCC, 463). God himself entered human history by becoming one of his creatures, while all the time remaining the Creator of the universe.

Why did the Word become flesh? (see CCC, 456–460). The *Catechism of the Catholic* Church lists four reasons:

1. The Word of God became flesh to save us from sin, death, and eternal separation from God. He did so by

What Do You Know about Jesus?

Before studying this chapter, test some of your knowledge about Jesus. Answer the following questions. (The answers are on page 66.)

1. True or False: The Incarnation refers to God becoming flesh in the person of Jesus.
2. Which of the following is not a book of the New Testament: (a) Daniel, (b) Luke, (c) James, (d) Timothy?
3. True or False: The title *Christ* means "Messiah" or "anointed one."
4. True or False: The "brothers and sisters" of Jesus referred to in the Bible were other children of Jesus' mother Mary.
5. According to Catholic teaching, Jesus Christ has: a) two natures, two persons; b) one nature, two persons; c) one person, two natures; d) one nature, one person.
6. True or False: Jesus came to abolish the Law of Moses.
7. True or False: The Paschal Mystery refers to the Life, Death, Resurrection, and Ascension of Jesus.
8. The following parable of Jesus best illustrates his teaching on love: (a) The Mustard Seed, (b) The Good Samaritan, (c) The Talents, (d) The Rich Fool.
9. When Jesus calls God "Abba" in the New Testament, he is calling him: (a) Friend, (b) Lord, (c) Father, (d) Spirit.
10. True or False: The Jewish people as a whole are responsible for the Death of Jesus.

Background Information

Biblical Concordance

If your students have not yet been introduced to the use of a biblical concordance, this lesson is a good place to do so. A biblical concordance is a helpful tool for Scripture study allowing students to easily locate a Scripture passage by looking up just one word. Concordances also allow students to evaluate which words or phrases are common to various books of the Bible. They can easily find comparisons in the use of a particular word or phrase and note whether concepts were more or less prevalent in the Old or New Testament.

Your school library should have one or more that you can borrow for classroom use. These books are typically large and very heavy, and also somewhat costly, so it is not practical to ask each student to have his or her own. Instead, keep one or more in the classroom and have small groups of students share them or take turns using them. For the Individual Assignment in Extending the Lesson on page 45 of this text, consider photocopying the page (or pages) on which the listing for "Christ" appears, particularly if you have only one or very few concordances available for use.

As many translations of the Bible are available online, the search engine for these websites also serves the same function as a concordance. See, for example, www.biblestudytools.net and www.biblegateway.com.

---

reconciling us with God by atoning for our sins. Christ gave his life so that we could live.

2. "The Word became flesh *so that thus we might know God's love*" (*CCC*, 458). Jesus Christ, as truly human, is able to show us the true nature of God.

3. God took on human flesh to be our model of holiness. Jesus shows us how to imitate him: to love one another as he has loved us (Jn 15:12).

4. God became human to make us sharers in his divine nature.

In the Apostles' Creed, Catholics profess belief in the Incarnation, saying, "I believe in Jesus Christ, his only Son, our Lord." Each of these titles—*Jesus, Christ, Son of God,* and *Lord*—reveals unique and profound truths about the Incarnation. The subsections that follow explore these truths based on each of these titles.

Jesus

The personal name *Jesus* comes from the Hebrew word *Yehoshua* (Joshua), which means "God saves," "God is Salvation," or simply, "Savior." Thus God's own name is present in the person of his Son. The angel Gabriel revealed this name to Mary (Lk 1:31), thus signifying Jesus' identity and mission. From his conception, God had destined that Jesus would save the world from sin and death.

The Gospels of Matthew and Luke tell us Jesus was born in Bethlehem in Judea during the reign of King Herod the Great, perhaps around the year 4–6 BC. (When changing the Roman calendar to correspond with the birth of Jesus, the monk Dionysius Exiguus made a mistake of several years in his calculations. Herod the Great died in 4 BC, so Jesus must have been born some time

before then.) He was raised by his mother, Mary, and foster father, the carpenter Joseph, in the town of Nazareth in Galilee. According to most scholars, Jesus began his preaching and healing ministry in the "fifteenth year of Tiberius Caesar's reign" (from AD 27–28), after being baptized by John the Baptist in the Jordan River. After a period of trial in the desert, Jesus chose twelve close followers called *Apostles* and had many other disciples as well. Jesus proclaimed the coming of God's Kingdom (reign). Because of his preaching, deeds, and claims, Jesus ran afoul of the Jewish religious leaders who claimed he was committing *blasphemy*, that is, claiming to make himself equal to God. Therefore, he was handed over to Roman authorities and ended up "suffering under Pontius Pilate, was crucified, died, and was buried." The story did not end there, however. Jesus Christ is risen from the dead.

Christ

Christ (*Christos* in the Greek) translates the Hebrew title *Messiah.* The Messiah was the "anointed one of Yahweh" through whom all of God's promises to the Chosen People were fulfilled.

Many Jews of Jesus' time were expecting the Messiah to be a political leader who would throw off the yoke of the Romans and restore Israel to its position of glory. Although Jesus accepted the title Christ when he asked his Apostles his true identity (Mt 16:13–17), he had to reinterpret the meaning of the title for them. Jesus understood that the Messiah's role was to suffer in accomplishing the Father's will of ushering in the Kingdom.

After the Resurrection, Christians took a new look at Jesus' life. They saw that he was anointed with the Spirit of God to accomplish Salvation through a life of suffering service. He accomplished

Christ
A title for Jesus meaning "the anointed one." In Greek, the word *Christos* translates the Hebrew *Messiah.*

Salvation
God's forgiveness of sins, accomplished through the mercy of Jesus Christ, resulting in the restoration of friendship with God.

Extending the Lesson

Individual Assignment: Ask the students to look up the word "Christ" in a biblical concordance. (Words are listed alphabetically, as in a dictionary.) If you have photocopied the page(s) (see Background Information, page 44), pass out the copies.

One of the first things students should notice is that the title Christ is never used in two of the four Gospels and only rarely used in the other two. On the other hand, Paul's letters make extensive use of the title. Have the students choose at random a few passages from Paul's letter to the Romans that include the title Christ. Ask individuals to read the passages aloud and then, as a class, try to determine whether Paul is using the title generally—to explain to a gentile audience the role of the Messiah—or specifically—to identify Jesus as the Messiah.

Have students look up the following passages to see examples of how the early Church understood Jesus' role as priest, prophet, and king: Hebrews 9:11–14; Luke 4:14–21; and Philippians 2:9–11.

Individual Assignment: Have students use a variety of methods to create collages, posters, or other visual artistic representations of one symbol or image of Jesus. They should choose one that is particularly meaningful to them, one that they are familiar with through their own relationship with Jesus. Next, have the students prepare and give a two-minute speech explaining their poster and why they chose the particular image or symbol they illustrated.

- **Direct Instruction:** Put the word "Incarnation" on the board. Then explain that due to controversies in the early Church over Jesus' true nature, the Nicene Creed explains more fully what Christians believe to be true of Jesus. Write out the following on the board or an overhead projector:

  I believe in one Lord, Jesus Christ, the Only begotten Son of God, born of the Father before all ages. God from God, Light from Light, True God from True God, begotten, not made, consubstanstial with the Father. Through him all things were made.

- **Class Assignment:** Review the four reasons the Word became flesh on pages 42–43. Have the students create an acronym to help remember them. One suggestion might be SKID: God became flesh to **S**ave us (S); so we might **K**now God's love (K); so we can **I**mitate him (I); and to make us sharers in the **D**ivine nature (D).

- **Writing Assignment:** Ask your students to consider why it is important that God became a human being. The textbook lists four reasons. Assign as an essay or journaling topic the questions: Which of these reasons most moves you? Which is most inspiring to you? Allow brief time for the students to work on their answers to these questions in class.

- **Class Activity:** Continue the lesson with reference to the text subsections "Jesus," "Christ," "Son of God," "Lord," and "Other Titles and Symbols for Jesus" (pages 43–45). Have the students create nametags using index cards. On each nametag have them write, "Hi, my name is . . ." then copy one title of Jesus for each one. On the back have them write a brief description of the title and its meaning. After the students have completed making the cards, have them tape a nametag on their shirts. Invite the students to walk around introducing themselves to one another and telling each other about who they are (their titles). Repeat this multiple times and have the students wear different nametags.

- **Direct Instruction:** Focus on the title "Christ" (see pages 43–44) and its threefold office of priest, prophet, and king. Review the definitions in the final paragraph of the subsection and have each student paraphrase the definitions in their own words.

- **Direct Instruction:** Related to the text subsection "Other Titles and Symbols for Jesus" (pages 44–45), take a few moments to brainstorm as many different images or symbols of Jesus as they can. Some that you might include are the Good Shepherd, the Vine, the Teacher, the Judge, Christ the King, the High Priest, the Light of the World, the Cornerstone, the Son of Man, the Son of David, and the Suffering Servant.

- **Direct Instruction:** Also, consider asking the students: "What is the scriptural basis for the following titles of Jesus: The Good Shepherd, the Alpha and the Omega, and the Judge? For each one, explain what the title reveals about Jesus and its significance to you." Share the following answers:

  - The Good Shepherd—John 10:11–14. This title expresses Jesus' intimate knowledge of each of us and his care for us. It is because he knows and cares for us that he is willing to die for us. We should not be afraid that he will ever abandon us because we belong to him. (Answers regarding personal significance will vary.)

  - The Alpha and the Omega—Revelation 22:12–13. This title reminds us that Jesus is truly one with God. He is the beginning and the end, around at the beginning and still with us to the end. (Answers regarding personal significance will vary.)

  - The Judge—Matthew 25:31–46. In the parable of the Judgment of the Nations, Jesus returns to determine who has earned a place in Heaven and who will go off to eternal punishment. Remembering that Jesus will be judging our behavior keeps us honest with ourselves about whether or not we are truly following him. (Answers regarding personal significance will vary.)

For Review Answers (page 45)

1. The Incarnation is God's choice to become a human being, to "take on human flesh" in the person of Jesus Christ.

2. God became human in order to save us from sin, death, and eternal separation from himself. He became human in order to provide a model of holiness for us to follow. He became human so that we would know his love, and so that we, too, would be able to be like God and take on his divine nature.

3. The name *Jesus* means "Savior" or "God saves." This name is appropriate because it reveals his purpose; it testifies to the meaning of his coming.

4. *Christ*: The word means "Messiah" or "Savior." It is more a title than a name, identifying Jesus as the one through whom all of God's promises to his people would be fulfilled. *Son of God*: This title expresses Jesus' role as the Second Person of the Trinity. *Lord*: This was the word used by the Jews in the place of God's unpronounceable name. To call Jesus "Lord" is equivalent to calling him God. *Son of Man*: This title emphasizes Jesus' humanity (Dan 7:13). *Suffering Servant*: This title describes Jesus' actions through his Passion and Death, his willingness to suffer and die to bring about God's will for our salvation.

his task through his threefold office of *prophet, priest,* and *king.* A prophet is one who speaks for God; a priest is a mediator between God and humans. A king is a leader and ruler. As prophet, Jesus spoke for his Father and shared the full message of Salvation. As priest, Jesus offered his life for all of us on the altar of the cross. Today he continues to fulfill the role of High Priest at each celebration of the Eucharist. As king, Jesus is the rightful ruler of the universe, one who rules gently and compassionately. He uses the power of love and service to attract followers to his way.

Son of God

The Gospels repeatedly make the truth that Jesus was the unique Son of God very clear. For example, at both his Baptism and Transfiguration, the Father calls Jesus his "beloved Son." Peter proclaims Jesus to be "the Messiah, the Son of the living God" (Mt 16:16). And Jesus himself clearly says that he is the Son of God (Jn 10:36): "The Father and I are one" (Jn 10:30).

Jesus' Father is the first Person of the Blessed Trinity. Jesus Christ is the natural Son who shares in God's very nature. Human beings, on the other hand, are God's adopted children.

Lord

In the New Testament, *Lord* had various meanings. For example, it could refer to a ruler or someone with great power. It was also used as a polite and respectful form of address, much like "sir."

However, the title *Lord* when referring to Jesus proclaims his divinity. The Greek translation of the Old Testament used the word *Kyrios* ("Lord") to render the most sacred name *YHWH* ("I am"), which God revealed to Moses. Pious Jews never said the most holy name of God. Therefore, to call Jesus Lord (*Kyrios*) is to state that he is God!

The simple statement that "Jesus Christ is Lord" is the earliest and shortest Christian creed. Jesus proved he was God during his ministry through his miracles. "He demonstrated his divine sovereignty by works of power over nature, illnesses, demons, death, and sin" (*CCC,* 447).

Jesus has the same sovereignty as God, and his Death and Resurrection have won eternal life for humanity, a gift only God can grant. Jesus is the one *true* Lord and the only Lord deserving our total allegiance.

Other Titles and Symbols for Jesus

Besides the titles of Jesus revealed in the Creed, there are other titles and symbols for Christ that come from the New Testament and early Church that tell more about him.

Jesus upset many of his contemporaries by rejecting their idea of the Messiah as a conquering, earthly ruler. He chose instead to be a *Suffering Servant* who took on the sins of his people and redeemed them. "The Son of Man did not come to be served but to serve and to give his life as a ransom for many" (Mt 20:28).

Jesus often used the title *Son of Man* when he referred to himself. Its Old Testament roots are a vision described in Daniel 7:13: "I saw One like a son of man coming, on the clouds of heaven." On the one hand, the title emphasizes Jesus' humanity, one who is like us and will suffer for and serve all people. On the other hand, Son of Man describes Jesus as the judge through whom God will fully establish his Kingdom at the end of time.

Several symbols for Jesus developed in the early Church. They also reveal Christian belief about Christ and have roots in Scripture:

"I am the Alpha and the Omega,' says the Lord God, 'the one who is and who was and who is to come, the almighty'" (Rev 1:8). From the book of Revelation, these are the first and last letters of the Greek alphabet, signifying that Jesus is the beginning and end of our lives.

INRI

On top of the cross, posted in Hebrew, Latin, and Greek, was the crime for which Jesus was crucified (Jn 19:19–20). *INRI* is an abbreviation of Jesus' crime in the Latin language: I=Jesus N=of Nazareth R=King I=of the Jews.

Homework Assignment

1. Complete one of the For Reflection assignments on page 45.

2. Complete the For Review questions on page 45.

3. Read the text section "Evidence for Jesus and His Life" (pages 45–49).

For Enrichment

Individual Assignment: During times of persecution in the early Church, Christians created artwork to symbolically represent Jesus Christ and the truths of their faith. Find images of these symbols found most frequently in the catacombs and share them with the students. These symbols included: a fish (Greek, ICHTHYS, or Jesus Christ, Son of God, Savior), the Chi-Rho, the Alpha and Omega, the anchor, the Good Shepherd, the "*orante*" praying figure, a dove, a phoenix, a peacock, a ship, palm branches, and a vine.

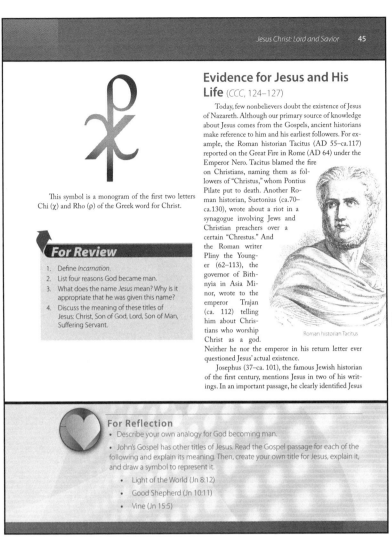

This symbol is a monogram of the first two letters Chi (χ) and Rho (ρ) of the Greek word for Christ.

Evidence for Jesus and His Life (CCC, 124–127)

Today, few nonbelievers doubt the existence of Jesus of Nazareth. Although our primary source of knowledge about Jesus comes from the Gospels, ancient historians make reference to him and his earliest followers. For example, the Roman historian Tacitus (AD 55–ca.117) reported on the Great Fire in Rome (AD 64) under the Emperor Nero. Tacitus blamed the fire on Christians, naming them as followers of "Christus," whom Pontius Pilate put to death. Another Roman historian, Suetonius (ca.70–ca.130), wrote about a riot in a synagogue involving Jews and Christian preachers over a certain "Chrestus." And the Roman writer Pliny the Younger (62–113), the governor of Bithynia in Asia Minor, wrote to the emperor Trajan (ca. 112) telling him about Christians who worship Christ as a god. Neither he nor the emperor in his return letter ever questioned Jesus' actual existence.

Josephus (37–ca. 101), the famous Jewish historian of the first century, mentions Jesus in two of his writings. In an important passage, he clearly identified Jesus

Roman historian Tacitus

For Review

1. Define *Incarnation*.
2. List four reasons God became man.
3. What does the name *Jesus* mean? Why is it appropriate that he was given this name?
4. Discuss the meaning of these titles of Jesus: Christ, Son of God, Lord, Son of Man, Suffering Servant.

For Reflection

- Describe your own analogy for God becoming man.
- John's Gospel has other titles of Jesus. Read the Gospel passage for each of the following and explain its meaning. Then, create your own title for Jesus, explain it, and draw a symbol to represent it.
  - Light of the World (Jn 8:12)
  - Good Shepherd (Jn 10:11)
  - Vine (Jn 15:5)

Evidence for Jesus and His Life (page 45–49)

Objectives

In this lesson, the students will:

- identify the non-Christian sources for our knowledge of Jesus and his early followers;
- recognize the importance of the New Testament, specifically the Gospels, as our primary source of knowledge about the life and teaching of Jesus;
- categorize specific books of the New Testament as Gospels, Acts of the Apostles, Pauline Letters, Catholic letters, and the Revelation of John;
- explain the process by which the Gospels came to be written.

Preview

This lesson discusses the evidence for Jesus' life on earth, cited not only from the Gospels but also from historical sources outside of Christianity. In addition this lesson shares the development of the Gospel in three stages, from the life of Jesus, to the oral sharing of the Good News, to the actual recording of the Gospels by the evangelists.

Resources

Printed Materials

Brown, Raymond E. *An Introduction to New Testament Christology*. Mahwah, NJ: Paulist Press, 1994.

An outstanding introduction to the development of Christian faith.

Drane, John William. *Introducing the New Testament*, rev. ed. Minneapolis: Fortress Press, 2001.

Lavishly illustrated and delightfully written. A wonderful introduction by a balanced Protestant scholar.

Fitzmyer, Joseph, S.J. *A Christological Catechism*. New Revised and Expanded Edition. Mahwah, NJ: Paulist Press, 1991.

An excellent and insightful book that belongs on the shelf of every high school catechist.

Harrington, Daniel J., S.J. *Who Is Jesus? Why Is He Important? An Invitation to the New Testament*. Franklin, WI: Sheed & Ward, 1999.

A popular overview of the New Testament by a respected scholar and a clear writer. Book-by-book analysis that highlights what each New Testament writer has to say about Jesus.

Hughes, John Jay. *Stories Jesus Told: Modern Meditations on the Parables*. Liguori, MO: Liguori, 1999.

Excellent commentary on some of the key parables.

Meier, John P. *A Marginal Jew: Rethinking the Historical Jesus*. New York: Doubleday, 1991, 1994, 2001.

Simply the best work by a Catholic author on the historical Jesus. If you read only one scholar on the historical Jesus, these are the books for you. Outstanding and highly regarded by all in the scholarly community. Volume 1 sets out the critical method Meier uses to pursue the historical Jesus and sketches his cultural, political, and familial background. Volume 2 contrasts Jesus with John the Baptist, establishes him as an eschatological prophet in the line of Elijah, and gives a lengthy treatment to Jesus' miracles. Volume 3 studies the various groups around Jesus and profiles groups like the Pharisees, Sadducees, Essenes, Samaritans, and so forth. Add these books to your personal library.

O'Collins, Gerald. *Interpreting Jesus*. New York/Ramsey: Paulist Press, 1983.

An orthodox, outstanding, clearly written exposition on Jesus. Highly recommended.

continued on page 52

Bell Ringers

- **Student Presentation:** Allow time for the students to share the titles they came up with to describe Jesus and the accompanying symbol to describe it (see page 46). Go over the answers to the For Review questions on page 45.

- **Group Discussion:** Check the students' progress on the Ongoing Assignments. Consider allowing students to meet with others who are working on the same assignments to discuss their progress, successes, and difficulties to this point.

- **Prayer Experience:** Provide an opportunity for the students to pray using images you have collected as well as those they have created for Jesus. Post all of the students' work and the artwork you have found around the classroom. Then ask the students to move quietly to stand in front of one of the posters that illustrates a title for Jesus that is unfamiliar to them. Ask them to use the posters as icons, focusing their imagination on the understanding of Jesus that comes through the image or symbol they have chosen. Ask them to consider what that image or symbol teaches them about Jesus, how it changes their reaction to him, and what it teaches them about him. After about five minutes of silent reflection, give the students a few moments to record their thoughts and reactions in their journal using the Prayer Reflection text and questions from page 66.

as a wise man, teacher, and wonderworker who made converts and was killed by Pontius Pilate. Another example from Jewish tradition is the collection of writings known as the *Talmud*, which states that Jesus existed. Had Jesus never lived, undoubtedly rabbis would have tried to disprove the Christian belief in Jesus' existence. But to the contrary, those non-Christians took for granted that he had lived.

A most convincing argument against the charge that Christians invented the historical Jesus is simply to ask: "What did they have to gain by doing so?" There

parable
A favorite teaching device of Jesus in which he told a short story with a striking, memorable comparison that taught a religious message, usually about some aspect of God's Kingdom.

was nothing to gain politically or economically. In fact, according to tradition, all the key witnesses of Jesus' public life (the Apostles), except John, met martyrdom for their testimony about Jesus.

Centrality of the Gospel

The best source for proving Jesus' existence is the New Testament itself. Its entire focus is Jesus Christ: his acts, teachings, Passion, Death, glorification, and the Church he started under the

guidance of the Holy Spirit. The heart of the Bible is the Gospels, the principal source on the life and teaching of Jesus Christ. The Gospels reveal a genius who taught with unique insight. For example, his parables are unparalleled stories proclaiming God's Kingdom. They are vivid, powerful, life-giving, and original. Also,

1. Jesus taught that God is Abba/Father and that we can pray to God using this intimate term.
2. He taught that God's reign is in our midst.
3. He taught that we should love our enemies.

These unique teachings and many others like them strongly lead us to conclude the historical reality of a remarkable, one-of-a-kind teacher.

For Christians, reading and praying with the Gospels is a necessary way to meet and know Christ. St. Jerome, who translated much of the Bible into Latin, said, "Ignorance of Scripture is ignorance of Christ."

Contents of the New Testament (CCC, 102; 124–125; 128–130; 134; 140)

Jesus is the New Testament (or New Covenant) with all humanity. His law is the law of love that requires a change of heart. He is the perfect prophet who fulfilled all prophecies. The New Testament writings show how his words and his actions reveal God's active presence in the world: saving, redeeming, and healing people. Jesus' life and ministry fulfilled all the Old Testament prophecies concerning his birth, his teaching and healing, his rejection by the leaders, his Passion, Death, and Resurrection.

The New Testament continues and fulfills the Old Testament; it does not contradict it. The Old Testament tells us about God's covenant with his Chosen

---

Audiovisual Materials continued from page 41

Greatest Story Ever Told

Filmed against the stunning background of the red-cliff mesas of Utah, this film stars the Swedish actor Max von Sydow. Light imagery is used to great effect. The portrayal of Lazarus' raising from the dead against the background music of Handel's *Messiah* is stunning. Distracting, though, are the cameo appearances of Hollywood stars that appear frequently as bit players. John Wayne as the Roman solider who pronounced "Truly, this was the Son of God" toward the end of the film often evokes laughter from today's viewers. Von Sydow's impeccable appearance, mesmerizing Swedish accent, and piercing blue eyes present an unearthly, controlled, mystical Christ who is easy to admire but hard to warm up to. Jesus' divinity is clearly stressed (1965; 199-minute feature film, Amazon.com).

How Jesus Died: The Last 18 Hours

A stunning medical account of Jesus' sufferings at Calvary (35-minute video, Videos with Values).

Islam

Explores the Judeo-Christian roots of Islam and its phenomenal expansion in the centuries after Mohammad's rise in the seventh century (58-minute video, Ecufilm.)

Jesus

A widely distributed film on the life of Jesus that is very faithful to the Gospel of Luke. Used with success with students for years. Brian Deacon stars as Jesus. Based on the Gospel of Luke and promoted by evangelical Christians, this film does a fine job presenting the Gospel and a human Jesus who laughs, dances at wedding parties, and enjoys being with his disciples. The film shows a human Jesus, yet one who is still divine and sure of his mission. The most marketed of any film made about Jesus, it has been used for mission outreach throughout the world and dubbed in more than 600 languages. It has its own website where students can watch a preview of the film online: www.jesusfilm.org/ (1979; 120-minute feature film, Ignatius Press).

Jesus

Stars Jeremy Sisto, who presents a human, attractive Jesus who loves, laughs, enjoys children, gets angry at the death of Joseph, and shows fear in the face of his Passion. However, his mother knows more about his identity than he does. Further, he shows way too much reluctance about embracing his ministry. Today's youth find this portrayal interesting, believable, and easy to discuss in light of the Gospels (2000; 173-minute CBS made-for-TV movie, Amazon.com).

continued on page 63

People. The New Testament reveals that our loving God has extended his Salvation to all people. A collection of various books, the New Testament's primary purpose is to announce the fulfillment of God's promises in Jesus Christ, his Son. The New Testament consists of:

The Gospels. The Gospels testify to Salvation in Jesus Christ. They contain facts about the historical Jesus and testify to Christian faith about Jesus' Passion, Death, Resurrection, and Ascension. Written by Evangelists ("proclaimers of the Good News"), their primary intent is to preach Jesus' miracles and teachings and recount the Paschal Mystery of his Passion, Death, and Resurrection that has won for us Salvation. The Gospels also present some reliable biographical material about Jesus. The Gospels are named for the Evangelists Matthew, Mark, Luke, and John.

Acts of the Apostles. Written by Luke as a continuation of his Gospel, the Acts of the Apostles recounts the history of the Church from Pentecost Sunday until the arrest of St. Paul in Rome around AD 63. It is often grouped with the Gospels.

The New Testament Letters. Most of the New Testament letters, or epistles, were written by St. Paul or attributed to him. All of the epistles highlight the importance of faith in Jesus Christ. The New Testament Letters are: Romans, 1 and 2 Corinthians, Galatians, Ephesians, Philippians, Colossians, 1 and 2 Thessalonians, 1 and 2 Timothy, Titus, Philemon, and Hebrews.

The Catholic Letters. These epistles encourage the universal ("catholic") Church to remain faithful to Jesus and to live Christian lives. They are: James, 1 and 2 Peter, 1, 2, and 3 John, and Jude.

Evangelists
The four Evangelists refer to the authors of the four Gospels: Matthew, Mark, Luke, and John. The word *evangelist* means "one who proclaims in word and deed the Good News of Jesus Christ."

Background Information

More Historical Evidence for the Life of Jesus

Cornelius Tacitus (ca. AD 55–117), a Roman historian, included in his *Annals* a detailed description of the Great Fire in Rome, which included the rumor circulated immediately after the fire that it had been started on the order of the Emperor Nero. Tacitus neither confirms nor denies this rumor, but he does suggest that the rumor itself was the reason for the beginning of Nero's persecution of the Christians:

> But all human efforts, all the lavish gifts of the emperor, and the propitiations of the gods, did not banish the sinister belief that the conflagration was the result of an order. Consequently, to get rid of the report, Nero fastened the guilt and inflicted the most exquisite tortures on a class hated for their abominations, called Christians by the populace. Christus, from whom the name had its origin, suffered the extreme penalty during the reign of Tiberius at the hands of one of our procurators, Pontius Pilatus. . . . An immense multitude was convicted. . . . Mockery of every sort was added to their deaths. Covered with the skins of beasts, they were torn by dogs and perished, or were nailed to crosses, or were doomed to the flames and burnt, to serve as a nightly illumination, when daylight had expired.

Teaching Approaches

- **Class Discussion:** Choose a famous person who is no longer living but whom your students would know (e.g., Mother Teresa, Martin Luther King Jr., Cesar Chavez), and ask your students what direct proof they could bring to you of that person's existence: for example, birth and death certificates, photos, film of the person, voice recordings, personal witnesses who knew the person when they were still living, etc. Discuss with your students what kind of evidence would constitute proof that the person actually lived and did the things for which they have become famous.

  ◆ Then suggest a much more ancient person, such as Joan of Arc or Alexander the Great. Would the kind of proof they could offer change? Would your standards for what constituted convincing evidence change? How?

  ◆ Continue with a discussion of the historical evidence that exists for the life of Jesus. Have the students note examples from the text. Also see the Background Information on page 49.

- **Class Activity:** Refer to the text subsections "Centrality of the Gospel" and "Contents of the New Testament" (pages 46–48). Have students fold a sheet of paper in half twice to create four equally sized boxes. Have them label the top of the boxes Gospels, Paul's Letters (New Testament Letters), Catholic Letters, and Other. Have the students copy the names of the books that belong to each category based on the Student Text. Then, have them write the page number of each of the books as they are found in your class set of bibles (or their personal bibles) to show that they can locate each book. Give them some time to memorize which books belong to which category; then test them on their knowledge. Write the names of five books of the Bible on the board and have them write the categories of each on a piece of scrap paper. Continue quizzing the students until they feel they have mastered the information. Consider playing a review game as well.

- **Direct Instruction:** Refer to the text section "The Formation of the Gospels." Remind students of the lesson in the previous chapter that focused on the intimate relationship between Scripture and Tradition (pages 24–25). The notes from that lesson are reprinted here so that you can review them with your students:

  ◆ Immediately after Christ's Death and Resurrection, the Apostles began to share with each other and with others the stories they remembered about Jesus' life and teachings.

- The Apostles began to spread Jesus' message to others in Jerusalem and in the gentile communities in neighboring regions.

- Letters containing teachings about Jesus and his message were written from the Apostles and other leaders of the early Church to different communities of Christians.

- Nearly one hundred years after Jesus' Death and Resurrection, the Gospels began to be written, based on the stories that had been handed down orally. There were many different Gospels, written by many different followers of Jesus.

- Gradually, over the next two hundred years, some of the letters and Gospels began to fall into disuse and were understood to contain errors or misunderstandings of the faith, while others became more and more accepted by Christians throughout the world.

- The accepted letters and four of the Gospels became known as the books of the New Testament and remain important and valuable to Christians today. They are accepted as the inspired Word of God.

- **Direct Instruction:** Discuss the three forms of preaching used by the Apostles during the second stage of formation (oral tradition): *kerygma, didache, liturgy,* and *diakonia.* Have the students read the three passages listed next and discuss which form of preaching most likely formed the story as it is told in the Gospel:

  - *Luke 4:16–19.* This passage was most likely formulated as part of the *kerygma* preached to unbelievers, both within and outside the Jewish community. It is a proclamation of Jesus' place in salvation history, as the fulfillment of prophecies well known to the Jewish community. For non-Jews, it is an introduction to the Good News—that God has come into the community to do good to those who are most in need.

  - *Matthew 5:1–12.* The Beatitudes are clearly a collection of Jesus' teachings recorded in the Gospels. They come out of the *didache,* the oral tradition passing on the words and teachings of Jesus that help people begin to understand what kind of life Jesus is leading us to.

  - *John 6:52–58.* This section of the Bread of Life Discourse is clearly expressing the Church's teaching about the meaning of the Eucharistic Liturgy. Recording this teaching in John's Gospel, and putting the words in Jesus' mouth ensures that the meaning of the liturgy will not be lost or corrupted later on.

catechesis
A process of "education in the faith" for young people and adults with the view of making them disciples of Jesus Christ.

The Revelation to John. This is a highly symbolic work also known by its Greek name—"the Apocalypse." It encourages Christians under persecution to remain faithful to Jesus Christ.

The Formation of the Gospels *(CCC, 124–127)*

The Gospels contain the principal teachings of Jesus and about his life. The Church teaches that there were three stages in their formation.

Stage 1: The Historical Jesus (4/6 BC–AD 30/33)

The first stage of Gospel formation was the very life of Jesus. Jesus was born around 4 to 6 BC, lived a typical Jewish life of the time, came onto the public scene probably in AD 28, preached and

worked miracles, and was crucified in Jerusalem by the Roman prefect, Pontius Pilate, either in AD 30 or 33.

His early disciples, at first frightened and confused, claimed to have seen Jesus after his Death and burial. They were convinced that he was alive and glorified as God's Son and present to them by the power of the Holy Spirit. Their hearts burned with love and joy over his Resurrection.

Stage 2: Oral Tradition (AD 30/33–50)

The disciples begin to live in light of the Resurrection of Jesus. With the help of the Holy Spirit, they now knew that Jesus was the Messiah, the Promised One, the Son of God, and the Lord. The Apostles remembered Jesus' command to "Go into the whole world and proclaim the gospel to every creature" (Mk 16:15). Their preaching took four forms and is the centerpiece of the oral tradition:

1. *Kerygma (preaching to unbelievers).* To aid them in this proclamation, the disciples begin to assemble collections of material about Jesus—for example, miracle stories, parables, and the Passion narrative. Later Evangelists drew on these sources to help compose their Gospels.

2. *Didache ("teaching").* The *Catechism of the Catholic Church (425–429)* teaches that the center of all catechesis must be Jesus Christ. This is true today, and it was also true for early converts to Christ. Catechesis literally means to "sound down," that is, to repeat the message and explain it in more depth. "[Catechesis] is to seek to understand the meaning of Christ's actions and words and of the signs worked by him" (*Catechesi Tradendae,* No. 5, quoted in *CCC,* 426). To aid in this instruction, lists of sayings of Jesus, for example, the

For Enrichment

Individual Assignment: Students benefit from learning to find and read original source material. As an extra credit assignment, challenge them to find references to Jesus in Tacitus's and Josephus's writings. They can use a library, an online search engine, or any other means to locate the material, but do not give them any more information to work with than is found in their textbook. It will not be enough for them to find the reference quoted in another work. Urge them to keep trying until they find a complete translation of the original work.

- Tacitus's entire account of the Great Fire and of the persecution of the Christians can be found online at http://classics.mit.edu/Tacitus /annals.11.xv.html.

- Flavius Josephus's reference to Jesus can be read in his book, *Jewish Antiquities,* Book XVIII, Chapter iii, which can be found at www .perseus.tufts.edu.

Sermon on the Mount, were probably assembled at this time.

3. *Liturgy* ("participation in the work of God"). The celebration of the Eucharist helped shape many of the Jesus stories that the Christian community preserved, for example, Jesus' words at the Last Supper, the Lord's Prayer, and the story of Jesus' Passion.

4. *Diakonia* (or service). Christ came to serve us, humbling himself in order to win our Salvation. In imitation of the Lord, early Christians served others, especially the poor, weak, and sick. People noticed the loving service of Jesus' followers and were attracted to his Church.

The primary interest of the early preachers and teachers' was to interpret the *meaning* of the key events and sayings of Jesus. They did not set out to offer a complete biography of Jesus. What they remembered, saved, and proclaimed was the heart of Jesus' message—related to the teachings of the Jewish faith and adapted to the audiences who heard it.

The preaching about Jesus based on oral traditions carried on well into the second century, even after the Gospels were written.

Stage 3: The New Testament Writings

(AD 50–ca.120)

The final stage of Gospel formation was the actual writing of the four Gospels and the other New Testament writings, the earliest of which were letters of St. Paul. Concerning the Gospels, many scholars believe that Mark's was written between 68 and 73, Matthew's and Luke's perhaps between 80 and 90, and John's in the 90s. Guided by the Holy Spirit, the four versions of the one Gospel of Jesus Christ all tell the truth about our Lord and Savior.

The oral preaching had to be committed to writing because Jesus was not coming back during the lifetimes of the first-generation Christians, as many of them expected. Eyewitnesses to Christ's life on earth began to die. It became increasingly necessary to preserve in a more accurate manner the apostolic testimony concerning Jesus, especially to combat false teachings that were starting to circulate about Jesus. Christians needed a written record of their beliefs—hence, the New Testament. This written record of the Apostles' preaching served as an aid to both worship services and for the instruction of new converts, much in the same way the Gospels are used today for the same purposes.

For Review

1. What is our primary source of knowledge about Jesus Christ?
2. What kinds of writing appear in the New Testament? Give examples of each.
3. Name the three stages of Gospel formation.
4. What forms did the preaching of the Apostles take in the period of oral tradition?
5. Give two reasons why the Good News about Jesus Christ finally took written form.

For Reflection

The following saying is attributed to St. Francis of Assisi because it expresses how he lived his life as Christ's ambassador: "Preach the Gospel at all times. Use words if necessary."

- Write your own catchy phrase to express what this quotation means.
- List three ways you can "preach the Gospel" through the deeds you perform on an ordinary school day.

Homework Assignment

1. Complete the For Review questions on page 49.

2. Complete in writing the For Reflection questions about St. Francis of Assisi on page 49.

3. Read the entire text section "Mysteries of Christ's Life" (pages 50–57).

- *Luke 22:24–30*. Jesus solves a dispute among the disciples by teaching them to be humble servants of others. This passage is likely an indication of the *diakonia* (service) that the early disciples were known for and which the Acts of the Apostles corroborates.

For Review Answers (page 49)

1. Our primary source of knowledge about Jesus comes from the four Gospels of the New Testament.

2. *The Gospels* (Matthew, Mark, Luke, and John) are evangelical stories about Jesus' life, teaching, Passion, Death, and Resurrection intended to recount the Paschal Mystery. They contain limited reliable biographical information about Jesus. The *Acts of the Apostles* is an account of the early growth of the Church. The New Testament letters are those that were written by Paul or attributed to him. They highlight the importance of faith in Jesus Christ. Examples include: Romans, 1 and 2 Corinthians, Galatians, Ephesians, Philippians, Colossians, 1 and 2 Thessalonians, 1 and 2 Timothy, Titus, Philemon, and Hebrews. The Catholic letters are directed to the universal Church and often contain exhortations to remain faithful to Christ and to live properly as Christians. They are identified by their reputed author: James; 1 and 2 Peter; 1, 2, and 3 John; and Jude.

3. The three stages of gospel formation are the historical Jesus, the oral tradition, and the writing of the New Testament.

4. The preaching of the Apostles took the form of *kerygma* (preaching to unbelievers), *didache* (teaching), *liturgy* (participation in the work of God), and *diakonia* (service).

5. Answers may include the realization that Jesus was not coming back during the lifetimes of first-generation Christians and as eyewitnesses to Christ's life began to die, they needed accurate testimony of the Apostles to combat false teachings. The written record of the Apostles also served as an aid for worship services and for the instruction of new converts.

Mysteries of Christ's Life

(pages 50–57)

Objectives

In this lesson, the students will:

- summarize Jesus' life story and his important teachings and miracles.
- compare and contrast the beginning of the four Gospels.
- defend the dogma of the perpetual virginity of Mary.
- summarize the main points of Jesus' proclamation of the Good News.

Preview

In this rather long section students will need their own copies of the New Testament to accompany almost every part. This entire section will likely be covered over several sessions. Some of the assignments may be completed as homework. Also, consider supporting the material in the text with an opportunity for the students to view a movie of the Life of Christ from the list on page 41. Be sure to preview the movie before you show it to the students and prepare a list of questions they can answer while they watch. Or plan for places to pause the movie and ask the questions orally before continuing.

Bell Ringers

- **Class Activity:** Give the students three minutes to recall and write down every event of Jesus' life. When the time is up, draw a blank timeline on the board. Have students share their answers and direct you to write the event in the correct spot on the timeline (no dates are needed). Do not correct students if they are wrong, but allow other students to correct each other. Consider constructing a timeline using paper and post it on the wall instead. Reference this timeline throughout this section.

- **Class Discussion:** Collect and discuss the answers to the For Review questions on page 49 and the Reflection Writing Assignment on St. Francis of Assisi.

Teaching Approaches

- **Direct Instruction:** Read or summarize the opening text section under the main heading "Mysteries of Christ's Life" (page 50). Introduce the section by defining the word "mystery" in context of the Life of Christ:

  - God is a mystery because is he is so great, omnipotent, and perfect that the human mind can never totally grasp his infinity.

  - The second meaning of mystery refers to God's saving plan that was gradually revealed in human history.

Mysteries of Christ's Life (CCC, 512–518; 561–562)

What is meant by the term *mystery* related to the life of Christ? God is a mystery because he is so great, omnipotent, loving, and perfect—the human mind can never totally grasp his infinity, even in Heaven. Second, the word *mystery* (in Greek, *mysterion*) in the New Testament refers to God's saving plan that was gradually revealed in human history.

There is an intimate connection between these two understandings of mystery. The God who is a mystery is the same God who chose to reveal himself in human history. God most fully revealed himself when he became man in Jesus Christ. It follows, therefore, that everything about Jesus—his deeds, works, teachings, Passion, Death, and Resurrection—all reveal a loving, infinite God of mercy.

Several mysteries of Christ's life will be explained in the subsections that follow.

Jesus' Early Life (CCC, 512–534; 563–564)

The Infancy Narratives. Each Evangelist had a particular audience and theological perspective in mind when he wrote his version of the Gospel. For example, Mark wrote for Gentile Christians and stressed Jesus as the Suffering Servant. Matthew wrote for a Jewish Christian audience and emphasized Jesus as the New Lawgiver. Luke highlighted Jesus as the Universal Messiah, and his audience, too, was Gentile Christians. John's Gospel, written many years later, reflects a more developed theology and presents Jesus as God's unique Word who came to be the Way, Truth, and Life.

These different perspectives reflect how Matthew and Luke present the birth of Jesus. For example, Matthew tells us about the visit of the angel to Joseph (Mt 1:18–25); Luke reports an annunciation by the angel Gabriel to Mary, Christ's mother (Lk 1:26–38).

Also, note Jesus' birth stories in Luke 1:1–2:52 and Matthew 1:1–2:23. Each Evangelist drew on two very different traditions to record Jesus' birth. However, what is remarkable is on how many basic facts the Gospels agree. For example,

- The principal persons mentioned are Jesus, Mary, and Joseph.
- Mary was a virgin. By freely consenting to God's action in her life, Mary became the Mother of God and our spiritual mother. She was open to God, serving as a model for all Christians who are to bring Christ into the world.
- The king reigning at the time of Jesus' birth was Herod.
- Jesus' conception was by the Holy Spirit.
- Jesus was born in Bethlehem.
- Jesus received his name before his birth.

 Printed Materials continued from page 47

———. *Interpreting the Resurrection*. New York: Paulist Press, 1988.

Offers an excellent defense of the traditional belief in the Resurrection.

Perkins, Pheme. *Reading the New Testament*. Second Edition. Mahwah, NJ: Paulist Press, 1988.

A solid one-volume introduction to the New Testament books and themes. Highly recommended.

Rausch, Thomas P. *Who Is Jesus?: An Introduction to Christology*. Collegeville, MN: Liturgical Press, 2003.

Up-to-date overview of contemporary views of Jesus.

Reiser, William. *Talking about Jesus Today: An Introduction to the Story behind Our Faith*. New York and Mahwah, NJ: Paulist Press, 1993.

A remarkable retelling of the Jesus story by a college teacher who successfully relates the historical Jesus to the lives of contemporary young people. The book challenges the reader to answer this question: "What are we prepared to do with Jesus?"

Senior, Donald. *Jesus: A Gospel Portrait*. Second Edition. New York, Mahwah, NJ: Paulist Press, 1992.

This has become a classic work by a well-respected scholar.

Sloyan, Gerald. *Jesus in Focus: A Life in Its Setting*, rev. ed. Mystic, CN: Twenty-Third Publications, 1994.

Insightful reading from a respected Catholic author.

- Jesus was descended from David.
- The family settled in the town of Nazareth.

The mysteries of Jesus' life in these chapters of Matthew and Luke reveal much about Jesus and his mission.

First of all, Jesus was born in poverty. He came to the world as one of the lowly and poor. He allowed the shepherds to see him first. Pious Jews like the Pharisees derisively referred to shepherds as "people of the land." Their occupation would not allow them to keep faithfully the religious rituals demanded by the Law. Yet Jesus came to call people such as these.

Next, Jesus' *circumcision* incorporated him into the Chosen People. He submitted to the Jewish law as a

PROFILE OF FAITH: EARLY FOLLOWERS OF JESUS

Jesus had many disciples during his public life. A disciple is a follower, someone who accepts the teachings of someone and then helps spread them through actions and words. From among his disciples, Jesus chose Twelve Apostles to be the official witnesses of his public life and his Death and Resurrection, and the caretakers of the mysteries of God. Four of them—brothers Peter and Andrew and brothers James and John—were fisherman. Another, Matthew, was a tax collector. We don't know what the other Apostles did before they met Jesus, but tradition does tell us that they preached about the Good News far and wide after Jesus' Ascension. With the exception of John son of Zebedee, often identified as the "Beloved Disciple," all the Apostles were put to death for their faith in Jesus Christ.

The Gospels tell us about other followers of Jesus. The most prominent and faithful one was Mary, the Blessed Mother. She perfectly fits Jesus' definition of a disciple as one who hears the word of God and acts on it (Lk 8:21). Jesus also had many women disciples, for example, Mary and Martha of Bethany, who were the sisters of his friend Lazarus, whom Jesus raised from the dead. Women played an important role in Jesus' ministry, providing for his needs while he preached in Galilee and even following him to Jerusalem. Unlike the frightened Apostles who deserted him at the time of his crucifixion, women disciples stayed with Jesus as he hung on the cross, witnessed his Death, and visited his grave. One of the most prominent of these disciples was Mary Magdalene, from whom Jesus drove out seven demons (Lk 8:2). According to the Gospels of Matthew and John, she was the first to see the Risen Lord. Jesus instructed her to tell the Apostles about the Resurrection, thus making her "the apostle to the Apostles."

Common people flocked to Jesus to hear the Gospel. They crowded houses and synagogues to listen to his teachings and followed him into the countryside to hear his preaching. Jesus showed his compassion by healing their maladies and by performing other miracles for them like that of the multiplication of the loaves and fishes.

Even prominent Jews like the Pharisee Nicodemus and a man of wealth, Joseph of Arimathea, became Jesus' disciples. Both were members of the Sanhedrin, the seventy-one-member supreme council of the Jewish people. Joseph successfully requested that Pontius Pilate release Jesus' body to him, providing the crucified Savior with a rock-hewn tomb.

Read the following passages. Answer the questions about Jesus' disciples.
1. *Matthew 10:1–15.* List the Apostles. Name three things Jesus instructed the Apostles to do.
2. *Luke 8:1–3.* Name three women followers of Jesus.
3. *Luke 10:38–42.* What was Martha complaining about? What did Jesus tell her?
4. *John 3:1–21.* What did Nicodemus not understand about Jesus' teaching?
5. *John 20:11–18.* Why did Jesus tell Mary Magdalene not to hold onto him?
6. *Luke 19:1–10.* Why was Zacchaeus despised by so many? What was the sign that he became a true disciple of Jesus?

Profile of Faith Scripture Answers (page 51)

1. The Apostles are Simon called Peter, Andrew, James, John, Philip, Bartholomew, Thomas, Matthew, James, Thaddeus, Simon the Cananean, and Judas Iscariot. Jesus instructs them to go to the "lost sheep of the house of Israel," proclaim the Kingdom of Heaven, cure the sick, raise the dead, cleanse lepers, drive out demons, and take very little.

2. Mary Magdalene, Joanna, and Susanna

3. She complained that her sister did not help her serve the guests. Jesus told her not to worry, but to sit and listen to him like her sister Mary.

4. Nicodemus did not understand the meaning of being born again.

5. Jesus had not yet ascended to his Father.

6. Zacchaeus was despised because he was a wealthy tax collector, but he proved his loyalty as a disciple by giving half of his possessions to the poor and promising not to steal from anyone.

Point out that many mysteries of Christ's life will be the subject of this long text section.

- **Writing Assignment:** Have the students think for a moment about something they would like to persuade their friends to do with them, something that would be fun for all of them but which they have never done before: perhaps going on a weekend camping trip, or watching all six *Star Wars* movies back to back, or forming a new student club. It can be something silly or serious; it doesn't matter as long as it is something safe. Ask them to take five minutes to write a note in which they try to persuade their friends to do this activity with them. Now ask them to write another letter persuading their parents to let them do what they have planned.

- **Class Discussion:** Ask: "How are the two letters similar? How are they different? Why were they written differently?" Connect this discussion to the material in the text describing the differences in the four Gospels (page 49). Each writer had a different audience and a different focus or theme, so their Gospels are somewhat different. However, they had much in common because the subject matter was the same—the Good News of Jesus Christ.

- **Group Activity:** Have the students get into small groups and outline the historical information about Jesus that can be gleaned from one of the Gospels. Use Chapter 2, Handout 1 "Questions about Jesus" (starting on page 285 and also online at www.avemariapress.com), which lists a series of questions that can be answered based on a particular Gospel. Some of the questions may not have answers in all four Gospels. Respond simply, "No information given" in that case. When the groups have finished the exercise, have them partner with three students from other groups who focused on the other three Gospels and compare their answers. Finally, discuss the differences and why the evangelists might have differed.

- **Direct Instruction:** Spend some time looking at the two infancy narratives in detail. Outline them with your students and try to connect the differences between them with the different audiences and themes Matthew and Luke had in mind. Distribute Chapter 2, Handout 2 "The Infancy Narratives" (starting on page 285 and also online at www.avemariapress.com) to each student to help with this activity. Make sure the students can distinguish between the two infancy narratives before moving on.

- **Writing Assignment:** Draw students' attention to the feature "Profile of Faith: Early Followers of Jesus" on page 51. Ask the students to reread and summarize the information as a class. Then, assign the six Scripture questions to be completed in class or as homework. See page 53 for answers.

- **Class Discussion:** Draw students' attention to the Explaining Your Faith feature (Did Jesus have brothers and sisters?) on page 52. Review the term dogma and explain why Church Tradition holds that Mary was a virgin even after giving birth to God. Ask the students to reread and cite the evidence to support Mary's perpetual virginity (the Gospels do not mention Mary giving birth after Jesus and "brothers" could mean "cousins" in Greek). You might also suggest that Joseph, who apparently has died by the time Jesus was a man, may have had children before marrying Mary.

- **Individual Assignment:** Note the text section "Jesus' Public Life" (pages 53–55). Two events mark the beginning of Jesus' public life. Both are examples of the teaching Jesus did as much with his actions as with his words. Review his baptism by having students read all four accounts of it in the Gospels (Mt 3:13–17; Mk 1:9–11; Lk 3:21–22; Jn 1:29–34). Have them note the similarities and differences between each of them. Provide some guidance with the following questions:

  - Who sees the sky open? *(Matthew: Jesus; Mark: Jesus; Luke: unclear, possibly everyone present; John: no one)*

  - Who sees the Holy Spirit descending in the form of a dove? *(Matthew: Jesus; Mark: Jesus; Luke: unclear, possibly everyone present; John: John the Baptist)*

  - Who hears the Father's voice? *(Matthew: everyone present; Mark: possibly everyone present; Luke: unclear, possibly everyone present; John: John heard the Father previously, telling him the dove would be a sign of the presence of the chosen one)*

Epiphany
The feast that celebrates the mystery of Christ's manifestation as the Savior of the world.

Virgin Birth
A Church dogma that teaches that Jesus was conceived through the Virgin Mary by the power of the Holy Spirit without the cooperation of a human father.

model of humility. At the Epiphany, when the Magi from the East visited him, Jesus manifested himself as the Savior of all people. Likewise, Jesus' *presentation in the Temple* revealed him to be the firstborn son who belongs to God. The old prophets Simeon and Anna recognized him as the long-expected Messiah, blessed God for being allowed to see him, and predicted the perfect sacrifice on the cross that the adult Jesus would endure for our Salvation (the sword of sorrow that would pierce Mary's heart).

Two other mysteries from Jesus' infancy—the *flight into Egypt* and the *slaughter of the innocents*—show how the forces of evil war against Jesus, but also reveal how God protects the Son who will save all people.

Jesus lived a hidden life of humble obedience in Nazareth. His obedience to his family contrasts with Adam's disobedience to God. It points to Jesus' obedience to his heavenly Father. He learned a trade from Joseph and grew in knowledge about his Jewish religion. He also regularly attended the religious festivals in Jerusalem. At one of them, he astounded the teachers by his keen knowledge. The finding in the Temple represents Jesus' total consecration to his mission as the Father's Son. Luke's Gospel reports that Jesus grew quietly in wisdom, age, and favor with God and with people (Lk 2:52). Truly, his humility during his "hidden years" shows us how to pray, live, and suffer for our faith.

 Explaining Your Faith

Did Jesus have brothers and sisters?

In a few places, the Gospels mention so-called "brothers and sisters" of Jesus. For example, Mark 6:3 mentions by name four brothers of Jesus and some sisters. Does this mean that Jesus had blood siblings and that Mary had other children?

Since the first century, Catholics have believed that Mary was always a virgin and that Jesus did not have other siblings. Both Scripture and Tradition support this teaching. The Gospels share that Mary was a virgin when she miraculously conceived Jesus by the power of the Holy Spirit (Mt 1:20 and Lk 1:34–35). This is the dogma of the **Virgin Birth**. The Tradition of the Church has always held that Mary was a perpetual virgin. The Fathers of the Church, early influential Church theologians whose writings give us great insights into truths of the faith, taught that the virginal conception was God's work, a mystery of Salvation. The Virgin Birth reveals that Jesus is truly God Incarnate; thus, he is both divine and human. The Gospels make no mention that Mary herself had children after the birth of Jesus.

The Gospel passages that refer to Jesus' so-called brothers and sisters use a word that also means "cousins" or "some other distant relation of the same generation." Even in our day, some cultures refer to cousins and close relatives as brothers and sisters. Interestingly, the Gospels identify two "brothers" of Jesus—namely, James and Joseph—as the sons of another Mary, a follower of Christ (Mt 27:56).

Thus, both the biblical evidence and Church Tradition argue strongly for the virginity of Mary and the special intervention of God in the conception of Jesus. Remember what Jesus said about his true relatives: "For whoever does the will of my heavenly Father is my brother, and sister, and mother" (Mt 12:50).

Background Information

Various Forms of Abuse

Related to the lesson on "bearing one's cross" it may be opportune to mention the issue of abuse. There have been times when people were encouraged to put up with abuse, to remain in an abusive situation because it was "part of their cross." This is not so. There is a difference between tolerating a person who has annoying habits, or responding respectfully to a parent's legitimate authority, and allowing oneself to be continually injured. Domestic violence, child abuse, and sexual abuse unfortunately are all a part of our society. The following are some statistics on domestic violence that you may want to share with your students:

- Nearly one in three adult women experience at least one physical assault by a husband or boyfriend during adulthood.
- An average of 28 percent of high school and college students experience dating violence at some point.
- Victims of dating violence report the abuse takes many forms: insults, humiliation, monitoring the victim's movements, isolation of the victim from family and friends, suicide threats, threats to harm family or property, and physical or sexual abuse. Their abusers also blamed them for the abuse or used jealousy as an excuse.
- Among adolescent abusers, 25 to 33 percent reported that their violence served to "intimidate," frighten," or "force the other person to give me something."

More information about abuse issues, and in particular about prevention, may be found at the following websites: www.endabuse.org, www.domesticviolence.org, and www.ncadv.org.

Jesus' Public Life

As God-made-flesh, everything about Jesus' life on earth reveals the Father. Reflecting on Jesus' teachings and the events of his life teaches us much about God and his love for us. Jesus is the model for human living. His humility, his way of dealing with suffering and persecution, his love for all including enemies, his compassion, and his other human qualities can teach us how to live. Jesus' public life begins with his baptism by John the Baptist, whom God sent to prepare the way for him.

By submitting to John's baptism, Jesus accepted and launched his mission to be God's Suffering Servant. At his baptism, the Holy Spirit descended on Jesus in the form of a dove. A heavenly voice proclaimed Jesus to be the beloved Son, thus revealing him as the Messiah and God's only Son. At his baptism, Jesus

- showed perfect submission to the Father's will,
- foreshadowed the baptism of his Death for the remission of our sins,
- and served as the model for our own baptism.

According to Luke's Gospel, after Jesus' baptism, the Holy Spirit led him into the desert to pray, fast, and prepare himself for his difficult mission ahead. During this forty-day retreat, Jesus was tempted by Satan. The letter to the Hebrews reveals that Jesus' temptations help him identify with humanity:

For we do not have a high priest who is unable to sympathize with our weaknesses, but one who has similarly been tested in every way, yet without sin. So let us confidently approach the throne of grace to receive mercy and to find grace for timely help. (Heb 4:15–16)

Like us, Jesus was tempted; though he never gave in to his temptations nor sinned. Jesus' response to temptations are the opposite of Adam's and show him to be the New Adam. By repudiating Satan, Jesus remained faithful to God.

Unlike the Chosen People who turned from God many times during their history, Jesus was God's obedient servant. He showed that he would be a Suffering Servant Messiah, not a typical earthly ruler.

When he emerged from the desert, Jesus began to preach the Good News of God's Kingdom. The essence of his message is found in Mark 1:15: "This is the time of fulfillment. The kingdom of God is at hand. Repent, and believe in the gospel." The heart of Jesus' message was that God's Kingdom was coming in Jesus' very person. This message requires an immediate response: repentance and faith in him. Jesus taught using vivid and memorable parables like the Parable of the Good Samaritan; in short, pithy aphorisms ("But many who are first will be last, and the last will be first" [Mt 19:30]); and in life-giving discourses like the Sermon on the Mount.

Jesus was a teacher who lived what he preached. His unconditional love for the poor and needy, the sick, women, foreigners, children, sinners, enemies, and the marginalized showed that God's Kingdom was indeed present in him.

Most dramatically, Jesus proclaimed the Gospel through the Paschal Mystery—his Passion, Death, Resurrection, and Ascension. This mystery of total love reveals to us that Jesus Christ is the way

Paschal Mystery
The saving love of God most fully revealed in the Life and especially the Passion, Death, Resurrection, and glorious Ascension of his Son, Jesus Christ.

- **Individual Assignment:** Draw the students' attention to the five main points of Jesus' proclamation of the Good News beginning on page 54. Use Chapter 2, Handout 3 "The Kingdom of God" (starting on page 285 and also online at www.avemariapress.com) to explore in more depth the things Jesus taught about the Kingdom of God. Then choose some or all of the other points of Jesus' proclamation of the Good News to emphasize.

- **Direct Instruction:** *God is a loving Father.* Remind students of Jesus' instructions to his disciples to call God "Abba." Read the parable of the Prodigal Son (Lk 15:11–32) with your class. Then have them describe the kind of father Jesus illustrates in this parable. Remind them of the work they did in the previous chapter on this topic.

- **Class Discussion:** *God is merciful.* Brainstorm with your class a list of people they know who are currently in need of God's mercy. Include general categories of people such as "children with cancer," "the homeless," or "people in prison," but also include some personal, specific individuals known to them, such as "my grandfather who has Alzheimer's" or "my neighbor whose spouse just died." (Be sure to include yourself and your students in some way!) Challenge them to come up with ways they might show God's mercy to the people they have listed, especially those they know personally.

- **Direct Instruction:** *Jesus is present with his Church.* Jesus' presence in his Church will be looked at in more detail in Chapter 4. For now it is enough to list the many different ways Jesus is present in the Church: in his disciples, the baptized; in the Eucharist; in the special authority he gave to Peter and Peter's successors; in the actions of his priests and bishops, such as forgiving sin; and in the presence of the Holy Spirit whom he sent to empower us to live Christian lives.

- **Prayer Experience:** *To accept Jesus is to accept the cross.* The lesson of the cross is a difficult one. Give your students an opportunity to consider the difficult or unpleasant parts of their lives, the things that "tick them off," and list them privately. Ask them to think about how they usually respond to those things—with anger, frustration, denial, avoidance, procrastination, a sense that it isn't fair, resentfulness, etc. Now ask them to think about needs in the world that are important to them—perhaps they are concerned about hunger, or the environment, or racial justice, etc. Have them write a short prayer that they can say whenever they are faced with one of their crosses, offering their willingness to suffer their cross for the good of whatever they have expressed is important to them. Then encourage them to copy that prayer and post it wherever they are most likely to face their cross—on their binder if they find studying distasteful, in their bedroom if they are tired of arguing with their parents about how messy it is, on a piece of paper stuffed in their mitt if they think the baseball coach unfairly singles them out for criticism. Recognizing our crosses as crosses can make it easier to bear them, as can offering our suffering for a good we believe in.

- **Group Activity:** Continue with the text section "Miracles of Jesus" (page 55) and the Knowing Christ through Scripture feature "Jesus the Miracle-Worker and Storyteller." Divide your class into eleven groups, assigning one of the miracles or parables listed in the exercise on page 56 to each group. Give the groups some time to prepare short skits in which they present the miracle or parable along with the information requested in the exercise. Thus, for the expulsion of the demon in Luke 4:31–37, the students' skit should explain the problem—a man was possessed by a demon who recognized Jesus as the Son of God—Jesus' solution—sending the demon out of the man—and the people's reaction—they are awed, they spread the word of him to friends and neighbors. Students might also imagine the reaction of the man who is no longer possessed. As each group presents their skit, the other students should take notes on the three elements the skits are intended to include.

- **Journal Assignment:** Have your students read at least one of the three stories of the Transfiguration (Mt 17:1–8; Mk 9:2–8; Lk 9:28–36). Allow the students to reflect on a "mountaintop" experience in their own lives, a time when they were aware of God's presence in an unusually clear way. Did they, like Peter, want to stay there? Was/is it possible for them to share the experience with others or was/is it too personal so that they feel it might be very difficult to make others understand? What happened when they "came down from the mountain?" What part of the experience have they been able to retain? Give students the opportunity to journal about their responses to these questions.

Kingdom of God
The reign of God proclaimed by Jesus and begun in his Life, Death, and Resurrection. It refers to the process of God reconciling and renewing all things through his Son, to his will being done on earth as it is in Heaven.

to Salvation. If we allow the Holy Spirit to join us to the Lord, the Blessed Trinity will adopt us into the divine family. Jesus teaches an important lesson: "I am the vine, you are the branches. Whoever remains in me and I in him will bear much fruit, because without me you can do nothing" (Jn 15:5).

The main points of Jesus' proclamation of the Good News include:

- *God's Kingdom is here.* The Kingdom of God is God's power and active presence, his saving activity in the entire universe, in Heaven and on earth. We can see God's presence in love, forgiveness, healing, compassion, works of justice, and creative goodness. Jesus himself is the divine agent of the Kingdom that is present in him. His miracles of healing the spiritual, physical, and psychological illnesses of people are a principal sign of the Kingdom. Jesus taught that the Kingdom's presence might appear small now and that the forces of evil will resist it, but its growth is inevitable. One day it will transform all of humanity.

- *God is a loving Father.* The Father's love reveals itself in his sending his Son to live with and die for us. We can approach our loving Father with simple, childlike confidence and trust that he will answer our prayers. This loving Father is incredibly merciful, like the generous father in the Parable of the Prodigal Son (Lk 15:11–32), who accepted back his wayward son and forgave his judgmental one.

- *God is merciful.* Jesus is the very image of the compassionate God. "The Father and I are one. . . . [T]he Father is in me and I am in the Father" (Jn 10:30, 38). We must be other Christs, by spreading his Good News. We do this by forgiving others—even our enemies—and caring for all, especially the poor and outcast. To allow God's Salvation to touch our own hearts means we must turn from our sins and put on Jesus Christ.

- *Jesus is present in his Church.* With God the Father, he has sent the Holy Spirit to empower us to live lovingly. Jesus promised that he would remain with us until the end of time. One way he does this is through his Body, the Church, which he established through the Apostles. He gave special authority to Peter and his successors (the bishops in communion with the Pope) to guide the Church in the truth. The bishops and their coworkers, priests, continue Jesus' saving activity, for example, by forgiving sin in his name and by celebrating the Eucharist. They also serve as teachers and leaders who govern the Church.

Extending the Lesson

Group Activity: Have students, working together in small groups, choose one of the infancy narratives and write their own original skit/drama based on it. Many Christmas pageants performed in elementary schools and churches include elements from both Matthew and Luke—they have shepherds and kings. Be sure your students choose just one and stick to it. When they present their skits, it should be clear upon which Gospel it is based. You can do this as a long-term project, aiming for a larger-scale production complete with costumes, well-rehearsed speeches and staging, music if desired, etc. Or you may make it simpler, devoting less time to it and focusing on the script more than the presentation.

As an alternative, allow the students to put themselves in the position of the original writers of the Gospels. They must first identify a modern audience whom they are trying to teach about Jesus' true identity. Then, they should choose from those elements of the two infancy narratives and other traditions expressed in carols and hymns about Jesus' birth, and combine them in their own narrative or skit in a way that they think will be persuasive to their chosen audience.

Jesus also remains present in the members of the Church who become incorporated into his Body at Baptism. Furthermore, he gives to us his very self—body and blood—in the Eucharist. Finally, he lives in us through the gift of the Holy Spirit, who dispenses many gifts that empower us to live a Christian life. The Church continues to preach and exemplify God's Kingdom. It is the seed of the Kingdom.

· *To accept Jesus is to accept the Cross.* To follow Jesus requires living a moral and loving life of serving others. We must turn our backs on sin and the world's false values that promise an empty happiness. A Christian life requires self-denial and sacrifice. We must imitate Jesus: "Whoever wishes to come after me must deny himself, take up his cross, and follow me" (Mt 16:24). Christ promises we will never be alone when we sacrifice for him:

Come to me, all you who labor and are burdened, and I will give you rest. Take my yoke upon you and learn from me, for I am meek and humble of heart; and you will find rest for your selves. For my yoke is easy, and my burden light. (Mt 11:28–30)

A life of service means dying to selfishness, but it leads to an eternal life of happiness.

Miracles of Jesus (CCC, 547–550)

Jesus performed many miracles to accompany his words. These mighty works, wonders, and signs revealed that God's Kingdom was present in his very person. They prove that he is the Messiah, the Son of God.

Jesus' miracles were signs of the messianic age. These signs freed some people from earthly problems and evils, but they did not abolish all human suffering. Their purpose was to show Jesus' power over sin. His exorcisms demonstrated his control over demons. All of his mighty works foreshadowed his great victory won by his Death and Resurrection. This victory over the power of sin, Satan, and death won us eternal life.

Living the Teaching of Jesus

Read the following teachings of Jesus. Determine which teachings are (a) most difficult for you to live and (b) most difficult for contemporary society to live. Explain why.

· *Self-denial.* "If anyone wishes to come after me, he must deny himself and take up his cross daily and follow me" (Lk 9:23).

· *Love.* "Do to others whatever you would have them do to you" (Mt 7:12).

· *Peace.* "But seek first the kingdom (of God) and his righteousness, and all these things will be given you besides. Do not worry about tomorrow; tomorrow will take care of itself" (Mt 6:33–34).

· *Humility.* "But many that are first will be last, and (the) last will be first" (Mk 10:31).

· *Simplicity.* "Take care to guard against all greed, for though one may be rich, one's life does not consist of possessions" (Lk 12:15).

· *Prayer.* "Ask and it will be given to you; seek and you will find; knock and the door will be opened to you" (Mt 7:7).

Devise a strategy of putting the virtue of humility into practice this coming week. For example, allow someone to get in line before you. Or in a discussion, quietly pay attention to every word the other people are saying. Or make a point to praise the achievement of a classmate. Or humbly learn from a mistake you made without putting blame on others or some external situation. Write in your journal what you learned about yourself after practicing the virtue.

For Enrichment

Individual Assignment: Have the students research more about the official Church teaching on the virgin birth of Christ and the perpetual virginity of Mary. Encourage them to cite evidence related to the discussion on whether or not Jesus had brothers or sisters from the Explaining Your Faith feature on page 52.

Homework Assignment

1. Complete the "Living the Teaching of Jesus" assignment on page 55 by writing a short response to the questions and the strategy for the coming week.

2. Complete the For Review questions on page 57.

3. Read the text section "Christ Died for Our Sake" (pages 57–61).

4. Continue working on the Ongoing Assignments from pages 65–66.

Knowing Christ through Scripture

Answers (page 56)

Miracles

Cure of the leper (Mt 8:1–4): leprosy; Jesus healed him; Jesus had great healing powers and he remained loyal to Mosaic Law

Blind man of Jericho (Mk 10:46–52): Bartimaeus is blind and poor, and the crowds will not let him come to Jesus; Jesus heals him; this showed that Jesus shows no partiality

Cure of the demoniac (Lk 4:33–37): a man is possessed by an unclean spirit; Jesus exorcises the demon; the crowds wondered at his power and the news spread about him

Expulsion of demons in Gadara (Mt 8:28–34): two people were possessed by demons; Jesus drove them out; the local town was afraid and asked Jesus to leave

Calming of the storm (Mk 4:35–41): the Apostles' boat is in danger of sinking from a storm; Jesus calms the wind and sea; the Apostles were in awe

Feeding of the 5,000 (Lk 9:10–17): a large crowd followed Jesus to a deserted place with no food; Jesus feeds them with five loaves of bread and two fishes; the witnesses may have recognized that Jesus was the bread of life

Lazarus (Jn 11:1–44): Jesus' friend has died; he raises him from the dead; through this event, people would believe that the Father sent Jesus

Jairus's daughter (Lk 8:41–42; 49–56): Jairus's daughter has died; Jesus raises her from the dead; her parents were astounded

Parables

Prodigal Son (Lk 15:11–32): Jesus was insulted for welcoming sinners to eat at his table.

The Judgment (Mt 25:31–46): We must treat the least in our midst as if they were Jesus.

Meal at Simon's House (Lk 7:36–50): Jesus came to seek out the sinners and provide for them the forgiveness of sins. The sinful woman will love Jesus more than the Pharisee because her sins are greater.

1. Answers will vary, but might include that the poverty and presence of the shepherds at his birth indicates God's welcome of the poor as his people; that the arrival of the Magi is meant to show God's intention to save all people, Gentile and Jew alike; that his circumcision indicates his belonging to the Chosen People and his humility, which we are called to imitate; that his flight into Egypt and the slaughter of the innocents are evidence of the evil ranged against Jesus and the power with which God protects him.

2. The Church teaches, on the basis of both Scripture and Tradition, that Mary had no other children besides Jesus. References to his "brothers" in the Scriptures use a word that was commonly meant to include cousins and other close family relations.

3. Jesus submitted to John's baptism as a sign of his acceptance of his mission to be God's Suffering Servant.

4. The term *Gospel* means "Good News" and refers both to Jesus' preaching of the Kingdom and to the good news of our salvation in Jesus himself. It is also the title we use for the four New Testament books that contain the primary source of our knowledge about Jesus.

5. Jesus taught that the Kingdom of God was in our midst and that it requires faith and repentance on our part in order for us to belong to it. The most important sign of God's Kingdom is his limitless mercy.

6. Answers will vary, but should be based on the following: *God is a loving Father.* God's love was revealed in his sending his Son to redeem us. Through Jesus we have been adopted as God's children; thus, we can also approach him in faith that he will care for us and answers our prayers for our good. *God is merciful.* Jesus' compassion teaches us that God's mercy is endless. We are to pass that mercy we receive from him on to others. *Jesus is present in his Church.* Jesus promised to be with his disciples always, "wherever two or three are gathered" in his name. He gave authority to Peter and the other Apostles to guide the Church and to continue his ministry. He also remains present in the baptized, in the Eucharist, and through the presence of the Holy Spirit. *To accept Jesus is to accept his cross.* Following Jesus requires sacrifice and self-denial and service to others.

7. Jesus performed miracles as a sign that God's Kingdom was present in him.

8. Jesus told parables to convey important truths about God's love and the Kingdom of God. Answers will vary regarding the meaning of each parable, so be generous in reviewing the responses.

Transfiguration of Jesus
(CCC, 554–556)

Jesus revealed his divine glory before Peter, James, and John up on a high mountain. His face "shone like the sun and his clothes became white as light" (Mt 17:2). By doing so, he was giving a foretaste of the Kingdom. In this special revelation, two Old Testament figures—Moses and Elijah—also appeared. Their presence recalls how the Law (given to Israel through Moses) and the prophets (Elijah was a great prophet) had announced the sufferings of the Messiah. This vision also reveals all three persons of the Blessed Trinity: the Father (in the voice); the Son; and the Holy Spirit (in the shining cloud).

KNOWING CHRIST THROUGH SCRIPTURE

Jesus the Miracle Worker and Storyteller

The Gospels tell us that that Jesus was both a miracle worker and a storyteller. His miracles helped reveal his identity as God's Son and showed how the Kingdom of God was breaking into human history. They reveal his compassion and love for all. Jesus' parables were short stories drawn from ordinary life that conveyed important truths about God's love and the Kingdom of God. Many of them contain the very heart of the truths Jesus came to reveal about God and humanity.

Turn to the Gospels now and do the following exercises.

Miracles
Jesus' miracles can be divided into four categories: healings, exorcisms (expelling demons), nature miracles, and raisings from the dead. Read and report on these elements of each miracle: 1) the problem, 2) how Jesus solved it, and 3) the meaning (what the miracle meant for the person involved or for those who witnessed it).

Healings
- Cure of the leper (Mt 8:1–4)
- Blind man of Jericho (Mk 10:46–52)

Exorcisms
- Cure of the demoniac (Lk 4:33–37)
- Expulsion of demons in Gadara (Mt 8:28–34)

Nature Miracles
- Calming of the storm (Mk 4:35–41)
- Feeding of the 5,000 (Lk 9:10–17)

Raisings from the Dead
- Lazarus (Jn 11:1–44)
- Jairus's daughter (Lk 8:41–42; 49–56)

Parables (CCC, 546)
Jesus' parables challenge us to accept God's reign and imitate Jesus' life of loving service for others. Read each parable below. Write your answers to the questions.

Prodigal Son (Lk 15:11–32)
- What situation caused Jesus to tell this story?

The Judgment (Mt 25:31–46)
- What must we do for others?

Meal at Simon's House (Lk 7:36–50)
- List two ways this passage exemplifies Jesus' message.

Extending the Lesson

Prayer Experience: Use the list of people in need of God's mercy that you have generated during the lesson to create an intercessory prayer service with your students. Working in small groups or individually, have the students write intercessions such as those used in the General Intercessions of the Mass. Chapter 2, Handout 4 "Intercessory Prayer Service" (starting on page 285 and also online at www.avemariapress.com) contains an invitation to prayer and a concluding prayer for you, as well as sample forms for the intercessory prayers. Choose one form that you think will work well for your students and ask them all to use the same one in crafting their prayers. This gives structure and a sense of congruity to the prayer service. Check the prayers to be sure they are all appropriate before proceeding with the prayer service.

This prayer can be offered in the informal space of your classroom with the simple preparation of having the students clear their desks or work areas of any distractions and turn their chairs to face in one direction. You may or may not choose to dim the lights to help deepen the sense of difference between prayer and regular class time. Read the invitation to pray and then have the students read the intercessions they have written. End with the concluding prayer.

Writing Assignment: Ask the students to write a brief essay describing their response to Jesus' miracles. Do they see evidence of God's Kingdom in Jesus because of his ability to work these miracles? Which miracle do they find the most amazing? Why? How do they feel about Jesus when they think about the miracles he performed?

Christ Died for Our Sake

(pages 57–61)

Objectives

In this lesson, the students will:

- explain the meaning of Jesus' Passion and Death.
- recognize the sinfulness of anti-Semitism and our obligation to treat all people as our brothers and sisters since we share one Father.
- provide evidence for the Resurrection.
- define the Paschal Mystery, Ascension, Pentecost, and Parousia.

Preview

One goal of this lesson is to help students think seriously about the possibility of their own death so that they can understand the sacrifice Jesus made in giving up his life for us. You may wish to decorate the room with images of penance and the Passion and Death of Christ for the opening part of this lesson. Then, as the lesson proceeds, evolve into the celebration of Easter using Easter colors (gold and white are the liturgical colors) and Easter theme decorations, regardless of the current season.

Reproduction of student textbook page 57:

For Review

1. What are two religious lessons about Jesus learned from his birth and infancy?
2. Explain the meaning of the so-called "brothers and sisters" of Jesus. Who were they?
3. Why did Jesus submit to the baptism of John?
4. What is meant by the term *Gospel*?
5. What did Jesus teach was the meaning of the "Kingdom of God"?
6. Name and explain two of Jesus' key teachings.
7. Why did Jesus perform miracles?
8. Why did Jesus tell parables? Explain the meaning of one of them.

For Reflection

How do you imagine Jesus' hidden years in Nazareth? What kind of teenager do you think he was?

Christ Died for Our Sake (CCC, 456–463; 599–623)

Shortly after the revelation of Jesus' true identity in the Transfiguration, he went to Jerusalem, where he was handed over by Jewish authorities to the Romans and put to death. The sacrifice that Jesus made through his Life, Death, and Resurrection repairs the broken relationship between God and man. It bestows God's blessings, grace, and life on humankind and adopts us into God's family. The salvation won by Jesus on the cross brings forgiveness for our sins and redeems us from sin, evil, and death.

Jesus alone is our Savior. As Peter proclaimed, "There is no salvation through anyone else, nor is there any other name under heaven given to the human race by which we are to be saved" (Acts 4:12).

Jesus Suffered Under Pontius Pilate

(CCC, 624–637)

Jesus shared human nature by undergoing the perfect sacrifice for us. The New Testament explains that Jesus' Death was a *Redemption*, that is, a "ransom" that defeated the powers of evil. He took on our guilt by substituting for us, by dying the death we deserve. He did so to buy our freedom with his eternal, divine love.

Jesus' Death was for all people in all ages. He took our sins to the cross and became the New Adam before the Father. The life he freely surrendered became a perfect instrument of God's love, a gift that opened eternal life to us. His obedient acceptance of suffering and death gives people the hope of an eternal life where there will be no suffering or death.

The Apostles' Creed proclaims the reality of Jesus' Death by crucifixion, perhaps the most painful form of capital punishment ever devised. The executioner was the Roman official Pontius Pilate.

The following events led to the Death of Jesus Christ:

Jesus offended certain Jewish teachers and leaders because of how and what he taught and who he was. In addition, Jesus associated with sinners and extended God's forgiveness to them. In doing so, he was claiming to be God himself. His forgiving of sins, expelling of devils, curing on the Sabbath, and teaching on certain ritual purity laws brought him the charge of being a blasphemer and a false prophet. Finally, he predicted that the temple of his body would be destroyed and rebuilt in three days (see Jn 2:14–22). This was to be a sign of the last days. Certain witnesses who heard this teaching interpreted Jesus' prediction as an attack on the Jerusalem Temple, claiming that he was involved in

Jesus Christ: Lord and Savior **57**

Background Information

A Saint Who Gave Up His Life for Others

In a very real way St. Maximilian Kolbe relived Jesus' sacrifice, giving up his own life to save another. Maximilian was a priest in Poland during the Nazi occupation. The monastery that he had founded sheltered more than three thousand Polish refugees, approximately two-thirds of whom were Jews. Eventually he was arrested for his anti-Nazi position and sent to Auschwitz, the German death camp. Maximilian volunteered to take another prisoner's place when the guards were seeking ten prisoners to execute in retaliation for one prisoner's escape, and submitted to two weeks of starvation, deprivation, and cruelty at the hands of the Nazis before he was given a lethal injection and cremated. His feast day is August 14. More information about Fr. Kolbe can be found at http://myhero.com/myhero/hero.asp?hero=mkolbe and www.catholic-forum.com/saints.

Extending the Lesson

Individual Assignment: Unfortunately, hate crimes against Jewish people continue to this day. Anti-Semitism is at the root of numerous cases of vandalism every year (such as, youth spray-painting swastikas on the walls of Jewish synagogues or Jewish-owned businesses). You might want to have your students do some research to find out if there have been instances of hate crimes against Jewish people in your local community recently. Start with reports in your local newspapers or by contacting your local police department. Then your students might want to brainstorm some possible ways they could stand in solidarity with the Jewish people who suffered these crimes—by writing letters expressing their sorrow over what occurred, by volunteering to help clean up any offensive graffiti in the community, etc.—their response will depend upon the type of crime that has been committed in your local community. For statistics on the incidence of anti-Semitic hate crimes in the United States check the following websites: www.fbi.gov/ucr/ucr.htm (the FBI's website containing information on federal hate crime statistics), www.hatewatch.org, and www.tolerance.org. (These sites also contain lots of ideas about how ordinary citizens can help. You might make one of their suggestions a class project.)

- **Direct Instruction:** Check the homework assignments from the previous lesson.
- **Individual Activity:** Ask the students to make a list privately of all the things they enjoy about their life, things that they expect to continue to enjoy for another week, month, or year (i.e., their friends, their favorite class, their club/team/charity activities, etc.). Then ask them to list things they hope to enjoy in the future (i.e., summer vacations, graduation, holidays, their sixteenth or eighteenth birthday, getting a driver's license, etc.). How would they feel if someone told them that none of that was going to happen? Or that it would happen, but without them?
  - Next ask them to consider what Jesus' lists would have looked like. Make a class answer list on the board. What did he enjoy? What did he look forward to? What would he have hoped for? What did he give up?
  - Ask them what they think motivated Jesus to be willing to die so that people would be able to experience God's love. This can be a class discussion or a written response.
- **Direct Instruction:** Introduce the text section by reading the introductory material under the heading "Christ Died for Our Sake" (page 57).

Teaching Approaches

- **Individual Assignment:** Read the story of the Passion in Matthew 26:36–27:61. Have your students list all of the things that Jesus suffers during his Passion: the inner turmoil he contends with in the garden, the betrayal by one of his friends, the reviling of the crowd, the pain of the physical punishments, and his death on the cross. Be as specific as possible. Include elements from the other Gospels as your students are aware of them—for example, his mother's presence and his last words to her (Jn 19:26–27).

revolutionary activity. Such a misrepresentation of Jesus' intent was threatening to some Jews who had an economic and religious interest in the Temple.

Under Jewish law, death was the penalty for religious crimes like these. At the time, however, the Romans occupied Palestine. Under Roman law only the Roman prefect could inflict the death penalty. Therefore, some Jewish authorities, acting out of ignorance and a lack of faith, turned Jesus over to the Roman prefect, Pontius Pilate, for execution as a political criminal and potential threat to Caesar's authority.

Thus, Pontius Pilate, the Roman prefect of Judea, Samaria, and Idumea from AD 26 to 36, sentenced Jesus to death, perhaps in April of the year AD 30 (or 33). Reading the Gospel accounts leaves one with the impression that Pilate thought Jesus was innocent. But by condemning Jesus, Pilate took the easy route of avoiding the truth.

A tragic historical *reality* has been to blame the Jewish people as a whole for the Death of Jesus. The complex trial of Jesus shows that only a *few* Jewish leaders and Pilate put Jesus to death. Jesus even offered forgiveness to those who condemned him while on the cross. The real authors and instruments of Jesus' crucifixion are sinners, that is, each of us, because it was for our sins that Jesus died.

Jesus freely offered his Life to liberate us from our sins and to bestow eternal life on us. He underwent the excruciating torments of the most painful form of death devised by human beings out of his immense love for us.

Joseph of Arimathea, a member of the Sanhedrin, received permission to bury Jesus. A prominent disciple, Nicodemus; Jesus' mother, Mary; and Mary Magdalene witnessed the place of burial, thus signifying that Jesus was truly dead. According to Matthew's Gospel, Pilate even stationed a guard at the tomb to prevent the disciples from stealing Jesus' body.

> Christ's death was a real death in that it put an end to his earthly human existence. But because of the union which the person of the Son retained with his body, his was not a mortal corpse like others, for "it was not possible for death to hold him" (Acts 2:24) and therefore "divine power preserved Christ's body from corruption."⁶ (*CCC*, 627)

The Apostles' Creed professes that the dead Christ went to the abode of the dead (*Sheol* in Hebrew, *Hades* in Greek) to proclaim the Good News to the just who were awaiting the Messiah.

Extending the Lesson

Prayer Experience: Take an on-campus field trip to the chapel to experience the Stations of the Cross. Many excellent resources are available for the Stations, some designed specifically for teens, such as *Stations for Teens*, published by Saint Mary's Press, or *Everyone's Way of the Cross*, published by Ave Maria Press. Choose readers in advance and allow them to practice beforehand so that the meditations will go smoothly.

If you do not have access to the Stations either in your campus chapel or a nearby church, extend this section by having the students create their own Stations. They might do living Stations, re-creating the scene as a tableau with students taking on various roles. Or they could re-create the Stations artistically, through sculpture, bas-relief, line drawings, or paintings. It could also be done as simply as having the Station numbers appear on crosses marking out a path through the school campus.

In this case, consider using *The Biblical Way of the Cross*, published by Ave Maria Press. This set of reflections is based on the Way of the Cross introduced by Pope John Paul II in 1991 in which each station is taken directly from Scripture. The Stations of the Scriptural Way of the Cross, with Scripture references, are listed on Chapter 2, Handout 5 "Scriptural Way of the Cross" (starting on page 285 and also online at www.avemariapress.com). This book is also available as an iPhone App. If students have an iPhone or iPod Touch, have them download it for free to use in their personal prayer lives or during this prayer experience.

The most important event in Salvation History took place on the third day following Jesus' Death, the first day of the week. That event was the Resurrection of Jesus.

On the Third Day He Rose Again (CCC, 638–653; 656–667)

The Resurrection of Jesus was a real event. The disciples did not expect anything to occur. In fact, they hid in Jerusalem, fearful that they themselves might be arrested. When the women reported they had seen the empty tomb and the Risen Lord, the Apostles at first did not believe. (The empty tomb does not of itself produce faith, but it is a concrete historical sign, a pointer toward belief that the Father brought his Son back to life.)

The Apostles and other disciples believed in the Resurrection when they actually *saw* Jesus. The New Testament lists many witnesses: Simon Peter, the head of the Apostles; the other Apostles; more than five hundred men and women and St. Paul himself, as he reported in 1 Corinthians 15:5–8; James, the leader of the Jerusalem Church; the disciples on the road to Emmaus; and various women, including Mary Magdalene at the tomb and his mother in the Upper Room. These real meetings of the Risen Lord

completely transformed the disciples from frightened and disillusioned followers of the historical Jesus into bold eyewitnesses who proclaimed the Good News that "Jesus is Lord!" Their testimony, aided by the Holy Spirit's gifts of faith and fortitude, led many of them to die for their belief that Jesus Christ rose from the dead.

Death was defeated for all time at Jesus' Resurrection. Salvation for humankind has been won. Christ conquered Satan and destroyed the power of death. We no longer fear death. Jesus is the gateway to Heaven and eternal life.

In his Resurrection, Jesus was fully restored to life. As the *Catechism* teaches, "In his risen body he passes from the state of death to another life beyond time and space" (CCC, 646). Jesus' human body was gloriously transfigured, filled with the Holy Spirit, into an incorrupt, glorious, immortal body "seated at the right hand of the Father."

Through the ages, some have tried to explain away Jesus' Resurrection by arguing against it in some way. Some of their misconceptions include the belief that it was a:

- *reanimated corpse*, that is, a body like Lazarus's come back to life that would eventually die again;
- *poetic way* of saying that Jesus' soul was immortal;
- *reincarnation*, a belief that the human soul is reborn time and again into new bodies;
- *psychological explanation* made up by the Apostles, who were trying to say that the *cause* of their teacher would live on.

Rather, an accurate view of the Resurrection follows:

Faith in the Resurrection has as its object an event which is historically attested to by the disciples, who really encountered the Risen One. At the same time, this event is mysteriously transcendent insofar as it is the entry of Christ's humanity into the glory of God. (CCC, 656)

The Resurrection is proof of Jesus' divinity. The Resurrection of the crucified Christ shows that he was truly the Son of God and God himself. The Resurrection further reveals the unending communion of God as Trinity: the Father who glorifies the Son; the Son whose sacrifice merits his exaltation; and the Holy Spirit who is the Spirit of life and Resurrection. Raised to a glorious body and filled with the power of the Holy Spirit,

Background Information

Works of Mercy

Corporal Works of Mercy
- Feeding the hungry
- Giving drink to the thirsty
- Clothing the naked
- Visiting the imprisoned
- Sheltering the homeless
- Visiting the sick
- Burying the dead

Spiritual Works of Mercy
- Admonishing sinners
- Instructing the ignorant
- Advising the doubtful
- Comforting the sorrowful
- Forgiving all injuries
- Bearing wrongs patiently
- Praying for the living and the dead

- **Class Discussion:** It may be difficult for your students to realize that Jesus was willing to suffer all of this for *them*. Encourage them to consider their emotional reaction to this truth. Give them opportunities to express their feelings about what was done to Jesus orally, in writing, through art, or in whatever way you think would be most beneficial to your students.

- **Direct Instruction:** Refer to the part of the text beginning with, "The following events led to the Death of Jesus Christ" on page 57. Over the centuries, Christians uncomfortable with the reality that our own sinfulness is the reason for Jesus' Death have sought to focus blame elsewhere, most notably on the Jews. As a result, centuries of persecution of the Jews have marred the history of the Church and Western civilization, culminating in the Holocaust. Researching the Holocaust might help your students understand the grave significance of allowing anti-Semitism to flourish unchecked (see Background Information on page 60).

- **Writing Assignment:** Imagine that a young child asks you, "Who killed Jesus?" What would you say and why? Then, discuss the answers as a class.

- **Class Discussion:** Transition into the text section "On the Third Day He Rose Again" (pages 59–60). Have the students share stories from their own lives of the best "good news" they ever got. (Begin with an example of your own.) Ask them whether it was a surprise. Did they have trouble believing it? What finally convinced them it was true?

- **Class Discussion:** Read the different accounts with your class, pointing out the people who were surprised, who had trouble believing, and the events that convinced them (Mt 28, Mk 16, Lk 24, Jn 20). Ask students to offer arguments to support that the Resurrection event actually occurred based on the information in the Student Text and the Scripture passages they read. Ask them to discuss what is most convincing to them.

- **Direct Instruction:** Review the final two subsections together. Discuss the important terms from the section "He Ascended into Heaven and Will Come Again" (page 60): Ascension, Pentecost, and Parousia, or the Second Coming. In your discussion of the Parousia, stress that the Catholic Church teaches that we must always be prepared for the return of Christ precisely because *no one* knows when he will return.

- **Journal Assignment:** Read Matthew 25:31–46, "The Judgment of the Nations," to your class. This parable explains the basis upon which our lives will be judged when Jesus Christ returns. Have your students list all the ways they can remember having fed, given drink to, clothed, sheltered, visited, or welcomed those in need in their journals. Do they remember opportunities that they had to do these things but refused?

- **Writing Assignment:** Challenge your students to list the twelve corporal and spiritual works of mercy, which are based on this text. The list can be found in the Background Information later.

- **Class Discussion:** Ask your students to suggest places in your school or local community where they see needs such as those in the lists of corporal and spiritual works of mercy. Brainstorm ways that young people might answer those needs. Try to develop a class plan to meet at least one local need as a class project.

For Review Answers (page 61)

1. Christ's Death and Resurrection repairs the broken relationship between God and man and bestows God's blessings, grace, forgiveness, redemption, and life to all humankind.

2. Pontius Pilate sentenced Jesus to death, but responsibility for the death of Jesus lies with all of us because it was to liberate us from our sins that he submitted to death.

3. Belief in the Resurrection is essential because it marks the defeat of death and is the evidence of our salvation. Jesus' Resurrection is evidence of his divinity, the power he holds over life and death. His Resurrection completes the repair of our relationship with God and gives us hope for our own rising and eternal life with God.

4. The *Paschal Mystery* is the saving love of God revealed in the Life, Passion, Death, Resurrection, and Glorification of his Son, Jesus Christ.

5. The *Parousia* is the Second Coming of Christ, when, at the end of time, he will return to judge the living and the dead and to establish God's Kingdom of justice, love, and peace. We must remain ready and look forward to this event, preparing ourselves by maintaining our relationship with God and working to build up the Kingdom in any way we can by promoting peace and justice and love in the world through our own efforts.

Parousia
The Second Coming of Christ, when the Lord will judge the living and the dead.

He Ascended into Heaven and Will Come Again (CCC, 668–670)

The Resurrection forms part of the Paschal Mystery, the saving event that includes

Jesus Christ has definitively conquered sin and death.

What effect does Christ's Resurrection have on humanity? Jesus' Passion, Death, and Resurrection repair our friendship with God. His Resurrection restores humanity, freeing us from our slavery to sin, death, and suffering. It gives us hope for our own rising after death and for eternal life with the Blessed Trinity.

No longer limited by space and time, Christ lives and reigns forever. He lives in his Body, the Church, and in a special way in the powerful signs of love he has given his Church—the sacraments. For example, by the power of the Holy Spirit, the Lord comes to us at Baptism, forming us into his own image. In the Sacrament of Confirmation, the Holy Spirit strengthens us with spiritual gifts to live like Christ. And we experience the Lord's forgiveness in the Sacrament of Penance, experience his healing touch in the Anointing of the Sick, and receive his help to live loving lives of service in Holy Orders and Holy Matrimony.

In a special way, Jesus is alive in the Eucharist. There the Risen Lord comes to us in the forms of bread and wine. We receive Christ to become Christ for others. The Lord meets us in each other and, in a special way, in the least of those in our midst—the poor, victims of discrimination, the powerless, the suffering, the lonely.

Jesus' Death (Good Friday) and his descent to the dead (Holy Saturday) and his glorification. Jesus' glorification consists of the Resurrection (Easter Sunday), the Ascension into Heaven (forty days after Easter), and Pentecost (fifty days after Easter).

The Ascension of Jesus refers to the time when Jesus stopped appearing to the disciples in visible, human form. The Ascension indicates a difference between the way the glory of the Risen Christ was revealed and that of "Christ exalted to his Father's right hand" (*CCC*, 660). Being seated at his right hand means that Christ now glorifies the Father as the incarnate Son of God, that he continually intercedes for us with the Father, and that it is the beginning of the Messiah's Kingdom, one that will have no end.

Pentecost is the day on which the Holy Spirit descended on the Apostles and gave them the power to preach with conviction the message that Jesus is Risen and is Lord of the universe. The feast of Pentecost is often known as the "birthday of the Church."

The Creed proclaims with great confidence the Parousia, that is, Jesus' arrival in glory at his Second Coming. The world we know will end at that time. All of God's creatures everywhere will acknowledge that Jesus is Lord. The glorious Lord Jesus will then fully bring about the Father's Kingdom of justice, love, and peace. Jesus told us that the exact time this will take place is hidden in God's almighty plan. However, we are always to be ready. "Be watchful! Be alert! You do not know when the time will come" (Mk 13:33).

He Will Judge the Living and the Dead (CCC, 678–679)

According to Matthew 25:31–46, at the Parousia the Son of Man will judge the living and the dead based on how loving we were toward others. Did we feed

Homework Assignment

1. Complete the For Review questions on page 61.

2. Read the text section "What We Believe about Jesus" (pages 61–64).

3. Continue working on the Ongoing Assignments, pages 65–66.

Background Information

The Holocaust

During World War II, an estimated 6 million Jews were put to death by the Nazis. This is probably the worst example of anti-Semitism in history, and it is tempting to lay the blame entirely at Hitler's feet, but his policies had their roots in the religious persecution of the Jews in all of Europe over the preceding centuries. For a wealth of information about the Holocaust and some excellent teacher's guides, check out the US Holocaust Memorial Museum Website, www.ushmm.org.

the hungry and give drink to the thirsty? Did we welcome strangers and minister to the poor, the sick, the imprisoned? If we can answer yes to his questions, then our reward will be beyond what we can possibly imagine. Jesus' instructions to us are simple:

I give you a new commandment: love one another. As I have loved you, so you also should love one another. This is how all will know that you are my disciples, if you have love for one another. (Jn 13:34–35)

The second to last verse of the Bible is a prayer to the Lord that he might return right away: "Amen! Come, Lord Jesus!" (Rv 22:20). This is a most appropriate prayer for Christians. In faith, we know who Jesus really is and what he has done for us. Who would not want him to come soon?

For Review

1. Explain what Christ's Death and Resurrection accomplished for us.
2. Historically, who is responsible for the Death of Jesus? In what way is every person the real author of Christ's crucifixion?
3. Why is belief in the Resurrection of Jesus Christ essential for Christians?
4. Define *Paschal Mystery*.
5. What is the Parousia? How can we prepare for it?

For Reflection

Prayerfully read the account of Jesus' Passion, Death, and Resurrection in Matthew's Gospel, chapters 26–28. Imagine that you are one of the persons who is mentioned in the account (examples: Peter, an arresting soldier, Caiaphas, Pilate, Simon of Cyrene, one of the criminals hanging next to Jesus, a bystander under the cross, etc.). Write a description of what happened from the point of view of that person.

What We Believe about Jesus (CCC, 464–483)

The Church defined several of its beliefs about Christ in response to heresies (false teachings) that arose about Jesus in the early years. The first major heresy concerning Jesus—*Gnostic Docetism*—held that God could not have actually taken on human flesh and that Jesus only *appeared* to be a man. It would follow, then, under this belief, that Jesus only *appeared* to suffer and die for us. If that were so, then it would only *appear* that we are saved!

Another heresy, promoted by a priest named Arius, denied the true divinity of Jesus. *Arianism* taught that God the Father created Jesus as the greatest of creatures but that Jesus was not equal to God (not of the same "substance"). Once again, if Arius were correct, then our

heresy
An obstinate denial after Baptism to believe a truth that must be believed with divine and Catholic faith, or an obstinate doubt about such truth.

What We Believe about Jesus
(pages 61–64)

Objectives

In this lesson, the students will:

- identify the two major types of heresies concerning Jesus—one denying his humanity, the other denying his divinity.
- describe the dogmatic teachings about Jesus that the Church formulated in response to these heresies.
- describe the beliefs about Jesus in other religions.

Preview

Often, the Church's beliefs were officially defined in response to a heresy, or false teaching, that arose during its history. This text section provides concise summaries of the Church's response to heresies formulated during early Church councils. The section also briefly outlines beliefs about Jesus in other religious traditions, an important consideration for our time.

Audiovisual Materials continued from page 48

Jesus of Nazareth

The acclaimed Zeffirelli film with an all-star cast. Robert Powell portrays Jesus. Jesus is dignified, idealistic, in control, polished, and visionary. The film does a good job showing Jesus as one Divine Person with two natures. It neither overemphasizes his divine nature nor his human nature, as films have a tendency to do. The miracles are handled tastefully, showing how the Father worked through his Son (371-minute feature film on VHS or DVD format, widely available, for example, Ignatius).

Jesus: The Complete Story

Produced in 2001, this is a good series that focuses on many archaeological sites that figure in Jesus' ministry. The second segment on Jesus' mission tends to stress more a political motivation for Jesus' healings and teachings. Segment 3 tries to reconstruct Jesus' face and reveals the mechanics of crucifixion. However, this segment also unduly raises issues about the historicity of the Resurrection. Use with care. The series might be good background for the teacher. Fr. Jerome Murphy-O'Connor was one of the consultants for the series (150-minute BBC/Discover Channel video production on three videos of approximately 50 minutes each, Critics' Choice).

Jesus and His Times

A favorite three-part series produced by *Reader's Digest*. Supportive of traditional teachings about Jesus. The segments are entitled "The Story Begins," "Among the People," and "The Final Days." Each segment is approximately an hour long (173 min. total, Critics' Choice, Questar).

Jesus: The New Way

An excellent series produced by Dr. Tom Wright, noted British biblical scholar who accepts the basic gospel message about Jesus, unlike so many of those in the Jesus Seminar who have a particular ax to grind. Segments could be used successfully with students or purchase for teacher background. Segment 6 on the Resurrection is probably the best segment of all. A good counteract to the previous citation (six one-half-hour programs on two videotapes with script, teacher's guide, and student worksheets, Vision Video/Gateway Films).

The Passion of the Christ

The acclaimed and controversial Mel Gibson movie starring Jim Caviezel as Christ. Never has a Jesus film garnered more notice. If you have not seen it, be sure you do. However, the violence is too intense for a younger audience. It is also recommended that any scenes with such violence not be shown in a high school classroom or that parental permission be sought beforehand.

Bell Ringers

- **Class Discussion:** Call on the students to discuss the For Review questions on page 64.
- **Class Activity:** Set up a small balance scale on a table at the front of the class. Have near it two piles of objects of different sizes and weights, such as one pile of thumbtacks and one of nickels, or one pile of paperclips and another of small pebbles. Challenge the students to exactly balance the scales. Refer to the balancing exercise to introduce the trouble with heresies in the early Church. The Church was constantly being challenged to "keep the balance" between those who wished to emphasize Christ's divinity and those who insisted on his humanity. Through the centuries the Church has consistently preached that Jesus was both, equally human and divine, and has resisted any tendency to promote one nature over the other. Look at the heresies mentioned in the text to determine which way they were leaning.

Salvation would be void since only God can save us.

A later heresy—*Nestorianism*—taught that Christ was *two* persons and that Mary was the mother of the human Jesus, not the divine Jesus. *Monophysitism* held that Christ's divine nature absorbed his human nature, thus in effect destroying Jesus' true humanity.

Answering the Heresies

To respond to these false ideas, Church leaders, under the guidance of the Holy Spirit, convened a series of ecumenical (worldwide) councils to define carefully the nature of Jesus Christ. These councils were Nicaea (325), Constantinople I (381), Ephesus (431), Chalcedon (451), Constantinople II (553), Constantinople III (680), and Nicaea II (787). They provide the following foundational dogmatic teachings about Jesus Christ:

- *Jesus is the only Son of God.* Mary was Jesus' human mother, but the First Person of the Blessed Trinity is Jesus' Father. Jesus is God the Father's natural son; we humans are adopted children.
- *Jesus Christ is true God, "God from God, Light from Light."* Like the Father, the Son possesses a divine nature. Proceeding from the Father, the Son is of one substance with the Father. Just as light is identical to the light from which it comes, Jesus Christ is true God.
- *Jesus is "begotten, not made, one in Being with the Father."* The always-existing Son "proceeds" from the Father. Forever he proceeded, and he always will proceed. The Son was not generated by God the Father the way human fathers generate their children. In other words, the Son was not created, that is, made by the Father.

    To underscore this point, the Council of Nicaea distinguished between *begotten* and *created*. The Father begets the Son and creates the world. In other words, the Son *always* existed. He always was in relationship to the Father from whom he proceeds. The Father was always the Father; the Son was always the Son. The prologue to John's Gospel states this: "In the beginning was the Word [the Son], and the Word was with God, and the Word was God" (Jn 1:1).
- *All things were made through the Son.* The Son always existed with the Father and shares his nature. Thus, he also shares in the creation of the world (cf. Jn 1:2–4).
- *There is only one Person in Christ, the Divine Person.* Person here is not meant in the modern sense of the word. Rather it refers to distinctions between the members of the Blessed Trinity. Jesus Christ is the Second

Person of the Blessed Trinity. Because this is so, "everything in Christ's human nature is to be attributed to his divine person, not only his miracles but also his sufferings and even his death" (*CCC*, 468).

- *Mary is truly the Mother of God.* She truly conceived God's Son.
- *There are two distinct natures in the one Person of Christ.* Jesus has a divine nature and a human nature. He is perfect in divinity and perfect in humanity. Jesus Christ is true God and true man.
- *Jesus has a human intellect and a human will.* However, Jesus' human intellect and will are perfectly attuned and subject to his divine intellect and will, which he has in common with the Father and the Holy Spirit.
- *In Jesus, God truly shared our humanity.* The human and divine natures in the one Person of Jesus are so perfectly united that it is right to say that the incarnate Son of God truly suffered, died, and rose from the dead for us.

One of the most important professions of faith concerning Jesus comes from the Council of Chalcedon in AD 451. It reads:

We all with one voice teach the confession of one and the same Son, our Lord Jesus Christ: the same perfect in divinity and perfect in humanity, the same truly God and truly man, of a rational soul and a body; consubstantial with the Father as regards his divinity, and the same consubstantial with us as regards his humanity; like us in all respects except for sin; begotten before the ages from the Father as regards his divinity, and in the last days the same for us and for our Salvation from Mary, the virgin Godbearer as regards his humanity; one and the same Christ, Son, Lord, only-begotten, acknowledged in two natures which undergo no confusion, no change, no division, no separation; at no point was the difference between the natures taken away through the union, but rather the property of both natures is preserved and comes together into a single person and a single subsistent being; he is not parted or divided into two persons, but is one and the same only-begotten Son, God, Word, Lord Jesus Christ, just as the prophets taught from the beginning about him, and as the

Lord Jesus Christ himself instructed us, and as the creed of the fathers handed it down to us.[7]

What Other Religions Believe about Jesus

Today, in our ever-shrinking world, it is important to understand how other religions besides Christianity understand Jesus. What follows are some beliefs of some of the other major religions about Jesus Christ.

- *Judaism.* Jesus, of course, was a Jew. The Christian faith was born out of Judaism, many believers in the early Church were Jews. However, most Jews in the first century did not accept Jesus of Nazareth as the Messiah or the Son of God. Today, most Jews believe that Jesus existed. Some hold that he preached a message of reform similar to the Pharisees but that he never claimed to be God. They reject the belief that Jesus was the Son of God who died to save us. They also do not accept that he was the Messiah, whom they believe will be an earthly king who will establish peace throughout the world. Many Jews today await the coming of the Messiah.
- *Islam.* The Islamic faith acknowledges the existence of Jesus. Muslims hold Jesus to be one of the great prophets, like Moses. They also accept that he was a miracle worker who cured people of sickness and brought them back to life. However, Muslims do not believe that Jesus is God and the Savior of humanity. They claim he did not die during the crucifixion or rise from the dead. They have high regard for Jesus' Mother and even hold that Jesus' birth was miraculous. But they do not consider Mary to be the Mother of God. For them, God's (Allah's) final revelation came not in Jesus Christ but in their scripture known as the Qur'an and that Muhammad, not Jesus, was Allah's greatest and last prophet.
- *Eastern Religions.* Hindu beliefs about Jesus vary. Some think he was a fable; others consider him a normal man; still others suggest he was an *avatar* (an incarnation of one of the Hindu gods). Many believe he was a wise guru (teacher) who may have come to India during his "hidden years" to learn Hindu beliefs. A leading figure of the twentieth century, Mahatma Gandhi, saw in Jesus a great teacher, a man of peace who taught humans how to resist evil through

Homework Assignment

1. Review the material in Chapter 2.
2. Read the Chapter Quick View on pages 64–65.
3. Complete the Ongoing Assignment(s) on page 65–66.

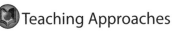

Teaching Approaches

- **Direct Instruction:** Write the names of the heresies described on pages 61–62: gnostic docetism, Arianism, Nestorianism, and monophysitism. Invite four students to come to the board and write the description of each heresy. Elaborate on the inaccuracies of each heresy.
- **Individual Assignment:** Have the students divide the list of responses to the various heresies given in the text on pages 61–62 into lists of those that reinforce belief in *Christ's humanity*, those that bolster confidence in *Christ's divinity*, and those that explicitly insist upon *both*.
- **Individual Assignment:** Have the students label each dogmatic teaching about Jesus Christ with one of the heresies on pages 61–62. Which teachings specifically rejected each heresy? When students are finished, review their work as a class.
- **Writing Assignment:** Ask the students which heretical tendency they think is most prevalent today. Are people more likely to see Jesus as too human and overlook or forget that he is God? Or are they more likely to have trouble relating to the Second Person of the Trinity, the Messiah, because he is divine and thus too different from themselves? Have them write answers of their own, defending Christ's humanity and his divinity, to the tendency they feel is most prevalent now.
- **Class Assignment:** Read the confession of Chalcedon as a class. Then invite students to make connections between the confession and the dogmatic teachings described on pages 62–63.
- **Class Assignment:** Have the students reread the section "What Other Religions Believe about Jesus." For each religion, have them list the beliefs they accept about Jesus and the beliefs they reject about him. Review their work as a class.

For Review Answers (page 64)

1. *Gnostic docetism* claims that Jesus only appeared to be human but did not in fact really take on human flesh. To counter this heresy, the Church proclaims that Jesus had both a divine and a human nature. He is true God but was also true man. He had a human intellect and human will, and because of this it is true to say that God truly shared in our humanity. *Arianism* is a heresy that claims Jesus was not truly divine, merely the greatest of God's creatures. In response, the Church asserts that Jesus is begotten of the Father, not made by him, that he is true God, of the same substance of the Father; that Jesus is just one person—the Son of God, the Second Person of the Trinity—with two natures, divine and human; that all things were made through him, thus showing his eternal existence with the Father and his taking part in the creation of the world.

2. *Judaism*: Jews believe that Jesus was a Jewish teacher, similar to a Pharisee, but not the Messiah or the Son of God. *Islam*: Muslims acknowledge that Jesus was a great prophet and miracle worker, however, they do not believe that he is God and Savior. *Hinduism*: Hindu beliefs about Jesus vary. They believe that he was a normal man, or an avatar, or a teacher. *Buddhism*: Some Buddhists believe that Jesus could have been a *Bodhisattva*, but they have no special belief about him.

nonviolent means. However, he rejected the belief that Jesus was the unique Son of God.

Most Buddhists have no special belief about Jesus, but some say he could have been a *Bodhisattva*, a compassionate being who has attained Enlightenment but dedicates his life to helping others attain happiness.

For Review

1. List and discuss several Church doctrines that counteract the heresies of Docetism and Arianism.
2. Discuss beliefs about Jesus held by any two of the great world religions.

For Reflection
Compose a three-sentence statement of your personal beliefs (that is, your personal creed) about Jesus.

CHAPTER QUICK VIEW

- The distinctive sign of Christian faith is belief in the Incarnation, God's Son taking on human flesh in Jesus Christ. (page 42)
- The name *Jesus* means "Savior" or "God saves." Jesus' titles reveal his identity and the meaning of his coming. (pages 43–45)
- Ancient Roman and Jewish writers attest to Jesus' existence, while the Gospels provide unshakable evidence of a remarkable person behind them—Jesus of Nazareth. (pages 45–46)
- *Gospel* means "Good News." It refers to Jesus' preaching of the Kingdom, to the Good News about Jesus himself, and to the four written Gospels, which are our primary source of knowledge about Jesus. These inspired documents resulted from a three-stage process that included the life of Jesus (4–6 BC to AD 30–33), a period of oral tradition, and the written Gospels themselves, which were composed between AD 50 and 120. (pages 48–49)
- Reflecting on the mysteries of Jesus' life will help us better understand his meaning for us. (page 50)
- The doctrine of the Virgin Birth holds that Jesus was conceived by the power of the Holy Spirit and born of the Virgin Mary. We further believe that Mary was perpetually a virgin. (page 52)
- Jesus taught that God's Kingdom is in our midst and that it requires faith and repentance on our part. The principal sign of God's reign is his limitless mercy. (page 54)
- To follow Jesus means to pick up a cross, to die to self for love of him and others. (page 55)
- Jesus promised he would always remain with us by power of the Holy Spirit. Thus, we can meet Jesus today through the Church, the sacraments, prayer, the Bible, and each other, especially the "least" of our brothers and sisters. (pages 54–55)
- Jesus saved us through his Paschal Mystery of love. He freely chose to sacrifice his life to redeem us and to allow us to participate in God's own life. (pages 57–60)
- Jesus really died, was laid in a new tomb, and on Holy Saturday went to the abode of the dead to proclaim the Gospel to the righteous ones awaiting the arrival of the Savior. (pages 57–59)
- Jesus really rose from the dead. Jesus' Resurrection is the basis of our Christian faith. (pages 59–60)

Chapter 2 Review Lesson

Objectives

In this lesson, the students will be able to:
- define the vocabulary words highlighted in Chapter 2.
- use the Chapter Quick View to review the key ideas in this chapter.
- prepare for the Chapter 2 Test.

Preview

This session is reserved to allow the students to review the main content in Chapter 2. Time is also reserved for the students to share their completed Ongoing Assignments.

Bell Ringers

- **Class Presentations:** Allow the opportunity for the students to share their Ongoing Assignments with their classmates.
- **Class Activity:** Give students three minutes to list the most important events of Jesus' life (again). Afterward, ask them if they did better this time than the first time they attempted the assignment.

Extending the Lesson

Student Presentations: If any student worked on Ongoing Assignment #4 (mini-service project to aid the hungry) on page 66, allow them to share their work and point out any ways the other classmates can help in this area.

- At the Parousia, Jesus will come again to establish God's Kingdom fully and to judge the living and the dead. (pages 60–61)
- Various early heresies like Docetism, Arianism, Nestorianism, and Monophysitism in one way or another denied either Jesus' humanity or divinity. Early ecumenical councils were convoked to combat these false teachings and taught foundational dogmatic statements about Jesus. (pages 61–63)
- Other major world religions acknowledge Jesus and have varying beliefs about him. (pages 63–64)

Learning the Language of Faith

Test your knowledge of important terms that you have learned in this and the previous chapters. Match the following terms with the definitions below. You will not use all the terms.

Terms
- A. Blessed Trinity
- B. Catholic
- C. Christ
- D. Dogma
- E. Epiphany
- F. Evangelist
- G. Gospel
- H. Heresy
- I. Immanence
- J. Incarnation
- K. Kingdom of God
- L. Magisterium
- M. Original Sin
- N. Parable
- O. Parousia
- P. Paschal Mystery
- Q. Religion
- R. Salvation
- S. Virgin birth

Definitions
1. Christ's manifestation as the Savior of the world
2. Saving love of God revealed in the Passion, Death, Resurrection, and Ascension of Jesus Christ
3. Messiah
4. The official teaching authority of the Church
5. God's forgiveness of sins accomplished in Jesus Christ
6. Gospel writer
7. God became man in Jesus Christ
8. Denial of a truth of the Catholic faith
9. The second coming of Christ
10. A term meaning "Good News."

Ongoing Assignments

As you cover the material in this chapter, choose and complete at least three of these assignments.

1. Interview three Catholics of different ages, genders, cultures, and the like. Ask them about their faith in Jesus Christ. For example, how they pray to Jesus, how they meet Jesus in others, their favorite Gospel stories, and how they have personally experienced Jesus.
2. Note the similarities and differences in how each Gospel reports Jesus' baptism. Read:

   - Mark 1:9–11
   - Matthew 3:13–17
   - Luke 3:21–22
   - John 1:29–34

   Answer the following questions related to each passage: Who sees the sky open? Who sees the Holy Spirit descending in the form of a dove? Who hears the Father's voice?

Teaching Approaches

- **Individual Assignment:** Continue to use the memory cards (see page 34) to review vocabulary words with the students. Add the words from this chapter to each deck as before. In your review games, use all of this chapter's words and as many from the preceding chapter as you think the students need to review.

- **Individual Assignment:** The Chapter Quick View is provided to help your students review the chapter material. While it is helpful for the students to read and study the list, more creative use of the list might help students to retain the information. For this chapter, have the students review the summary list and then choose five statements from the list that they think are the most important for them to remember about Jesus. These should be things they think will affect their relationship with God in Jesus Christ, or that will make a difference in how they live out their faith in their life. There are no right or wrong choices, but students should be encouraged to think this through carefully and be able to explain why they chose the things they did.

- **Individual Assignment:** Have the students work on the Learning the Language of Faith questions on page 65. When they have finished, allow them to check their answers with a partner or go over them as a class.

Homework Assignment

Study for the Chapter 2 Test.

Learning the Language of Faith Answers (page 65)

1. E. Epiphany
2. P. Pashcal Mystery
3. C. Christ
4. L. Magisterium
5. R. Salvation
6. F. Evangelist
7. J. Incarnation
8. H. Heresy
9. O. Parousia
10. G. Gospel

Chapter 2 Test Lesson

Objectives

In this lesson, the students will:

- take a test on their knowledge of the material in Chapter 2.
- preview the main themes to be covered in Chapter 3.

Preview

This session is reserved for the Chapter 2 Test. Allow all or nearly all of the class period for test taking. Have them write their responses to the Prayer Reflection on page 66 after completing the test.

Teaching Approaches

- **Chapter Test:** Pass out a copy of the Chapter 2 Test (starting on page 285 and also online at www .avemariapress.com) to each student. Allow enough time for the students to complete the test. Collect each test as the students finish.
- **Prayer Experience:** As the students complete the test, have them work on the questions from the Prayer Reflection on page 66. If there is time, lead a short meditation on the icon on page 66. Invite students to focus on the image and allow their minds to wander in prayer based on the expressions they see.

---

3. After researching on the Internet, create a PowerPoint presentation on one of the following or a topic of your own:
   - The mysteries of Jesus' Life
   - Stations of the Cross: traditional and updated
   - Jesus in art through the ages
   - A tour of important places in the Holy Land

4. Devise a miniservice project to aid the hungry, thus responding to one of the corporal works of mercy in Matthew 25:35–36. The project can involve direct service (for example, preparing a meal yourself) or indirect service (for example, collecting food to deliver to the community food bank).

5. Read the Gospel of Mark in one sitting. Design prayer cards or another art medium using ten of your favorite passages from the Gospel.

6. Depict in any art form your image of what you think Jesus may have looked like.

7. Prepare a report on one or more of the Apostles.

8. Research in more depth what one of the world's major religions believes about Jesus Christ.

9. With your classmates, prepare a skit of one of the parables.

10. In an artistic representation, design a crucifix that has a collage of pictures that depict the suffering of the world that Christ has redeemed by his Death on the cross. Be prepared to explain the symbolism.

11. Create a two-page (with graphics) newsletter that covers the events Jesus' birth as reported in Luke's Gospel (Lk 2:1–40).

Prayer Reflection

Recite the famous Jesus Prayer in front of an icon of Christ. One version of the Jesus Prayer goes this way: "Lord, Jesus Christ, Son of the Living God, have mercy on me, a sinner." Note how it includes all the titles discussed in this chapter. It also emphasizes Jesus' role as our Savior.

The word *icon* in Greek means "image." When we pray before icons, we are putting ourselves in the presence of the holy person or entering into the religious mystery that is portrayed.

 This icon of Jesus points to a famous passage from John's Gospel: "I am the light of the world. Whoever follows me will not walk in darkness, but will have the light of life" (Jn 8:12).

- *Reflection:* How has Christ brought light to your life? List five ways you bring light to those around you.
- *Resolution:* Consciously look for ways that Christ's presence is alive in the world.

Answers to "What Do You Know about Jesus?" (page 42): 1-T, 2-a, 3-T, 4-F, 5-c, 6-F, 7-T, 8-b, 9-c, 10-F.

Chapter 2 Test Answers (110 total points)

Part 1: Matching (2 points each)

1. B
2. H
3. D
4. F
5. G
6. A
7. K
8. A
9. C
10. D
11. C
12. A
13. B
14. A
15. D

Homework Assignment

1. Read the Chapter 3 Outline on page 69 and the opening text section of Chapter 3, "The Holy Spirit Is God" (pages 70–71).

2. Examine the Ongoing Assignments on pages 92–93.

Part 2: Multiple Choice (2 points each)

16. C

17. B

18. A

19. C

Part 3: True or False (3 points each)

20. F

21. T

22. T

23. F

24. F

25. T

Part 6: Fill-in-the-Blank (3 points each)

26. the Gospels (New Testament)

27. Paschal Mystery

28. Evangelist

29. Incarnation

30. Mary

Part 7: Short Answer (3 points each)

31. the first two letters in the Greek term (*Christos*) for Christ

32–34. Accept any three teachings that actually come from Jesus. Make sure your students' explanations match their choices.

35–37. Answers may include: God became flesh to save us; so we might know God's love; so we can imitate him; and to make us sharers in the divine nature.

38–40. Stage 1: the period of the historical Jesus; Stage 2: oral tradition; and Stage 3: the Gospels were committed to writing.

41–43. Answers may include: the same people are mentioned (Jesus, Mary, and Joseph); Mary's virginity; King Herod; conception by the Holy Spirit; Jesus was born in Bethlehem; Jesus received his name before his birth; Jesus was descended from David; the family settled in Nazareth.

3 The Holy Spirit and the Blessed Trinity

Overview of the Chapter

You are probably familiar with the story of St. Augustine who was one day walking along the beach while contemplating the mystery of the Blessed Trinity. He saw on the seashore a young boy with a bucket, going back and forth pouring water into a little hole. The great saint asked, "What are you doing?" The boy confidently replied, "I am putting the water of the ocean into this hole." Immediately it dawned on Augustine that what *he* was trying to do was to put the infinite God into his finite mind.

The lesson we can learn from St. Augustine, who wrote more eloquently about the Blessed Trinity than perhaps any Church theologian, is that no human can possibly fathom the absolute mystery that is God. Yet, as religious educators, we must help our students begin to reflect on the Blessed Trinity. As the *Catechism of the Catholic Church* teaches:

> The mystery of the Most Holy Trinity is the central mystery of Christian faith and life. It is the mystery of God in himself. It is therefore the source of all the other mysteries of the faith, the light that enlightens them. It is the most fundamental and essential teaching in the "hierarchy of the truths of faith." The whole history of salvation is identical with the history of the way and the means by which the one true God, Father, Son, and Holy Spirit, reveals himself to men "and reconciles and unites with himself those who turn away from sin." (234)

The Holy Spirit and the Blessed Trinity

To the Father, through the Son, in the Holy Spirit is the underlying theme of this chapter, which treats both the Holy Spirit and the doctrine of the Trinity. After an opening exercise on the seven gifts of the Holy Spirit, the chapter presents an overview of how the Holy Spirit was present in the Old Testament, in the New Testament, and most specifically in the life and ministry of the Son of God. The next section discusses the meaning of the name *Holy Spirit* and explains various titles and symbols of the Spirit, including fire, tongues of fire, anointing with oil, water, hand, dove, finger of God, and cloud and light.

The chapter then discusses how the Holy Spirit is present in the Church and in the life of the individual Christian. For example, he is the Life Giver who showers his grace on us, forms us as Church, enables us to proclaim Jesus as Lord, and dispenses his many gifts—gifts that sanctify and help us serve the Church and gifts that result in spiritual fruit. The Spirit can be found in the Scriptures, Tradition, the Magisterium, the sacraments, prayer, the lives of the saints, and so forth. For example, the Spirit was found in the life of a Spirit-filled leader of the Church—Blessed Pope John XXIII who was inspired by the Spirit to assemble the Second Vatican Council.

Since Jesus and the Holy Spirit reveal the awesome truth of the nature of God, this chapter is a logical place to discuss the dogma of the Blessed Trinity. The discussion begins with the many references in the New Testament to the three Divine Persons. It then moves on to a discussion of the theology of the Blessed Trinity, distinguishing between the Immanent Trinity (God's own inner life) and the Economic or Salvific Trinity (God's activity in human history). Terms like *substance*, *Person*, and *relation* are defined before presenting essential dogmatic formulations: There is only one God. There are three distinct Persons—Father, Son, and Holy Spirit—in the one God. The Divine Persons have distinct relationships with one another. Finally, the divine missions of the Blessed Trinity—creation, salvation, and sanctification—are summarized.

You might highlight this Trinitarian dynamic so your students can understand better their relationship to each person of the Trinity. One suggestion is to have them pray in an appropriate way to each person of the Blessed Trinity as you progress through the course. An attempt is made in this chapter to show the dynamic relationship that exists between the individual Christian and each Person of the Blessed Trinity. The Father is our loving Abba who gives us life and calls us into union with him. The Son is our Lord Jesus Christ who saves, reconciles, and invites us to share resurrected life in eternity. The Holy Spirit is God's vital presence, a Spirit of love, who has spoken through the prophets but continues to speak today through the Scriptures, the Church, and incredibly through the lives of individual Christians. The Spirit draws us into the divine community of love.

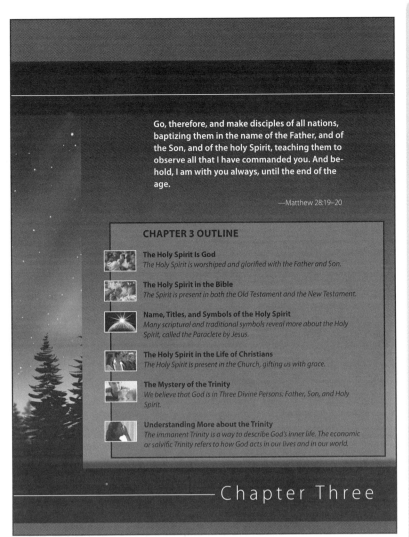

Go, therefore, and make disciples of all nations, baptizing them in the name of the Father, and of the Son, and of the holy Spirit, teaching them to observe all that I have commanded you. And behold, I am with you always, until the end of the age.

—Matthew 28:19–20

CHAPTER 3 OUTLINE

The Holy Spirit Is God
The Holy Spirit is worshiped and glorified with the Father and Son.

The Holy Spirit in the Bible
The Spirit is present in both the Old Testament and the New Testament.

Name, Titles, and Symbols of the Holy Spirit
Many scriptural and traditional symbols reveal more about the Holy Spirit, called the Paraclete by Jesus.

The Holy Spirit in the Life of Christians
The Holy Spirit is present in the Church, gifting us with grace.

The Mystery of the Trinity
We believe that God is in Three Divine Persons: Father, Son, and Holy Spirit.

Understanding More about the Trinity
The immanent Trinity is a way to describe God's inner life. The economic or salvific Trinity refers to how God acts in our lives and in our world.

Chapter Three

Resources

 ## Audiovisual Materials

Christ Incognito: Classic Insight Dramas: Jesus B.C., The Day Everything Went Wrong, The Man Who Mugged God

> *Jesus B.C.*: "God calls a family meeting and summons his son 'Chris,' and his Holy Ghost 'Grace,' to discuss how best to deal with his new creation, man" (video, Paulist Press).

He Will Send You the Holy Spirit

> The Fountain Square Fools enact the meaning of confirmation. Part 1 underscores Confirmation as a sacrament of initiation, affirmation of faith (in ourselves and the Church), and a sacrament of the Holy Spirit. Part 2 treats the gifts of the Holy Spirit, the call of Christian witness, and the Rite of Confirmation (40-minute video, Paulist Press).

Mystery of Faith, The Trinity (previously published in the "Images of Grace" Series)

> Demonstrates how the doctrine of the Trinity is the central Christian teaching (video, Paulist Press).

The Mystery of God

> "Beautiful location photography from around the world is combined with story-telling, dramatizations and expert narrative to provide a fascinating, coherent explanation of how the Catholic faith views the Trinity." Leader's guide included (three 30-minute videos, Videos with Values).

> The Video with Values website describes each tape this way:

> **Vol. 1 Father:** How to recognize God's presence in our world and lives. Segments on the Nicene Creed, Baptism, and marriage are included, along with an African folktale about the creation and the story of Abraham and Sarah.

continued on page 74

Chapter Outline
- The Holy Spirit Is God
- The Holy Spirit in the Bible
- Name, Titles, and Symbols of the Holy Spirit
- The Holy Spirit in the Life of Christians
- The Mystery of the Trinity
- Understanding More about the Trinity

Advance Preparations

Note the Ongoing Assignments, including which projects will be assigned and the date(s) they will be due.

The Holy Spirit Is God (ST pages 70–71)
- A clip of the movie *Rain Main* for the Video Presentation on page 72.

The Holy Spirit in the Bible (ST pages 72–75)
- The song "Breath of Heaven" by Amy Grant or another suitable song for the Prayer Experience on page 74.
- Arrange for one or two guest speakers for the Guest Speakers activity on page 77.

Name, Titles, and Symbols of the Holy Spirit (ST pages 76–79)
- Blank index cards, to be used to add to the memory cards created in previous chapters, for the Group Activity on page 79.
- Poster board, glue, old magazines, scissors, colored markers, and other art supplies, or have computers available, for the Group Activity on page 81.
- Arrange for a science teacher to visit the class for the Guest Speaker activity on page 81.

The Holy Spirit in the Life of Christians (ST pages 80–83)
- One of the Chicken Soup series books, such as *Chicken Soup for the Teenage Soul*, for the Direct Instruction on page 84.

The Mystery of the Trinity (ST pages 83–86)
- Three candles and a lighter or matches for the Direct Instruction on page 87.
- Copies of Chapter 3, Handout 1 "Understanding the Creeds" (starting on page 285 and also online at www.avemariapress.com) for the Individual Assignment on page 88.
- A clip of the television program *Joan of Arcadia* for the Video Presentation on page 88.

Understanding More about the Trinity (ST pages 87–90)
- Blank index cards for the Class Activity on page 89.
- Copies of Chapter 3, Handout 2 "Trinity: One God, Three Persons" (starting on page 285 and also online at www.avemariapress.com) for the Individual Assignment on pages 91–92.
- Created debate position cards for the Class Discussion on page 92.

Chapter 3 Review Lesson
- Optional items listed in Student Presentations on page 94.

Chapter 3 Test Lesson
- Copies of the Chapter 3 Test (starting on page 285 and also online at www.avemariapress.com).

The Holy Spirit Is God (pages 70–71)

Objectives

In this lesson, the students will:

- recognize the Holy Spirit as God and an equal person of the Blessed Trinity.
- list and define the gifts of the Holy Spirit.

Preview

The Holy Spirit has sometimes been called the "forgotten" person of the Trinity. This chapter provides an opportunity for students to clarify their understanding of the Holy Spirit, to become more conscious of the Holy Spirit's action in their lives, and to learn to seek out guidance from the Holy Spirit more consistently. This first section also includes a separate feature that introduces the students to the gifts of the Holy Spirit.

 Bell Ringers

- **Class Discussion:** Read the Gospel passage from Matthew 28:19–20 on page 69 together as a class. Ask the students to clearly explain what Jesus is asking of them when he says to:
  - go
  - make disciples
  - baptize in the name of the Father, Son, and Holy Spirit
  - teach all he has commanded
  - know that he is with us

- **Writing Assignment:** Have students answer the following question in their journals: "The spirit of people like Martin Luther King Jr. and Mahatma Gandhi continues to inspire their followers today. How is their spirit different from the Advocate Jesus describes in John 14 quoted on page 70?"

Teaching Approaches

- **Class Discussion:** Ask students to recall a time when they were frightened and were given courage by another, or were sad and were brought to joy by someone else's actions. Have one student read Acts 2:1–41 aloud. Remind them of the fear the Apostles felt at Jesus' Death, and that before Pentecost the Apostles were staying together in the Upper Room out of fear of being killed. How were the Apostles transformed by the action of the Holy Spirit?

- **Class Discussion:** Have one of the students summarize the opening story about Julio Franco. Note that the Spirit of Jesus, the Paraclete, motivated Julio to continue to work hard long into his career. Ask the students to make connections between this story and the translation of Paraclete in the Karre language. What do these stories reveal about the Holy Spirit?

The Holy Spirit Is God (CCC, 243–248; 689–690)

The forty-nine-year-old Julio Franco retired in 2008 after twenty-three years in Major League Baseball. His statistics are quite impressive. A three-time All Star, he was the oldest player, at age forty-eight, to hit a home run in the majors and against a star pitcher at that, Randy Johnson. He was also the oldest player in the history of the sport to steal a base.

With all the scandals involving baseball players using drugs like steroids to give them a competitive advantage, it was only natural that Franco would also be accused of using them. When a retired outfielder by the name of Andy Van Slyke made that charge, Julio revealed the true source of his longevity on the baseball diamond:

Tell Andy Van Slyke he's right—I'm on the best juice there is. I'm juiced up every day, and the name of my juice is Jesus. I'm on his power, his wisdom, his understanding. Andy Van Slyke is right, but the thing he didn't mention was what kind of steroids I'm on. Next time you talk to him, tell him the steroid I'm on is Jesus of Nazareth.[8]

When he was a young man, Julio, a native of the Dominican Republic, lived a wilder, more carefree life. But in his thirties he realized that God had given him a talent and it was his responsibility to treasure and develop it. The result was a long, productive career.

Jesus brought new life to Julio Franco and his baseball career, and he brings life to us. Jesus has given himself to us by sending us the Holy Spirit, whom he called the Paraclete. When Bible translators were trying to translate the word *Paraclete* into the Karre language of equatorial Africa, they had a hard time finding the right word. But one day, they met some porters who were carrying bundles on their heads. They noticed that one of the men did not carry anything. They assumed he was the boss who was directing the others. However, when they questioned him, they discovered that he had a special job. He was there to help anyone who became exhausted. He would pick up the load and carry it for them. His name in the Karre language was "the one who falls down beside us." The translators had discovered the Karre name for the Holy Spirit.[9]

After the Ascension, Jesus did not abandon his followers. Jesus was true to his word that after his suffering, Death, and Resurrection, he would send a Helper to them:

And I will ask the Father, and he will give you another Advocate to be with you always, the Spirit of truth, which the world cannot accept, because it neither sees nor knows it. But you know it, because it remains with you, and will be in you. . . . The Advocate, the holy Spirit that the Father will send in my name—he will teach you everything and remind you of all that (I) told you. (Jn 14:16–17, 26)

After his Resurrection and Ascension, Jesus' glorified body is no longer visible, but he remains present to us through the power of the Holy Spirit. The Holy Spirit is the very presence of the Risen Lord, the Spirit of love who *always* existed with the Father and Son.

In the Nicene Creed, Catholics profess that the Holy Spirit is "Lord and giver of life." The Council of Constantinople (381) taught as a point of dogma, "With the Father and Son, he is worshiped and glorified." The Holy Spirit is neither a creature (like an angel) nor an impersonal force. He is the Lord God. The Spirit's primary mission is to adopt us into the divine family and to unite us to Christ Jesus. By uniting us to the Son, we are drawn to the Father. This formula says it well: "To the Father through the Son in the Holy Spirit." The Holy

---

Background Information

The Church's Relationship with the Holy Spirit

The *Catechism of the Catholic Church* explains the Church's relationship with the Holy Spirit this way:

> The apostolic faith concerning the Spirit was confessed by the second ecumenical council at Constantinople (381): "We believe in the Holy Spirit, the Lord and giver of life, who proceeds from the Father." By this confession, the Church recognizes the Father as "the source and origin of the whole divinity." But the eternal origin of the Spirit is not unconnected with the Son's origin: "The Holy Spirit, the third person of the Trinity, is God, one and equal with the Father and the Son, of the same substance and also of the same nature. . . . Yet he is not called the Spirit of the Father alone, . . . but the Spirit of both the Father and the Son." The Creed of the Church from the Council of Constantinople confesses: "With the Father and the Son, he is worshipped and glorified." (245)

Extending the Lesson

Video Presentation: Show a clip of the movie *Rain Main* (popular release) in preparation for the Group Activity on pages 73–74. Dustin Hoffman portrays brilliantly a man with autism and the struggle he experiences.

Spirit is our interior teacher who keeps us united in Christ: "And no one can say, 'Jesus is Lord,' except by the holy Spirit" (1 Cor 12:3).

This chapter will also explain the central mystery of our faith—the doctrine of the Blessed Trinity and how the Holy Spirit relates to the other Persons in the Trinity.

Paraclete
Another name for the Holy Spirit that means "advocate, defender, or consoler."

Gifts of the Holy Spirit

The Holy Spirit offers the gifts we need to live Christ-like lives. Traditionally, the Church lists seven **gifts of the Holy Spirit**, qualities that the Old Testament prophet Isaiah (see Is 11:2–3) said would identify the Messiah. Jesus Christ lived each of these gifts perfectly.

These gifts are showered on us by the Holy Spirit at Baptism and Confirmation, and Catholics are given the grace to use these same gifts to draw others to Christ. The traditional seven gifts of the Holy Spirit are *wisdom, understanding, counsel, fortitude, knowledge, piety,* and *fear of the Lord.*

Read the following definitions of the gifts of the Holy Spirit. Write about how one of the gifts is particularly evidenced in your life. Also write about how another of the gifts of the Spirit needs more work in your life.

- *Wisdom* is looking at reality from God's point of view. Having wisdom involves praying before making decisions and seeking guidance from those with more experience.
- *Understanding* involves taking the time to uncover the deeper meaning of faith and the mysteries of God's magnificent creation.
- *Knowledge* is the grace to see how God is working in our lives, especially in the areas of great moral decisions.
- *Counsel (right judgment)* helps us to form our conscience in light of Church teaching. We do this by praying and consulting other people before deciding on moral issues.
- *Fortitude* is the strength to follow our own convictions in the face of peer pressure. It also involves openness to suffering for the Lord.
- *Piety (reverence)* is respect we show to the Lord through praise and worship. Respecting the dignity and worth of others is another important expression of this gift.
- *Fear of the Lord (wonder and awe)* is the gift of the Spirit that helps us to show concern about the reality of sin in our life and to avoid anything that might alienate us from God and others.

gifts of the Holy Spirit
An outpouring of God's gifts that enable us to live a Christian life. The traditional gifts of the Holy Spirit are wisdom, understanding, knowledge, counsel (right judgment), fortitude (courage), piety (reverence), and fear of the Lord.

For Reflection
- Name the greatest joy you have ever experienced.
- What does it mean to say that the Holy Spirit is the "giver of life"?

Background Information

St. Thomas Aquinas on the Importance of Belief in the Trinity

In his *Summa Theologica*, Thomas Aquinas stated, "It is impossible to believe explicitly in the mystery of Christ without faith in the Trinity, for the mystery of Christ includes that the Son of God took flesh, that He renewed the world through the grace of the Holy Spirit, and, again, that he was conceived by the Holy Spirit." (*Summa Theologica*, part II of part II, question 2, article 8).

Homework Assignment

1. Choose one gift of the Holy Spirit that you feel you have been given in a special way and one that you would like to increase, and write a brief paragraph about it.

2. Complete, in writing, answers to the For Reflection questions on page 71.

3. Read the text section "The Holy Spirit in the Bible" (pages 72–75).

- **Direct Instruction:** Explain to students that the doctrine of the Trinity is difficult for humans to imagine. However, the fact that it is hard for us to imagine something does not mean that it does not exist. Explain that in this chapter we will work to increase our understanding of the Trinity and students will seek out images to help them comprehend the Trinity more completely.

- **Direct Instruction:** Review the importance of the Nicene Creed and the Apostles' Creed in clarifying our Catholic beliefs. Because they are so familiar to us, we can say them without truly thinking about their importance. The quotations from the Nicene Creed and the Council of Constantinople on page 70 are clear evidence that the early Church saw the Holy Spirit as equal with the Father and the Son and as someone Christians need to recognize and turn to in our lives.

- **Direct Instruction:** Point out the separate feature, "Gifts of the Holy Spirit," on page 71. Have students read Isaiah 11:2–3. Remind them that Church tradition is firmly rooted in Scripture. The list of the gifts of the Holy Spirit comes from this and other biblical passages that reveal the Spirit's role in human history.

- **Individual Assignment:** Have the students close their books and attempt to define each of the seven gifts of the Holy Spirit. When they are finished, have them open their books again and check their definitions against the definitions on page 71. Then, have them attempt to memorize all seven gifts of the Holy Spirit before moving on.

- **Group Activity:** In order to be able to benefit from the gifts, students need to understand them, recognize their value, and seek them out in real-life situations. Divide students into groups of three or four. Describe the following scenarios for them, and have them discuss and write down how each of the gifts of the Spirit could be helpful in each situation. How might the outcome be different if a person ignored the gifts of the Spirit?

    ◆ A family has a child with severe autism. Autism causes people to have difficulty processing information; they have trouble coping with change, often have difficulty expressing empathy for others, and may act out unpredictably. The family has three other children, and it is difficult to meet the needs of all of their children. A social worker has recommended that the child with autism be placed in a residential facility. The parents have called a family meeting to discuss their options.

    ◆ A woman in her sixties is in an automobile accident. Her injuries are severe, and the doctors say her chances of recovery are remote. She has been unconscious and on a respirator for ten days. Her family has limited financial resources. Her son suggests that the family ask the hospital to remove the respirator.

The Holy Spirit in the Bible
(pages 72–75)

Objectives

In this lesson, the students will:
- demonstrate an improved understanding of the nature and action of the Holy Spirit.
- recall examples of the Holy Spirit's presence in the Old and New Testament.

 Preview

This section demonstrates the scriptural basis for belief in the Holy Spirit. It recounts the saving action of the Spirit from the beginning of the Old Testament, and shows Jesus' response to the Spirit in his life. Although the Jewish people did not think of the Holy Spirit as a person distinct from the Father, they celebrated the action of the Spirit in their history. In the New Testament, the concept of the Holy Spirit became more and more distinct. Beginning each section of this class with a prayer based on a Scripture passage on the Spirit will help make their learning about the Holy Spirit more concrete.

 Bell Ringers

- **Class Discussion:** Call on students to share from their homework how particular gifts of the Holy Spirit are evidenced in their lives and how other gifts need more work in their lives.
- **Prayer Experience:** Open with a short prayer. Play Amy Grant's "Breath of Heaven" (or another suitable piece of music). Invite students to bring any concerns they may have before the Holy Spirit. Close with a spontaneous prayer to the Holy Spirit or a prepared prayer read by the teacher or a student.

The Holy Spirit in the Bible

The Holy Spirit "spoke through the prophets." He guided the biblical authors to reveal God's Word and gives us the gifts that we need to accept God's Revelation and live a Christ-filled life. In Salvation History, the Holy Spirit seems hidden, but this is only because the Holy Spirit does not speak of himself. He is like the mysterious power of electricity, always present but out of sight to provide the power to operate electrical appliances.

theophany
An appearance or manifestation of God to humans.

The Holy Spirit in the Old Testament (CCC, 103–108; 687; 702–730)

Before the coming of Christ and the Holy Spirit's descent on Pentecost Sunday, the Father and the Holy Spirit had

a joint, hidden mission. Today, with the light of faith and the Spirit's help, the Church searches the Old Testament to discover the Spirit's active presence in Salvation History where he prepared for and promised us the Messiah. The Old Testament biblical authors often use the Hebrew word *ruah* (wind or breath) to speak of God's mysterious, powerful, and life-giving presence in creation and at work among the Chosen People. Over time, the Old Testament gradually came to reveal the Holy Spirit in more personal terms.

The Church discovers the active presence of the Holy Spirit in several ways.

In creation (Gn 1:2) and in giving the breath of life to Adam and Eve (Gn 2:7), the Spirit brings life to the world and keeps the world in existence. By the power of the Holy Spirit, God forged a covenant with the Chosen People through Abraham. Eventually, a Messiah was born among Abraham's descendants.

To Moses, God showed himself by the power of the Holy Spirit, for example, in the theophany that revealed God's presence as in the burning bush and one in the clouds that led the people through the desert. God's Spirit helped the Israelites keep the Law. The Law served as a teacher to lead people to Christ, but it could not save them. It made people aware of how sinful they were and how impossible it is to obey God's law without the help of the Holy Spirit.

The Spirit inspired kings like David to rule in Yahweh's name. But after David's time, the Chosen People drifted away from the Law and ignored God's covenant. God's spirit "anointed" Israel's prophets like Elijah (2 Kgs 2:9) and Elisha (2 Kgs 2:15), who spoke on God's behalf by instructing people to remain faithful to the covenant. The sinfulness of the Israelites eventually led them to exile

For Enrichment

Individual Activity: Have students write a news story describing the Pentecost event but setting it in modern-day America. Where would the Apostles be hiding? Why would they be afraid? To whom would they speak after being transformed by the Holy Spirit? What would be the likely response?

 Audiovisual Materials continued from page 71

Vol. 2 Jesus: How God is revealed to us in the person of Jesus, the meaning of Christmas, and the "radical ethic" Jesus preached at Sermon on the Mount are featured along with the story of "Jairus' Daughter."

Vol. 3 Spirit: The stories of how the Blessed Virgin Mary answered the Spirit's call, and the Native American tale of "The Wind and the Rain" are combined with other metaphors and images to give a rich description of the powerful presence of the Spirit in everyday life.

Spirit Alive in Community

From the *Sealed with God's Spirit* Catholic Update series, this program shows the Holy Spirit's active presence "in the lives of Christians when they celebrate, worship, learn and serve together as members of the Body of Christ" (St. Anthony Messenger Press).

Will You Carry the Light?

Used to prepare teens for Confirmation, this brief video helps the viewer reflect on how the Holy Spirit is present in each Christian whose mission is to be the light of Christ to others. A Study Guide is included (20-minute video, Harcourt).

in Babylonia. It was then that the Holy Spirit sustained them until they could return to the Promised Land. He continually spoke through the prophets who promised that one day the Messiah would come to rule them.

The Suffering Servant Songs of Isaiah reveal the Messiah's qualities. They also prophesy the Lord's Passion and his Death, the necessary prelude for his unleashing the Spirit of life on all humans:

> Yet it was our infirmities that he bore, our sufferings that he endured. . . .
>
> But he was pierced for our offenses, crushed for our sins,
>
> Upon him was the chastisement that makes us whole,
>
> by his stripes we were healed. . . .
>
> Though he was harshly treated, he submitted and opened
>
> not his mouth;
>
> Like a lamb led to the slaughter or a sheep before the shearers,
>
> he was silent and opened not his mouth. . . .
>
> Because of his affliction he shall see the light in fullness of days;
>
> Through his suffering, my servant shall justify many,
>
> and their guilt he shall bear.
>
> Therefore I will give him his portion among the great,
>
> and he shall divide the spoils with the mighty,
>
> Because he surrendered himself to death
>
> and was counted among the wicked;
>
> And he shall take away the sins of many,
>
> and win pardon for their offenses. (Is 53:4–5, 7, 11–12)

Not until Jesus Christ came was the Holy Spirit fully revealed as a separate, distinct Person of the Blessed Trinity.

The Holy Spirit in the New Testament
(CCC, 689–693; 717–732; 743; 745–746)

Pentecost, originally a Jewish harvest festival celebrated fifty days after Passover, was the day the Holy Spirit descended on Christ's disciples hiding in the Upper Room in Jerusalem, the place of the Last Supper. The Acts of the Apostles, written by the Evangelist Luke, records how on that day the Holy Spirit came down with power on the early Christians. The Spirit's presence gave the early Church the courage to proclaim the Gospel of Jesus Christ to the ends of the earth.

The Apostles, the Blessed Mother, and some women were praying, trying to make sense of the events leading to our Lord's Death and Resurrection:

> Suddenly there came from the sky a noise like a strong driving wind, and it filled the entire house in which they were. Then there appeared to them tongues as of fire, which parted and came to rest on each one of them. And they were all filled with the holy Spirit and began to speak in different tongues, as the Spirit enabled them to proclaim. (Acts 2:2–4)

Scripture Search

Read the following Old Testament passages. Summarize briefly the main point about God's Spirit that the passage expresses.

1. Genesis 1:1–2; 2:7
2. Isaiah 11:1–3
3. Isaiah 61:1–2
4. Ezekiel 36:26–28
5. Ezekiel 37:1–14

Teaching Approaches

- **Direct Instruction:** Read the opening text under the heading "The Holy Spirit in the Bible" (pages 72–75). Note the comparison of the power of the Spirit to the power of electricity. Ask the students to suggest other similar comparisons for the Holy Spirit.

- **Direct Instruction:** Summarize the text subsection "The Holy Spirit in the Old Testament" (pages 72–73). Be sure to define and discuss the term *theophany*. Refer to the accompanying references from the *Catechism of the Catholic Church* as time permits.

- **Class Discussion:** List the names of various Old Testament figures, including Adam and Eve, Abraham, Moses, David, Elijah, Elisha, and Isaiah. Call on students randomly to cite evidence that the Holy Spirit was at work in the lives of each of these individuals.

- **Class Assignment:** Work in groups of five to complete the Scripture Search on page 73. First have each student read and write their own summaries of each passage. Then, have the groups take turns sharing with one another their own summaries (possible answers are on page 75 of this text).

Resources

 Internet Links see www.avemariapress.com

Scripture Search Possible Answers (page 73)

- *Genesis 1:1–2; 2:7:* The Spirit was present from the beginning of creation. The Spirit brought the first humans to life and continues to sustain us and all living things today.

- *Isaiah 11:1–3:* The Spirit inspired Isaiah and the Jewish people to look forward to a Messiah. He also described the Messiah so we would be able to recognize him when he did appear.

- *Isaiah 61:1–2:* Isaiah is speaking of Jesus in this passage. The Holy Spirit was making the vision of the Messiah clearer. Jesus has come to show God's tender love to all, particularly to those who suffer.

- *Ezekiel 36:26–28:* This passage describes the impact the Holy Spirit has on those who are willing to let him into their hearts. The Holy Spirit helps us to be open and kind and willing to see what God asks of us in loving God and those around us.

- *Ezekiel 37:1–14:* This passage uses vivid imagery, which is fairly unfamiliar to contemporary readers. Ezekiel is describing the power of the Spirit to bring life and hope even when it seems that all hope has been lost.

- **Direct Instruction:** Continue with the text subsection "The Holy Spirit in the New Testament" (pages 73–74). This section focuses on the Pentecost event. The message is that the Holy Spirit is able to bring about dramatic transformation in people's lives, sometimes almost instantaneously. Share some information about "speaking in tongues." The students may not be aware that this gift is still witnessed today. Consider having the students do an Internet search on the phenomenon of speaking in tongues in present-day America.
- **Group Activity:** Have students gather in five small groups. Assign one Gospel to each of four groups; assign the Acts of the Apostles to the fifth group. Have the groups work together to find and cite as many references for the Holy Spirit as they can and record them on one common paper. Call time after ten minutes and find out which group was able to find the most references.
- **Class Discussion:** Summarize many of the examples of how the Holy Spirit was with Jesus through his whole life (see pages 74–75). Review the terms Advocate and Paraclete in the text. Ask students to give examples of times when they have needed a helper who would guide them and give them comfort. Lead a discussion on how the Holy Spirit could make a difference to them today. When someone has come to their aid in the past, is it possible the Holy Spirit inspired that person to help them?
- **Class Discussion:** Have students review Jesus' instructions to Nicodemus in John 3:5–8. What does it mean to be born again? Some Christian denominations believe this to be a once-in-a-lifetime event that can be clearly identified and remembered. In general, Catholics see this as an ongoing lifetime experience that follows our one baptism. Lead a discussion on how students see themselves as having changed in positive ways since the beginning of their high school years.
- **Writing Assignment:** Before the session concludes, check students' understanding by having them complete an "exit card" necessary to leave class. Have them identify three examples of the Holy Spirit in both the Old and the New Testaments. Check their answers quickly and review before the next class.

Immediately afterward, the Apostles went to proclaim the Gospel to the crowds in *tongues*, that is, the many languages of the various people who were gathered there. Remarkably, Jewish pilgrims from all around the Roman Empire understood them. At first the crowds were skeptical; in fact, they thought the Apostles were drunk. But Peter assured them that they were quite sober—after all, it was only nine in the morning. Peter explained that what was happening was clearly promised by the prophet Joel:

"It will come to pass in the last days," God says,

"that I will pour out a portion of my spirit upon on all flesh.

Your sons and daughters shall prophesy,

Your young men shall see visions,

your old men shall dream dreams. . . .

and it shall be that everyone shall be saved who calls on the name of the Lord." (Acts 2:17, 21)

Pentecost fulfilled Jesus' promise to send the Holy Spirit. On that day, 3,000 people were baptized. By the end of the first century, the Gospel had been preached to every corner of the Roman Empire. Today, the same Holy Spirit remains alive in the world and in the Church, bringing Christ's Salvation to all people everywhere.

John's Gospel tells how Jesus sent the Holy Spirit to the Apostles on Easter Sunday. Jesus greeted his Apostles with peace and then commissioned them by saying, "As the Father has sent me, so I send you. . . . Receive the holy Spirit. Whose sins you forgive are forgiven them, and whose sins you retain are retained" (Jn 20:21–23).

God breathed life into Adam and Eve at the beginning of human history. After his Resurrection, Jesus recreated his disciples by giving them the life of the Holy Spirit, a life as God's children. A major emphasis of John's Gospel is to show how the Church is to continue Jesus' work of Salvation.

Jesus Is Filled with the Holy Spirit

The Holy Spirit accompanied Jesus through his whole life. The Church was able to recognize this through the eyes of faith. For example:

- The Holy Spirit enabled Mary to conceive Jesus, thus bringing God's Son into our midst. He is *Emmanuel*—"God-with-us."
- The Holy Spirit helped John the Baptist to prepare people for the "way of the Lord."
- The Holy Spirit was at Jesus' baptism, led him into the desert for prayer and fasting, and sustained him there in his battle with Satan.
- Jesus began his preaching ministry in Nazareth filled with the Spirit's power (Lk 4:14). Jesus testified that the Spirit was upon him, anointing him to preach Good News to the afflicted, proclaim liberty to captives, give sight to the blind, and let the

Background Information

The Bible Is Written under the Inspiration of the Holy Spirit

According to the Second Vatican Council document *Dogmatic Constitution on Divine Revelation (Dei Verbum)*,

the divinely revealed realities, which are contained and presented in the text of sacred Scripture, have been written down under the inspiration of the Holy Spirit. For Holy Mother Church relying on the faith of the apostolic age, accepts as sacred and canonical the books of the Old and the New Testaments, whole and entire, with all their parts, on the grounds that, written under the inspiration of the Holy Spirit, they have God as their author, and have been handed on as such to the Church herself. (Chapter III, number 11)

oppressed go free (Lk 4:16–21). Jesus' miracles of healing, driving out demons, raising from the dead, and showing power over the forces of creation were all done through the power of the Holy Spirit.

- In his public ministry, Jesus gradually revealed the mystery of the Holy Spirit. Examples include his instructions to Nicodemus (Jn 3:5–8), conversation with the Samaritan woman (Jn 4:10, 14, 23–24), and his teaching about the Eucharist (Jn 6:27, 51, 62–63).
- Jesus promised to send the Holy Spirit (Jn 14:16–17, quoted on page 70). In this promise, Jesus referred to the Holy Spirit by the name Advocate or Paraclete. A paraclete is a helper who will give aid and comfort. Jesus is all of these, but he promised to send *another* Paraclete—"the Spirit of truth" who will live in us and guide us to the truth.

Finally, the Holy Spirit remained with Jesus even up to his Death and Resurrection. When the soldier stabbed Jesus with a spear, blood and water gushed out of the wound (Jn 19:34). This symbolizes the life and waters of the Holy Spirit flowing out to the world. Through the Spirit, God raised Jesus from the dead. Our Risen Lord has a spiritual, glorified body. As resurrected Lord, Jesus is, through the power and presence of the Holy Spirit, the invisible head of his Body, the Church. The Holy Spirit gives the Church life and directs it in Christ's continuing work of Salvation.

When the Father sends the Son, he also sends the Holy Spirit. The Son and Holy Spirit have a joint but distinct mission. It is Christ Jesus who is visible, the image of God; however, it is the Holy Spirit who reveals him to us.

For Review

1. List and briefly describe the seven gifts of the Holy Spirit.
2. Name three ways the Holy Spirit was active in Salvation History before the coming of Christ.
3. What happened on the feast of Pentecost?
4. List and briefly discuss four ways the Holy Spirit was active in the life of Jesus.
5. Define *Paraclete*.

For Reflection

Write or share of a time when the Holy Spirit's gift of fortitude empowered you to do the right thing.

For Review Answers (page 75)

1. The seven gifts of the Holy Spirit are:
   - *Wisdom* – looking at reality from God's point of view
   - *Understanding* – uncovering the deeper meaning of faith
   - *Counsel* – forming a right conscience in light of Church teaching
   - *Knowledge* – grace to see God working in our lives
   - *Fortitude* – the strength to follow our convictions
   - *Piety* – respect we show God through praise and worship
   - *Fear of the Lord* – our concern to avoid sin

2. The Holy Spirit was present, for example, in the act of creation, in God forging the covenant with Abraham, in the theophany of the burning bush, and in the actions of the prophets.

3. On the feast of Pentecost, the disciples were filled with the power of the Holy Spirit and were given new courage and power to speak. Some external signs of this event were the appearance of tongues of fire over the heads of the disciples and their ability to speak in foreign languages.

4. Jesus was conceived by the power of the Holy Spirit; the Holy Spirit inspired St. John the Baptist; the Holy Spirit was with Jesus when he was tempted in the desert; the Holy Spirit was with Jesus in his public ministry.

5. *Paraclete* is a helper who will give aid and comfort.

Homework Assignment

1. Complete the For Review questions on page 75.
2. Read the text section "Name, Titles, and Symbols of the Holy Spirit" (pages 76–79).

Extending the Lesson

Guest Speakers: Arrange for one or both of the guest speakers to accompany the information in this lesson. For example, have someone speak to the class who has had a profound conversion experience. These experiences can be triggered by a wide variety of events: retreats, a death or other loss, a relationship with a faith-filled person, and even, occasionally, time spent in prison. Have the person tell their story and then explain what it is like to live out their new life on a daily basis. Allow time for student questions, and be sure to take time to process in the following class. Your speaker could be an adult or an older student. Campus ministers, parish youth directors, and students may be able to suggest possible speakers.

Or, have a speaker from a denomination that exercises the charismatic gifts of the Holy Spirit. It would be important that this person be known to the teacher; some members of these denominations are critical of Catholic beliefs, and it is important that the visit improve understanding and tolerance.

Name, Titles, and Symbols of the Holy Spirit (pages 76–79)

Objectives

In this lesson, the students will:

- identify and define the names and titles for the Holy Spirit.
- list several symbols for the Holy Spirit and make connections with their origins in Scripture.
- explain why the symbols are connected with functions of the Holy Spirit.

 Preview

The previous section described the growing awareness and understanding of the Holy Spirit throughout salvation history. This section deals more directly with our attempts to understand who the Holy Spirit is. Each of the names and symbols in this section is simply an attempt to grasp the essence of the Spirit. Words and images are always limited, but they can help us get a little closer to understanding the Holy Spirit and recognizing the ways the Spirit is active in our lives.

 Bell Ringers

- **Class Discussion:** Check and collect all of the students' homework assignments. Call on students to share their answers with the class after collecting their work.

- **Individual Assignment:** Review the previous lesson's presentation of the Holy Spirit in Scripture. Have students turn to the Knowing Christ through Scripture feature on page 78. After they read the information about the Holy Spirit in the Acts of the Apostles, have them complete the Scripture questions. When they have completed the questions, discuss the answers as a class.

Teaching Approaches

- **Class Discussion:** Write the following question on the board: **"Who is the Holy Spirit?"** Based on what students have learned so far, develop a definition/description of the Holy Spirit to compare to the names and symbols discussed in this section. If necessary, remind them of the Spirit's role in Scripture as a springboard for the discussion.

- **Class Discussion:** "Awesome" is another word for holy. Ask students to think of times when they have been struck by awesome sights, such as watching stars at night, encountering mountains or the ocean, etc. What feelings do they have at that moment? Do they feel small and yet at the same time important? These encounters are a taste of what it is like to experience the holiness of God. We and our lives are put into perspective in a very positive way.

Name, Titles, and Symbols of the Holy Spirit (CCC, 691–701)

You are probably familiar with the terms that make up the proper name of the Third Person of the Blessed Trinity—*holy* and *spirit*. *Holy* refers to God's total uniqueness from his creatures; he alone is "totally other"; he is awesome and beyond what we can grasp. God is the only all-holy one. *Spirit* is also an interesting word. Teams or student bodies are sometimes spoken of as having "spirit." The word *spirit* also refers to the real sense of something, as in the expressions "keeping to the spirit of the law" or "living the spirit of '76." Many religions refer to God as the "Great Spirit" because they recognize that he is the source of life and the one who keeps everything in existence.

Recall the Hebrew word *ruah*, which is translated as "spirit." *Ruah* means "breath, life, wind, air." The biblical authors used *ruah* 379 times to depict God's actions in Salvation History. For example, the spirit (*ruah*) in the image of driving wind hovers over the dark, chaotic waters at creation. In the first creation account (Gn 1:1–2:4a), the Spirit is linked with God's Word; it brings light, order, and life into existence. In the second creation account (Gn 2:4b–25), God breathes the "breath of life" into Adam after making him from clay (Gn 2:7). This breath of life is God's gift to us, God's Spirit in us that enables us to live and to communicate with and love God.

When Christians join the terms *Holy* and *Spirit* together, they are clearly following Jesus' revelation about the Third Person of the Blessed Trinity. The Holy Spirit is of the same "substance" (nature) as the Father and the Son. The Holy Spirit is the breath (Spirit) of the Father with whom Jesus is totally filled. The Spirit is active in the Word. He is the gift given by the Father and Son to all of Jesus' followers to do in us what he did in Jesus. He is what St. Paul also refers to as the Spirit of the promise, the Spirit of adoption, the Spirit of Christ, the Spirit of the Lord, and the Spirit of God.

As you saw above, Jesus gives the Holy Spirit the titles of Paraclete and the Spirit of truth. *Paraclete* reveals the Holy Spirit's role in our lives. He consoles, acts as an advocate, and defends us.

Symbols of the Holy Spirit

Some other scriptural and traditional symbols for the Holy Spirit are explained below.

Fire

God appeared to Moses in a burning bush—a symbol of divine holiness. He led the Israelites through the desert by pillars of fire, helping to purify the people and make them holy. Fire also punishes the wicked, as in the destruction of Sodom. Fire in both cases represents the transforming energy of the Holy Spirit.

Fire also gives light. Jesus calls himself the Light of the World. His followers are to be light as well, leading

Resources

Printed Materials

Bracken, Joseph. *What Are They Saying about the Trinity?* New York: Paulist Press, 1979.

    A still-useful introduction to recent theology on the Trinity.

Congar, Yves, O.P. *I Believe in the Holy Spirit*. Milestones in Catholic Theology. Trans. David Smith. New York: Crossroad/Herder & Herder, 1997.

    A definitive treatment on the Holy Spirit by one of the twentieth century's leading theologians.

Dodds, Bill. *The Seeker's Guide to the Holy Spirit: Filling Your Life with Seven Gifts of Grace*. Chicago: Loyola, 2003.

    Dodds is a clear and interesting writer. All the books in this series are informative.

Downey, Michael. *Altogether Gift: A Trinitarian Spirituality*. Maryknoll, NY: Orbis Books, 2000.

    His insights on God as love are insightful and appealing to the modern reader.

Fortmann, Edmund J. *The Triune God*. Philadelphia: Westminster Press, 1972.

    A key modern work on the doctrine of the Trinity.

Hunt, Anne. *What Are They Saying about the Trinity?* Mahwah, NJ: Paulist Press, 1998.

    An easy-to-read overview of recent trends in the study of the Trinity.

Kaspar, Walter. *The God of Jesus Christ*. Trans. Matthew J. O'Connell. New York: Crossroad, 1986.

    A highly respected book by a highly respected theologian who is now a cardinal.

continued on page 87

others to him and to the Gospel's truth. Thus, he gives the Holy Spirit to his disciples to empower them to enlighten the world. The Holy Spirit is our inner light to help us see Jesus and burn with love for him and others.

Tongues of Fire

The tongue enables us to speak. Jesus spoke God's truth because he was filled with the Holy Spirit. His words forgave sin, brought about cures, controlled the forces of nature, and brought the dead back to life.

The Spirit whom Jesus gives to his disciples enables us to reverse the prideful confusion brought to humanity at the time of the Tower of Babel (Gn 11:9). The Holy Spirit makes its possible for us to proclaim Christ Jesus, to speak the truth, and to create community in the Lord's name.

Anointing with Oil

The New Testament associates anointing with oil with being anointed with the Holy Spirit. The title *Christ* means "anointed one." The Sacraments of Baptism and Confirmation both use oil to express the gift of the Holy Spirit who makes Catholics anointed ones of the Anointed One. Also, those baptized men who receive the Sacrament of Holy Orders are anointed with holy chrism "as a sign of the special anointing of the Holy Spirit who makes their ministry fruitful" (*CCC*, 1574). The symbol of the *seal*, as in the expression "The Father has set his seal on Christ," is related to the symbol of anointing. Baptism, Confirmation, and Holy Orders bring about an indelible character through the anointing of the Holy Spirit in these sacraments.

Symbols for the Holy Spirit

Identify which symbol of God's Spirit or presence is depicted in the following passages. Then use any art medium to devise a symbol for the Holy Spirit based on one or more of the passages.

1. Exodus 19:18
2. Psalm 104:30
3. Ephesians 5:6–20
4. Revelation 21:6

Background Information

The *Catechism of the Catholic Church* clearly outlines how the Holy Spirit is represented in name, titles, and symbols:

The proper name of the Holy Spirit

"Holy Spirit" is the proper name of the one whom we adore and glorify with the Father and the Son. (691)

Titles of the Holy Spirit

Paragraphs 692–693 highlight many titles of the Holy Spirit, including "Paraclete," the one used by Jesus.

Symbols of the Holy Spirit

Paragraphs 694–701 highlight the following symbols of the Holy Spirit:

Water

Anointing

Fire

Cloud and light

The seal

The hand

The finger

The dove

- **Class Discussion:** Athletic teams and their fans often try to quantify "spirit" and "play with spirit." Schools themselves often talk about "improving school spirit." Brainstorm with students the qualities and behavior that indicate strong team spirit or strong school spirit. How would your school rate in showing qualities and behavior consistent with the Holy Spirit? Have students develop a checklist of qualities that would appear in a school community guided by the Holy Spirit. Where do they see their school as being strong? Where do they see need for growth?

- **Group Activity:** Summarize the material under the heading "Name, Titles, and Symbols of the Holy Spirit" (page 76) and "Symbols of the Holy Spirit" (pages 76–79). Have students work in pairs to study and remember some of the names, titles, and symbols for the Holy Spirit. Besides the names and symbols listed in the rest of the section, terms to remember include holy, Spirit, Advocate, Paraclete, ruah, the gifts of the Holy Spirit, theophany, Pentecost, fire, tongues of fire, anointing with oil, water, hand, and dove. Have them create "memory cards" to help remember the definitions. For each term/name have them create two cards: one with the term, name, or symbol and the other with the definition. When they have finished making the cards, allow them to play a memory game with all the cards face down on their desks. Students may turn over two cars per turn to match the term with its definition. If they make a match, they may keep the cards. The player with the most cards wins.

- **Direct Instruction:** Fire, oil, and water are important symbols throughout the Old and New Testaments. Explain to students the immediate and critical importance these held in Jesus' time and why these symbols were appropriate for the Holy Spirit.

  - *Fire* was the only source of heat other than the sun. People needed to gather fuel for fires and keep a fire burning so that they would not be required to go to a neighbor to begin a new fire or begin it anew themselves. Fire was also their only source of light in the darkness. Like fire, the Holy Spirit is the light within each of us and, like fire, it transforms us.

  - *Anointing with oil* may be one of the most difficult symbols for students to grasp. Anointing with oil was used in Jewish and other cultures as a symbol of designating a person for a mission. Throughout the missionary journeys of Jesus and his Apostles, the Gospels and the Acts of the Apostles explain that they were led by the Spirit. Have students brainstorm rituals and symbols that are used on various teams to "pass the baton" from one year's captains to the next. Explain the similarities between these traditions and the ancient tradition of anointing with the Holy Spirit.

- ◆ *Water*, a scarce commodity in many areas of the world, needs to be carried by hand in primitive cultures. Water is the source of life. In parts of the world where water is abundant, it may also be difficult for students to understand the power of this symbol. Flooding can also be a catastrophic issue in many parts of the world. For this reason Jesus made a connection between the water, the source of life and death, and the Holy Spirit, which brings us new life through baptism.

- **Class Discussion:** Continue with the discussion of other symbols mentioned in the text. Have students reflect on the power of touch in people's lives. Ask for examples of ways in which touch soothes, comforts, or strengthens people: massage, hugs, an encouraging pat, etc. Reflect on the importance of touch in babies' lives: babies, human or animal, that are not held and touched can develop what is called "failure to thrive" syndrome; some even give up and die. The symbol of hands calls to mind the importance and power of touch in encouraging and guiding all people.

KNOWING CHRIST THROUGH SCRIPTURE

Acts—The Gospel of the Holy Spirit

The Holy Spirit plays a prominent role in the Acts of the Apostles, so much so that Acts has sometimes been called "the Gospel of the Holy Spirit." The Holy Spirit is the Third Person of the Blessed Trinity. He speaks to the disciples in Acts, for example, instructing Peter to meet the servants of the Gentile centurion Cornelius (Acts 10:19) and inspiring elders to serve their flock (Acts 20:28).

Jesus continues his work through the Holy Spirit. The Spirit is Christ's gift to his disciples, the one who creates the Church, a community of love, sharing, and prayer (Acts 2:43–47). The Holy Spirit empowered Jesus' earliest followers to open up the gospel message to all people—for example, to the hated Samaritans (Acts 8:14–24) and eventually to non-Jews, the Gentiles (Acts 10:44–48). It was the Holy Spirit who led the Church leaders at the Council of Jerusalem to accept Gentiles into the Church without their having to submit to all the regulations of the Jewish religion, especially the law of circumcision (Acts 15:28–29).

The Holy Spirit enabled the early Church to witness bravely and without fear on behalf of Christ and his Gospel. This was true even in situations where the authorities had the power of life and death over the disciples:

> As they prayed, the place where they were gathered shook, and they were all filled with the holy Spirit and continued to speak the word of God with boldness. The community of believers was of one heart and mind, and no one claimed that any of his possessions was his own, but they had everything in common. With great power the apostles bore witness to the resurrection of the Lord Jesus, and great favor was accorded them all. (Acts 4:31–33)

Read the following selections from Acts to see how the Holy Spirit helped create the Church and give it the courage to preach the Gospel of Jesus Christ. Answer the questions that follow:

Acts 2: Pentecost
- What were the signs of the coming of the Holy Spirit?
- After giving his testimony about Jesus, what did Peter tell the first converts they had to do?
- Describe the life of the early believers.

Acts: 6:5–7:60: The Martyrdom of Stephen
- Why were Stephen's opponents unable to counteract his testimony?
- Discuss two ways Stephen's death was similar to Jesus' Death.

Acts 9: The Conversion of Saul
- Why was Saul going to Damascus?
- What happened to him on the way?
- What did Ananias and Barnabas do for Saul?

Acts 10: Peter and Cornelius
- What is the meaning of Peter's dream?
- What was the sign that Gentiles were meant to become members of the Church?

Acts 15:1–35: The Council of Jerusalem
- What question was taken up at the council?
- What position did Peter take at the meeting?
- What was the final decision reached at the council under the inspiration of the Holy Spirit?

Knowing Christ through Scripture Answers (page 78)

Acts 2: Pentecost
- A noise like a wind, tongues of fire, speaking in tongues
- He told them to repent and be baptized.
- "They devoted themselves to the teaching of the apostles, and to the communal life, and to the breaking of the bread, and to the prayers." They also sold their possessions to divide them among them according to their need.

Acts 6:5–7:60: The Martyrdom of Stephen
- Because he spoke with wisdom and the Spirit
- Like Jesus, Stephen was accused of blasphemy by elders and scribes, condemned by false witnesses, and before his death he forgave them for his death and proclaimed, "Lord, receive my spirit" just as Jesus had said, "Father, into your hands I commend my spirit."

Acts 9: The Conversion of Saul
- Saul was going to Damascus to arrest Christians.
- On his way he encountered the Risen Christ.
- Ananias healed and baptized Saul, and Barnabas defended him before the Apostles.

Acts 10: Peter and Cornelius
- Peter's dream meant that the Gentiles would not be forced to follow Jewish laws regarding unclean foods.
- The Gentiles received the Holy Spirit.

Acts 15:1–35: The Council of Jerusalem
- Whether it was necessary to be circumcised to be saved
- Peter agreed that circumcision was not necessary, but that all were "saved through the grace of the Lord Jesus."
- Circumcision was not necessary, but Gentiles should refrain from worshiping idols, unlawful marriage, and eating meat of strangled animals.

Water

Water can represent both death and life. Too much water causes floods that lead to destruction and death, yet we need water to live. Images of both death and life appear in the Bible in connection with water. For example, God punished humanity in the time of Noah by sending the Flood. But God also created the world out of the watery chaos and sent springs of water to the Chosen People in the desert.

Jesus associated water and the Spirit when he said to Nicodemus, "Amen, amen, I say to you, no one can enter the kingdom of God without being born of water and Spirit" (Jn 3:5). This refers to the Sacrament of Baptism, which brings about our death to our old life of sin and our rebirth to eternal life. The waters of Baptism initiate us into Christ's body, the Church, and bestow on us the gift of the Holy Spirit.

Hand

Jesus healed through touch. His Apostles healed in his name as well. And they passed on the Holy Spirit through the imposition of hands. This sign is used in the sacraments (at the laying on of hands) to signify the giving of the Holy Spirit.

Dove

In the Old Testament, a dove released by Noah returned to the ark with an olive tree branch to show that the floodwaters were receding. The dove is a symbol of life. In biblical times the dove was also used as a purification offering for the poor (for example, Lk 2:24).

In the Gospel stories of Jesus' baptism, the Holy Spirit descends on him in the form of a dove. This image of a descending dove brings to mind God's Spirit hovering over the waters at creation. A dove also signifies gentleness, virtue, and peace—gifts that we receive when we are united to the Holy Spirit.

Two other symbols of the Holy Spirit mentioned in the *Catechism of the Catholic Church* are the *finger* of God that writes the divine law on our hearts and the *cloud and light* that reveal the saving God, yet veil the divine glory.

For Review

1. Define *ruah*. Give an example of how ruah applied to the presence of the Holy Spirit in the Old Testament.
2. List and explain four other scriptural images of the Holy Spirit besides ruah.

For Reflection

Study this image of the Holy Spirit. What do you think it represents? Note your interpretation of it in your journal.

- **Class Discussion:** For more detail on the symbol of the dove, have the students read the story of Noah in Genesis 6:9–7:22. Ask: Why is the dove seen as a symbol of peace? Where else have students seen the dove used as a symbol of peace?
- **Journal Assignment:** Read each of the passages in the Symbols for the Holy Spirit activity on page 77. Write the symbol mentioned in your journal. Draw your own symbol based on each of these images based on each passage.
- **Group Activity:** Divide the class into small groups. Give a piece of poster board, glue, old magazines, scissors, colored markers, and any other art supplies you wish to each group. Have them work together to find and draw images that represent the Holy Spirit. If the students have laptops, have them create a collage using a computer program like Microsoft Publisher.

For Review Answers (page 79)

1. *Ruah* means breath. At creation, God breathed life into Adam and Eve.

2. The Holy Spirit appeared as *fire* in the burning bush set before Moses, in the punishing fire of Sodom, the baptism of Christ, and in the tongues of fire present at Pentecost. *Water* is a symbol of the Holy Spirit. The power of water is demonstrated in the flood that punished humans and in the water of baptism and the water that God gave to the Chosen People as they were wandering in the desert. *Oil* is another symbol of the action of the Holy Spirit. Jesus was spoken of as the Anointed One. The *dove* is a memorable symbol of the Holy Spirit. The dove appears in the Old Testament as a sign to Noah that the earth is again safe, and the Holy Spirit appears as a dove when Jesus is baptized as a sign of Jesus being filled with the Holy Spirit.

Homework Assignment

1. Continue working on the Ongoing Assignment(s).
2. Complete the For Review questions on page 79.
3. Read the text section "The Holy Spirit in the Life of Christians" (pages 80–83).

Symbols for the Holy Spirit Answers (page 77)

1. *Exodus 9:18:* The Spirit is symbolized by the call of a trumpet coming forth from clouds surrounding Mount Sinai.
2. *Psalms 104:30:* The Holy Spirit is shown through the creation and renewal of the earth and its people.
3. *Ephesians 5:6–20:* The Spirit is shown when people move out of darkness into a life lived in the light. People who are filled with the Spirit are full of gratitude and praise for God.
4. *Revelation 21:6:* Those who live in the Spirit will never be thirsty, for they drink from an everlasting source of the water of life.

Extending the Lesson

Guest Speaker: Invite a science teacher to give the students a presentation on matter and energy. The Genesis account of the creation, with the Holy Spirit bringing life and order to the universe, has some similarities to the way in which energy animates matter. Facilitate a discussion about the ways in which a scientific understanding of the world can meld with a theological understanding of the world.

The Holy Spirit in the Life of Christians (pages 80–83)

Objectives

In this lesson, the students will:

- describe the need for the Holy Spirit in our lives.
- distinguish between the gifts, charisms, and fruits of the Holy Spirit.
- list and explain the ways in which the Holy Spirit works in the Church.
- explain the role Pope John XXIII played in the renewal of the Church.

Preview

This section focuses on the action of the Holy Spirit in everyday life. It describes the work of the Holy Spirit in the life of the Church as well as the lives of individuals. The Holy Spirit produces qualities of character, particularly love. Other qualities are the gifts and the fruits of the Spirit. Charisms are particular abilities given to individuals to contribute to the welfare of the community. Finally, the section lists the various means by which the Holy Spirit is active in the Church.

Bell Ringers

- **Class Discussion:** Allow a few minutes for the students to share their responses to the For Review questions on page 79.
- **Prayer Experience:** Have the class work to memorize the "Come, Holy Spirit" prayer (below). Ask them to sit with a partner and take turns testing each other by reciting the words to the prayer. When completed, recite the prayer together with the class.

> Come Holy Spirit, fill the hearts of your faithful.
> Enkindle in us the fire of your love.
> Send forth your Spirit and we shall be created
> And you will renew the face of the earth.
> Let us pray:
> > O God, who by the light of the Holy Spirit did instruct the hearts
> > of your faithful,
> > Grant that by that same Holy Spirit we may be truly wise and
> > ever enjoy his consolation, through Christ our Lord,
> > > Amen.

The Holy Spirit in the Life of Christians (CCC, 733–742; 747; 976, 1485; 1830–1832; 1845)

The Holy Spirit makes us Christians: "No one can say 'Jesus is Lord,' except by the Holy Spirit" (1 Cor 12:3). The Holy Spirit also makes a difference in our lives as Christians. How? First, the Holy Spirit is the great Life Giver. He teaches, directs, and strengthens the Church through the Magisterium so that we may serve as compassionate and wise servants of the Gospel. He lives in each believer, too, as our internal teacher. He inspires us to recognize Christ, and he showers on us many gifts to lead Christlike lives.

As Life Giver, the Holy Spirit is God's grace to us. *Grace* is a traditional theological term that means "good will, benevolence, or gift given." When we are baptized, the Holy Spirit comes to us. Filled with the Holy Spirit, we are justified before God. Justification means our sins are forgiven and we are able to enter into a right relationship with God through faith in Jesus Christ. This justification begins a lifelong healing process, a conversion or turning to God that leads to eternal life and makes it possible to share in God's own life.

Think about this miracle of God's gift to us—sharing his own life, a life of perfect love. The Holy Spirit actually adopts us into the divine family. We become children of God and brothers and sisters to Jesus. We share in Christ's own eternal Life because the Spirit of God lives in and loves through us:

> As proof that you are children, God sent the spirit of his Son into our hearts, crying out, "Abba, Father!" So you are no longer a slave but a child, and if a child then also an heir, through God. (Gal 4:6–7)

By living in Christians, the Holy Spirit forms the Church, which is the very Body of Christ and Temple of the Holy Spirit. His presence gives life to the Church, builds it up, and sanctifies it. The Holy Spirit uses the Church to draw us to Christ, to reveal the good things the Lord has done for us, and to make present the Paschal Mystery of Christ's love. This is done most wonderfully through the holy Eucharist, in which we share God's own life. The liturgy is a unique sign of the Blessed Trinity's close friendship with us.

The Holy Spirit showers on individual Christians and on the Church many gifts to help us live like Jesus Christ. These gifts build up the Church. They include:

1. *Gifts that make us holy.* These are the seven gifts of the Holy Spirit listed in the exercise on page 71: wisdom, understanding, knowledge, counsel (right judgment), fortitude, piety (reverence), and fear of the Lord. These gifts make it easier for us to respond to the Holy Spirit's promptings.
2. *Gifts that serve the Church.* St. Paul lists other gifts that are meant to build up the body of Christ, the Church

For Enrichment

Individual Assignment: Have students do an Internet search on the following charisms of the Holy Spirit: faith healing, miracle working, prophecy, discernment, speaking in tongues, and interpreting tongues. They will discover a range of sources, some of them more credible than others. Have students evaluate the reliability of their sources, based on the sponsorship of the website and the plausibility of the information. This can lead into a discussion of miracles and students' opinions on whether miracles happen today.

(see 1 Corinthians 12:4–11). Each of these special gifts is known as a charism. The charisms Paul mentions include wisdom, knowledge, faith, healing, miracle working, prophecy, discernment, speaking in tongues, and interpreting tongues.

3. *Gifts that result in spiritual fruit.* St. Paul also names some fruits of the Holy Spirit, perfections that result from the Holy Spirit living in us. These are the firstfruits of eternal glory (see Galatians 5:22–23). Church tradition lists them as charity, joy, peace, patience, kindness, goodness, generosity, gentleness, faithfulness, modesty, self-control, and chastity.

All these gifts of the Spirit are related to one another. When these gifts are present in our lives, they show that we are one with Christ Jesus, the true vine (see John 15:1). The Holy Spirit is the Spirit of Love, God's great gift to us through Jesus:

> "God is Love" and love is his first gift, containing all others. "God's love has been poured into our hearts through the Holy Spirit who has been given to us" (Rom 5:5). (*CCC*, 733)

Of all the gifts of the Spirit, love is the greatest of all. Love is given to us freely. We cannot earn it. We do not deserve it. It is pure gift. God does not give love to us because we are good. We are good because God loves us and lives in us. We know love in this way:

> Love is patient, love is kind. It is not jealous, (love) is not pompous, it is not inflated, it is not rude, it does not seek its own interests, it is not quick-tempered, it does not brood over injury, it does not rejoice over wrongdoing but rejoices with the truth. It bears all

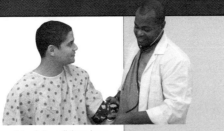

things, believes all things, hopes all things, endures all things. (1 Cor 13:4–7)

Where the Holy Spirit Is Present (*CCC*, 683–690; 742–743)

With the descent of the Holy Spirit on Pentecost Sunday, the Paschal Mystery was completed and the mystery of the Blessed Trinity was fully revealed. The Holy Spirit brings the Church into existence. As the Church's Advocate, he sustains it in many ways. The *Catechism of the Catholic Church* (688) teaches that the Holy Spirit actively works in the Church in:

- the Scriptures, which he inspired;
- Sacred Tradition, witnessed to throughout the ages by the Church Fathers;
- the Magisterium of the Church, that is, the Holy Father and the bishops whom the Holy Spirit guides in their roles as teachers and servants of God's people;
- the sacraments, both words and symbols, which put us in contact with the Risen Lord;
- prayer, where he continually intercedes for us;
- the many gifts and ministries that build up Christ's Body, the Church;
- the signs that go with the Church's apostolic and missionary life;
- and the saints, whose lives over the centuries witness to the presence of

grace
God's gift of friendship and life that enables us to share his life and love.

charism
A special gift of the Holy Spirit that helps us build up the Church, Christ's Body. Some of these gifts are the ability to express wisdom and knowledge, healing, prophecy, and discernment of spirits (see 1 Corinthians 12:4–11).

fruits of the Holy Spirit
Perfections that result from living in union with the Holy Spirit. They are love, joy, peace, patience, kindness, generosity, faithfulness, gentleness, modesty, self-control, and chastity (see Galatians 5:22–23).

Background Information

Pope John XXIII's Post–World War II Efforts

After World War II was over, there was tremendous tension in countries that had been occupied by the Nazis. Some citizens had chosen to help the occupiers, while others risked and lost their lives to continue to resist the Nazis. Those who had remained neutral or who had worked with the resistance were understandably resentful of those who had helped the Nazis out of fear or for personal gain. Following up on the example of Pope Pius XII (1939–1958), Blessed Pope John XXIII showed great skill and compassion in order to be able to help the people of France and other countries to begin to live and work together in a united way. These skills also made it possible for him to bring together different groups in the worldwide Church to come to common agreement on important changes within the Church.

Teaching Approaches

- **Direct Instruction:** Summarize some of the main points in the text section "The Holy Spirit in the Life of Christians" (pages 80–83). Begin by defining the Holy Spirit as God's grace to us and following up with definitions on grace and justification (write on board):
  Grace is "God's gift of friendship and life that enables us to share his life and love."
  Justification means that our sins are forgiven and we are able to enter into a right relationship with God through faith in Christ.

- **Individual Assignment:** Have the students fold a blank sheet of paper twice to create three equal sections. Have them label the sections "Gifts of the Holy Spirit," "Charisms," and "Fruits of the Holy Spirit." First have them define each type of gift and write where they came from (Is 1:2–3; 1 Cor 12:4–11; and Gal 5:22–23). Then, have them list the many gifts that are included in each group. Note that some of the gifts fall into more than one category. Ask students to cite differences between the different groups of gifts so that they will be able to distinguish between them.

- **Group Activity:** Regarding the fruits of the Holy Spirit, form groups of six and assign each person two of the fruits to define in their own words and tell an example of how a person they either know or know of has lived out this fruit. Allow time for the students to formulate their answers before the discussion. At the end of the discussion time, list the fruits on the board and call on volunteers to share some sample definitions and examples.

- **Class Discussion:** Love is the greatest gift of the Holy Spirit. Read 1 Corinthians 13:4–7 on page 81 to the students. Have the students suggest several large and small conflicts in the world today. Summarize these on the board. Then, ask: How might these conflicts be resolved if St. Paul's description of love is followed?

- **Direct Instruction:** Continue with the text subsection "Where the Holy Spirit Is Present" (pages 81–82). Review each of the elements listed on pages 81–82 of the text. Students may be unfamiliar with some terms. Clarify that *Tradition* means the collected teaching of the Church through the centuries. Also:
  - A quick diagram of the hierarchy of the Church and a review of the local bishop(s)' names and residences may help students understand the role of the Magisterium.
  - Some students may not know the names or purposes of all the sacraments. A quick review can be helpful.

- Many students do not know of the Church's work outside their own parish or school. Students can brainstorm the variety of ways the Church serves the local community and the world.

- The signs of the Church may be new to most students and will be studied in more depth in the following chapter.

- **Class Activity:** Have the students work individually or in groups to develop a visual diagram of the elements listed on page pages 81–82 (Scriptures, Tradition, etc.) Call for a summary by asking the students to explain how these elements interrelate with one another.

- **Individual Assignment:** If the students have prepared flash cards, have them add the fruits and charisms of the Holy Spirit, as well as the list just covered, to their stack of review cards. Give students time to drill one another on this information.

- **Direct Instruction:** Read or summarize with the class the story of Blessed John XXIII as recounted on page 82. Have the students suggest a timeline of the key events in Blessed Pope John XXIII's life and add at least three non-Church events that happened during this time (e.g., assassination of John F. Kennedy [1963] or the launching of the civil rights movement [1950s to early 1960s]). *Extra Credit:* Have the students do the assignment listed at the end of the article on Pope John, that is, reading from one or more Internet sites to be able to list three interesting facts about his life.

- **Direct Instruction:** Summarize the role cited by the Second Vatican Council fathers on the role of the Holy Spirit at the council (see page 83). For example, write the following on the board:
  The Spirit dwells in the Church and in the hearts of the faithful.
  The Spirit prays on their behalf.
  The Spirit equips and directs the Church with his fruits.

the Holy Spirit, his holiness, and his continuing work of Salvation.

The Holy Spirit is for living the Christian life. The Spirit's greatest gifts received in Baptism offer faith to proclaim Jesus as our Lord and Savior, adoption into God's own family, and the privilege of being able to address God as Abba, Father.

PROFILE OF FAITH: BLESSED POPE JOHN XXIII, SPIRITUAL MASTER

Blessed Pope John XXIII was born in northern Italy on November 25, 1881. The fourth of fourteen children, his baptismal name was Angelo Giuseppe Roncalli. He entered the seminary in 1892 and began a practice of making spiritual notes, which he continued his whole life. They have been published in one of the great spiritual classics of the twentieth century, *Journal of a Soul.*

Roncalli was ordained to the priesthood in 1905, pursued further studies, and eventually became a professor of Church history in his home diocese of Bergamo, Italy. He was a popular preacher, known for his profound but simple spiritual insights. At this time, he also became secretary to his bishop.

During World War I, he served in the medical corps and was chaplain to wounded soldiers. These experiences convinced him that war was one of humanity's greatest evils. After the war, he was ordained a bishop (1925) and sent as the Vatican's delegate to Bulgaria. In 1935, he was appointed apostolic delegate to Turkey and Greece. His thirty years of service as Church diplomat taught him an openness to people of different faiths and cultures. His years in the Near East brought him in contact with the separated Eastern Churches, which led to his strong commitment to work for Church unity.

During World War II, Archbishop Roncalli was instrumental in helping thousands of Jews escape Nazi persecution. He also served as a papal ambassador to France. There his gentle and tactful skills helped smooth over relations with French citizens who were at odds with collaborators of the Nazi occupation.

Because Archbishop Angelo Roncalli was good at making all kinds of people friends of the Church, Pope Pius XII made him a cardinal in 1953. The Pope soon appointed him head of the important Diocese of Venice, where Cardinal Roncalli was loved and admired by the people of the Church there.

Surprising to most observers because of his age, the college of cardinals elected the seventy-seven-year-old Cardinal Angelo Roncalli Pope in 1958. He took the name John and soon became one of the most beloved Popes of all time. His visits to prisons, hospitals, and Roman parishes, and his down-to-earth, simple, and humble manner won for him the name Good Pope John.

Remarkably, in late 1961 Pope John XXIII called the Second Vatican Council (1962–1965), a major undertaking since cardinals, bishops, and other leading Christians would have to travel to Rome. This was a surprise because everyone thought Pope John would be a transitional Pope who would not have any major achievements during his reign. The Pope attributed inspiration for the council to the Holy Spirit. Its purpose, he said, was *aggiornamento,* that is, to update and to renew the Church, to produce a "new Pentecost" that would revitalize the Church and let it speak its Gospel message to today's world. The Second Vatican Council produced sixteen documents that renewed the liturgy, explained the role of the Church in the modern world, and advanced the cause of Christian unity. Unfortunately, Pope John XXIII died of painful stomach cancer in 1963 and was only involved in the first session of the council. (His successor, Pope Paul VI reconvened and completed the council.)

Today, the Church of the twenty-first century is still trying to put the reforms of Vatican II into practice as a way to achieve Christian unity. Pope John XXIII was beatified in 2000. Beatification, a major step on the road to being canonized a saint, declares that a holy person like John XXIII lived a life led by the Holy Spirit.

Research more information on Blessed Pope John XXIII. Write three interesting facts you learned about his life from your reading.

Homework Assignment

1. Continue working on the Ongoing Assignments (pages 92–93).

2. Complete the For Review questions on page 83.

3. Read the text section "The Mystery of the Trinity" (pages 83–86).

Extending the Lesson

Direct Instruction: Grace is a fairly abstract concept, which can be difficult for students to grasp. Select a passage from one of the *Chicken Soup* books; *Chicken Soup for the Teenage Soul* can be particularly appropriate. Choose a passage that describes an incident where someone seemed overwhelmed or at a dead end and then from somewhere found the strength and insight to do what needed to be done. Explain that these are examples of grace in our lives. Encourage students to share any similar stories they may have.

Guest Speaker: Ask a person who is extensively involved in serving the poor or powerless, whether as a volunteer or as a professional, to speak to the class. Ask the person to explain their work and what leads them to continue to spend their time in this way. Ask them to recount ways in which they see God's presence among their coworkers and those they serve.

The Second Vatican Council on the Role of the Holy Spirit

When the work which the Father gave the Son to do on earth (cf. Jn 17:4) was accomplished, the Holy Spirit was sent on the day of Pentecost in order that He might continually sanctify the Church, and thus, all those who believe would have access through Christ in one Spirit to the Father (cf. Eph 2:18). He is the Spirit of Life, a fountain of water springing up to life eternal (cf. Jn 4:14; 7:38–39). . . . The Spirit dwells in the Church and in the hearts of the faithful, as in a temple (cf. 1 Cor 3:16; 6:19). In them He prays on their behalf and bears witness to the fact that they are adopted sons (Gal 4:6; Rm 8:15–16, 26). . . . He both equips and directs [the Church] with hierarchical and charismatic gifts and adorns [it] with His fruits (cf. Eph 4:11–12; 1 Cor 12:4; Gal 5:22). (*Dogmatic Constitution on the Church*, 4)

• How have you experienced the Holy Spirit working in the Church?

For Review

1. Define *grace*.
2. How is the Holy Spirit grace to Christians?
3. What is the Holy Spirit's greatest gift to us?
4. List the three categories of gifts of the Holy Spirit.
5. Discuss five ways the Holy Spirit is active in the world today.

For Reflection

Think about someone in your family, parish, or school who exemplifies in a powerful way one of the charisms of the Holy Spirit. Write up a short profile of this person and how they use this gift for the benefit of others.

The Mystery of the Trinity

(*CCC*, 235; 237; 261–263; 265)

The dogma of the Blessed Trinity is a mystery in the strictest sense, that is, a mystery of God himself. By *mystery*, the Church is not talking about a problem that can be solved as, for example, a math problem can be. Rather, mystery is a truth of the faith that is knowable but inexhaustible. It is knowable only because God revealed it to us. It is, however, a reality beyond our full comprehension. Its significance is so profound that the human mind and human words can never fully plumb its depths.

Jesus Reveals the Trinity

Why do we believe God is a Trinity of Persons? Why do we believe that the one God, with one divine nature, is three Divine Persons: Father, Son, and Holy Spirit, with the Son proceeding from the Father and the Holy Spirit proceeding from the Father and the Son? Simply, we believe that God is Trinity because of our knowledge of and relationship with Jesus Christ.

Background Information

The Holy Spirit's Presence in the Lives of Christians

In the Second Vatican Council document *Lumen Gentium* (*The Dogmatic Constitution on the Church*), the presence of the Holy Spirit in the lives of Christians is explained:

> When the work which the Father gave the Son to do on earth was accomplished, the Holy Spirit was sent on the day of Pentecost in order that He might continually sanctify the Church, and thus, all those who believe would have access through Christ in one Spirit to the Father. He is the Spirit of Life, a fountain of water springing up to life eternal. To men, dead in sin, the Father gives life through Him, until, in Christ, He brings to life their mortal bodies. The Spirit dwells in the Church and in the hearts of the faithful, as in a temple. In them He prays on their behalf and bears witness to the fact that they are adopted sons. The Church, which the Spirit guides in way of all truth and which He unified in communion and in works of ministry, He both equips and directs with hierarchical and charismatic gifts and adorns with His fruits. By the power of the Gospel He makes the Church keep the freshness of youth. Uninterruptedly He renews it and leads it to perfect union with its Spouse. The Spirit and the Bride both say to Jesus, the Lord, "Come!" Thus, the Church has been seen as "a people made one with the unity of the Father, the Son and the Holy Spirit." (4)

The Mystery of the Trinity

(page 83–86)

Objectives

In this lesson, the students will:

• explain the theological meaning of the term "mystery."

• cite examples of scriptural support for the doctrine of the Trinity.

• explain the new understanding of God that Jesus brought to his disciples (e.g., God as Abba, the feminine qualities of God).

Preview

This section shifts focus from the Holy Spirit to the Trinity as a whole, particularly a review of God as Father and Jesus as Son in the New Testament. It addresses the ways in which the understanding of Three Persons developed throughout Jesus' ministry. It addresses the notion of mystery and new images of God revealed by Jesus, such as God as Abba and the feminine qualities of God. This section provides a scriptural basis for the next, more doctrinal lesson on the Trinity.

Bell Ringers

- Point out the section title "The Mystery of the Trinity," and review the meaning of mystery as it applies here by reading the opening paragraph.

- **Class Activity:** Have students explore more of the various meanings of the term "mystery." Give them two minutes to write down everything that comes to their mind when they think of the word mystery. Then, invite students to come to the board and share what they have written.

- **Direct Instruction:** Discuss the responses and clarify how the definition of mystery when it is applied to God is different from the mystery of literature. Explain that the Trinity is a mystery, much in the same way that love is a mystery. The human heart is a mystery; to some degree, we are mysteries to ourselves.

Teaching Approaches

- **Direct Instruction:** Use a demonstration to remind the students how three parts can make up a whole and, in fact, be the whole. For example:

    ◆ show a shamrock with three leaves making up the entire shamrock

    ◆ describe how a man can be a father to his son, a son to his father, as well as a husband to his wife

    ◆ show three types of cola of one product (e.g., diet, caffeine free, cherry) explaining all can still be described as Coke or Pepsi, etc.

    Connect the discussion to the fact that Three Persons—Father, Son, and Holy Spirit—make up the one God.

- **Class Discussion:** Page 84 of the text describes Jesus as "so fully attuned to God." What does it mean to say a person is attuned to another person? Have students think of examples of people who are attuned to another person: a parent with a child, two people in love, good friends who know one another very well. Brainstorm the behaviors and attitudes that reveal this attentiveness to the other person. Have the students give examples of when Jesus demonstrated this same attentiveness to the Father. Remind the

In Jesus we see a person so fully attuned to God that in faith we say that this one-of-a-kind person is God himself. Jesus' words hold truth: "Whoever has seen me has seen the Father" (Jn 14:9). We also believe God's testimony at Jesus' baptism: "This is my beloved Son, with whom I am well pleased" (Mt 3:17).

The Apostles and other believers were certain that the God of their ancestors was at work in a unique way in his Son, Jesus. Later, after Jesus' Resurrection, they experienced the same God in the Holy Spirit who lives in Christ's followers. This Advocate, who was poured out on the disciples on Pentecost Sunday, impelled them to go out and preach the Gospel they learned from Jesus. Thus, they preached that God reveals himself as a loving Father whose love for humans is bottomless. At the same time, they announced that God also reveals himself as an incredibly loving Son, Jesus Christ, a Savior who frees us from sin and death. Finally, they spread the Good News that God also reveals himself as a Spirit of love, a Holy Spirit who dwells in believers with the fullness of the Risen Christ's life.

Thus, we believe in the Blessed Trinity because of the things Jesus teaches about who God really is. The Father shows his immense love for us by sending his only beloved Son and the Holy Spirit. Through them, he teaches us his own intimate life. However, God not only wants to share information about who he is; he wants to share his very life with us. Through Baptism "in the name of the Father and of the Son and of the Holy Spirit," we are invited to partake in a mysterious way in the life of the divine family here on earth and after death in an eternal life of happiness and love.

New Testament Evidence for God as Father (CCC, 238–242)

Many religions call God "Father" in the sense of a creator who loves his children. The Jewish faith also invokes God as a father in that Yahweh created the world, fathered the covenant with the Chosen People, gave the Law, and served as their ruler. Israel also saw God as the "father of the poor" who cared for and protected the defenseless.

Jesus, however, was unique in his teaching about Abba/Father. He taught that the Father of the Chosen People was *his* Father, an eternal Father to him, the unique Son who shared God's own nature. To stress his unique relationship with God, the Lord spoke of "*My*

heavenly Father" (Mt 15:13). In contrast, to us he says, "*Your* heavenly Father" (Mt 5:45). Jesus also taught that God is eternally the Father by his relationship to the Son and vice versa: No one knows the Son except the Father, and no one knows the Father except the Son and anyone to whom the Son wishes to reveal him (Mt 11:27).

For this reason, the Apostles referred to Jesus as the Word of God, the very image of the invisible God. And the early Church council at Nicaea (AD 325) defined that Jesus was *consubstantial* with the Father, that is, having the same nature as God. *Jesus is God.*

Time and again Jesus revealed that God the Father was incredibly loving. He expressed his own unity with the Father in his use of *Abba*, a simple term of endearment meaning "daddy." Jesus told his followers to address God as Abba when they pray. Parables like the Lost Coin, the Lost Sheep, and the Lost Son all reveal God to be loving beyond what we can imagine (Lk 15). Jesus' healing miracles reveal a compassionate God. Most significantly, Jesus reveals a Father who gives us his own selfless Son for our Redemption. The Father saves us through this Son, Jesus Christ, in the Holy Spirit. The Father brought his beloved Son back to life, and, through him he promises Resurrection to all who believe. As St. Paul writes, "Thanks be to God who gives us the victory through our Lord Jesus Christ" (1 Cor 15:57).

Background Information

The Father and the Son Are Revealed by the Holy Spirit

For more information, see the *Catechism of the Catholic Church*, paragraphs 243–246.

Explaining Your Faith:

If God is our Father, does this mean that God is male?

Scripture most often talks about God as Father. Jesus taught us to say "Our Father" when he taught us the Lord's Prayer. Still, it is important to remember that God is pure spirit, neither male nor female. Therefore, we can be sure that God possesses to an infinite degree the traits we associate with both fathers and mothers—creativity, leadership, nurture, sustenance, compassion, tenderness, availability, acceptance, guidance, and love. There is no limit to God's parental love for us.

It is acceptable to refer to God's parental tenderness using images of motherhood. By doing so, we emphasize God's closeness and gentle love for us.

Jesus himself used feminine images when teaching about God's love, for example, by comparing God to a woman who rejoiced when she found a lost coin (Lk 15:8–10) or when he expressed his own desire to gather the people of Jerusalem "as a hen gathers her young under her wings" (Mt 23:37).

The medieval mystic Julian of Norwich wrote that the notion of God as Mother increases our understanding of God's love for us. Consider, for example, how much a mother suffers to give birth to her child. While we know that no earthly mother is perfect, most mothers love and accept their children, do their best to protect them, and forgive them easily.

The Holy Spirit Reveals the Father and Son *(CCC, 243–244)*

Every page of the New Testament proves the divinity of Jesus. For example, Jesus' many miracles attest to God working through and in him. His teaching authority is another sign of his divinity. The Resurrection of Jesus is the great sign that Jesus is God. Filled with the power of the Holy Spirit, the witnesses to the Risen Jesus proclaim him Lord and God. When Thomas probes Jesus' wounds, he is the first to say aloud: "My Lord and my God" (Jn 20:28).

An earlier Gospel reference to Jesus' divinity and that of the Father and the Spirit occurs at Jesus' baptism. The Gospel of Mark describes the incident:

More about the Mystery of the Trinity

An ancient Church creed, the Athanasian Creed, teaches the following about the Mystery of the Trinity:

Now this is the Catholic faith: We worship one God in the Trinity and the Trinity in unity, without either confusing the persons or dividing the substance; for the person of the Father is one, the Son's is another, the Holy Spirit's is another; but the Godhead of the Father, Son, and Holy Spirit is one, their glory equal, their majesty coeternal. (*Athanasian Creed*, quoted in *CCC*, 266)

- Devise a symbol for the Holy Trinity that you can use in a short lesson to teach primary-age children (grades 1 to 4) about the Mystery of the Trinity. Work with a religious education program or Catholic school to be able to present your lesson as part of their regularly scheduled class.

Printed Materials continued from page 78

O'Collins, Gerard. *The Tripersonal God: Understanding and Interpreting the Trinity*. New York: Paulist Press, 1999.

An excellent recent work on the Trinity. Highly recommended.

Pasco, Rowanne, and John Redford, eds. *Faith Alive: A New Presentation of Catholic Belief and Practice*. Mystic, CT: Twenty-Third Publications, 1990.

A good resource written in a lively, interesting style. Short chapters by a variety of contributors. The late Cardinal Suenens, an influential figure at the Second Vatican Council, composed Chapter 6 on the Holy Spirit.

Rahner, Karl, S.J. *Foundations of Christian Faith*. Trans. William V. Dych. New York: Crossroad/Herder & Herder, 1978.

Excellent treatment of the doctrine of God. Requires careful reading, even though Rahner wrote the book as an introductory piece.

———. *The Trinity*. Introduction, Index, and Glossary by Catherine Lowery Lacugna. New York: Crossroad/Herder & Herder, 1997.

A recent edition of the famed brief but powerful Rahner treatise on the Trinity. Excellent introduction by the late acclaimed Catherine Lacugna.

Ratzinger, Joseph Cardinal. *Introduction to Christianity*. Trans. J. R. Foster. San Francisco: Ignatius Press, 1990.

Theological reflection on the Apostles' Creed. Chapter 5 is a challenging and insightful discussion of the Trinity.

Schreck, Alan. *Hearts Aflame: The Holy Spirit at the Heart of Christian Life Today*. Ann Arbor, MI: Charis Books, 1995.

students that we believe in the Holy Trinity because Jesus taught us to understand God in this way.

- **Class Discussion:** Continue with the subsection "New Testament Evidence for God as Father" (page 84). The people of the Old Testament understood God as their Father, but they did not have any awareness that the Father also had a divine Son. Draw out students' understanding of this by challenging their awareness of teachers' lives. Many students do not consider their teachers to have personal lives, particularly teachers who are not young and single. Ask students to tell any stories they may have about encountering a teacher in another setting: at a mall, a concert, or at church. If no one has a story, ask them what their reaction would be. Brainstorm the variety of roles teachers may have in their lives: son or daughter, parent, friend, active citizen, etc. Our first, limited knowledge of a person is not necessarily wrong—it is just limited. Jesus was not disregarding the Jewish people's understanding of God; he was expanding on it.

- **Direct Instruction:** The term *consubstantial* (see page 84) addresses the belief that Jesus has the same nature as God, that he is God. Three candles can provide a visual illustration. Begin by lighting one candle and drawing students' attention to the flame. Then light two other candles; the flame separates into three, but it has its origins in the first flame. It is possible to rejoin the flames and extinguish the other two flames. Remind students that *no* visual representation or explanation, including this one, can fully or even accurately, communicate the mystery of the Trinity.

- **Class Discussion:** Read or summarize the answer to the question "If God is our Father, does this mean God is male?" (page 85). Brainstorm with students the traditional masculine and feminine traits associated with parenting, such as protectiveness for fathers and nurturing for mothers. Facilitate a discussion on whether students see those expectations as having changed or blended for their own fathers and mothers. Do they see further change when they become parents? Encourage them to see the advantages of attributing the traditional feminine as well as the masculine qualities to God.

- **Direct Instruction:** Read the subsection "The Holy Spirit Reveals the Father and Son" and the passage from Mark 1:10–11 on page 86 that describes how the Father, Son, and Spirit were all present at Jesus' baptism. Remind the students, too, that the Holy Spirit always existed with the Father and Son and that it is the Spirit that helps us adore God the Father.

- **Individual Assignment:** Read or summarize the feature "More about the Mystery of the Trinity" (page 85). Distribute copies of Chapter 3, Handout 1 "Understanding the Creeds" (starting on page 285 and also online at www.avemariapress.com). Have the students compare and contrast the language about the Trinity in these three creeds. Discuss their answers as a class.
- **Individual Assignment:** Have the students consider how they would help second graders see the difference that the Trinity makes in their lives. Have students present their lesson plans to the class.

For Review Answers (page 86)

1. The Trinity is a mystery in that it is a reality beyond our full comprehension, like trying to pour the ocean into a small hole in the beach. (page 83)

2. Jesus reveals the Trinity through his words and actions, for example (pages 83–84):
   - "Whoever has seen me has seen the Father" (Jn 14:9)
   - "No one knows the Son except the Father, and no one knows the Father except the Son and anyone to whom the son wishes to reveal him" (Mt 11:27).
   - At Jesus' baptism, the Father's words, "This is my beloved Son, in whom I am well pleased" (Mt 3:17).
   - "You will receive power when the Holy Spirit comes on you (Acts 1:8).

3. The Father was present in the words, "This is my beloved Son in whom I am well pleased." The Holy Spirit was present in the form of a dove, signifying in a visual way God's unique presence with Jesus. (pages 85–86)

4. Answers will vary, but should express the oneness and intimacy of God in Three Persons in some way.

Extending the Lesson

Video Presentation: Show a clip of the television program *Joan of Arcadia*. Joan, a high school student, experiences God speaking to her in a variety of appearances. Facilitate a discussion on the image of God that is portrayed through Joan's conversations: Do the students see God as caring? scolding? immediate? etc. How does this image compare with the Father as described in the text and Scripture passages?

On coming up out of the water he saw the heavens being torn open and the Spirit, like a dove, descending upon him. And a voice came from the heavens, "You are my beloved Son; with you I am well pleased." (Mk 1:10–11)

This important passage refers to all three Divine Persons of the Blessed Trinity. It also points to how Jesus was filled with the Spirit as he began his public ministry. God's Spirit worked with the Lord as he taught, performed miracles, and underwent the Paschal Mystery for our Salvation. The full Mystery of the Blessed Trinity was revealed at Pentecost, when the Father and Son sent the Holy Spirit. As the *Catechism of the Catholic Church* teaches:

> The Spirit will now be with and in the disciples, to teach them and guide them "into all the truth." The Holy Spirit is thus revealed as another Divine Person with Jesus and the Father. (CCC, 243)

The Holy Spirit *always* existed with the Father and the Son. He attracts us to the Son and enables us to proclaim him our Lord and Savior. The Holy Spirit also helps us adore God the Father, the source of all the good gifts the gracious Triune God showers on us.

For Review

1. In what way is the dogma of the Blessed Trinity a *mystery*?
2. How does Christ reveal God as Father, as Son, and as Holy Spirit?
3. How were the Three Persons of the Trinity present at Jesus' baptism?
4. Explain how you understand a God in Three Persons, the Blessed Trinity.

For Reflection

- Reflect on how you experience God in your own life. Describe some qualities of God's love that you associate with fatherhood. Describe other qualities of God's love that you associate with motherhood.
- Read the following Gospel passages to see some of the things Jesus said about God the Father. Write your answers to the questions.

  Matthew 18:19–20: What does Jesus tell us to do? What is the payoff?
  Matthew 18:21–35: What is the point of this parable?
  Luke 11:1–13: What will the Father do for us if we follow Jesus' teaching?

Homework Assignment

1. Continue work on the Ongoing Assignments (pages 92–93), nearing completion.

2. Complete the For Review questions and For Reflection questions on page 86.

3. Read the text section "Understanding More about the Trinity" (pages 87–90).

For Enrichment

Individual Assignments: Have students rewrite the Lord's Prayer using language consistent with Jesus' advice to address God as "Daddy." Have the students evaluate the prayers produced, based on whether the revised prayers stay true to the original meaning of the prayer while still keeping an informal, intimate tone throughout.

Understanding More about the Trinity *(CCC, 232–233; 236)*

"In the name of the Father and of the Son and of the Holy Spirit. Amen." Catholics are familiar with the Sign of the Cross, a formula that begins many Catholic prayers and worship. The large Sign of the Cross—made with our right hand touching our forehead, chests, and shoulders—professes that our minds, hearts, and entire beings are under the power of our holy Redeemer. The small Sign of the Cross—made with the thumb on the forehead, lips, and over the heart—petitions the Triune God to bless our thoughts, words, and desires. The Sign of the Cross in each form is a clear profession of faith in the Blessed Trinity.

More detail about the formula: we are baptized in the *name* of the Father and the Son and the Holy Spirit, not in their *names*. There is only *one* God. But there are three Divine Persons in this one God. How can this be: three-in-one? Recall again that we are dealing with a strict mystery of God. Trying to understand God's inmost nature is like looking directly into the blinding sun.

To help our understanding, Jesus Christ and the coming of his Holy Spirit have revealed to us that God is a Trinity of Persons. So our human minds, guided by the Spirit, have struggled to explain, even if in a partial way, this profound truth of our faith. Great Church Fathers like St. Augustine and famous theologians like St. Thomas Aquinas distinguish between two aspects of God when speaking about the Trinity: *theology* and *economy*. *Theology* (from the Greek word *theos*, meaning "God") refers to God's own inner life as Trinity. God's inner life is referred to also as the *immanent Trinity* (how God exists in God). *Economy* means the many works God has performed to reveal and communicate his divine life. This understanding is also called the *salvific Trinity*. By reflecting on God's works, we learn something about who God

really is. The better we understand who God is, the more clearly we see and understand all of his works.

The Immanent Trinity: God's Own Inner life *(CCC, 245–256; 264)*

When the Trinity is explained in terms of God alone without any reference to human beings, this is known as the immanent Trinity, meaning "existing completely within." Early Church councils and Church Fathers considered how best to address the mystery of the Trinity. Three important terms that developed were:

1. *Substance*—a word that means "nature" or "essence." When we say that the Father has the same substance or nature as the Son and the Holy Spirit, we are proclaiming that God is *one* divine being.
2. *Person* refers to the distinctions among the Father, Son, and Holy Spirit.
3. *Relation* designates that the Father, Son, and Holy Spirit are distinct because of their relationships.

Using this vocabulary as background, the Church teaches three important truths about God's own inner life:

1. *There is only one God.* The Blessed Trinity is one God, that is, one divine being, possessing a divine substance or nature.
2. *There are three distinct Persons—Father, Son, and Holy Spirit—in one God.* "Person" in the Trinity refers to distinctions between the members (and not in the sense of human persons). Thus, there are not three separate consciousnesses in God. There is only one, simple, divine being. There are not three separate intelligences or wills in the one God. When one Person of the Trinity acts, the other two Persons also act. Each person is *distinct* but does not act separately from the others. God is one, a community-in-unity. The Divine Persons are inseparable in both what they do and in what they are, loving us with the same love and knowing us with the same knowledge.
3. *The Divine Persons have distinct relationships with one another.* Our faith is in one God with three Divine Persons who are really distinct from one another. In a mysterious way, we can say "God is one but not solitary" (*Fides Damasi*, quoted in *CCC*, 254). The Divine Persons are distinct in their relations of origin. The Church explains the relationships among the three Persons of the Trinity this way:

Background Information

Understanding the Immanent Trinity

As human beings, our awareness of ourselves grows as we mature. But at this point students know themselves, and hopefully, accept themselves. This is the closest comparison to God's knowledge of Himself (which is the Son) and loving Himself (which is the Spirit.)

Understanding More about the Trinity *(pages 87–90)*

Objectives

In this lesson, the students will:

- explain the significance of the large and small Signs of the Cross.
- compare and contrast the Three Persons of the Trinity.
- distinguish between two aspects of God when speaking about the Trinity: theology and economy.
- learn about the meaning of the Immanent Trinity and the Economic or Salvific Trinity.

Preview

This section introduces students to a more detailed theological understanding of the Trinity. Immanent Trinity means "existing completely within." In other words, how does God exist in God? The Persons Father, Son, and Holy Spirit, though distinct, do not act apart. The second way of understanding is known as Salvific Trinity or Economic Trinity. In this approach we know God by what he does, how he acts in our lives and in the world.

 Bell Ringers

- **Direct Instruction:** Collect and discuss the For Review questions and For Reflection questions from page 86.
- **Class Activity:** Have the students each write down one fact they have learned in another subject area (e.g., mathematics, history, English, etc.) on an index card. Collect the cards and randomly distribute them to all the students. Then have them sit with a partner. Have the partners communicate one of the messages to another pair without using words or written language. After the assigned time is up, find out how successful the students were in getting their message across.
- **Direct Instruction:** Compare this activity to God trying to communicate with the world. Much of God's Revelation occurs through God's actions rather than directly through words, although in Scripture God does communicate through words. When we speak of the Economy of the Trinity, we are referring to understanding the Trinity through God's actions in the world. Point out that there is another way to talk about Trinity: God's own understanding of himself.

Teaching Approaches

- **Prayer Experience:** The Sign of the Cross is a powerful symbol, which is often prayed in a rush and overlooked. Guide students through a slow, meditative enactment of each Sign of the Cross. Two possible scripts for this prayer are:

In the name of the Father,
    the Creator who set into motion the stars and
        the planets,
    who placed the oceans and the
        mountains,
    who brought each of us into existence
    and upholds us at this very moment,
and the Son,
    the Redeemer who became one of us,
    who taught us in word and example
    who suffered and celebrated with us
    who died for us and rose to save us,
and the Holy Spirit
    who remains in our hearts
    who guides and strengthens us
    who comforts and challenges us
    who will be with us to the end,
                                Amen.

May the Lord be in our minds,
    in all of our thoughts about ourselves and
        those around us,
    in our understanding of the world and its
        workings
    in our beliefs about God and our place in His
        creation
in our words,
    in what we say to others
    and in what we say to ourselves
and in our hearts
    in our struggles to love
    and our struggles to forgive,
    in our decisions to be generous
    and our willingness to repent when we have
        been unkind.
                                Amen.

- *The Father.* The First Person of the Trinity is absolutely without origin. From all eternity he "begets" the Son, the Second Person of the Trinity. The Son proceeds from the Father. There was never a time when the Son did not proceed from the Father.

- *The Son.* We can think of the Father's begetting the Son as God knowing himself perfectly. The Father expresses himself perfectly to himself, and this is the Son, the Word of God. Thus, the Son is the Father's perfect, divine expression of himself. They are one, yet distinct.

- *The Holy Spirit.* The relationship of the Father and Son is a perfect relationship. The Father and Son love each other with an eternal, perfect, divine love. The love *proceeds* from the Father and the Son and is the Third Person of the Trinity, the Holy Spirit. The Holy Spirit proceeds from both the Father and the Son as the perfect expression of their divine love for each other. Thus, the Holy Spirit is the Spirit of Love between the Father and the Son; the Spirit binds them into a community of unity.

In a classic expression of faith, the Athanasian Creed expresses the relationships of the three Persons of the Trinity this way:

> The Father is not made by anyone, nor created, nor begotten. The Son is from the Father alone, not made, not created, but begotten. The Holy Spirit is from the Father and the Son, not made, not created, not begotten, but proceeding. . . . The entire Three Persons are co-eternal with one another and co-equal, so that . . . both Trinity in Unity and Unity in Trinity are to be adored.

The Economic or Salvific Trinity (CCC, 257–260; 267)

In the economic or salvific Trinity we know God by what he does, how he acts in our lives and in the world. God reveals the Trinity to us through his works in Salvation History, especially Christ's Incarnation and the gift of the Holy Spirit. Our own Christian living in union with God strengthens our belief that our one God relates to us as Father, Son, and Holy Spirit.

We meet God through creation—its beauty and greatness, its intricate design and awesome power. Jesus teaches us that we can address our Creator God as Abba,

Father. He is merciful, filled with love for us, and compassionate beyond what we could possibly hope for.

A second way we experience God is through God-made-flesh, Jesus Christ. He is Emmanuel, "God-with-us." Through the teachings, actions, miracles, and Paschal Mystery, we have met God in Jesus Christ. In Christ, we have experienced God with a human face.

Third, we experience God as the Holy Spirit, who gives us life and directs us to live Christ-filled lives. He joins us to Jesus Christ, who in turn takes us to his heavenly Father. "To the Father, through the Son, in the Holy Spirit." The Holy Spirit is the love of God that was promised by Jesus to always remain with the Church.

God has communicated himself to humanity in three distinct ways. It is the same, one, mysterious God who reveals. But he does so through three distinct Persons or relationships—Father, Son, and Holy Spirit—each of whom works as one.

Thus, all Three Persons of the Blessed Trinity are involved in the common work of Salvation. However, each Person performs this common work according to his unique personal property.

Trinitarian Symbols

Many images try to express the Mystery of the Triune God.

The Shield of the Trinity
The translation reads this way: "The Father (*Pater*) is (*est*) God (*Deus*); the Son (*Filius*) is God; and the Holy Spirit (*Spiritus Sanctus*) is God." Thus, God's unity is professed. Equality among the persons is symbolized by the equilateral triangle. And the distinction between each Person of the Trinity is again conveyed by the Latin: the Father is not (*non est*) the Son or the Holy Spirit; and the Son is not the Father or the Holy Spirit; and the Holy Spirit is not the Father or the Son.

The Shamrock
The legendary story is told that when St. Patrick was preaching to the pagans in Ireland, he was challenged to prove how God could be one being yet three Persons. St. Patrick picked a shamrock and asked whether he held up one leaf or three leaves. "If three, then why one stem? If one stem then why three leaves?" Those who questioned him could not answer. St. Patrick responded, "If you cannot explain such a simple mystery as a shamrock, how can you hope to understand such a profound one as the Blessed Trinity?"

Tree and Sun
St. John Damascene taught two famous images for the Trinity. The first is a tree, where the Father is the root, the Son the branches, and the Spirit the fruit. The substance of each (root, branch, and fruit) is all the same—that of a tree yet there is distinction. So with the Trinity. Each Person has the fullness of the divine nature, yet there is distinction. One God, Three Persons. His second image was that of the sun. The Father is the sun, the Son is the rays, and the Holy Spirit is heat. Distinction but all the same substance.

Assignment
- Read each of the following quotations about the Blessed Trinity. Then write at least two of your own quotations that describe the Trinity.

> God is the beginning, the middle, and the end of every good. But the good cannot become active or be believed in otherwise than in Jesus Christ and the Holy Spirit.
>
> —St. Mark the Ascetic

> The Trinity is our maker. The Trinity is our keeper. The Trinity is our everlasting lover. The Trinity is our endless joy.
>
> —Blessed Julian of Norwich

> The Spirit works, the Son fulfills his ministry, and the Father approves; and man is thus brought to full Salvation.
>
> —St. Irenaeus

Background Information

Distinction of Persons of the Holy Trinity
As the *Catechism of the Catholic Church* explains:

> The divine persons are really distinct from one another. "God is one but not solitary." "Father," "Son," "Holy Spirit" are not simply names designating modalities of the divine being, for they are really distinct from one another: "He is not the Father who is the Son, nor is the Son he who is the Father, nor is the Holy Spirit he who is the Father or the Son." They are distinct from one another in their relations of origin: "It is the Father who generates, the Son who is begotten, and the Holy Spirit who proceeds." The divine Unity is Triune. (254)

Homework Assignment

1. Complete the Ongoing Assignment(s) (pages 92–93). Plan to share and turn them in at the next class session.

2. Write answers to the For Review questions on page 90.

3. Study for the Chapter 3 Test.

- **Journal Assignment:** Have students reflect on the differences and similarities between their own inner and outer lives. Have each student write down a list of things that belong to our inner lives (emotions, thoughts, moods, beliefs, etc.) and our outer lives (hobbies, arguments, service work, etc.). Humans sometimes experience inconsistencies between our inner and our outer lives: we say things we don't mean, and make choices we don't want. With God, the inner and outer lives are perfectly consistent. All of God's actions, for example, are consistent with God's love for us, even when we don't understand the reason for the actions.

- **Direct Instruction:** Continue with the text subsection "The Immanent Trinity: God's Own Inner Life" (pages 87–88). Focus primarily on the three important truths that arise from our attempts to understand God's own inner life:
  - There is only one God (one *substance*).
  - There are three distinct *persons*—Father, Son, and Holy Spirit in one God.
  - The Divine Persons have distinct *relationships* with one another.

- **Direct Instruction:** In reviewing the term *substance* with students, remind them of the example of the flame. The flame, whether appearing as one or as three, has the same substance—oxidizing molecules. The term *nature* is used in conversation when we talk about human nature, animal nature, and the like. Also, remind students that it is not possible for us to imagine everything that exists—reality is not limited by our ability to visualize something. The three separate Persons of God, which do not have separate consciousness as we humans have separate consciousness, falls into this category. As humans, we tend to think in concrete, material terms; the Trinity is a spiritual reality and so both greater and less concrete than most of what we encounter.

- **Class Discussion:** Have students turn to St. John Damascene's image of the sun and its rays on page 89. This image can provide some help for this difficult concept. The Father is the sun, the Son is the rays, and the Holy Spirit is heat. Facilitate a discussion about the similarities between this image and the Trinity. There is no sun without rays or heat, no heat without rays or sun. None of the elements precede any of the other elements.

- **Individual Assignment:** Distribute copies of Chapter 3, Handout 2 "Trinity: One God, Three Persons" (starting on page 285 and also online at www.avemariapress.com). Based on what they have learned so far, have students write the differences (what makes each Person distinct) in the other sections of the circle and the similarities (what makes God one substance) in the triangle in the middle. Have students refer back to Chapter 3, Handout 1 "Understanding the Creeds" (from the Individual Assignment on page 88) for additional information that can be entered into each category. Some similarities should include the singular consciousness, life givers, love, coeternal, and they are all worshiped. As you move on, have students add to their responses.

- **Class Discussion:** Review the text subsection "The Economic or Salvific Trinity" (pages 88–90) with students; you may want to have them read it again out loud. Put three columns on the board labeled "Father," "Son," and "Holy Spirit," and have students list the types of actions associated with each.

- **Class Discussion:** Note from the text definitions for the terms *creation*, *redemption*, and *sanctification*. Facilitate a discussion with students on ways in which we partake in God's action as Creator, Redeemer, and Sanctifier. How do we create new things, physically, emotionally, or spiritually? How do we "redeem" another person when we forgive a friend or help someone right a wrong? How do we inspire people to love better, to be more courageous or generous?

- **Direct Instruction:** Review the Trinitarian Symbols in the feature on page 89. Also, draw on the board this symbol of interlocking rings

and have the students offer possible explanations of it.

- **Class Activity:** Have the students work on the assignment on page 89 individually. Create a blog or class wiki on the Internet. Have students add their quotations to the blog or wiki, and have students comment on their classmates' quotations.

divine missions of the Blessed Trinity
The special roles in Salvation History attributed to each member of the Trinity: the Father is the Creator, the Son is the Savior, and the Holy Spirit is the Sanctifier. The whole plan of Salvation is the common work of the three divine Persons who possess one and the same nature.

Therefore, we attribute creation, and its continual existence, to God the Father.

Salvation is attributed to the Son, who became human to reveal the Father's merciful love.

And to the Holy Spirit we attribute sanctification, that is, the work of making us holy and Godlike.

Creation, Salvation, and sanctification are known as the divine missions of the Blessed Trinity. Although we attribute creation to the Father, Salvation (Redemption) to the Son, and sanctification to the Holy Spirit, we must remember that all three Persons of the Trinity act as one and are fully present in all the missions.

In contemplating the Mystery of the Blessed Trinity, we come to know a God of incredible love who draws us into union with him. God is a Father who has lovingly created us, a Son who gave his life so that we might have eternal life, and a Spirit of love who enables us to love, that is, to imitate the very nature of God.

God loved us into existence and wants us to love. As the Church has taught for centuries, our goal in life is to get to know, love, and serve the Blessed Trinity in this life and to be united with God for all eternity. Prayer helps us to accomplish our destiny: *to the Father through the Son in the Holy Spirit*.

Jesus and the Holy Spirit reveal that God is a community-in-unity. We allow the Triune God to live in us when we approach him with others and reach out in love to our brothers and sisters. When we love others, we are imitating the Triune God, who is love. An important lesson of Christian living is that we go to God together with other people. It is the Church that we join with on our journey to God. The Church is the prime means the Lord uses to continue his work of Salvation in a world that desperately needs it.

For Review

1. Explain the meaning of the Sign of the Cross.
2. To what do the terms *substance* and *person* refer when talking about the Blessed Trinity?
3. Identify the term *economic* or *salvific Trinity*.
4. Identify the term *immanent Trinity*.
5. What are the divine missions of the three Persons of the Blessed Trinity?

For Reflection

List seven qualities of love as described in the following passage. Then give an example of each quality from your own life and lives of your friends.

"God is Love" (1 Jn 4:8, 16) and love is his first gift, containing all others. "God's love has been poured into our hearts through the Holy Spirit who has been given to us" (Rom 5:5). (*CCC*, 733)

Extending the Lesson

Class Discussion: Have students engage in a fishbowl debate about the Trinity. During a fishbowl discussion, only a designated number of students, seated in chairs in the middle of the room, are allowed to speak. Students who wish to speak need to tap an active member on the shoulder and take his or her place in the fishbowl.

Distribute cards to each student, assigning him or her a position to uphold during the discussion. Positions will include:

- Christians who believe in the Trinity
- Uncatechized person who does not know about the Holy Trinity
- Christians who believe Jesus is God but do not know about the Holy Spirit

Have all students take time to prepare their positions, including finding Scripture passages to back up their statements as they apply. Allow time for each person to present his or her position before others in the circle are allowed to respond.

CHAPTER QUICK VIEW

- The seven gifts of the Holy Spirit are wisdom, understanding, knowledge, counsel, fortitude, piety, and fear of the Lord. (page 71)
- Working in union with God the Father, the Holy Spirit had an active but hidden role in Salvation History before the coming of the Messiah. (page 72)
- The Holy Spirit came in power on the feast of Pentecost, giving the Apostles the courage to proclaim that Jesus is Lord and Savior. (pages 73–74)
- Sharing a joint mission with the Son of God, the Holy Spirit was present throughout the ministry, Life, preaching, miracle working, Passion, Death, Resurrection, and glorification of Jesus Christ. (pages 74–75)
- Images of the Holy Spirit include *breath, wind, fire, tongues of fire, water,* and the *dove.* (pages 76–79)
- The Holy Spirit adopts us into God's family, enabling us to call God Abba/Father. He justifies us, forgives our sins, and enables us to love as other Christs. (page 80)
- The Holy Spirit is the Paraclete, our advocate before God, a helper and consoler. He is the Spirit of Truth who testifies to the Lord. (page 75)
- Jesus is head of the Church, his Body. The Holy Spirit is the soul of the Church and gives it life. We can find him in the inspired Sacred Scriptures, Church Tradition, the Fathers and Magisterium of the Church, the sacraments, prayer, various gifts and ministries, the apostolic and missionary life of the Church, and the witness of the saints through the ages. (pages 81–82)
- The Holy Spirit is God, the Third Person of the Blessed Trinity. He is the Giver of Life who is equal in dignity to the Father and Son. Christians should worship and glorify him. (page 85)
- Jesus revealed to us in the power of the Holy Spirit that God is a Blessed Trinity. This is a strict mystery that could only be revealed by God. Our minds can never fully grasp it. (pages 83–84)
- Jesus revealed that God the Father is his unique Father. (page 84)
- Jesus' miracles, teaching, and Paschal Mystery show that he is God's unique Son. He and the Father are one. (pages 84–86)
- The early disciples discovered God's presence in the Holy Spirit (an Advocate and Comforter) who came on Pentecost Sunday as Christ had promised. (page 84)
- We are baptized in the *name* of the Father, Son, and Holy Spirit, not the *names.* There is only one God. (page 87)
- Reflecting on God's inmost life (theology) reveals God's works (the divine economy). Reflecting on God's saving works sheds light on his inner nature. (page 87)
- God is one divine being. The Three Persons in this one God—Father, Son, and Holy Spirit—are distinct in their relations. From all eternity, the Father generates the Son. The Son is always begotten by the Father. The Holy Spirit proceeds as the love between the Father and the Son. (pages 87–88)
- The missions of the Blessed Trinity refer to God's saving action for us. This is also known as the divine economy (work) on our behalf. Creation is attributed to the Father, Redemption to the Son, and sanctification to the Holy Spirit. However, God is one divine being. Therefore, all three Divine Persons are involved in the common work of God's saving plan. (page 90)

For Review Answers (page 90)

1. There is both a large and small Sign of the Cross. The large Sign of the Cross is made by the right hand touching the forehead, chest, and shoulder, signifying our dedication to God in our minds, hearts, and entire beings. The small Sign of the Cross is traditionally said before the reading of the Gospel at Mass. In this gesture, we form the Sign of the Cross on our foreheads, lips, and heart, asking God to open our minds, our words, and our desires to his inspiration.

2. *Substance* refers to the one nature or essence of God. *Person* refers to the distinctions among the Three Persons of the Trinity, but it does not indicate a separate consciousness that exists among different human persons.

3. The *Economic* or *Salvific Trinity* refers to the Trinity's action in the world. It refers to the different experience humans have of the Persons in the Trinity.

4. *Immanent Trinity* refers to the internal reality of the Trinity, the nature of God, and the relationships among the Persons of the Trinity.

5. The Father is the Creator, bringing the world into existence and continuing to hold it in existence. The Son is our Redeemer, who became a human person to teach us the way to the Father and who suffered, died, and rose to save us from our sins. The Holy Spirit is the Sanctifier, who remains with us, transforming us and giving us the power to grow in God's life.

Chapter 3 Review Lesson

Objectives

In this lesson, the students will be able to:
- review the main content of Chapter 3.
- share and display Ongoing Assignments.
- study for the Chapter 3 Test.

Preview

Give students the opportunity to review the chapter terms and concepts. Also allow time for the students to share and display their Ongoing Assignments (suggestions listed next).

Bell Ringer

1. **Class Discussion:** Call on students to answer the For Review questions on page 90 and answer any additional questions related to the Trinity.

2. **Individual Assignment:** Have the students transform the Chapter Quick View points into possible test questions. Then, have them exchange the questions with a partner to answer the questions.

Teaching Approaches

- **Student Presentations:** Use the following suggestions for sharing and displaying each of the Ongoing Assignments from pages 92–93:
  - Set up a display on a bulletin board or on the wall for the collages.
  - Make copies of the prayer and give them to each student so they can pray these words prior to taking the Chapter 3 Test.
  - Call on students to offer a brief synopsis of their reports.
  - Allow students to summarize their findings. Or, if possible, arrange for one of the adults interviewed to speak in person to the class.
  - Call on students to offer a brief summary of information they discovered about the Second Vatican Council.
  - Set up a table where the quotations from Pope John XXIII can be displayed.
  - Allow students to briefly summarize what they found out about Native American beliefs in God.
  - Provide students with the opportunity to present the PowerPoint presentations about the Blessed Trinity.
  - Allow students to lead the class in prayer using the prayers to the Blessed Trinity from Catholic websites.
- **Individual Assignment:** Have students complete the Learning the Language of Faith assignment on page 92 and then review their answers as a class.
- **Class Discussion:** Have the students close their notebooks and textbooks. Quiz them using the For Review questions at the end of each section and the highlighted vocabulary words from Chapter 3.
- **Individual Assignment:** Allow time for individual study. Encourage the students to study and commit to memory the Chapter Quick View information on page 91.
- **Prayer Experience:** Recite the prayers written by those who did Ongoing Assignment 3 on page 93.

Learning the Language of Faith

Complete each sentence below by choosing the correct answer from the list of terms given here. You will not use all of the terms.

Catholic	heresy
charism	immanence
charity	Kingdom of God
covenant	monotheism
Deism	Paraclete
dogma	Paschal Mystery
Epiphany	Sacred Tradition
fruits of the Holy Spirit	theological virtue
gifts of the Holy Spirit	theophany
grace	Virgin Birth

1. God's gift of friendship and life that makes it possible for us to share his life and love is known as ____.
2. A ____ is a central truth of Divine Revelation that Catholics are obligated to believe.
3. God's appearance to Moses in a burning bush is known as a ____.
4. Perfections that result from living in union with the Holy Spirit are known as ____.
5. God's saving love most fully revealed in the Passion, Death, Resurrection, and Ascension of Jesus Christ is the ____.
6. Fortitude and wisdom are two ____.
7. When you are blessed with a special gift to help build up Christ's Body, the Church, you are blessed with a ____.
8. On the feast of the ____, we celebrate the manifestation of Jesus Christ as the Savior of the world.
9. The Holy Spirit is a ____, our Advocate, who helps us live the Christian life.
10. Faith is a ____.

Ongoing Assignments

As you cover the material in this chapter, choose and complete at least three of these assignments.

1. Make a collage from newspapers and magazines to represent how the Holy Spirit is active in the world today, especially in works of justice and love.
2. Read Luke 4:14–30. Answer the following questions:
   - Where does this take place?
   - Which Old Testament prophet is Jesus quoting?
   - What is he claiming when he comments on this passage?
   - How do the people first react?
   - Why do they change?
   - What do they wish to do to Jesus?

   Write about a time when speaking the truth got you in trouble.

Homework Assignment

1. Reread Chapter 3.
2. Study for the Chapter 3 Test.

3. Compose a prayer to the Holy Spirit designed to help students who are preparing for a test. Share with your classmates.

4. Report on the life of a Spirit-inspired person who made a difference in people's lives. For example: Dorothy Day, Archbishop Oscar Romero, or Mother Teresa.

5. Interview several adults who were brought up in the pre–Vatican II Church. Ask them how the liturgy and parish life were different. Report to the class.

6. Research the writings of Blessed Pope John XXIII. Write at least five meaningful quotations from any of his texts.

7. List three traits your mother (or another important woman in your life) possesses that you think are holy. Explain the difference it makes to your image of God to know that he possesses those same traits to infinite degree.

8. Write an essay about the seven gifts of the Holy Spirit. Address (1) what the gifts mean to you, (2) how the gifts are part of your life, and (3) how you can share the gifts with others.

9. Prepare a PowerPoint presentation on how the Blessed Trinity and the Holy Spirit have been depicted in art through the ages.

10. Find online from Catholic websites at least two prayers to the Blessed Trinity. Reproduce one by creating a colorful prayer card with the text of the prayer and an appropriate graphic.

Prayer Reflection

Prayer of St. Augustine to the Holy Spirit
Breathe into me, Holy Spirit,
that my thoughts may all be holy.

Move in me, Holy Spirit,
that my work, too, may be holy.

Attract my heart, Holy Spirit,
that I may love only what is holy.

Strengthen me, Holy Spirit,
that I may defend all that is holy.

Protect me, Holy Spirit,
that I may always be holy. Amen.[10]

- *Reflection:* Describe how the Holy Spirit is with you now.
- *Resolution:* Pray this prayer before starting your first class at school during the coming several weeks.

Homework Assignment

1. Read the Chapter 4 Outline on page 95 and the opening text section of Chapter 4, "Where Christ Is, There Is the Church" (pages 96–97).

2. Examine the Ongoing Assignments on pages 121–122.

Chapter 3 Test Lesson

Objectives

In this lesson, the students will:
- be tested on the material in Chapter 3.
- complete a written and meditative Prayer Reflection.
- preview the material in Chapter 4.

Preview

Plan to allow a majority of the period for test taking. However, prior to the test explain to the students that they will be working on the Prayer Reflection on page 93 and it, too, should be completed by the end of the period.

Teaching Approaches

- **Prayer Experience:** Pray aloud the "prayers for test taking" completed as part of Ongoing Assignment 3 on page 93.
- **Chapter Test:** Distribute one copy of the Chapter 3 Test (starting on page 285 and also online at www .avemariapress.com) to each student. Allow enough time for the students to complete the test. Collect the finished tests as they are completed.
- **Prayer Experience:** As the students complete the exam, have them write a "letter to God" as suggested in the Prayer Reflection. As time allows, also instruct the students to write a response to the letter from Jesus' or the Father's viewpoint. Check to see that the students completed the assignment, but do not collect them. As time permits, allow for optional sharing of the letters to God or sharing any enrichment assignments the students worked on during this chapter.

Chapter 3 Test Answers

Part 1: Matching (4 points each)

1. D	5. C
2. E	6. F
3. A	7. G
4. B	

Part 2: True or False (4 points each)

8. F	12. T
9. T	13. F
10. F	14. F
11. T	15. T

Part 3: Multiple Choice (4 points each)

16. B	18. A
17. A	19. D

Part 4: Short Fill-ins (4 points each)

20. grace

21. Paraclete

22. Blessed Trinity

Part 5: Short Essay (12 points possible)

23. There are many possible answers here. For example, in the Scriptures and Sacred Tradition, in our official Church teachers, through the sacraments, in private and public prayer, in the countless gifts the Holy Spirit showers on members of Christ's body, in the saints, in each of us through our baptismal gifts, and so forth.

4 The Church: The Body of Christ

Overview of the Chapter

With the scandals in the Catholic Church hitting the headlines and airwaves in an unprecedented way in recent years, religious educators and others who have given their lives to the Church often feel great sadness. But recall the image of St. Boniface who compared the Church to a great ship being pounded by incessant waves. The challenge is not to abandon ship, but to work all the harder to keep it on course. Catechists do their part to stay the course by inviting students to become a vital part of the Church and help steer it to the future. Our young people also belong to the Church. They are its future. The gifts that the Holy Spirit has showered on them will help the Church weather its current problems.

The chapter begins by asking students to reflect on their image of the Church. It then defines the Church as a worshipping community, a local gathering, and the worldwide gathering of believers—all of whom "belong to the Lord" and are "called out" by him. Following the lead of the *Catechism of the Catholic Church* (754–757), the chapter then examines the Church as a mystery of God's love, which is, at the same time, a visible society and spiritual community, organized hierarchically and the mystical body of Christ, an earthly community with heavenly riches. Various images are presented as multifaceted ways to begin to understand this mystery: Bride of Christ, pilgrim, flock, and vineyard. But four images predominate in this section of the chapter: Church as Sacrament, Church as People of God, Church as Body of Christ, and Church as Temple of the Holy Spirit.

Chapter 4 then turns to membership in the Church (hierarchy, laity, those in consecrated life) and its various ministries that derive from sharing in Christ's role as prophet, priest, and king. The prophetic role of the Magisterium and papacy are discussed in some detail in this section. Then, the ideal characteristics already present in the Church but not yet fully revealed are examined. These are the four traditional "marks" of the Church: one, holy, catholic, and apostolic (see *CCC*, 813–865).

The topic of ecumenism is a fitting way to conclude this chapter. In this section, the Church's teaching about non-Christians and the Protestant and Orthodox Churches is presented, including the question of salvation outside of the Church. In many ways this section is the culmination of the question guiding the entire chapter: what makes the Catholic Church distinct from other communities, other denominations, and other religions?

The Church: The Body of Christ

Resources

 ### Audiovisual Materials

AD

Re-creates the turbulent years following the Death of Christ. Acclaimed TV mini-series depicts the years AD 30–69. Comes with a 52-page study guide for a twelve-week course (three tapes, 360 minutes, Ignatius Press).

Entertaining Angels

Tells the story of Dorothy Day's life as an activist Marxist journalist who converted to Catholicism and devoted her life to serving the poor (111-minute video, Ignatius Press).

Faith Unconquered

Chronicles the roots of the early Church after Jesus' Resurrection. Details the lives of four Christian martyrs who lived in Rome during these years, including that of St. Clement (52-minute video, Questar).

Great Souls: Mother Teresa

Shot on location and told from the viewpoint of those who knew Mother Teresa, this inspiring story shows how God can use one person to do good in the most troubling of circumstances (56-minute video, Ignatius Press).

Great Souls: Pope John Paul II

Traces the life and character of one of history's greatest popes (56-minute video, Ignatius Press).

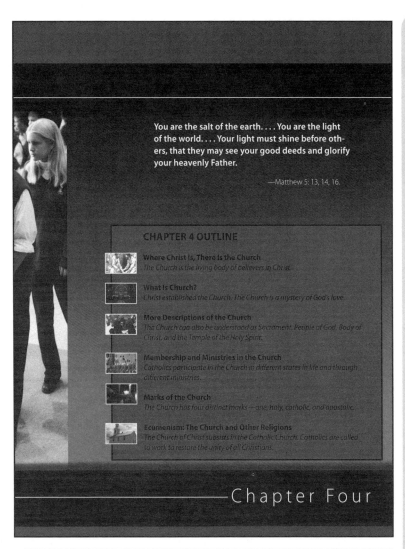

You are the salt of the earth. . . . You are the light of the world. . . . Your light must shine before others, that they may see your good deeds and glorify your heavenly Father.

—Matthew 5: 13, 14, 16.

CHAPTER 4 OUTLINE

Where Christ Is, There Is the Church
The Church is the living body of believers in Christ.

What Is Church?
Christ established the Church. The Church is a mystery of God's love.

More Descriptions of the Church
The Church can also be understood as Sacrament, People of God, Body of Christ, and the Temple of the Holy Spirit.

Membership and Ministries in the Church
Catholics participate in the Church in different states in life and through different ministries.

Marks of the Church
The Church has four distinct marks—one, holy, catholic, and apostolic.

Ecumenism: The Church and Other Religions
The Church of Christ subsists in the Catholic Church. Catholics are called to work to restore the unity of all Christians.

Chapter Four

 Audiovisual Materials continued

Inside the Vatican
A beautifully scripted and filmed inside look of how the Vatican works on a day-to-day basis. Narrated by Martin Sheen. Students watch this excellent production rather attentively (90-minute DVD, National Geographic Film, Critics' Choice, Ignatius Press).

Malcolm X
A 1992 biographical film about African American activist Malcolm X (202-minute DVD, Amazon.com).

Monasteries
Features seven Christian monasteries around the United States, depicting the life of prayer of various orders of monks (45-minute video, Ignatius Press).

Peter & Paul
The acclaimed film that traces the adventures of these two towering figures. Study guide is available (195-minute DVD, Amazon.com).

Remember the Titans
A *Rudy*-like football film that shows how unity is achieved despite racial tensions and diversity. Could exemplify the Church's marks of oneness and catholicity (114-minute feature film, Ignatius Press, Critics' Choice, Amazon.com).

The Twelve Apostles
Who were these humble tradesmen Jesus chose? Depicts how the Twelve took the message of Jesus around the world after the Resurrection (100-minute video produced by the History Channel, Ignatius Press).

Chapter Outline

- Where Christ Is, There Is the Church
- What Is Church?
- More Descriptions of Church
- Membership and Ministries in the Church
- Marks of the Church
- Ecumenism: The Church and Other Religions

Advance Preparations

Assign the Ongoing Assignments early in the chapter to allow the students enough time to complete their work.

Where Christ Is, There Is the Church (ST pages 96–98)
- A video clip on the persecution of the Church for the Video Presentation on page 99.

What Is Church? (ST pages 98–100)
- Religious objects and a paper bag for a game of twenty questions for the Class Activity on page 100.
- Magazines to be used to create a collage for the Individual Activity on page 102.
- A video clip of the Pope on his travels around the world (e.g., *Great Souls: Pope John Paul II* on page 96) for the Video Presentation on page 100.
- Arrange access to a computer lab for the *Researching Rural Issues* Background Information on page 101.

More Descriptions of Church (ST pages 100–105)
- Arrange for a guest speaker from the school counseling department for the Guest Speaker activity on page 104.
- Copies of articles from the Catholic Relief Services website (www.crs.org) for the Extending the Lesson Group Discussion on page 104.

Membership and Ministries in the Church (ST pages 106–112)
- Arrange for a catechumen or recent neophyte to speak to the class for the Guest Speaker activity on page 109.
- A box for prayer intentions for the Prayer Experience on page 111.

Marks of the Church (ST pages 112–116)
- Art materials, including markers, crayons, and magazines, for the Class Activity on page 116.
- A piece of music for the Prayer Experience on page 117.
- Arrange for a guest speaker from a diocesan office, a religious order, or a former lay missionary for the Guest Speaker activity on page 115.

Ecumenism: The Church and Other Religions (ST pages 117–120)
- Copies of Chapter 4, Handout 1 "The Church as Sacrament Pop Quiz" (starting on page 285 and also online at www.avemariapress.com) for the Individual Assignment on page 119.

- Copies of phone books or other directories for churches for the Class Activity on page 119.
- A clip from the movie *Malcolm X* for the Video Presentation on page 121.

Chapter 4 Test Lesson
- Copies of the Chapter 4 Test (starting on page 285 and also online at www.avemariapress.com).

Where Christ Is, There Is the Church (pages 96–98)

Objectives

In this lesson, the students will:
- create a class definition of the Church based on prior experience and understanding.
- reflect on the obstacles that stand in the way of sharing the Good News.

Preview

This section is an introduction to the chapter on the Church. The chapter opener offers a thought-provoking analogy of "Basin Theology" that should springboard a discussion of the obstacles to evangelization. This section lays the groundwork for a more complete and theological understanding of the Church.

Bell Ringers

- **Writing Assignment:** Have students list the names of churches (Protestant and Catholic), synagogues, mosques, or temples if applicable that they pass in their everyday lives. What do they know about the beliefs and practices of these places of worship? In what ways are they similar to Catholicism? In what ways are they different? Do students have friends who worship in these places? Discuss their answers as a class.

- **Group Discussion:** Assign the "Share the Good News" feature (pages 97–98). First, read through the eight descriptions of Church with the students. Next, call on several students to share which two descriptions of Church best fit their idea of Church and explain why. Finally, have the students work in triads to write their definition of Church. Call on representatives to share definitions with the class. Record a sampling of the definitions, working toward a class definition of Church. Note its comparison with the definition of Church on page 96.

- **Class Discussion:** Compare the class definition of Church with the definition in the analogy of Church with a missing "u." In what way does this analogy fit into the context of their definition?

Where Christ Is, There Is the Church

A recent convert to Christianity was talking to his pastor. He said, "You know, the practice of our faith really comes down to Basin Theology."

The pastor was confused and asked, "What do you mean by Basin Theology?"

"Well," said the new Christian, "do you remember what Pilate did when he had the chance to set Jesus free, a man he knew was innocent? He asked for a basin and then washed his hands, symbolizing that he was denying any responsibility for the Death of Jesus. He did what was expedient and involved no risk to his position or his reputation. He knew what was right but was too cowardly to do it.

"In contrast," continued the convert, "recall what Jesus did. At the Last Supper, the night before he died, he also asked for a basin. But he used it to wash the feet of his disciples. He, the Son of God, showed what it means to serve. He set an example for all of us."

This "Basin Theology" challenges followers of Jesus to choose what their role will be in the Church, the community that Jesus formed to continue his work. Will we be like Pilate, who washed his hands and dodged responsibility? Or will we be like Jesus and get down on our knees to serve others?

This is an important choice because every person has a role to play in Christ's Church. Consider the word "CH_ _CH." Notice what is missing: U R ("you are"). The word *Church* that is used in the northern European languages is based on the Greek words *kyriake*

evangelization
To bring the Good News of Jesus Christ to others.

Church
The Body of Christ, that is, the community of God's people who profess faith in the Risen Lord Jesus and love and serve others under the guidance of the Holy Spirit. The Roman Catholic Church is guided by the Pope and his bishops.

oikia, which we translate "the family of the Lord." This interesting word shows that one of the most important things to understand about the Church is that it is a family, a family that is meant to carry on the Gospel message and work of Jesus Christ, our Lord and Savior. Each person in this family is important and has a role to play.

The family of the Lord needs each of us because the work of the Church is never done. Each generation needs to hear and be invited to respond to the good news of Jesus Christ. Jesus gave this very command to the Church before ascending to Heaven:

> Go, therefore, and make disciples of all nations, baptizing them in the name of the Father, and of the Son, and of the holy Spirit, teaching them to observe all that I have commanded you. And behold, I am with you always, until the end of the age. (Mt 28:19–20)

The main way the Church fulfills Christ's command is through evangelization. The Church is able to do the task of preaching the Gospel because it is a living body of believers who are grafted onto Jesus Christ as branches are to a vine. The Church is Christ's presence in the world. He is with us to help us carry on his work. As St. Ignatius of Antioch wrote, "Where there is Christ Jesus, there is the Catholic Church."

Consider again how appropriate the family image is when applied to the Church. Like our own family, the Church loves us, accepts us, and contributes to our development. The Church is also our Mother. Like a good mother, the Church nurtures and sustains us through life. Because of the human element in the Church, sometimes the members of the Church shirk their responsibilities,

For Enrichment

Writing Assignment: Have the students create a list of people they depend on each day. Then point out that our lives are a network of relationships of people cooperating to achieve goals. Explain that the Church is like this, too, a network of people who help each other on the journey to God.

Background Information

The Church Was Foreshadowed from the World's Beginning

God created the world for the sake of communion with his divine life, a communion brought about by the "convocation" of men in Christ, and this "convocation" is the Church. (*CCC*, 760)

The Church throughout the World

The Vatican II document *Dogmatic Constitution on the Church* says "all the faithful scattered throughout the world are in communion with each other in the Holy Spirit so that 'he who dwells in Rome knows those in most distant parts to be his members'" (Chapter II, #13).

just like Pilate did. Nevertheless, Jesus' presence in the Church by the power of the Holy Spirit guarantees her ultimate success. It is the Holy Spirit who encourages us to be a vibrant, loving, open, and welcoming Catholic community willing to serve Christ Jesus and other people. We must all ask ourselves these questions: Will we be missing in action or will we imitate our Lord? Which basin will we pick up—the one that shuns responsibility or the one that commits us to serving Christ and others?

This chapter will focus on several aspects of the Roman Catholic Church: a definition, its images (for example, Mystery, Sacrament People of God, Body of Christ, Temple of the Holy Spirit), its requirements for membership, its ministries, its marks (one, holy, catholic, apostolic), and its reaching out to other Christians in its ecumenical efforts.

The Roman Catholic Church is home to many, including perhaps you. It is a place where we are treated the best and often grumble the most. As in any family, we are accepted and loved without question. This is the Church.

For Reflection
- What would you say to Catholics who get so mad at human failings in the Church that they decide to leave the Church?
- How do you find the Church like a home?

Share the Good News

St. Paul, known as the Apostle to the Gentiles, encourages all followers of Jesus Christ to spread the Gospel far and wide. This task doesn't come without great challenges. Satan presents obstacles in our way. In the Letter to the Ephesians, St. Paul draws on imagery from the military to explain ways we can overcome these challenges:

Finally, draw your strength from the Lord and from his mighty power. Put on the armor of God so that you may be able to stand firm against the tactics of the devil. . . . Therefore, put on the armor of God, that you may be able to resist on the evil day and, having done everything, to hold your ground. So stand fast with your loins girded in truth, clothed with righteousness as a breastplate, and your feet shod in readiness for the gospel of peace. In all circumstances, hold faith as a shield, to quench all (the) flaming arrows of the evil one. And take the helmet of salvation and the sword of the Spirit, which is the word of God. With all prayer and supplication, pray at every opportunity in the Spirit. To that end, be watchful with all perseverance and supplication for all the holy ones. (Eph 6:10–11, 13–18)

Examine how well you are preparing to defend the Good News of Jesus against the obstacles that stand in your way. Read each of the descriptions below. Choose and share examples of any two on the list that you are doing well. Then, comment on two you do not do as well. Reflect on and explain things you can do to improve in those areas.

1. *Draw your strength from the Lord.* I turn to Jesus in good times and in bad. I ask for his help.
2. *Put on the armor of God.* I go to Mass and receive Holy Communion every Sunday and every Holy Day of Obligation. I turn to the Sacrament of Penance for forgiveness.

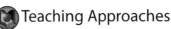

Teaching Approaches

- **Class Discussion:** Read or summarize the introductory text on pages 96–97. Ask one of the students to describe the meaning of "Basin Theology." Discuss which group most teens fall into: Pilate, who washed his hands and dodged responsibility, or Jesus, who washed his disciples' feet and served others?

- **Direct Instruction:** Relate the opening quotation from Matthew 5:13–14, 16 with the definition of evangelization on page 96. Ask the students how evangelization involves letting their "light shine" before others (page 102).

- **Journal Assignment:** Review the feature "Share the Good News" about St. Paul, the "Apostle to the Gentiles." Have students read this section and then choose two ways of sharing the Good News that they are doing well and two that they could improve. Remind the students of the concept of "Basin Theology" and ask them to relate this concept to the activities described in this feature.

Extending the Lesson

Video Presentation: Show a clip of a video on the persecution of the Church (see, for example, *Faith Unconquered*, on page 96). An understanding of the scope of persecution throughout history is helpful for students who are challenged to spread the Good News today. It also reveals the resiliency of the Church.

Homework Assignment

1. Read the text section "What Is Church?" (pages 98–100).

2. Note all the Ongoing Assignments on pages 121–122. Plan to participate in Assignment 5 with classmates and complete any one of the other assignments individually.

Background Information

The Unity of the Church

The Church knows that she is joined in many ways to the baptized who are honored by the name of Christian, but do not profess the Catholic faith in its entirety or have not preserved unity or communion under the successor of Peter. Those "who believe in Christ and have been properly baptized are put in a certain, although imperfect, communion with the Catholic Church." *With the Orthodox Churches* (ital. in *CCC*), this communion is so profound "that it lacks little to attain the fullness that would permit a common celebration of the Lord's Eucharist." (*CCC*, 838)

What Is Church? (pages 98–100)

Objectives

In this lesson, the students will:

- explain the ways in which the Church is a mystery.
- illustrate and describe the meaning of the images of the Church.
- evaluate definitions of the Church.

Preview

This section introduces students to some of the definitions of Church. Because Church is a mystery, there is no one definition or image that can completely describe its meaning. This section provides a foundation for the more specific and theological discussion of Church to follow.

Bell Ringers

- **Class Activity:** Play a game of twenty questions related to items associated with being Catholic or with a Catholic Tradition: for example, rosary beads, a holy card, a parish bulletin, a book about a saint, a religious medal. Hide the item in a paper bag. Divide the class into two sides of the room. Show the item to one team and allow them to field "yes or no" questions from the other side. Score points based on the amount of questions it takes to guess the item (e.g., twenty points if guessed after one question to one point if guessed after twenty questions).
- **Class Discussion:** After the activity, discuss with the students how some of these items reveal the richness of the Tradition of the Catholic Church. Note that many of these items are called "sacramentals" because they represent a deeper reality that is a part of the Church's faith but not quite fully sacraments, which actually bring about what they represent.

Teaching Approaches

- **Direct Instruction:** Review the opening paragraph descriptions of the word Church as "family of the Lord" or "belonging to the Lord." Highlight the three ways Catholics use the word Church today on pages 98–99:
  - The Church is a community of Catholics who assemble to worship.
  - The Church is a local gathering of Catholics in a particular neighborhood.
  - The Church is a worldwide gathering of those who have faith in Jesus Christ.
- **Journal Assignment:** In many parts of the country, geographic parish boundaries are no longer observed as closely as in the past. Ask students to write in their journals about their family's decision to belong to a parish, if their family participates in parish life. Why did their family choose that parish? What do they see as the strengths of their parish?

3. *Stand fast in truth.* I am unafraid of the consequences of being an honest person as Jesus was when he admitted to Pilate his true identity.
4. *Clothed in righteousness.* I am a dependable person. I keep my commitments. Others know me as reliable.
5. *Feet shod in readiness for the Gospel of peace.* I willingly share my belief in Jesus Christ with other people.
6. *Faith is my shield.* I believe in Jesus' promise to be with me always.
7. *Helmet of salvation and sword of the Spirit, which is the word of God.* I sincerely desire to know more about my faith.
8. *Pray at every opportunity in the Spirit.* I pray every day. I ask the Holy Spirit for his strength to live a Christian life.

What Is Church? (CCC, 751–752; 777)

Recall that the word *church* is derived from the Greek words for the "family of the Lord." Another way to translate this same word is "belonging to the Lord." This is an apt description when we consider that Jesus Christ is the head of his Body, the Church, and we are its members. We "belong to the Lord" because we are attached to him the way an arm is to the body. As the head of the Church, Jesus gives his Body direction and vision. And it is the Holy Spirit who is the soul of the Church. The Spirit lives in the baptized and showers on them the gifts we need to be holy, alive, and Christlike. Indeed, without Jesus Christ and the Holy Spirit, there would be no Church.

Church also translates the Greek word *ekklesia,* meaning "those called out, convocation, or assembly." Old Testament authors used this term for God's Chosen People. Being chosen means having a special task or mission. Christians are chosen to worship and to proclaim Jesus Christ as Lord, to live a sacramental life of holiness, and to join in a life of fellowship and service for the sake of God's Kingdom.

"I am going to church." "My church is St. Patrick's." "We are the Church." These three expressions reveal how Catholics use the word *church* today. Each of these expressions has a rightful place:

- The Church is the community of Catholics who assemble to worship. Catholics do this in a superb way when they come together to celebrate the Eucharist.

Extending the Lesson

Video Presentation: Show a clip of a video of the Pope on his travels around the world (e.g., *Great Souls: Pope John Paul II* on page 96). Footage of a World Youth Day event can also be particularly powerful for students. Help the students reflect on the presence of the Church in the larger world, including people of almost every country on earth.

Guest Speaker: If you have a peer ministry program at your school, invite a peer minister to speak to your students. You might also invite a junior or senior who is active as a leader in his or her home parish. Ask them to include the idea of *ekklesia,* or being called out with a special mission, as part of the presentation. How did the young person decide to be a leader? How does he or she see this as a part of being a follower of Jesus, a member of the Church?

For Enrichment

Student Presentations: Many parishes began as ethnic parishes, a haven where immigrants could find support and speak their own language. In many cities, Catholic churches were built close together, each parish serving a different immigrant group. This is why many parishes are forced to close or consolidate today. As immigrant groups moved to the suburbs, the inner-city ethnic parishes dwindled in numbers. Have students research more about their parish or church's foundation and history and present their findings to the class.

Receiving Holy Communion, Catholics are united to the Lord so that they can become the Lord for others.

- The Church is the local gathering of Catholics in a particular neighborhood. For most of us, this means our parish.
- The Church is also the worldwide gathering of those who have faith in Jesus Christ. The Holy Spirit unites people around the world into the People of God, under the leadership of the Pope and bishops.

The Church as a Mystery of God's Love (CCC, 758–780; 880)

In the previous chapter, the term *mystery* was used to describe the Blessed Trinity. Divine mysteries, like the Trinity, both reveal and conceal God's ways, which are not our ways, yet in these mysteries God has somehow blessed us with the truth of his divine plan. The Church is another mystery of our faith. She is both a means and a goal of the great mystery of God's love for us. Each Divine Person of the Blessed Trinity was involved in preparing for the Church and helping her come into existence.

God the Father created the world so that human beings could be united with the Blessed Trinity. Creation, therefore, foreshadowed the Church. The Father prepared for the Church in Old Testament times when he called Abraham and formed a people. Israel was the sign of the Church that was to come.

In God's own time, he sent the Son to accomplish his plan of Salvation. As part of this plan, *Jesus Christ established the Church*—a direct result of preaching the coming of God's reign and his own Paschal Mystery of selfless love. The Church celebrates the Paschal Mystery of Salvation in its sacraments, especially the holy Eucharist. The Church, built by

Christ on Peter and the Twelve Apostles, "is the Reign of Christ already present in mystery" (*The Dogmatic Constitution on the Church*, No. 3, quoted in *CCC*, 763).

Finally the Holy Spirit came on Pentecost to make the Church holy and to lead her in its mission of preaching the Good News of Salvation to all people. The Holy Spirit gives us—both the Magisterium and each Catholic—the gifts we need to do what Christ commanded, that is, to "[proclaim] and [establish] among all peoples the Kingdom of Christ and of God" (*The Dogmatic Constitution on the Church*, No. 5, quoted in *CCC*, 768). Thus, each Person of the Blessed Trinity had a role in the planning of the Church and in her coming into historical reality.

St. Augustine defined *mystery* as "a visible sign of an invisible grace." Pope Paul VI described the Church as a reality filled with God's hidden presence. Both of these definitions point to two essential ingredients in the Church: the human and the divine, the visible reality that we can see along with the spiritual reality that brings us God's life. With the eyes of faith, we proclaim that in the Church, Heaven and earth come together. The Church is at the same time:

- a visible society and a spiritual community,
- a society organized hierarchically and the mystical body of Christ,
- and an earthly community blessed with heavenly riches.

mystery
A reality filled with God's invisible presence. This term applies to the Blessed Trinity's plan of Salvation in Jesus Christ, the Church that is his Body, and the sacraments.

Homework Assignment

1. Complete the For Review questions on page 100.

2. Read the text section "More Descriptions of Church" (pages 100–105).

3. Begin a log of the sufferings—big and small—that are endured daily. Keep the log for one week. See "The Teaching of the Documents" feature on page 102.

Background Information

Researching Rural Issues

Your county extension agency, or other Web-based resources, can be useful in providing information on farming and gardening in city schools where students have limited access to this information. If you have access to a computer lab, students could search for information on these topics as a class. Knowledge of rural issues is important for urban students in future work on caring for the environment and other aspects of Catholic social teaching.

If student families are not involved in a parish, the same question can be asked about participation at the school.

- **Direct Instruction:** Continue with the text subsection "The Church as a Mystery of God's Love" (pages 99–100). Review the descriptions of mystery and Trinity from the previous chapter. Note roles of the each Person of the Holy Trinity in establishing the Church.

- **Class Discussion:** Direct students to the For Reflection questions on page 100. Possible points of discussion may include:

  - The *Catechism of the Catholic Church* says, "Grace is *favor*, the *free and undeserved help* that God gives us to respond to his call to become children of God, adoptive sons, partakers of the divine nature and of eternal life" (1996). The Church is one of the concrete ways in which God helps us respond to his call, encouraging and supporting us, pointing the way to a life lived with God.

  - The Church is made up of human beings, inspired by God and trying to follow God. Some concrete ways in which the human and divine meet are the sacraments, where God touches people, often at critical times in their lives; the teaching of the Church, where the Holy Spirit inspires, particularly through the infallible teachings of the Pope; the corporal and spiritual works of mercy; and work for social justice, bringing the reign of God into present-day life.

- **Class Discussion:** Review the image of Church as the *Bride of Christ*. Have students brainstorm the qualities of a good marriage. Invite students to tell stories about people they know who have strong marriages. Ask students to explain ways in which Jesus' relationship with the Church is similar to the relationship between spouses (love, care for one another's welfare, knowing the other person well, being willing to sacrifice for the good of the spouse, lifelong commitment, etc.).

- **Journal Assignment:** Review the image of Church as *pilgrim*. Explain the idea of pilgrim and pilgrimage to students. Ask them to list in the journals the ways in which we would live differently if we were conscious of being pilgrims. How would this awareness change our attitude toward material things? Success or failure in academics or careers? What makes it difficult for us to remember this image in our society?

- **Direct Instruction:** Review the image of Church as a *farm*. Brainstorm with students all the tasks that are involved in tending a garden in your area. If anyone in the class has experience with a farm, have them describe the work involved in growing and cultivating crops. What are the qualities a farmer or gardener needs to be successful (e.g., diligence; hard work; knowledge of plants, soil, and climate; love for the work; patience; etc.)? How are these similar to the qualities God shows in caring for the Church?

- **Class Discussion:** Review the image of Church as a *vineyard.* Those who tend vineyards and orchards also need to prune in order to bring about maximum yield. Pruning involves cutting away excess growth in order to open a plant or tree to light, to make better use of nutrients, and to produce larger, but perhaps fewer, fruits. Ask students for examples of times when God does similar work in our lives, perhaps taking away something in order to make room for something more important to grow.

- **Individual Activity:** Have students create a collage of the images of the Church on page 100 using pictures from magazines or the Internet. On the back of their collages, have them describe the meaning of each of the images. You might suggest that they begin each description with something like, "The Church is like a . . . because . . ." You might also suggest that students create an illustrated mind-map to describe the images of the Church.

For Review Answers (page 100)

1. Students should include both the idea of the People of God and the specifically Catholic belief in a group led by the hierarchy. "Church" as a term used to designate a building or a worship service is spelled in lowercase letters.

2. The Church is a mystery because it is a reality—God's presence among us—that exceeds our ability to understand. While we can see the people and the actions of the Church, God's action in guiding and inspiring the Church is beyond our ability to grasp in its entirety.

3. Images may include:
- *Family* – the Church is intimately connected as a family is connected.
- *Marriage* – Christ will care for the Church forever, as a bridegroom cares for his bride.
- *Pilgrim* – the Church is a community on its way to Heaven.
- *Building* and *farm* – Christ planted his disciples and continues to cultivate the Church today.
- *Flock* – the Church is led by Christ, the Good Shepherd.
- *Vineyard* – Christ is the source of life for the branches (the Church).

Because the Church is a mystery where the human and divine meet, Scripture uses many vivid images to describe the Church; for example: Bride of Christ, pilgrim, God's building and farm, the flock of Christ, Christ's vineyard, God's family, and our mother. Each of these adds to our understanding and appreciation of the mystery of the Church. For example:

- In the imagery of St. Paul, the Church is in a *marriage union with Christ.* In this union, Christ Jesus is the bridegroom; the Church is the Bride of Christ. The purpose of this wedding between Christ and his Church is to bring us to God and thus make us holy. The Bridegroom loves his Bride so much that he gave his life for her. He will care for her (the Church) forever.
- The Church as *pilgrim* teaches us that the Church is a community on its way to a final destination—heaven.
- The *building and farm* images remind us that Jesus Christ has planted his disciples and that he still cultivates the Church like a farmer tending his crops.
- The Church as *flock* calls to mind our sacrificing Good Shepherd. It is his voice we must listen to in order to remain safe from perils.
- The *vineyard* image stresses that Christ alone gives life and fruitfulness to the branches.

For Review

1. Explain two translations for the word *Church.*
2. Why is the Church called a *mystery*?
3. Name and explain any two images of the Church.

For Reflection
- What does it mean to say that the Church is "a visible sign of invisible grace"?
- Describe concrete ways the human and divine elements of the Church meet.

sacrament
An outward (visible) sign of an invisible grace. An efficacious symbol that brings about the spiritual reality to which it points. This term applies to Christ Jesus, the great sign of God's love for us; to the Church, his continuing presence in our world; and to the Seven Sacraments.

More Descriptions of the Church

In addition to the images of the Church related to mystery, the *Catechism of the Catholic Church* highlights four other descriptions of the Church: *Sacrament, People of God, Body of Christ,* and *Temple of the Holy Spirit.* Following is a brief discussion of each of these descriptions. It is important to remember as you examine each of the descriptions that none of them defines the Church. The images we use to describe the Church never completely answer the question of what the Church is, either individually or even taken together. Ultimately, the Church remains a mystery, never fully explained or defined.

The Church Is a Sacrament
(CCC, 774–776; 780)

Mystery and sacrament are intimately connected. The Greek word for mystery translates to the Latin term *sacramentum.* The term *sacrament* refers to a

Background Information

More on the Mystery of the Church

The Second Vatican Council document *Dogmatic Constitution on the Church* (Lumen Gentium) states that "all men are called to this union with Christ, who is the light of the world, from whom we go forth, through whom we live, and toward whom our whole life is directed" (Chapter 1, no. 3).

The mystery of the holy Church is manifest in its very foundation. The Lord Jesus set it on its course by preaching the Good News, that is, the coming of the Kingdom of God, which, for centuries, had been promised in the Scriptures: "The time is fulfilled, and the kingdom of God is at hand." In the word, in the works, and in the presence of Christ, this kingdom was clearly open to the view of men. The Word of the Lord is compared to a seed which is sown in a field; those who hear the Word with faith and become part of the little flock of Christ, have received the Kingdom itself. Then, by its own power the seed sprouts and grows until harvest time. The Miracles of Jesus also confirm that the Kingdom has already arrived on earth: "If I cast out devils by the finger of God, then the kingdom of God has come upon you." Before all things, however, the Kingdom is clearly visible in the very Person of Christ, the Son of God and the Son of Man, who came "to serve and to give His life as a ransom for many." (Chapter 1, no. 5)

very special kind of sign or symbol. An ordinary symbol is something concrete (something we can perceive with our senses) that points to another reality. For example, a stop sign uses shape, color, and a word to point to the *idea* of stopping. However, the stop sign does not *cause* a driver to stop. Let's say your school mascot is a tiger to represent strength, speed, intelligence, and vitality. But your school mascot does not *make* the student body strong, fast, smart, or filled with school spirit.

A sacrament is also a symbol, but one different from those described above. A sacrament is an *efficacious* symbol, which means that it brings about what it points to and embodies the very reality that it represents. Hence, a sacrament is a concrete reality that, in some way, *is what it represents*.

Thus it is accurate to say that *Jesus is the prime sacrament of God's love.* Jesus not only points to God; he is God. He not only symbolizes God's love; he is God's love. He is what he represents. He is the first and most important sacrament of all. "Whoever has seen me has seen the Father" (Jn 14:9). He makes concrete God's love for us. Jesus takes us to the Father by remaining with us in his Body, the Church, where he remains hidden but very active by the power of the Holy Spirit.

A sacrament, because it is a mystery, has both visible and invisible aspects to it. This is true of the Seven Sacraments: each sacrament is a visible or outward sign of God's grace. Sacraments both point to a spiritual reality *and* actually bring it about. For example, the Eucharist not only signifies communion with the Risen Lord and one another, it really accomplishes it. When we receive the consecrated bread and wine—the Body and Blood of Christ—we come into real union with the Lord and are united in him with one another.

This term *sacrament* also applies to the Church. Because of the presence of Jesus and his Holy Spirit in the Church, it too is a sacrament, a meeting place of Heaven and earth. It is a special sign that both contains and communicates the invisible, divine reality to which it points. The Church is a visible sign of Christ Jesus in our world. A famous quote from the Second Vatican Council says it this way: "The Church, in Christ, is like a sacrament—a sign and instrument, that is, of communion with God and of unity among all men" (*Dogmatic Constitution on the Church*, No. 1, quoted in *CCC*, 775).

Three important truths are revealed here by our understanding of Church as sacrament:

1. People from all over the world come together in the Church to be united to God. In the Holy Spirit, the Church is joined to Jesus, who takes us to the Father.

2. Because we come together in the Catholic Church, the Church is also a sign of the unity of all humankind. This fact encourages us to give up hate for love, war for peace. Love and sharing help promote unity. Our final goal in life is to be in union with God and each other. The Church is a sign that points to that final union.

3. God uses the Church as an instrument to bring about Salvation to the entire world. Mother Teresa of Calcutta once described herself as a pencil in God's hand. The Church is also an instrument God uses to bring about the unity, Salvation, and holiness he desires for all his people. Here is where the seven individual sacraments come into play. They are the special signs that help bring God's saving love to us. They not only point to the spiritual realities of Salvation—healing, forgiveness, communion with God, and the like—but they also actually bring about these spiritual realities because they are efficacious signs.

People of God (CCC, 781–786; 802–804; 849–854)

People of God is another description of the Church from the *Catechism*. The People of God is marked by several distinct characteristics:

1. It is of God, not the property of any one people.
2. One becomes a member of this People not by physical birth, but by baptism "of water and spirit."
3. This Church has Jesus Christ as its head.
4. The People of God have dignity and freedom as children of God.
5. The Law the People of God are obliged to follow is the new law of love: "to love as Christ loved."
6. The mission of the People of God is to be the salt of the earth and the light of the world, a beacon of Salvation for all.
7. The destiny of the Church is God's Kingdom, which will be brought to perfection at the end of time.

The People of God are those who are baptized and acknowledge that Jesus Christ is Lord and Savior. This includes not only those who are ordained (the clergy) or

Resources

 Internet Links see www.avemariapress.com

Resources

 Printed Materials

Burns, Robert A., O.P. *Roman Catholicism: Yesterday and Today*. Chicago: Loyola University Press, 1992.

> Good analysis of some contemporary developments in the Church by looking at the history of the past four centuries. Balanced treatment.

Cunningham, Lawrence S. *The Catholic Faith: An Introduction*. New York: Paulist Press, 1987.

> A college-level text that provides a sound introduction to the Catholic faith.

Dues, Greg. *Catholic Customs & Traditions: A Popular Guide*. Revised and expanded edition. Mystic, CT: Twenty-Third Publications, 1992.

> Make sure your school library has a copy of this book. You may wish to assign short research projects out of it and similar books.

Dulles, Avery, S.J. *Models of the Church*. Expanded edition. Garden City, NY: Image Books, 1991.

> A classic work on ecclesiology. If there is one book to read on this topic, this is it.
> *continued on page 109*

More Descriptions of Church
(pages 100–105)

Objectives

In this lesson, the students will:

- list and explain the images of Church as Sacrament, People of God, Body of Christ, and Temple of the Holy Spirit.
- recognize that mystery and sacrament are intimately connected.
- describe the tasks and challenges of the Church as People of God.
- explain the image of the Church as the Body of Christ.
- describe how the Church is the Temple of the Holy Spirit.

Preview

This text section is likely to be challenging to students because the images used are quite abstract. For some students, they may also be unfamiliar. The section also provides an opportunity to review and reinforce some of the lessons on the Trinity and the Holy Spirit taught in the previous chapter.

Bell Ringers

- **Direct Instruction:** Check the students' answers to the For Review questions on page 100. Collect and record as appropriate.
- **Class Activity:** Randomly assign each student the name of a classmate. Have them write a description of the person they have been assigned to, beginning with vague points ("He has brown hair.") and ending with more specific points ("She volunteers at the homeless shelter once per month."). Then, have a few students read their descriptions out loud. Ask the class whether that description completely describes the person. Point out that no matter how we try, we can never completely capture a person in words. In the same way, descriptions of the Church are an attempt to convey the reality of the Church, but they can never completely capture the complexity or beauty of the Church.
- **Writing Assignment:** Have students turn to the For Reflection feature on page 105. Read about the two images presented in the quotations from St. Boniface and the *Catechism*. Have the students create five other similes to describe the Church as they see it. Have the students share their similes in groups or as a class.

Teaching Approaches

- **Writing Assignment:** Have the students develop an outline of the main points of the subsection "The Church Is a Sacrament" (pages 100–102). When they have completed the assignment, allow them to get into pairs to compare their outlines and clarify any misunderstandings.

- **Direct Instruction:** Note the definition of sacrament on page 104 and the connection to *mystery*. Also point out how a sacrament is an efficacious symbol. Have the students share an example. Ask the students to explain how the term "sacrament" applies to both Jesus and the Church.

- **Class Discussion:** Have the students name the Seven Sacraments. For each, have them write the symbols used to celebrate the sacrament and the important reality each symbol represents. (See below for a basic chart.)

  Discuss with students the ways in which the sacraments bring about a new reality as well as showing the reality that exists. Ask the students to identify how the Church fits into this framework based on the text. They should identify a united people as the symbols of Heaven, salvation, and communion with God.

- **Direct Instruction:** Focus on the text section "The People of God" (pages 101–103). Introduce the characteristics of the People of God on page 101.

- **Group Discussion:** Form four groups for a jigsaw discussion. Give each group responsibility for detailing ways that teenagers can best handle the four tasks and challenges of being a People of God on pages 102–103: message, community, service, and worship. Encourage them to make their suggestions specific to their peer groups. When they finish, have one member from each group join members from each of the other groups to form a group of four. Have them share with their small group what was discussed in their larger group.

- **Direct Instruction:** The description of the Church as the "Body of Christ" may be more familiar to the students. Point out the various types of examples included in this section (e.g., vine, 1 Cor 12:12–13; Christ as the Bridegroom).

- **Writing Assignment:** Have the students examine St. Paul's treatment of the Church in his letters. Refer to the Knowing Christ through Scripture feature on page 104. Have students read each passage and answer the questions on notebook paper. Collect and review their responses as a class.

- **Guest Speaker:** Arrange for a guest speaker from the school counseling department to speak to students about talents and challenges in the areas of academics and career. Ask the speaker to give students some concrete advice about recognizing and developing their interests and talents, such as thinking outside the box and listening to the feedback of others while still being true to their own desires.

- **Journal Assignment:** In response to the speaker or

laity
All the members of the Church who have been initiated into the Church through Baptism and who are not ordained (the clergy) or in consecrated life. The laity participate in Jesus' prophetic, priestly, and kingly ministries.

liturgy
The official public worship of the Church. The sacraments and the Divine Office constitute the Church's liturgy. The Mass is the most important liturgical celebration.

are in consecrated life, but the laity as well. Therefore, each person in Christ's Church has fundamental dignity. Because we are joined to Christ, we share his priestly, prophetic, and royal office (see pages 107–111). This makes us missionaries, ones sent by Christ armed with the gifts of the Holy Spirit to proclaim the Gospel to the ends of the world: "As the Father has sent me, so I send you" (Jn 20:21). As Catholics, we are to be ambassadors of Christ's love, letting his light shine through. Just as salt flavors food, we are to live in such a way that we enhance the world with our Christian love. The tasks and challenges of the Church's mission as People of God include:

Message. We must preach the Gospel in word and deed. Even in today's world of mass communications, some people have not heard the Good News of God's love in Jesus Christ; others have heard it only in a garbled way. The Church must never cease to proclaim that Jesus is Lord, that the Kingdom is present in our midst, that we must repent, believe, and be baptized. This timeless message must always be a central focus of the Church.

Community. To be an effective sign of the Gospel, nonbelievers must see it in action—a community that actually lives its faith, hope, and love. A loving Church is like a magnet drawing others to the Good News of Jesus Christ. Love is not optional for disciples of Christ. Jesus commands, "Love one another. As I have loved you, so you also should love one another" (Jn 13:34).

Service. It is often said, "Service is the price we pay for the space we occupy." To occupy a place at Christ's table means Catholics must help one another, especially the least in our midst. Catholics must imitate Christ, who washed his disciples' feet at the Last Supper and gave his life for all people on Calvary. Non-Catholics will find the Church believable especially when Catholics walk the road that Jesus walked—a way of obedience, simplicity, poverty, and self-sacrificing love, even unto death.

Worship. Worship is a humble admission that God gives us everything: our very life and all the many gifts he has showered on us. He is worthy of our praise, adoration, and gratitude. When we celebrate liturgy, the official public prayers and rituals of the Church, we are engaged in the most important work of the Church. (*Liturgy* in Greek means

The Teaching of the Documents

The Head of this Body is Christ. He is the image of the invisible God and in Him all things came into being. He is before all creatures and in Him all things hold together. . . . All the members ought to be molded in the likeness of Him, until Christ be formed in them.

—*Dogmatic Constitution on the Church*, No. 7

One way to model Christ is to accept and offer all suffering that comes your way to Christ and his cross. In a notebook or journal, keep a log of the sufferings big and small that you endure each day. Keep the log for one week. At the end of each day write a prayer offering these hardships to God.

Sacrament	Symbols	Reality Represented
Baptism	Water, salt, chrism	New life in grace
Penance	Confession, absolution	Forgiveness, reconciliation
Eucharist	Bread and wine	Nourishment, unity with Jesus
Confirmation	Imposition of hands	Full life in the Holy Spirit
Matrimony	Vows	Union in marriage
Holy Orders	Imposition of hands	Priesthood in the Church
Anointing of Sick	Anointing, oil	Healing of spirit and body

Extending the Lesson

Group Discussion: Catholic Relief Services is the international aid organization for the Catholic Church. They have an excellent website (www.crs.org), which is frequently updated. Catholic Relief Services is an impressive example of how the Church is a force for love and peace in the world today. Duplicate one or two articles from the site that illustrate the Church's presence in Asia, Africa, or South America and have students react to them in groups.

"work of the public.") God's work of Salvation takes place in the liturgy, especially in the Eucharist, which both celebrates and creates the Church. Liturgy is the source of our union with the Lord and each other. It is the wellspring of our love. It inspires us to be other Christs, "to become in deed what we proclaim in creed."

Body of Christ (CCC, 787–796; 805–808)

We have all experienced the rewards of a group coming together socially, to work for a common goal, or to support one another after a tragedy. Human solidarity is important. Common and shared efforts by a group of like-minded people can accomplish much; on the other hand, each individual has a role to play with his or her unique talents.

The Church is also a communion of people with God, a "mystical communion," the Body of Christ. At the Last Supper Jesus used this vivid image: "I am the vine, you are the branches. Whoever remains in me and I in him will bear much fruit, because without me you can do nothing" (Jn 15:5). The vine gives life to its branches as Christ gives life to his disciples. By the power of the Holy Spirit, Jesus is united closely with the Church. This unity is achieved in a special way in the holy Eucharist. Through the Eucharist, Christ lives in us and we in him. We receive the Body and Blood of Christ Jesus to take him into the world to others.

The Body of Christ imagery for the Church was also used by St. Paul. When Paul (who was also known as Saul before his conversion) was on his way to Damascus to persecute Christians, the Risen Lord appeared to him and asked, "Saul, Saul, why are you persecuting me? . . . I am Jesus, whom you are persecuting" (Acts 9:4–5). By hunting down followers of Christ, he had been persecuting the Lord himself. Many years after his conversion, Paul wrote to the Christian converts in Corinth:

As a body is one though it has many parts, and all the parts of the body, though many, are one body, so also Christ. For in one Spirit we were all

baptized into one body, whether Jews or Greeks, slaves or free persons, and we were all given to drink of one Spirit. (1 Cor 12:12–13)

Christ is the head of this body, the Church. We are its members. Baptism incorporates us into the Body of Christ. The Holy Spirit unites us into a single body where each of us has an important role to play regardless of race, color, nationality, and sex. Being a part of Christ's Body, the Church, stresses the great dignity, value, and worth each of us has. St. Paul also wrote, "Now you are Christ's body, and individually parts of it" (1 Cor 12:27). Because of Christ, we are linked to one another, and in a special way to poor, persecuted, and suffering people. "Christ and his Church . . . together make up the 'whole Christ'" (CCC, 795).

Each Catholic is important to the health of the Body of Christ. We each have our role to play as prophets, teachers, healers, assistants, administrators, and so forth. Jesus unites himself and his saving acts to our own actions. Though we are one with Jesus, he is still distinct from us. He is the Bridegroom; the Church is his bride.

For Enrichment

Student Presentation: Have students attend Mass in a parish that serves an immigrant population or a community with a different ethnic background from their own. Have the students present to the class their observations about similarities and differences in their worship experience.

as an assignment on its own, have students journal about what they envision their role to be within the Body of Christ. What do they have to offer the world on behalf of the Church? What special skills do they bring to spreading the Good News?

- **Class Discussion:** Check the students' progress on the log of sufferings they have experienced in the past few days (from the Homework Assignment on page 100). Point out that there are often lessons in suffering, which are missed if we simply push through it or try to ignore it. Acceptance of unavoidable suffering helps us to be at peace even in the midst of pain. Some students may reveal exceptionally difficult or risky situations in response to this assignment. Be prepared to respond and refer the student to professional resources if appropriate.

- **Direct Instruction:** Review with the students their notes on the Holy Spirit from Chapter 3. Then read or summarize the text subsection "Temple of the Holy Spirit" (page 105).

Extending the Lesson

Journal Assignment: Have the students write in their journals about the gifts they see in themselves. Brainstorm first with students about "categories" of gifts: academic, leadership, physical, musical/artistic, moral, etc. Facilitate a discussion with the students about what they are doing to develop their gifts.

Work with students on the difference between a practical, logical approach to recognizing gifts and the spiritual process of discerning gifts. Discerning involves praying in an open manner, asking God to reveal something to us. Encourage students to take some time in prayer as a way of recognizing their own, perhaps hidden, gifts to the world. Affirm the validity of both the practical and the spiritual approaches; they are complementary, not mutually exclusive.

A truly Christian exercise of gifts involves consciously acknowledging that our gifts have been given to us by God the Father and relying on the inspiration of the Holy Spirit to develop and share them. Have students reread the assigned text concerning Jesus' commissioning for public ministry. Lead a prayer dedicating the classes' gifts to God and asking for strength. The prayer could be:

> God,
> Thank you for the gifts and talents you have given me,
> Both recognized and yet unknown.
> Please give me the courage and generosity
> To develop my gifts and share them with those around me.
> Send me mentors and examples
> To show me how I can use them to serve you.
> I ask this in Jesus' name. Amen.

Knowing Christ through Scripture

Answers (page 104)

1 Corinthians 15:12–28
- Christ's Resurrection

Romans 5:6–11
- Christ died for us while we were still sinners.

Romans 8:14–17
- We can call God "Abba, Father!"

Philippians 2:5–11
- Humility

Romans 3:21–31
- Grace brings justification.

Colossians 3:5–17
- Christians should do everything in the name of the Lord Jesus.

1 Corinthians 12:12–30
- Although we are all different, each member of the Body of Christ serves a different but equally important role.

1 Corinthians 11:17–34
- There is division within the Corinthian church causing some to eat and get drunk during the Lord's Supper while others go hungry. Paul instructs them to eat before they celebrate the Eucharistic feast.

His love for his bride moves him to send his Holy Spirit to shower us with the gifts we need to be faithful to him, to be effective body-builders, and to be worthy preachers of the Gospel. Although we may be endowed with different gifts according to the part we are to play, we all have been given the gift of love. It is the greatest gift of all and puts tremendous responsibility on us to do what Christ wants us to do.

KNOWING CHRIST THROUGH SCRIPTURE

St. Paul's Message about Christ and His Church

St. Paul was the early Church's greatest missionary, taking the Gospel to the ends of the Roman Empire and preaching it to the Gentiles. His epistles contain deep and important theological insights into Jesus Christ and the Church. Among Paul's recurring themes in his writings are the following:

- Jesus Christ is the Savior. He is the Lord of the universe. Our Salvation takes place through him.
- The heart of the Gospel is the Death, Resurrection, and Glorification of Jesus Christ.
- We will participate in the Resurrection of Jesus Christ.
- Salvation is a free gift of God that requires faith. We cannot earn it.
- Christians are bound together in one Body, the Church, of which Jesus is the head. We become sons and daughters to God through Baptism, which unites us with God's Son.
- The Holy Spirit is the life of the Church who enables us to call God Abba, Father.
- As brothers and sisters of Jesus, we should treat each other with dignity. We must love.
- Following Jesus means that we must suffer for him gladly.

Read the following passages. Identify from the themes above which are being discussed in the particular passage. Then answer the questions.

1 Corinthians 15:12–28
- What is the basis of Christian faith?

Romans 5:6–11
- How did God prove his love?

Romans 8:14–17
- What does the Spirit enable us to do?

Philippians 2:5–11
- What virtue of Christ should Christians imitate?

Romans 3:21–31
- What brings about justification?

Colossians 3:5–17
- How should Christians live their lives?

1 Corinthians 12:12–30
- In what way is each Christian valuable?

1 Corinthians 11:17–34
- What problem was troubling the Corinthians? How did St. Paul solve it?

Background Information

More on the Sacramental Character of the Church

In *The Face of Christ in the Face of the Church* (available online at www.vatican.va/roman_curia/congregations/csaints/documents/rc_con_csaints.doc_20021210_martins-rosto-de-cristo_en.html), the sacramentality of the Church and the role of the People of God are explained this way:

> The Dogmatic Constitution *Lumen gentium* begins by affirming two basic teachings: "Christ is the light of all nations. Hence this most sacred Synod, which has been gathered in the Holy Spirit, eagerly desires to shed on all men that radiance of his which *brightens* the countenance of the Church. This it will do by proclaiming the Gospel to every creature" (*Lumen gentium*, n. 1). The Conciliar document emphasizes the sacramental character of the Church: she "in Christ, is a kind of *sacrament* or sign of intimate union with God, and of the unity of all mankind." In speaking of the People of God, the text returns to this concept: "God . . . has established . . . the Church, that for each and all she may be the *visible sacrament* of this saving unity" (*ibid.*, n. 9). (2)

Temple of the Holy Spirit (*CCC*, 747; 797–801; 809–810)

The Holy Spirit dwells in the Church, the Body of Christ, to give it life. He is present in the Risen Lord Jesus, the head of the Body of Christ, and in each individual member. The Holy Spirit is the soul of the Church. He builds it up, gives the Church life, and makes each of us holy by uniting us to Christ Jesus. Because of the Spirit's presence, we can call the Church the Temple of the Holy Spirit. This Temple—the Church—is "the sacrament of the Holy Trinity's communion" with us (*CCC*, 747); that is, because the Holy Spirit dwells in the Church, the Church both symbolizes and brings about God's presence and his union with his people. The Church is the place in which God's people are united to God and become "perfect, just as your heavenly Father is perfect" (Mt 5:48). The Church is "a people brought into unity from the unity of the Father, the Son, and the Holy Spirit" (*CCC*, 810).

The Holy Spirit works through the Church and its members to continue the work of Salvation. The Spirit uses the sacraments, holy Scripture, and various graces and virtues to help us do good works for others. The Spirit also gives charisms (special gifts) to individual Christians who are to use them under the direction of the Magisterium to build up the Body of Christ.

For Review

1. Define *sacrament*. How is Christ a sacrament? How is the Church a sacrament?
2. Name four tasks that the Church as the People of God must perform to fulfill their Christ-given commission.
3. Explain the image of the Church as the Body of Christ. How does this image highlight the dignity of each Christian?
4. How is the Church the Temple of the Holy Spirit?

For Reflection

Consider the following two quotations:

The Church is like a great ship being pounded by the waves of life's different stresses. Our duty is not to abandon ship, but to keep her on her course.

—**St. Boniface** (ca. 680–754)

The Church has no other light than Christ's; according to a favorite image of the Church Fathers, the Church is like the moon, all its light reflected from the sun.

—*Catechism of the Catholic Church*, 748

Compose five other "the Church is like . . ." similes that describe the Church as you see it.

For Review Answers (page 105)

1. A sacrament is an outward sign of an invisible grace. Both Christ and his Church are sacraments because they are visible and tangible, they point us and draw us toward a reality that is invisible, and because in themselves they hold that reality—God's presence in the world.

2. The Church, as the People of God, must preach the Gospel message, be active in the community, serve others, and worship God.

3. The Church is the Body of Christ because of the close unity members share with Christ and with one another. The image of the body reminds us of the diversity among members, such as arms, legs, and eyes, while at the same time maintaining unity through our source, Christ. Our union with Christ gives us the guidance and strength to do many things we would be unable to accomplish on our own.

4. The Church is the Temple of the Holy Spirit because by the Spirit's presence the Church is a source of grace to the world. The Holy Spirit works through the sacraments, Scripture, gifts, and graces to transform the members of the Church and to make the Kingdom of God present.

Homework Assignment

1. Complete the journal log of experiences of large and small suffering.

2. Complete the For Review questions on page 105.

3. Read the text section "Membership and Ministries in the Church" (pages 106–112).

4. Continue working with classmates on Assignment 5 of the Ongoing Assignments (pages 121–122). Also, continue work on the individual Ongoing Assignments that you chose.

Extending the Lesson

Group Discussion: Divide the class into small groups. Ask students to develop a list of qualities and behaviors that a school would have if it was truly functioning as a Christian community. Have them include all members of the community in their list: administrators, teachers, parents, and coaches, as well as students. What do they see as their school's greatest strengths? What do they see as the areas where the school needs to grow? What can they do about the areas of growth? Invite students to make a commitment to take one step toward bringing about better community, by either affirming a strength that already exists or addressing a weakness. Have students report on their commitments at a future date.

Membership and Ministries in the Church (pages 106–112)

Objectives

In this lesson, the students will:

- compare and contrast teams or clubs and the Church.
- define the terms *hierarchy, laity and consecrated*, and *religious life*.
- explain the requirements for being a member of the Church.
- describe the roles of Church as priest, prophet, and king and apply them to the life of the Church today.
- identify misunderstandings about the teaching of papal infallibility.

Preview

This section introduces students to the structure of the Church and members' participation in the life of the Church. Information on the role of the hierarchy, laity, and vowed religious forms a foundation for later work on vocation and answering God's call in one's own life. The section describing the roles of priest, prophet, and king merit particular care, since students may not be aware of their participation in those roles and need encouragement to see the practical implications for their lives.

Membership and Ministries in the Church (CCC, 871–873; 897–900; 914–934; 944–945)

Who is a Catholic? What makes a person a member of the Church? And once a member, what privileges and responsibilities does a person have?

First, members of the Catholic Church are those baptized Christians

- who accept Jesus as their Lord and Savior,
- who accept the entire system and means of Salvation Christ left with the Church (including union with the Pope and bishops),
- and who devote themselves to continuing Christ's work of Salvation according to their situation in life.

Second, Catholics minister (serve) God in the Church in different ways. Each person is called to one of the three categories of membership in the Church: the hierarchy, the laity, or the consecrated life.

hierarchy
The official, sacred leadership in the Church made up of the Church's ordained ministers—bishops, priests, and deacons. The symbol of unity and authority in the Church is the Pope, the Bishop of Rome, who is the successor of St. Peter.

The hierarchy is the order of ministry established by Jesus Christ on the Apostles and their successors. It includes the Pope and bishops and their coworkers, priests. The hierarchy has three essential roles: to teach the faith truthfully and fully; to sanctify the members of the Church, especially through the celebration of the sacraments; and to govern the Church wisely as loving shepherds who serve humbly in imitation of Christ.

The laity includes any baptized Catholics who have not received Holy Orders nor belong to a Church-approved religious state. The laity has the special call to be involved in the social, political, and economic affairs of the wider human community and to direct them according to God's will. Laymen and -women are to be light of the world and salt of the earth.

Those in *consecrated* or *religious life* can be members of the hierarchy or laypeople and include hermits, consecrated virgins, secular institutes, different apostolic societies, and men (brothers) and women (sisters) in religious orders like the Jesuits, Franciscans, Dominicans, Benedictines, and so forth. Those living

Extending the Lesson

Guest Speaker: Invite a member of a religious order to speak to the class. Ask the speaker to talk about his or her discernment of religious vocation, the difference between men and women religious and diocesan priesthood (the vows of poverty, chastity and obedience, community life) and the work they currently engage in.

Background Information

Electing a New Pope

When a pope dies there is a period of mourning. The cardinals from around the world gather in Rome and seclude themselves during the selection process. A secret vote is taken. If there are not enough votes to select a new pope, the ballots are mixed with straw and then burned; the gray smoke escapes through a special chimney. When a new pope has been selected, the ballots are burned alone, producing a white smoke for the crowd waiting outside. The new pope chooses a name and appears at a window, blessing the crowd. This event played out in April 2005 with the passing of Pope John Paul II and the election of Pope Benedict XVI.

in religious life serve as a special gift to their fellow Catholics. They are a unique witness to the Lord's union with his Church and thus are a sign to the world that God's Salvation is taking place in our midst. Other distinctive traits of those in consecrated life are their public profession of the evangelical counsels of poverty, chastity, and obedience; their commitment to liturgical celebration; and their living a shared life in common.

Third, Baptism into the Church makes each Catholic a child of God with equal dignity. Furthermore, it conveys a share in Christ's roles as priest, prophet, and king. The priestly (sanctifying), prophetic (teaching), and kingly (governing) ministries are all essential for building up Christ's Body and extending his saving works to all people. Catholics participate in these three offices in several ways. By Baptism, you share in the priesthood of Christ. You offer yourself with him in his sacrifice to the Father. By the gift of faith, you share in the prophetic ministry by becoming witnesses of Christ's truth to the world. And in your service to those in need, you share in Christ's kingship. In suffering, you join with the royalty of his suffering on the cross.

Each of these ministries is examined in more detail in the subsections that follow.

Priest (CCC, 893; 901–903; 941)

The Church shares in Christ's priesthood, his work of sanctification. Jesus came to invite us into friendship with the Blessed Trinity, to give us a life of love and holiness. When he founded the Church, he formed a priestly people to bring Salvation to the ends of the earth. Our vocation as members of Christ's body is to help bring others to Christ.

What is a priest? A priest is a mediator between God and people. A priest offers sacrifice to God. A priest helps people

on the path to holiness. These definitions apply perfectly to Jesus Christ, the High Priest. Jesus brought God to us and takes us to God. It is his sacrifice on the cross, his Death and Resurrection, his glorification that make us holy by power of the Holy Spirit. He is the perfect mediator between God and humankind. The letter to Hebrews says of Jesus, the Son of God:

> For we do not have a high priest who is unable to sympathize with our weaknesses, but one who has similarly been tested in every way, yet without sin. So let us confidently approach the throne of grace to receive mercy and to find grace for timely help. (Heb 4:15–16)

Though some men have a Christ-given vocation (call) to Holy Orders, by virtue of our Baptism, each of us is called to holiness. We are great in God's eyes not because of the special gifts we have been given, but rather because of how much we love him and other people. While a student, you can share in Christ's priestly ministry by dedicating school work, family life, prayer, involvement in sports and other recreational activities, and even your disappointments to Christ. When offered to God in the Eucharist, the activities of your daily life are united to Christ's Paschal Mystery, the source of all holiness. You can also do so on a daily basis simply by making a morning prayer to God, offering all your activities of the coming day to him as a gift of love.

evangelical counsels
Vows of personal poverty, chastity understood as lifelong celibacy, and obedience to the demands of the community being joined, which are professed by those entering the consecrated life.

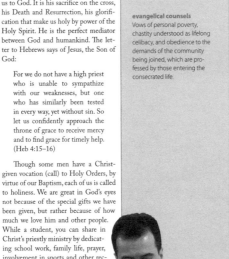

Bell Ringers

- **Direct Instruction:** Check the students' answers to the For Review questions on page 105. Pay particular attention to the students' understanding about the Church as Body of Christ.
- **Student Presentations:** Call on representatives from small groups working on Ongoing Assignment 5 (small service project, page 121) to report on their group's progress. Record on the board some of the experiences the students have had to this point.
- **Guest Speaker:** Invite a catechumen or recent neophyte to speak with the class on (1) why they chose to enter into full communion with the Catholic Church, (2) the qualifications for membership in the Church, and (3) the occasions when he or she first felt welcomed in the Catholic Church.

Printed Materials continued from page 103

Haughton, Rosemary. *The Catholic Thing*. Springfield, IL: Templegate, 1997.

Rosemary Haughton is one of the most brilliant and insightful Catholic theologians on the scene today. This book will give you a sense of what it means to be a Catholic while preserving the notion of Church as mystery.

Higgins, Gregory C. *Twelve Theological Dilemmas*. Mahwah, NJ: Paulist Press, 1991.

One of the issues Higgins addresses in this fine book is a chapter related to Christianity and world religions. Includes a great deal of background information to elicit views on both sides of twelve issues.

Koch, Carl. *A Popular History of the Catholic Church*. Winona, MN: St. Mary's Press, 1997.

Easy-to-read overview of Church history.

Kresta, Al. *Why Do Catholics Genuflect?* Ann Arbor, MI: Servant Books, 2001.

The Catholic radio broadcaster answers questions asked about Catholic beliefs, practices, and customs. Popular apologetics.

Madrid, Patrick. *Pope Fiction: Answers to 30 Myths and Misconceptions about the Papacy*. San Diego, CA: Basilica Press, 1999.

McBrien, Richard. *The Church: The Evolution of Catholicism*. San Francisco: HarperOne, 2009.

Fr. McBrien offers a thorough examination of the study of ecclesiology with a special treatment on the Second Vatican Council.

O'Collins, Gerald, S.J., and Mary Venturini. *Believing: Understanding the Creed*. New York/Mahwah, NJ: Paulist Press, 1991.

Theological and personal reflections on the Apostles' Creed. Engaging style where the authors react to each other's insights. Fr. O'Collins is a noted theologian; Mary Venturini is a journalist and mother.

Perko, Michael, S.J. *Catholic & American: A Popular History*. Huntington, IN: Our Sunday Visitor, Inc., 1989.

Relies heavily on Hennesey and Dolan, but also contains many interesting and novel insights. Fr. Perko, a professor of educational history, sketches some wonderful portraits of leading American Catholics, notably, Junipero Serra, Charles Carroll, John Carroll, Sister Blandina Segale, John Ryan, and Dorothy Day.

Pichler, Tony, and Chris Broslavick. *Service Projects for Teens: 20 Plans that Work*. Dayton, OH: Hi-Time/Pflaum, 2001.

Rasmussen, Martha. *The First 2000 Years: A Popular Survey and Study Guide to Church History*. San Francisco: Ignatius Press, 2003.

continued on page 118

Teaching Approaches

- **Class Discussion:** Facilitate a discussion about what it means to belong to a specific community. For example, when people belong to a team, they show up for practices together, share the goal of winning and improving as players, follow the coach's instructions, and try to do their best to contribute to the team. Some players are more committed than others, but they are all members of the team. Have the students compare Church membership with membership on a team or in a club. What are the similarities? What are the differences? Refer the students to the privileges and responsibilities of Church membership on pages 106–107 of the text. Point out that:

  - Similarities include friendship, common goals and activities, the opportunity to be coached and to improve skills and abilities, potential for disciplinary action, etc.

  - Differences include the lack of divinely inspired leadership and the goals of competing and winning.

- **Individual Assignment:** Quiz the students on the roles in the Church: hierarchy, laity, and consecrated life. Have students number a sheet of paper 1–10. Have the students identify which of the three groups each of the following falls into (answers are on page 111 of this text):

  1. Pope
  2. Fr. [insert name of a priest they know]
  3. married couples
  4. deacons
  5. monks
  6. young children
  7. nuns
  8. Bishop [insert name of the local bishop]
  9. hermits
  10. you, the teacher

If you should marry, the love you have for your spouse will be united to Jesus in the Sacrament of Matrimony. Your marriage can be a great source of holiness. Your mutual love, which is open to the sharing of the great gift of life, will result in the *domestic Church*, the unit called the family. Your family will become a miniature Church, in which moms and dads have a unique ministry to lead their children on the path of holiness.

Laymen and -women can also serve God's people in certain ministries. For example, they can read the Holy Scripture at Mass or serve as special ministers of the holy Eucharist.

To assist him in leading others to holiness, Jesus established the ministerial or hierarchical priesthood. The ministerial or hierarchical priesthood is received by bishops and priests through the Sacrament of Holy Orders. The ministerial priesthood serves the common priesthood and is directed at unfolding the baptismal grace of all Christians. It is the means by which Christ builds up and leads his Church.

The Church's ruling office shows the way to serve Christ with humility and love. However, it is the role of the bishops and their coworker priests to respond to Jesus' command to baptize, celebrate the Eucharist, pray, help the poor and outcast, and forgive sins in his name.

Prophet
(CCC, 874–882; 888–892; 936–939; 904–906; 935; 942)

Because Baptism gives us a share in Christ's teaching (prophetic) ministry, each member of the Church is called to be a prophet, that is, one who proclaims the Gospel in both word and deed. Teens fulfill this prophetic call in many ways. For example, an opportunity may present itself when a peer wonders why you do not do drugs or engage in premarital sex. Your good example speaks volumes. Living a Christlike life is often the best form of Gospel preaching. St. Francis of Assisi is credited with saying, "Preach the Gospel always. Use words if necessary."

In the future you might serve the Church in a special way by training to be a catechist or religion teacher. If you become a parent, you will have the responsibility to pass on the Good News of Jesus to your children. Jesus told his disciples to preach the Gospel to the ends of the earth (see Mt 28:19–20). This makes us all missionaries. The history of Christianity has given us many models of how to preach Christ effectively to others.

For example, in the twentieth century, Mother Teresa of Calcutta taught others to see Christ in the poor and suffering. Another example is the lay missionary Jean Donovan, who left a comfortable life to serve the poor in El Salvador. For her prophetic witness, she and three religious sisters were martyred.

The Pope, bishops, and priests have been given a special prophetic role. Their role is deeply connected with Church Tradition. Jesus gave the Church the duty to teach authentically and proclaim truthfully the Gospel as it appears in both Scripture and Tradition. The word *tradition* means "handing on." When he established the Church on Peter, Jesus himself promised to be with his Church in a special way until the end of time. As the founder, Jesus is the source of ministry in the Church. He is the one who gives the Church its authority, mission, orientation, and goal.

At the same time, Christ established a hierarchy of leadership to guarantee that the essential jobs of teaching, governing, and sanctification would take place in his Church. The hierarchy is a sacred leadership that receives its ministry of service from the Lord himself. The Pope, bishops, priests, and deacons do not act on their own authority. They continue the service of Peter and the Apostles whom Jesus appointed to carry on his work of Salvation. Their role is to preserve authentic tradition and spread the true Gospel as taught by Jesus Christ.

The Pope has a unique role in the Church because he is the successor of Peter. He is a symbol of unity and has primacy over the whole Church. The Holy Father is the Vicar of Christ. We base this belief on Christ's own teaching, given after Peter proclaimed that Jesus is the Messiah, the Son of the Living God:

For Enrichment

Individual Assignment: Assign students to research one religious order. Some possibilities are:

- Jesuits
- Franciscans
- Dominicans
- Benedictines
- Crosiers
- Christian Brothers
- Resurrection
- Sisters of St. Joseph

Students should research the founder, the particular charism of the order, their current work, and their projected future. This can also be an opportunity for students to learn about the challenge of supporting elderly members of religious orders as numbers of religious decrease across the country.

Blessed are you, Simon son of Jonah. For flesh and blood has not revealed this to you, but my heavenly Father. And so I say to you, you are Peter, and upon this rock I will build my Church, and the gates of the netherworld shall not prevail against it. I will give you the keys to the kingdom of heaven. Whatever you bind on earth shall be bound in heaven; and whatever you loose on earth shall be loosed in heaven. (Mt 16:17–19)

The Pope and bishops exercise their prophetic (teaching) role in the follow ways, through:

1. *Magisterial teaching.* The Pope and bishops usually teach through the ordinary Magisterium of the Church. Recall that *Magisterium* refers to the teaching office of the Church. The task of the Magisterium is to proclaim the Gospel, build up Christian love and service, and see to the proper administration of the sacraments and other spiritual and temporal benefits offered by the Church. The Church's magisterial teaching can be found in encyclicals, pastoral letters, sermons, and the like. Because Christ gave the hierarchy the right to teach, Catholics give religious assent to magisterial teaching through prayerful listening and obedience.

2. *Ecumenical councils.* The Pope and bishops together form the College of Bishops. The bishops must truthfully preach the Gospel in union with the Pope and each other. The bishops' authority comes from Christ and can only be exercised in union with the Pope since he is Peter's successor and the head of the College of Bishops. Ecumenical (worldwide) councils bring the Pope and bishops together to offer unified teachings. The Pope has a special role as the sign of unity when the bishops speak as one. As the Bishop of Rome, Peter's successor must be a living sign of unity in Christ for the universal Church, both for the bishops' and all God's People. His voice with the bishops' is Christ's own voice teaching the Church today.

3. *Infallibility.* Christ promised that he would remain with the Church until the end of time. Therefore, when it comes to essential matters of faith and morals, the Church is infallible. Infallibility means that a certain doctrine (teaching) is free from error.

Guided by the Holy Spirit, the College of Bishops, in union with the Pope, can exercise the gift of infallibility when teaching about or protecting Christ's revelation on matters of belief or morality. They do this in a special way when they gather together and teach with the

infallibility
A gift of the Spirit whereby the Pope and bishops are preserved from error when proclaiming a doctrine related to Christian faith or morals.

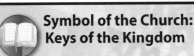

Symbol of the Church: Keys of the Kingdom

The key is a symbol of the authority to forgive sin in the name of Jesus. Two keys signify the authority to open Heaven for sinners who repent or lock out sinners who refuse to turn to the Lord. Research and report on the history of this symbol.

- **Direct Instruction:** Continue with the text subsection "Priest" on pages 107–108. Make sure to explain the differences between the Christ-given vocation (call) to Holy Orders and the vocation of all the baptized to holiness. Explain to students some of the functions that currently belong to:
  - *ordained priests*: celebrating the sacraments of Eucharist and Penance; being pastor of a parish.
  - *ordained priests and deacons*: preaching at Sunday liturgies; witnessing the Sacrament of Matrimony; administering the Sacrament of the Sick.
  - *bishops*: administering the sacraments of Holy Orders and Confirmation; being the pastor of a diocese.
  - *lay people*: under special circumstances, administering the Sacrament of Baptism; participating in the Sacrament of Matrimony.

  Point out that bishops, for example, can perform all the functions of lay people (except to receive the Sacrament of Matrimony) but that lay people cannot perform the functions reserved for priests or bishops.

- **Writing Assignment:** Review the concept of the family as the domestic Church. Ask students to list ways in which parents can help their children to develop a strong faith in God. Ask them also to describe strategies that they think are not helpful in encouraging faith or that were appropriate when they were younger but are not as effective today. How would they try to pass their faith on to their own children?

Roles in the Church Answers (page 110 of the TWE)

1. hierarchy
2. hierarchy
3. laity
4. hierarchy
5. consecrated life
6. laity
7. consecrated life
8. hierarchy
9. consecrated life
10. varies

Extending the Lesson

Prayer Experience: One role of a priest is to be a mediator between God and people. An important way in which all people can perform this function is by praying for one another. Place a box for prayer intentions in the classroom. Invite students to place prayer intentions in the box. Some students may place confidential intentions in the box that they would not mention aloud in class. Include prayer for the intentions in the box into class prayer. If the school has a chapel, the intentions could be transferred to a place in the chapel on a regular basis. Periodically invite students to share answers to prayer, to encourage and affirm the serious role of interceding for one another.

- **Direct Instruction:** Continue with the text subsection "Prophet" (pages 108–110). Explain the three ways listed in the text that the pope and bishops exercise their prophetic teaching:
  - Magisterial teaching
  - Ecumenical councils
  - Infallibility

  Question the students on each of these areas and have them explain more about their meanings.

- **Direct Instruction:** Point out the illustration of the "keys of the kingdom" on page 109. Explain to students that the references to the keys and to binding and loosing refer to the Sacrament of Penance. Through this sacrament, God has given clergy the grace to forgive sins through the power of the Holy Spirit.

- **Class Discussion:** Have students summarize the text, clarifying their understanding of papal infallibility. Question the students as to their understanding of which teachings of the Magisterium would be candidates for infallibility. For example, "Jesus is fully human and fully divine" is a matter of faith; the Pope's position on a specific war being fought in the world would not be.

Pope in an ecumenical council. Individual bishops can also proclaim Christ's teaching infallibly when they teach collectively around the world, always united to the Holy Father.

Papal infallibility refers to the special gift given to the Pope as the supreme teacher and pastor of the universal Church. He exercises this gift when he teaches *ex cathedra* ("from the chair" of St. Peter), that is, using his Christ-given authority as the successor of St. Peter. The Holy Father teaches infallibly: when he teaches as pastor of all the faithful, is proclaiming a definitive doctrine pertaining to faith or morals, and does so intending to use his full authority in an unchangeable decision.

While the teaching of the Pope is the teaching of the apostolic faith and without error, infallible *definitions* are rare. The most recent occurrence is Pope Pius XII's 1950 declaration of the dogma of our Blessed Mother's Assumption into Heaven. Because Christ promised to remain with his Church through the

canon law
The official body of rules (canons) that provides for good order in the Catholic Church.

Holy Spirit and not lead it astray, Catholics owe the obedience of faith to infallible statements. Recall that an obstinate

denial or doubt by a baptized Catholic of some divine or Catholic truth is heretical.

Infallibility does not mean that the Pope is free from sin or mistakes. He is not infallible on matters not pertaining to faith, for example, if he were to propose a solution to a particular political debate or conflict between two nations. The Pope's personal opinions, like anyone else's, can be wrong. Infallibility refers solely to the Pope's gift as successor of Peter to teach correctly Christ's revelation. This is especially true when some core belief is under attack, thus causing confusion among believers. The purpose of the gift of infallibility is not to inflate a particular person's self-image. Its purpose is to build up the body of Christ and to give the Church certitude about Christ's revelation.

King (CCC, 894–896; 908–913; 943)

Jesus is called Christ, the King, reminding us that he is the source of all authority (Mt 28:18). The definition of a king is one who is a ruler, regent, and person with authority. Christ shares his teaching and ruling authority with the hierarchy to guarantee that the Church is able to accomplish its mission of bringing Christ's Salvation to the ends of the earth.

The sole purpose for the Church's ruling office is to help people grow in faith and holiness. Canon law is another term for the Church's precepts and rules that help Catholics live as loving members of Christ's Body. Catholics give respectful obedience to these Church laws, as well as to the legitimate commands of the Pope and bishops.

Jesus, the Good Shepherd, is the model of the kingly role taken on by Church leaders: "I am the good shepherd. A good shepherd lays down his life for the sheep" (Jn 10:11). At the Last

Background Information

The Relationship between the Laity and the Ordained

The *Dogmatic Constitution on the Church* (Lumen Gentium) addresses the connectedness between the laity and the ordained:

> Though they differ from one another in essence and not only in degree, the common priesthood of the faithful and the ministerial or hierarchical priesthood are nonetheless interrelated: each of them in its own special way is a participation in the one priesthood of Christ. The ministerial priest, by the sacred power he enjoys, teaches and rules the priestly people; acting in the person of Christ, he makes present the Eucharistic sacrifice, and offers it to God in the name of all the people. But the faithful, in virtue of their royal priesthood, join in the offering of the Eucharist. They likewise exercise that priesthood in receiving the sacraments, in prayer and thanksgiving, in the witness of a holy life, and by self-denial and active charity. (Chapter II, no. 10)

Supper he told his Apostles, "If I, therefore, the master and teacher, have washed your feet, you ought to wash one another's feet" (Jn 13:14). Humble service, even unto death, is the ideal for those exercising authority in the Church.

Laypeople also share in Christ's kingly ministry. Catholics are to engage in works of self-denial (for example, fasting) to help become masters of sin in ourselves and in the world around us. Laypeople are also to engage in works of justice to help extend God's Kingdom on earth. When invited by bishops or priests, they can serve on various councils, parish finance committees, advisory boards, and the like so the organizational Church can function more smoothly.

Explaining Your Faith

Can non-Catholics get to Heaven? (CCC, 846–848)

Jesus Christ is present in his Body, the Church. Jesus alone is the one mediator between God and humans. He alone is the Savior and the way to the heavenly Father. The Acts of the Apostles puts it this way: "There is no Salvation through anyone else, nor is there any other name under heaven given to the human race by which we are to be saved" (4:12).

Where do we meet the Savior today? We meet him in an explicit way only through his Body, the Church. As people search for Salvation, Christ will draw them to his Body, the Church, because it is the living sign and sacrament of God's love. It witnesses to the way God has shown his love and achieved the Salvation of humans through his beloved Son, Jesus Christ. The Church's Christ-given mission is to show people the way to the Lord.

Jesus himself taught that people need faith and Baptism (Jn 3:5). Because of Jesus' own instruction, the Church teaches that anyone who knows "that the Catholic Church was made necessary by God through Jesus Christ, [and] would refuse to enter her or to remain in her could not be saved" (*Dogmatic Constitution on the Church*, No. 14).

But what about people who have never had the Gospel preached to them? Or what about those who have a distorted picture of our Savior because of false teachings they have heard? Can such people be saved?

The Church teaches that honest seekers after God, who through no fault of their own have never heard of Christ or his Church, can attain Heaven if they respond to the graces God gives them and live according to the dictates of their consciences. Even atheists who, "without blame on their part, have not reached an explicit knowledge of God, but who strive to live a good life, thanks to his grace," can attain Salvation because of God's goodness and love (*Dogmatic Constitution on the Church*, No. 16).

The Holy Spirit can mysteriously draw people into God's Kingdom. God's love and grace embrace all people who must seek God's Kingdom as they know it. Everyone must live with as much love as they possibly can because God, simply, is love. "God is love, and whoever remains in love remains in God and God in him" (1 Jn 4:16).

However, a person must be sincere. If someone truly knows the truth of the Gospel that has been given to him or her as a gift, then this person should recognize and accept the necessity of the Church for Salvation. It would be a serious sin for someone who has received the gift of faith to reject the Body of Christ, the Church, because this person would be rejecting Christ himself. Jesus himself taught, "Whoever listens to you listens to me. Whoever rejects you rejects me. And whoever rejects me rejects the one who sent me" (Lk 10:16).

Homework Assignment

1. Complete the For Review questions on page 112.

2. Read the text section "Marks of the Church" (pages 112–116).

Extending the Lesson

Class Activity: Have students enact a simulation of a Church council. Select a topic of current Church concern for the council to consider, or select an issue that is under discussion at your school. Divide the class into groups ("dioceses") and select a "bishop" to come as a representative of each group. Each small group will have a discussion, and then the "bishop" will prepare to join the council. Remind the students that councils are a distinct form of democracy in that the bishops today are not elected. Bishops may invite groups to advise them on an issue, but they are not bound by the advice of these groups. Select a person to act as "Pope" and preside over the council. Seat the "bishops" in the center of the room, and have them briefly discuss the topic at hand. Conclude with a general discussion about how the process is similar to how Church councils function.

- **Class Activity:** Distribute copies of the following quotation or post it on the board. Suggest that this statement is a response to the question "Is the Pope infallible?" on an online questions forum like Yahoo! Answers. *"Yes, the Catholic Church teaches that only the Pope is infallible. He is divinely inspired so that everything he teaches is God's truth. This is a manmade fallacy since the Pope is a sinner like everyone else in the world. Everything that the Catholic Church teaches is wrong since it comes from a man."* Make sure the students can point out the following misunderstandings:

  - The Pope is not the only one who can teach infallibly. The College of Bishops, in union with the Pope, can also exercise the gift of infallibility.

  - Everything the Pope teaches is not infallible. He exercises the gift of infallibility when teaching *ex cathedra*, as the pastor of the faithful, on matters of faith and morals, and when he intends to use his full authority in an unchangeable decision.

  - Yes, the Pope is not free from sin, but this does not affect his ability to teach infallibly.

  - Infallible definitions are rare, so to reject the entire Catholic Church's Tradition based on the infallibility of the Pope is going too far.

- **Class Discussion:** Beginning the text subsection on "King" (pages 110–111) and the Church's authority, have the students consider the value of authority in their lives, in their local communities (including their families and schools), and in the world at large. Ask the students to suggest examples in each of these areas of the positive value of authority.

For Review Answers (page 112)

1. People can be members of the Church as hierarchy, lay people, or vowed religious. The hierarchy includes priests, bishops, cardinals, and the Pope. Vowed religious have made solemn promises of poverty, chastity, and obedience, and live as members of religious communities. Lay people are all married and single members of the Church.

2. Priestly ministry refers to the work of bringing people to holiness, prophetic ministry involves teaching, and kingly ministry refers to governance within the Body of Christ. The members of the hierarchy have special responsibility for these roles, but lay people share in these privileges and responsibilities as well.

3. In Matthew 16:17–19 Jesus tells Peter "upon this rock I will build my Church . . . I will give you the keys to the kingdom of Heaven."

4. Infallibility is the principle that when the Pope speaks on essential matters of faith and morals, with the full authority of his role, the Holy Spirit will protect him from error in that teaching.

Marks of the Church (pages 112–116)

Objectives

In this lesson, the students will:
- identify and explain the four marks of the Church.
- recognize that the Blessed Trinity is the source of unity in the Church.
- explain that Christ and the saints are the model for the Church's holiness.
- recall the four ways that the Church is catholic or universal.
- describe three ways the Church remains apostolic.

Preview

This text section explains the essential marks of the Church as one, holy, catholic, and apostolic. The introduction reminds us of the "already but not yet" nature of the Kingdom; the Church is called to embody these four qualities, but in reality is yet imperfect.

For Review

1. List the three categories of membership in the Church. Briefly describe each.
2. How do Catholics share in Christ's priestly, prophetic, and kingly ministries?
3. Identify the Gospel passage that shows that Jesus Christ intended a sacred leadership in his Church.
4. Define *infallibility*. Under what conditions does the Church teach infallibly?

For Reflection

As one who shares in Christ's kingly role of service, share three concrete ways you have shown your care for others.

marks of the Church
Four essential signs or characteristics of Christ's Church that mark her as his true Church. The Church is one, holy, catholic, and apostolic.

Marks of the Church
(*CCC*, 811–812; 853)

The Church has four characteristics or marks to help us understand more about what the Church is, who she includes, and what her mission is. These marks—one, holy, catholic, and apostolic—build up the faith of Catholics. They can also help attract nonbelievers to the Church.

The marks of the Church are present in the Church, but at the same time they also challenge the Church to live up to her true identity. They point to Christ and the Holy Spirit working in the Church. But because the members of the Church are sinners, the marks are not always visible to the waiting world. For example, the Church is holy because of the Lord, but she is the home of sinners who sometimes betray him. The Church is one because of the Blessed Trinity living

Extending the Lesson

Class Activity: Explain to students that before the Second Vatican Council, Mass was celebrated in Latin everywhere on earth. A Catholic could go to Mass anywhere and experience essentially the same liturgy as in his or her home country. The unity of expression was powerful; the disadvantage was that few people understood Latin. If available, play a recording of liturgical music recorded in another language.

in her, but the presence of various Christian denominations show a wounded unity. The Church is catholic and open to all people, yet individual Catholics can at times act superior to others. The Church is apostolic, yet certain Catholics are exclusionary, preferring to keep the Gospel to themselves. The Church, individually and collectively, needs to constantly repent of her sins. In this way, the marks of the Church will be bright beacons to help bring others to Christ.

One (CCC, 812–818; 820; 866)

The Blessed Trinity is the source of unity in the Church. The Church is one because of its founder and source, Jesus Christ, and its soul, the Holy Spirit. Also, Christ continues to pray for unity in his Church (see Jn 17:20–21).

Love (charity) is the spiritual reality that unites the Church's members into one body. In addition, there are visible bonds of unity in the Church, namely:

- *profession of one faith,* which goes back to the time of the Apostles (for example, the Apostles' Creed and the Nicene Creed);
- *divine worship celebrated in common,* especially the Seven Sacraments;
- the *succession of the bishops* from the time of the Apostles to today through the power of the Sacrament of Holy Orders.

Just because the Church is one does not mean that there is a rigid sameness in the Church. The Lord has blessed the different members of his Body with many different gifts. Because of the differences in God's People, the Church allows for various local and cultural expressions of the faith, for example, celebrating Mass in the language of the people. As another example, various nationality groups have customs and devotions that appeal to their history, for example, the strong devotion to Our Lady of Guadalupe in Mexico or to the Black Madonna in Poland. These practices contribute to the Church's diversity within her unity.

Holy (CCC, 823–829; 853; 867)

Again, Christ is the model for the Church's holiness. In addition, Jesus and God the Father have sent the Holy Spirit to sanctify the Church, to unite her members to the Triune God who alone is holy. We profess that the Church is holy because the Holy Spirit

lives in her. She is the "holy People of God," and its members are "saints" (meaning, "holy ones").

God uses the Church to bring his life and light into the world, to sanctify the Church and her members. He has given the Church "the fullness of the means of Salvation," that is, all that we need to become holy. These include:

- the scriptural Word of God (the Bible), apostolic Tradition, the writings of great saints and theologians, and the Church's teaching office;
- the Church's liturgy, which includes the sacraments, especially the holy Eucharist;
- correct and complete confession of faith;
- full sacramental life;
- ordained ministry;
- apostolic succession;
- the many different ways of praying practiced by Catholics through the ages.

For Enrichment

Student Presentations: Assign students to research one of the following: Our Lady of Guadalupe, the Black Madonna, the custom of Las Posadas, or the Day of the Dead celebration in Guatemala. Have students report briefly on their findings to the class.

Extending the Lesson

Guest Speaker: Invite a speaker to address students about missionary activity. This could be someone from a diocesan office, or a religious order, or a former lay missionary. Or, show a video of people engaging in missionary activities for the Church. Many religious orders such as Maryknoll have videos highlighting their work; these are usually available at reasonable prices.

Bell Ringers

- **Class Discussion:** Ask the class to name qualities that are common to successful families. Point out to students that these are the "marks" by which we know that a family is healthy and loving. Then ask students to consider whether any family is capable of living these qualities perfectly. Clearly, no family is able to be patient, supportive, generous, etc., at all times. So these qualities also are ideals that families aspire to grow toward. The marks of the Church are similar to these characteristics in their "already but not yet" presence in our midst.

- Check the students' answers to the For Review questions they completed for homework.

Teaching Approaches

- **Direct Instruction:** Introduce the "Marks of the Church" section by reading or summarizing the opening text on pages 112–113. Then move right into coverage of the individual marks of the Church, beginning with the subsection "One" (page 113).

- **Direct Instruction:** Quiz the students orally to make sure they know that three visible bonds of unity in the Church are:
  - profession of one faith
  - divine worship celebrated in common
  - succession of the bishops

- **Direct Instruction:** Draw a diagram for the students illustrating the succession of bishops from Jesus' time to today. The central "trunk" of the succession is from Peter to Pope John Paul II; include recent Popes Pius XII, John XXIII, Paul VI, and John Paul II. Show the many branches indicating the growing Church over the centuries. Draw the beginning of your own diocese, reminding students the first bishop was commissioned by the Pope and assigned to the diocese. End with the names of your current bishop.

- **Class Discussion:** Continue with the text subsection on holiness (pages 113–114). Ask the students to play word association with "holy." Some of their connotations may be negative, since the term "holy" is not commonly used in conversation and can indicate a person who is boring, out of touch, or self-righteous. Remind students that the true meaning of the term is solid and positive and is modeled in the life of Jesus.

- **Prayer Experience:** Refer to the definitions of saints covered in the text. Explain more about the canonization process and Catholics' devotion to saints, especially Mary, the Mother of God. Explain the tradition of praying to saints, as some of them may be confused. Asking a saint to pray for us is similar to asking a friend or teacher to pray for us, with the difference that a saint is an exceptionally holy person who we know is with God in Heaven.
  - Pray a litany to the saints. Have each student recite the name of their patron or favorite saint and have the class respond with, "Pray for us."
  - Encourage students, if they like, to choose a saint whose life inspires them and to ask the saint to pray for the student on a regular basis.

- **Class Activity:** Provide art materials to begin the section "Catholic" (page 114). Have the students work together as a class to create one large (or several smaller) murals representing the universal nature of the Church as described in the text. You should include markers and crayons, along with

---

114   Our Catholic Faith

St. André Bessette

Catholic
From a Greek word meaning "universal" or "general." The Catholic Church is the Christian community that is one, holy, apostolic, and catholic—that is, open to all people everywhere at all times and that preaches the fullness of God's Revelation in Jesus Christ.

Though the Church is holy, we, the members of the Church, are both holy and sinful. We are always in need of conversion. We are pilgrims, that is, people on the way to meet God in Heaven. Holiness is something we must achieve, with God's help and grace.

However, despite the sins of its individual members through the ages, the Church has always had models of holiness. Their Christian witness was heroic, leading Church leaders to canonize some of them as saints worthy of our admiration and imitation. The process of *canonization* declares that certain holy men and women are with the Lord in Heaven and can serve as models of holiness. Saints can intercede for us while we are still on our earthly journey. The greatest saint of all is our Blessed Mother, Mary, the Mother of God. "In her, the Church is already the 'all-holy'" (*CCC*, 829).

What the saints teach us is just what Jesus taught: that the way to holiness is to love God above all and to love our neighbor as ourselves for the love of God.

Catholic (*CCC*, 830–835; 868)

Catholic means "general" or "universal," a word first applied to the Church by St. Ignatius of Antioch, a bishop who was martyred around 110. The Church is catholic or universal in four ways:

1. As the head of the Church, Christ's presence gives the Church the *fullness* of the means of Salvation: a complete and correct confession of faith, an ordained ministry that goes back to the Apostles, and a full sacramental life, especially the gift of the Eucharist.

2. The Church follows Jesus' command to go out to all nations, preaching to all people at all places in all times.

No matter who a person is, the Church invites everyone to become a member.

3. The Church teaches everything that Christ taught. Therefore, throughout her history, people from every geographic, ethnic, racial, and cultural group have professed the same faith and worshiped the same Lord.

4. Each local diocese, united under its bishop, is also catholic because of its union with the Holy Father in Rome. The worldwide Church shows her catholicity in many different cultures, liturgical rites, and spiritual disciplines and traditions.

Christ's presence in the Church guarantees that the Church will always be catholic. But Catholics must continue to preach the Gospel in all times and places for it to remain a universal Church. This means the Church, of its nature, is *missionary*. A missionary is one who is sent to accomplish a certain task. The task is Christ-given: to bring the Gospel in word and deed to all people. We do so best when we allow the love of Christ to shine through us, when we work and pray to restore Christian unity, and when we respectfully engage in dialogue with those who have not accepted Christ's Salvation.

Apostolic (*CCC*, 857–865; 869)

The Church is apostolic because she continues the faith of the Apostles, those Christ especially chose and sent forth to proclaim the Gospel to all people. The Church remains apostolic in three ways:

1. It is the Church that Christ founded on the Apostles.

2. With the guidance of the Holy Spirit, the Church continues to hand on the teaching of the Apostles, without changing anything essential through the ages.

For Enrichment

Individual Assignment: Have students research the life of a canonized saint in the Church. If their baptized name is a saint's name, have them research their patron saint. In their report, have the students list three characteristics that they consider to be particularly holy in their chosen person.

---

3. The Church continues to be taught, made holy, sanctified, and led by the College of Bishops, whom Christ appointed to be the successors of the Apostles. The Holy Father and the bishops can trace themselves in an unbroken line of succession to the Twelve Apostles.

By definition, an Apostle is an "ambassador," or "one who is sent." The Pope and bishops are sent to continue to preach, govern, and sanctify. But all members of Christ's body share in the *apostolate* of preaching and living Christ's Gospel. The success of our Christ-given mission depends on our wise use of the gifts and talents that the Holy Spirit has given to us. It also depends on our remaining close to the Lord by our participation in the Eucharist.

Apostle
One "sent" to be Christ's ambassador, to continue his work. In its widest sense, the term refers to all of Christ's disciples, whose mission is to preach his Gospel in word and deed. Originally, it referred to the Twelve whom Jesus chose to help him in his earthly ministry. The successors of the Twelve Apostles are the bishops.

PROFILE OF FAITH: ST. TERESA OF AVILA, BUILDER OF THE CHURCH

St. Teresa of Avila was a woman who made the most of her individual gifts to build up the Body of Christ. A woman of enormous intellectual ability, Teresa entered the Carmelite Incarnation convent in Avila, Spain, when she was twenty. At this time in Church history, convents were almost like finishing schools for young ladies, allowing a lot of freedom, for example, visiting, dancing, entertaining, wearing jewelry, and eating fine foods. At first, Teresa joined in the casual routine of her fellow nuns.

However, Teresa also prayed regularly and performed penance. Gradually, over the course of years, she deepened her spiritual life. She began to experience a close, mystical relationship with Jesus, one which gave her deep spiritual experiences. She developed an intimate friendship with the Lord. Later, she would teach that an excellent way to pray is to imagine talking to Jesus as to a close friend. Her familiarity with Jesus allowed her to scold him. One day, her cart turned over on the road while she was engaging in a good deed. She said to the Lord, "No wonder you have so few friends! Look how you treat them!"

Teresa's friendship with Jesus Christ moved her to reform her Carmelite order of nuns. She left her original convent and set up a reformed convent of thirteen nuns who wanted a simple, austere life. Eventually, her experiment was so successful that she traveled throughout Spain and set up scores of convents that adopted her strict rule. Her Discalced (shoeless) Carmelites lived an austere life of poverty, withdrawal from the world, and intense prayer. Eventually her reforms resulted in a separate order. Her good example encouraged a Carmelite priest, St. John of the Cross, to initiate similar reforms in his own order.

Teresa's profound writings on the spiritual life have been a major gift to the Church. Notable are her *Autobiography*; her *Way of Perfection*, which describes the Christian life; and her *Interior Castle*, which outlines the various steps involved in contemplative prayer.

St. Teresa of Avila is a Doctor of the Church. Read these famous words of St. Teresa:

You Are Christ's Hands

Christ has no body now on earth but yours,
no hands but yours, no feet but yours,
Yours are the eyes through which must look out
Christ's compassion on the world;
Yours are the feet with which he is to go about doing good;
Yours are the hands with which he is to bless men now.

Background Information

The Four Marks of the Church in the Catechism

The four marks of the Church are outlined in these paragraphs:

- One (813)
- Holy (823–824)
- Catholic (830–831)
- Apostolic (857)

Homework Assignment

1. Complete the For Review questions on page 116.

2. Read the text section "Ecumenism: The Church and Other Religions" (pages 117–120).

magazines with photos of people from around the world.

- **Class Discussion:** Share the three ways listed in the text (pages 114–115) that the Church remains apostolic. Point out that an Apostle's role is to be an ambassador of Christ to the world. Ask the students to consider how they can do this in their lives. Use the following exercises to help them imagine ways:

  ◆ Have them imagine that they have been given a formula for making a drug that arrests the development of HIV. They have been assigned to pass that information on to as many people as possible across the world. They are only allowed to have ten written copies of the formula, and cannot use any other means of communication other than demonstration and verbal explanation. How would they get the word out to as many people as possible, and still make sure that the formula was correct? If they were living in a remote country and were told about the formula, how would they verify that they had the correct information?

  ◆ Point out to students that the idea of apostolic succession is a similar way of verifying the accuracy of a message that was first given so many years ago. Remind them of the interdependence of the people out in the field, spreading the word, with those at the center of the network maintaining the accuracy of the information.

- **Journal Assignment:** Read the Profile of Faith feature on St. Teresa of Avila (pages 115–116). Write a journal entry in response to St. Teresa's advice on topics such as flexibility and self-criticism. Be specific in application of her advice. Facilitate a discussion on the reflections.

- **Prayer Experience:** Close the period with a prayer based on St. Teresa's reflection *You Are Christ's Hands*. Choose a piece of calming music to set the mood in the classroom. Have a student read St. Teresa's reflection, and then invite students to consider the ways in which they have had the opportunity to be Christ's presence over the last week. Conclude with something like the following:

  Loving God,

  You have given us the example of women and men like St. Teresa of Avila. Give us generous and open hearts to find your path for us. Help us be willing to see you in others and make you present to those around us. Thank you for the gift of this day and all the opportunities it holds for us.

  Amen.

For Review Answers (page 116)

1. The Church is one, holy, Catholic, and apostolic.

2. The visible bonds of unity; the ways in which we can see the unity within the Church; or the profession of common faith, worship celebrated in common, including the sacraments, and the succession of bishops from the time of the Apostles to today.

3. The Church is holy because of the means given her to bring members to holiness: Scripture, Church teaching, liturgy, prayer and sacraments, profession of faith, and ordained ministry. While the Church never achieves perfect holiness, both the call and the means are provided at all times.

4. The Church is catholic because it is universal. It is universal in its invitation to all people in all parts of the world, and it is catholic in the fullness of its teaching.

5. The Church is apostolic because it was founded by the Apostles of Jesus. We rely on their teaching to guide the Church in today's world.

On Self-Criticism:

Be kind to others, but severe on yourself.

On Flexibility:

Never be obstinate, especially in unimportant matters.

On Prayer:

All the beginner has to do . . . is to labor and be resolute and prepare himself with all possible diligence to bring his will into conformity with the will of God.

Don't imagine that if you had a great deal of time you would spend more of it in prayer. Get rid of that idea! Again and again God gives more in a moment than in a long period of time, for his actions are not measured by any time at all.

On Jesus:

If we never look at him or think of what we owe him and of the death which he suffered for our sakes, I do not see how we can get to know him or do good works in his service.

Write a one-page reflection essay about St. Teresa of Avila and her teaching.

For Review

1. Name the marks of the Church.
2. List the visible bonds of unity in the Church.
3. How is the Church *holy*?
4. In what sense is the Church *catholic*?
5. How is the Church *apostolic*?

For Reflection

Who is a model of holiness for you? Write a short profile of this person and how his or her life inspires you to be more Christlike in your own life.

Printed Materials continued from 109

Ratzinger, Joseph Cardinal. *Called to Communion: Understanding the Church Today*. San Francisco: Ignatius Press, 1996.

Smith, Huston. *The World's Religions*. San Francisco: HarperSanFrancisco, 1991.
A highly respected introduction to comparative religions.

Sullivan, S.J., Francis A. *Salvation Outside the Church: Tracing the History of the Catholic Response*. Wipf & Stock Publishers, 2002.
Extensive summary of the Church's tradition regarding the question of salvation outside the Church.

Sullivan, S.J., Francis A. *The Church We Believe In: One, Holy, Catholic, and Apostolic*. Mahwah, NJ: Paulist Press, 1999.

Tillard, J.M.R., O.P. *The Bishop of Rome*. Wilmington, DE: Michael Glazier, 1983.
Examines the role of the papacy in the Church.

Ecumenism: The Church and Other Religions

(CCC, 813–819; 866)

The true Church of Jesus Christ *subsists* in the Catholic Church. This means that in the Catholic Church can be found the *fullness* of the means of sanctification that Christ left with us. Also, in the Catholic Church (with the Orthodox Churches) is the apostolic succession traceable to St. Peter. The Pope is the symbol and servant of unity who provides leadership and direction when troublesome conflicts and disruptive differences arise in the Church.

Because of human sin, the Church historically has not always shown perfectly the various marks that set her off as Christ's Bride: one, holy, catholic, and apostolic. For example, a study of Christianity reveals that there is a lack of perfect unity in the Church, the unity Christ willed for it. The various Christian denominations resulted from *heresy*, that is, false teaching that denied essential truths of the Catholic faith; *apostasy*, that is, the denial of the faith; or *schism*, that is, a break in Church unity resulting from the failure to accept the Pope as the Vicar of Christ. Historically, there is enough blame to assign to all sides of the controversies that resulted in the various ruptures in Christ's Body. It is wrong to blame people living today for these divisions. Unity among Christians is rooted in Baptism, even among those who are not professed Catholics. As the fathers of the Second Vatican Council taught, "Justified by faith in Baptism, [they] are incorporated into Christ; they therefore have a right to be called Christians, and with good reason are accepted as brothers

by the children of the Catholic Church" (*Unitatis redintegratio*, 3).

Although we affirm that the Catholic Church possesses all the means of sanctification that Jesus Christ intended for us to have, there are also many means of holiness that can be found *outside* of the Catholic Church. These include:

1. Scripture, the written Word of God;
2. the life of grace;
3. faith, hope, and charity, and other gifts of the Holy Spirit.

In the words of the Second Vatican Council:

> The brethren divided from us also carry out many of the sacred actions of the Christian religion. . . . [T]hese actions can truly engender a life of grace. (*Decree on Ecumenism*, No. 3)

Role of Ecumenism

(CCC, 820–822)

Every Catholic is called to be involved in some way in the work of ecumenism, that is, the movement that works to restore the unity of Christ's Church.

ecumenism
The movement, inspired and led by the Holy Spirit, that seeks the union of all Christian religions and eventually the unity of all peoples throughout the world.

Background Information

Vatican II on the Church and Other Faiths

In the Second Vatican Council document *Unitatis Redintegratio (Decrees on Ecumenism),* the relationship between Catholics and other faiths is addressed:

> Even in the beginnings of this one and only Church of God there arose certain rifts, which the Apostle strongly condemned. But in subsequent centuries much more serious dissensions made their appearance and quite large communities came to be separated from full communion with the Catholic Church—for which, often enough, men of both sides were to blame. The children who are born into these communities and who grow up believing in Christ cannot be accused of the sin involved in the separation, and the Catholic Church embraces upon them as brothers, with respect and affection. For men who believe in Christ and have been truly baptized are in communion with the Catholic Church even though this communion is imperfect. The differences that exist in varying degrees between them and the Catholic Church—whether in doctrine and sometimes in discipline, or concerning the structure of the Church—do indeed create many obstacles, sometimes serious ones, to full ecclesiastical communion. The ecumenical movement is striving to overcome these obstacles. But even in spite of them it remains true that all who have been justified by faith in Baptism are members of Christ's body, and have a right to be called Christian, and so are correctly accepted as brothers by the children of the Catholic Church.

Ecumenism: The Church and Other Religions (pages 117–120)

Objectives

In this lesson, the students will:

- express a basic understanding of the relationships among various Christian and non-Christian groups.
- define ecumenism.
- identify the work of ecumenism today.

Preview

This section outlines the relationships among Catholics and other Christian and non-Christian faiths. It is an opportunity to reinforce for students the respect the Church holds for those of other faiths, and to strengthen a balanced perspective on the similarities and differences among believers. Students can be invited to become more aware of the diversity of religious beliefs in their community, and of the differences they are likely to encounter when they leave high school and move into a broader community.

Bell Ringers

- **Individual Assignment:** Administer Chapter 4, Handout 1 "The Church as Sacrament Pop Quiz" (starting on page 285 and also online at www.avemariapress.com), which highlights material in the chapter to this point. Collect and grade (answers are on page 120 of this text).
- **Class Discussion:** Through class sharing, check the answers to the For Review questions from page 116.
- **Class Activity:** Provide students with several copies of the Yellow Pages or other directory from your area. If you live in a small town, secure copies from a larger town if possible. Have students look through the category "Churches" to see the number and range of Christian churches present in your area. Point out to students that Jewish worshipping communities would be listed under "Synagogues" and other faiths might be listed under "Temples." Note if there are non-Christian listings under the listing for "Churches."

Teaching Approaches

- **Direct Instruction:** Put the term **ecumenism** on the board. After taking suggestions as to the meaning, write the definition as found on page 117: "the movement that works to restore the unity of Christ's Church."
- **Writing Assignment:** Next, write the following on the board: **Christian**, **Catholic**, **Muslim**, **Jewish**, **Orthodox**, **Protestant**, **Methodist**, **Lutheran**,

Non-denominational. Have students copy the terms in their notes, and then briefly write everything they know about each of these terms. Have them refer to their list as the lesson progresses, updating for accuracy.

- **Class Discussion:** Discuss the differences among the words heresy, apostasy, and schism with students. Have students also share what might be the actions of people engaged in heresy, apostasy, or schism on sports teams. The goal of the discussion is to make these terms concrete for students, so feel free to use other examples.

- **Class Discussion:** Continue the lesson based on the text subsection "Role of Ecumenism" (pages 117–118). Invite students to share their experiences with people of other denominations or faiths. If non-Catholic students are in your class and are comfortable, ask them to describe their worship experiences and the beliefs of their community.

- **Individual Activity:** Read or have the students read the commonalties between the Catholic Church and Protestant and Orthodox churches on page 118 of the subsection "The Church and Non-Catholic Christians: Protestant and Orthodox Churches" (page 118). Point out that the clearest element that Catholic, Protestant, and Orthodox churches share is belief in Jesus. Ask students to come up with a definition of what it means to be a Christian. Their definition should include trust in Jesus and attempting to live a life modeled in his life, as well as belief in certain principles about who Jesus is.

118   Our Catholic Faith

Great Schism
A major break between the churches of the West (centered in Rome) and the East (centered in the city of Constantinople). The Roman Church had added the expression "and the Son" to the article of the Nicene Creed referring to the Holy Spirit ("he proceeds from the Father and the Son") without seeking approval from a Church-wide council of bishops.

Protestant
A baptized Christian who believes in Christ but who does not accept all the teachings of the Catholic Church. Protestant communities first came into existence during the Reformation in the sixteenth century.

The Holy Spirit is working among all Christians today helping them to achieve a closer unity to our Lord and Savior. Catholics are invited as individuals and communities to join in ecumenical efforts. An important first step is to live a holy life of love as taught in the Gospels. Catholics can pray with our Christian brothers and sisters that the Holy Spirit may guide our efforts for Christian unity. Catholics can also study the truths of the Church so that they can share with others without prejudice or the negative judgment of others. In addition, Catholics can learn about other Christian denominations from personal research and talking with their members with the goal of promoting unity through increased understanding. Finally, working with other Christians in service and social justice projects can be a major step in furthering ecumenical understanding.

In recent history, Catholic and other Christian scholars have engaged in ecumenical dialogues at the highest levels. These efforts have fostered mutual understanding and produced common professions of faith. The Church is committed to continuing these dialogues.

The Church and Non-Catholic Christians: Protestant and Orthodox Churches

Protestant and Orthodox faith communities "have a certain, although imperfect communion" (*CCC*, 838) with the Catholic Church. We have much in common with them that is to be respected and praised, namely:

- faith in the Blessed Trinity;
- acceptance of the Bible;
- prayer and grace;
- the theological virtues of faith, hope, and love;
- the gifts of the Holy Spirit;
- the Sacrament of Baptism;
- a commitment to God's Kingdom and the desire to live a moral life.

The Catholic Church and the Orthodox churches have a deep communion. Our basic beliefs and traditions up to the Great Schism (1054) are the same. Catholics accept as valid all seven of their sacraments and recognize that they have a legitimate hierarchy and priesthood. Our major difference involves the role of the Pope, whom Orthodox Christians do not accept as having primacy over the whole Church. However, major ecumenical strides have been made in recent years.

The Catholic Church and Non-Christians (*CCC*, 836–845; 870)

Jesus Christ invites everyone to belong to the one, holy, catholic, and apostolic Church. Catholics, other Christians, and all people to whom God extends the gift of Salvation in different ways belong to or are ordered to the unity found in the Catholic Church. However, full membership in the Catholic Church belongs to:

those who, possessing Christ's Spirit, accept her entire system and all the means of Salvation given to her, and through union with her visible structure are joined to Christ, who rules her through the Supreme Pontiff and the bishops. This joining is effected by the bonds of professed faith, of the sacraments, of ecclesiastical government, and of communion. (*Dogmatic Constitution on the Church*, No. 14)

However, even baptized Catholics are not *guaranteed* Salvation. Catholics must live loving, Christlike lives to

---

Chapter 4, Handout 1 "The Church as Sacrament Pop Quiz" Answers

Matching

1. G
2. H
3. D
4. B
5. A
6. C
7. F
8. E

Short Essay

9. The four marks of the Church are one, holy, catholic, and apostolic. Explanations should reflect text material on pages 113–115.

10. The hierarchy is the order of ministry established by Jesus Christ on the Apostles and their successors. The laity includes any baptized Catholics who have not received Holy Orders and do not belong to a Church-approved religious state. Those in *consecrated* or *religious life* can be members of the hierarchy or lay people and include hermits, consecrated virgins, secular institutes, different apostolic societies, and men (brothers) and women (sisters) in religious orders. See pages 106–107 for more explanation.

11. Protestant and Orthodox faith communities "have a certain, although imperfect union" with the Catholic Church. We have much in common with them that is to be respected and praised, namely, faith in the Blessed Trinity; acceptance of the Bible; prayer and grace; the theological virtues of faith, hope, and love; the gifts of the Holy Spirit; the Sacrament of Baptism; and a commitment to God's Kingdom and the desire to live a moral life.

12. The Greek word for mystery translates to the Latin term *sacramentum*. The term *sacrament* refers to a special kind of sign or symbol.

120   OUR CATHOLIC FAITH **TEACHER'S WRAPAROUND EDITION**

be members of Christ's Church, not only in body, but in heart and soul as well.

For its part, the Church finds much to admire in other religions, finding in them elements of holiness and truth. For example, the Catholic Church esteems the Jewish faith as the spiritual parent of Christianity (see page 63). And the Islamic faith is monotheistic, honors Jesus as a great prophet, and recognizes Mary, his mother (see page 63).

There are many other non-Christian religions, including Hinduism and Buddhism. God's grace extends to all people since God made everyone and destined all for eternal life with the Blessed Trinity. Therefore, the Church accepts whatever is true and holy in each person. The Church

> looks with sincere respect upon those ways of conduct and life, those rules and teachings which, though differing in many particulars from what she holds and sets forth, nevertheless often reflect a ray of that Truth which enlightens all men. (*Declaration on the Relationship of the Church to Non-Christian Religions*, No. 2)

The Church respects nonbelievers since they too are made in God's image and likeness. In a way known to God alone, he offers his grace to them.

A traditional image of the Church is that of an ark, a seaworthy vessel. Christ, the captain of the ship, and the Holy Spirit, who provides the friendly breezes, help us navigate the rough seas that we encounter on our earthly pilgrimage on the way to our eternal destiny. The Church must respectfully listen to and learn from people of other faiths. However, Christ has sent us on a mission to proclaim in deed and word his Gospel to a world that seeks the meaning of life. If we do so faithfully and with loving hearts, the members of Christ's Body can help all God's children see the truth and goodness that God has placed in their hearts. It can help lead them to the greatest adventure of all: eternal happiness with our loving God, won for us by our Lord and Savior, Christ Jesus.

For Review

1. What was the Great Schism?
2. Define *ecumenism*. What part can individual Catholics play in the ecumenical effort?
3. What does the Church teach about Protestant and Orthodox Christians?
4. What does the Church teach about non-Christian religions?
5. Is it possible for a nonbeliever to be saved? Explain your answer.

For Reflection

The following sign was seen in front of a parish church building: *"You are not too bad to come in, and not too good to stay out."* Compose your own "catchy" sign inviting passersby to attend Mass in your parish community.

Homework Assignment

1. Complete the Ongoing Assignments and be prepared to share them at the next session.
2. Read the Chapter Quick View on pages 120–121.

Extending the Lesson

Individual Assignment: Have students visit the website www.seedsof peace.org. This is an organization that sponsors summer camps for young Palestinians and Israelis to spend time together in Maine, learning about one another's worlds and finding ground to build partnerships. While not specifically ecumenical, this is an excellent example of bridge-building efforts such as those listed on pages 117–119 of the text. Stories and photos from this site can bring the process of learning about and partnering with people of different backgrounds to life.

Video Presentation: Play a clip from the movie *Malcolm X* (popular release) that depicts Malcolm's pilgrimage to Mecca and offers both beautiful photography and a voice-over explaining the impact of Islam on Malcolm X's life.

- **Direct Instruction:** Explain the difference between *faith* and *denomination* to students. Judaism and Islam are faiths or religions different from Christianity; while all three believe in one Creator God, the differences in belief are so substantial that they are referred to as separate faiths. Denomination refers to a subgroup that shares many core beliefs with others within that group. Baptist, Lutheran, and Methodist are examples of different Christian denominations.

- **Class Discussion:** Refer to the text subsection "The Catholic Church and Non-Christians" (pages 118–119). Ask students to list what aspects of Catholicism are important to drawing closer to God but not available to non-Christians. Examples are the sacraments and the life and teaching of Jesus. Ask students to brainstorm ways in which people of other faiths are taught about God and the ways God wants us to live our lives.

- **Class Discussion:** Refer to the Explaining Your Faith feature on page 111 titled "Can non-Catholics get to Heaven?" Have students outline the response to the question as it is presented in the text. Using their responses, create a class outline of the response on the board and discuss the Church's answer.

  - Students can be aided in grasping this concept by drawing on the analogy of medical or nutritional guidelines. In order for humans to sustain life, we need to eat foods that sustain our bodies and receive proper medical care when we are injured or ill. Many people do not know the principles of sound nutrition, or live in places where they do not have knowledge of medical practices. Those people can live good and loving lives, but they will not be able to have the fullness of experience or length of life that would be available to them under other circumstances. This fact is not a judgment on their intelligence or moral character; they simply do not have access to the best resources. Similarly, people who have not heard of Jesus in an effective way are cut off from the knowledge and strength that come from a relationship with Jesus. God continues to sustain them, but their lives are lacking in some important ways. It is not judgmental to recognize what other people may be missing, just as it is not judgmental to recognize that some people do not have access to proper information and resources for caring for their bodies.

  - *Note:* This topic holds the potential for hurt among students, particularly those who are not Catholic or who have loved ones who are not Catholic. It is important to be particularly alert to comments or body language in the classroom that might be disrespectful to students who either affirm or disagree with this teaching.

For Review Answers (page 119)

1. The Great Schism occurred in 1054, and was a split between the Eastern and Western portions of the Church. The Orthodox Churches of the East hold the same core teachings, apostolic succession, worship, and sacraments as the Roman Catholic Church.

2. Ecumenism is the work of bringing Christian Churches back into unity with one another. Catholics can be active in this work by learning more about Catholic and non-Catholic teachings, and by building individual and community relationships between Catholics and non-Catholics.

3. The Church affirms the common beliefs held by all Christians, such as faith in the Blessed Trinity, the Scriptures, prayer and grace, the Sacrament of Baptism, and gifts and virtues. At the same time, the Church recognizes the important differences in beliefs among Christian churches.

4. The Church recognizes the ways in which people of non-Christian religions pursue holiness and truth. The Church also affirms the dignity of all persons. At the same time, the Church affirms the important truths that are not accepted by non-Christians, such as the divinity and message of Jesus and the authoritative teaching of the Church.

5. God extends love and grace to all people. The Church teaches that anyone who, through no fault of their own, has not heard the message of Jesus, and who responds to God's grace by living life according to their conscience, will be welcomed into Heaven.

Chapter 4 Review Lesson

Objectives

In this lesson, the students will be able to:
- summarize the work they did on the Ongoing Assignments.
- prepare for the Chapter 4 Test.

 Preview

Allow some time at the beginning of the class period for the students to share or display work they have done on any of the Ongoing Assignments. Save a bit more time for a summary of the group activity. The students should also write answers to the Learning the Language of Faith questions and then share their answers with others in the class.

 Explaining Your Faith

How can we be sure that the teachings of the Church actually come from God and are not made up by our leaders?

Before ascending into Heaven, Jesus himself promised his Apostles that he would remain with his Church until the end of time. Christ also gave the Church a share in his own infallibility, preserved in the Magisterium. The Church's Sacred Tradition assures us that the doctrines of the Church come from God. Christ entrusted his teachings to St. Peter and the Apostles. They then passed on those beliefs through those that came after them. Down through the centuries, it was the Pope and bishops, that is, the successors of St. Peter and the Apostles, who carefully transmitted the truths that Christ taught for our Salvation. The *Catechism of the Catholic Church* assures us:

The mission of the Magisterium is linked to the definitive nature of the covenant established by God with his people in Christ. It is this Magisterium's task to preserve God's people from deviations and defections and to guarantee them the objective possibility of professing the true faith without error. Thus, the pastoral duty of the Magisterium is aimed at seeing to it that the People of God abide in the truth that liberates. To fulfill this service, Christ endowed the Church's shepherds with the charism of infallibility in matters of faith and morals. (*CCC*, 890)

CHAPTER QUICK VIEW

- The Church is a mystery of God's love that the Blessed Trinity uses as a means and goal in the plan of Salvation. (pages 99–100)
- Jesus is the first sacrament of God's love, the visible image of God, who *is* God. The resurrected Lord lives on in the Church to continue his work of Salvation. It is correct to call the Church a sacrament, a special sign that points to and brings about our union with God, through Jesus Christ, in the Holy Spirit. (pages 100–101)
- Scripture gives us many images of the Church including these: People of God, Body of Christ, Bride of Christ, and the Temple of the Holy Spirit. (pages 100–105)
- All members of the Church—hierarchy, laity, and those in consecrated life—share in Christ's prophetic, priestly, and kingly ministries. (pages 106–111)
- Christ established a special role in the Church for the hierarchy, those in Holy Orders. He endows this sacred leadership with the offices of teaching, sanctifying, and governing the Church. He also blesses the Church with the gift of infallibility, which safeguards the truth when the Pope and bishops united to him, teach in matters of faith and morals. Catholics owe the obedience of faith to the infallible teachings of the Magisterium. (pages 108–110)
- The four marks of the Church—one, holy, catholic, and apostolic—help us recognize its nature and attract nonbelievers to it. (page 112)

For Enrichment

Journal Assignment: There is a tradition within Judaism called "The 100 Blessings." A common beginning to Jewish prayers is, "Blessed are You, O Lord our God, King of the Universe." This prayer is a litany, which begins with this phrase and then lists a blessing bestowed by God. Have students write this phrase in their journals, and then list fifty blessings they have received.

 Homework Assignment

1. Complete all of the For Review questions on page 119.
2. Study for the Chapter 4 Test.

- God wills the Salvation of everyone and invites everyone to belong to the one, Catholic Church. Rejecting the truth of the Church would be seriously wrong for a person who knows that Christ intended the Church as the sacrament of Salvation. The true Church of Jesus Christ "subsists" in the Catholic Church, governed by the Pope and bishops in union with him. (page 117)
- In cooperation with the Holy Spirit, ecumenism works for unity among Christians. A spirit of repentance and self-renewal, prayer, study, communication, and shared service help foster Christian unity. (pages 117–118)
- Out of respect, the Catholic Church acknowledges what is good, holy, and true in other religions. However, blessed with the Gospel of Salvation, the Church must continue its missionary role of proclaiming the Good News of Jesus Christ to nonbelievers. (pages 118–119)

Learning the Language of Faith

Test your knowledge of important terms that you have learned in this chapter and previous chapters. Write your answers to the following questions.

1. Explain the connection between being an apostle and the task of evangelization.
2. What is the Great Schism?
3. How does the Holy Father exercise the charism of infallibility?
4. What is the relationship between the hierarchy and the Magisterium?
5. Name two things you can do to further the cause of ecumenism.
6. What are the evangelical counsels? Who professes them?
7. Who belongs to the Catholic Church?
8. What is another name for Church law?
9. What are the four marks of the Church? Briefly explain the meaning of each.
10. Explain how the word *sacrament* can be applied to both Jesus Christ and his Church.

Ongoing Assignments

As you cover the material in this chapter, choose and complete at least three of these assignments.

1. In today's world, on which issues should the Church take a prophetic stand? Name the issue and a focused plan for what you think the Church should do.
2. Use any art medium to create a new, modern image of the Church. Be sure to include both a divine and human dimension in this image.
3. Research the mission of a Church-sponsored organization (for example, school, hospital) and how it fulfills it. Interview the director of this organization or invite a representative to speak to your class.
4. Read and report on Chapter 2 of the *Dogmatic Constitution on the Church*. You can find this document using its Latin title, *Lumen Gentium*, online at www.rc.net/rcChurch/vatican2/lumen.gen. This chapter takes up the theme of the Church as the People of God.
5. Jesus reminded his disciples that they are the light of the world and the salt of the earth. Christians should make a difference. With other students in your class, devise a small service project. Here are some examples:
   - Collect food for the needy.
   - Begin a tutoring program for younger students.
   - Help elderly people with household chores in your neighborhood.
   - Volunteer to help organize receptions to celebrate sacramental celebrations in your parish.
   - Participate in a pro-life awareness day.
   - Visit shut-ins or those in nursing homes.

 Bell Ringers

- **Student Presentations:** Call the small groups that worked together on Ongoing Assignment 5 to come before the class one at a time to share their experience serving others. Focus the presentations in each of the following areas:
  - the preparation the project entailed
  - rewarding and challenging experiences from the event itself
  - most interesting or unusual memory of the event
  - ideas for participating in this service area in the future

  Encourage more than one person from each group to speak about their experiences.

- **Student Presentations:** Continue with a focus on having the students display or share any of the other Ongoing Assignments they worked on. Consider the following procedures for each project:
  - Call on students to share the key issue they perceive the Church should take a prophetic stand on and one idea for what the Church and people their own age can do.
  - Display the modern images of the Church in the classroom or in a display case elsewhere in the school.
  - If there is time for the director of a Church-sponsored organization to speak to the class in this period, reserve at least ten minutes. If not, consider keeping it until the end of the testing session or for one of the opening sessions of Chapter 5.
  - Collect and grade the report.

Learning the Language of Faith Answers (page 121)

1. *Apostle* means "one sent" and refers to the people that Jesus chose to continue his work. These people and their successors, the bishops, continue the work of *evangelization* by spreading the Good News and bringing Christ into the world.
2. The *Great Schism* was a major break within the Catholic Church between the West (Rome) and East (Constantinople) over the phrase "and the Son" in the Nicene Creed.
3. The Holy Father exercises the charism of *infallibility* when speaking *ex cathedra*, or as the pastor of all the faithful, when proclaiming a definitive doctrine pertaining to faith or morals, and when he intends to use his full authority to make an unchangeable decision.
4. The term *hierarchy* refers to any ordained leader within the Church and includes the *Magisterium*, the teaching office of the Church made up of the Pope and the College of Bishops.
5. Answers will vary, but may include attending non-Catholic worship services in addition to the weekly attendance of Catholic Mass, inviting others to attend Mass, and researching and participating in national ecumenical movements.
6. The *evangelical counsels* are the vows of poverty, chastity, and obedience taken by those participating in consecrated life.
7. The Catholic Church is made up of baptized individuals who participate as members of the hierarchy, laity, or vowed religious.
8. Church law is called *canon law*.
9. The Church is one (united in profession of faith, worship, and leadership), holy (containing the fullness of the means of salvation), catholic (universal or open to all nations and cultures), and apostolic (founded on the Apostles and their successors and led by the Holy Spirit).
10. *Sacraments* are visible and efficacious signs of invisible grace. Jesus Christ is the prime sacrament in that he is God, whom he represents. Similarly, the Church is the presence of Christ on earth and a symbol of the unity of the Blessed Trinity.

Teaching Approaches

- **Direct Instruction:** Read and review the Chapter Quick View on pages 120–121.
- **Group Activity:** Have the students work in pairs to complete the Learning the Language of Faith questions on page 121. Allow time for the students to share their answers with each other. Make sure each student records all of the answers to use for study.
- **Class Discussion:** Challenge the students to think critically about what they learned about the Church in this chapter. Discuss the ways that the Church is set apart or "called out" of the world. How is it different from teams, clubs, or other communities? What do the images of the Church reveal about the mystery of the Church?

Chapter 4 Test Lesson

Objectives

In this lesson, the students will:
- be tested on the material in Chapter 4.
- complete a written and meditative Prayer Reflection.
- preview the material in Chapter 5.

Preview

Allow plenty of time for the students to complete the Chapter 4 Test (starting on page 285 and also online at www.avemariapress.com). At the end of the test, as the students finish, have them read the Prayer Reflection and answer in writing the three questions that follow.

Teaching Approaches

- **Chapter Test:** Distribute the Chapter 4 Tests. Instruct the students to work alone and to turn in completed tests as they finish.
- **Journal Assignment:** Before the students begin, tell them that when they have finished the test they are to read the Prayer Reflection on page 122 and complete in writing the two questions that follow in their journals.
- **Prayer Experience:** Recite together with the class the Prayer for Guidance by St. Teresa of Avila on page 122. Have the students reflect individually on what to do for another person in Christ's name.

6. Prepare a report on a topic of interest:
   - Write a profile of an important event or interesting person from your diocese.
   - Do a biographical sketch of one of the Church's current cardinals.
   - Write a report on the history of the Vatican.
   - Read and report on one of Pope John Paul II's or Pope Benedict XVI's World Youth Day speeches.
   - Write a profile of Catholic youth in America today.
   - Report on a current news event that involves the Church on a continent other than North America.
7. Attend Mass at two different parish churches in your diocese other than your own home parish. Report on your experience of the liturgy. Obtain copies of the parish bulletin and report on something interesting happening in each parish.
8. Prepare a PowerPoint presentation on how St. Paul has been presented in art. Consult the following web page: www.jesuswalk.com/philippians/artwork-st-paul.htm.
9. View the classic film *Chariots of Fire*. Report on how Eric Liddell, a 1924 Olympic runner from Scotland, lives the theme of St. Paul about "running the race" of faith. The film is a good commentary on Galatians 2:20: "I live, no longer I, but Christ lives in me; insofar as I now live in the flesh, I live by faith in the Son of God who has loved me and given himself up for me."
10. Report on a Catholic martyr of the twentieth or twenty-first century.
11. Do a short report on one of the following Protestant denominations: Lutherans, Presbyterians, or Methodists. Construct a list of beliefs Catholics share in common with the denomination. Make another list to indicate differences.

Prayer Reflection

St. Teresa of Avila's Prayer for Guidance
Lord, grant that I may always allow myself to be guided by You,
always follow Your plans,
and perfectly accomplish Your Holy Will.
Grant that in all things,
great and small, today and all the days of my life,
I may do whatever You require of me.
Help me respond to the slightest prompting of Your Grace,
so that I may be Your trustworthy instrument for Your honor.
May Your Will be done in time and in eternity—
by me, in me, and through me. Amen.

- *Reflection*: How important is God in *your* life? What do St. Teresa's words mean to you?
- *Resolution*: Seek out God's will for your life. Act on what you discover.

Homework Assignment

1. Preview Chapter 5.
2. Read the opening text section of Chapter 5, "Eternal Destiny" (pages 126–127).
3. Examine the Ongoing Assignments on pages 150–151.

Chapter 4 Test Answers

Part 1: Matching (4 points each)

1. B

2. C

3. A

4. D

Part 2: Multiple Choice (4 points each)

5. E

6. C

7. D

8. A

9. E

10. A

11. D

12. A

Part 3: True/False (4 points each)

13. F

14. T

15. T

16. F

17. T

18. F

Part 4: Fill-ins (4 points each)

19. evangelical counsels

20. "one sent"

21. canon law

22. hierarchy

Part 5: Short Answer (4 points each)

23. a major break in the unity of the Church between the East (centered in Constantinople) and the West (centered in Rome)

Part 6: Short Essay (8 points are possible)

24. The Catholic Church is different from other communities, clubs, or teams in that it is an assembly of people "called out" and together representing the greater mystery of salvation and unity with God. It is the People of God, called to bring Good News to the World. It is the Body of Christ, diverse yet unified and representative of Christ in the world. It is the Temple of the Holy Spirit, led by God and made holy by the Holy Spirit. Unlike other denominations and faiths, the Catholic Church includes the fullness of the means to salvation, particularly in the apostolic leadership and the sacraments.

5 Communion of Saints, Forgiveness of Sins, **Eternal Life**

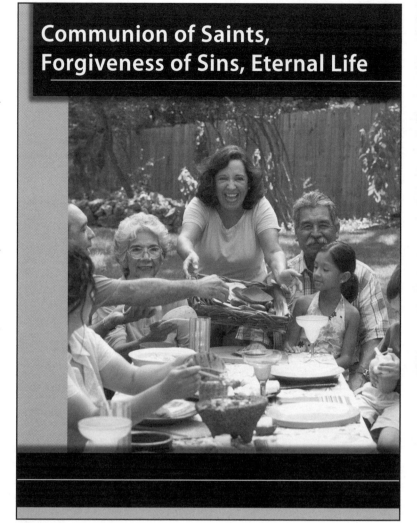

Communion of Saints, Forgiveness of Sins, Eternal Life

Overview of the Chapter

An old tombstone bears this epitaph:

> Pause, Stranger, when you pass me by,
> As you are now, so once was I.
> As I am now, so you will be,
> So prepare for death and follow me.

Someone who read these words inscribed this reply below them:

> To follow you I'm not content,
> Until I know which way you went.

The unknown observer had it right. Death sums up our lives and asks: "Where have you been? Where are you going?"

Chapter 5 takes up the final articles of the Apostles' Creed, topics like the Communion of Saints, the Blessed Mother as the greatest of the saints, forgiveness of sin, and topics in eschatology. These are all interrelated. The chapter begins with the doctrine of the Communion of Saints, which includes our unity in holy things and the unity among holy persons—the pilgrim Church, the Church suffering, and the Church triumphant. Ours is a spiritual family united in the Spirit of Jesus Christ. In this family those who have attained the prize of Heaven pray for us, and we on earth continue to remember those in Purgatory. Devotion to the saints—especially imitating their virtues and praying to them to intercede for us—is a distinctive characteristic of Catholic faith. (An exercise is included on patron saints and students are directed to research the life of a favorite saint.) St. Francis de Sales advised that we make friends with the saints, using words of praise and tenderness in our prayers so they will be with us as we leave this life and enter eternity.

This is, in fact, what we pray for when we pray the Hail Mary. We beseech our Blessed Mother, the greatest of the saints and the Christian par excellence, to pray for us and to be at our side at the hour of our death, just as she stood under the Cross, faithful to her Son to the end. The chapter highlights Mary by discussing her special role in salvation history and by examining Church dogmas about her, including her Immaculate Conception, the virginal conception of Jesus, her titles of Mother of God and Mother of the Church, and her Assumption into Heaven. Special devotions to Mary are reviewed, especially the Rosary, which serves as the Prayer Reflection at the end of the chapter.

The next section of the chapter reviews the Creed's teaching about one baptism for the forgiveness of sin, distinguishes between Original Sin and actual sin that can be either mortal or venial, and lists the capital sins (vices). It also sets forth Church teaching on the necessity of confessing post-baptismal mortal sin in the Sacrament of Penance.

To die separated from God is the greatest consequence of mortal sin and affects our eternal destiny. The chapter's last section explains Catholic belief about the "last things," namely, death, a profound mystery; the resurrection of the body; the particular judgment; Heaven, Hell, and Purgatory; and the last or general judgment. These are important topics that interest students greatly. The *Catechism of the Catholic Church* tells us:

> The Christian Creed—the profession of our faith in God, the Father, the Son, and the Holy Spirit, and in God's creative, saving, and sanctifying action—culminates in the proclamation of the resurrection of the dead on the last day and in life everlasting. (988)

An important point to make while teaching this material is that our judgment takes place right now. As catechists, we must help our students see that what we do has significant, eternal meaning. For example, our acts of Christian love help form us into Christ's image, making us recognizable to the Lord as one of his own. Acts of self-denial for others help determine our eternal destiny. Of course, this theme of love for others is countercultural in a society that glorifies instant gratification.

Chapter 5 concludes the study of the Apostles' Creed. It is appropriate to end this section of the text by explaining the meaning of the word *Amen*—"so be it, I agree, certainly, it is firm."

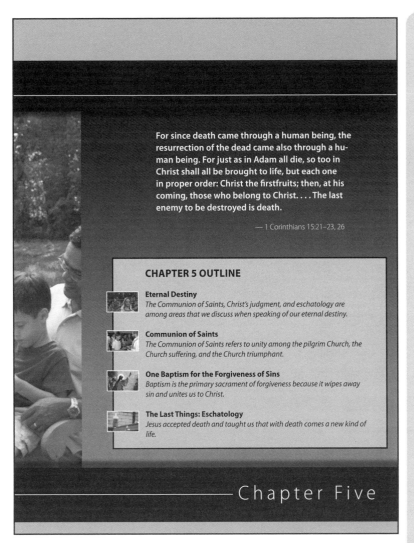

For since death came through a human being, the resurrection of the dead came also through a human being. For just as in Adam all die, so too in Christ shall all be brought to life, but each one in proper order: Christ the firstfruits; then, at his coming, those who belong to Christ. . . . The last enemy to be destroyed is death.

— 1 Corinthians 15:21–23, 26

CHAPTER 5 OUTLINE

Eternal Destiny
The Communion of Saints, Christ's judgment, and eschatology are among areas that we discuss when speaking of our eternal destiny.

Communion of Saints
The Communion of Saints refers to unity among the pilgrim Church, the Church suffering, and the Church triumphant.

One Baptism for the Forgiveness of Sins
Baptism is the primary sacrament of forgiveness because it wipes away sin and unites us to Christ.

The Last Things: Eschatology
Jesus accepted death and taught us that with death comes a new kind of life.

— Chapter Five

Resources

Audiovisual Materials

The Bucket List
Comedy starring Morgan Freeman and Jack Nicholson about two terminally ill men who meet in a hospital and decide to create and complete a list of things to do before they die (97-minute DVD video, Amazon.com).

Damien
Winner of the Peabody Award, this film tells the story of the saintly Fr. Damien, the Leper priest of Molokai (90-minute VHS video, Ignatius Press).

Don Bosco
Starring Ben Gazzara, this film tells the story of this popular saint who went into the streets to rescue children. Heart-warming life of a saint with a wonderful sense of humor (113-minute VHS video, Ignatius Press).

The Gift of Hope: The Tony Melendez Story
An inspiring story about Tony Melendez, who was born without arms because his mother was prescribed thalidomide. Tony sings and plays guitar with his feet. After playing for the Pope, his uplifting life of a modern-day hero became known worldwide (42-minute video, Ignatius Press, Amazon.com).

Heaven & Hell
Subtitled "Biblical Images of the Afterlife," the video uses dramatic recreations, art of the masters, and computer graphics to depict Heaven and Hell (60-minute video, Questar).

continued on page 141

Chapter Outline

- Eternal Destiny
- Communion of Saints
- One Baptism for the Forgiveness of Sins
- The Last Things: Eschatology

Advance Preparations

Assign the Ongoing Assignments early in the chapter to allow the students enough time to complete their work.

Eternal Destiny (ST pages 126–127)
- A clip from the movie *The Bucket List* for the Video Presentation on page 128.

Communion of Saints (ST pages 127–134)
- Images of the saints, as detailed in the Preview on page 129.
- A small votive candle for the Prayer Experience on page 132.
- Copies of Chapter 5, Handout 1 "Marian Doctrine" (starting on page 285 and also online at www.avemariapress.com) for the Class Assignment on page 133.
- Copies of Chapter 5, Handout 2 "Litany of the Blessed Virgin Mary" (starting on page 285 and also online at www.avemariapress.com) for the Prayer Experience on page 134.
- Copies of Chapter 5, Handout 3 "Your Patron Saints" (starting on page 285 and also online at www.avemariapress.com) for the Individual Assignment on page 130.
- Copies of Chapter 5, Handout 2 "Litany of the Blessed Virgin Mary" (starting on page 285 and also online at www.avemariapress.com) for the Individual Assignment on page 131.

One Baptism for the Forgiveness of Sins (ST pages 134–138)
- Copies of Chapter 5, Handout 4 "The Good News of God's Forgiveness" (starting on page 285 and also online at www.avemariapress.com) for the Writing Assignment on page 136.
- The same muddied mirror from the Chapter 1 Class Activity on page 33, for the Direct Instruction on page 137.
- One of the suggested videos from the resource list on page 127 for the Video Presentation on page 139.

The Last Things: Eschatology (ST pages 139–148)
- An image of the Last Judgment by Michelangelo on the wall of the Sistine Chapel for the Class Discussion on page 142.
- Copies of Chapter 5, Handout 5 "Seven-Day Calendar" (starting on page 285 and also online at www.avemariapress.com) for the Individual Activity on page 143.
- Blank index cards for the Class Activity on page 146.

- Clips of the movie series *Left Behind* or copies of the novels for the Direct Instruction on page 148.
- Arrange for a trained bereavement minister for the Guest Speaker activity on page 143.
- Seeds, cups, soil, and a full-grown plant for the Direct Instruction on page 144.

Chapter 5 Review Lesson
- Copies of Chapter 5, Handout 6 "Word Search" (starting on page 285 and also online at www .avemariapress.com) for the Individual Assignment on page 152.
- Copies of Chapter 5, Handout 7 "Chapter Quick View Review" (starting on page 285 and also online at www.avemariapress.com) for the Class Activity on page 152.

Chapter 5 Test Lesson
- Copies of the Chapter 5 Test (starting on page 285 and also online at www.avemariapress.com)

Eternal Destiny (pages 126–127)

Objectives

In this lesson, the students will:
- reflect on their life goals and what they would like their last words to be.
- make predictions about the meaning of the topics of this chapter: death, Heaven and Hell, Mary and the Communion of the Saints, and our final judgment.

Preview

Death and dying are difficult subjects to discuss, particularly for students who have recently lost a family member or close friend. Be sure you are aware of any such losses among your students and are sensitive to those students' reactions to the subject matter.

Bell Ringer

- **Journal Assignment:** Write the following Journal Assignment on the board for students to work on as they arrive: **"The five most important things I want to accomplish with my life are . . ."**
- **Class Discussion:** Ask volunteers to share some of their life goals. If necessary, share some of your own to get the conversation started. Use this discussion to introduce the chapter topics, and what should be each student's most important goal, getting to Heaven. Ask the students if they think the goals they have written help them get to Heaven. Ask students to share ways they might adapt some of their goals to redirect themselves toward Heaven.

Eternal Destiny

In the Hail Mary, we ask the Blessed Mother to pray for us always and, in a special way, at the time of our death:

Holy Mary,
Mother of God,
pray for us sinners now,
and at the hour of death.
Amen.

It is a great blessing that we have the Mother of God to intercede for us at the critical time of our last moments on earth. It is the hope of every Christian to die in the friendship of Christ like those saints reported by Paul Thigpen in his book *Last Words: Final Thoughts of Catholic Saints and Sinners*. For example, the following saints died with these words on their lips:

- St. Joseph of Cupertino (1603–1665), a Franciscan friar and mystic, died saying, "Praised be God! Blessed be God! May the holy will of God be done!"
- St. Teresa Benedicta of the Cross (1891–1942), a Jewish convert, a renowned philosopher who became a Carmelite nun, wrote a short note to her sisters while awaiting death at the Nazi death camp in Auschwitz: "I am content about everything. . . . *Ave crux, spes unica.* [Hail to the cross, our only hope.]"

- St. Francis Borgia (1510–1512), a Spanish courtier who became father general of the Society of Jesus, when asked on his deathbed if he wanted anything, responded, "I want nothing but Jesus."
- St. Catherine of Siena (1347–1380), a great saint, mystic, and Doctor of the Church, after receiving the last anointing, repeatedly said, "I have sinned, O Lord; have mercy upon me! Holy God, have mercy upon me!"
- St. John Bosco (1815–1888), who founded religious orders to care for poor and neglected boys and girls, shouted encouragement to his boys at the end of his prolonged illness: "Pray! Pray, but with faith—with living faith! Courage, courage! Onward, ever onward!"
- Bl. Miguel Pro (1891–1927) was a Mexican priest who was arrested and martyred by staunchly anti-Catholic government officials. Facing the firing squad, he had a crucifix in one hand and a rosary in the other. He stretched out his hands like Christ's on the cross, and declared: "*Viva Cristo Rey!*" "Long live Christ the King!"
- Bl. Elizabeth of the Trinity (1880–1906), a French Carmelite nun and spiritual writer, just moments before she died, said, "I am going to Light, to Love, to Life!"[11]

These last quotations of the saints remind us that the single most important goal in life here on earth is to get

Homework Assignment

Read the text section "Communion of Saints" (pages 127–134).

For Enrichment

Video Presentation: Show the students an excerpt from the movie *Bucket List* with Morgan Freeman and Jack Nicholson. Have students consider adapting their life goals to create a "bucket list" themselves to do at sometime in their future.

to Heaven. Thanks to Jesus and the Salvation he has won for us and to the grace of the Holy Spirit, this is a reachable goal for us. This chapter examines three topics related to our eternal destiny:

- The doctrine of the Communion of Saints will be explored, including what the Church teaches about Mary, the Queen of Saints and the Mother of God.
- This chapter also addresses Christ's judgment at the end of time and its

relationship with the doctrine of the forgiveness of sins.

- Finally, topics that deal with eschatology, a Greek word that means "study of the last things," will be covered. The area of eschatology includes death; judgment (both particular and general); Christ's Second Coming; Heaven, Hell, and Purgatory; and the resurrection of the body and eternal life.

Communion of Saints
The unity in Christ of all those he has redeemed—the Church on earth, in Heaven , and in Purgatory.

eschatology
A study of and teaching about the "last things" (death, judgment, Heaven , Hell, Purgatory, the Second Coming of Christ, and the resurrection of the body).

Heaven
Perfect life of supreme happiness with God and the Communion of Saints for all eternity.

For Reflection

- What would you like your last words on earth to be?
- If you were to die soon, what three things of value that you have accomplished so far would you like to present to Jesus when you meet him in eternity?
- What words to describe your life would you like to be engraved on your tombstone?

Communion of Saints (CCC, 946–962)

Think about how you feel just after you have eaten a good meal. The food was delicious and you didn't overeat. Likely, your whole body is satisfied. Conversely, think of how miserable you feel when you have a bad toothache. Your whole body seems in pain due only to one small tooth. It is like this with Christ's Body, the Church. Jesus is the head, and we are the members. When something good happens to one member, it is communicated and shared with the others. You may have experienced this in your own family. If your parent or sibling is rewarded for something they did, the whole family shares in the glory. In God's family, each person also shares in the spiritual benefits of the other members. How true this is especially with Christ. He freely shares

his goodness and graces with each person.

These ideas form the basis of the doctrine of the Communion of Saints, that is, unity in holy things and unity among holy persons.

Members of the Church share many "holy things" in common:

- the Catholic faith;
- the graces of the sacraments, especially the Eucharist also known as *Holy Communion*;
- the spiritual benefits that come from the special gifts (charisms) the Holy Spirit has given to us;
- material goods shared among all people and especially poor people in our midst;

Resources

 Printed Materials

Bauer, Judith A., ed. *The Essential Mary Handbook: A Summary of Beliefs, Practices, and Prayers.* Liguori, MO: Liguori Publications, 1999.

Blancy, Alain, Maurice Jorjon, and Dombes Group. *Mary in the Plan of God and in the Communion of Saints: Toward a Common Christian Understanding.* Foreword by Joseph Fitzmyer, S.J. Mahwah, NJ: Paulist Press, 2002.

Borchard, Therese Johnson. *Our Blessed Mother: Mary in Catholic Tradition.* New York: Crossroad/Herder and Herder, 2000.

Bunson, Matthew, Bunson, Margaret, Bunson, Stephen, and Dolan, Timothy. *Our Sunday Visitor's Encyclopedia of Saints.* Huntington, IN: Our Sunday Visitor, 2003.

Cantalamessa, Raniero. *Mary: Mirror of the Church.* Trans. Frances Lonergan Villa. Collegeville, MN: Liturgical Press, 1992.

Mary's life, words, and deeds are presented as models of imitation for modern believers.

Dodds, Bill. *The Ride of Your Life: A Road Trip for Catholic Teens.* Ann Arbor, MI: Charis, 2002.

Entertaining supplemental reading for your students. Written in the language of young people, Dodds compares our life's journey to a road trip. Lots of good tips on how to stay on course and live a life in the Catholic Church.

Ellsberg, Robert. *The Saints' Guide to Happiness.* New York: North Point Press, 2003.

Excellent spiritual reading for teachers and other searchers.

continued on page 130

Teaching Approaches

- **Class Discussion:** Have the students reread the last words of the saints on page 126. Have them choose the quotation that they like the best; then go around the room having them read their favorite quotation out loud. Then, discuss these quotations and ask students to share what they think is similar and profound about all of them.
- **Journal Assignment:** Have students reflect on these words as well as their life goals from the Bell Ringer assignment. What would they like their last words to be? Have them write these words in their journals. If there is time, have them share what they have written with a partner.
- **Writing Assignment:** Review the introduction to the topics in this chapter. Have students make predictions about what they think the chapter will be about. Record their responses on the board. Have them skim through the chapter, observing the subsection titles, features, and pictures. Then, have them write three learning goals that they would like to reach based on the content of the chapter. For example, "I would like to know what Heaven is like" or "I would like to . . ."

Communion of Saints

(pages 127–134)

Objectives

In this lesson, the students will:

- describe the three groups that make up the Communion of Saints.
- explain the role of the saints in the life of the Church.
- explain why and how Catholics venerate the saints.
- develop or deepen their own devotion to the saints.
- defend the Catholic teachings about the Virgin Mary.

Preview

For visual learners, pictures, posters, books with illustrations, prayer cards, statues, and other physical representations of the saints may be more helpful than encyclopedia entries or short biographies like those in *The Lives of the Saints*. Try to have as many saints as possible visible in your classroom throughout the time you are working on this chapter. Offer students extra credit points if they bring in prayer cards, small statues, or pictures of saints that they have at home.

Bell Ringers

- **Writing Assignment:** Have students complete the following in as many words as possible:
  - The Church is like . . .
  - Heaven is like . . .

- **Direct Instruction:** Have students share their responses. Remind them that the Church, which is a sacrament, represents and brings about Heaven on earth. The Church and Heaven are similar in that they both express a *communion*, a unity of persons, and both are united in the Communion of Saints.

For Enrichment

Individual Assignment: Use Chapter 5, Handout 3 "Your Patron Saints" (starting on page 285 and also online at www.avemariapress.com) to help students find and begin to research their own patron saints. You may make this research assignment as simple or as complex as you choose, but be certain that the students explain why they chose the saint they did and what qualities or virtues the saint has that they would like to emulate. Make sure the students visit the websites listed online at www.avemariapress.com as they research information about their patron saints.

---

128   Our Catholic Faith

Purgatory
The state of purification that takes place after death for those who need to be made clean and holy before meeting the all-holy God in Heaven.

- the fruits that come from working together for a just society;
- the communion that results from charity, the power of love that unites Catholics to Jesus Christ and each other by the power of the Holy Spirit.

Communion of Saints also refers to the unity among these three groups of people:

- the *pilgrim Church* (those of us who are living on earth today, also known as the "Church militant");
- the *Church suffering* (those undergoing purification in Purgatory);
- the *Church triumphant* (the blessed in Heaven).

The Catholic doctrine of the Communion of Saints is an extension of the belief that the Church is a community of faith united by the Holy Spirit at Eucharist. The Risen Lord is present in his word proclaimed at Mass and in the liturgy of the Eucharist under the forms of bread and wine. By the power of the Holy Spirit, the Risen Lord, the source of all holiness, binds and sanctifies the Church into a communion of the faithful.

All members of the Church—those alive today and those who have died—make up one big family united in the Spirit of Christ Jesus. Family members depend on each other. Such is the case in God's family bound together in love. Family members must communicate to grow and thrive. In God's family, prayer is the supreme way to keep alive a relationship with our Christian brothers and sisters.

Jesus taught, "Whatever you ask for in prayer with faith, you will receive" (Mt 21:22). This is why the Church encourages us to pray and offer up our good works for each other, both for those on

Personal Plan for Sainthood

Enact a plan for living life to the fullest, using your gifts, and reaching your potential. Seven potential steps for discerning your future are listed below. Write a sentence for each step, explaining how each can help you enact a plan to live a holy life worthy of sainthood.

1. Dream
2. Temper Your Dream with Realism
3. Plan
4. Seek Advice
5. Pray
6. Act on Your Decision
7. Evaluate

📖 Printed Materials continued from 129

Ghezzi, Bert. *Mystics and Miracles: True Stories of Lives Touched by God*. Garden City, NY: Doubleday, 2002.

Enjoyable and inspiring reading from a master storyteller.

Hayes, Zachary. *What Are They Saying about the End of the World?* New York: Paulist Press, 1983.

A good survey on the issue.

Kreeft, Peter J. *Everything You Ever Wanted to Know about Heaven, but Never Dreamed of Asking*. San Francisco: Ignatius Press, 1990.

In the style of C.S. Lewis, the brilliant author takes an entertaining and informative look at Heaven. Easy-to-read and thought-provoking blend of classical and modern views.

———. *Love Is Stronger than Death*. San Francisco: Ignatius Press, 1992.

Lewis, C.S. *The Screwtape Letters*. San Francisco: HarperSanFrancisco, 2001.

Lewis's fictional collection of letters from one demon to his student. Typical brilliance from Lewis. Useful for a discussion of Christian values and human vices.

Martin, James S.J., *My Life with the Saints*. Chicago, IL: Loyola Press, 2006.

Although not meant to be a reference book about the saints, the popular Catholic author Fr. Jim Martin presents his semi-autobiographical account of his life with many great saints of the Catholic Church.

O'Connor, Edward D., C.S.C. *The Catholic Vision*. Huntington, IN: Our Sunday Visitor, Inc., 1992.

An excellent introduction to the Catholic faith. You will find chapter 21 on grace and sin and chapter 28 on eschatology good background reading for this chapter of the text.

continued on page 133

earth and those souls in Purgatory. The prayers of the faithful on earth help those in Purgatory reach the goal of Heaven as their prayers can help us here on earth. We also derive great benefit from the saints in Heaven who continue to pray for us to our heavenly Father. We believe that they can offer the merits of their good works for us through Christ, who alone is the one Mediator and Savior.

Once we get to Heaven, we will be amazed at how much good others have done for us through their prayers, love, and good works. The Catholic doctrine of the Communion of Saints really stresses how we are related to all members of God's family. With Jesus, we are never alone.

Devotion to the Saints (CCC, 828; 956–957; 963)

The early Church called itself a community of saints. The word *saint* comes from the Latin word *sanctus*, which means "holy." Every member of Christ's Body has a call to holiness. Christ has given his Church all the means necessary to attain holiness: the Holy Spirit, the many gifts and graces of the Spirit, and the sacraments, especially the Eucharist.

The example of canonized saints can help all friends of Christ on the path to holiness. Canonized saints are those whose lives have been meticulously examined by Church authorities and declared to be heroic and exemplary. By imitating their virtues and honoring them through prayerful devotion, we are praising God's own holiness and love. It is important to note that Catholic devotion to saints involves *veneration*, not *worship*. Catholics worship God alone. Out of respect and honor, Catholics pray to the saints to petition God the Father, to be go-betweens on our behalf. Because of their extraordinary goodness, saints have a deep, personal, and loving relationship with God.

Many saints in Heaven have not made the official list of canonized saints. Undoubtedly many of them include your own relatives. The feast day of this great multitude of saints is All Saints' Day, November 1, a holy day of obligation. It is exciting to know that those living on earth are still in communion with their relatives and friends who have gone before them. In the distant future you might have great-great-grandchildren who will pray for *your* heavenly help as they try to live Christlike lives here on earth. It is our fervent hope to be among that number of countless heroic good women and men who are with God in Heaven.

True devotion to the saints involves studying their lives and imitating their virtues. They were flesh-and-blood people who proved their worth by rising to the challenge of the Christian life. They are worthy of imitation. St. John Bosco said, "The history of the Church teaches us that the greatest saints are those who professed the greatest devotion to Mary." This is so because she is the greatest saint of all, the Mother of God. On the cross, Jesus gave her to the Church. He told his beloved disciple, John, "Behold, your mother" (Jn 19:27). This makes Mary the Mother of the Church. A mother's love is very special. When you stay close to Mary, you will inevitably stay close to her Son.

Mary, the Greatest Saint (CCC, 511; 964–965; 967–969; 973)

Mary the Mother of God plays a special role in Salvation History. She said yes to God's plan to send his Son to accomplish Salvation for humankind. Mary did not understand how she was to conceive a child; however, her faithful response showed that she was willing to work with her Son from the very beginning in his mission of Salvation.

She and Joseph then raised Jesus in a loving, prayer-filled home. They taught and cared for him. When Jesus came on the public scene, Mary continued to witness to and support him, even as he experienced his arrest, suffering, and Death on the cross. In addition, she was a steadfast disciple who prayed with the Apostles

Background Information

Familiar Artistic Expressions of Saints

Artistic representations of the saints often include symbols that help us to identify which saint is being depicted. For instance, St. Joseph is shown with carpentry tools; St. Agnes is almost always accompanied by a lamb; St. Peter holds the keys to Heaven and is often standing on a rock; St. Francis of Assisi is shown with animals, especially a lion and a lamb; St. Thérèse of Lisieux appears with roses; and St. Thomas Aquinas holds a book and quill. When your students research their patron saint, you may want them to try to find out what symbols are used to identify them and why. If they do the "family saint" activity, encourage them to choose symbols to represent the family member they have researched and to include artwork in their report.

Extending the Lesson

Individual Assignment: Allow each student to choose one description of Mary from the Chapter 5, Handout 2 "Litany of the Blessed Virgin Mary" (starting on page 285 and also online at www.avemariapress.com) to represent in a drawing or painting. Do not allow more than one student to choose any one description. When the drawings are complete, post them around the room and have the students walk by them, praying the litany silently as they pass each picture.

Teaching Approaches

- **Direct Instruction:** Use the following two analogies to express the mystery of the Communion of Saints:

  - Ask students to reflect on all the different groups of people they would consider members of their school community and list them on the board. They should come up with a comprehensive list, including students, parents, alumni, teachers, staff (like the secretary, librarian, etc.), coaches, etc. Point out that their school community consists of more than the people who are currently students and teachers. Draw out the parallels between the saints who have gone before us to Heaven and the alumni who have graduated yet still remain an important part of the school community.

  - Suggest that the Communion of Saints is also like social networking websites on the Internet. Different people belong to different groups, but they all belong to the same site. They are all united under one organization although they log in from different computers, in different places, and even different countries and may never even see each other.

- **Class Discussion:** Have the students identify and define the three groups of people who are understood to make up the Communion of Saints: the pilgrim Church, the Church suffering, and the Church triumphant. Test their knowledge by having them suggest possible examples of people who would be in each group. *Note*: They may suggest family members who have died. This is perfectly fine. Remind them that although we do not know how they were judged, we should continue to pray for them and ask for their prayers for us.

- **Journal Assignment:** Draw the students' attention to the feature "Personal Plan for Sainthood." Remind them that everyone is called to become a saint. Have them write a sentence for each step in their journals.
- **Prayer Experience:** Begin a "prayer partner" activity. Explain that asking a saint to pray for us is, in many ways, similar to asking a friend to pray for us. As a journaling assignment for the next week, ask them to record their prayers for a classmate. Assign names at random, perhaps by having the students draw them from a box, checking to make sure they do not draw their own name. At the end of the week, invite the students to reveal their prayer partners and to share with them the prayers they have recorded.
- **Class Discussion:** Continue with the text subsection "Devotion to the Saints" (page 129). Point out the differences between the definitions of veneration and worship regarding our relationship to saints. Ask students to share responses they would give to someone who accused Catholics of worshipping saints.
- **Prayer Experience:** As in Chapter 4, a litany of saints would be an appropriate prayer experience for this lesson. Dim the lights in your room and have the students clear their desks of any distractions. Moving around the room in an orderly fashion, have each student say aloud the name of their favorite saint or patron saint (see For Enrichment activity on page 132) with the rest of the class responding: "Pray for us." Students can pass a small votive candle around to designate the next speaker if that helps you keep order and ensure that no one is skipped or goes out of turn. Close with the whole class saying "All holy men and women, pray for us. Amen." *Note*: Litanies are intended to be long. If you have a class of fewer than eighteen to twenty students, have the students choose two saints and go around the classroom twice.

Immaculate Conception
The Church dogma that holds that the Blessed Mother, by a special grace from God and by virtue of her Son's merits, was preserved immune from all stain of Original Sin from the very first moment of her human existence. This feast is celebrated on December 8, a holy day of obligation.

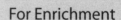

in the upper room awaiting the descent of the Holy Spirit in power on Pentecost Sunday. Throughout her life, Mary obeyed God's will; she fully cooperated with our Lord's work of Salvation; she generously responded to the graces of the Holy Spirit. All of these qualities make her the perfect model of Christian faith and love.

Because of her example, the Church honors Mary with many titles, all of which tell us something about what we believe about her. Mary is Our Lady, the Mother of God, the Immaculate Conception, the Blessed Mother, the Mother of the Church, Ever Virgin, the Queen of Heaven and Earth. Mary is a loving Mother; she continues to plead for us before her Son. This is why the Church prays to her using these titles: Advocate, Helper, Benefactress, and Mediatrix.

Because of her special role in Salvation History, the Church teaches certain truths about Mary. The most important of these truths are explained below.

Immaculate Conception (*CCC*, 490–493; 508; 722)

Mary, from the first moment of her conception, was preserved immune from Original Sin. This also means that from the first moment of her existence, Mary was full of grace, that is, free of any alienation from God caused by Original Sin. She had a special role in God's work of Salvation. Therefore, God graced her with this divine favor in anticipation of

her son's Death and Resurrection. We celebrate this doctrine each year on December 8, the Feast of the Immaculate Conception, a holy day of obligation. Many people wrongly believe that this feast day celebrates Jesus' conception, but in fact it celebrates the gift of grace of Jesus' Salvation offered to Mary from the very beginning of her life.

In addition, Mary was so close to God that she did not commit any personal sins. She lived a blameless life, the most blessed of all human beings. The angel Gabriel proclaimed to her, "The Lord is with you" (Lk 1:28). As the Mother of God, Mary is all-holy.

Virgin Mary (*CCC*, 484–489; 494; 496–499; 502–503; 510; 723)

The Apostles' Creed statement that Jesus was born of the Virgin Mary proclaims that God took the initiative in the Incarnation. God alone is the Father of Jesus Christ. Jesus was conceived by the Holy Spirit and born of the Virgin Mary, who remained a virgin "before, in, and after" the birth of the Lord.

This virginal conception of Jesus is God's work, beyond "all human understanding and possibility" (*CCC*, 497). We can understand its true meaning only with the gift of faith. From all eternity, God chose Mary to be Jesus' mother. She was a true daughter of Israel, in a line of holy women who helped prepare for her mission of cooperating with God's plan of Salvation. Her response of "May it be done to me according to your word" (Lk 1:38) helped God's plan of Salvation bear fruit.

Mother of God, Mother of the Church (*CCC*, 495; 501; 509; 724–726; 963)

The Holy Spirit inspired the early Church to teach that Jesus is *one* Divine Person possessing both a divine nature

For Enrichment

Student Presentation: The Student Text points out that many saints in Heaven have not been canonized by the Church. Expand on this by having students research a "family saint." Ask them to interview members of their family, asking them about a family member who has died and who they are reasonably certain is with God in Heaven. Who was this person? What was special about them? How did they show or express their faith? Can they identify the feast day for this person? (A saint's feast day is usually the date of his or her death.) In presenting this assignment, you could give students a few options:

- They could write a brief biography of their family's saint, including as much detail about the person's life of faith as possible—especially stories that show the person's virtues.
- They might represent the person artistically, including symbols that relate to their life and their unique expression of faith in and love for the Lord (see Background Information on page 131).
- They could write a prayer asking their family saint for help in attaining the virtues that this person exhibited during his or her lifetime.

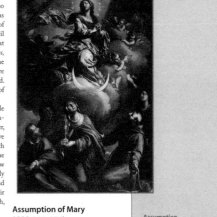

and a human nature. The Church also has consistently taught that Jesus was divine from the very first moment of his conception. This is why the Council of Ephesus (AD 431) proclaimed that Mary is "Mother of God" (*Theo-tokos*, "bearer of God"). Because Mary is the mother of Jesus Christ, it is therefore proper to call her the Mother of God. This title for Mary is supreme to any of her other titles.

Jesus' words to his disciples, while hanging on the cross "Behold, your mother" (Jn 19:27), make Mary our Mother, too. She is a spiritual mother whose love for her Son and for us helps bring birth to believers in the Church. She is also the Mother of the Church. Mary is a new Eve who cooperated fully with the Holy Spirit to bring Christ into the world and people to Christ. Children imitate their mothers. By giving Mary to the Church, Jesus wants Catholics

- to learn from her—her fidelity, obedience, compassion, love, and prayerfulness;
- to know what great things he does for those he loves;
- to have a perfect model of holiness;
- to see what an image of God's love looks like.

Assumption of Mary
(*CCC*, 966; 974)

In his official words defining the doctrine of the Assumption in 1950, Pope Pius XII said, "The Immaculate Mother of God, the ever Virgin Mary, having completed the course of her earthly life, was assumed body and soul into heavenly glory." This doctrine is based on Christian belief from the earliest years of the Church. It connects two realities:

Assumption
The Church dogma that teaches that the Blessed Mother, because of her unique role in her Son's Resurrection, was taken directly to Heaven when her earthly life was over. The feast of the Assumption on August 15 is a holy day of obligation.

Our Lady of Perpetual Help

The picture of *Our Lady of Perpetual Help* is an icon (or holy image) of Mary. It has been venerated by both Eastern- and Western-rite Christians for centuries. The archangels Gabriel and Michael are holding the instruments of the Lord's Passion as the Child Jesus looks on and grasps his Mother's hand. The Mother of God looks at us with quiet sorrow in her face. Like all good Marian art, we are drawn into the picture so that we end up focusing on Jesus. Mary serves this function; she attracts and points us to Jesus, her Son, our Lord and Savior.

- **Individual Assignment:** Read and discuss the life of St. John Bosco presented in the Profile of Faith feature on pages 133–134. Have students compose intercessory prayers to St. John Bosco in their journals based on what they read and discussed. Consider having students complete the research assignment suggested within the feature.

- **Class Assignment:** "Mary, the Greatest Saint" (pages 129–132) is the focus of the next text subsection and this part of the lesson. Divide your class into four small groups (eight if you have a large class) and assign each group one of the following topics: the Immaculate Conception, the Virgin Mary, the Mother of God and of the Church, or the Assumption. Each group should review the material in the text and any supplementary information you can provide and then present that material to the class.

  ◆ The presentations should include a faith response to the material as well as the "facts." That is, the presentation should express the difference this belief about Mary makes for believers. Use Chapter 5, Handout 1 "Marian Doctrine" (starting on page 285 and also online at www.avemariapress.com) to help direct the students' efforts.

  ◆ While the groups are presenting the information, students should take notes at their desks especially recording the basis of the teaching in Scripture, relevant Church documents, and the implications that the teaching has on beliefs about Mary and Jesus.

Background Information

Our Lady of Perpetual Help

The picture, painted on wood, with a background of gold, was brought to Rome in the fifteenth century by a merchant who put in his will that the picture should be kept in a church and exposed for public devotion. Originally it was kept at the church of San Matteo Via Merulana. When the French invaded Rome in 1812 the church was destroyed and the picture disappeared for over forty years. It was rediscovered in an oratory of the Augustinian fathers at Santa Maria in Posterula in 1865. Pope Pius IX, who had prayed before the picture as a boy, ordered it returned to the new church in Rome, St. Alphonsus. In places other than the United States, the Our Lady of Perpetual Help image is known as "Our Lady of Perpetual Succor."

Printed Materials continued from page 130

O'Donnell, John S.J., *A Faith You Can Live With: Understanding the Basics.* Franklin, WI: Sheed & Ward, 1999.
> A marvelous overview of "the basics." Good discussion of the Apostles' Creed in Chapter 1 of the book.

Phan, Peter. *Responses to 101 Questions on Death and Eternal Life.* Mahwah, NJ: Paulist Press, 1997.
> Good, general overview.

Redford, John. *What Is Catholicism? Hard Questions—Straight Answers.* Foreword by Avery Dulles. Huntington, IN: Our Sunday Visitor, 1999.
> Apologetic in tone, this book gives good answers to challenging questions on Original Sin (pp. 52–55), Hell, Purgatory, and the Beatific Vision (pp. 72–79).

Sheen, Fulton J. *The Seven Capital Sins.* New York: Alba House, 2000.
> Perennial wisdom from a great communicator.

- **Direct Instruction:** In connection with the text subsection "Veneration of Mary" (page 132), Remind the students of the difference between veneration and worship. Be sure that they understand that the honor and respect given to those things we venerate is not the same as the worship that we give to God alone. If necessary, analyze each part of the "Hail Mary" prayer noting how all of it praises God through Mary. For example, she is full of grace because the Lord is with her. She is holy because she is the Mother of God. We ask for her prayers to her Son for us as sinners.

- **Individual Assignment:** Test the students' knowledge on the Catholic teachings about Mary. Read these statements to the class and have them indicate whether they are true or false on a sheet of paper:

  1. Jesus' birth is called the "Immaculate Conception."
  2. Mary was a virgin when she gave birth to the Son of God, but she may have had children with Joseph afterward.
  3. Mary's soul is in Heaven, but her body is buried in the Holy Land.
  4. Catholics worship Mary.

  All answers are false. Discuss the answers and have students explain why each answer is false. Have them correct each statement by rewriting them in their notes.

- **Prayer Experience:** Note the assignment on page 132, "Praying with Mary." Discuss the ways the students may participate in the Church's veneration of Mary. Ask: Have you ever participated in a May crowning? Are there special celebrations on the holy days that honor Mary, such as the Feast of the Immaculate Conception or the Assumption? If not, can your class think of ways to begin those traditions? Assign it as either a small group or individual homework assignment. If you did the litany of saints prayer experience in the last section and it was well received, or if you did not but would like your students to experience the litany prayer form, you can introduce your students to the Litany of the Blessed Virgin Mary via Chapter 5, Handout 2 "Litany of the Blessed Virgin Mary" (starting on page 285 and also online at www.avemariapress.com).

1. Mary's unique role as God's mother preserved from Original Sin.
2. The reality of our final resurrection in Christ.

Mary was preserved from death's decay. Because she is the mother of the Savior, Mary is the first to share in the Lord's Resurrection. We celebrate this feast on August 15 as a holy day of obligation, a celebration that reminds us of our own joyous resurrection if we stay united to Mary's Son, Jesus Christ.

Veneration of Mary
(*CCC*, 970–972; 975)

It is a hallmark of our Catholic faith to venerate Mary. Praying to and honoring Mary increases our love for her and helps us to imitate her virtues, especially her life of total commitment to Jesus.

Giving Mary special honor is not meant to hide Jesus' role as our one Mediator. Mary does not have the power to answer our prayers on her own; only God has that power. We pray to Mary because she is our Mother, too. We ask for her help since she is in Heaven and knows how to praise God and offer prayers on our behalf. When Mary and other saints lived among us, they followed God's will and did good for others. In Heaven, they continue to cooperate with God by doing good for those of us on earth and in Purgatory.

We should never forget that Mary's motherly role is to help us pay attention to Jesus, our unique Redeemer. Her good qualities make her a special human being, a mother who attracts us to her Son. All good Marian art—like Michelangelo's *Pietà*—draws our attention not to her, but to her Son. This points to her role in the Mystery of Salvation: she gives her Son to humanity. She leads us to him. She shows us how to live in response to him. She intercedes on our behalf, like she did for the young married couple in Jesus' first miracle at the wedding in Cana (see Jn 2:1–12).

There are many devotions to Mary. The most popular is the Rosary, which includes vocal prayers and meditation on the mysteries of Christ's life. The most repeated prayer in the Rosary is the beloved Hail Mary. Other popular Marian devotions include the Angelus, the First Saturday devotion, the Litany of the Blessed Mother, and various novenas.

Praying with Mary

Read more about the following devotions. Choose one of the devotions and make it part of your own prayer:

1. the Angelus
2. First Friday devotion
3. a novena to Mary

Background Information

The Communion of Saints Is a Living Organ

In the Second Vatican Council document Lumen Gentium, the idea of the Communion of Saints is addressed:

> Christ, the one Mediator, established and continually sustains here on earth His holy Church, the community of faith, hope and charity, as an entity with visible delineation through which He communicated truth and grace to all. But, the society structured with hierarchical organs and the Mystical Body of Christ, are not to be considered as two realities, nor are the visible assembly and the spiritual community, nor the earthly Church and the Church enriched with heavenly things; rather they form one complex reality which coalesces from a divine and a human element. For this reason, by no weak analogy, it is compared to the mystery of the incarnate Word. As the assumed nature inseparably united to Him, serves the divine Word as a living organ of salvation, so, in a similar way, does the visible social structure of the Church serve the Spirit of Christ, who vivifies it, in the building up of the body. (Chapter I, no. 8)

For Review

1. Define *eschatology*.
2. What three groups does the Communion of Saints embrace?
3. What advantages are there for being devoted to the saints?
4. Briefly explain the following Marian doctrines: Immaculate Conception, Ever Virgin, Mother of God, and Mother of the Church.
5. Why does the Church honor Mary?

For Reflection

Consider the following definition of a saint: "A saint is: a mind—through which Christ thinks; a voice—through which Christ speaks; a heart—through which Christ loves; a hand—through which Christ helps." What are specific ways you can apply this definition to your own life as Jesus' disciple?

PROFILE OF FAITH: ST. JOHN BOSCO, FATHER AND TEACHER OF THE YOUNG

St. John Bosco, whom Pope John Paul II called "Father and Teacher of the Young," was born in the Piedmont area of Northern Italy in 1815. His father died when he was only two. Raised by his mother, he had a difficult childhood, often having to serve as a shepherd to help the family finances. But he was a bright, energetic, and religious boy. As a youth he learned magic tricks and acrobatics. He used these skills to attract both children and adults to him and then, after his performance, would discuss religion with them.

John was ordained a priest in 1841 and settled in Turin, Italy, where peasants flocked to find work. One day while visiting the prisons of the city, *Don* ("Father") Bosco learned of the deplorable fate of orphans who would today be called "street children." He was especially appalled by the evil influences that tempted them. It became clear to him that his life work would be to care for them with love and compassion. Before long, he established homes known as oratories where the boys could live in a safe and secure environment, learn trades like tailoring and shoe-making, engage in wholesome recreation, learn music, and, most important, grow in knowledge and love of the faith. In the early years of his ministry, he was greatly aided by his mother, who sold her home and jewelry to help support the first home for boys.

Don Bosco placed his work under the patronage of St. Francis de Sales, a beloved saint who was known for his patience and gentleness, virtues that Don Bosco wanted his teachers to imitate. Priest friends assisted Don Bosco at the beginning of his work, but they had their own parish work to attend to. So Don Bosco began to select certain of his students who might be good priests. He helped counsel them and gave them a good education. In 1859, he and twenty-two of his young men formed the Salesian Society to carry on his work. In the 1870s, with St. Mary Domenica Mazzarello, he cofounded the Daughters of Mary Help of Christians (the Salesian Sisters) to engage in similar work with poor girls that the Salesian priests and brothers do for boys.

Various biographies of St. John Bosco tell of many prophetic dreams he had throughout his life. God used these dreams to guide his work. The most important one took place when he was nine, when he dreamed of a field of

---

Homework Assignment

1. Complete in writing the For Review questions on page 133.

2. Read the text section "One Baptism for the Forgiveness of Sins" (pages 134–138).

Resources

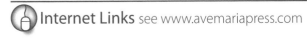

Internet Links see www.avemariapress.com

For Review Answers (page 133)

1. Eschatology is the study of and the Church's teaching about the "last things": death, judgment, Heaven, Hell, Purgatory, the Second Coming of Christ, and the resurrection of the body.

2. The Communion of Saints includes all those redeemed by Christ—those in Heaven, in Purgatory, and still on earth. These three groups are also referred to as the *pilgrim Church*, the *Church suffering*, and the *Church triumphant*.

3. Devotion to the saints gains for us the benefit of their good example as well as their intercession on our behalf. By imitating their virtues we, too, can rise to the challenge of living a truly Christian life.

4. *Immaculate Conception*: the belief that Mary was conceived without Original Sin. God granted her this grace in anticipation of Jesus' Death and Resurrection. *Ever Virgin*: this belief is connected to our belief in the Incarnation. God alone is Father to Jesus. *Mother of God*: this is a proper title for Mary because Jesus was both human and divine from the moment of his conception. His divinity was not assumed at some later point. Therefore, Mary, his mother, is the Mother of God. *Mother of the Church*: Mary is the spiritual mother of all Christians. She gives us a good example to follow and imitate—her fidelity, obedience, compassion, love, and prayerfulness.

5. The Church honors Mary because she leads us to Christ through her example and through her intercessions on our behalf.

One Baptism for the Forgiveness of Sins (pages 134–138)

Objectives

In this lesson, the students will:
- differentiate between venial and mortal sin.
- identify the seven deadly sins.
- examine their conscience in preparation for receiving the Sacrament of Penance.

 Preview

If it is possible to arrange for a class celebration of the Sacrament of Penance, this would be a good time to do it, particularly if you are currently in the middle of or approaching the seasons of Advent or Lent. Be sure that in addition to the liturgical, communal celebration there is opportunity for individual confession. The celebration of Penance would entail an extra class period separate from the lesson for this session.

 **Bell Ringers**

- **Class Discussion:** Ask the students: "Do you find it easier to forgive someone or to accept someone's forgiveness?" Call on one student to be "on the spot" in front of the class to answer the question by being as specific as possible.

- **Writing Assignment:** Chapter 5, Handout 4 "The Good News of God's Forgiveness" (starting on page 285 and also online at www.avemariapress.com) provides a list of Scripture references that relate to the question of forgiveness. Ask your students to look up the passages, summarize them briefly on the worksheet, and then choose the one passage that to them best expresses "Good News." Ask them to explain their choice either orally or in writing.

---

cursing and misbehaving children. In the dream, Jesus told John that he would have to use gentleness and kindness to win over the unruly youth—a dream that eventually led him to his life's work years later. St. John was also known in his life as a miracle worker, one who multiplied food and cured blindness. He was also a renowned author of pamphlets that clearly explained Catholic doctrines and countered the attacks and misunderstandings of anti-Catholics. One of his most important books was his biography of one of his students—St. Dominic Savio (1842–1857), who died as a young teen.

When Don Bosco died in 1888, there were 1,400 Salesians and 250 Salesian houses in Europe and South America. Today, there are 40,000 members of the Salesian family who work among poor and abandoned youth on six continents in more than 120 countries.

- Read and report about something of St. John Bosco not covered in this text.
- Research the work of the Salesians and report on one aspect of their ministry.
- Research and report on the life of St. Dominic Savio.

One Baptism for the Forgiveness of Sins

(CCC, 976–987)

Jesus forgave sins. This was at the heart of his ministry. Irish author Alice Carey wrote, "Nothing in this lost world bears the impress of the Son of God so surely as forgiveness." For example, imagine the impression Jesus made on the penitent woman who burst into Simon the Pharisee's house. Her rejoicing must have been great when Jesus said, "Your sins are forgiven" (Lk 7:48).

Or consider the reaction of the paralytic who heard Jesus proclaim, "Child, your sins are forgiven" (Mk 2:5). When some Pharisees heard this announcement, they harshly criticized Jesus, mumbling that only God could forgive sin. To the astonishment of all, Jesus proceeded to cure the paralyzed man. In doing so, Jesus revealed his divine identity and the source of his power to forgive sin.

Jesus' proclamation of the Good News of God's forgiveness for sinners even occurs at the height of his crucifixion, when Christ forgave his executioners: "Father, forgive them, they know not what they do" (Lk 23:34).

Forgiveness of sins was an essential part of Jesus' earthly ministry and deeply connected to his saving actions. Because of this, Jesus instructed his disciples to continue to forgive sins in his name: "Receive the holy Spirit. Whose sins you forgive are forgiven them, and whose sins you retain are retained" (Jn 20:22–23). The Apostles' Creed recognizes this by linking the forgiveness of sin to three other articles of faith: the Holy Spirit, the Church, and the Communion of Saints.

Background Information

Development of the Sacrament of Penance

The Sacrament of Penance goes by many different names, including penance, reconciliation, and confession. It has also taken many different forms as our understanding of it has deepened. It has always been clear that the Church retained Christ's power to forgive sin. Early on, it was thought that this could happen only once in a person's life. Baptism forgave all sins, but for serious sins committed after baptism, confession had to be made to the bishop and penances were both severe and public. For periods sometimes over a year, penitents were denied admission to Mass or any gathering of Christians. They had to give evidence publicly of their repentance, and only after their lengthy penance was served would absolution be granted. For this reason many converts to Christianity chose to wait until they neared death to be baptized.

Penance first began to look more like the sacrament we celebrate today in the seventh through eleventh centuries in Ireland. Celtic missionary priests and monks would travel from village to village, talking with people privately and assigning penances. The next time the priest came through, the people would let him know they had completed their penance and they would be absolved.

In obedience to the Lord, who united forgiveness of sin to faith and Baptism, the early Church preached repentance and the need for faith and Baptism in the name of the Triune God. On Pentecost Sunday, Peter proclaimed, "Repent and be baptized, every one of you, in the name of Jesus Christ for the forgiveness of your sins; and you will receive the gift of the holy Spirit" (Acts 2:38).

Baptism is the primary sacrament of forgiveness because it wipes away sin and unites us to Christ Jesus. A major effect of Baptism is the complete forgiveness of both Original Sin and one's personal offenses. In the rite of Baptism, new Christians renounce sin in their lives. (In the Baptism of infants, the godparents and parents renounce sin for their children.) Though Baptism does indeed forgive all sins, the graces of Baptism do not free the person from the weakness of human nature and the inclination to sin in the future. Unfortunately, people do commit sins after Baptism. And some of the sins are serious enough to be mortal, that is, deadly. The effects of mortal sin are terrible: killing the person's relationship with God, separating him or her from the other members of Christ's Body, and alienating the person from himself or herself.

The Types of Sin

The Church distinguishes between two kinds of sin: *Original Sin* and *actual sin*. *Original Sin* is the term used to describe the prideful disobedience of Adam and Eve and the effects of this disobedience that all humans inherit. Although the "forbidden fruit" story in Genesis 3 is symbolic, the nature of the Original Sin of the first humans was a deliberate act of disobedience against God. This turning from God's love brought with it alienation from God, self, others, and God's beautiful creation. Separation from God's love and the resulting loss of sanctifying grace are the worst spiritual

effects of Original Sin. Physical suffering and death are the worst physical effects of Original Sin.

A simple glance at the daily newspaper or a self-examination into one's own heart reveals that we are born into a sinful state. The entire human community bears the wounds of Original Sin. Violence, terrorism, prejudice, drug addiction, sexual aberration, anger, hatred, exploitation of the poor, and our own weak tendencies to give into temptation—all these testify to the existence of a condition of sin into which we are all born.

sin
An offense against God through a violation of truth, reason, and conscience.

Teaching Approaches

- **Individual Assignment:** Give the students the opportunity to research how sin is presented in the New Testament using the Knowing Christ through Scripture feature on page 138. Review their answers as a class before moving on.
- **Direct Instruction:** Write the following terms highlighted in the text section "One Baptism for the Forgiveness of Sins" (pages 134–138) on the board. Refer to them throughout the lesson. As they apply, call on students to offer definitions in their own words and from the text:
  - sin
  - Original Sin
  - actual sin
  - venial sin
  - mortal sin
  - capital sins
  - vices

By the end of the lesson, make sure that the students can differentiate between the meanings of these terms.

- **Direct Instruction:** In the Chapter 1 Class Activity on page 33, a mirror and mud were used to explain the effect of Original Sin and subsequent actual sin on our souls. Bring a muddied mirror to class again to review that material with your class. Continue to use the mirror to explain Baptism by pouring water over the mirror to wash away the mud. You can also use the mud to differentiate between venial sin (stain a small portion of the mirror) and mortal sin (cover it completely).

For Enrichment

Individual Assignment: If your class has time for a longer project, consider asking them to research the history and development of the Sacrament of Penance. You might assign small groups to look into different historical periods such as the New Testament period, the second and third centuries, the fourth through sixth centuries, the seventh through eleventh centuries, the Dark Ages, the period of the Reformation, pre–Vatican II, and post–Vatican II. Each group should find some way to present their findings to the class. A skit in which they act out the form of the sacrament would be particularly appropriate.

- **Individual Assignment:** In addition to the visual lesson of the mirror, have the students write definitions of the words listed on the board into their notes. Then, have them draw a Venn diagram in their notes and label the two circles "venial sin" and "mortal sin." Review the responses as a class. Make sure they can explain the three requirements for an act to be categorized as a mortal sin.
- **Writing Assignment:** Quiz the students on the capital sins on page 136, also known as the seven deadly sins, that can lead to mortal sin. Suggest that they memorize these vices using an acronym such as: "**G**oo**GL**e **PEAS**" for greed, gluttony, lust, pride, envy, anger, and sloth.

venial sin
Actual sin that weakens and wounds our relationship with God, but does not destroy divine life in our souls.

vices
Bad habits or dispositions (like pride) that turn us from the good and incline us to commit evil.

capital sins
Sins that are the root of other sins and vices. There are seven capital sins: pride, covetousness, envy, anger, gluttony, lust, and sloth.

Original Sin entered the world through two people, Adam and Eve. But the Gospel proclaims that the perfect life and loving sacrificial Death of one person, Jesus Christ, the Son of God, have conquered sin. Through Jesus, God has redeemed humanity, offering each person forgiveness and birth into a new life. It is this life of grace that God bestows at Baptism. God frees the baptized from Original Sin. But this does not make the person perfect. The new Christian remains weak and in need of the support, encouragement, and prayers of fellow Christians. The Church gives Catholics many helps—primarily the sacraments—to fortify us to live a Christian life.

Actual sin is personal, individual sin. It is an act, word, or desire contrary to eternal law. "To commit a sin" is to do something evil, knowingly and willingly. Actual sins diminish us as persons and damage our relationships with God, others, and self. Sin offends reason, truth, and right conscience. The root of all sin is within the human heart.

Actual sins include:

- *Freely chosen bad attitudes or inordinate desires.* An example of a "bad attitude" is prejudice, which often causes hateful feelings toward others. Lust—defined as a "disordered desire for or inordinate enjoyment of sexual pleasure" (*CCC*, 2351)—is an example of an inordinate desire.
- *Failures to act.* Examples include sins of *omission* like failing to help a person who falls sick while we pass by.
- *Actions (including words) directed against God, neighbor, or self.* Examples include sins of *commission* like stealing, cheating, lying, or misusing the gift of sexuality.

Sins differ in their degree. Venial sin refers to "lesser sins" that are a stumbling block on the path of following Jesus. They typically involve slight matters. Venial sins also occur when full consent of the will is lacking or ignorance is present in the sinner. Venial sins are *not* deadly sins. Unlike mortal sin, they do not destroy sanctifying grace, friendship with God, charity, or eternal happiness. The theft of a small item, a sarcastic word, and not praying regularly are examples of venial sins.

Venial sin is something Catholics should try to eradicate from their lives. The danger of all sin is that we can become attached to it. Repeating the same sinful acts can give a foothold to vices, bad habits that turn a person from love. These vices, especially the so-called deadly or capital sins—*pride, envy, anger, sloth, greed, gluttony,* and *lust*—can lead to mortal sin. Venial sin also weakens love,

Extending the Lesson

Class Activity: It is important for students to be able to identify areas of sinfulness in their own lives and in their community. There are a number of ways to help the students with this. Ask them to keep a "sin book"—a notebook in which they write down every single sin they witness or commit for at least one day and up to a week.

You could also simply brainstorm with them in class for a few minutes asking them to list some sins that they have witnessed or have committed themselves. Be sure they do not use names or identifying characteristics—just have them use the word "someone." You may need to "prime the pump" with a few examples of your own to get them started.

Once you have a good lengthy working list, ask the students which of these sins they think might be mortal sins. Remind them that only God knows for sure the intent of the person, but they can say, "If the person intended x, then this was a mortal sin."

If the students keep a "sin book," and if you are able to arrange a time for the Sacrament of Penance for your class, be sure they bring the books with them. They can use the books to examine their conscience prior to receiving the sacrament. If you cannot arrange for the sacrament, consider offering some kind of credit to those students who seek the sacrament on their own in the coming weeks.

attaches us to created goods rather than God, and merits temporal punishment.

Mortal sin is the most serious kind of sin. Mortal sins include attitudes, desires, or actions (or failures to act) that kill our relation to God and others. Mortal sins destroy love in the human heart by breaking God's law. To sin mortally, the sin must include:

- *Grave matter.* For example, murder, adultery, and apostasy are serious, gravely wrong actions.
- *Sufficient reflection.* This means that the person knows full well that what he or she proposes to do is seriously wrong, but does it anyhow.
- *Full consent of the will.* This means that the person commits the sinful action with freedom and not under the influence of limiting factors like force, fear, or blinding passion.

The Church teaches that just as it is possible for us to love, human freedom also makes it possible for us to sin mortally. Mortal sin results in the loss of love and deprives the sinner of sanctifying grace. If a person does not repent and receive Christ's forgiveness and dies in a state of mortal sin, he or she will merit eternal separation from God—Hell. A Christian should do everything possible with God's help to avoid mortal sin or to repent immediately and ask for God's forgiveness if he or she should commit deadly sin.

Forgiveness of Post-Baptismal Actual Sins

Because of their gravity, mortal (deadly) sins kill a person's relationship with God and others. The Church teaches that Christ forgives these sins through the Sacrament of Penance. Jesus knew of our human weakness. This sacrament (also known as confession or reconciliation) is a "second baptism" in which the Church proclaims once again Christ's forgiveness

of the contrite sinner. Through this sacrament of forgiveness, the Lord gave the Apostles and their successors the power of the keys of the Kingdom. This authority enables bishops and priests to forgive sins committed after Baptism in the Lord's name.

Sin is a turning away from God and God's family. To be forgiven, we need to convert once again and renounce our sin with sincere and contrite hearts. Having *contrition* for our sins means that we are truly sorry for them. There are three signs of true contrition. First, we must have a sincere intention to avoid sin in the future. Second, we must also avoid what we know can cause us to sin, that is, the "near occasions" of sin. Third, as far as possible, we must try to repair any harm our sins have caused. For example, a person who has cheated on a test must firmly resolve not to do so again. This means never again making a cheat sheet or sitting next to a classmate who is known to copy answers. Also, the person must own up to the past cheating incident and accept the grade that was truly deserved.

When a repentant sinner approaches a priest in the Sacrament of Penance, Christ reaches out to pronounce his forgiveness; he removes the person's sins and brings him or her back into communion with the Church.

mortal sin
A serious violation of God's law of love that results in the loss of God's life (sanctifying grace) in the soul of the sinner. To commit mortal sin, there must be grave matter, full knowledge of the evil done, and full consent of the will.

Hell
Eternal separation from God that results from a person dying after freely and deliberately choosing to act against God's will (that is, not repenting of mortal sin).

- **Prayer Experience:** Summarize the text subsection "Forgiveness of Post-Baptismal Actual Sins" (page 137). This part of the text emphasizes the importance of the Sacrament of Penance. If you have been able to arrange for a separate session to allow for celebration of the sacrament, allow time for the students to review and prepare at this time.
- **Video Presentation:** Show one of the suggested videos about the Sacrament of Penance listed among the resources starting on page 127. Stop the video periodically to expand upon what is said and relate it to the information in the text.

Homework Assignment

1. Write some talking points for the For Reflection entry on page 148. Be prepared to discuss these issues at the next session.

2. Continue working on the Ongoing Assignments (pages 150–151).

3. Read the text section "The Last Things: Eschatology" (pages 139–148).

4. Complete a detailed written report on Hinduism as called for in the assignment on page 150.

Background Information

Pope John Paul II on the Meaning of Repentance

In his homily on Ash Wednesday, February 25, 1998, Pope John Paul II explained the importance of true repentance:

> The psalmist does not stop at confessing his own sins and asking forgiveness for them; he especially hopes for interior renewal from the Lord's goodness: *"Create in me a clean heart, O God, and put a new and right spirit within me"* (Ps 50 [51]:10). Illumined by the Spirit about the devastating power of sin, he asks to become a new creature, to be, in a certain sense, created anew.

> This is the grace of Redemption! Faced with the sin that defiles the human heart, the Lord bends over his creature to renew the saving dialogue and to open for him new prospects of life and hope. Particularly during the Lenten season the Church reflects deeply on this mystery of salvation.

> To the sinner who wonders about his situation and whether he can still obtain God's mercy, today's liturgy replies with the Apostle's words from the Second Letter to the Corinthians: *"For our sake he made him to be sin who knew no sin, so that in him we might become the righteousness of God"* (2 Cor 5:21). In Christ, the heavenly Father's boundless love for each person is proclaimed and offered to believers. (2)

For Review Answers (page 138)

1. Forgiving sins was at the heart of Jesus' ministry, connected to his saving actions and an integral part of the "Good News" he proclaimed even from the cross.

2. *Original Sin* refers both to the disobedient act of Adam and Eve and to the effects of that disobedience inherited by all human beings.

3. The results of Original Sin include our alienation from God, God's creation, other people, and our own selves. Separation from God is the worst spiritual effect; physical suffering and death the worst physical effects of Original Sin.

4. Actual sins are those personal sins committed by individuals. An actual sin is any act, word, or desire that is contrary to God's eternal law. There are different types of sins, which include: *freely chosen bad attitudes or excessive desires*, such as racial prejudice, which causes hateful feelings (and often actions) against others; *sins of omission*, such as any failure to act for the good of another when the need is obvious and pressing; and *sins of commission*, such as any direct actions against God, neighbor, or self, including lying, cheating, stealing, or misusing the gift of one's sexuality.

5. A venial sin is an actual sin that weakens our relationship with God. Although venial sins do not destroy our relationship with God, they are obstacles to faith that can weaken our capacity to love, cause us to become attached to created goods rather than to God, and create bad habits that lead to mortal sin. Mortal sins are serious sins that result in the loss of God's life and grace in the soul of the sinner. These sins must involve serious issues, such as murder, adultery, or apostasy; there must be sufficient reflection such that the person knows full well that they are doing wrong but they do it anyhow; and there must be full consent of the will, that is, the person must commit the action freely, uninfluenced by force, fear, or blinding passion.

6. Actual sins are forgiven through the Sacrament of Penance, when the sinner is sincere and contrite. This means the person must truly intend not to sin again, they must avoid the people or situations that lead to sin, and they must try to repair the harm done by the sin.

KNOWING CHRIST THROUGH SCRIPTURE

The New Testament on Sin

Jesus is our Savior. He came to forgive our sins. When he was criticized for eating with sinners, he said, "Those who are healthy do not need a physician, but the sick do. I have not come to call the righteous to repentance but sinners" (Lk 5:31–32). At the Last Supper, he told us the purpose of his sacrificial death—the redemption of all sinners: "This is my blood of the covenant, which will be shed on behalf of many for the forgiveness of sins" (Mt 26:28).

Jesus hated sin, but he loved sinners. He knew all too well the terrible effects of sin. Read the following passages related to sin that come from Jesus himself or his early disciples, like St. Paul. Write responses to the questions.

Mark 7:21–22
- According to Jesus, what are sins that originate in the human heart?

John 8:34 and John 9:29–41
- What happens when we commit a sin?

John 8:1–11
- What point is Jesus making in verse 7?
- What two important points are made in verse 11?

Romans 13:8–14

Galatians 5:19–21

Ephesians 4:25–31

Colossians 3:5–9
- Construct a list of ten sins that followers of Jesus should avoid based on the readings above.

Colossians 3:12–17
- What are three things Christians should do to counteract sin?

1 John 3
- What must Christians do to show that we belong to Jesus Christ?

For Review

1. What role did forgiveness play in Jesus' ministry?
2. Define *Original Sin*.
3. What are some effects of Original Sin?
4. Define *actual sin*. Discuss three general types of actual sin.
5. Distinguish between *venial sin* and *mortal sin*.
6. How does one obtain forgiveness of sins committed after Baptism?

For Reflection

- Share your favorite Gospel story of Jesus' forgiveness.
- Among your peer group, what are considered the most serious kinds of sins?

Knowing Christ through Scripture Answers (page 138)

Mark 7:21–22
- Evil thoughts, unchastity, theft, murder, adultery, greed, malice, deceit, licentiousness, envy, blasphemy, arrogance, folly

John 8:34 and John 9:29–41
- We become slave to sin; we become blind.

John 8:1–11
- We are all sinners and should not accuse others of sinfulness.
- God does not condemn us, but loves us unconditionally. We should, as a result, sin no more because of his great love.

Romans 13:8–14; Galatians 5:19–21; Ephesians 4:25–31; Colossians 3:5–9
- Students should list the Ten Commandments or variations of these commandments based on the readings.

Colossians 3:12–17
- Forgive others, let Christ dwell within us, and do everything in the name of Christ. (Other answers may be acceptable based on the reading)

1 John 3
- Keep Christ's commandments and love one another.

The Last Things: Eschatology (CCC, 1002–1003; 1005–1014; 1016–1019)

Everyone faces death, the separation of the immortal soul from the body. St. Athanasius said that it is natural to fear death, but if we put our faith in the cross of Christ, we can despise what we naturally fear. How so? St. Bernard of Clairvaux said, "Death is the gate of life." The Catholic faith holds that with death comes a new type of life. Jesus taught, "I am the resurrection and the life; whoever believes in me, even if he dies, will live, and everyone who lives and believes in me will never die" (Jn 11:25–26).

It is natural to die: "There is an appointed time for everything, and a time for every affair under the heavens. A time to be born, and a time to die" (Eccl 3:1–2). Scripture also teaches that death is a penalty for sin. God did not originally intend for people to die. St. Paul explained how Adam turned from God, thus infecting humanity with death: "Therefore . . . through one person sin entered the world, and through sin, death, and thus death came to all, inasmuch as all sinned" (Rom 5:12).

Had sin not touched humanity, we would be immune to bodily death. Christ rescued humanity from its natural fate. He has conquered death. The Second Vatican Council teaches:

> Although the mystery of death utterly beggars the imagination, the Church has been taught by Divine Revelation, and herself firmly teaches, that man has been created by God for a blissful purpose beyond the reach of earthly misery. In addition, that bodily death from which man would have been immune had he not sinned will be vanquished, according to the Christian faith, when man who was ruined by his own doing is restored to wholeness by an almighty and merciful Savior. (*The Church in the Modern World*, No. 18)

Jesus' own acceptance of his Death is a model for all. In the Garden of Gethsemane, Jesus was anxious about his impending Death. He prayed, "Abba, Father, all things are possible to you. Take this cup away from me, but not what I will but what you will" (Mk 14:36).

This prayer and his impending Death were Jesus' final acts of total self-giving to the Father. As his followers, we are called to imitate him. Though it is natural to fear dying, in faith we recite with Jesus, "Father, into your hands I commend my spirit" (Lk 23:46).

Death is a profound mystery. But Christian faith reveals that Jesus Christ has conquered death. Christ has won an awesome victory, giving us hope that death is an entrance into an eternal life of union with the Triune God of love. Baptism unites Catholics with the Risen Lord; in a mysterious way the baptized already participate in his heavenly life. The Eucharist nourishes Catholics with Christ's heavenly life.

The fervent hope of all is that we will rise on the last day with Christ in his glory. But this can only occur if we die in union with him. We only have one life to

The Last Things: Eschatology
(pages 139–148)

Objectives

In this lesson, the students will:

- express their own feelings and fears about death.
- develop their own plan for living with the end things in mind.
- compare and contrast Heaven, Hell, and Purgatory.
- differentiate between particular judgment and general judgment.

Preview

This is the final section in the series of chapters devoted to the Apostles' Creed. Make sure students understand the Catholic position on life after death, especially in comparison to Protestant beliefs in the Rapture and the denial of the resurrection of the body. Challenge students to elevate their understandings of Heaven and Hell to a theological understanding in relation to the loving God.

Audiovisual Materials continued from page 127

Heroes of Faith

Produced by Heart of the Nation, this video profiles the lives of eleven prominent Christians who have overcome obstacles, both internal and external, to grow in their faith in God, and come to a place of deeper and more profound faith in God. Those profiled are Father Lawrence Martin Jenco, Father Tom Takahashi, Orel Hershiser, Fred Rogers, Flannery O'Connor, Dave Brubeck, Natzih Rizk, St. Francis of Assisi, Jean Donovan, Dorothy Day, and Martin Luther King Jr. Study guide included (60-minute video, Harcourt).

Joseph: Man Closest to Christ

Examines Jesus' foster father as a prayerful worker and exemplary model of manhood (60-minute video, Ignatius Press, Videos with Values).

Mother Teresa: The Legacy

The official film of the occasion of her beatification in Rome (54-minute video, Videos with Values).

The Sacrament of Reconciliation

Beginning with the experience of sin and guilt, it explains why the sacrament is a unique gift from God. Examines the Rite of Reconciliation in detail (90-minute video, Argus).

Sacrament of Reconciliation, The Past and Present

Examines the history of the sacrament from biblical times to the present (39-minute video, Twenty-Third Publications).

Saints Gallery

The narrator uses classical art and exciting stories to recount the lives of some of the great saints (Videos with Values).

Volume I: Heavenly Heroes: Joan of Arc (Warrior), St. Joseph (Father and Husband), St. Martin de Porres (Dominican Brother), St. Elizabeth Seton (Mother and Nun), St. Martin of Tours (Soldier), and St. Elizabeth of Hungary (Princess) (35 minutes).

Volume II: Founders of religious orders: Features St. Ignatius Loyola, St. Francis of Assisi, St. Angela Merici, St. Benedict, and St. Eugene de Mazenod (40 minutes).

Volume III: Saints for All Seasons: Mary-Queen of Saints, St. Patrick, St. Nicholas, St. Valentine, St. Mary Magdalene (40 minutes).

Volume IV: Early Church Leaders: St. Peter, St. Clare of Assisi, St. Thomas Aquinas, St. Catherine of Siena, and St. Paul (43 minutes).

Volume V: Great Women: Thérèse of Lisieux, Edith Stein, and Kateri Tekakwitha.

continued on page 142

Bell Ringers

- **Class Discussion:** People often suggest the expression that they are living in Heaven and Hell on earth. Have the students write a description of the type of life that might be described as "Heaven on earth" or "Hell on earth." Afterward, have students discuss what these descriptions might suggest about how people will experience Heaven and Hell after death.

- **Class Discussion:** Have students observe the popular image of the Last Judgment by Michelangelo on the wall of the Sistine Chapel. What does the image express about the people who will go to Heaven or Hell? Have students choose a few of the figures and try to guess what they think the artist is trying to show.

live and one death to experience; there is no reincarnation. This is why Christ instructed us always to be ready, to live each day as though it were our last. This truth is a powerful motivator to help us live purposeful and loving lives today. St. John Vianney observed, "Life is given us that we may learn to die well, and we never think of it. To die well we must live well."

Thinking about your own death can help you resolve to live more lovingly in the present. What if today were your last day to live? How loving would your

thoughts, words, and deeds be if you believed that Christ would judge you in the next few hours? Living this way always, you would not only live an exciting, love-filled Christian life, you would attract many people to the Lord Jesus and his great news of Salvation.

If we imitate Jesus in his love of others, then we need not fear death. Jesus Christ wants us to befriend him in this life so that we can live joyfully with him in eternity. This is not only the Good News of the Gospel, this is the greatest news we could possibly want to know.

Heaven

For we brought nothing into the world, just as we shall not be able to take anything out of it.

—1 Timothy 6:7

To the good man to die is gain. The foolish fear death as the greatest of evils, the wise desire it as a rest after the labors and the end of ills.

—St. Ambrose

Do one of the following:
- Write a short story about Heaven.
- Design your image of Heaven using any art medium.

resurrection of the body
The Christian belief that when Christ comes again, he will reunite the bodies of every human with their souls.

The Resurrection of the Body (CCC, 988–1001; 1004; 1015–1017)

God created humans with a body (flesh). God's Son, the Word of God, took on a human body (flesh) to redeem it. Furthermore, the resurrection of the body (flesh) completes the creation and Redemption of human flesh. These interlocking truths of the resurrection of the body and the gift of everlasting life are fundamental beliefs, based on our faith in the Lord's own Resurrection. A hallmark sign of following Jesus is to witness

to Christ's Resurrection, proclaiming to the world the great news that we will rise with and through him.

At death the human soul separates from the body, which will corrupt. It is immediately after death that God will judge us. Then, when Christ comes again, by the power of his own Resurrection, the most Blessed Trinity will raise our bodies. Our resurrected bodies will be made incorrupt, and they will join again with our souls. St. Paul uses a vivid image of the Roman triumphal procession to describe the Lord's Second Coming. When the trumpet of God blasts, God

---

Audiovisual Materials continued from page 141

St. Clare of Assisi and the Poor Clares

    A documentary about this extraordinary woman and her community of cloistered nuns (70-minute video, Ignatius Press).

St. Francis Assisi

    Filmed in Umbria, this Oriente Occidente Production shows the authentic sites where Francis lived, worked, prayed, and died (30-minute video, St. Anthony Messenger Press).

The Song of Bernadette

    The timeless story of Mary's appearance to a humble girl at Fatima, Portugal (156-minute DVD, Ignatius Press, Amazon.com).

Tuesdays with Morrie

    A made-for-TV dramatization based on Mitch Albom's book of the same name. Stars Jack Lemmon. Shows how to die with dignity (89-minute DVD, Ignatius Press, Amazon.com).

What Catholics Believe: Reconciliation

    Overview of the sacrament (30-minute video, Oblate Media).

will take both living and dead up into the clouds "to meet the Lord in the air" (1 Thes 4:17). Later, Good News awaits us: "The one who raised the Lord Jesus will raise us also with Jesus and place us with you in his presence" (2 Cor 4:14).

Our Catholic faith holds that God will raise from the dead all people on the last day. How God will accomplish this is unknown to us, but we trust his Word that he will make our bodies incorruptible when they reunite with our souls. To describe this mysterious transformation, St. Paul used the analogy of the seed:

But someone may say, "How are the dead raised? With what kind of body will they come back?" You fool! What you sow is not brought to life unless it dies. And what you sow is not the body that is to be but a bare kernel of wheat, perhaps, or of some other kind; but God gives it a body as he chooses, and to each of the seeds its own body. . . . It is sown corruptible; it is raised incorruptible. It is sown dishonorable; it is raised glorious. It is sown weak; it is raised powerful. It is sown a natural body; it is raised a spiritual body. If there is a natural body, there is also a spiritual one. (1 Cor 15:35–38; 42–44)

The most important quality of the resurrected body will be immortality; we will never die again. St. Paul lists other attributes of the resurrected body: imperishable, glorious, powerful, and spiritual. Theologians have interpreted these traits to mean that we will never feel pain. The resurrected body will shine brightly, reflecting the glory of the Beatific Vision, that is, "seeing God." Material creation will not hinder us; for example, we will be able to move about easily and swiftly.

Finally, our spirits will control our glorified bodies.

Related to the resurrection of the body is our belief that God will transform material creation in Christ. We simply cannot imagine what God has in store for us. However, it makes sense that he has created a suitable environment where our resurrected, glorified bodies will thrive for eternity.

The belief in the resurrection of the body should encourage a great respect for your own body and for the bodies of other people. Our human existence includes the possession of both a soul and a body. They come from God as gifts and will return to glorify him. When we care for and respect our bodies, including those of the most helpless among us (like unborn babies), we are expressing profound respect and gratitude to a loving God, who made us as a composite being of body and soul.

The Catholic-held belief in the resurrection of the body contrasts sharply with many other religions that teach an afterlife of the soul alone. Catholic belief goes much deeper in teaching that the whole person—body and soul—will survive death.

Beatific Vision
Seeing God face-to-face in Heaven, the source of our eternal happiness; final union with the Triune God for all eternity.

Teaching Approaches

- **Individual Activity:** The best way to relieve all our fears about death is to focus on Christ and on living our life as he commanded—with love.

  - Ask your students to imagine for a moment that when they are judged by Christ at the end of their life *only the next 7 days will count*. Pass out copies of Chapter 5, Handout 5 "Seven-Day Calendar" (starting on page 285 and also online at www.avemariapress.com) and have the students plan their next seven days with love in mind. To begin they should write in all the appointments they know they have—school, practices, work, time for homework, Mass, youth group, co-curricular activities, etc. How will they meet these responsibilities? What will they do to make themselves better people? To help their families and school community? For each appointment have them write one virtue they want to put into practice while they are completing that task.

  - Reteach the lesson from Chapter 2 (on pages 60–61)—they will be judged by how they feed the hungry, give drink to the thirsty, clothe the naked, etc. How can they do those things over the next seven days?

  - Review the students' plans to be sure they are practical and realistic. Then ask them to take their plans home and try to live them out over the next seven days. They should take a few minutes each day to evaluate how they did on that day. At the end of the seven days, discuss with the class how they did. Challenge them to make a new plan for the next seven days and to follow it even though it is not an assignment.

Extending the Lesson

Guest Speaker: One of the corporal acts of mercy is to bury the dead; one of the spiritual acts of mercy is to comfort the grieving. Both of these find expression in the Church through the work of bereavement ministers. Many parishes and dioceses today have specially trained bereavement ministers who are available to offer support to family members and communities who are grieving the death of a loved one. They offer support by helping to plan funerals, rosaries, and wakes for the deceased; by hosting receptions and providing hospitality to the mourners who need a place to gather to share stories and memories of the person who is gone; and by organizing support groups for family members who need help as they go through the process of grieving.

Invite one of these trained ministers to come to your class and share some of their experiences with your students. You will want to help the speaker prepare by giving them some questions or topics you would like them to address beforehand. Some questions that might be of interest are:

- What do bereavement ministers do?
- Why are funerals important?
- Can you share a story about a time you saw a person's faith might comfort them when a loved one dies? What comfort does the Catholic faith offer to those who have experienced the death of a loved one?
- If our friend loses a loved one, how can or should we express our sorrow, our concern, and our love for our friend? Are there things we should not say or do?

You should also ask the students what they would like to know.

- **Individual Activity:** Have the students list, in order, a series of events that will occur after we die based on Catholic theology. Have them be as specific as possible. Suggest that they create multiple lists for different types of people. Afterward, create a master list as a class. Later, compare this list to what the students will learn in this section.
- **Direct Instruction:** Summarize the subsection "The Resurrection of the Body" (pages 140–141). Make sure that you dispel the misunderstanding about life after death that only includes the resurrection of the soul. Note that Jesus himself rose from the dead body and soul, and his body ascended to Heaven along with his soul. If we follow him in his Resurrection, then we, too, will rise, body and soul.
- **Direct Instruction:** Knowing that we will have the bodies that God gave us forever has a profound impact on the way we treat ourselves. Have the students list five ways that you respect and take good care of your body. Then, list five ways you respect and take care of other people's bodies.

particular judgment
The individual's judgment right after death, when Christ will rule on one's eternal destiny to be spent in Heaven (after purification in Purgatory, if needed) or in Hell.

Particular Judgment (CCC, 1020–1022; 1051)

An immediate judgment after death is based on Divine Revelation. This particular (individual) judgment will determine whether we go to Heaven immediately, need purification in Purgatory, or must suffer the punishments of Hell and eternal damnation. St. Paul writes:

> For we must all appear before the judgment seat of Christ, so that each one may receive recompense, according to what he did in the body, whether good or evil. (2 Cor 5:10)

Jesus himself referred to the particular judgment in the Parable of the Rich Man and Lazarus (Lk 16:19–31). Because of his selfish lifestyle and neglect of the starving Lazarus, the rich man suffered the fires of Hell. In contrast, Lazarus went to a peaceful resting place.

If we live a just and loving life, we have nothing to fear when we die. God is a God of justice *and* mercy. God's judgment is based on whether we loved him and love our neighbor as ourselves. God is not out to trick us at the particular judgment. There will be no surprises. People know if they have lived loving and God-centered lives or not. The famous poet Dante Alighieri said it well:

> If you insist on having your own way, you will get it. Hell is the enjoyment of your own way forever. If you really want God's way with you, you will get it in heaven.

One way to consider the "day of judgment" is to think of it as our permanent decision to accept or reject Jesus Christ. But Scripture reveals another judgment, at the end of time. It will be a final judgment, when there will be final victory over evil.

RIP

RIP is a familiar acronym that translates a short prayer asking God to remember the deceased: *Requiescat in pace*, "May he/she rest in peace."
Another Latin phrase, *Sic transit gloria mundi* ("Thus passes the glory of the world"), reminds us that we have only a brief time to make our mark. Time speeds quickly by. What the world holds important may not be so in God's eyes.

Reflect on your own life and where it is going. Write your responses to the following three questions posed by St. Ignatius of Loyola (1491–1556):

1. What have you done for Christ?
2. What are you doing for Christ?
3. What will you do for Christ?

For Enrichment

Direct Instruction: During the discussion on the resurrection of the body, try to make visible Paul's metaphor of the seed, which must die in order to be reborn as a full-grown plant. Bring to class on the day of this lesson a handful of large bean seeds and a full-grown bean plant. If you have a green thumb, plant a few seeds and grow them yourself. Be sure to start early so that your plants have time to grow well. If not, a quick trip to a nursery will be helpful. You may want to have your students participate by growing their own seeds in plastic cups. If they fill the cups with moistened paper towels and push the seeds down the outside edge, they will be able to watch the seed being transformed into a plant. Later, show the bean seeds and full-grown plant you have brought to class or by directing the students' attention to their own cups. Just as the seed is "intended" to become a healthy and beautiful plant (that is its purpose), so are their bodies destined for resurrection.

Extending the Lesson

Direct Instruction: For the final subsection "Amen" (pages 147–148), you will want to take the time to celebrate all that your class has experienced and learned thus far. To prepare, make a list of all the different activities and exercises that you remember doing with the class over the last five chapters. Try to think of something each student did or said that impressed you. You might choose to write these compliments in a personal letter to each student, or you may just want to make notes that will help you to compliment each student's contribution during the following lesson.

Heaven, Purgatory, Hell (CCC, 1023–1037; 1052–1058)

At death, all people receive the rewards for their life. Those who have done good merit eternal reward, and those who have died separated from God receive their chosen punishment. Catholic doctrine explains that there is an eternal life that we will spend in Heaven or Hell. The reward of Heaven is eternal life spent in union with God and all those who share in God's life. Hell is eternal separation from God.

The existence of Heaven and Hell take very seriously the reality of human freedom. If we use our freedom properly, then we will choose our own eternal destiny—a joyous life with our loving, Triune God. On the other hand, if we decide to model ourselves into heartless, unloving, selfish people, then God will respect our decision. When we choose self over God, then we have *chosen* Hell. Our God respects our freedom and will give us what we want. But God generously rewards freedom that is used properly. Victor Hugo wrote, "Good actions are the invisible hinges of the doors of heaven."

Many images try to capture the differences between Heaven and Hell. One comes from a legend that tells of a man who dreamed of both of them. In his first dream he found himself in a magnificent palace where countless millions gathered around eight-foot-high tables overflowing with food. However, there was a problem. Although the spoons they had were long enough to reach the food, they were way too long to put the food into their mouths. Despite this, everyone was extremely happy and satisfied because they used their spoons to feed their neighbors and friends. Everyone was feeding others; everyone was being fed.

The man's second dream was like the first. Again, there was a very tall table replete with delicious food. But the people were upset, angry, frustrated, and bitter. Why? They tried to feed themselves. So fixed were they in their selfish mindset, it never occurred to them to feed those around them.

Heaven

Heaven is the name for our union with the loving, Triune God, the Blessed Mother, and all the angels and saints, including our relatives and friends who have lived a God-centered life. Those who reach Heaven will live with Christ Jesus forever. They will enjoy the Beatific Vision, that is, seeing God face-to-face, as he really is,

Jesus' Death and Resurrection have given us access to Heaven. In Heaven we will be fully incorporated into Christ. Although we will have perfect communion with him and his loved ones, we will both retain and find our true individual identity as his brother or sister. We will continue to fulfill God's will in Heaven and will reign with Christ Jesus forever.

contemplating his heavenly glory. In Heaven, "[God] will wipe every tear from their eyes, and there shall be no more death or mourning, wailing or pain, (for) the old order has passed away" (Rv 21:4).

The pleasures and happiness in store for us in Heaven are beyond human imagination. Scripture uses many images to help describe them, for example, wedding feast, light, life, peace, paradise, the Father's house, and heavenly Jerusalem.

Even these cannot begin to describe Heaven. As St. Paul's first letter to the Corinthians explains, "What eye has not seen, and ear has not heard, and what has not entered the human heart, what God has prepared for those who love him" (1 Cor 2:9). There is no goal more worthwhile than getting to Heaven. We should always keep it before our eyes and resolve not to do anything foolish enough to jeopardize our attaining it.

- **Class Activity:** Divide the class into two teams of equal size. Divide your chalkboard in half as well. Assign one team to fill one half of the board with ways in which our society respects and cares for our bodies. Assign the other team to fill the other half with ways in which our society does not respect or take good care of our bodies. On one side of the board the students will come up with things like research into cures for various diseases, promoting healthy diets, exercise clubs, seatbelts, speed limits, etc. On the other side they might list things like too much junk food, inadequate access to health care for the poor, drug use/abuse, promiscuous sex, abortion, rape, child abuse, etc.

- **Direct Instruction:** Related to the text subsection on the "Particular Judgment" (page 142), read with the class the story of Lazarus and the rich man with your students (Lk 16:19–31). Compare this parable with the separation of the sheep and the goats from Matthew 25:31–46. Help your students to make the connection between the rich man and the people who did nothing to feed the hungry, clothe the naked, care for the ill, etc. These stories reveal the basis on which we will be judged.

Background Information

Explaining More about Eschatology

In his book *Catholicism* (HarperCollins), Fr. Richard P. McBrien explains:

> Eschatology is that area of theology which is directly concerned with the "study of the last thing(s)." The "last thing" is God, or, more precisely, the final manifestation of the reconciling, renewing, and unifying love of God. The "last things" are various moments or stages in the final manifestation process: death, particular judgment, heaven, Hell, purgatory, Second Coming of Christ, resurrection of the body, general judgment, consummation of all things in the perfection of the Kingdom of God. . . . At the very least, eschatology provides a wider context for the discussion of every other theological question, for eschatology is about the Kingdom (or "reign") of God." (1101)

- **Class Activity:** Pass out index cards to each student. Have them complete the "RIP" exercise on page 142, listing the information called for the imaginary obituary. On the back of the index card have them answer the other two requests (i.e., supposing they were to die next week vs. at age sixty-five). Have the students meet in groups of six to eight, and have them exchange index cards and read each other's imaginary obituaries. Then allow time for them to discuss and ask questions about anything that they read.

- **Group Activity:** Summarize the text subsection "Heaven, Purgatory, and Hell" on pages 143–145 paying particular attention to the legend about the man's dreams of Heaven and Hell. Point out that there is a saying about Heaven and Hell: **"It is Heaven all the way to Heaven and Hell all the way to hell."** Write this saying on the board and ask your students what they think this means. Use class time to discuss ways in which we choose to live in Heaven or Hell every day. Split the class into groups of four to five students. Ask each group to choose a secretary who keeps a list of the group's ideas and a spokesperson who will report to the entire class. First, ask the groups to describe Heaven. Not so much what it looks like, but what it feels like. How do people in Heaven feel about being there? How do they feel about/toward the other people who are also there? What feelings accompany the presence of God? Allow the spokespeople from each group to share a summary of their group's ideas. Do the same with hell—asking first what it feels like to be there and then what activities create those emotions. Finally, ask the students to suggest some experiences that can be considered purgatorial. What experiences, though painful, bring us closer to God, or open our eyes to see God's action in the world?

St. John Vianney (1786–1859) reminds us of a powerful truth: "Our home is Heaven. On earth we're like travelers staying at a hotel. When you're away, you're always thinking of going home."[12] May we always remember our true home—the one to which God calls us.

Purgatory

Purgatory is the name for the state of being of the final purification of those who die in God's grace and friendship. Purgatory is also called the "Church suffering."

The existence of Purgatory is rooted in the Bible. For example, Judas Maccabeus and his soldiers prayed for the martyred Jews they might be released from their sins (see 2 Mc 12:39–46). Church Tradition has interpreted certain New Testament passages as referring to a place of a "cleansing fire" after death. From the first centuries, the Church has honored the dead by offering the Eucharist for them and encouraging the faithful to pray for them. In addition, the Church has recommended almsgiving, indulgences, and acts of penance for the "poor souls in Purgatory."

The doctrine of "purification," or Purgatory, makes sense. To embrace an all-loving God, we must be free of any imperfection in our own capacity to love. Only a clean person can enter Heaven to embrace the all-holy God. Not everyone who dies has cleansed himself or herself of his or her venial sins or any punishment due sins that are present at death. To a degree, on our earthly journey we can accomplish this process of purification.

However, dying to our attachment to sin and our selfishness is a long and painful process.

Purgatory involves both a joyful and painful process of letting go of sin. Those undergoing purification are happy that the Lord has promised them Heaven. At the same time, they need to leave behind their selfish attachments before meeting the all-holy God. This painful process of "letting go and letting God" may be what is meant by the "fires of Purgatory." The process of purgation might be one of "burning" with sorrow and shame over a sinful life, and a profound wish to be united to the loving, good, saving God. To be separated from the Lord whom they love so deeply brings suffering to our brothers and sisters in Purgatory. However, when their purgation is complete, their suffering will end as they enter into the bliss of Heaven.

We belong to the Communion of Saints, so we should never forget to pray for those in Purgatory and ask for their prayers as well. We can honor our relatives who have gone before us by praying for them and offering our good works and sacrifices on their behalf. Then, when they make it to Heaven, they will be sure to remember us before God.

Hell

To die in mortal sin without repenting and accepting God's merciful love means remaining separated from him forever by one's own free choice. This is the meaning of Hell. The principal punishment of Hell is separation from our loving God who created us for love, life, joy, and happiness—our deepest yearnings that only God can satisfy. Christian tradition speaks of the "fires of Hell." These describe the loss of love, self-hatred, and the total loneliness that results from failure to love God above all others and our neighbor as we do ourselves for the love of God. Those in Hell grieve over their eternal punishment, suffer spiritually and physically, and give up all hope of Salvation.

God does not predestine anyone for Hell. God made us to love him. However, for those who freely choose to commit mortal sin by refusing to love God, and die without repenting of their lack of love, their own free choice will forever separate them from God.

Scripture and Church Tradition both affirm the existence of Hell. For example, Jesus

For Enrichment

Individual Assignment: Have the students complete the assignment "Heaven" (page 140) by choosing and completing either one of the choices listed.

Writing Assignment: Ask the students to complete a creative writing assignment in which they imagine what their own particular judgment will be like. They can write in prose or poetry or a dialog—anything to get across how they imagine their own judgment. What will this judgment look and feel like? Who will be there? Will there be a conversation or just a pronouncement? What do they imagine?

referred several times to Gehenna (Hell). In the parable of the sheep and goats (Mt 25:41–46), Jesus condemns to Hell those who fail to respond to those in need. On another occasion, Jesus offered this stern warning:

The Son of Man will send his angels, and they will collect out of his kingdom all who cause others to sin and all evildoers. They will throw them into the fiery furnace, where there will be wailing and grinding of teeth. (Mt 13:41–42)

The existence of Hell flows from the belief that God is a loving God who made us truly free. God respects our freedom, even if, out of pride, we choose to reject God's love, grace, and mercy. God forever showers his love on us; his mercy is always there for us to embrace. Nevertheless, a person can be hard hearted and stiff-necked, adamantly selfish and unloving. People can and do commit mortal sin. Having created us free beings, God respects our freedom.

God does not send us to Hell; unrepentant mortal sin does. We cannot say for sure who is in Hell because we do not know for sure who has defiantly turned their backs on God. Jesus warns us not to judge others lest we be judged ourselves. What we can do is to pray to repent and accept God's love and forgiveness.

If we live a life loving God and others, we should not let the existence of Hell frighten us unduly. If we have turned from our sins as Christ calls us to do, and struggle to live with love in our hearts, then we should trust and believe that Christ Jesus will save us. He is a merciful, loving Savior who will always forgive us if we repent. His Father is our Abba, who loves us more tenderly than any human mother or father possibly could.

However, we should take Hell's existence seriously. It challenges us to live responsibly, to repent of our sins, and to reform our lives in the image of Jesus. It reminds us to live a good life *right now* because we never know when we will die.

Differentiating Heaven and Hell

Complete each of the following activities:

- Read the Parable of the Weeds (Mt 13:24–30, 36–43) and the Parable of the Net (Mt 13:47–50). Write your own interpretation of these parables based on what they are saying about God's judgment.
- C. S. Lewis contrasted Heaven and Hell using images like the ones below. Create at least four more images of your own to contrast Heaven and Hell.

Hell is . . .	Heaven is . . .
an unending Church service without God	God without a Church service
gray, and so are its inhabitants	full of colors and all colors of people
full of clocks and telephones	full of only those possessions you gave away on earth
sex without pleasure	pleasure without sex

- Lewis also wrote, "The safest road to Hell is the gradual one—the gentle slope, soft underfoot, without sudden turnings, without milestones, without signposts." What did Lewis mean? Is he correct? Offer evidence one way or the other.

- **Individual Assignment:** Assign the "Differentiating Heaven and Hell" activities (page 145). If there is time, have the students work on this assignment in class. Or, assign this for homework.
- **Direct Instruction:** Take a few moments to dispel misunderstandings about Purgatory (page 144). Explain that people in Purgatory will only go to Heaven. These people have not died in a state of mortal sin, but are happy that the Lord has promised them Heaven. Purgatory is a purification process that is needed so that we are able to see God in the Beatific Vision. Purgatory is not so much a punishment as it is a cleansing before meeting God face to face.
- **Class Discussion:** Have the students summarize the text section "The Last or General Judgment" (page 146), especially with an understanding of the term "parousia." Ask students to make comparisons between particular judgment (page 142) and general judgment. List these differences on the board.
- **Group Activity:** Divide the class into two groups. Ask each group to write a one-act play based on the parable of the judgment of the nations, when Jesus separates the saved who have served him in their brothers and sisters, and the damned. Ask them to write dialog that fleshes out the Scripture passage more fully.
  - Scripts should be submitted to you, checked, and returned before students choose parts and begin rehearsing.
  - When the groups are ready, have them perform the plays either at the current session or, more likely, in a future session. If possible, record their plays using a digital camera or tape recorder.

Extending the Lesson

Individual Activity: To add to the "RIP" exercise on page 142, have the students list ten to twenty adjectives they would want their friends and family members to use if they were writing their eulogy. Narrow the list to the five most important words or phrases. Next, have them think of one thing they could do tomorrow to give people reason to use each of those words. Do one of them each day for three to five days. At the end of the week, review the assignment with the students. How did they do?

- **Direct Instruction:** Summarize the Explaining Your Faith feature "Do Catholics Believe in the Rapture and that Jesus Will Return Any Day Now?" If possible, show clips of the movie series *Left Behind* or bring in the novels from your local library. Summarize the response in the text and ask for students to share what they think about the answer.

- **Class Activity:** Conclude this long section of the text and coverage of the Apostles' Creed with the subsection that focuses on the word "Amen" (pages 147–148). To do so, re-create the Apostles' Creed on the board by asking students to each write one line. Ask for a volunteer to write the first line and then another to write the next, and another the next. Each volunteer may also correct previous lines if they feel something was left out or in the wrong order. If your students have laptops at their desks, have them attempt this activity using a wiki or Google Docs, but make sure they do not look up the text online. When you have finished and the entire prayer is on the board, ask the students which activities and lessons they remember best in relation to each part of the Creed. What did they learn? How did they experience God? How did they experience the Christian community? What brought them joy?

last (general) judgment
Jesus Christ's judgment of the living and the dead on the last day, when he comes to establish God's Kingdom fully.

The Last or General Judgment (*CCC*, 1038–1050; 1059–1060)

The events of the last day of human history are known as the last or general judgment. On that day, the resurrection of the just and unjust will take place and the Risen, Glorified Lord will come again (see the *Parousia*, pages 60–61). Christ, who is Truth itself, will reveal each person's relationship with God. Finally, everyone will recognize God's saving plan in Christ Jesus. The Son of Man, in the presence of all the angels, will separate the sheep from the goats (Mt 25:31–32).

As to *when* this will take place, only the Father knows. When the day comes, however, everyone will see "that God's justice triumphs over all the injustices committed by his creatures and that God's love is stronger than death" (*CCC*, 1040). Followers of Christ look forward to this day of final judgment because the unity with God that our hearts yearn for will be accomplished. Furthermore, on this day God will transform and restore the entire physical universe. Along with a transformed humanity, "the new heavens and new earth" will share in Christ Jesus' own glory. Since we do not know the exact hour of Christ's return and our final judgment, we should always be ready. The time to live a Christlike life is now.

Today we have a glimpse of our future life because Christ has already launched the Kingdom of God. Despite the sinful forces at work in the world to undermine God's saving love, his loving grace is very much alive to help attract people to our Triune God. The Spirit gives Catholics the power and the mission of cooperating with Christ's work of freeing people. He strengthens us with virtues like fortitude to work tirelessly as peacemakers. We can work for justice by

helping people attain their God-given rights. We also cooperate in Christ's plan when we promote human solidarity and respect the dignity of every human being. In a special way, we promote the Kingdom of God when we extend mercy to the weak, poor, and defenseless.

The Holy Spirit gives us the virtue of hope. It helps us look forward to the glorious day of Christ's Second Coming. It helps us pray the prayer that concludes the entire Scriptures: "Amen! Come, Lord Jesus! The grace of the Lord Jesus be with all" (Rv 22:20–21).

Extending the Lesson

Individual Assignment: There are many excellent fictional works that deal with the subject of Heaven in some way. Assign a book report to be completed by your students. You can either give them a list of books to choose from or assign one book for the whole class to read. Choose from one of the following or another that you have read:

- *The Last Battle*, by C.S. Lewis. This is a children's book from his Narnia series. It depicts the end times of Narnia and the author's fictional vision of Heaven (and more briefly, Hell).
- *The Five People You Meet in Heaven*, by Mitch Albom. This is an adult book, but appropriate and readable for high school ages as well.
- "Revelation" from *Everything That Rises Must Converge*, by Flannery O'Connor. This is a short story in which a woman who is confident she is "good people," is confronted with a vision in which she sees all those she considers herself "better than" on their way to Heaven before her.
- *The Great Divorce*, by C.S. Lewis. This is a short novel, accessible to teens and more mature than the Narnia series. It makes clear the truth that the damned choose their exile in hell.

Explaining Your Faith

Do Catholics believe in the Rapture and that Jesus will return any day now?

This question is often asked because of the recent Left Behind series of novels and books. The series began with a book telling how Christ came to lift up millions of "good" people and takes them to Heaven in an event known as the Rapture. Those "left behind" had to contend with the Antichrist and his battle for their souls in the next seven years. The last book in the series rewrites the book of Revelation as a thriller about the end of the world and the sudden disappearance of millions of Christians.

These novels are the product of biblical fundamentalist theology that is severely at odds with Catholic teaching about the end of the world and the coming of Jesus. (One characteristic of fundamentalism is to read the Bible literally with little regard to literary types.) In truth, the Book of Revelation is a beacon of hope to Christians under persecution. Its basic message is that if we remain faithful to Christ, we will share in his heavenly kingdom. Catholic theology, therefore, looks with hope to the day of our Lord's return. In contrast, opinions like those in the Left Behind novels present a harsh and judgmental God at odds with the scriptural portrait.

We should be wary about fundamentalist interpretations about the end of the world, for example, by distrusting claims of certain sects that periodically try to predict when the final battle between good and evil will take place. We should also ignore those who make scary predictions about the world's end. Some people, consciously or not, exploit the natural fear we have of the unknown. Their "secret" knowledge of the future gives them a type of control over others.

Catholic teaching holds that, yes, Christ will come again to judge the living and the dead (Mt 12:36). But since Jesus is a loving Savior, we should not fear this day (Jn 3:17). We should, however, prepare for Judgment Day by serving others (Mt 24:42–44). The Church does not pretend to know when the world will end or the nature of the events preceding it.

As our loving Mother, the Church directs us to the teaching of Jesus himself. When the Apostles asked him when the world would end, Jesus replied, "But of that day or hour, no one knows, neither the angels in heaven, nor the Son, but only the Father" (Mk 13:32).

Jesus teaches that we should always be ready by living a Christian life right now (Mk 13:33). Needless worry about the future is pointless, accomplishing nothing. Jesus instructs us to set our hearts on God's Kingdom first and to trust in God's saving justice. Everything else will take care of itself (Mt 6:33–34). It is hard to improve on this formula for a happy, productive Christian life.

Amen (CCC, 1061–1065)

Amen is the traditional way we end our prayers, including the Apostles' Creed. Amen is also the word that ends the Bible. Amen means "so be it, I agree, certainly, it is firm." Amen comes from the Hebrew word for "believe." Thus, when we say Amen, we are making an act of faith, proclaiming the truth of what we pray and celebrate. Amen summarizes our heartfelt conviction and expresses our solidarity with it.

Jesus often said Amen to stress that what he was about to teach was trustworthy, that it came from his Father. God the Father also said Amen when he sent us his Son. The Lord is indeed the yes of God's saving love for us.

Finally, death is really an Amen to our lives. For Christians who have "fought the good fight," death is a state that readies us for eternity. If we live struggling to do right, trying to love, repenting of our sins, trusting in Jesus—then our death is not something to fear.

Amen
A Hebrew word for "truly" or "it is so," thus signifying agreement with what has been said. New Testament and liturgical prayers and creeds and other Christian prayers end with *Amen* to show belief in what has just been said.

- **Journal Assignment:** Give them a few minutes to reflect in their journals on which parts of the Creed they are most confident of and which parts they may find more challenging. Remind them that prayer is a way of asking for increased faith so when they have doubts or are confused about their faith, that is the time to pray even harder.
- **Prayer Experience:** Close by praying the Apostles' Creed together, ending with a resounding "Amen!"

Background Information

The Mystery of Death

The Vatican II document *Pastoral Constitution on the Church in the Modern World (Gaudium et Spes)* addresses the mystery of death:

> While the mind is at a loss before the mystery of death, the Church, taught by divine Revelation, declares that God has created man in view of a blessed destiny that lies beyond the limits of his sad state on earth. Moreover, the Christian faith teaches that bodily death, from which man would have been immune had he not sinned, will be overcome when that wholeness which he lost through his own fault will be given once again to him by the almighty and merciful Savior. (Chapter I, no. 18)

For Review Answers (page 148)

1. The doctrine of the resurrection of the body means that we believe that God will reunite our souls and our bodies on the last day. Our resurrected bodies will be different from our present bodies. Most significantly, they will be immortal so we will never die again.

2. Catholic belief opposes reincarnation because Scripture reveals that we only die once and then meet God in judgment. Also, Christians believe in the goodness of God's creation—including the human body. We believe that our bodies will be resurrected— this is incompatible with a belief in reincarnation. Reincarnation also supposes that eventually a soul will "get it right" and save itself through purification and enlightenment, but the Church teaches that Jesus alone has the power to save us. We cannot save ourselves.

3. The Beatific Vision refers to our seeing God face to face in Heaven. It is our final destiny—union with the Triune God for all eternity.

4. Purgatory is the place or process where we are purified of any remaining sinfulness before attaining Heaven.

5. Hell is eternal separation from God.

6. At the Second Coming of Christ, the truth of our relationship with God will be revealed, our bodies will be resurrected, the just will be admitted to Heaven, and the unjust condemned to Hell for eternity.

7. Amen comes from the Hebrew word for "believe." It means "so be it, I agree, certainly, it is so." Saying "Amen" at the end of a prayer confirms our agreement and participation in the prayer.

8. "Amen" is a fitting end to the Apostles' Creed because it confirms our belief in everything we have just said.

9. The belief in the Rapture is based on the fundamentalist interpretation of the Book of Revelation. Catholics look in hope to the day of the Lord's return, unlike those who believe in the Rapture, which is characterized by a harsh, judgmental God and the coming of the evil Antichrist.

Rather, it is a fitting end to our lives, a yes to the life of a disciple about to enter eternity.

Catholic beliefs about the "last things" assure us that God has the final word. Our end in this life is but the birthday to an eternal life with the Lord. The doctrines of the resurrection of the body, judgment, and life everlasting teach that everything we do, or fail to do, has significance. If we choose Jesus and stay close to him in this life, then we can embrace these comforting words of St. Paul:

And when this which is corruptible clothes itself with incorruptibility and this which is mortal clothes itself with immortality, then the word that is written shall come about: "Death is swallowed up in victory. Where, O death, is your victory? Where, O death, is your sting?" The sting of death is sin, and the power of sin is the law. But thanks be to God who gives us the victory through our Lord Jesus Christ. Therefore, my beloved brothers, be firm, steadfast, always fully devoted to the work of the Lord, knowing that in the Lord your labor is not in vain. (1 Cor 15:54–58)

For Review

1. What is the meaning of the doctrine of the resurrection of the body?
2. Explain why Catholic belief opposes reincarnation.
3. Identify the term *Beatific Vision*.
4. Describe the nature of Purgatory.
5. What is Hell?
6. What will happen at the Second Coming of Christ?
7. What is the meaning of the word *Amen*?
8. Why is saying Amen an appropriate way to end the Apostles' Creed?
9. Why don't Catholics believe in the Rapture?

For Reflection

Imagine your own particular judgment. What three questions would you want Jesus to ask you as you enter eternity? How would you answer them?

Homework Assignment

1. Complete any unfinished in-class assignments from this lesson.

2. Complete the For Review questions on page 148.

3. Complete the chosen Ongoing Assignments on pages 150–151.

4. Begin to study for the Chapter 5 Test.

CHAPTER QUICK VIEW

- Those alive on earth (the Church militant), those suffering in Purgatory (the Church suffering), and the blessed ones in Heaven (the Church triumphant) make up the Communion of Saints. (page 128)
- Christ calls all of us to be saints, that is, to be holy. (page 129)
- The Church canonizes some saints to declare that they lived lives of heroic Christian witness. We honor the saints when we imitate their virtues and pray to them, asking them to intercede for us. (page 129)
- Mary is worthy of our devotion as the holiest of all humans. Her faith in becoming the Mother of God, her loving service of her Son, and her response to the Holy Spirit make her the supreme example of what a Christian should be. (pages 129–132)
- Mary is the Mother of God and our Blessed Mother, too. She is the Mother of the Church who prays for us always. (pages 130–131)
- *Original Sin* resulted from the prideful disobedience of Adam and Eve. All humans suffer the effects of this first sin, including the loss of God's friendship, physical suffering, and death. Jesus has conquered Original Sin and makes it possible for us to be united once again with our loving God. (pages 135–136)
- *Actual sin* is personal, individual sin. It can be an act, word, or desire contrary to God's law. *Venial sins* partially reject God. *Mortal sins* kill our relationship with God and others. To sin mortally there must be grave matter, sufficient reflection, and full consent of the will. (pages 136–137)
- The Apostles and their successors have the Christ-given power to forgive sin in his name, a major component of his saving activity. The Church follows Christ's command to forgive sin through the Sacraments of Baptism and Penance (reconciliation or confession). (page 137)
- Baptism forgives all sin. The Sacrament of Penance forgives post-baptismal sin of sincere and contrite sinners. (page 137)
- Death, introduced by Adam's sin, is a great mystery. But Christ Jesus overcame death through the Paschal Mystery of his Death on the cross and his Resurrection. If we die united to Jesus Christ, God will raise us on the last day to share in his glory. (pages 139–140)
- Our bodies will rise to an incorruptible, eternal life joined to our souls in the resurrection of the dead. (pages 140–141)
- When we die, we will appear before God for a particular judgment that will determine if we enter Heaven, Purgatory, or Hell. (page 142)
- Heaven is eternal union with God. Purgatory is a place or state of purification for those who die in God's friendship but need to be cleansed of their attachment to sin before meeting the all-holy God. Hell is eternal separation from God. (pages 143–145)
- Only the Father knows the day and hour of Christ's Second Coming. On that day of general judgment, Christ will reveal the truth of every person's relationship with God. The just will find their reward in Heaven; the unjust will go to Hell. (page 146)
- When we say "Amen", we are professing anew our faith in what has just preceded. Jesus is the great Amen of God's love for us. (pages 147–148)

Chapter 5, Handout 6 "Word Search" Answers

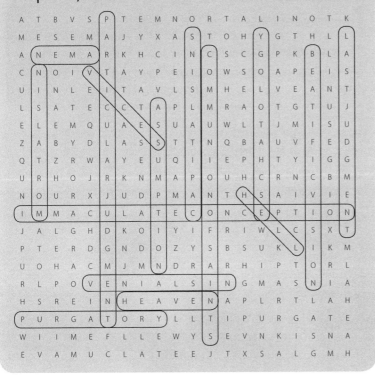

Chapter 5 Review Lesson

Objectives

In this lesson, the students will be able to:

- recall the definitions of the highlighted terms in Chapter 5.
- study and review the Chapter 5 material by focusing on the Chapter Quick View.

Preview

Chapter 5 is loaded with material. A review lesson can help you to slow down the pace, check assignments, show videos, and the like, as well as begin to help the students review the Chapter 5 material in preparation for the Chapter 5 Test. Design the lesson to fit your needs. Use as many or as few of the options listed here.

Bell Ringers

- **Class Discussion:** Have the students assess their progress in this chapter. Refer to the goals they set for themselves in the first lesson and have them evaluate their progress. Did they master the material to the degree that they hoped? Do they now know what they hoped to learn at the beginning of the chapter? Have students share their progress with the class.
- **Student Presentations:** Allow time for the students to report on or share any assignments they have been working on throughout this chapter with the exception of the Ongoing Assignments, which will be covered in more detail as the lesson proceeds.

Teaching Approaches

- **Student Presentations:** Use the following suggestions for sharing and displaying each of the Ongoing Assignments from pages 150–151:

1. Review Church teaching and Catholic belief on the afterlife. Then allow students who worked on the teachings of the other major religions to comment on the differences. Collect the reports.
2. Call on students who worked on this report to give brief answers on why Mary is disciple par excellence. Collect the reports.
3. Call on students to work together to list a summary point by point on the board of the canonization process.
4. Have the students share their experience in small groups.
5. Allow sharing of this experience. If this was done as a class project, assign a reflection paper on what the students found to be the rewards and challenges of living the corporal mysteries.
6. Review the meaning of the word "Amen," then allow students to share their findings.
7. Invite the students who chose to practice the corporal work of mercy "clothe the naked" to share their experiences.

8. Review the titles and teachings about Mary with the class. As students show their PowerPoint presentations, have them make connections with the images to the lessons they learned about Mary in this chapter.

- **Individual Assignment:** Consider having students review the vocabulary terms for this chapter in the following ways:
  - If the students have begun using memory cards (page 34) to review vocabulary, have them add the words from this chapter to each deck as before.
  - Have students complete the sentences in the Learning the Language of Faith feature on page 150.
  - Chapter 5, Handout 6 "Word Search" (starting on page 285 and also online at www.avemariapress.com) can be used by your students as a study tool as well. Answers are on page 151 of this text.

- **Class Activity:** The Chapter Quick View is provided to help your students review the chapter material. While it is helpful for the students to read and study the list, more creative use of the list might help students to retain the information.
  - Send the students on a "treasure hunt" through the chapter to identify the pages on which the information in each summary point can be found.
  - Chapter 5, Handout 7 "Chapter Quick View Review" (starting on page 285 and also online at www.avemariapress.com) contains a reprint of the Quick View with some of the key words and phrases missing. You can use this as a quiz to help the students evaluate areas they need to study more carefully or as a simple study sheet. If they are able to fill in all of the blanks easily, they should be ready to do well on the Chapter Test.

Chapter 5 Test Lesson

Objectives

In this lesson, the students will:
- take a test on the material in Chapter 5.
- pray for family members and friends who have died.
- introduce the material in "Part II: We Hope: Celebrating the Christian Mystery."

Preview

Though the session can be used for clearing up loose ends and collecting assignments from Chapter 5, most of the session should be reserved for the students to work on the Chapter 5 Test.

Teaching Approaches

- **Chapter Test:** Have the students clear their desks. Pass out the Chapter 5 Test. Allow most of the class period for the students to complete the test.

Learning the Language of Faith

Complete each sentence by choosing the correct answer from the list of terms below. You will not use all of the terms.

actual sin	last judgment
Ascension	Magisterium
Assumption	mortal sin
Beatific Vision	Original Sin
capital sins	Parousia
Communion of Saints	particular judgment
dogma	Paschal Mystery
ecumenism	resurrection of the body
eschatology	Salvation
evangelization	sin
general judgment	venial sin
Immaculate Conception	vices
Incarnation	Virgin Birth
infallibility	

1. When we get to Heaven, we will have the ____; that is, seeing God face-to-face.
2. The doctrine of Mary being born without Original Sin is known as the ____.
3. ____ are bad habits.
4. In order to commit ____, what we do must be seriously wrong and involve the complete agreement of our will.
5. The ____ takes place immediately after death.
6. ____ studies the "last things," including the doctrines of Heaven and Hell.
7. The Church Triumphant, the Church Militant, and the Church Suffering belong to the ____.
8. When the Blessed Mother died, her body was taken to Heaven. This is known as the doctrine of the ____.
9. Lust is one of the ____.
10. The teaching about Purgatory is a ____ of the Catholic Church, that is, a teaching of the highest authority.

Ongoing Assignments

As you cover the material in this chapter, choose and complete at least three of these assignments.

1. Research and report on what one of the following religions teaches about the afterlife: Judaism, Islam, Buddhism, Hinduism, or a Native American religion.
2. Write an essay titled "Mary, the First Disciple." Support reasons for stating that Mary is the Christian disciple *par excellence*.
3. Research the process of canonization in the Roman Catholic Church. Briefly summarize the requirements of each step leading to sainthood.
4. Read the account of the adulterous woman in John 8:1–11. Then do each of the following:
   - Rewrite this story from the viewpoint of the woman or one of her accusers whom Jesus challenged.
   - Write of a time when someone forgave you. What did you feel at the time? How did this forgiveness affect your relationship?

Homework Assignment

1. Study for the Chapter 5 Test.
2. Complete any unfinished assignments from Chapter 5.

Learning the Language of Faith Answers (page 150)

1. Beatific Vision
2. Immaculate Conception
3. vices
4. mortal sin
5. particular judgment
6. eschatology
7. Communion of Saints
8. Assumption
9. capital sins
10. dogma

5. Devise a project to put two of the corporal works of mercy—visiting the sick and buring the dead—into practice. For example: (1) visit a nursing home and talk to the lonely patients there; (2) do chores for an elderly neighbor; (3) set up for a luncheon (through your parish's hospitality committee) for the family members and friends of a deceased parishioner after the funeral Mass and burial.

6. Examine the following ten "Amen" sayings of Jesus in the Gospel of John. Write out each saying and then explain the point that Jesus is making in his pronouncement.

- John 3:3
- John 3:5
- John 5:24
- John 6:47–48
- John 6:53
- John 8:58
- John 10:7
- John 12:24
- John 13:20
- John 16:23

7. Devise a project with classmates to put into practice one of the corporal work of mercy—clothe the naked. Sponsor a clothing drive to collect gloves, underwear, socks, and hats for homeless people. Donate the items to a shelter.

8. Create a PowerPoint presentation on how Mary has been depicted in art through the ages or one that depicts the mysteries of the Rosary. Share with the class.

Prayer Reflection

The teaching on Purgatory is based on the practice of praying for the dead. "From the beginning the Church has honored the memory of the dead and offered prayers in suffrage for them, above all in the Eucharistic sacrifice, so that, thus purified, they may attain the beatific vision of God" (CCC, 609). Make a commitment to pray for family members and friends who have died. Use this traditional prayer:

A Prayer for Our Dear Departed[13]
O God Jesus, Whose loving Heart was ever troubled by the sorrows of others, look with pity on the souls of our dear ones in Purgatory. O Thou Who didst "love Thine own" hear our cry for mercy, and grant that those whom Thou hast called from our homes and hearts may soon enjoy everlasting rest in the home of Thy Love in Heaven. Amen.

V. Eternal rest grant unto them, O Lord.
R. *And let perpetual light shine upon them.*
V. May they rest in peace. Amen.

- *Reflection:* Who is a deceased friend or relative who needs your prayers?
- *Resolution:* Commit to one day per week to remember these people by name in prayer.

Homework Assignment

Read the Part II introduction, "We Hope: Celebrating the Christian Mystery" (pages 154–157).

- **Journal Assignment:** After turning in their tests, have the students write a response to the Reflection question and Resolution in the Prayer Reflection feature on page 151 in their journals.
- **Student Presentations:** Collect any unfinished assignments from Chapter 5. If there is time, allow the students to report on the assignments.
- **Prayer Experience:** Recite together the "A Prayer for Our Dear Departed" on page 151. Ask students to share the names of the people they would like to pray for before closing with an Our Father.

Chapter 5 Test Answers

Part 1: Multiple Choice (4 points each)

1. D

2. C

3. D

4. B

5. C

6. B

Part 2: True or False (4 points each)

7. F

8. F

9. F

10. F

11. T

12. F

13. T

14. T

15. F

16. T

17. T

Part 3: Short Fill-ins (4 points each)

18. venial sin

19. Communion of Saints

20. "truly"; "it is so"; "I believe"

21. consent of the will

22. pride

23. eschatology

Part 4: Short Essay (8 points are possible)

24. Answers should describe (1) particular judgment, (2) Purgatory (possibly), (3) Heaven/Beatific Vision, (4) resurrection of the body, (5) general or last judgment, (6) Heaven/Beatific Vision

We Hope:

Celebrating the
Christian Mystery

Part II: We Hope: Celebrating the Christian Mystery

Objectives

In this lesson, students will:

- explain how participating in the liturgy is our participation in God's work.
- explain ways that the Blessed Trinity is at work through the Church's liturgy.
- describe the effects and function of the sacraments.
- identify the Seven Sacraments.

Preview

Part II of the text is devoted to the celebration of the Christian Mystery. The introduction to this section explains the term *liturgy* and how the Church's liturgy is the action of the whole Body of Christ through which the Blessed Trinity works. The sacraments are the principal liturgical actions. They are "efficacious symbols," that is, effective signs that convey sanctifying grace and particular sacramental graces. They should be received worthily. Baptism, Confirmation, and Holy Orders are mentioned as conferring a "sacramental character." Spend the lesson covering the material on pages 154–157 of the Student Text. Also, consider showing one of the films suggested in the resources for Chapter 6 as part of this lesson.

🪃 Bell Ringers

- **Direct Instruction:** On the board, draw a shovel buried in the ground with its handle sticking up. Or, take the class outside and show them a shovel handle sticking up from the ground with the spade buried below the earth. After they guess what is below ground, explain that Jesus is like that. He points beyond to what we can see to the mystery of the Holy Trinity.

- **Class Discussion:** Introduce Part II, explaining that the lessons will define sacraments and liturgy as well as take a look at the individual sacraments divided in areas of initiation, healing, and service. Call on students to name the sacraments in each of these categories. List them on the board as they call them out.

📖 Teaching Approaches

- **Direct Instruction:** The opening of the text section "The Liturgy" (pages 154–155), reminds us that the Holy Spirit uses the liturgy to gather the Church together to (write on the board):
  - celebrate;
  - pray;
  - worship;
  - proclaim the Gospel;
  - live out the Paschal Mystery.

  Discuss each of these points. Then focus on what it means to "live out the Paschal Mystery."

- **Direct Instruction:** Explain that Paschal Mystery refers to Christ's saving actions through his Passion, Death, Resurrection, and Ascension. The liturgy celebrates the Paschal Mystery of our Salvation. Christ continues his work of redemption through the liturgy. Through the liturgy all Christians are incorporated into Christ.

Our Participation in God's Work

Part 2 of *Our Catholic Faith* discusses how Catholics celebrate our faith in Christ. The liturgy is our participation in God's work of Salvation. The Seven Sacraments are efficacious (truly effective) signs of God's grace. Celebrating the liturgy, especially the Eucharist, is central to our membership in the Body of Christ.

By celebrating the sacraments, we are trusting that our Lord continues to do his work. We show confidence that he uses the sacraments to help us on our journey to eternal life. The sacraments also strengthen our faith in God, who provides for us and increases in us the virtue of love, God's own life in us.

The Liturgy (CCC, 1066–1069; 1073–1076; 1135–1144; 1187–1188)

The word *liturgy* means a "public work" or "people's work." Today, this term refers to the Church's prayerful participation in and celebration of God's work—our Redemption and Salvation. Liturgy is the Church's official public worship. Christ continues his work of Salvation through, in, and with the liturgy. It is the source of the Church's power.

"Liturgy is the 'action' of the *whole Christ*" (*CCC*, 1136). This means that those of us on earth celebrate the liturgy in union with the saints in worshiping our loving Trinity. Since Baptism gives every Christian a share in Christ's priesthood, all are actively involved when participating in any liturgy. However, through the Sacrament of Holy Orders, the Holy Spirit empowers some members to serve as celebrants (leaders) of liturgy. In addition, there are other various special ministries at liturgies, for example, readers, commentators, servers, and choir members.

Through the Holy Spirit, Jesus makes his saving actions present to us in the liturgy. In the liturgy, we join Christ in his own prayer to the Father in the Holy Spirit. Also, especially in the Eucharistic liturgy and the other sacraments, we meet the living God, the source of our life, joy, and happiness. The Holy Spirit uses the liturgy to gather us together as members of Christ's body to celebrate, to pray, to worship God, to proclaim the Gospel, and to live out the Paschal Mystery in our own lives.

The Liturgy and the Blessed Trinity (CCC, 1077–1112)

The Blessed Trinity is at work through the Church's liturgy in the following ways:

1. God's People bless, praise, adore, and thank *God the Father* for all his gifts and blessings given in creation. We especially acknowledge the gift of Salvation won for us through his beloved Son and the gift of the Holy Spirit who has adopted us into the divine family.

2. Jesus promised to be with his Church as its head. One way *God the Son* is present to us through the liturgy, both in the priest who leads the worship and in the assembled community, but especially in the Eucharist, the bread and wine that become Christ's Body and Blood through the action of the Holy Spirit. The Risen Lord continues to speak to the Church through Scripture, and he dispenses his graces through the sacraments. Christ also joins the Church to the heavenly liturgy celebrated by the angels and saints, giving us a foretaste of our eternal destiny.

3. *God the Holy Spirit* is active in many ways in the liturgy. He prepares the worshiping community to meet Christ by recalling God's work in the Old Testament (for example, the Exodus and Passover) and by helping us to pray the psalms. It is the Spirit who invites us to meet the Lord Jesus in the liturgy and enables us to participate in the Lord's Paschal Mystery. This happens in a special way in the epiclesis (invocation prayer) of the Eucharist. In this prayer, the priest petitions God the Father to send the Holy Spirit to transform ordinary bread and wine into the Body and Blood of Jesus Christ. Finally, the Holy Spirit is the source of our unity in Christ and in each other. He empowers us to bring Jesus' love into the world.

Sacraments (*CCC*, 1113; 1115–1116; 1118–1124; 1128–1134; 1145–1162; 1189–1192; 1996–1999; 2002–2003; 2023)

The principal liturgical actions in the Church are the sacraments. A *sacrament* is an efficacious symbol, that is, an effective or powerful sign that causes what it points to. A sacrament is what it represents. An ordinary symbol like a stop sign points to the *idea* of stopping; it does not cause it. In contrast, a sacrament like Baptism actually brings about the rebirth that the baptismal waters signify. Because Baptism is an effective sign, it actually washes away sin and really brings about spiritual rebirth into God's family.

We already studied how the term *sacrament* fits both Jesus and the Church. Jesus points to God's love; at the same time he *is* God's love for us who has reconciled the world to his Father. Jesus' Incarnation is the primary

sacrament of our Salvation. His Death on the cross shows how great God's love is for us. The mysteries of his Life serve as the foundation of what he gives to us in the sacraments, through the ministers of the Church. The Church is also a sacrament, an effective sign that continues his work of Salvation. The Holy Spirit gives life to the Church, and we can meet Jesus in the Church. The Lord Jesus continues to speak to us through his Word proclaimed. And through his Church, he calls each of us to be effective signs of his love. We, too, are to be sacrament people, that is, light to the world. Our faithful lives of love and service point the way to Christ and his Father.

Christ instituted the Seven Sacraments, special powers that flow from his Body, the Church. They are effective, symbolic actions of Christ that not only point to divine life, but actually convey it to the members of Christ's body. Some important truths about the sacraments include the following:

1. *The sacraments are signs.* Comprised of body and soul, humans express and perceive spiritual realities through signs and symbols. God reaches out to us through created, material realities. For example, most people first learned of God's love through the warm affections of their parents. Christ uses many signs and symbols to help us celebrate his Paschal Mystery of love and to communicate God's life to us. The mysteries of Christ's Life—from

- **Direct Instruction:** Point out the ways that the Blessed Trinity is at work through the Church's liturgy on pages 154–155. God the Father is the source of the liturgy in the same way he is the source of creation. Christ, at the Father's right hand, pours out the blessings of the Holy Spirit through the sacraments. The Holy Spirit enlightens our faith and inspires our response to the liturgy as Church.

- **Direct Instruction:** Check the students' understanding of the liturgy and the Trinity's involvement in the liturgy with a quick writing assignment. Have students write a one-sentence definition of liturgy and three sentences describing the ways each of the Persons of the Trinity are active in the liturgy. Collect these and scan through them to see what needs to be reviewed in the following lesson.

- **Direct Instruction:** Continue with the text subsection "Sacraments" (pages 155–157). Distinguish between signs and symbols. Signs can be defined as "anything that points to something else" and symbols as "special signs that convey deep meanings." The deeper meaning of symbols, like sacraments, calls forth both conscious and unconscious feelings and thoughts.

Extending the Lesson

Video Presentation: As time permits consider showing a video that presents an overview of liturgy and the sacraments, for example, *Understanding the Sacraments* (part of the Catholic Update Video series, St. Anthony Messenger Press, 30 minutes). This presentation shows various Catholics testifying what celebrating the sacraments means to their lives.

- **Individual Assignment:** Have students create a mind-map of the truths of the sacraments from pages 155–157 one by one:
  - ◆ Sacraments are signs.
  - ◆ Sacraments are efficacious.
  - ◆ Sacraments convey grace.
  - ◆ Each sacrament conveys sacramental grace.
  - ◆ Baptism, Confirmation, and Holy Orders convey a sacramental character.
  - ◆ Sacraments require proper dispositions on our part.
- **Individual Assignment:** Have students read and respond to each of the Scripture passages in the Knowing Christ through Scripture feature "Jesus Christ Is Present in the Sacraments" on page 157.

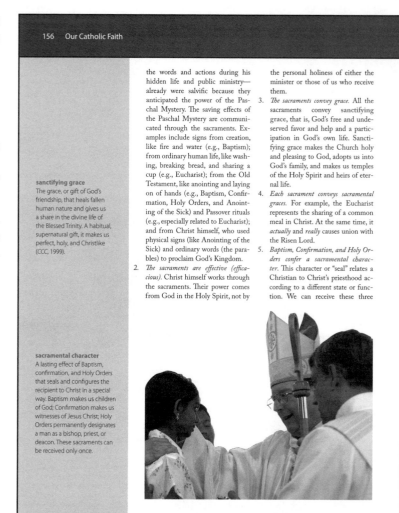

the words and actions during his hidden life and public ministry—already were salvific because they anticipated the power of the Paschal Mystery. The saving effects of the Paschal Mystery are communicated through the sacraments. Examples include signs from creation, like fire and water (e.g., Baptism); from ordinary human life, like washing, breaking bread, and sharing a cup (e.g., Eucharist); from the Old Testament, like anointing and laying on of hands (e.g., Baptism, Confirmation, Holy Orders, and Anointing of the Sick) and Passover rituals (e.g., especially related to Eucharist); and from Christ himself, who used physical signs (like Anointing of the Sick) and ordinary words (the parables) to proclaim God's Kingdom.

2. *The sacraments are effective (efficacious).* Christ himself works through the sacraments. Their power comes from God in the Holy Spirit, not by the personal holiness of either the minister or those of us who receive them.

3. *The sacraments convey grace.* All the sacraments convey sanctifying grace, that is, God's free and undeserved favor and help and a participation in God's own life. Sanctifying grace makes the Church holy and pleasing to God, adopts us into God's family, and makes us temples of the Holy Spirit and heirs of eternal life.

4. *Each sacrament conveys sacramental graces.* For example, the Eucharist represents the sharing of a common meal in Christ. At the same time, it *actually* and *really* causes union with the Risen Lord.

5. *Baptism, Confirmation, and Holy Orders confer a sacramental character.* This character or "seal" relates a Christian to Christ's priesthood according to a different state or function. We can receive these three

sanctifying grace
The grace, or gift of God's friendship, that heals fallen human nature and gives us a share in the divine life of the Blessed Trinity. A habitual, supernatural gift, it makes us perfect, holy, and Christlike (CCC, 1999).

sacramental character
A lasting effect of Baptism, confirmation, and Holy Orders that seals and configures the recipient to Christ in a special way. Baptism makes us children of God; Confirmation makes us witnesses of Jesus Christ; Holy Orders permanently designates a man as a bishop, priest, or deacon. These sacraments can be received only once.

Extending the Lesson

Individual Assignment: Offer another definition of symbol to pull these elements together: "a symbol is a sign (an outward reality) that represents an invisible (spiritual) reality." Ask the students to test this definition against the following examples:

- a wedding ring
- a present given to a loved one
- an alma mater
- a crucifix
- a photo of a loved one
- an autograph of a personal hero
- a nation's flag
- the color blue
- a candle
- a hug

Call on volunteers to offer their opinion of each item based on the definition of symbol.

KNOWING CHRIST THROUGH SCRIPTURE

Jesus Christ Is Present in the Sacraments

The Seven Sacraments make present the values and loving actions of Jesus. Read the following New Testament passages to discover how Jesus met people in their time of need. Note (1) which sacrament each set of passages refers to and (2) which value of Jesus appears in the passage.

- Matthew 9:35–38 and Matthew 28:16–20
- John 6:47–58 and Luke 22:14–20
- John 2:1–11
- Luke 12:8–12 and John 16:5–16
- Luke 7:36–50 and John 20:19–23
- Mark 8:22–26 and Mark 1:40–45
- Matthew 3:13–17 and John 3:3–8

sacraments only once because the Holy Spirit uses them to configure us to Christ and the Church in an *indelible* way.

6. *Sacraments require proper dispositions on our part.* If we want the sacraments to bear fruit in us, we must receive them worthily. We must have faith and use the gifts God gives to us through the sacraments.

Christ continues his work of preaching the Good News and establishing his Father's Kingdom through his Church. The Holy Spirit has helped the Church identify the Seven Sacraments as privileged signs and liturgical actions that build up the Kingdom of God in a special way. These signs are "by the Church" because the Church is Christ's sacrament in the world. At the same time, they are also "for the Church" because they help make the Church. They do so by revealing to people the Mystery of the Blessed Trinity's union of love with us through Christ. The Seven Sacraments are Baptism, Confirmation, Eucharist, Penance, Anointing of the Sick, Matrimony, and Holy Orders.

For Review

1. What is the *liturgy* of the Church?
2. How is each of the Divine Persons at work through the Church's liturgy?
3. What does it mean to call a sacrament an "efficacious symbol"?
4. How is Jesus a sacrament?
5. In what way is the Church a sacrament?
6. What is *sanctifying grace*?
7. What does a *sacramental character* do? Which sacraments confer a sacramental character?

For Reflection

Describe a person who is an exemplary Christian. What qualities does this person have that make him or her an effective sign of Christ? Discuss how you can grow in these same qualities.

Knowing Christ through Scripture

Answers (page 157)

Matthew 9:35–38 and Matthew 28:16–20
- Sacrament: Holy Orders
- Values: leadership, mercy, charity, compassion

John 6:47–58 and Luke 22:14–20
- Sacrament: Eucharist
- Values: faith, hope, charity, sacrifice,

John 2:1–11
- Sacrament: Matrimony
- Values: faith, obedience, love

Luke 12:8–12 and John 16:5–16
- Sacrament: Confirmation
- Values: faith, courage

Luke 7:36–50 and John 20:19–23
- Sacrament: Reconciliation
- Values: forgiveness

Mark 8:22–26 and Mark 1:40–45
- Sacrament: Anointing of the Sick
- Values: compassion, mercy

Matthew 3:13–17 and John 2:2–8
- Sacrament: Baptism, Confirmation
- Values: faith, hope

For Review Answers (page 157)

1. The liturgy is the Church's prayerful participation in and celebration of God's work.

2. The *Father* is at work through the liturgy by the recognition of his gifts, particularly Salvation. The *Son* is present in the priest and in the assembled community, but especially in the Eucharist. The *Holy Spirit* prepares the worshiping community, enables them to participate in the Paschal Mystery, makes the sacraments efficacious, and is the source of unity in Christ and each other.

3. As an "efficacious symbol," a sacrament is an effective or powerful sign that causes what it points to.

4. Jesus points to God's love, at the same time he *is* God's love.

5. The Church is an effective sign that continues his work of Salvation. The Holy Spirit gives life to the Church. Jesus is present in the Church. We point the way to Christ and God the Father.

6. Sanctifying grace is a gift of God's friendship that heals fallen human nature and gives us a share in the life of the Blessed Trinity.

7. Sacramental character relates a Christian to Christ's priesthood according to a different state or function. Baptism, Confirmation, and Holy Orders confer Sacramental Orders.

Homework Assignment

1. Complete the For Review questions on page 157.

2. Complete the For Reflection question on page 157.

3. Read the opening text section of Chapter 6, "Our Need for Signs and Symbols" (pages 160–161).

4. Read the list of Ongoing Assignments on pages 180–181.

6 The Sacraments of Initiation

Overview of the Chapter

Chapter 6 turns to the Sacraments of Initiation. It begins by summarizing the early Church's celebration of these sacraments as a unity that culminated on the Easter Vigil.

The section on Baptism starts with an analysis of its etymology. It then discusses infant Baptism and the baptismal symbols of water, oil, the white garment, and candle that appear in the rite. The effects of Baptism are discussed, and the fate of unbaptized babies is explained.

Confirmation completes the sacramental grace of Baptism. Its effects and its biblical and historical roots are discussed, including the differences between the Western and Eastern Rite ways of performing the sacrament. Like Baptism, the Rite of Confirmation is summarized in this chapter.

The chapter then turns to the Holy Eucharist. The *Catechism of the Catholic Church* teaches:

> The Eucharist is the heart and the summit of the Church's life, for in it Christ associates his Church and all her members with his sacrifice of praise and thanksgiving offered once and for all on the cross to his Father; by this sacrifice he pours out the graces of salvation on his Body which is the Church. (1407)

After discussing the Old Testament roots and Gospel references to the Eucharist, the chapter explains the significance of the various names used for this central sacrament that completes our Christian initiation. They include Eucharist, Lord's Supper, breaking the bread, Eucharistic assembly, Holy and Divine Liturgy, Most Blessed Sacrament, Holy Sacrifice, Holy Communion, and Holy Mass. As part of the explanation of these sacramental names, the effects of the sacrament are discussed and the term *transubstantiation* is defined.

The chapter outlines the order of the Mass, briefly treating the meaning of each part. An exercise asks students to locate the readings for a coming Sunday and prepare a short homily based on them.

The chapter concludes with a short discussion of the liturgical year and sacramentals.

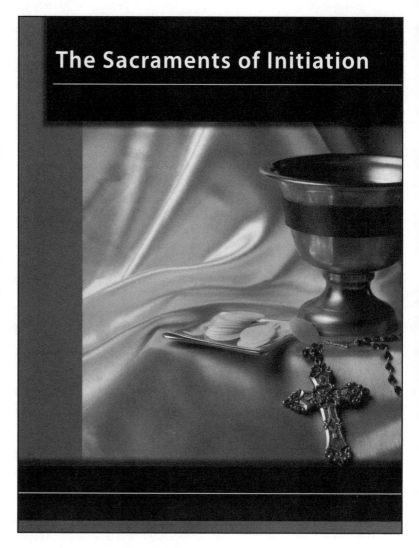

The Sacraments of Initiation

Resources

🔘 Audiovisual Materials

Eucharist: A Celebration of Life

A Teleketics classic that uses images like clouds, rain, flowers, a laughing child, and the aged to depict how they are all bound together with the Eucharist (9-minute video, St. Anthony Messenger Press).

Moving On: Responding in the Spirit

Tells the story of a family that moves into a new home next door to a Vietnam veteran scarred by memories of the past. The family must heed Christ's call to love him as a neighbor. Shows the need to heed our baptismal call to respond to the promptings of the Holy Spirit and live Christlike lives. Study guide included (20-minute video, Videos with Values).

Ritual: The Language of Worship

Depicts the origin of the ritual from human history, the early Christian Church, and down through the centuries. Barry Brunsman, O.F.M., explains the beauty and profound meaning of the liturgy (67-minute video, Videos with Values).

Sacraments: Celebrations of God's Life

A presentation of the seven rites of the Catholic sacraments is presented (60-minute video, Harcourt).

Sacraments: God's Amazing Grace

A three-tape video set that covers all Seven Sacraments in seven segments. Bishop Paul Zipfel introduces each tape. Also includes the upbeat music of Jesse Manibusan. With study guide (seven 8-10-minute segments on three video tapes, Videos with Values).

continued on page 173

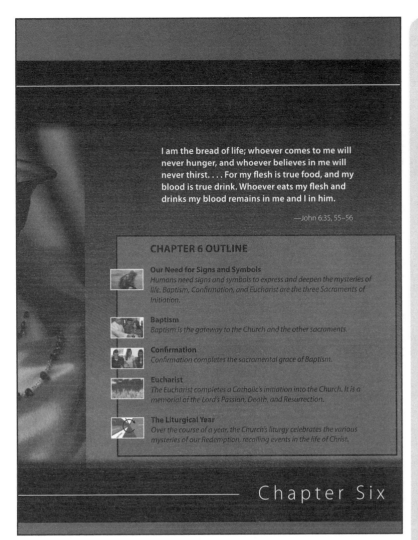

I am the bread of life; whoever comes to me will never hunger, and whoever believes in me will never thirst. . . . For my flesh is true food, and my blood is true drink. Whoever eats my flesh and drinks my blood remains in me and I in him.

—John 6:35, 55–56

CHAPTER 6 OUTLINE

Our Need for Signs and Symbols
Humans need signs and symbols to express and deepen the mysteries of life. Baptism, Confirmation, and Eucharist are the three Sacraments of Initiation.

Baptism
Baptism is the gateway to the Church and the other sacraments.

Confirmation
Confirmation completes the sacramental grace of Baptism.

Eucharist
The Eucharist completes a Catholic's initiation into the Church. It is a memorial of the Lord's Passion, Death, and Resurrection.

The Liturgical Year
Over the course of a year, the Church's liturgy celebrates the various mysteries of our Redemption, recalling events in the life of Christ.

Chapter Six

Resources

 Internet Links see www.avemariapress.com

Resources

 Printed Materials

Bausch, William J. *A New Look at the Sacraments*. Mystic, CT: Twenty-Third
    Publications, 1983.
    Very clearly written. Still remains fresh after many years.

Champlin, Joseph. *Special Signs of Grace*. Collegeville, MN: Liturgical Press, 1986.
    Focus is on the revised rites and relating each sacrament to the real lives of real
    people.

Cooke, Bernard. *Sacraments and Sacramentality*. Mystic, CT: Twenty-Third
    Publications, 1994.
    An excellent introduction that argues for the central role of sacramentality in
    human life. Well articulates Jesus as the sacrament of the Father and the Spirit-
    led Church as Jesus' sacrament that expresses his actions through the Seven
    Sacraments.

Driscoll, Jeremy. *What Happens at Mass*. Chicago, IL: Liturgy Training Publications,
    2008.
    A short and profound explanation of the Mystery of the Mass, focused specifically
    on the work of the Trinity through the liturgy.

continued on page 182

Chapter Outline

- Our Need for Signs and Symbols
- Baptism
- Confirmation
- Eucharist
- The Liturgical Year

Advance Preparations

Review all the long- and short-term assignments for Chapter 6, including the Ongoing Assignments suggestions on pages 179–180. Determine how many assignments you will give and when they will be due.

Our Need for Signs and Symbols (ST pages 160–162)
- Art supplies, such as poster board and markers for the Class Assignment on page 163.
- Arrange for an adult convert to speak to the class for the Guest Speaker activity on page 162.

Baptism (ST pages 163–165)
- Blank index cards for the Individual Assignment on page 166.
- Copies of Chapter 6, Handout 1 "Renewing Your Baptismal Promises" (starting on page 285 and also online at www.avemariapress.com) for the Prayer Experience on page 165.

Confirmation (ST pages 166–169)
- Copies of Chapter 6, Handout 2 "Comparing Christian Churches" (starting on page 285 and also online at www.avemariapress.com) for the Direct Instruction on page 170.

Eucharist (ST pages 169–175)
- Blank index cards for the Group Activity on page 176.
- Copies of Chapter 6, Handout 3 "Seder Meal Script" (starting on page 285 and also online at www.avemariapress.com) for the Individual Assignment on page 173.

The Liturgical Year (ST pages 175–177)
- Copies of a blank calendar for the Individual Activity on page 178.
- Poster board, an X-ACTO knife, and tape for the Individual Activity on page 177.

Chapter 6 Test Lesson
- Copies of the Chapter 6 Test.

Our Need for Signs and Symbols (pages 160–162)

Objectives

In this lesson, the students will:

- recognize rituals, signs, and symbols in religious and secular life.
- explain the process of initiation into the Church, particularly through the Rite of Christian Initiation of Adults (RCIA).
- define sacrament, catechumen, catechumenate, neophyte, and Rite of Christian Initiation of Adults.

Preview

This opening section of Chapter 6 introduces signs and symbols in comparison to the way that sacraments function in the Church. It also introduces the Sacraments of Initiation, the main subject of the chapter. The students are provided with a brief overview of the initiation process for adults through history. Related to the discussion of symbols, the students will also be asked to create for themselves a "coat of arms" to represent much of their own lives.

Bell Ringers

- **Group Activity:** Ask the students to work in small groups to create rituals that celebrate one of the following events:
    - acceptance into college
    - being named all-conference in high school athletics
    - the induction of a student into a national honor society
    - the life of a classmate who has died

    Explain that the rituals should contain the following elements: symbols, gestures, words appropriate to the occasion, and music. Allow time for the groups to discuss and work on one of these events and also time for the groups to share their rituals.
- **Class Discussion:** Discuss the value of rituals. Compare and contrast the students' rituals to the rituals that are a part of Mass.

 Teaching Approaches

- **Class Discussion:** Have one of the students summarize the meaning of the opening story about the soldier. Discuss what it means to be present to one another and how God is present to us.
- **Class Discussion:** Help to summarize the subsection "Sacraments of Initiation" (pages 160–161). The section explains concisely the history of adult initiation and the meaning of terms like catechumen and neophyte. Ask the students to speculate why after Christianity became legal the number of infant baptisms increased dramatically.

Our Need for Signs and Symbols

A famous story tells about a soldier who asked his commanding officer to allow him to go out to a battlefield to retrieve his wounded friend. The superior refused the request because he knew that it was highly likely that the soldier's friend was already dead. "Besides," the commanding officer warned, "I don't want the enemy shooting at you, too."

Nevertheless, the soldier went out, thereby disobeying a direct command. An hour later he returned mortally wounded, carrying the corpse of his friend.

The officer said to the dying soldier, "Your foolish gesture surely was not worth the effort."

The loyal friend answered, "But, sir, it definitely was. When I got to my friend, he was still alive. And he said to me, 'Jim, I was positive you'd come.'"

This story illustrates an important quality of friendship: *being present to another*. God the Father revealed his friendship for us by sending his beloved Son, Jesus Christ, to win to us—through his Passion, Death, and Resurrection—eternal life. Jesus remains with us today, through his Body, the Church. And he has given us the gift of the Holy Spirit, who empowers us to be Jesus for each other. Our Lord has also left us the Seven Sacraments as special signs of his presence and his friendship.

Jesus fully understands human nature and our need for signs that remind us that someone loves and cares for us, much like Jim needed to experience a final time the presence of his friend. That is one of the principal reasons Christ left his Church the sacraments, special symbols of God's love and important signs of grace and divine friendship. St. Augustine of Hippo defined *sacrament* as a "visible sign of an invisible reality, a visible sign of invisible grace." Through the sacraments, we both *perceive* and *receive* the invisible grace of God's own life. Through them, we experience the Good News of God's love.

Chapter 6 focuses on three sacraments that initiate us into God's People: Baptism, Confirmation, and the Eucharist. In Chapter 7, the Sacraments of Healing and Ministry will be discussed.

Sacraments of Initiation (CCC, 1229–1233; 1247–1249; 1275)

The three Sacraments of Initiation are Baptism, which brings new life in Christ; Confirmation, which strengthens the new life; and the Eucharist, which nourishes Catholics with Christ's Body and Blood. Together they "gather in" God's people and make us members of Christ's Body, the Church. These sacraments give us the life of Christ and bestow the gift of the Holy Spirit so that we can be Christ for others.

In the early Church most converts were adults. Christian initiation was seen as a journey that took place

Extending the Lesson

Class Discussion: Have students brainstorm everything that comes to mind with the word "Christmas" and write their answers on the board. Take several items individually, such as presents, food, decorations, and Christmas trees, and ask students to describe their own family traditions. Ask students to write down what they consider to be the true meaning of Christmas. Have students share their answers with the class, and list their answers on the board. Next, ask students to reflect on how the physical traditions of Christmas help put families in touch with, or sometimes get in the way of, the true meaning of Christmas. Finally, ask students to consider what December 25 would be like without the concrete, physical expressions that have been developed.

Guest Speaker: Have an adult convert speak to the class about the decision to become a Catholic and the RCIA process. Have students prepare classes ahead of time to ask the speaker after the presentation. Local parishes may be able to provide the name of someone willing to address the class.

in stages. It was a serious decision to become a Christian because people had to renounce sin and take on a new life in Christ. There was also a real danger of being persecuted or martyred, as Christianity was illegal through three centuries. A person studying to become a Christian was known as a catechumen. This same term is used today. Catechumens had sponsors who helped them prepare through a three-year period of prayer, fasting, and self-denial before becoming members of the Church. The catechumenate (period of preparation) coincided with the Paschal Mystery of Christ's Death and Resurrection. Finally, after a forty-day period of prayer and formal instruction in the faith during Lent, when the catechumens learned the creed and the Lord's Prayer, they received all three Sacraments of Initiation at the Easter Vigil, Holy Saturday.

During the first three centuries, the bishop was the main celebrant of the initiation sacraments. After questioning the candidates to see if they were seriously committed to Christlike lives, he anointed them with oil. The candidates then disrobed and were plunged into the baptismal waters three times, each time expressing their faith in the Triune God. When they emerged from the water, their five senses were anointed and the Holy Spirit was invoked. This anointing was the Sacrament of Confirmation. The new Catholics (called neophytes) received white garments to symbolize a new life in Christ. They also received candles to remind them of their new vocation to be the light of Christ. After common prayers and the sharing of a sign of peace, the Eucharist was celebrated. At this liturgy, the neophytes received their first Holy Communion

Following the legalization of Christianity in AD 313, most Catholics were baptized in infancy. Today, Holy Communion is typically received at age seven, the age of reason. However, when adults seek conversion, the Second Vatican Council has restored the ancient way of initiating adults into the Church. Its distinct steps, consisting of four periods and three stages, are found in the *Rite of Christian Initiation of Adults* (RCIA).

Each of the Sacraments of Initiation examined in detail throughout the rest of this chapter.

catechumen
An unbaptized person who is preparing to receive all of the Sacraments of Christian Initiation.

neophytes
Those newly received into the Church through the Sacraments of Initiation at the Easter Vigil.

Coat of Arms

Create a personal coat of arms that symbolizes for you some of your goals, values, and dreams. Divide it into five sections. Draw simple pictures or find illustrations that capture the following:

1. Your idea of success
2. Your concept of love
3. Your most noteworthy achievement
4. Your attitude toward Jesus
5. The biggest obstacle that stands in the way of your growth

---

Background Information

Signs and Symbols Explained

Recognizing man's need for signs and symbols as a reminder that he or she is loved, Jesus left the Church the sacraments, special symbols of God's love, important signs of grace and divine friendship. St. Augustine of Hippo defined sacrament as a "visible sign of an invisible reality, a visible sign of invisible grace." Some of the Church's signs and symbols are explained in the *Catechism of the Catholic Church*, including in paragraphs 1145–1148, 1150, and 1152.

For Enrichment

Individual Assignment: Have the students interview a staff person in a parish who works with RCIA, infant Baptism, or Confirmation preparation and describe the process their parish has for preparing candidates. What is asked of the person, or of the parents, in order to receive the sacrament or be received into the Church? If non-Catholic students are in the class, they can ask the same questions at their own place of worship.

(One of the main reasons was that the sheer number of people interested in being baptized increased. Another reason was the awareness of Original Sin and the desire to be forgiven of it through Baptism.)

- **Journal Assignment:** Speak more about initiation rituals the students are aware of. For example, brainstorm with students the groups to which they belong: family, neighborhood, school, church, team, activity, friends, etc. Then have students choose one group and write answers to the following questions in their journals:
    - How were you taught the way to behave in that group?
    - How were you welcomed into that group?
    - What traditions does the group have (e.g., family reunions, pre-game or pre-activity rituals, school pep rallies)?
    - How do those traditions communicate the identity of the group to its members?
    - Facilitate a discussion about the importance of initiation, formal or informal, in developing a group that possesses spirit and identity.

- **Class Discussion:** Ask students who have attended Easter Vigil services to share remembrances and impressions. Ask questions like: Do any of their parishes practice Baptism of immersion? Do the catechumens wear white garments? What ages are the catechumens in their parish? Why do some people only receive Confirmation? When does Confirmation take place in the ceremony? Who were the sponsors? What seemed to be their role?

- **Group Activity:** Review the feature "What Is RCIA?" Have students write the names of the RCIA's four periods, three liturgical rites, and their descriptions on separate note cards (a total of fourteen cards). In pairs or groups of three, have students try to connect the periods and rites with their definitions and place them in correct chronological order. Do this until all of the students have shown proficient mastery of the information.

- **Class Assignment:** Using art supplies like poster board, markers, and the like, follow the directions on page 161 and draw a personal coat of arms. Share the finished projects. Display them in the classroom.

For Review Answers (page 162)

1. Sacraments make us holy, build up Christ's body, and give worship to God.

2. The Sacraments of Initiation are Baptism, Confirmation, and Eucharist.

3. Adults joining the Church, who were called catechumens, spent three years in prayer, fasting, and self-denial to prepare for entering the Church. A sponsor helped them through this period. After spending Lent in prayer and study of the faith, they received Baptism, Confirmation, and Eucharist at the Easter Vigil.

4. The four periods of the RCIA process are precatechumenate, catechumenate, purification and enlightenment, and mystagogy.

Baptism (pages 163–165)

Objectives

In this lesson, the students will:

- describe the meaning, history, and scriptural roots of Baptism.
- list the symbols of Baptism and describe their meaning.
- explain the effects of Baptism.
- summarize the Church's teaching on what happens to those who are not baptized.

Preview

This section of the text covers the history, scriptural roots, and effects of Baptism, the first of the Sacraments of Initiation. Through Baptism, a person is incorporated into Christ and the Church. The baptized is configured to Christ and given an indelible spiritual mark of his or her belonging to Christ. The character, or mark, can never be erased, even if sin prevents the graces of Baptism from leading the person to salvation. These teachings, along with some of the symbols associated with the sacraments, and special issues pertaining to infant Baptism and questions about what happens to unbaptized children are addressed in this section.

Bell Ringers

- **Class Discussion:** Call on a student to be "on the spot" and come before the class to respond to the following:
  - Are you glad your parents had you baptized as an infant? Why or why not?
  - To me, being a Christian means . . .
  - To me, being a Catholic means . . .

What is RCIA?

RCIA is the acronym for the Rite of Christian Initiation of Adults, the process for nonbaptized men and women entering the Catholic Church. This process includes four periods and three major liturgical rites. A brief explanation of each follows.

The *precatechumenate* is the period when persons show an interest in the Catholic faith and begin a period of inquiry into the faith. After they begin to grow in preliminary knowledge of the Gospel and want to continue the faith journey, the Church welcomes them in a *Rite of Acceptance into the Catechumenate*.

In the *catechumenate*, the catechumens study the Catholic faith in a deeper way, usually under the guidance of a Christian sponsor. This period can last for months or even years as the catechumens grow familiar with the Christian life, study the Bible, and participate fully in the Liturgy of the Word. This period concludes with a *Rite of Election*, which takes place on the first Sunday of Lent. The rite is celebrated by the bishop or his appointee, usually at the cathedral of the diocese. At this point the catechumens become known as "the elect."

The elect prepare for Baptism and full reception into the faith community through prayer and fasting during the *purification and enlightenment* period. On the third, fourth, and fifth Sundays of Lent there are special rituals and prayers for the elect known as the *scrutinies*. These rites help the elect to reflect on what it means to be a follower of Jesus Christ, to root out sin in their life, and to grow in holiness. This period ends at the Easter Vigil with the *Rite of Initiation*, when the elect are baptized, confirmed, and receive Holy Communion for the first time as full members of Christ's Body.

There is another stage after the Easter Vigil. *Mystagogy* is a time of catechesis that takes places from Easter to Pentecost. During this period of further instruction, the neophytes, supported by the parish community, study more deeply the mysteries of the faith, that is, those signs of God's love that are present in the Church's sacramental life. Pentecost Sunday concludes the RCIA process. By this time the new Catholics have selected some way to serve God's People and build up the Church. Theirs is now the full responsibility of a disciple of Christ.

RCIA—The acronym that designates the Rite of Christian Initiation of Adults, which consists of four periods and three major liturgical rites. It is the process that prepares adults for entrance into the Catholic Church leading up to the reception of the Sacraments of Initiation at the Easter Vigil.

For Review

1. What is the purpose of the sacraments?
2. Name the Sacraments of Initiation.
3. Discuss how the initiation process took place in the early Church.
4. What are the four periods in the RCIA process?

For Reflection

"Deciding to become a Christian can be risky business in today's world." Share some of the ways this statement could be true.

Homework Assignment

1. Look over and choose at least one of the Ongoing Assignments to work on (pages 179–180). The assignments will be due at the session prior to the Chapter 6 Test.

2. Complete the For Review questions on page 162.

3. Read the text section "Baptism" (pages 163–165).

4. Find out information on your godparents and the meaning of your Christian name (see the For Reflection questions, page 165).

Background Information

Water in the Creation Accounts

The Hebrew word for spirit is *ruah*, which is translated as "breath" or "wind." In Genesis, God breathes his Spirit into the lifeless form of Adam. God's breath (wind) also dries the land. Blowing from the ocean, it brings water and coolness, refreshment, and rain. God's life-giving breath and saving waters symbolize God's care for his people.

Baptism (CCC, 1214–1228; 1276–1277)

The word *baptism* comes from a Greek word that means "to plunge" or "to immerse" into water. This symbolic drawing and drawing up again from the water reminds us that a new Catholic enters into Christ's Death and then rises to a new life of grace.

The Sacrament of Baptism has its roots in Scripture. The Old Testament foreshadows this sacrament. For example, in the creation account in Genesis, the Spirit of God overshadows the waters to bring life to the earth. This prefigures how today the Holy Spirit imparts new life at Baptism. Another Old Testament example comes in the story of the renewal of the earth following the Great Flood (see Gn 9). The New Testament tells how Jesus himself was baptized (see, for example, Mt 3:13–17). Also, before ascending to Heaven, Jesus commanded:

Go, therefore, and make disciples of all nations, baptizing them in the name of the Father, and of the Son, and of the holy Spirit, teaching them to observe all that I have commanded you. (Mt 28:19–20)

Beginning with the Day of Pentecost, the Church has preached the need for Baptism. Through Baptism, Catholics participate in the Death, burial, and Resurrection of Christ.

Infant Baptism (CCC, 1234–1245; 1250–1256; 1278; 1282; 1284)

The Church has baptized infants from its earliest days. The practice of infant Baptism shows that Salvation is a pure gift of Christ's grace that extends even to children. The practice of infant Baptism makes clear that the Church relies on the faith of the parents,

godparents, and all the Church to ensure that infants are baptized in a faith-filled environment where they learn about the faith they have received.

Most infant Baptisms take place on Sunday, often as part of the Sunday liturgy. Even when not held as part of Mass, Baptisms should always take place in a company of believers. The rite of Baptism begins with a greeting from the ordinary minister of the sacrament (priest, deacon, or bishop). The baptismal rite includes an instruction to the parents and godparents to raise the child in a Christian home, a welcoming of the child, a proclamation of God's Word, and prayers of exorcism to free the child from sin and Satan's power. The child is anointed with the Oil of Catechumens to proclaim that he or she is to be joined to Christ, the Anointed One. After the baptismal waters are blessed, those assembled recite their baptismal vows, and the parents and godparents state that they desire Baptism for their child. Next comes the essential rite of Baptism: the minister pours water on the head of the child three times (or immerses the child in water three times) and pronounces the words, "N., I baptize you in the name of the Father, and of the Son, and of the Holy Spirit."

After the baptism, the crown of the head is anointed a second time with sacred Chrism (perfumed oil), a white garment is placed on the child, and a lit candle is held by one of the parents. The celebrant touches

essential rite
That portion of the liturgical celebration of a sacrament that is strictly necessary in order for the sacrament to be valid.

Chrism
Blessed by the bishop, this perfumed oil is used for anointing in the Sacraments of Baptism, Confirmation, and Holy Orders. It represents the gift of the Holy Spirit.

For Enrichment

Individual Assignment: Have students design a certificate that could be presented to parents or catechumens at Baptism. The certificate should welcome the new Catholic into a particular parish, affirm the support provided by the community, and explain briefly the meaning of the sacrament. The certificate should include appropriate graphics to mark the importance of the occasion.

Extending the Lesson

Prayer Experience: Distribute copies of Chapter 6, Handout 1 "Renewing Your Baptismal Promises" (starting on page 285 and also online at www.avemariapress.com). Ask students to read the promises silently, considering their meaning. Then ask them to consider what the areas of greatest temptation or struggle are for them in their lives today. Finally, invite the class to renew their promises. Remind students that they should consider this seriously and only speak aloud those statements they truly believe.

• **Prayer Experience:** Display the symbols of Baptism described on page 164. Try to focus an explanation and reflection on each of the symbols for each class session you study Baptism. For the first day, begin with this prayer:

> Loving God,
>
> At the beginning of creation you made water, without which we cannot have life. You gave us lakes and oceans, which provide us with food and whose beauty calms our hearts. You make the rain, which brings fields and gardens to life. You give us water to drink and to cleanse ourselves. Help us be grateful for this gift in our lives. Give us the grace as individuals and as a community to care for the water in our environment and use it wisely.
>
> Amen.

Teaching Approaches

• **Direct Instruction:** Summarize the opening text on page 163. Read Genesis 1 aloud, noting water's place in the two stories of creation.

• **Class Discussion:** Next, have students read Genesis 8:1–9:17 silently. Call on students to respond to the following questions:

1. How is the role of water different in this story than in the Genesis creation accounts? (Water both takes away and restores life.)

2. What similarities do you see with this story and Baptism? (The waters in each wash away sin and bring new life.)

• **Direct Instruction:** Continue with a discussion of the subsection "Infant Baptism" (pages 163–164), including the symbols of Baptism. Point out that the Rite of Baptism for children includes an instruction to parents and godparents to raise the child in a Christian home, a welcoming of the child, a proclamation of God's Word, and prayers and exorcisms to free the child from Satan's power. Also mention that in an emergency, the essential rite of Baptism may be performed by any baptized Christian. Have students memorize the essential rite: pouring water on the head three times and pronouncing the words of Baptism. It is highly unlikely that anyone in the room will be called on to perform a Baptism, but knowing they can administer this sacrament can increase students' sense of full membership in the Church.

• **Class Discussion:** Ask the students to describe an ideal environment for a young Catholic to grow up strong in faith. Ask: "How can the parents, extended family, godparents, and parish best help a young person understand, live, and accept the faith?" Print ideas on the board.

- **Direct Instruction:** Share more information on each of the symbols of Baptism and the truths they reveal. Original Sin and its understanding relates to the practice of infant Baptisms. Point out why it is crucial to understand the doctrine of Original Sin: without understanding the doctrine of Original Sin, the Mystery of Christ is undermined. When we understand that we all come into the world as sinners, we realize that we need and are assured the grace of salvation that comes through Jesus Christ. Point out that godparents and our Christian names are also vital symbols of Baptism.

- **Group Discussion:** Allow the students to share with a partner their answers to the For Reflection questions on page 165 that they did for homework. Then take a sampling of the responses from volunteers. Also offer that years ago, Catholic names were almost exclusively saints' names; biblical names were uncommon. This question can provide a transition to the lesson on Confirmation, in that many students are or will be participating in Confirmation preparation, where they will be asked to choose a name for themselves.

- **Individual Assignment:** Have students create flash cards from blank index cards to help them remember the symbols of each of the sacraments. On one side have them draw the symbol and on the other have them write the name of the sacrament and the meaning of the symbol in relation to the sacrament.

- **Individual Assignment:** Read and explain each of the "effects of Baptism" listed on page 164. Have students write "Baptism" on the left side of a piece of notebook paper. On the right side have them list the effects of the Sacrament of Baptism from memory with arrows drawn to each one from the word "Baptism." Have them check their answers when they are finished.

- **Class Discussion:** Focus on the gift of sanctifying grace. Ask the students to think of examples of ways in which sanctifying grace could be apparent in their lives. Examples include help in patience with family members (love), inner strength or a timely conversation in times of doubt (belief), and an unexpected kindness from someone in a time of discouragement. Remind students that it is easy to miss the opportunity to respond to God's grace if we are not alert to its presence. A comparison is being unaware of background music that is being played softly if we are surrounded by noise or distractions.

- **Individual Assignment:** Note the question posed in the Explaining Your Faith feature on page 165.

the ears and mouth of the child and prays that the child will hear the Gospel and proclaim God's word. Everyone recites the Lord's Prayer, after which the celebrant concludes the ceremony by blessing the parents and everyone assembled.

The various symbols used in Baptism reveal important spiritual truths about its meaning:

Water. Water represents cleansing. It also symbolizes death to an old life of sin and rebirth into a new life with Christ Jesus. Jesus told Nicodemus that Jesus himself was living water, the source of all life. In Baptism we are reborn to a new life with Jesus Christ. Original Sin is washed away, and we inherit eternal life as adopted children of God.

Oil. In the ancient world, oil was used to anoint kings and queens to show that they were set apart from others. The natural symbol of oil also represents healing and protection. The title *Christ* means "anointed one." The oils of Baptism (Chrism) represent that we have been anointed in Jesus. We belong to him. We share in his Life and Salvation. We receive the Holy Spirit, who protects, guides, and strengthens us. We also share in

Christ's priestly and kingly ministries, sent by him to preach the Good News of God's Kingdom. We also help him in his healing ministry by serving others, especially the poor in our midst, and by working toward the unity of a wounded human community.

White garment. When early Christians came out of the baptismal pool, they donned new white robes to represent rising with Christ. Today, the white cloth symbolizes "putting on Christ" (Gal 3:27). It is a symbol of purity, happiness, and a new identity of living in union with the Lord.

Candle. The baptismal candle, lit from the Easter candle, reminds us how Christ is the light of the world and that his followers should be Christ's light to others.

Effects of Baptism (CCC, 1262–1274; 1279–1280)

The Sacrament of Baptism is the gateway to the Church and the reception of the other sacraments. It has many effects, including:

1. Baptism forgives both Original Sin and personal sin and remits all punishment due to sin. However, some consequences of sin remain, for example, suffering, weakness of character, inclination to sin (traditionally called *concupiscence*), and death.

2. Baptism gives us birth into a new life in Christ. It makes us children of God and temples of the Holy Spirit.

3. Baptism confers sanctifying grace, the grace of justification. This enables us to believe, hope, and love. Baptism also brings the Holy Spirit and the Spirit's gifts that enable us to grow in holiness and goodness.

4. Baptism initiates and incorporates us into Christ's Body, the Church. It empowers us to share in Christ's priestly ministry of worship and service. Baptism joins us to all Christians, even to those who are not yet fully united to the Catholic Church.

5. Baptism seals Christians with an indelible spiritual *character* that marks us as belonging to Christ. This is why Baptism can be received only once and should never be given to someone who has already been baptized. This baptismal character consecrates us for Christian worship and binds us to the Lord. If we live our baptismal promises, Christ has promised a resurrected body and a life of happiness with God and all his people forever.

Background Information

Baptism of Desire

The *Catechism of the Catholic Church* states:

> As regards *children who have died without Baptism*, the Church can only entrust them to the mercy of God, as she does in her funeral rites for them. Indeed, the great mercy of God who desires that all men should be saved, and Jesus' tenderness toward children which caused him to say: "Let the children come to me do not hinder them," allow us to hope that there is a way of salvation for children who have died without Baptism. All the more urgent is the Church's call not to prevent little children coming to Christ through the gift of holy Baptism. (1261)

Homework Assignment

1. Complete the For Review questions on page 165.

2. Read the text section "Confirmation" (pages 166–169).

Explaining Your Faith

Can unbaptized babies be saved?

Baptism is necessary for Salvation because Jesus himself said to the Pharisee Nicodemus, "Amen, amen I say to you, no one can see the kingdom of God without being born from above" (Jn 3:3).

Traditionally the Church has taught that there are three forms of Baptism: baptism of water (through the Sacrament of Baptism), baptism of blood (the death of martyrs who died for their faith before being baptized), and baptism of desire. *Baptism of desire* refers to catechumens who die before receiving the sacrament. Their turning from sin, desire to be baptized, and life of charity assure them of the Salvation the sacrament conveys. Baptism of desire also applies to all those good people who have not been given the gift of faith but whose lives show that they would have accepted Jesus Christ had they been given the chance on earth to know him.

The Church trusts that God's infinite and mysterious mercy will touch unbaptized babies because God wants everyone to be saved. Jesus himself showed tender love to children (Mk 10:14). However, since Divine Revelation does not specifically address the question of unbaptized infants, the Church asks parents to baptize their infants as soon as possible.

For Review

1. What are some of the Old and New Testament scriptural roots for Baptism?
2. What is the essential rite of Baptism?
3. List and discuss the meaning of three important symbols used in Baptism.
4. Discuss four effects of receiving the Sacrament of Baptism.

For Reflection

- Who are your godparents? Interview your parents and ask why they chose them to be your spiritual parents.
- Research the meaning of your Christian name. If you are named after a saint, do a short report on his or her life. Interview your parents as to why they chose your name.

Background Information

Baptism Is the Gateway to the Church and the Other Sacraments

The support and love of the entire Christian community is a vital element of any baptism. As the catechumen begins his or her journey through the catechetical process, it is the responsibility of the community to be present and sponsor as a whole those who are making their way. The *General Directory for Catechesis* stresses this point:

> The catechesis given in the catechumenate is closely linked with the Christian community. From the moment of their entry into the catechumenate, the Church surrounds catechumens "with her affection, her care, as though they are already her children and joined to her: indeed, they belong to the family of Christ." Thus the Christian community assists "candidates and catechumens during their initiation process. . . ." (237)

The answer contains explanations of three forms of Baptism: baptism of water, baptism of blood, and baptism of desire. The third form helps to answer the question about whether unbaptized babies can go to Heaven (see Background Information on page 166). Have the students create pictures to help them remember the meaning of each form of Baptism.

- **Prayer:** Conclude any of the Baptism lessons with the following prayer:

> Holy Spirit, we have been anointed in baptism and begun our journey through this life. Oil symbolizes your presence within us and your protection, guidance, and strength, which is with us every day. Help us listen to your voice and rely on your help. Thank you for your constant presence, in ourselves and those around us. Amen.

For Review Answers (page 165)

1. Baptism is strongly rooted in Scripture. In the Old Testament, the Holy Spirit overshadows the waters at the time of creation before the Father brings life from the waters. God renewed life on the earth after the devastation of the Great Flood. In the New Testament, John the Baptist baptized Jesus; the Holy Spirit descended on him, and Jesus began his public ministry in the power of the Spirit. Jesus instructed his disciples to baptize all those who heard the Good News and decided to follow.

2. The essential rite of Baptism is the pouring of water on the forehead (or immersing the person) while saying the words, "I baptize you in the name of the Father, and of the Son, and of the Holy Spirit."

3. The symbols of Baptism are water, oil, white garment, and candle. Water represents cleansing and the passage through death into life. The oil represents healing and protection and the catechumen's new, expanded life as a person joined to Jesus. The white garment is a sign of a new identity, pure, happy, and united with Christ. And the candle is a reminder that Christ and his followers are light to the world.

4. Baptism forgives original and personal sin, although the consequences of sin remain. Baptism gives new life in Christ. Baptism confers sanctifying grace, the presence of the Holy Spirit, and the gifts of the Spirit. Baptism incorporates us into the Body of Christ and unites us with all other Christians. Baptism confers an indelible character on the soul.

Confirmation (pages 166–169)

Objectives

In this lesson, the students will:

- list and explain the requirements for receiving Confirmation.
- describe the process of preparing for and receiving Confirmation.
- explain the history of the sacrament.
- describe the similarities and differences with Confirmation as celebrated in Eastern Rite Churches.

Preview

This section builds on the concepts introduced in the section on Baptism. Because students may be in the process of preparing for Confirmation, there is particular opportunity to provide a solid foundation for their reception of the sacrament. Confirmation is a sacrament that celebrates the special outpouring of the Holy Spirit on the baptized in the same way that the Spirit once came to the Apostles at Pentecost. Confirmation "completes" Baptism in that it, too, imprints an indelible spiritual mark on the soul. Confirmation brings about an increase and deepening of baptismal grace.

 Bell Ringers

- **Prayer Experience:** Pray this prayer from the Rite of Confirmation as an opening to the lessons on the sacrament:

    All-powerful God, Father of our Lord Jesus Christ,

    by water and the Holy Spirit

    you freed your sons and daughters from sin and gave them new life.

    Send your Holy Spirit upon them

    to be their helper and guide.

    Give them the spirit of wisdom and understanding,

    the spirit of right judgment and courage,

    the spirit of knowledge and reverence.

    Fill them with the spirit of wonder and awe in your presence.

    We ask this through Christ our Lord.

- **Journal Assignment:** Explain that the gifts of the Spirit listed in the prayer are taken from Isaiah 11:1–5. Ask the students to briefly write answers to the following questions in their journals:

    1. What do these gifts mean to me?

    2. How can I share them with others?

- **Class Discussion:** Allow time for writing. Then call on several students to share their responses to each question.

Confirmation (CCC, 1285; 1302–1311; 1316–1317; 1319)

The Sacrament of Confirmation completes the sacramental grace of Baptism. Every Catholic who has been baptized, and yet not confirmed, should receive this sacrament. In the Western Church, once a person has reached "the age of discretion," he or she can be confirmed. However, in danger of death, even children should be confirmed. A candidate for this sacrament must profess the faith, be in the state of grace, intend to receive the sacrament, and be prepared to be a witness for our Lord Jesus Christ.

Today the Sacrament of Confirmation is often received in the teen years to help represent a teen's increasing personal commitment to faith. In preparation for the sacrament, teens learn more about the Holy Spirit and how to use the Spirit's many gifts to serve the Church, including their own parish. Prayer and the Sacrament of Penance are also part of the preparation for the sacrament. Those to be confirmed also choose a Confirmation sponsor to accompany them in preparation and at the rite. It is most appropriate that this be one of their baptismal godparents. The effects of the Sacrament of Confirmation include:

- the full outpouring of the Holy Spirit, which makes it possible for us to cry out, "Abba! Father!";
- binding us more closely to the Church and more firmly to Christ;
- increasing the gifts of the Holy Spirit in us, especially his strength to spread and defend the Christian faith by word and deed.

Confirmation, like Baptism, imprints an indelible spiritual mark on the soul, and so can be received only once. The sacramental character consists of marking Christians with the seal of the Holy Spirit, giving them the power to witness to the Lord. This completes the common priesthood of the faithful received in Baptism.

Biblical Roots and Historical Dimensions (CCC, 1286–1292; 1297; 1312–1314; 1318)

Like the other sacraments, Confirmation is rooted in the Bible. For example, the Old Testament prophets promised that the Spirit would rest on the coming Messiah. At Jesus' Baptism, the Spirit did indeed rest on him. The Holy Spirit was present throughout Jesus' life. Examples include his conception by the power of the Spirit, his public ministry of teaching and healing in union with the Spirit, and his promises to send the Holy Spirit to the Church.

The origin of the Sacrament of Confirmation is found in the apostolic laying on of hands. Acts 19:1–6 tells the story of a group of new disciples who had been baptized by John the Baptist. Paul taught them about Jesus and baptized them in Jesus' name. When he laid hands on them, the Holy Spirit came upon them. They received special charisms, or gifts of the Spirit, namely

Extending the Lesson

Individual Assignment: Write the following words in a column on the board: Scripture, morality, sacraments, the Trinity, life and teaching of Jesus, liturgy, prayer, Catholic social teaching, Church structure, Mary and the saints, afterlife, the Mass, the commandments. Have students rate their current level of knowledge about each area on a scale of 1 to 10, with 10 being "extremely well informed." In what areas do they particularly see a need for growth?

For Enrichment

Individual Assignment: Have students do a brief research paper on the practice of bar mitzvahs and bat mitzvahs in the Jewish faith. Have them answer the following questions:

- What does it mean to be an adult in the Jewish faith? What privileges and responsibilities are included?
- What is the preparation for participating in a bar mitzvah or bat mitzvah? (This will vary, depending on whether the participant is a member of an Orthodox, Conservative, or Reform congregation.)
- What is the ceremony like, and what is a typical family celebration afterward?
- How are the preparation, ceremony, and effect of a bar mitzvah or bat mitzvah similar to the Sacrament of Confirmation? How are they different?

the gifts of tongues and prophecy. An anointing with perfumed oil (Chrism) signifies the gift of the Holy Spirit. Chrism is related to the name Christian, meaning "anointed" of Christ, who was himself anointed with the Holy Spirit.

In the early Church, Baptism and Confirmation were part of the adult initiation process that climaxed at the Easter Vigil liturgy, with the bishop presiding. In these early years, children probably joined their parents in the initiation process. Whole households became Christian together. As Christianity grew, infant baptisms multiplied. Because it became increasingly difficult for the bishop to be present at every Baptism, priests were allowed to baptize. However, the bishop wished to retain some role in the initiation process.

In the Western Church the custom grew of the bishop at some later date "confirming" the baptismal commitment of Christians baptized as infants. This practice emphasizes that each Christian is in communion with the bishop who guarantees and serves Church unity, catholicity, and apostolicity. By the thirteenth century, the Church saw the wisdom of teaching youngsters

more about their baptismal commitment. Therefore, the time of preparation to receive Confirmation became a good time to give them further instructions in the faith.

Therefore, in the Western Church, the bishop was and is the ordinary minister of Confirmation for those who were baptized as infants. Confirmation takes place some time after a person reaches the age of reason, generally between seven and sixteen years. For a serious reason, the bishop can delegate priests to confirm. In the case of adult baptism, or Christian converts being accepted into the Catholic Church, the priest who baptizes or receives them also confirms them at the Easter Vigil. And any priest can administer Confirmation when there is danger of death.

Eastern Rite Churches administer all three initiation sacraments at the same time, including for infants. This stresses the unity of Christian initiation. In the Eastern Rites, the priest confirms the new Christian after Baptism and then celebrates the first Eucharist. However, the priest confirms only with *myron* (or Chrism) that has been blessed by a bishop. This signifies the special bond with the bishop resulting from Confirmation.

Confirmation and the Holy Spirit

Read the following Scripture passages that cite the Holy Spirit. Answer the questions that accompany each reading.

- *Ezekiel 36:24–28.* What does Yahweh promise to the Chosen People?
- *John 14:15-17.* What quality of the Holy Spirit does Jesus emphasize in his promise?
- *Mark 1:9–11.* When does the Holy Spirit descend on Jesus?
- *Romans 8:14–17.* What does the Holy Spirit enable us to do?
- *Galatians 5:22–23.* What qualities will a person who lives in the Spirit have?

The Rite of Confirmation (CCC, 1293–1296; 1298–1301; 1320–1321)

Like Baptism, Confirmation usually takes place during Eucharist, thus stressing the unity among the Sacraments of Initiation. The Confirmation liturgy begins with a renewal of baptismal promises and a profession of faith by those to be confirmed (*confirmands*). The bishop then extends his hands over them and invokes the outpouring of the Holy Spirit. The essential rite follows:

The minister *anoints the forehead of the confirmand with sacred Chrism* (in the Eastern Churches, the other sense organs as well), *lays on his hand, and recites the words: "Be sealed with the Gift of the Holy Spirit."* (In the Eastern Churches, the minister says, "The seal of the gift that is the Holy Spirit.")

A sign of peace concludes the rite, thus signifying unity with the bishop and the Church.

Background Information

Confirmation Completes the Sacramental Grace of Baptism

Unlike baptism, which can be received as an infant, the Sacrament of Confirmation must be received when a candidate is able to profess the faith, be in the state of grace, intend to receive the sacrament, and be prepared to witness to our Lord Jesus Christ.

Pope John Paul II spoke of how the Sacrament of Confirmation "perfects baptismal grace":

> . . . A renewed appreciation of the Holy Spirit's presence focuses our attention especially on the Sacrament of Confirmation (cf. *Tertio millennio adveniente*, n. 45). As the *Catechism of the Catholic Church* teaches, "it perfects baptismal grace; it . . . gives the Holy Spirit in order to root us more deeply in the divine filiation, incorporate us more firmly into Christ, strengthen our bond with the Church, associate us more closely with her mission, and help us bear witness to the Christian faith in words accompanied by deeds" (n. 1316).

Through the seal of the Spirit conferred by Confirmation, the Christian attains his full identity and becomes aware of his mission in the Church and the world. "Before this grace had been conferred on you," St Cyril of Jerusalem writes, "you were not sufficiently worthy of this name, but were on the way to becoming Christians" (*Cat. Myst.,* III, 4: *PG* 33, 1092). (*L'Osservatore Romano*, #1, Oct. 7, 1998)

Teaching Approaches

- **Direct Instruction:** Summarize the opening text section under "Confirmation" (page 166). List the four requirements for receiving the sacrament on the board:
  - Profess the faith.
  - Be in the state of grace.
  - Intend to receive the sacrament.
  - Be prepared to witness to Jesus Christ.

- **Class Discussion:** Ask the students to tell what each of these requirements means in their own words. Some students may be ambivalent about being confirmed. Adolescent faith is frequently filled with doubt. This can be an opportunity to affirm their questioning as a form of faith. Catholics are often very private about their faith. Facilitate a discussion about recent opportunities they may have had to witness to their faith in word or example.

- **Individual Assignment:** Use the following questions to quiz the students' knowledge of the information in the text subsection "Biblical Roots and Historical Dimensions" (pages 166–167). Have the students write their responses on scrap paper and check answers with a partner when completed.

1. What is the origin of the Sacrament of Confirmation? (*the apostolic laying on of hands on those who had been baptized*)

2. What happened when hands were laid on the baptized? (*The Holy Spirit came upon them and they received special charisms.*)

3. How did Baptism and Confirmation become separated? (*It became more difficult for the bishop to be at every Confirmation.*)

4. Who is the ordinary minister of the sacrament in the Western Church? (*the bishop*)

5. How does the Eastern Rite celebrate Confirmation? (*All three initiation sacraments are celebrated together. The priest confirms using myron that has been blessed by a bishop.*)

- **Writing Assignment:** Read the Scripture passages listed in the assignment "Confirmation and the Holy Spirit" (page 167). Write answers to each accompanying question (answers are on page 170 of this text).

- **Direct Instruction:** Continue with the text subsection "The Rite of Confirmation" (pages 167–168). Emphasize the essential rite of Confirmation on page 167:
  - anointing on the forehead with sacred chrism
  - the minister's (bishop's) laying on of hands
  - the recitation of the words "Be sealed with the Gift of the Holy Spirit"

If students created flash cards for the symbols of Baptism, have them add oil, laying on of hands, and the words of Confirmation to their stack of cards.

- **Class Discussion:** Because oil is not a symbol that has significance in contemporary life, it may be difficult for students to grasp its impact. Ask them to come up with examples of symbolic gestures that confer a new role on a person. Examples can be the swearing in of the president or a judge, the passing of a gavel to a new student council president, coming-of-age traditions in indigenous cultures, and the exchange of vows and rings in a wedding ceremony. List the ideas on the board, and then draw the comparison between these traditions and the Rite of Confirmation.

- **Direct Instruction:** Introduce the information on Eastern Rite Churches (page 168). To expand on the information in the text with the online links, have the students fill in Chapter 6, Handout 2 "Comparing Christian Churches" (starting on page 285 and also online at www.avemariapress.com). Possible answers are on page 170 of this text.

Confirmation and the Holy Spirit

Answers (page 167)

- *Ezekiel 36:24–28* God promises a secure relationship with him, which will result in the Jewish people's transformed lives. They will be protected from harm, they will love one another, and they will live in obedience to God's laws.

- *John 14:15–17* Jesus emphasizes the truthfulness of the Spirit. This is not simply refusing to tell lies, but rather an understanding of the world as it really is. For example, a spirit of truth would help people see that material things do not bring happiness. It would free people to share their resources and value other people for their uniqueness and not their possessions or accomplishments.

- *Mark 1:9–11* The Holy Spirit descended on Jesus at his Baptism, the beginning of his public ministry.

- *Romans 8:14–17* The Holy Spirit enables us to be children of God and heirs of Heaven. The Holy Spirit releases us from fear and allows us to enter fully into our relationship with God.

- *Galatians 5:22–23* Those who live in the Spirit are blessed with the fruits of the Spirit: love, joy, peace, patience, kindness, goodness, faithfulness, gentleness, and self-control.

rite
The manner or form of celebrating a particular sacrament and performing other Church rituals like blessings. The term also refers to the principal historical rituals in the Catholic Church, for example, the Roman Rite or the Byzantine Rite.

The anointing with oil in Confirmation represents total consecration to Christ, a sharing in Jesus' mission. The newly confirmed person is charged with bringing forth in word and deed "the aroma of Christ." The Confirmation anointing permanently marks the Christian with the seal of the Holy Spirit. In Confirmation, we are sealed totally to Jesus Christ to be servants of his Gospel forever.

Eastern Rite Churches

What do we mean when we refer to Eastern Rite Churches? Eastern Rite Churches are Catholic Churches following one of the six rites derived from the ancient traditions of Christian churches that were centered in Constantinople (modern Greece). Eastern Rite Churches are in communion with the Pope and the Latin or Western Church.

The term **rite** refers to a special way of doing the liturgy, but it also refers to a variety of traditions including a married clergy, special sacramental traditions like confirming baptized infants and giving them the Eucharist, and the use of ancient languages in liturgies. Eastern Rite Churches have their own version of canon law (Church law) and are governed by a patriarch.

The Eastern Rite Churches are also called "Eastern Catholic Churches" or "Uniate Churches" (meaning in union with the Roman Catholic Church). There are more than ten million Eastern Catholics. They belong to one of these six rites: Byzantine, Alexandrian or Coptic, Syriac, Armenian, Maronite, and Chaldean. There are subdivisions within each of these rites along national or ethnic lines. Numerically, the largest group of Eastern Catholics belongs to the Byzantine Rite.

- Read and report on one of the Eastern Rite Churches listed above.

Chapter 6, Handout 2 "Comparing Christian Churches" Handout Possible Answers

	Roman Catholic	Eastern Rite	Orthodox	Protestant
Baptism	Infant	Infant	Infant	Infant/adult
Eucharist	Yes, weekly	Yes, weekly In communion with Catholic; given to infants	Yes, weekly Given to infants	Perhaps
Confirmation	Yes	Yes, in infancy	Yes, in infancy	Perhaps
Scripture	Roman Catholic Canon	Same as Roman Catholic canon	Same as Roman Catholic canon	Delete seven Old Testament books
Clergy	Celibate male	Married male	Married male	Married, some female
Hierarchy	Pope, bishops, priests	Patriarch, bishops, priests	Patriarch, bishops, priests	Some have bishops

For Review

1. When is Confirmation ordinarily administered in the Western Church?
2. List three effects of the Sacrament of Confirmation.
3. Who is the ordinary minister of the Sacrament of Confirmation in the Western Church? In the Eastern Church?
4. List three scriptural roots of Confirmation.
5. Explain the essential rite of Confirmation.
6. Explain three meanings of anointing with the oil of Confirmation.
7. Name three rites in the Eastern Catholic Churches.

For Reflection

List one of the virtues St. Paul mentions in Ephesians 4:1–6 and discuss how you can put it into practice during the coming week either at home or at school.

Eucharist (*CCC*, 1322–1344; 1356–1397; 1409–1412; 1414–1418)

The Eucharist completes a person's Christian initiation. It unites the new Catholic to Christ's sacrifice on the cross, a sacrifice of praise and thanksgiving to the Father. Through this wondrous gift, Christ continues to pour out his saving graces on the members of his Body, the Church.

The Eucharist has its roots in Scripture. The Old Testament foreshadowed the Eucharist when the priest Melchizedek offered God bread and wine (Gn 14:18), when the Jews celebrated Passover to commemorate the Exodus from slavery (Ex 12:1–20), and when God gave manna to the Chosen People in the desert (Ex 16:4–35).

In the Gospels, Jesus' multiplication of the loaves and his changing of water into wine at Cana prefigured

Homework Assignment

1. Complete the For Review questions on page 169.
2. Complete one of the reports suggested with the "Eastern Rite Churches" feature on page 168.
3. Write a homily based on the upcoming Sunday readings. See "Preparing a Homily" (page 174).
4. Read the entire text section "Eucharist" on pages 169–175.

For Review Answers (page 169)

1. In the Western Rite Church, Confirmation is normally administered between the ages of seven and sixteen.
2. The effects of the Sacrament of Confirmation are the full outpouring of the Holy Spirit, binding us more closely to the Church and to Christ, and increasing the gifts of the Holy Spirit. In particular, the gift of Pentecost, the ability to courageously share the Gospel, is increased.
3. The ordinary minister of the Sacrament of Confirmation in the Western Rite Church is the bishop. In the Eastern Rite Church, Confirmation is administered with Baptism to infants by the priest. However, the priest uses chrism that has been blessed by the bishop.
4. The scriptural roots of Confirmation include the prophets' promise that the Spirit would rest on the Messiah, which was exemplified at Jesus' baptism. Jesus promised to send the Holy Spirit to be with the Church when he left. In the Acts of the Apostles, we read of the Apostles' practice of laying hands on people and praying for the full release of the Holy Spirit in them.
5. The essential rite of Confirmation is anointing the forehead, laying on hands, and reciting the words "Be sealed with the Gift of the Holy Spirit."
6. Anointing with the oil of Confirmation represents total consecration to Christ, the charge to represent Christ in word and deed, and the permanent mark of being sealed with the Holy Spirit.
7. The rites of the Eastern Catholic Churches include married clergy, confirming baptized infants, giving infants the Eucharist, and the use of ancient languages in liturgies. Eastern Catholic Churches include Byzantine, Alexandrian or Coptic, Syriac, Armenian, Maronite, and Chaldean.

Eucharist (pages 169–175)

Objectives

In this lesson, the students will:

- explain the various names for the Eucharist.
- describe the two main parts of the Mass, the Liturgy of the Word and the Liturgy of the Eucharist.
- categorize the parts of the Mass.
- appreciate the importance of the Eucharist in their lives and increase their devotion to the Eucharist.

Preview

This section expands students' understanding of the Eucharist, which they experience in school and parish life. The challenge is to break through their familiarity with the sacrament and help them see the Eucharist in a new light. Even students who attend Mass regularly may not be able to identify the various parts of the Mass. This section can help enrich students' participation in the Eucharist and understand that the Eucharist is indeed the "sacrament of sacraments."

---

the institution of the Eucharist. Moreover, Jesus made direct reference to the Eucharist in John's Gospel (6:53–59) when he declared the importance of eating his body and drinking his blood, a hard teaching that caused some disciples to leave him. The Lord established the Eucharist at the Last Supper in the context of the Jewish feast of Passover. He took unleavened bread, blessed and broke it, and gave it to his Apostles, saying:

"This is my body, which will be given for you; do this in memory of me." And likewise the cup after they had eaten, saying, "This cup is the new covenant in my blood, which will be shed for you." (Lk 22:19–20)

KNOWING CHRIST THROUGH SCRIPTURE

Jesus at Meals

Read the following Gospel passages about Jesus' participation at meals during his earthly ministry. Answer the questions that follow.

Matthew 9:9–13, Luke 7:36–50, and Luke 19:1–10
- What common theme runs throughout these passages?

John 21:1–14
- What was the purpose of this meal?

John 13:1–17
- What important lesson is Jesus teaching here?

John 6:52–59
- What does Jesus promise in this passage? Explain why this is such an important passage for Catholic teaching about the Eucharist.

Various Names for the Eucharist

We can never fully understand the Eucharist, since it is such a rich mystery of God's love for us. But by reflecting on some of its various names, we can begin to appreciate it more.

Eucharist

The term *Eucharist* in Greek means "thanksgiving." In this sacrament, we thank God for his gifts of creation, Redemption through our Lord and Savior Jesus Christ, and sanctification in the Holy Spirit.

Lord's Supper

The term *Lord's Supper* brings to mind the Last Supper. Jesus chose a Passover meal to launch the events of our Salvation. A meal is a universal symbol of friendship

and life. The Eucharist is Christ coming to us as our greatest friend and Savior and giving us a share in his own divine Life.

Breaking the Bread (cf. Acts 2:42)

The Apostles recognized Jesus in the *breaking of the bread* (Lk 24:35), a symbol for sacrificing and sharing. We are to be broken like the Lord as we serve others. We receive the bread of life to become the bread of life for others.

Eucharistic Assembly

Eucharistic assembly emphasizes how we celebrate the Eucharist in the midst of the assembled Church. Validly ordained priests are the only ones who can preside at this Eucharistic assembly to consecrate the bread

---

Extending the Lesson

Individual Assignment: Take the students through Chapter 6, Handout 3 "Seder Meal Script" (starting on page 285 and also online at www.avemariapress.com). See also Ongoing Assignment 2, on page 179. This script highlights the similarities and makes connections between this ceremony and the format of the preparation of gifts at Mass. These similarities illustrate in a concrete way the scriptural and Jewish roots of our celebration of Eucharist. Have students circle the similarities or make note of them in the margin and review their suggested similarities as a class. Consider celebrating a simple Seder meal during class.

Knowing Christ through Scripture Answers (page 170)

Matthew 9:9–13, Luke 7:36–50, and Luke 19:1–10
- Jesus spent particular attention to reach out to the sinners and outcasts of society, with whom he often ate meals.

John 21:1–14
- To show the disciples (and us) that Jesus will continue to be present at communal meals.

John 13:1–17
- Jesus is present in his disciples who will serve rather than be served.

John 6:52–59
- Jesus promises that those who eat his flesh and drink his blood will have eternal life. This is important because it shows that the Eucharist is the source and summit of the Catholic faith.

and wine so that these ordinary species can become the Body and Blood of the Lord (*CCC*, 1411).

Holy and Divine Liturgy

The Eucharist is the very heart of the Church's liturgical life. The term *liturgy* means "people's work." The *holy and divine liturgy* of the Eucharist is the supreme worship we can give God, "the source and summit of the Christian life" (*Dogmatic Constitution on the Church*, No. 11). This is why Church law requires Catholics to attend Mass on Sundays and holy days. The Sunday obligation comes from Jesus himself, who told us to break bread in his name. Weekly Mass attendance joins us to our brother and Savior Jesus Christ and to one another in worship of the Father.

Most Blessed Sacrament

The Eucharist is the *Most Blessed Sacrament*. The consecrated Eucharistic species reserved in the tabernacle also go by this name. The essential signs of the Eucharistic sacrifice are wheat bread and grape wine. In the Eucharistic liturgy, the priest consecrates bread and wine by invoking the blessing of the Holy Spirit. He does so with the words of Jesus himself: "This is my body, which has been given up for you . . . This is the cup of my blood . . ."

Holy Sacrifice

The word *sacrifice* means "to make holy." The Eucharist is a memorial of our Lord's Passion, Death, and Resurrection. It makes present Christ's sacrifice and includes the offering of the Church. The shedding of his blood on Calvary was Christ's supreme act of love. It makes us holy and pleasing to God because:

1. Jesus is the High Priest and the victim who offers himself through the celebrant and the assembly in praise,

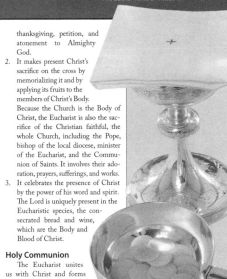

thanksgiving, petition, and atonement to Almighty God.

2. It makes present Christ's sacrifice on the cross by memorializing it and by applying its fruits to the members of Christ's Body. Because the Church is the Body of Christ, the Eucharist is also the sacrifice of the Christian faithful, the whole Church, including the Pope, bishop of the local diocese, minister of the Eucharist, and the Communion of Saints. It involves their adoration, prayers, sufferings, and works.

3. It celebrates the presence of Christ by the power of his word and spirit. The Lord is uniquely present in the Eucharistic species, the consecrated bread and wine, which are the Body and Blood of Christ.

Holy Communion

The Eucharist unites us with Christ and forms us into his Body, the Church. In the Eucharist "the Body and Blood, together with the soul and divinity, of our Lord Jesus Christ and, therefore, *the whole Christ is truly, really, and substantially* contained" (*CCC*, 1374, quoting the teaching of the Council of Trent). This presence of Christ in the consecrated species of bread and wine is called the "real presence." Exactly how Jesus is present in the consecrated bread and wine is a mystery. The term *transubstantiation* expresses that at the consecration of the Mass the reality (the substance) of the bread and wine change into the reality of Jesus—his risen, glorified Body and Blood, even though the appearances of bread and wine remain. The Lord is present whole and entire in each species

transubstantiation
The term used to describe what happens at the consecration of the bread and wine at Mass when their entire substance is turned into the entire substance of the Body and Blood of Christ, even though the appearances of bread and wine remain. The Eucharistic presence of Christ begins at the moment of consecration and endures as long as the Eucharistic species subsist.

 Audiovisual Materials continued from page 160

Teen Discipleship

From the *Sealed with God's Spirit* Catholic Update series, this program shows "Catholic youth how their Christian baptismal commitment comes alive in service to others" (St. Anthony Messenger Press).

Understanding the Sacraments

This Catholic Update video includes a story, witness, and teaching segment and concludes with a music video reflection. Stresses that sacraments "are not so much objects as events, not simply something we receive, but something we are" (30-minute video, St. Anthony Messenger Press).

A Walk through the Mass

Cardinal Donald Wuerl gives a step-by-step presentation of the Mass in five sections, providing descriptions of what is being done, as well as the reasons for the actions. Citations from the *Catechism of the Catholic Church* are given (54-minute video, Our Sunday Visitor Press).

A Walk through the Mass

A Catholic Update video that explores the meaning behind the Eucharist and explains the four principal parts of the Mass (30-minute video, St. Anthony Messenger Press).

Why Catholics Do What They Do (In Church)

Examines the meaning of signs and symbols like candles, water, gestures, and crosses that we use in our Catholic rituals (28-minute video, Videos with Values).

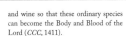 **Bell Ringers**

- **Class Discussion:** Brainstorm with the students "reasons why teenagers go to Mass" and print their responses on the board. Likewise, have them list "reasons why teenagers do not go to Mass" and print these on the board as well. Sample answers for going to Mass may include: it's a sin to miss Mass, it makes me feel good, and my parents expect me to. Sample answers for not going to Mass might be: it's too early in the morning, my parents do not go, and it's boring. Refer to the second For Reflection question on page 175. Ask students to share how they would respond.

- **Journal Assignment:** Next have the students write in their journals an entry entitled "Why I Go to Mass" or "Why I Don't Go to Mass" while incorporating some of the responses into their answer.

 Teaching Approaches

- **Group Activity:** Introduce the section "The Eucharist" (pages 169–175). Point out the Scripture references of the roots of Eucharist. Have the students work with a partner and divide up the following passages:
  - Genesis 14:18
  - Exodus 12:1–20
  - Exodus 16:4–35
  - John 6:53–59

  Have each person read their assigned passages and then explain their connection to Eucharist to their partner.

- **Individual Assignment:** Have students read and respond to the questions in the Knowing Christ through Scripture feature "Jesus at Meals" on page 170. When students have completed the answers, discuss them as a class.

- **Class Discussion:** Use the following discussion points to take the students through each of the various names for the Eucharist on pages 170–173:
  - *Eucharist* What are some things that you are thankful for? Also, have the students prepare a list of causes for gratitude in their lives. Encourage them to bring a mental list the next time they go to Mass or to their place of worship and to consciously give thanks at that time.

  - *Lord's Supper* Describe a meal you shared in which you were able to experience the presence of someone not physically with you?

  - *Breaking the Bread* What does it mean, practically, for you to be "bread of life" for others? Facilitate a discussion with students on what it means to be broken. How does being generous and patient or telling the truth "break" us?

- *Eucharistic Assembly* Why is the assembly lacking when any members are absent from the celebration of Eucharist?

- *Holy and Divine Liturgy* When are times during Mass you feel most united with Christ? With your neighbors?

- *Most Blessed Sacrament* The Eucharist is adored, even after the Mass is concluded. When is a time you feel the need to sit in prayer before the Blessed Sacrament?

- *Holy Sacrifice* What are elements of the Mass that remind you of Jesus' sacrifice on the cross? Ask students to write down a definition of sacrifice. Answers are likely to center on giving something up to attain a greater good: we make sacrifices at Lent; a parent may sacrifice time, money, and even life for the good of a child; students sacrifice sleep or fun activities in order to make good grades. This understanding of sacrifice is true, but not complete. To make something holy goes beyond giving things up: it is a unique kind of result.

- *Holy Communion* What are the benefits of receiving Holy Communion? (Have the students recite from pages 172–173 of the text.) Because of the Catholic belief in transubstantiation, Catholics show great reverence for consecrated bread and wine. Before Vatican II, lay people were not allowed to touch a chalice because it held the Body and Blood of Jesus. Ask students to pay attention the next time they attend Mass for how the sanctity of Holy Communion is preserved: consumption of wine after distribution of Communion, locking consecrated hosts in the tabernacle, etc. Have them report back to class the following Monday.

- *Holy Mass* How do you respond to the charge to "go in peace to love and serve the Lord?" Some Orthodox Churches use the term "Divine Liturgy" instead of the word "Mass." Have students write a dismissal rite. Advise students to make their dismissal instructions concrete and directed to current conditions in their community. For example, "When you leave, be polite to other cars that are also exiting the parking lot. Be patient with your family members when you get home. Bring dinner to your elderly neighbor who is sick. Bring peace to those you touch at school or at work . . ."

- **Class Activity:** Form students into teams of three. On a small piece of paper, write each of the names of the Eucharist; make three copies of each title. Distribute the sheets evenly among the groups. Have groups take turns sending a representative to the board to visually depict a name for the Eucharist while the class tries to guess the correct answer.

PROFILE OF FAITH: BLESSED KATERI TEKAWITHA, STRONG IN FAITH

Kateri Tekawitha was born in 1656 near Auriesville in upstate New York. Her father was a Mohawk chief and her mother an Algonquin Indian who had converted to Christianity. When she was four years old, her parents and younger brother died of smallpox, a disease that also struck Kateri, scarring her face and impairing her eyesight. Because of her poor vision, she was nicknamed *Tekawitha*, meaning "she who bumps into things."

When she was about eight, she was adopted by relatives who opposed her Christianity. The family moved to another village near present-day Fonda, New York. In her teen years, Jesuit missionaries came to her village. Both her family and tribe opposed the Catholic influence, but this did not deter Kateri, who began to meet with a priest who taught her the faith, how to pray, and how to live as a disciple of the Lord. When she was twenty, she was baptized on Easter Sunday. She took the baptismal name of Catherine (*Kateri* in the Mohawk language).

Kateri met scorn and derision from her fellow villagers for her conversion to the faith. Eventually she fled to the Mission of St. Francis Xavier, a settlement of Christian Indians near present-day Montreal, Canada, where she lived the remaining years of her life. She took a vow of perpetual virginity and engaged in good works by caring for the elderly and the sick and teaching prayers to children. She also lived a prayerful life and was profoundly devoted to the Blessed Sacrament, the Blessed Mother, and the Cross of Christ. Her devotion to the Eucharist was inspirational. Each morning she would go to the chapel at four and remain there until the last Mass.

In the last years of her life, Kateri patiently suffered greatly from serious illness. She died on April 17, 1680, shortly before her twenty-fourth birthday. Her final words on earth were, "Jesus, I love you." Witnesses to her death testified that the smallpox scars on her face disappeared and her face became lovely and radiant.

Shortly before her death, Kateri promised that in Heaven she would continue to pray for and love her friends. The priest who took care of her during her final illness and others reported that Kateri had appeared to them. Healing miracles were attributed to her.

In 1980, Pope John Paul II beatified Kateri Tekawitha. She is the first Native American declared Blessed, the last step to canonization. The courage she displayed in living her Christian faith despite obstacles remains an inspiration to us today. She is known as the "Lily of the Mohawks." The Church celebrates her feast day on July 14 and, along with St. Francis of Assisi, honors her as the patroness of ecology and the environment.

- Read and report in more detail about Blessed Kateri Tekawitha.

from the moment of consecration for as long as the Eucharistic species subsist (see *CCC*, 1377).

The Church encourages us to receive *Holy Communion* every time we participate in a Eucharistic liturgy. (The bare minimum, though, is at least once a year, if possible during the Easter season.) However, we must receive Holy Communion worthily, that is, we be must in the state of sanctifying grace.

The Eucharist communicates God's very life to us by giving us the Risen Lord himself who, by power of the Holy Spirit, binds us together and makes us the Church. Among the many graces of Holy Communion are:

- spiritual life and nourishment
- cleansing from *past* sins by wiping away venial sin and preservation from *future* mortal sins (The Sacrament of Penance is the proper sacrament to gain forgiveness of mortal sin. The Eucharist is the sacrament for those who are in the state of sanctifying grace, in full communion with the Church.)
- a greater commitment to the poor, because when we receive Christ in Holy Communion, we must recognize him in the poorest people in our midst

For Enrichment

Class Discussion: Read and discuss the life of Kateri Tekawitha. Note that she is the first Native American to be declared "blessed." Have students cite three reasons why in her life she exemplified a Christlike life. Invite students to spend some time researching more about Blessed Kateri.

Writing Assignment: Have the students write an essay entitled "My Favorite Celebration of Eucharist" while focusing on the specific elements that made it a special celebration.

Extending the Lesson

Class Discussion: Review with students the practice of spending time in the presence of the Blessed Sacrament. If possible, show the students photographs of monstrances in different styles, from simple to very ornate. Ask them to describe the message about Jesus conveyed through the different types of design. Very formal, jeweled designs accentuate the majesty of Jesus; more simple designs tend to accentuate Jesus' close presence among us. If the school has a Eucharistic chapel, take students to the chapel for a visit.

- an increase in the theological virtues of faith, hope, and love and strengthening of the gifts and fruits of the Holy Spirit
- spiritual energy for our earthly pilgrimage, a foretaste of Heaven, and union with the Blessed Mother and the saints in Heaven

In sum, the Eucharist puts us in touch with the saving effects of the Paschal Mystery, the eternal life that Jesus' sacrifice has won for us.

Holy Mass

The term *Holy Mass* derives from the sending forth in the dismissal rite (in Latin, *Ite missa est*). We are to become for others the Christ we receive in the Blessed Sacrament of the Eucharist.

The Celebration of Mass (CCC, 1345–1355; 1408)

The Mass consists of two major parts—the *Liturgy of the Word* and the *Liturgy of the Eucharist*. In the Liturgy of the Word we hear God's Word and are called to respond to it. The Liturgy of the Eucharist celebrates the Paschal Mystery of Jesus Christ's love for us. The order of the Mass is as listed in the following subsections.

Introductory Rites

Entrance and Greeting. The Mass begins with the congregation standing and singing an appropriate song. The celebrant and people make the Sign of the Cross. The priest greets the people.

Penitential Rite. To worship with a pure heart, we acknowledge our sinfulness and ask for God's forgiveness.

Gloria. A prayer of praise and thanksgiving to the Triune God is shared.

Opening Prayer. The priest offers a prayer of supplication, which recalls the Mystery of Salvation proper to the day or feast.

Liturgy of the Word

The First Reading and *Responsorial Psalm.* Typically, the first reading comes from the Old Testament. Its theme is similar to the message of the Gospel. The psalm response, either sung or recited, shows that we plan to take God's Word to heart.

Second Reading and *Alleluia* or *Acclamation.* The second reading usually comes from one of St. Paul's letters and often deals with a problem facing followers of Jesus.

It is not explicitly connected to the other readings. The Alleluia verse is our resounding yes to God's Word.

Gospel. The most important reading is from a Gospel, thus linking us to the Word of God, Jesus the Lord. Standing is a sign of reverence. Signing ourselves with a small cross on the forehead, lips, and heart symbolizes our commitment to make God's Word come alive in what we think, say, and do.

Homily. The celebrant or another priest or deacon preaches the homily to apply Scripture to our lives.

The Creed. Our profession of faith in the Nicene Creed expresses our common belief. It binds us more closely as a community.

General Intercessions. Here we pray with confidence that the Lord will take care of our needs and those of our world.

Liturgy of the Eucharist

Offertory. The bread and wine are brought to the altar in procession. The prayer said over these gifts tells of God's goodness that we now offer back to God. The congregation offers a Sunday collection to support the Church's ministries and those who are in need.

The Eucharistic Prayer. This prayer is the heart of the Eucharistic liturgy. The *preface* (an introductory prayer) reminds us of our duty to thank the Father through Jesus Christ in the Holy Spirit. The entire congregation assents to the preface by singing or reciting a hymn of

- **Direct Instruction:** Continue with a presentation on the two major parts of the Mass—the Liturgy of the Word and the Liturgy of the Eucharist (pages 173–174). It is best to take the students through each part of the Mass with a brief explanation of each.
- **Direct Instruction:** Focus on the homily. Explain the connection between the theme of the first reading and of the Gospel. Point out that a purpose of the homily is to apply this theme to the lives of the particular congregation being addressed.
- **Student Presentation:** Reserve time for all of the students to share all or part of their prepared homilies, first with a partner or in a small group, and then by calling on selected volunteers to share with the entire class. Move around the room to make sure all of the students completed the assignment, but refrain from grading specifically on content.
- **Individual Assignment:** Distribute copies of any of the Eucharistic prayers to the students available online at http://catholic-resources.org/ChurchDocs/EP.htm. Help the students to identify and underline:
  - the epiclesis
  - the words of institution
  - intercessions for peace and various intentions of the community
  - the doxology leading to the Great Amen

Background Information

The Eucharist Is the Source of the Church's Life

In his address to a general audience on April 8, 1992, Pope John Paul II addressed the Eucharist as the source of the Church's life:

According to the Second Vatican Council the truth of the Church as a priestly community is realized through the sacraments; it comes to fulfillment in the Eucharist. Indeed, we read in *Lumen Gentium* that the faithful, "Taking part in the Eucharistic sacrifice, which is the fount and apex of the whole Christian life . . . offer the divine victim to God, and offer themselves along with it" (LG 11).

The Eucharist is the source of the Christian life because whoever shares in it receives the motivation and strength to live as a true Christian. Christ's sacrifice on the cross imparts to the believer the dynamism of his generous love. The Eucharistic banquet nourishes the faithful with the Body and Blood of the divine Lamb sacrificed for us and it gives them the strength to "follow in his footsteps" (cf. 1 Pet 2:21).

The Eucharist is the summit of the whole Christian life because the faithful bring to it all their prayers and good works, their joys and sufferings. These modest offerings are united to the perfect sacrifice of Christ. Thus they are completely sanctified and lifted up to God in an act of perfect worship which brings the faithful into the divine intimacy (cf. Jn 6:56–57). Therefore, as St. Thomas Aquinas writes, the Eucharist is "the culmination of the spiritual life and the goal of all the sacraments" (Summa Theol., III, q. 66, a. 6).

The Angelic Doctor also notes that the "effect of this sacrament is the unity of the mystical body [the Church], without which there can be no salvation. Therefore it is necessary to receive the Eucharist, at least by desire (in voto), in order to be saved" (III, q. 73, a. 1, ad 2). These words echo everything Jesus himself said about the necessity of the Eucharist for the Christian life: "Amen, amen, I say to you, unless you eat the flesh of the Son of Man and drink his blood, you do not have life within you. Whoever eats my flesh and drinks my blood has eternal life, and I will raise him on the last day" (Jn 6:53–54).

According to these words of Jesus, the Eucharist is a pledge of the resurrection to come, but it is already a source of eternal life in time. Jesus does not say "will have eternal life," but "has eternal life." Through the food of the Eucharist, Christ's eternal life penetrates and flows within human life.

- **Group Activity:** Have students create cards for a "Parts of the Mass" game in groups of two. Have them write the names of each part of the Mass on separate cards and number them in order on the back. Have them mix up the cards into a stack. First, have them categorize each card as "Liturgy of the Eucharist" or "Liturgy of the Word." Then, have them assemble the cards in order on their desks or on the floor. They should work in pairs to check their answers and compete if possible for the most correct responses.

For Review Answers (page 175)

1. In the Old Testament, Melchizedek offered God bread and wine. The Jewish people celebrated Passover with bread and wine, and God fed the Jews with manna in the desert. In the New Testament, Jesus' multiplication of the loaves and fishes prefigured the Eucharist.

2. Jesus instituted the Eucharist at the Last Supper.

3. The term *Eucharist* means "thanksgiving" in Greek.

4. *The Lord's Supper:* a meal of friendship and life
   Holy and Divine Liturgy: literally, people's work. The greatest work we can offer God.
   Holy Sacrifice: literally, to make holy. An emphasis on Jesus' sacrifice in redeeming us by his Death and Resurrection.
   Breaking the Bread: symbolizes sacrifice and sharing
   Blessed Sacrament: emphasizes Jesus' real presence in the consecrated bread and wine
   Holy Communion: nourishes us through our union with Christ
   Mass: we go in peace to love and serve

5. The effects of the Eucharist are spiritual life and nourishment; cleansing of past sins and preservation from future mortal sins; a greater commitment to the poor; an increase in the theological virtues of faith, hope, and love; and a strengthening of the gifts and fruits of the Holy Spirit.

epiclesis
The prayer that petitions God to send the Holy Spirit to transform the bread and wine offered at the Eucharistic liturgy into the Body and Blood of Jesus Christ. This term also applies to the prayer said in every sacrament that asks for the sanctifying power of the Holy Spirit.

praise called the *Sanctus* ("Holy, Holy, Holy").

The Church has four standard Eucharistic prayers, used on different occasions. Each of these prayers:

- invokes the power of the Holy Spirit (the *epiclesis*);
- recounts the words of institution spoken by Jesus at the Last Supper, remembers and acknowledges Christ's saving deeds (*anamnesis*), and offers the sacrifice of Jesus to the Father;
- contains intercessions that petition God for peace and various intentions of the whole community;
- concludes with the Great Amen in which we respond with a resounding yes, affirming we agree with what was prayed.

Communion Rite. The communion rite includes the Lord's Prayer, the prayer for deliverance, the prayer for peace, the sharing of a sign of peace, and the breaking of the bread while the *Lamb of God* is sung or recited. The congregation approaches the altar to receive the food of Salvation, God's heavenly gift to us—the Risen Lord. The communion rite closes with a prayer of petition on behalf of the community.

Concluding Rite

After any announcements, the Mass concludes when the celebrant blesses and dismisses the people. We are to "go in peace to love and serve the Lord" as the priest and others process out to the singing of an appropriate song.

Preparing a Homily

Locate the readings that will be used at next Sunday's liturgy. Read and summarize the main themes of the readings. Then, prepare a short outline of a talk you could give on these readings to a group of primary school students. *Hint:* Look for a central theme in the first reading and the Gospel. Arrange to share your homily in religious education class for the primary age you chose.

Homework Assignment

1. Complete the For Review questions on page 175.

2. Read the text section "The Liturgical Year" (pages 175–177).

3. Bring two sacramental objects to class (see page 177) and explain their meaning.

4. Continue working on the Ongoing Assignments due near the completion of the chapter.

For Review

1. Name some scriptural roots for the Eucharist.
2. When did Jesus institute the Eucharist?
3. What does the term *Eucharist* mean?
4. Briefly note an important truth that we can learn about the Eucharist when we speak of it as:
   - The Lord's Supper
   - Breaking the Bread
   - Holy and Divine Liturgy
   - Blessed Sacrament
   - Holy Sacrifice
   - Holy Communion
   - Mass
5. Name four spiritual effects of the Sacrament of the Eucharist.

For Reflection
- What was the most memorable liturgy you have ever participated in?
- What are some excuses teens give for missing Sunday Mass? How would you counter their excuses?

The Liturgical Year

(*CCC*, 1163–1173; 1193–1195)

Sunday is the Lord's Day, the day Christ rose from the dead. Sunday is the day that all Catholics are required to attend Mass. At the Sunday Mass we listen to God's Word, and the Paschal Mystery is made present to us. We thank God for our Savior Jesus Christ and receive him in Holy Communion. Sunday is also a time for us to celebrate family life and seek rest from work.

Over the course of a year, the Church's liturgy celebrates the various mysteries of our Redemption, including the Incarnation of Jesus Christ, the major events of his teaching ministry, his Ascension, the sending of the Holy Spirit on Pentecost, and the future anticipation of Jesus' Second Coming. The

Church's liturgical calendar is organized as follows:

- *Advent.* Advent prepares for Christ's coming. It begins at the end of November and lasts for four Sundays.
- *Christmas Season.* This period begins with Christmas, a feast that proclaims *Emmanuel,* "God is with us!" This joyful season also celebrates the feasts of the Holy Family, the Solemnity of Mary (January 1), and Jesus' Epiphany, or manifestation to the Magi. The season ends with the feast of the Lord's Baptism.
- *Ordinary Time 1.* Between the Christmas season and Lent, the Church does not celebrate any

Advent
The four-week season in the liturgical year that prepares for the coming of our Savior on Christmas.

For Enrichment

Individual Activity: Have the students make Advent calendars. A piece of poster board forms the basis for the calendar. Doors are cut into the poster board with an X-ACTO knife and labeled with numbers representing each day in Advent. The students can illustrate a passage from the daily Scriptures of the season for each door on a piece of paper approximately 2" x 3". Have them tape each sheet of paper to the back of poster board. As a service project, students could make several calendars and distribute them within your own or an elementary school.

The Liturgical Year (pages 175–177)

Objectives

In this lesson, the students will:
- identify the seasons of the liturgical year.
- create a liturgical calendar.
- describe the characteristics of each season and the colors and Scripture passages used during this time.
- list some sacramentals and explain their importance.

Preview

This section focuses on the scope of the Church's liturgical year. The preeminent Sunday is Easter. Every other Sunday the Church commemorates Easter and Christ's victory over sin and death. The other days and seasons of the liturgical year focus on the various Mysteries of Redemption. This section also defines and names sacramentals as objects, actions, prayers, and places that help people to remember Christ's presence.

Bell Ringers

- **Direct Instruction:** Provide an overview of the liturgical year using the chart on page 175 and the material on pages 175–176.
- **Journal Assignment:** Have the students reflect on their experience with each season of the liturgical year. Have them write about their memories of each season in their journal.
- **Class Discussion:** Have the students share their memories as a class. Discuss some of the most important events and themes that go along with each of the seasons based on the students' memories. Refer back to these memories as you progress through the lesson.

Teaching Approaches

- **Direct Instruction:** Summarize the main content of the text section "The Liturgical Year" (pages 175–177). Take the students through each of the seasons, mentioning key feasts and other aspects of the mysteries being celebrated.
- **Direct Instruction:** Take up in more depth each of the individual seasons as time allows. Review Advent traditions with students. Most are familiar with Advent wreaths and the meaning behind them; the candles represent the weeks of Advent; and the circular wreath represents eternity. A Jesse tree is made with a small, bare-branched tree. Throughout Advent, people hang symbols on the tree representing characters and stories from salvation history, such as Adam and Eve, Jonah and the whale, David's lyre, and the Ten Commandments.
- **Class Discussion:** Read Matthew 2:1–12, the story of the Epiphany. In many countries, gifts are

exchanged on Epiphany rather than on Christmas Day. Facilitate a discussion with students about the importance of this first manifestation of Jesus' identity to the world.

- **Writing Assignment:** Lent is a time of repentance and renewal. Have students each jot down five areas where they see teens in need of change. Encourage them to move beyond stereotypical, obvious answers. Remind them that failing to do something we should do can be as serious as committing a wrong action.

- **Direct Instruction:** Review the liturgies for each of the three days of the Triduum. Ask students to share their own experiences of these liturgies. Some families and parishes celebrate a Seder dinner on Holy Thursday. Review with students the distinctive parts of the Easter Vigil liturgy: kindling of the new fire, blessing of baptismal water, decorating and lighting the Easter candle. If desired, have students reenact portions of this liturgy.

- **Individual Activity:** Invite students to create liturgical calendars for the current year. Print out a set of blank calendar pages for each student. Have students perform an Internet search for the current year's dates of seasons and feast days. Have them label holy days of obligation and other important feast days and color all of the liturgical seasons according to the traditional colors associated with them. In the margins or at the top or bottom of the month in which a liturgical season begins, have students write a short explanation of the significance and themes that apply to that particular season. Collect these projects and check for accuracy. Either post them around the room or give them back to the students to use at home.

- **Direct Instruction:** Continue with a presentation on sacramentals (see pages 176–177). If possible, have a collection of objects that are sacramentals present for the students to see.

- **Class Discussion:** Also discuss blessings as sacramentals. Brainstorm with students the events, people, or places that can be blessed appropriately. Have the students create their own simple blessings.

- **Class Discussion:** To review, go through each category of sacramentals and ask the students to name one or more examples of each:
  - actions
  - objects
  - places
  - prayers

- **Class Discussion:** Call on students to display, share, and explain two of their favorite sacramentals (see page 177).

- **Prayer Experience:** If time allows, pray a decade of the Rosary, reviewing with the students how to pray it. Read the entire section on theRosary from the Catholic Handbook for Faith, pages 302–303.

Lent
A season of intensified prayer, fasting, and almsgiving in preparation of Christ's Resurrection and our Redemption at Easter. The season begins on Ash Wednesday and continues to Holy Thursday, a period of forty weekdays and six Sundays.

Triduum
The three-day-long liturgy that is the Church's most solemn celebration of the Paschal Mystery. It begins with the Mass of the Lord's Supper on Holy Thursday, continues through the Good Friday service, and ends on Holy Saturday with the conclusion of the Easter Vigil. Although it takes place over three days, the Triduum is considered one single liturgy.

sacramentals
Sacred signs (for example, objects, places, and actions) that resemble the sacraments. Through the prayers of the Church, spiritual effects are signified and obtained.

particular aspect of the Christian mystery. Rather, the readings take the Gospels in sequence: Matthew (Cycle A), Mark (Cycle B), and Luke (Cycle C). (John's Gospel is read during the Lenten and Easter season and for some of the Ordinary Time in Cycle B since Mark's Gospel is short.) Participating in the Sunday liturgy over a three-year period exposes us to much of the Gospel.

- *Lent.* The word *lent* comes from an Anglo-Saxon word for "spring." Beginning on Ash Wednesday, Lent prepares us for the solemn and joyful feast of Easter. Lent lasts six Sundays and forty weekdays, concluding on Holy Thursday with the celebration of the Lord's Last Supper.

  Historically, catechumens prepared for Baptism during Lent. Today's *Rite of Christian Initiation of Adults* continues this tradition by preparing the elect for the initiation sacraments of the Church. Lent also calls all baptized Christians to renew their own baptismal commitment through penance and prayer.

- *Triduum.* Easter is the center of the liturgical year and of the Christian faith. Easter celebrates our Redemption in Christ and his promise of everlasting life. It consists of a Triduum (three days): 1) sunset of Holy Thursday to sunset of Good Friday, 2) sunset of Good Friday to sunset of Holy Saturday, and 3) sunset of Holy Saturday to the sunset or Evening Prayer of Easter Sunday. Easter is celebrated on the first Sunday after the first full moon of the spring equinox and is thus a movable feast.

- *Easter season.* This joyful season consists of the fifty days from Easter to Pentecost Sunday. Readings focus on the themes of Resurrection and living a life of grace. The final ten days

of the Easter season celebrate the promise and gift of the Holy Spirit. Ascension Thursday occurs forty days after Easter. Pentecost Sunday (fifty days after Easter) celebrates the descent of the Holy Spirit, the event in Salvation History that inaugurated the Church.

- *Ordinary Time 2.* Ordinary Time resumes after the Easter season and proceeds to Advent and a new Church Year. Trinity Sunday is celebrated one week after Pentecost, and the feast of Corpus Christi one week later. The other Sundays in Ordinary Time look to the teaching and ministry of Jesus. Near the end of this period, the readings focus on the end of time and Christ's Second Coming. The feast of Christ the King is the last Sunday of the Church Year.

In addition, during the annual cycle of celebrating Christ's life, the Church honors Mary, Mother of God, with a special love. She is an excellent example of the faithful disciple who took Christ's words to heart. In the same way, the Church honors saints and martyrs as a way to provide us with models of Christian holiness.

Sacramentals (CCC, 1667–1679)

Sacramentals are sacred signs that resemble the sacraments. They include objects, actions, and prayers that help us become aware of Christ's presence. Sacramentals prepare us to receive the sacraments. The Church institutes and blesses these holy signs that can gain for us spiritual benefits through the Church's intercession. The spiritual value of sacramentals depends on our personal faith and devotion. This is not the case with the sacraments because our Lord works through them even when our faith is weak.

Extending the Lesson

Class Activity: In cooperation with the campus minister, have the class expand awareness of the liturgical year into the rest of the school. Choose appropriate spaces and have students decorate them in harmony with the season. This is an opportunity for students to become more aware of the colors of the liturgical year: purple for Advent and Lent, white for Christmas and Easter, and green for Ordinary Time.

Group Activity: Have the students work in small groups to develop a Lenten plan they think would actually help bring about some change in a person's life. For example, resolutions to be nicer to siblings rarely bring long-term results because they are vague and there is no accountability. Begin by asking students to recall changes they have made in the past and to recount what events or insights prompted the change. The plan should include a concrete change in behavior, a means of accountability, and perhaps an ongoing help in motivation.

Examples of sacramentals include *actions* like blessings (for example, of persons, meals, objects, and places), genuflections before the Blessed Sacrament, and the Sign of the Cross; *objects* like candles, holy water, statues and icons, blessed palms, rosary beads, relics, vestments, scapulars, church buildings, crosses, and religious medals; *places* like the Holy Land, Rome, Lourdes, places of pilgrimage, chapels, and retreat centers;

prayers like grace recited before meals; and *sacred time* like holy days, feasts of saints, and Fridays in Lent.

Besides the sacraments and the sacramentals, many other popular devotions enrich our lives as Catholics. They do not replace the liturgy; rather, they extend it. You are probably familiar with many of these; for example, the recitation of the Rosary, Stations of the Cross, and novenas.

icons
Religious images or paintings that are traditional among many Eastern Christians.

For Review

1. What are the main divisions in the Church year?
2. Define *sacramental*. Give five examples of sacramentals.

For Reflection

Using clip art from the Internet and a favorite passage from the Bible, create a religious bookmark. For tips on how to create bookmarks, type "bookmarks templates" into an Internet search engine.

Your Favorites

Share two favorite sacramentals with the class. Offer an explanation of their meaning.

Homework Assignment

1. Complete the Ongoing Assignment(s).

2. Complete the For Review questions on page 177.

3. Read the Chapter Quick View on page 178 and begin to review the content of the chapter.

For Review Answers (page 177)

1. The Church Year consists of Advent, Christmas, Ordinary Time, Lent, and Easter.

2. Sacramentals are sacred signs that resemble sacraments. Examples of sacramentals are holy water, the Sign of the Cross, shrines, feasts of saints, and prayer before meals.

For Enrichment

Individual Assignment: Have students research the history of American Easter traditions: the Easter bunny and hiding of eggs. Other students can research Lenten and Easter traditions in other countries. For example, many countries have processions honoring and reenacting the Way of the Cross. In some Eastern traditions, eggs are dyed bright red to commemorate Jesus' blood shed for us. Eastern European countries have highly symbolic decorations for Easter eggs; styles are distinctive to specific countries.

Background Information

Special Days in the Liturgical Year

Over the course of a year, the Church's liturgy celebrates the various mysteries of our redemption, recalling and commemorating events in the Life of Christ. The Church's calendar also includes feast days of various saints, celebrating their lives and contributions to the world and the faith. A list of saints' feast days can be found online at www.catholic.org/saints/calendar/.

The Second Vatican Council document *The Constitution on the Sacred Liturgy* explains:

> The Church has also included in the annual cycle days devoted to the memory of the martyrs and the other saints. Raised up to perfection by the manifold grace of God, and already in possession of eternal salvation, they sing God's perfect praise in heaven and offer prayers for us. By celebrating the passage of these saints from earth to heaven the Church proclaims the paschal mystery achieved in the saints who have suffered and been glorified with Christ; she proposes them to the faithful as examples drawing all to the Father through Christ, and through their merits she pleads for God's favors. (104)

Chapter 6 Review Lesson

Objectives

In this lesson, the students will be able to:

- recall the definitions of the highlighted terms in Chapter 6.
- review the main themes and content of Chapter 6.
- share Ongoing Assignments, including those of an enrichment nature.

Preview

The Review Lesson for Chapter 6 allows the students a chance to prepare for the Chapter Test, as well as to share their work on the long-term assignments for this chapter. Begin by providing an opportunity for the students to be quizzed on the vocabulary terms from this session.

Bell Ringers

- **Group Activity:** Assign the students into small groups of five or six. Have each group create a short quiz, crossword puzzle, word search, or the like using the vocabulary words from this chapter as well as forming questions based on the Chapter Quick View on page 178.
- **Direct Instruction:** When completed, ask for one neat copy of each group's project. Arrange for copies to be made of each group's project for every student in the class.

Teaching Approaches

- **Student Presentations:** Use the following suggestions for sharing and displaying each of the Ongoing Assignments from pages 179–180:

  #1: Collect the reports. Have the students write the symbolic meaning of water in each of the passages on the board.

  #2: Collect the reports. Call on students who worked on this assignment to summarize a few ways the Eucharist resembles the Jewish Passover.

  #3: Call on students to summarize some of the areas of liturgy they investigated. If they have brought any photos or items to class, allow time for them to share. Collect the reports.

  #4: Allow students to explain which churches they visited and what impressed them about their tours. Set up a display table for their photographs.

  #5: Allow for sharing. Note how Jesus ate with sinners. Call on a sampling of students to react to this. Collect the reports.

  #6 & #10: Display the symbols in the classroom.

CHAPTER QUICK VIEW

- St. Augustine of Hippo defined *sacrament* as "a visible sign of an invisible reality, a visible sign of invisible grace." (page 160)
- The sacraments are special signs of God's presence and friendship. (page 160)
- The Sacraments of Initiation are Baptism, Confirmation, and the Eucharist. (page 160)
- In the early Church, new converts entered a three-year period of preparation known as the *catechumenate* before receiving the three Sacraments of Initiation on Holy Saturday. (pages 160–161)
- Today, most in the Western Church are baptized as infants. Bishops, priests, and deacons are the ordinary ministers of Baptism. (page 163)
- The essential rite of Baptism includes the pouring of water (or immersion) and the words, "N., I baptize you in the name of the Father, and of the Son, and of the Holy Spirit." The main symbols of Baptism are water, oil, white garment, and candle. (pages 163–164)
- Baptism forgives Original Sin and personal sin, gives us new life in Christ, adopts us into God's family, and makes us a temple of the Holy Spirit. It confers sanctifying grace, incorporates us into the Church, and seals us with an indelible character that consecrates us in a unique way to our Lord and Savior. (page 164)
- The effects of the Sacrament of Confirmation include the full outpouring of the Holy Spirit, binding more closely to the Church and more firmly to Christ, and increasing the gifts of the Holy Spirit, especially the strength to spread and defend the Christian faith. (page 166)
- The sacramental character of Confirmation seals the recipient to the Holy Spirit and gives him or her the power to witness to the Lord. (page 166)
- The bishop is the ordinary minister of Confirmation for those who were baptized as infants. The essential rite of Confirmation includes the minister of the sacrament anointing the forehead of the one being confirmed with Chrism; the laying on of hands; and the recitation of the words, "Be sealed with the Gift of the Holy Spirit." (page 167)
- Jesus instituted the Eucharist at the Last Supper. *Eucharist* means "thanksgiving." In this sacrament we thank God for his many gifts, especially for Redemption through his Son and sanctification by the Holy Spirit. (page 170)
- We refer to the Eucharist as the Lord's Supper to recall his Passover that won our Salvation. (page 170)
- The Eucharist is also the holy and divine liturgy, the supreme worship we give God, "the source and summit of Christian life." By calling the Eucharist the Most Blessed Sacrament, we are acknowledging the presence of Christ in the consecrated bread and wine that we receive as Holy Communion. The Eucharist is also the Holy Sacrifice of the Mass. It is the sacrifice, offered by Jesus the High Priest and victim, that memorializes his Paschal Mystery. (page 171)
- When we receive Holy Communion, we receive the Body and Blood of our Lord Jesus Christ, who is truly, really, and substantially present under the form of bread and wine. (pages 171–172)
- The Eucharist gives us spiritual life; cleanses us from venial sin and helps preserve us from mortal sin; increases in us the theological virtues; gives us spiritual energy and a foretaste of Heaven; and unites us with the Blessed Mother and saints in Heaven. (pages 172–173)
- Catholics are called to celebrate the Eucharist each Sunday (or the Vigil Mass on Saturday evening) to commemorate the Paschal Mystery and to recall the Lord's Day—his Resurrection on Easter Sunday. (page 171)
- The Church Year consists of Advent, Christmas Season, Ordinary Time 1, Lenten Season, Triduum, Easter Season, and Ordinary Time 2. The center of the liturgical year and of our Christian faith is Easter. (pages 179—180)
- Sacramentals—including objects, actions, and prayers—resemble the sacraments and prepare us to receive them. Their spiritual value depends on our personal faith and devotion. (pages 176–177)

Extending the Lesson

Prayer Experience: St. Teresa of Avila wrote the following litany of thanksgiving to God. Pray it with the students to conclude the class period:

> May you be blessed forever, Lord, for not abandoning me when I abandoned you.
>
> — for offering your hand of love in my darkest, most lonely moment.
> — for putting up with such a stubborn soul.
> — for loving me more than I love myself.
> — for drawing out the goodness in all people, even including me.
> — for repaying our sin with your love.
> — for being constant and unchanging.
> — for your countless blessings on me and all your creatures.

Learning the Language of Faith

Choose the italicized term in parentheses is that best completes each sentence.

1. The holy oil used for anointing in the Sacraments of Baptism, Confirmation, and Holy Orders is known as (*charism/chrism*).
2. The prayer that asks for the sanctifying power of the Holy Spirit is the (*epiclesis/Epiphany*).
3. (*Actual/Sanctifying*) grace gives us a share in the divine life of the Blessed Trinity.
4. Those who are newly received into the Church through the Sacraments of Initiation are (*catechumens/ neophytes*).
5. The season of (*Lent/Advent*) prepares for Christ's Resurrection and our Redemption.
6. A (*right/rite*) is a manner of celebrating a particular sacrament.
7. RCIA is an abbreviation for the Rite of Christian Initiation for (*Adolescents/Adults*).
8. The Easter Vigil on Holy Saturday is part of the (*Good Friday/Triduum*) liturgy.
9. The change of the Eucharistic elements into the Body and Blood of Christ is described by the term (*transfiguration/transubstantiation*).
10. Icons are (*sacramental characters/sacramentals*).

Ongoing Assignments

As you cover the material in this chapter, choose and complete at least three of these assignments.

1. Read the following passages and note what water symbolizes in the particular context of the passage.

   - Exodus 17:2–7
   - Psalm 23:1–4
   - Ezekiel 47:1–12
   - Romans 6:1–5
   - Revelation 22:1–2

2. Prepare a report on the Jewish Passover meal. Note several ways the Eucharistic liturgy resembles it.
3. Research and report on a particular aspect of the liturgy (e.g., history, vestments, vessels). Search the Internet using the words "vestments" and "sacred vessels."
4. Make visits to several other Catholic churches. Take pictures of the altar, crucifix, and other appropriate signs and symbols inside the church. Prepare a presentation for your classmates.
5. Read the following passages from the Gospels. Summarize what took place when Jesus celebrated meals with others.

   - Matthew 9:9–13
   - John 21:9–17
   - Luke 7:36–50
   - Luke 19:1–10

6. Design an appropriate symbol for one of the sacraments.
7. Write a brief essay recounting a time that you felt the special presence of the Holy Spirit in your life, for example, the joy you experienced after a special achievement or the courage to do the right thing in a trying situation.
8. Research how initiation into the community takes place in another religion. Do further research on the Sacraments of Initiation and compare the two processes.
9. Interview a recent convert to the Catholic faith. Discover answers to the following questions:
   - What do you find attractive about Catholicism?
   - What do the Church and her sacraments mean to you?
10. Construct a banner to be used at a Baptism of an infant. Include several baptismal symbols.

Homework Assignment

1. Study for the Chapter 6 Test.

2. Complete any assignments from Chapter 6, including For Enrichment assignments that have not been finished.

3. Read the Prayer Reflection on page 180. Make a visit to the Blessed Sacrament and use the prayer approach suggested.

#7: Call on students to summarize their essays and witness to the Holy Spirit in their lives.

#8: Collect the reports. Have the students share the initiation rituals with the class, using pictures if possible. Discuss the similarities between these rituals and the Sacraments of Initiation.

#9: Call on students to share what they learned about the recent converts they interviewed.

#11: Display the pictures of human hands along with the lists they created in the classroom.

#12: Call on students to share their experiences at a parish that is not their own.

- **Individual Assignment:** Pass out copies of the review activities the small groups prepared as part of the Bell Ringer exercise. Assign each person to work on the same activity. Allow time, and then call on the group who prepared the activity to provide the correct answers. Continue with other activities in the same way.

- **Individual Assignment:** Have students work on the Learning the Language of Faith questions on page 179. Check their answers (answers are on page 181 of this text) and allow them to keep the assignment to study for the test.

Learning the Language of Faith
Answers (page 179)

1. chrism

2. epiclesis

3. sanctifying

4. neophytes

5. Lent

6. rite

7. adults

8. Triduum

9. transubstantiation

10. sacramentals

Chapter 6 Test Lesson

Objectives

In this lesson, the students will:
- take a test on the material in Chapter 6.
- share responses to the question, "Where is Christ in my life?"
- preview the material in Chapter 7.

Preview

A majority of the class period should be reserved for the Chapter 6 Test. As time remains, point to the Prayer Reflection and allow the students time to concretely answer the questions that follow.

Teaching Approaches

- **Chapter Test:** Pass out the Chapter 6 Test. Allow a majority of the class period for the students to work on the test.
- **Direct Instruction:** Collect any unfinished assignments from Chapter 6, including For Enrichment assignments the students may have worked on.
- **Prayer Experience:** Pray together the prayer attributed to Cardinal John Henry Newman. Assign two sides of the room to alternate reading line by line.
- **Class Discussion:** Have the students write several examples of how they witness Christ's presence in their lives. Allow time for sharing.

11. Many sacraments include gestures using the hands. With this in mind, do one of the following:
    - List fifteen positive and life-enriching activities done with human hands.
    - Create a collage of human hands doing life-giving tasks.

12. Attend Mass in a parish that is not your own. Pretend that you are an outsider observing the Eucharistic celebration for the first time. Report on the following topics:
    - How were the people involved? Describe their involvement or lack of involvement.
    - List and discuss five symbols that impressed you.
    - How friendly and welcoming were the people? Did you try to be friendly?

Prayer Reflection

A good spiritual practice is to visit our Lord in the Blessed Sacrament either in your school chapel or your parish church. Here are a few suggestions on how to approach our Lord:

1. St. Teresa of Avila suggested using a variety of images when praying to Jesus. For example, you can "speak to him as with a father, or a brother, or a lord, or as with a spouse; sometimes in one way, at other times in another" (*The Way of Perfection*, 28:3). Tell the Lord how your day is going.
2. Speak to Jesus as you would to your best friend. Tell him about what is worrying you. Settle down and let his healing presence calm your heart.
3. Simply sit in the presence of the Lord. There is no need to say anything because your friend knows you are there.
4. Recite the following communion prayer of the Venerable Cardinal John Henry Newman. It was recited daily after receiving Holy Communion by Blessed Mother Teresa of Calcutta and her Sisters of charity.

> Dear Jesus,
> help me to spread your fragrance wherever I go.
> Flood my soul with your spirit and life.
> Penetrate and possess my whole being so utterly
> that my life may only be a radiance of yours.
> Shine through me and be so in me that every soul I come in contact with
> may feel your presence in my soul.
>
> Let them look up and see no longer me, but only Jesus!
> Stay with me and then I will begin to shine as you shine,
> so to shine as to be a light to others.
>
> The light, O Jesus, will be all from you; none of it will be mine.
> It will be you, shining on others through me.
> Let me thus praise you in the way which you love best,
> by shining on those around me.
> Let me preach you without preaching, not by words but by example,
> by the catching force, the sympathetic influence of what I do,
> the evident fullness of the love my heart bears for you. Amen.[14]

- *Reflection:* How can the light of Christ shine through you?
- *Resolution:* This week share the Gospel in both words and action.

Printed Materials continued from page 161

The Essential Catholic Handbook on the Sacraments. A Redemptorist Pastoral Handbook. Liguori, MO: Liguori, 2001.

Guzie, Tad. *The Book of Sacramental Basics.* New York: Paulist Press, 1981.

> Excellent work on the meaning of sign and symbol. A good sourcebook for teachers.

Kelly, Liam. *Sacraments Revisited: What Do They Mean Today?* Mahwah, NJ: Paulist Press, 1998.

Martos, Joseph. *Doors to the Sacred: An Historical Introduction to Sacraments in the Catholic Church.* Tarrytown, NY: Triumph Books, 2001.

> If there is one book you should read on the historical background on the sacraments, this is it. It is simply outstanding—well researched, interesting, and balanced. Dr. Martos's bibliographies at the end of each chapter are worth the price of the book. This text also lists hundreds of additional works on the sacraments and related topics.

Mick, Lawrence E. *Understanding the Sacraments Today.* Collegeville, MN: Liturgical Press, 1987.

> Short, easy reading on each of the sacraments.

O'Neill, Colman E. *Meeting Christ in the Sacraments.* Alba House, 2002.

Osborne, Kenan. *Sacramental Theology: A General Introduction.* Mahwah, NJ: Paulist Press, 1994.

———. *Sacramental Guidelines: A Companion to the New Catechism for Religious Educators.* Mahwah, NJ: Paulist Press, 1995.

———. *The Christian Sacraments of Initiation.* Mahwah, NJ: Paulist Press, 1998.

> Excellent and clear author who writes on the historical, scriptural, and doctrinal sources for Baptism, Confirmation, and Eucharist.

Richstatter, Thomas, O.F.M. *The Sacraments: How Catholics Pray.* Cincinnati, OH: St. Anthony Messenger Press, 1995.

Roberts, William. *Encounters with Christ.* Mahwah, NJ: Paulist Press, 1985.

> Excellent, clear, short chapters that develop the sacramental theology out of the common human experience of encounter.

Stasiak, Kurt. *Sacramental Theology: Means of Grace, Ways of Life.* Catholic Basics. Chicago: Loyola, 2001.

Homework Assignment

1. Read the opening quotation on page 183 as well as the text section "The Power of Forgiveness in a Suffering World" (pages 184–187).

2. Preview the Ongoing Assignments on page 206.

Chapter 6 Test Answers

All questions are worth 4 points each.

Part 1: Multiple Choice

1. B
2. D
3. C
4. A
5. D
6. B
7. D
8. A
9. A
10. B
11. C
12. C

Part 2: True or False

13. T
14. F
15. F
16. F
17. F
18. T

Part 3: Short Fill-ins

19. thanksgiving
20. sanctifying grace
21. laying on of hands
22. transubstantiation
23. *examples:* candles, holy water, statues and icons, blessed palms, rosary beads, relics, vestments, scapulars, church buildings, crosses, religious medals

Part 4: Short Essay

24–25. Possible answers would include to receive our Lord himself; to receive spiritual life and nourishment; cleansing of sin; to receive the grace of a greater commitment to the poor; spiritual energy to live our life; union with the Blessed Mother, saints, and other Christians, etc. Accept any plausible personal reflection.

7 The Sacraments of Healing and Ministry

The Sacraments of Healing and Ministry

Overview of the Chapter

This chapter introduces the Sacraments of Healing—Penance and Anointing of Sick—and the Sacraments at the Service of Communion—Holy Orders and Matrimony. Concerning the Sacraments of Healing, the *Catechism of the Catholic Church* teaches:

> The Lord Jesus Christ, physician of our souls and bodies, who forgave the sins of the paralytic and restored him to bodily health, has willed that his Church continue, in the power of the Holy Spirit, his work of healing and salvation, even among her own members. This is the purpose of the two sacraments of healing. . . . (1421)

The discussion begins with an explanation of the various names for the Sacrament of Penance, namely, the Sacrament of Conversion, Confession, Forgiveness, and Reconciliation. The Rite of Penance is outlined and the acts of the penitent—contrition, confession, and satisfaction—as well as God's action, are explained. In the apologetics box, students are given some help to explain to others why Catholics confess to a priest.

After a brief history of the Sacrament of the Anointing of the Sick, students are asked to reflect on Jesus' healing ministry in the Gospels and their own experience of carrying crosses. An explanation of the rite follows, as well as a listing of the effects of this sacrament.

The *Catechism of the Catholic Church* reminds us that the sacraments of Holy Orders and Matrimony

> . . . are directed towards the salvation of others; if they contribute as well to personal salvation, it is through service to others that they do so. They confer a particular mission in the Church and serve to build up the People of God. (1534)

In the discussion of Holy Orders, the chapter makes a clear distinction between the common priesthood conferred on all baptized Catholics and the special role of the ordained ministry. The orders of the bishop, priest, and deacon are distinguished, and the special ministries and graces of each office listed. After a brief outline of the Rite of Ordination of a priest, the issue of clerical celibacy is covered.

The final section of the chapter treats the Sacrament of Matrimony. The text explains how God is the author of marriage who wrote marital love into our very nature. Jesus viewed marriage as sacred and taught the necessity of lifelong fidelity.

Resources

 ### Audiovisual Materials

The Church Celebrates the Reconciling God
A Catholic Update video from the "Reconciliation Series," this production focuses on the history, theology, and practice of the Sacrament of Reconciliation (27-minute video, St. Anthony Messenger Press).

Empty Cup
A docudrama that tells the story of a Franciscan who labors with the Indians in Bolivia (17-minute video, St. Anthony Messenger Press).

A Father and Two Sons
Produced by the American Bible Society, this video retells the story of the Prodigal Son (10-minute video, Harcourt).

Les Miserables
A motion picture rendition of Victor Hugo's popular novel and the musical (134-minute video, Sony Pictures).

Orthodox and Roman Catholic Christianity
Examines the interwoven history of these two branches of Christianity, explaining the doctrinal differences, and addresses the cultural influences on both (50-minute video, Insight Media).

Pardon and Peace
A modern retelling of the parable of the Prodigal Son (15-minute video, St. Anthony Messenger Press).

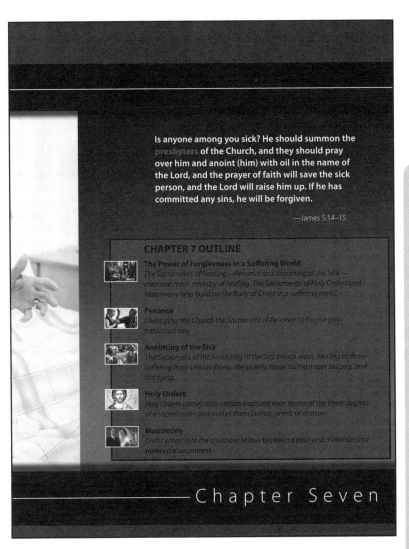

Is anyone among you sick? He should summon the presbyters of the Church, and they should pray over him and anoint (him) with oil in the name of the Lord, and the prayer of faith will save the sick person, and the Lord will raise him up. If he has committed any sins, he will be forgiven.

—James 5:14–15

CHAPTER 7 OUTLINE

The Power of Forgiveness in a Suffering World
The Sacraments of Healing—Penance and Anointing of the Sick—continue Jesus' ministry of healing. The Sacraments of Holy Orders and Matrimony help build up the Body of Christ in a suffering world.

Penance
Christ gave the Church the Sacrament of Penance to forgive post-baptismal sins.

Anointing of the Sick
The Sacrament of the Anointing of the Sick brings Jesus' healing to those suffering from serious illness, the elderly, those facing major surgery, and the dying.

Holy Orders
Holy Orders consecrates certain baptized men to one of the three degrees of a sacred order and makes them bishop, priest, or deacon.

Matrimony
Christ enters into the covenant of love between a man and a woman and makes it a sacrament.

Chapter Seven

 Audiovisual Materials continued

Reconciliation: Closing the Gap

This film helps students see how everyday conflicts can help them live in the loving example of Jesus. Gives a brief overview of the sacrament. Study guide (15-minute video, Harcourt).

Sacrament of Anointing: The Church's Prayer for the Sick

A Catholic Update Video presented by Fr. Tom Richstatter, O.F.M. Presents an overview of the Sacrament of Anointing of the Sick. Emphasizes its communal celebration and healing of the whole person—body, mind, and spirit (17-minute video, St. Anthony Messenger Press).

Resources

Internet Links see www.avemariapress.com

The effects of this sacrament of love are explained. The chapter discusses the difference between divorce, which cannot be permitted, and annulment, which is a declaration that what appeared to be a valid Christian marriage was not. It encourages students to learn how to be friends, since cultivating friendships is a great skill for learning how to prepare for the lifelong commitment that is Christian marriage.

Chapter Outline

- The Power of Forgiveness in a Suffering World
- Penance
- Anointing of the Sick
- Holy Orders
- Matrimony

Advance Preparations

Assign the Ongoing Assignments early in the chapter to allow the students enough time to complete their work.

The Power of Forgiveness in a Suffering World (ST pages 184–187)

- Copies of Chapter 7, Handout 1 "Student Panel Discussion Questions" (starting on page 285 and also online at www.avemariapress.com) for the Preview on page 186.
- A clip of the movie *Les Miserables* for the Video Presentation on page 187.

Penance (ST pages 187–190)

- Copies of Chapter 7, Handout 2 "Sacrament of Reconciliation Outline" (starting on page 285 and also online at www.avemariapress.com) for the Individual Assignment on page 190.
- Copies of Chapter 7, Handout 3 "Penance Service" (starting on page 285 and also online at www.avemariapress.com) for the Prayer Experience on page 190.
- Scrap paper, markers, and a small basket; a small table set with a candle, crucifix, and Bible; for the Prayer Experience on pages 189–190.

Anointing of the Sick (ST pages 191–193)

- Oil, a towel, and a bible for your demonstration of the Anointing of the Sick in Direct Instruction on pages 194–195.

Sacrament of Holy Orders (ST pages 194–198)

- Catholic magazines or periodicals for the Group Activity on page 197.
- Arrange for a priest and a deacon to speak to the class for the Guest Speakers activity on pages 197–198.
- A video showing an ordination in your diocese for the Video Presentation on page 198. Ordination Masses can be quite long (often two to three hours), so you will need to preview the video in order to identify

those sections you most want your students to see. If you are unable to find a video of a local ordination, a video called *Crossing the Threshold Celebration: June 1997 Ordination Liturgy* is available through the Resource Center of the Diocese of Helena at (406) 442-5820.

The Sacrament of Matrimony (ST pages 198–203)
- Arrange for a married couple from a local parish to speak to the class for the Guest Speaker activity on page 202.
- Copies of Chapter 7, Handout 4 "Who Can Marry?" (starting on page 285 and also online at www.avemariapress.com) for the Class Discussion on page 203.

Chapter 7 Review Lesson
- Blank index cards for the Class Activity on page 206.
- Copies of Chapter 7, Handout 5 "Word Search Puzzler" (starting on page 285 and also online at www.avemariapress.com) for the Individual Assignment on page 206.

Chapter 7 Test Lesson
- Copies of the Chapter 7 Test (starting on page 285 and also online at www.avemariapress.com).

The Power of Forgiveness in a Suffering World (pages 184–187)
Objectives

In this lesson, the students will:
- share their own experiences of the four sacraments covered in this chapter through a rotating panel discussion.
- defend against accusations that God is unjust for allowing suffering in the world.

Preview

One goal of this lesson is to take note of the students' current understanding of the sacraments presented in this chapter. Chapter 7, Handout 1 "Student Panel Discussion Questions" (starting on page 285 and also online at www.avemariapress.com), addressing the sacraments covered in this chapter, will help you to prepare for the rest of the lessons in this chapter. In addition, students will grapple with the question of why a good God allows suffering in the world.

The Power of Forgiveness in a Suffering World

Victor Hugo's famous novel *Les Misérables*, made into a musical and often depicted on the screen, tells the story of Jean Valjean, who was imprisoned for five years for stealing a loaf of bread to feed his starving family during a time of famine. Fourteen additional years were added to his term for his attempts to escape. Valjean's prison experience transformed him from an innocent youth to a hardened, tough, and bitter man.

After nineteen years, Jean was eventually released but forced to carry a yellow passport that identified him as a convict. During his flight he sought refuge at the home of a kind bishop, who fed him and gave him a warm bed to sleep in. After the bishop had retired for the night, Jean snuck into the bishop's pantry and stole some valuable silverware. As he was caught by the police and brought back to the bishop, Jean told the police that the bishop had given him the silverware as a gift.

The police were ready to throw Jean into prison for life but first wanted to disprove his story. The good bishop greeted Jean warmly. He expressed great delight that Jean had returned and told him that he had forgotten the candlesticks, worth 200 francs, as well. Jean was awestruck because the bishop told the police that he had given the silver to Jean as a gift. The police were satisfied and left Jean at the bishop's house.

The bishop looked into Jean's eyes and asked him to promise to use the money to become an honest man. Jean left the bishop's house pondering his words and the new life he was given.

The bishop's kindness in Hugo's famous novel exemplifies well the power of Christ's own forgiveness, a power that can melt hearts and help us live a Christian life. Jean Valjean allowed the power of forgiveness to transform him into a loving, kind man who ministered to other people. Christ calls all of his disciples to extend his love and to minister to others as well. He gave us the sacraments to help us live out the vocation he gave us:

1. Christ continues to show his compassion to us through the Sacrament

presbyters
Priests or members of the order of the priesthood who are coworkers with the bishop and servant to God's people, especially in celebrating the Eucharist.

bishop
A successor to the Apostles who governs the local Church in a given diocese and governs the worldwide Church in union with the Pope and the College of Bishops. A bishop receives the fullness of the Sacrament of Holy Orders.

Resources

Printed Materials

Champlin, Joseph. *Why Go to Confession: Questions and Answers about Sacramental Reconciliation*. Cincinnati, OH: St. Anthony Messenger Press, 1996.
   Helpful reading for students and teachers alike.

Doran, Kevin. *More Joy in Heaven! Confession, The Sacrament of Reconciliation*. Collegeville, MN: The Liturgical Press, 1988.
   A popular presentation. Chapter 4 gives a helpful examination of conscience that might suggest possibilities for your students. Written by an author who is also a sensitive confessor.

Ghezzi, Bert. *Sacred Passages: Bringing the Sacraments to Life*. Garden City, NY: Doubleday, 2003.
   Ghezzi offers a pedestrian yet thorough look at the sacraments.

Lawler, Michael G. *Symbol and Sacrament: A Contemporary Sacramental Theology*. New York: Paulist Press, 1987.
   A multidisciplinary study of the sacraments that draws on Rahner and Schillebeeckx. Challenging but outstanding.

Noll, Ray Robert. *Sacraments: A New Understanding for a New Generation*. Mystic, CT: Twenty-Third Publications, 2000.
   Comes with a CD-ROM with additional readings.

of Penance and the Sacrament of the Anointing of the Sick. He forgives our sins in the sacrament of conversion and helps suffering people with his graces in the sacrament of healing.

2. The Sacrament of Holy Orders calls men to minister to us in Jesus' place.

3. The Sacrament of Matrimony helps married couples be Christ to each other and their families.

Our common ministry often involves reaching out to others in times of sin and suffering. Anyone who looks at the cruelty and injustice in our world might be led to ask the following question: how can a good and loving God permit so much suffering and evil in the world? In answering this question, consider the following points:

1. *God is supremely good and loving, even in the midst of suffering.* Christ's own suffering and Death prove beyond any doubt God's immense love for human beings. Christ has redeemed us from our sins and won for us a share in God's own life for eternity. He has given us the Gift of the Holy Spirit and invites each of us into friendship with him. He continues to be present to us in the Catholic Church, the Body of Christ, and comes to us in the sacred liturgy, especially the Seven Sacraments. The Sacraments of Healing—Penance and Anointing of the Sick—continue Jesus' work of healing. These sacraments do not provide answers to why people must hurt, why people must suffer. Instead, they seek simply to heal the hurt and suffering that people are feeling.

2. *Suffering and evil are an unfortunate part of the human story.* God does not cause or send suffering. He is all-good and only brings about goodness. The *Catechism of the Catholic*

Church summarizes the dilemma this way: "Faith gives us the certainty that God would not permit an evil if he did not cause a good to come from that very evil, by ways that we shall fully know only in eternal life" (*CCC*, 324).

3. *God's created world is on a journey to perfection.* God could have created a finished and perfect world with no physical evil. But in God's goodness and wisdom, he decided to create a world that is in a process of becoming. It is not yet perfect. Nature's constructive and destructive forces exist side by side. The more perfect exists alongside the less perfect. "With physical good there also exists *physical evil* as long as creation has not reached perfection" (*CCC*, 310).

Just as a champion swimmer must put in countless tedious hours of hard practice to achieve renown, so the world undergoes pain to achieve the perfection God has in store. We cannot now appreciate the pain involved in this

Sacrament of the Anointing of the Sick
A Sacrament of Healing, administered by a priest to a baptized person, in which the Lord extends his loving, healing touch through the Church to those who are seriously ill or dying.

Sacrament of Holy Orders
The Sacrament of apostolic ministry at the Service of Communion whereby Christ, through the Church, ordains men through the laying on of hands. It includes three degrees: episcopate, presbyterate, and diaconate. Those who exercise these orders are bishops, priests, and deacons.

Sacrament of Matrimony
A Sacrament at the Service of Communion in which Christ binds a man and woman into a permanent covenant of love and life at the time of their freely given consent and bestows his graces on them to help them live as a community and as a loving family if he blesses them with children.

 Bell Ringers

- **Individual Assignment:** Read the opening quotation on page 183 from James 5:14–15. Have the students note three sacramental actions involved in the reading (i.e., the summoning of an ordained minister, the anointing of the sick, and the forgiveness of sins). Have the students note other examples in Scripture where presbyters were called to anoint the sick (see 1 Tm 5:17, Ti 1:5).

- **Video Presentation:** Show the beginning of the film version of *Les Miserables*. Have the students place themselves in the shoes of Jean Valjean. Have them discuss or describe in their journals what the experience of Jean Valjean must have been like.

Printed Materials continued

Osborne, Kenan, O.F.M. *A History of Ordained Ministry in the Roman Catholic Church*. New York: Paulist Press, 1988.

Osborne's series of books on the sacraments is outstanding, including this one. Highly recommended.

———. *Reconciliation & Justification: The Sacrament and Its Theology*. Mahwah, NJ: Paulist Press, 1990.

Summarizes the theme of justification from Paul's theology and traces the theological, historical, and liturgical developments from the beginning of Christianity to today.

Stravinskas, Peter M. J. *Understanding the Sacraments: A Guide for Prayer and Study*. San Francisco: Ignatius, 1997.

West, Christopher. *Good News about Sex and Marriage: Answers to Your Honest Questions about Catholic Teaching*. Ann Arbor, MI: Charis Books, 2000.

———. *The Theology of the Body for Beginners*. West Chester, PA: Ascension Press, 2004, 2009.

Provides a succinct and easy-to-read summary of John Paul II's catecheses on the Theology of the Body. It is a great theological background to the Church's teaching on Matrimony and Holy Orders.

Teaching Approaches

- **Class Discussion:** Summarize the answer to the question: "How can a good and loving God permit so much suffering and evil in the world?" Then, have students think of examples from their own lives, the news, or TV and movies that illustrate each point. Discuss their examples as a class. Have them share how they would respond to someone who made accusations that God was unjust for allowing suffering in the world. Have them decide which examples from their lives prove that God is not unjust.

- **Class Discussion:** Point out the Sacraments of Healing and Ministry that will be discussed in this chapter: Penance, the Anointing of the Sick, Matrimony, and Holy Orders. Hold a panel discussion with your students to look into the ways in which they have experienced or been touched by these sacraments, particularly as they relate to dealing with suffering or experiencing the witness of those who are married or ordained.

  - ◆ Choose four to five students to form the first panel. Ask for volunteers who have had a memorable experience of the Sacrament of Penance. Use the questions on the "Student Panel Discussion Questions" handout to get your panel discussion started. Allow students in the "audience" to ask respectful follow-up questions or to initiate new lines of questioning. After a few minutes, have each panel member choose someone who has been present for an Anointing of the Sick, either as a recipient or a witness, to replace himself or herself on the panel. Continue with more questions from the list on the resource page. Change panels and move on to questions about marriage and Holy Orders as on the handout. For these you need students who have personal relationships with people living out these sacraments; many of your students will have parents who are living out their marriage commitment, but it may be harder to find students who know a priest on a personal level.

  - ◆ As the panel members are answering questions, have one student in the class keep a list of any questions that the panel members struggle with or cannot answer. Refer to these questions as you prepare for later lessons so that you can help your students find ways to answer them.

- **Journal Assignment:** Read and explain the "Talents to Serve" assignments on page 186. First, read each New Testament passage as a class. Then, have students work on the questions individually by writing their answers in their journals.

The Student Page

The reproduced student page (page 186) contains:

growth process because innocent people suffer at the hands of nature. But we believe that in God's wisdom this growth is good both for individuals and humanity as a whole as we journey to perfection.

4. *The misuse of freedom is the cause of much moral evil.* Out of divine goodness, God created humans and angels as *intelligent* and *free* creatures, not unthinking puppets. The gifts of intellect and free will are what make us beings of tremendous dignity and not mindless robots. However, these two gifts require responsibility. We must freely choose to love God and others on our journey toward eternity. When we refuse to love, we sin. And sin brings about incredible evil and suffering.

Divine Revelation tells us that when some angels chose to sin, these fallen angels or devils unleashed evil in the world in opposition to God. Satan is known as the father of lies, a deceiver of the whole world. He and the other devils try to get humans to revolt against God through disobedience, that is, to sin. Satan acts in the world out of hatred for God; and "although his action may cause grave injuries—of a spiritual nature and, indirectly, even of a physical nature" (*CCC*, 395), his power is limited because he

and the other devils are only creatures. He cannot do anything to prevent the building up of God's reign. Unlike Jesus, who resisted the lies of Satan in the desert, humans from the time of Adam and Eve have given in to his deceptions, which have led to sin. And human sin—both Original Sin and actual sin—has resulted in terrible moral evils like war, rape, abortion, drug abuse, prejudice, and greed. God does not *cause* this moral evil. Humans, by misusing their freedom, are the cause. God *permits* moral evil, however, because God loves and respects the free creatures he has made. And in a way known only to God, he knows how to derive good out of all evil. (See the discussion on suffering and evil in the Explaining Your Faith section on pages 32–33.) As St. Paul wrote, "We know that all things work for good for those who love God" (Rom 8:28).

5. *Christian faith announces the Good News of Jesus Christ, who conquered the forces of evil.* Certainly the worst moral evil in the world was for humans to put to death the innocent God-man. Like any normal person, Jesus abhorred suffering and even asked his Father to remove it. But Jesus freely embraced the sufferings that unjustly came his way by submitting to his Father: "May your will be done."

Talents to Serve

Everyone has a vocation, a calling to bring Christ into the world. Examine your talents and your call to serve others by doing the following:

1. Read the following New Testament passages.
   - 1 Corinthians 12:4–11
   - Matthew 25:31–40
   - John 13:1–20

2. Reflect on your gifts. Choose one of your talents. How you can use it in the coming week to help someone at home, school, parish, or work? Write your answers to the following questions:
   - What is my talent?
   - How can I use it for others?
   - Who will benefit from my generosity?
   - What is my specific plan of action?
   - How can I check the results of my service?

Homework Assignment

1. Write answers to the For Reflection questions on page 187.

2. Read the text section "Penance" (pages 187–190).

3. Begin work on one of the Ongoing Assignments on page 206.

Extending the Lesson

Group Activity: Sometimes the best way to be sure that your students understand something is to ask them to teach someone else. Help your students to develop a lesson to use with second-grade students who are preparing to receive the Sacrament of Penance for the first time. Divide the class into groups and assign each group one of the terms used to describe the sacrament: *conversion, confession, forgiveness, reconciliation,* and *penance.* Each group should come up with an activity or game based on their term, that will help seven- and eight-year-olds understand something important about the sacrament. Remind your students that students in that age range do better with hands-on projects and do not like to sit still for long periods.

If possible, arrange for your students to try out their lessons and activities with second graders at a nearby parish or parochial school. If you are not sure your students are ready to lead a lesson themselves, perhaps you could arrange for them to assist in a local parish's religious education classes as the teacher's aide. This could be an excellent community service opportunity for your class.

God heard Jesus' prayer, not by saving Jesus *from* death, but by saving him *out* of death. Jesus' suffering, Death, and Resurrection have conquered the worst evil: death and separation from God. If we love as Jesus teaches us to do and join our sufferings to his, we will share forever in the Lord's superabundant, joy-filled Life. This is "Good News," actually great news, that can help us cope with the mystery of evil and suffering.

Jesus left us the Sacraments of Healing and Service to help us live a Christian life. For example, undoing much of the suffering in the world and making the world a better place to live are part of the effects of the Sacraments of Holy Orders and Matrimony. These two sacraments help build up Christian life. Both of them involve love and service, two essential features of our living together in the same Body of Christ.

This chapter presents the Sacraments of Healing and the Sacraments at the Service of Communion in more detail.

For Reflection

- How have you come to grips with the perennial question, "Why does God permit suffering?"
- Write of a time when some good came out of an "evil" that befell you.
- What are some questions you have about the Sacraments of Penance, Anointing of the Sick, Holy Orders, and Matrimony as you begin studying this chapter?

Penance *(CCC, 1422–1438; 1440–1446; 1461–1470; 1486–1495)*

Even though we receive new life in the Sacraments of Initiation, we still have a weakened human nature. We are still tempted to commit sin, a condition known as concupiscence. The Christian life requires lifelong conversion. That is why Christ has given the Church a sacrament of conversion called the **Sacrament of Penance**, a great help on our spiritual journey. For Catholics, individual and integral confession of our sins in this sacrament, followed by **absolution**, is the ordinary way of reconciliation with God and the Church. Jesus chose this sign of love to show, in a personal way, his merciful forgiveness to individual sinners.

The Sacrament of Penance is also called *conversion, confession, forgiveness,* and *reconciliation.* Each of these names reveals something important about this sacrament of healing.

As the sacrament of *conversion,* Penance takes seriously Jesus' call to repent, the first step in returning to our loving Father. A gift from the Holy Spirit, conversion or repentance helps us return to our Lord after we sin and to have the courage to begin anew. Conversion involves changing our lives by rooting out sin, by hating the evil we have committed, by firmly intending to sin no more, and by trusting in God's infinite mercy and grace.

The term *confession* highlights a key element of the sacrament—telling

Sacrament of Penance
A Sacrament of Healing, also known as reconciliation or confession, through which Christ extends his forgiveness to sinners, bringing about reconciliation with God and the Church. Its essential elements consist of the acts of the penitent (contrition, confession of sins, and satisfaction) and the prayer of absolution of the priest.

absolution
The prayer by which a priest, by the power given to the Church by Christ Jesus, pardons a repentant sinner in the Sacrament of Penance.

Background Information

The Sacrament of Penance goes by many different names, including penance, reconciliation, and confession. It has also taken many different forms as our understanding of it has deepened. It has always been clear that the Church retained Christ's power to forgive sin. Early on, it was thought that this could happen only once in a person's life. Baptism forgave all sins, but for serious sins committed after baptism, confession had to be made to the bishop, and penances were both severe and public. For periods sometimes lasting more than a year, penitents were denied admission to Mass or any gathering of Christians. They had to give evidence publicly of their repentance, and only after their lengthy penance was served would absolution be granted. For this reason, many converts to Christianity chose to wait until they neared death to be baptized.

Penance first began to look more like the sacrament we celebrate in Ireland in the seventh through eleventh centuries. Celtic missionary priests and monks would travel from village to village, talking with people privately and assigning penances. The next time the priest came through, the people would let him know they had completed their penance and they would be absolved. Later, books were developed to help priests determine what penances were appropriate for which sins.

Penance *(pages 187–190)*

Objectives

In this lesson, the students will:

- outline the meaning behind the various names for the Sacrament of Penance.
- describe the development of the present form of the Sacrament of Penance over time.
- defend the practice of confessing one's sins to a priest.
- receive the sacrament with friends in a communal celebration of the Sacrament of Penance followed by individual confession and absolution.

Preview

Much of the material in this section was first introduced in Chapter 5. If there was no time then to cover the supplemental information or to assign the longer research project, consider doing so now. Certainly, if you were not able to arrange an opportunity for your students to participate in a communal Rite of the Sacrament of Penance, you should do so now. See the information on page 299 to help the students to prepare.

Bell Ringers

- **Class Discussion:** Have a general sharing time based on the For Reflection questions on page 187. For the discussion on suffering, make sure to point out that though the answer is steeped in mystery, we do know that God in no way, directly or indirectly, is the cause of any moral evil. God permits evil, suffering, and death because he knows how to derive good from them. For question 3, create an ongoing list of questions to address during the course of this series of lessons on these sacraments.
- **Journal Assignment:** Have the students write about the last time they said they were sorry. The following are some questions they might consider:
  - To whom did you apologize and for what?
  - Why did you apologize? How did you know you needed to?
  - Were you truly sorry?
  - How did you feel before you apologized? After?
  - Were you forgiven?
  - Did you offer or need to do anything to "make up for" what you needed to apologize for?
  - What do you think would have happened if you had not apologized?

Teaching Approaches

- **Individual Assignment:** This section lends itself well to a lesson in taking notes in outline form. If your students are competent and experienced at using the outline form, simply assign them the task of outlining the entire section on the Sacrament of

Pennance (pages 187–188). Pass out Chapter 7, Handout 2 "Sacrament of Penance Outline" (starting on page 285 and also online at www.avemariapress.com). Point out that the outline is begun for them but is incomplete. (A sample completed outline is included on page 191 of this text.) Model how to outline the first section "A. *Conversion*," then have the students complete the rest on their own. Circulate around the room to check how well each student is following correct outlining procedures.

- **Group Activity:** Have students get into six (or three) groups. Assign each group one of the Scripture passages in the Knowing Christ through Scripture feature "Jesus and Forgiveness" (two groups for each passage). Have the students work together to create a presentation of the passage to the class. When students present each passage, have the rest of the students take note of how the passage involves healing, forgiveness, conversion, and reconciliation.

- **Individual Assignment:** Continue with the text subsection "Rite of Penance" (pages 188–189). Have the students outline this material using the same format as described on page 190. Review the students' outlines of this section. If you are going to ask students to do the longer research project described in the For Enrichment box on page 190, take time now to introduce it and clarify your requirements and expectations.

- **Prayer Experience:** Prepare the students to receive the Sacrament of Penance (whether or not the sacrament will available at school) by reviewing the form for individual confession found in the Catholic Handbook for Faith, page 299. Make available to them a variety of examinations of conscience that will help them to recognize areas of sinfulness in their lives that they want to confess and discuss with the priest during their reception of the sacrament. Many such examinations can be found online.

our sins to the priest. In this sacrament we also "confess," that is, praise God for the great mercy God extends to us.

Calling this sacrament the sacrament of *forgiveness* reminds us that God imparts pardon and peace through the priest's words of absolution. Sin is a great evil because it offends God's honor and love, causes a break in our union with God, disfigures the sinner who is made in God's image, and ruptures our relationship with other members of Christ's body, the Church. Only God can forgive sin. He gave us his Son whose major mission among us was to forgive sin and to associate with sinners to show how much God loves his wayward children.

Christ also gave the power to absolve, that is, to forgive sin, to the Apostles and their successors, a ministry carried on today by our bishops and priests (Mt 16:19). Through the formula of absolution, the bishop or priest proclaims God's forgiveness of the sinner. When the priest holds his hands over the penitent's head and recites the words, "I absolve you from your sins in the name of the Father, and of the Son, and of the Holy Spirit," Christ himself is giving us the sign we need to know that God forgives us.

The sacrament is called the sacrament of *reconciliation* because God's loving forgiveness:

- reconciles (unites) us with God and the Church, whom we have alienated by our sins;
- brings peace of conscience and spiritual comfort;

contrition
Heartfelt sorrow and aversion for sins committed, along with the intention of sinning no more. Contrition is the most important act of penitents, necessary for receiving the Sacrament of Penance.

- strengthens us to live the Christian life;
- takes away some of the temporal punishment due to sin;
- remits fully the eternal punishment that results from mortal sin;
- prepares us for our meeting with our Divine Judge when we die by teaching us how to repent, do penance, and have faith in a loving and merciful God.

Finally, the official name, the Sacrament of *Penance,* stresses that when we turn from sin, we must do penance and make satisfaction for the sins we have committed. A sign of inner conversion is being willing to do external actions of penance. Examples are fasting, prayer, and almsgiving—three traditional acts that express conversion in relation to self, God, and others. We can also express interior conversion by being peacemakers, praying for our neighbors, praying to the saints, receiving the Eucharist, doing other acts of charity like showing concern for the poor, and accepting the trials and sufferings that come into our lives.

Rite of Penance (CCC, 1447–1460; 1480–1484; 1491; 1497)

The way the Sacrament of Penance is celebrated has changed through the ages. In the earliest centuries, it was tied to rigorous public penances and often celebrated only once a lifetime. Around the seventh century, private, individual, devotional confession to a priest became the norm. This is the form we celebrate today. However, two essential elements of the sacrament were always present. They are:

1. The *acts of the penitent,* which include:
   - *Contrition*, which is genuine sorrow for one's sins, a detesting of them, and firmly resolving

Extending the Lesson

Prayer Experience: If you cannot have a penance service offering your students the opportunity for individual confession, use Chapter 7, Handout 3 "Penance Service" (starting on page 285 and also online at www.avemariapress.com) as a communal experience of our common need for forgiveness and reconciliation with one another.

For this Penance Service you will need a small piece of scrap paper for each participant (approximately the size of an index card), markers, and a small basket. You will want to arrange your prayer space in a way that is conducive to quiet reflection. You may wish to dim the lights and gather the students around a small table set with a candle, crucifix, and Bible. Pass out the scraps of paper and markers to the participants as they gather. Give them a moment to get seated and to settle themselves and then begin with a reading from Psalm 32. After the reflection portion, pass the basket around the room for the students to deposit their pieces of paper. Conclude by having the students read together the Concluding Prayer.

KNOWING CHRIST THROUGH SCRIPTURE

Jesus and Forgiveness

Read the following Gospel passages. Then write how each passage involves healing, forgiveness, conversion, and reconciliation.

- John 8:2–11 (woman caught in adultery)
- Mark 2:1–12 (cure of the paralyzed man)
- Luke 15:11–32 (parable of the loving father and two sons)

not to sin again. *Perfect* contrition is sorrow that comes from love of God. *Imperfect* contrition comes from other motives, for example, fear of punishment.

- *Confession* of one's sins, which takes place after examination of one's conscience in light of God's Word. Catholics are obligated to confess their mortal sins at least once a year or before receiving Holy Communion, which requires a state of grace. Although we are not required to confess venial sins, doing so helps us grow in the spiritual life.
- *Satisfaction*, also called penance, is part of the reparation sinners need to do. Examples include praying and doing works of mercy, service, and self-denial. We show we are truly sorry when we try to repair the harm our sins caused, for example, by returning stolen goods. Although absolution forgives our sins, it does not repair or make satisfaction for the harm our sins have caused.

2. *God's action*, which works through bishops and their priest coworkers who forgive sin in Jesus' name. Standing in place of the Good Shepherd, they also determine what type of penance to give to penitents.

The ordinary way we celebrate this sacrament today is through the anonymous or face-to-face confession of sins to a priest by an individual penitent. The liturgy involves a greeting and blessing by the confessor and a Scripture reading on God's forgiving love. The penitent then confesses his or her sins, making sure to mention any mortal sins committed since the last confession. The priest assigns a suitable penance, pronounces the words of absolution, and concludes with a prayer of praise and thanksgiving and a dismissal blessing.

A second form of this sacrament often takes place during certain liturgical seasons like Lent and Advent. Parishes then conduct a communal celebration of the Sacrament of Penance, which includes the opportunity for individual confession of sins to a priest and individual absolution.

In times of serious need, a priest may give general absolution after a general confession of sin by those assembled. However, those in mortal sin must intend to confess their sins individually as soon as possible.

- **Direct Instruction:** As you review the material in the Explaining Your Faith feature on page 190 ("Why do we have to confess our sins to a priest?"), refer back to the questions in the Bell-Ringer activity at the beginning of this section. Ask your students to compare and contrast their experience of saying "sorry" with the Sacrament of Penance. For instance:

> Saying our sins aloud is owning up to our actions, just as approaching someone we have hurt to say that we are sorry requires us to be honest about what we have done.

> When we say sorry but don't really mean it, our friend is not usually convinced—our apology is likely to be ineffective—just as going to confession is ineffective if we are not truly sorry for our sins.

> Sometimes when we say we are sorry, our friend is not ready to forgive us, but God is always waiting to forgive us and to welcome us back when we admit our mistakes.

Use the last question of the Bell Ringer activity (What do you think would have happened if you had not apologized?) to emphasize the importance of this sacrament to your students.

Chapter 7, Handout 2 "Sacrament of Penance Outline" Sample Answers

A. Conversion: the first step in returning to God
1. a gift of the Holy Spirit
2. requires changing our lives
3. rooting out sin
4. hating the evil we have committed
5. forming intention not to sin again
6. trusting in God's love and mercy

B. Confession: telling our sins to a priest
1. praising God for the great mercy shown to us

C. Forgiveness: reminds us God imparts pardon and peace through the priest's words
1. Sin is a great evil
2. offends God's honor and love
3. breaks our union with God
4. disfigures the sinner who ought to show forth God's image
5. ruptures our relationship with other members of God's Church
6. Christ gave power to forgive sins to Apostles and their successors

D. Reconciliation: recognizes God's loving forgiveness
1. reconciles us with God and the Church
2. brings peace of conscience/spiritual comfort
3. strengthens us to live a Christian life
4. takes away some of the temporal punishment due to sin
5. remits fully the eternal punishment resulting from mortal sin
6. prepares us to meet our Divine Judge

E. Penance: official name for the sacrament
1. making satisfaction for the sins committed
2. external acts done as a sign of inner conversion
3. traditional examples include: fasting, prayer, almsgiving
4. other examples include:
   a. being peacemakers
   b. praying for our neighbors
   c. praying to the saints
   d. receiving the Eucharist
   e. doing acts of charity for the poor
   f. accepting trials of our daily life

For Review Answers (page 190)

1. The name "the sacrament of *conversion*" emphasizes our continual need to repent and return to our Lord after we have sinned. Using the term *penance* to identify the sacrament focuses our attention on our need to make amends for the wrong that we have done, through some prayer or action. Our inner conversion is made visible and real through the action we are willing to perform. Calling the sacrament *confession* stresses the importance of naming our sins aloud to a priest and "confessing" God's great mercy that he offers to us in this sacrament. When we refer to the sacrament as the sacrament of *forgiveness*, we focus on God's great mercy and the peace and pardon he imparts to us through the priest's words of absolution. The word *reconciliation* is used because it is through this sacrament that we are reunited with God and the Church, which in turn brings us peace of conscience, strength to live the Christian life, relief of the temporal punishment due to sin, and complete remittance of the eternal punishment due to mortal sin.

2. Sin offends God's honor and love, causes a break in our union with God, disfigures the sinner who is made in God's image, and damages our relationship with others.

3. Absolution is the prayer that the priest, who has the power given to the Church by Christ, says to pardon a repentant sinner in the Sacrament of Penance.

4. When we receive the Sacrament of Penance worthily, we are reconciled with God and the Church, we receive peace of conscience and spiritual comfort, we are strengthened to live the Christian life, the temporal punishment that we are due because of our sin is lessened and the eternal punishment due any mortal sin is remitted fully, and we are prepared for our meeting with our Divine Judge when we die.

5. In the Sacrament of Penance the penitent does three things: he expresses contrition or true sorrow for his sins; he confesses those sins aloud to a priest, after making an examination of conscience; and he makes satisfaction for his sins by doing the penance assigned by the priest. God's action in the sacrament is expressed through the bishop or priest who forgives the penitent's sins in Jesus' name. The priest also determines the penance given to the penitent.

6. Answers will vary here, but may include the following:
- Confession helps us know the truth about ourselves.
- It helps us to hear Christ's forgiveness and the reassurance of his love.
- Because sin affects others, we need to be reconciled with the Church as well as with God.
- The sacrament helps us to grow in holiness.

Explaining Your Faith

Why do we have to confess our sins to a priest?

There are many possible answers to this question. But the key reason we should celebrate the Sacrament of Penance is to experience the gift of Jesus' forgiveness. Christ meets us in a special way in this sacrament. Confession enables us to experience firsthand the saving love of Christ that reaches out to us through his minister (the priest) and his Church. Other good reasons for confessing our sins to a priest include:

1. *Confession helps us know the truth about ourselves.* Everyone sins. Everyone carries guilt. Everyone needs to be honest. We all yearn to open ourselves to another. When we name our sins aloud to a priest, we own up to our darkest secrets. We accept responsibility for what we have done. Saying our sins aloud is an excellent sign of sincere contrition; it helps us overcome self-deception. Modern psychology tells us that confession is good for the soul. This is especially true in the Sacrament of Penance because it lifts burdens, forgives sins, relieves guilt, and gives us a fresh start on our spiritual journey.

2. *The sacrament helps us to hear Christ's forgiveness and reassurance of his love.* It is only human to want assurance of love and forgiveness when we have gone astray yet repented of our sins. Jesus understood this in his own ministry for he often *spoke* his word

of forgiveness. He continues to speak today through his Church's sacraments. A forgiving word spoken and heard brings joy and strengthens us to recommit ourselves to following the Good Shepherd.

3. *We need to celebrate reconciliation with others.* Though we often sin alone and privately, sin is never a private affair. Sin harms our relationship with God and others. When we confess, we acknowledge that our sins affect others and that we have become estranged from our brothers and sisters in faith. The celebration of the Sacrament of Penance is a public declaration that we want to reconcile with the Church. It is also an acknowledgment that our personal sin is linked with the sins of society. The sacrament heals our sinfulness and gives the graces to help transform our hearts. It also challenges us to heal and transform the sinful conditions in the world, to become part of the solution and not part of the problem.

4. *The sacrament helps us to grow in holiness.* All the sacraments strengthen friendship with God. Reconciliation sharpens our conscience, prods us out of our spiritual laziness, heals our spiritual weakness, and unites us more closely with God and our neighbors.

For Review

1. Explain the meaning of the Sacrament of Penance under each of these names: conversion, penance, confession, forgiveness, and reconciliation.
2. What are some results of sin?
3. Define *absolution*.
4. What are some of the effects of receiving the Sacrament of Penance worthily?
5. Briefly discuss the acts of the penitent and God's action in the Sacrament of Penance.
6. Name three good reasons to go to Confession.

For Reflection
Why is it important for you to go to confession?

Knowing Christ through Scripture Answers (page 189)

Look for examples of both physical and spiritual healing. Also, point out how the element of conversion is present both for the person who forgives the sin and the person whose sin is forgiven.

Homework Assignment

1. Complete the For Review questions on page 190.
2. Read the entire text section "Anointing of the Sick" (pages 191–193).
3. Continue work on the Ongoing Assignments, page 206.

Anointing of the Sick (*CCC*, 1499–1512; 1514–1515; 1526; 1528–1529)

Jesus Christ announced the coming of God's Kingdom. One way he showed that the Kingdom is present was through his compassionate healing ministry. Jesus cured blind and lame people, cleansed lepers, and brought the dead back to life. Jesus touched suffering people and healed their spiritual, psychological, and physical sicknesses.

After his Ascension, Jesus' earliest disciples obeyed his charge to continue his healing ministry by preaching repentance, casting out demons, and anointing and healing the sick. Today, the Lord continues to heal us through the prayers of the Church and through the sacraments, especially the Eucharist, and the Sacrament of the Anointing of the Sick. The Letter of James shows the roots of

the Sacrament of Anointing of the Sick (see page 183).

Anointing and praying for the sick were commonplace in the early Church (see, for example, Acts 9:34 and Acts 28:8–9). However, by the Middle Ages, this sacrament was usually administered only to those who were dying. The term for the sacrament became *extreme unction*, that is, the "last anointing" before death. Penance and viaticum ("food for the way"), the reception of a final Eucharist, come before the sacramental anointing of a dying person.

The liturgical reforms of the Second Vatican Council stress that the Sacrament of the Anointing of the Sick is for those suffering from serious illness, for the elderly, for those facing major surgery, as well as for the dying. And sick persons may repeat the sacrament if, after recovery, they fall ill again or if the original condition worsens.

viaticum
Holy Communion received by dying persons to help them pass over to God in the afterlife.

For Enrichment

Class Activity: As a follow-up to the Knowing Christ through Scripture assignment on page 192, consider the following. Research ways that the healings that Jesus performed in the Scripture passages listed in the text continue to happen among the poor in the world today. Begin by directing them to such organizations as:

- Doctors Without Borders (www.doctorswithoutborders.com)
- Shriner's Hospitals for Children (www.shrinershq.org/Hospitals/Main)
- The Plasticos Foundation (www.plasticosfoundation.org)
- Physicians for Peace: Walking Free (http://physiciansforpeace.org)
- Operation Smile (www.operationsmile.org)

All of these organizations offer medical services free to those who are unable to afford them. As your students research these organizations, ask them to list other ways patients who are treated by these groups are "healed" beyond the physical healing. Raising funds to support the work of one of these or a similar organization might be a valuable service project for your class. If they choose to do this, allow the students to select which program to support and how to raise funds. You might assign small groups to research the different organizations to find out what they do, for whom, where, and why and then present their findings to the class. After the presentations, the class will be able to vote for which organization they want to support.

It will help to motivate them if they set a goal for their fundraising and keep track of their earnings as they begin to collect money. They should plan to advertise throughout their school and, hopefully, wider community.

Anointing of the Sick
(pages 191–193)

Objectives

In this lesson, the students will:

- look at their own experience of illness and the things that helped them to heal.
- compare Jesus' healings in the New Testament and the effects of Anointing of the Sick.
- describe how the sacrament is carried out.

Preview

In this lesson, you will demonstrate the sacrament for your class since it is unlikely that many of your students have had any experience of it. You will need to bring a small amount of oil to use in place of the blessed oil that would be used by the priest. If you have a lightly scented oil, that would be best. Otherwise, a light olive oil or other salad oil will work fine. Have a clean towel to wipe the oil from your hands, and from your volunteer, after the demonstration. You will also need a chair for your volunteer "sick person" at the front of the class. Mark your bible ahead of time with the passage from James that opens this chapter so that you can find your place easily. Memorize the prayer the priest says over the ill person instead of reading from the textbook, or if necessary, copy it from the text onto a small piece of paper, which you can tuck into your pocket. Pause to give explanations of the different steps of the sacrament as you do them and ask often if there are questions.

Bell Ringers

- **Direct Instruction:** Collect the homework assignments. Check the students' progress on the Ongoing Assignments they are working on.
- **Journal Assignment:** Ask the students to spend a few minutes writing in their journals about a time they were sick enough to stay home from school for a few days. What was wrong? How did they feel physically? Emotionally? Who took care of them? What did this person do that made them feel better? Did they have visitors? How did that make them feel? Allow time for sharing.

Teaching Approaches

- **Direct Instruction:** Begin by exploring the scriptural roots of the Sacrament of the Anointing of the Sick by reading the following passages to the students and explaining each of the types of healing represented primarily in each:
  - Matthew 9:27–30 (*physical healing*)
  - Mark 9:14–27 (*spiritual healing*)
  - Acts 9:34 and Acts 28:8–9 (*healing in the early Church*)
  - James 5:14–15 (*prayer and Anointing of the Sick*)

- **Class Discussion:** Discuss the passages with your students and follow up with a discussion of the appropriate times a person might seek out the sacrament today. Also review the origins of the sacrament from the passage from the letter of James (page 183 of the Student Text).
- **Writing Assignment:** Allow time for students to complete the assignment in the Knowing Christ through Scripture feature "Jesus and His Healing Touch" (page 192)
- **Direct Instruction:** Continue with an explanation of the rites of the sacrament (see text subsection on page 192). *Use a volunteer from your class and act out the sacrament.* Be sure to tell them that you are just demonstrating what the sacrament might look like but that you are not performing the sacrament. The rest of the class should consider themselves "friends and family" of the "sick person," who have gathered to support that person with their prayers. In a real occurrence of the sacrament, they would be participants in the sacrament, not an audience watching it.
  - Begin by inviting everyone to recite an Act of Contrition together. The sacrament works to forgive sin, particularly if there is no opportunity for the Sacrament of Penance. Follow this with the Scripture reading you have marked (Jas 5:14–15 or another passage you have chosen that relates to healing). You might ask a student ("friend or family member") to read the passage.
  - Following the Scripture reading you will lay hands on the "sick person." Usually, the priest will place both hands firmly but gently on the person's head or shoulders. It is not appropriate to merely hold your hands above the person. The touch is an important part of the sacrament, a sign of Jesus' healing touch and a recognition of the human need to be touched. The priest will pray silently for the person during this time. Explain to the class that this is their time to pray silently for the person as well.
  - After a few moments of silent prayer you will begin to anoint the forehead and hands of the "sick person" while saying the following prayer aloud: "Through this holy anointing may the Lord in his love and mercy help you with the grace of the Holy Spirit. May the Lord who frees you from sin save you and raise you up." Remind your students of the symbolic properties of oil that you covered in the previous chapter: healing, strength, dedication to God.
  - After your demonstration, take a few moments to explain the changes that would happen if the person were receiving Penance and viaticum as well: the Sacrament of Penance would come first; then, the Eucharist would follow taking the place of the

KNOWING CHRIST THROUGH SCRIPTURE

Jesus and His Healing Touch

The Gospels give many examples of Jesus' power over sickness. Read the following passages. Summarize and comment on the meaning of each:

- Matthew 9:18–26
- Luke 7:1–10
- Luke 17:11–19
- John 4:46–54
- John 5:1–9
- John 9:1–7

Rite of the Sacrament of Anointing (CCC, 1513; 1516–1519; 1524–1525; 1530–1531)

Only priests and bishops may administer the Sacrament of the Anointing of the Sick. However, the prayerful support of the entire Church is important because it shows the unity of the family and friends with the sick person. When the sacrament takes place during Mass, the parish community is reminded in a special way to respond in love to those who are suffering. The essential elements of the sacrament include:

- the priest lays hands on the sick person(s);
- he prays for them in the faith of the Church;
- he anoints their forehead and hands (in the Roman or Latin Rite) or other body parts (in the Eastern Rite) with oil ideally blessed previously by a bishop (or, if necessary, by himself).

Latin Rite
The liturgical, legal, and customary traditions of the Church in the West, as distinct from the rites and practices of the Eastern Churches.

In the rite of the sacrament, an act of repentance precedes the Liturgy of the Word. This awakens the faith of the sick person and of the community to pray to the Lord for the Holy Spirit's strength. Next comes the laying on of hands. This is an important biblical sign of Jesus' loving touch and the outpouring of the Spirit of strength, love, and forgiveness. The prayer of the priest over the sick person invokes the grace of the Spirit:

Through this holy anointing may the Lord in his love and mercy help you with the grace of the Holy Spirit. May the Lord who frees you from sin save you and raise you up.[15]

In the Latin Rite—that is, in the Western Catholic Church's ritual tradition, which is the commonest rite in the Roman Catholic Church and the one with which we are most familiar in our country—the priest recites this prayer while anointing the forehead and hands of the sick person. Anointing with blessed oil symbolizes healing, strength, and special dedication to God.

This sacrament encourages those who are sick to overcome the alienation caused by sickness, to grow to wholeness through the illness, to identify with the sufferings of Jesus Christ, and to enter more fully into the Paschal Mystery.

Knowing Christ through Scripture Answers (page 192)

- Matthew 9:18–26 (a woman with a hemorrhage is healed when she touches Jesus' clothing)
- Luke 7:1–10 (Jesus is amazed at the faith of the Gentile; faith is connected to the healing of his slave)
- Luke 17:11–19 (Jesus prescribed a Jewish ritual healing, but the ten lepers were healed on the way; only one returns to thank Jesus)
- John 4:46–54 (Jesus heals a dying boy from a distance away)
- John 5:1–9 (Jesus heals on the Sabbath, showing that a good deed is worth more than obeying a law)
- John 9:1–7 (Jesus heals a blind man at the Pool of Siloam and explains sin did not cause his suffering)

Effects of the Sacrament of Anointing
(CCC, 1520–1523; 1527; 1532)

The effects of the Sacrament of the Anointing of the Sick include:

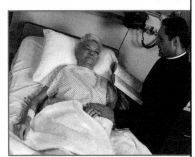

- the forgiveness of sin, if the sick person has not been able to obtain it through the Sacrament of Penance;
- spiritual healing, including the comfort, peace, and courage of the Holy Spirit to overcome the difficulties of this particular illness;
- physical healing when this will help the person in his or her condition before God;
- the union of the sick person more closely to Christ's redemptive Passion, which will benefit both the individual and the good of all God's people;
- for dying persons, the strength of the anointing and viaticum in the final struggle before entering eternity and meeting our loving God.

For Review

1. Identify these terms: *extreme unction, viaticum.*
2. How is the Sacrament of the Anointing of the Sick administered?
3. What are the effects of the Anointing of the Sick?

For Reflection

Think of a family member, friend, or neighbor who is ill. Pray for this person during the coming week. If possible, visit the person, give a call, or send a get-well card.

My Prayer for the Sick

Compose a short prayer for a sick or dying person whom you know personally. Recite it daily for their benefit.

Homework Assignment

1. Compose a short prayer for a sick or dying person and recite it daily (see page 193).

2. Complete the For Review questions on page 193.

3. Read the text section "Holy Orders" (pages 194–198).

second step noted earlier. After the reception of Eucharist, the Sacrament of Anointing would proceed with the third and fourth steps. Before you end this discussion, ask the students if they have any other questions.

- **Individual Assignment:** Check the students' understanding of the process of the sacrament by having them create a series of simple pictures, somewhat like a comic strip, that illustrates the events of the rite. Collect, check, and give them back to the students to review for the Chapter Test.

- **Class Discussion:** Ask students to make connections between the Rite of Anointing and the healing miracles in the Gospels. What did Jesus do that can also be found in the sacrament? Answers should include touch and forgiveness of sins.

- **Group Discussion:** Look over the section on the effects of the Sacrament of Anointing with your students (see page 193). Lead a discussion with them on the importance of each effect. To begin, divide the class into groups of four or five. Ask each group to list the effects in order of importance, with the first being the most important. Suggest that they base their rankings on what they would think if they were the ones receiving the sacrament. They should be prepared to explain their choices. As the groups present their lists to the class, seek explanation primarily for the most and least important positions, as these should be easiest for the students to explain. There are no necessarily right and wrong answers here. You are really looking for the explanation as to why do they think one effect is more important than the others.

- **Class Discussion:** Remind the students once again of the healing miracles in the New Testament. How are the effects of the Sacrament of Anointing of the Sick similar to the effects of Jesus' healing miracles?

For Review Answers (page 193)

1. *Extreme unction*, or the "last anointing," is the old name used for the Sacrament of the Anointing of the Sick, when it was primarily given just before death. *Viaticum*, "food for the way," is the name for the last reception of the Eucharist before the sacramental anointing of a dying person.

2. The Sacrament of the Anointing of the Sick is given by a priest who lays hands on the sick person, says prayers for them, and anoints their forehead and hands with oil that has been previously blessed by a bishop.

3. The sacrament forgives sin, offers spiritual healing to overcome the difficulties of the illness, provides physical healing when this will help the person in his condition before God, unites the sick person more closely to Christ's redemptive Passion, and, for dying persons, strengthens them in the final struggle before entering eternity and meeting our loving God.

Holy Orders

(pages 194–198)

Objectives

In this lesson, the students will:

- compare and contrast the activities of the three degrees of the Sacrament of Holy Orders.
- express appreciation for something they have learned from a priest.
- describe the key elements of the Sacrament of Holy Orders.
- describe the importance of clerical celibacy.

 ## Preview

Gather as many Catholic magazines or periodicals as you can before this class. Your school library may be able to give you past issues of your diocesan newspaper or of a national Catholic newspaper. Multiple issues of a weekly or biweekly Catholic magazine would be helpful as well. If your library needs the periodicals returned, be sure to caution your students to handle them carefully. You might also print out pages from diocesan websites that reveal the different activities priests are involved in.

Invite a priest and a deacon to come and share their experiences with your class. You will need to set this up probably a few weeks or even months in advance, as priests are often very busy and deacons often have secular jobs from which they will need to request time off. Ask them to prepare a ten-minute talk about what they do and the graces they have received to do it. Ask them to give one example of something that has made them particularly glad that they responded to God's call to the priesthood or diaconate. Also, ask them to be prepared to field questions from your class.

 ## Bell Ringers

- **Individual Activity:** Pass out small scraps of paper to your students and invite them to write down something good they have learned from a priest—either something he said that has stuck with them or something he has done that has been a good example to them. They do not need to know the priest personally. (If they are having trouble, remind them that they probably learned about a lot of priests when they studied saints in a previous chapter of this text.) They may write down more than one thing, but should use separate papers for each thing they write down.
- **Writing Assignment:** Invite your students to express their gratitude personally to a priest they know from their school, parish, or other area. Letter writing is a particularly good method, as it gives the students time and space to express themselves without embarrassment or feeling pressed for time, and it leaves the priest with something tangible that he can keep as a reminder that he has made a difference to a young person.

Holy Orders (CCC, 1533; 1536–1538; 1544–1553; 1591–1592)

Although all of us are called to serve others and our Baptism and Confirmation initiate us into the common priesthood of the faithful, the Lord saw a special need for certain members in the Church to "minister to the ministers." The ministerial or hierarchical priesthood is received by bishops and priests through the Sacrament of Holy Orders. Sacramental ordination consecrates certain baptized men to one of three degrees of a sacred order: *episcopacy* (bishops), *presbyterate* (priests), and *diaconate* (deacons). (Deacons do not participate in the priesthood, which Christ exercises through bishops and priests. More information on deacons follows on pages 195–196.) Bishops and their coworker priests lead the members of Christ's Body by helping unfold the graces of Baptism to all Christians. "Those who receive the Sacrament of Holy Orders are *consecrated* in Christ's name to feed the Church by the word and grace of God." (*CCC*, 1535, quoting *Lumen Gentium*, 11, §2). For this reason Holy Orders (along with Matrimony) is one of the Sacraments at the Service of Communion.

The ministerial priesthood continues the special ministry Jesus entrusted to the Apostles. It is essentially different from the common priesthood of the faithful. Through the ministerial priesthood, Christ himself becomes visibly present to the Church as its head and High Priest of his redemptive sacrifice.

Holy Orders confers a gift of the Holy Spirit that allows bishops and priests to exercise a "sacred power" of service on behalf of Christ for his Church. Bishops and priests must:

- proclaim and teach God's Word to all people,
- lead the Christian community in worship,
- guide and rule God's people by imitating Jesus' model of humble service.

Roles of the Ordained Ministers (CCC, 1539–1545; 1550; 1554; 1590; 1593)

The Jews, God's Chosen People, were "a kingdom of priests, a holy nation" (Ex 19:6). From among these special people, Yahweh chose the tribe of Levi to serve the nation at liturgical services. The priesthoods of Aaron and Melchizedek and the seventy elders also prefigured the ordained ministry of the New Covenant. Although in Old Testament times there was a special rite to consecrate priests, their sacrifices and prayers could not bring Salvation.

Christ fulfilled the Old Testament prefigurations of the priesthood. His unique sacrifice brought about our Redemption once and for all. He is the High Priest.

The Sacrament of Holy Orders is exercised in different degrees by those who have from the earliest times been called bishops, priests, and deacons. There are various New Testament roots of the Sacrament of Holy Orders. Examples include St. Paul writing to Timothy about the laying on of the hands of ordination (2 Tm 1:6)

Background Information

From the Common Priesthood to the Ordained Ministry

The common priesthood of the faithful extends to all who are baptized. Through our Baptism, we are called to serve others. For some, this call to serve others leads them to be a "minister to the ministers" in the Church and to receive Holy Orders and be ordained to the diaconate, priesthood, or episcopacy (bishops).

The call to the priesthood can come in unexpected ways for some. Cardinal Joseph Bernardin, the former archbishop of Chicago, wrote of his journey in his book Gift of Peace:

> . . . I became friends with a couple of young priests from my hometown parish. They took a great interest in me and eventually asked if I had ever thought about entering the priesthood. When I told them that I wanted to become a doctor, they approached the question a different way. They showed me that my interest in becoming a doctor indicated that I wanted to help people, to reach out to others. They proceeded to explain to me that I could also help people by becoming a priest. (85)

and reference to the office of bishop being a worthy way to serve God's people (1 Tm 3:1).

Just as the Eucharist makes present Jesus' saving sacrifice, so does Holy Orders make present Christ's priesthood. Jesus is really present through the priesthood of bishops and priests; therefore, we can be certain that his graces come to us when the sacraments are administered. Christ works through bishops and priests, despite their human weaknesses. Deacons help and serve bishops and priests.

Each of the three degrees of ordained ministry has a special role.

Episcopacy (CCC, 1555–1561; 1594)

Bishops receive the fullness of the Sacrament of Holy Orders, the "high priesthood." Consecration to the episcopacy confers a sacred character as a successor to the Apostles to take Christ's place as teacher (to instruct), as shepherd (to rule), and as priest (to sanctify). The Pope must approve the ordination of bishops, who may be consecrated only by other bishops. This practice shows how the order of bishops is a College of Bishops united with the Pope, the Bishop of Rome who is the visible bond of unity in the worldwide Church. Each bishop is the visible head of a local Church (diocese). With the College of Bishops, he serves the worldwide Church under the authority of Peter's successor, the Pope.

Presbyterate (CCC, 1562–1568; 1595)

Priests work alongside bishops as their helpers and extensions. Ordination to the presbyterate makes them members of the sacerdotal college around the bishop. (This is similar to the bishops forming a college around the Pope.) Priests also receive a sacramental character from the Holy Spirit to act in the person of

Christ. They do this most fully when they celebrate the Eucharist. Priests represent their bishops to their parishes and are joined to them in an intimate sacramental fellowship.

Diaconate (CCC, 1569–1571; 1596)

Deacons receive a sacramental character from ordination to the diaconate that configures them to Jesus Christ "to serve, not to be served." The bishop of a local diocese commissions deacons to serve. The reforms of the Second Vatican Council in the Latin Church allow married men to be ordained to the permanent diaconate.

Deacons are not priests, so they cannot celebrate the Eucharist, forgive sin in the Sacrament of Penance, or anoint the sick. Rather, they help bishops and priests at liturgies, distribute Holy Communion at Mass and to the sick, proclaim and preach the Gospel, witness and bless marriages, preside at funerals, and perform many other actions of service for God's People.

diaconate
The third degree in the hierarchy of Holy Orders. The diaconate is not a degree of the ministerial priesthood. Deacons are ordained ministers who assist bishops and priests in the celebration of liturgy, distribute communion, witness and bless marriages, proclaim and preach the Gospel, celebrate funerals, and perform various ministries of Christian charity, all under the authority of their bishop.

- **Direct Instruction:** Check the students' homework from the previous lesson and the progress they are making on the Ongoing Assignments, page 206.

Teaching Approaches

- **Group Activity:** Divide your class into groups of three to four students each. Give each group a mixed stack of periodicals and website pages that you have gathered (see the notes under Preview on page 196).
  - Have the students skim through the newspapers, magazines, etc., for examples of what bishops, priests, and deacons do. There should be articles covering a range of Church activities that directly involve each of these. Have the students make a list of everything they find. You might suggest that the students look carefully at the by-lines of the articles: they might be surprised to find priests working as journalists, columnists, editors, and publishers. They should also look at the advertisements, since many religious orders and organizations use diocesan newspapers to seek support in their various ministries.
  - Have each group report on their lists to the class. Try to list the activities under the headings of the three responsibilities of the ordained: (1) to proclaim and teach God's Word, (2) to lead the community in worship, and (3) to guide and rule God's people by imitating Jesus' model of humble service.
- **Prayer Experience:** Write a short prayer for vocations. Share with a partner. See also the idea for a prayer service for vocations in the "Extending the Lesson" panel on page 199.
- **Guest Speakers:** Use one class period before the visit from the priest and deacon to brainstorm

Extending the Lesson

Prayer Experience: As a brief prayer service, find a Prayer for Vocations promulgated for your diocese. Look on the diocesan website under "Office for Vocations" or call the Office for Vocations and ask for one. Print out copies of the prayer for your students and say the prayer together. You might choose to begin and end each class with this prayer for the entire time that you are studying Holy Orders. If you can't find one from your own diocese, you may use this one, written by Cardinal Roger Mahony and reprinted from the website of the Archdiocese of Los Angeles:

Prayer for Vocations
By Cardinal Roger Mahony

Good and gracious God,
you have called us through Baptism
to discipleship with your son, Jesus Christ,
and have sent us to bring the Good News of salvation to all people.
We pray you to grant us more priests, deacons, religious brothers and sisters, and lay ministers to build up your Church here in the diocese of __N.__ .
Inspire our young men and women by the example of Blessed Junipero Serra to give themselves totally to the work of Christ and his Church.

Amen.

Note: You will need to use the name of your own diocese and substitute the name of a well-known priest or religious person from your area for "Blessed Junipero Serra," who is important to the Church of Los Angeles because he was the founder of many of the California missions. If you cannot think of a priest or religious person who would be significant and recognized by your students to name in place of Fr. Serra, you may omit the entire phrase "by the example of __N.__ ."

questions that your students have about the roles of priests and deacons. (This presentation parallels the text subsection "Roles of the Ordained Ministers," pages 194–195.) Ask the students to record the list of questions they generate in their notebooks so that they will be able to remember the ones they really want to ask about when the priest and deacon visit. (If possible, providing this list to the priest and deacon who have agreed to come talk will help them to be prepared to answer anything the students might ask.)

- Introduce the visiting priest and deacon to your class. Ask your students to listen carefully while each of them describes their role in the Church and graces they have received that have allowed them to complete their tasks.

- After the speakers have finished, moderate a question-and-answer session. Students might ask follow-up questions based on what the priest and deacon shared in their opening talks, or they might use the questions that were brainstormed by the class earlier.

- As a follow-up activity, write thank-you notes to the speakers for coming and sharing their time with the class.

- **Individual Assignment:** Make sure students know the differences in ministries and graces of each of the three degrees (see chart on page 196). Quiz the students with simple statements and questions that are answered by writing *bishop, priest,* and/or *deacon.* Some questions may include:
  - Can perform all of the sacraments. (*bishop*)
  - Can be married. (*deacon*)
  - Can baptize people. (*bishop, priest,* and *deacon*)
  - Can perform the Sacrament of Anointing of the Sick. (*bishop* and *priest*)
  - Is the normal minister of the Sacrament of Confirmation. (*bishop*)
  - Is unable to preside at Mass. (*deacon*)
  - The spiritual "father" of a diocese. (*bishop*)
  - Is the bishop's extension into the diocese. (*priest*)

- **Video Presentation:** Summarize the section "Rite of Holy Orders" (page 197), focusing both on the text material and the *Catechism of the Catholic Church* citations. Next, show the video of a priest or bishop's ordination that you have prepared. Ask your students to take notes, listing the elements they see taking place that they do not recognize from a regular celebration of the Eucharist.

- **Direct Instruction:** After the video, go over the students' notes, discussing the different elements within the Rite of Holy Orders. Be sure to note the essential elements of valid ordination—that only a bishop may confer the sacrament on the ordained, and that the

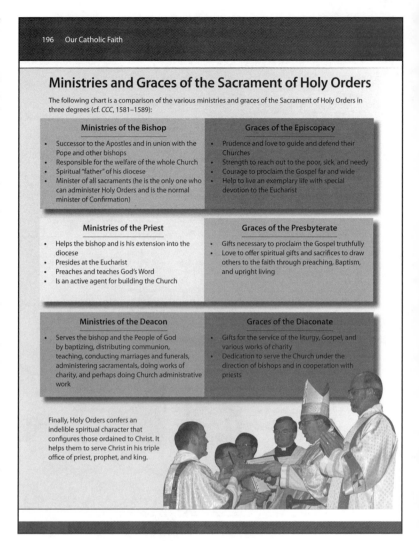

For Enrichment

Individual Assignment: Have your students research the process for ordination as a deacon in your diocese. Diocesan websites are a good place to start. They should find out what the pre-requirements are to be considered a candidate for the diaconate. They should look into what training and educational requirements there are. What are the commitments and promises that a deacon must make? Is his family involved in any way? Ask them to write a short paper on what they learn from their research.

Background Information

History of a Married Clergy

Celibacy has been a requirement for priests in the Roman Catholic Church only since the twelfth century. Prior to this, many priests and even bishops were married though the charism of celibacy was practiced in the Church since its beginning. The decision to require celibacy changed the form of the ministerial office of the priest but did not change its character. Thus, it would be possible for the Church to change that form once again and remove the requirement of celibacy.

Rite of Holy Orders (CCC, 1552; 1572–1578; 1597–1598; 1600)

The Sacrament of Holy Orders is administered within Mass, ideally on a Sunday and at the diocesan cathedral. It is good for God's people to be present at this sacrament because they are the ones to be served by the newly ordained ministers. Only validly ordained bishops have Christ's authority to ordain, thereby continuing the apostolic line begun from the earliest days of the Church.

The Church has the authority to ordain only baptized men. It does not have the authority to ordain women to the priesthood. Although in his earthly ministry Jesus greatly emphasized the dignity of women, Jesus chose only male Apostles. Not even the Blessed Mother was chosen to serve as an Apostle, bishop, or priest. The Apostles followed the example of Jesus when they chose only male collaborators to succeed them in the ordained ministry.

A theological reason for male-only ordination comes from the truth that sacramental signs, including persons and objects, should represent what they signify by natural resemblance. The priest is a sign of Christ, a representative of the Lord when he leads the Church in prayers to God. Because Christ was a male, the priest must also be male.

Priesthood is a gift of Christ to his Church. No one has a *right* to ordination because it is a call by God to serve the Church in a very special way. There are many other ways to serve in the Church for both men and women. Baptism gives us great dignity as God's adopted daughters and sons. The Holy Spirit showers us with many gifts and talents to bring God's love into the world to the millions of people who are desperate for it.

The essential sign for all three orders is the bishop's laying his hands on the head of the one to be ordained, followed by a prayer of consecration. This prayer asks the Holy Spirit to grant the special graces needed for bishops, priests, or deacons to serve God and his people with love and fidelity.

Clerical Celibacy (CCC, 1579–1580; 1599)

In the Latin Rite of the Catholic Church, priests and bishops (but not deacons) may not marry. Men who are married may be ordained deacons. However, they may not remarry if their wife dies. Nor can men ordained as deacons while single ever marry. Catholic priests observe celibacy to express freely their wholehearted commitment to serve both God and God's people. They follow this discipline because:

- By living a loving, celibate life for the sake of the Gospel, a priest is a living sign pointing to eternal life, when there will be no marriage.
- Jesus himself did not marry. By not marrying, a priest is imitating Jesus, who committed himself totally to doing God's will by serving others.
- Celibacy frees a person from family obligations and therefore allows priests or bishops to give themselves totally to the Lord.

celibacy
The state of being unmarried that priests and other religious choose in order to dedicate their lives totally to Jesus Christ and God's people.

laying on of hands is the essential sign of the sacrament. Review the symbolism of oil that you discussed in relation to Baptism and especially Confirmation. Ask: What does the anointing with oil of the priest's hands signify in Ordination? (See page 77.)

- **Class Discussion:** Review the material on clerical celibacy (pages 197–198) with your class. Call on a student to be "on the spot" and come before the class to defend one of the positive reasons listed in the text for the discipline of celibacy (e.g., "being able to give themselves totally for the Lord"). Choose other students to be on the spot to defend the same reason before moving on to the other three reasons listed on pages 197–198. As to the issue of a married priesthood, note the Background Information on the subject listed on page 198.

Homework Assignment

1. Complete the For Review questions on page 198.

2. Read the entire text section "Matrimony" (pages 198–203).

3. Write the essay suggested on page 199, "The Meaning of Christian Marriage," after reading the Scripture passages suggested.

For Review Answers (page 198)

1. Bishops are responsible for the welfare of the whole Church and can administer all of the sacraments. They are given prudence and love to guide and defend the Church, strength to reach out to the poor, and courage to proclaim the Gospel and help to live an exemplary life. Priests help the bishop to reach all of the people of the diocese, preside at Eucharist, preach and teach God's Word, and are active agents for the building up of the Church. They are given the gifts necessary to proclaim the Gospel truthfully, and love to offer spiritual gifts and sacrifices to draw others to the faith through preaching, Baptism, and the example of their living. Deacons serve the bishop and the People of God by baptizing, distributing Communion, teaching, conducting marriages and funerals, and doing works of charity. They are given the grace of dedication to serve the Church under the direction of the bishops and in cooperation with priests.

2. The Church does not ordain women because it does not have the authority to do so. Jesus chose only men as Apostles; therefore, the Church, through the ages, has followed Jesus' example in choosing only men as successors to the Apostles in the ordained ministry. Also, because the priest is a sign of Christ, he ought to bear a natural resemblance to Christ; therefore, he must be male.

3. The essential sign in the Rite of Ordination is the laying on of hands when the bishop puts his hands on the head of the one to be ordained. This is followed by a prayer of consecration asking the Holy Spirit to grant the graces needed for the newly ordained to serve God and God's people with love and fidelity.

4. An icon is an image of Jesus, Mary, or one of the saints used to teach believers about God and to help focus our minds when we pray or meditate.

The Sacrament of Matrimony

(pages 198–203)

Objectives

In this lesson, the students will:

- describe what it takes to have a successful marriage.
- explain the requirements for sacramental marriage in the Catholic Church.
- explain the difference between divorce and annulment.

 Preview

The most important element of the lesson on the Sacrament of Matrimony is the witness of a married couple. A couple involved in marriage preparation from a local parish would be an excellent choice. Also, consider recruiting the parents of a former student whom you know to have a good marriage and who are able to relate well to teens. You may choose to have just one couple, or a panel of married men and women, depending on who you have available to you.

Try to have at least one man and one woman prepare a five-minute talk focusing on their life as a married person, the graces they have been given through their marriage, how their marriage serves the larger community or how it helps them to serve the community, the challenges they have faced and what has helped them to overcome them, and any advice they would give to a couple thinking about getting married today.

198   Our Catholic Faith

- Giving up the blessing of a family witnesses dramatically the call Jesus makes to some of his followers. He said, "And everyone who has given up houses or brothers or sisters or father or mother or children or lands for the sake of my name will receive a hundred times more, and will inherit eternal life" (Mt 19:29).

For Review

1. What are some sacred roles and graces of each of the ordained orders (bishops, priests, and deacons)?
2. Why does the Church not ordain women?
3. What is the essential sign in the rite of ordination?
4. Define *icon*.

For Reflection

What would you think if your best friend said you would make a good priest, religious sister, or religious brother? Do you ever think that perhaps God might be calling you to the consecrated life or priesthood? If so, who would be a good person for you to talk to about it?

Matrimony

(CCC, 1601–1617; 1659–1661)

polygamy
Having more than one wife at the same time. It distorts the unity of marriage between a man and a woman and offends the dignity of women.

Christian marriage is a wonderful sign of God calling a man and woman to holiness through ordinary married life. Christ Jesus enters this covenant of love by making it a sacrament. Through it, he joins the couple to bless, sustain, and rejoice in their union. In this holy union the couple is committed to raise a family responsibly if God should bless them with children.

God is the source of marriage. Out of love, he created men and women in the divine image for the purpose of loving each other. Therefore, marriage is a vocation written into our very nature because a God of infinite love made us. Because of Original Sin, however, men and women need God's grace and help to live in the harmony he intends for us.

This understanding of marriage grew gradually throughout Salvation History. At first, polygamy (men taking more than one wife) and divorce were tolerated. However, in the book of Genesis, several divine truths about marriage were revealed, including:

For Enrichment

Individual Assignment: As a longer project, ask the students to interview family members or parishioners who have been married twenty years or more. They can use the lists they made in the Bell Ringer activity to help them decide whom to interview. The interviews should be recorded—preferably on videotape or with a digital camcorder. Some questions the students might ask are:

- When were you married?
- How old were you? And your spouse?
- How did you meet?
- How soon did you know you wanted to marry?
- What has been the best thing about being married?
- What has been the hardest thing about being married?
- Do you think it was easier or harder for people to stay married in your generation compared to today? Why?
- What advice do you have for young couples being married today?

- God made us male and female in the divine image. This established both human sexuality and marriage, both of which God declared to be "very good" (Gn 1:31). He commanded us to "be fertile and multiply; fill the earth and subdue it" (Gn 1:28).
- The second purpose of marriage is companionship between friends who share the same life and love. This is the meaning of the story where God creates Eve from Adam's rib. Genesis tells us they should cling to each other and become one body (see Gn 2:23–24). This means that from the beginning God intends a permanent, exclusive, monogamous relationship between man and woman who have been created in the divine image. This union helps the married couple overcome self-centeredness and opens them to each other, "to mutual aid and to self-giving" (*CCC*, 1609).

Later in Salvation History, prophets like Hosea and Malachi preach about marriage as an image of how Yahweh (the husband) loves his beloved people, Israel. He does so with great faithfulness. Other Old Testament books describe the qualities of an ideal wife, talk about how spouses should be faithful and tender, and see the affection between husband and wife in marriage as good, holy, and joyful.

In the New Testament, the Gospels tell us of Jesus' attendance at the wedding feast of Cana, acknowledging his love and support of the married couple and the institution of marriage. He saw that marriage is both natural and good. In his teaching ministry, Jesus also told us what his Father intended for marriage—it should be a permanent, exclusive love relationship. Therefore, he condemned divorce and remarriage, saying it was equivalent to adultery (Lk 16:18). Jesus also taught that lustful thoughts lead to sexual sins. Jesus stressed purity of heart. For example, men must treat women with respect, as equals, and as persons endowed with great dignity (see Mt 5:27–28).

The early Church learned from Jesus and thus viewed marriage as sacred. St. Paul, for example, taught that husbands must love their wives as they love their own bodies (Eph 5:28–32). In short, the Church saw in the union of a husband and wife a comparison to the union Christ, the Bridegroom, has with his Church, his Bride. St. Paul calls this a *mystery* (a word translated by St. Augustine as "sacrament"), an outward sign of Christ's love. Marriage, in fact, is a covenant, a total, lifelong commitment that mirrors Christ's love for his Church.

Jesus Christ is the Father's gift of love to us. He is the fulfillment of God's promises to humanity. The Lord we receive in the Eucharist makes us one, gives us many gifts, treats us as special individuals, and challenges us to serve others. A Christian marriage is like this open-ended commitment to love that the Father made with us in Jesus Christ. True, committed love brings forth life. So, too, in a marriage where God gives a husband and wife the privilege of procreating life. A Christian marriage is a unique way to live a Christlike life of love and service in the context of family living. Through this sacrament of love, Jesus and his Holy Spirit give the couple the graces they need to love each other with the same love he has for the Church. These graces lift up their human love, strengthen their indissoluble unity, and sanctify them on their journey to eternal life.

Wedding Liturgy

Listed below are some of the readings the Church suggests for the wedding liturgy. Read one selection from each group. Write a short essay based on the readings titled "The Meaning of Christian Marriage."

Old Testament
1. Genesis 1:26–28, 31a
2. Genesis 2:18–24
3. Tobit 8:5–10

New Testament
1. 1 Corinthians 12:31–13:8a
2. Ephesians 5:2a, 21–33
3. 1 John 3:18–24

Gospels
1. Matthew 5:13–16
2. Mark 10:6–9
3. John 15:12–16

Ask the panelists to also be prepared to answer questions from the students about marriage. Reassure them that you will work with the students on their questions beforehand so that none of the questions are improper or too personal. Do your best to get the students' questions to the panelists before they meet your students so that they can be comfortably prepared.

Bell Ringers

- **Writing Assignment:** Ask the students to tell about the couple they know that has been married the longest. Say: "Name some characteristics of their marriage that contributed to its longevity."
- **Group activity:** Continue with the feature on page 202, "Rules for a Successful Marriage." Have the students work in pairs or in small groups to complete a list of ten rules for preparing for a happy marriage. Plan to share some of these rules with the married people who speak with the class.
- **Student Presentations:** Call on several students to read their essays aloud, "The Meaning of Christian Marriage." Collect all the completed essays.

Chapter 7, Handout 4 "Who Can Marry?" Answers

- *José and Marina* can be married. José's first marriage, which ended with civil divorce, would be a problem except that his first wife has since died. Although Marina is not Catholic, she has been baptized and understands the lifelong commitment of marriage. Both are open to children. José will need to seek permission from the Church and will have to agree to raise any children the couple might have in the faith. The couple will also need to attend Marriage Preparation classes as the diocese requires. Many dioceses have special classes for couples like José and Marina who will be blending families.
- *Kristina and George* cannot be validly married at this time. Kristina is too young in most dioceses of the United States where eighteen years is the minimum age. Also, the couple does not want to have children, and Kristina's comments reveal that she does not consider marriage a lifelong commitment.
- *Peter and Mary Ellen* may be validly married, although it will require a dispensation from the Church since Peter is not Christian. They will need to attend marriage preparation classes, which, in many dioceses, will include special sessions for couples entering a "mixed marriage."

Teaching Approaches

- **Direct Instruction:** Trace the history and purpose of Christian marriage by reading the text under the main heading "Matrimony" (pages 198–199). Have the students share what they learned about marriage in the Old and the New Testaments. (Split Teaching Approaches 2–4 over one day followed by 5–6 on a second day.)

- **Guest Speaker:** Begin to prepare your students for the speakers who will come to talk to them about marriage. Allow time for the students to prepare questions for the married people who will participate on the panel. For example, "How do you know that someone is the right person you should marry?" or "What is the best thing about being married?" or "What is the hardest thing about being married?" or "How do you see God acting in or through your marriage?" If necessary, remind your students that the questions should not be so personal that the speaker will be unable to answer them comfortably.

  - Have the students work in groups to list their questions in order of the most commonly asked (questions that all the students in the group asked) to the least (questions that only one student wanted to know). Ask each group to choose a spokesperson to speak for the group and then have each group in turn read their list of questions to the class. Compile a master list, again in order of importance to your students, and assign the questions to individual students to ask during the panel discussion. Give this list to your speakers so that they will know in advance the kinds of questions the students will be asking.

  - On the day your panelists will be there, arrange your classroom so that the students will be able to see the speakers. Introduce each of the panelists to your students and then have your two speakers give their five-minute prepared talks. Following the talks, have the students ask their questions of the panel speakers. If you finish with the prepared questions, open the discussion to more questions that the students may have. Also make sure to have the students share their "rules for a successful marriage" they constructed as part of the Bell Ringer assignments. Be sure to thank the panelists for their time at the end. Follow up the panel discussion by asking the students to write thank-you notes to one or more of the speakers, telling them what made the most impression on the student from what the speaker said.

- **Direct Instruction:** Continue with a focus on the "Preparation for Marriage" subsection on page 200. Cover the following essential points in a lecture or outline for your class:

Preparation for Marriage (CCC, 1621–1637; 1662–1663)

The Church can administer the Sacrament of Matrimony only to a couple who are baptized, of a mature age, unmarried, not closely related by blood or marriage, and are able to give their free consent to marry. To give free consent, the couple must not be under any constraint (like fear or force) or blocked by any natural or Church law. The exchange of consent between the partners is the indispensable element that makes for a valid marriage. If freedom of consent is missing, then a true marriage never really exists.

To have true consent, the man and woman must commit to a lifelong covenant of love; be capable of sexual intercourse, which is the sign of mutual love and union; and be open to raising a family if God should bless them with children.

Because Christian marriage is a serious commitment, the couple should prepare for their future life together. Most dioceses today require engaged couples to attend marriage preparation classes to learn about the spiritual dimensions and practical aspects of married life. Also, if a Catholic is going to marry a non-Catholic Christian (known as a mixed marriage), Church authority must give permission. When a Catholic is going to marry someone who is not baptized, Church authority must give a dispensation for the marriage to be valid. In either case, the Catholic partner must promise to live his or her Catholic faith and to have the children baptized and raised in the Catholic faith. The non-Catholic partner is made aware of this pledge, but not required to make any promises. Both partners must know and not exclude the essential purposes and qualities of marriage.

The ministers of the Sacrament of Matrimony are the bride and bridegroom themselves. In the Latin Rite, the Sacrament of Matrimony usually takes place during Mass. The essential sign of the sacrament takes place after the homily when the bridal couple exchanges vows in the presence of the priest, two witnesses, and the assembled Church. They promise unconditional love—to be true in good times and bad, in sickness and in health, and to love and honor each other until death. The priest is the official witness of the Church who blesses the wedding rings, which serve as symbols of fidelity and unending love. A nuptial blessing takes place after the Lord's Prayer.

Effects of the Sacrament of Matrimony (CCC, 1638–1645; 1652–1658; 1664; 1666)

Because Christian marriage is a covenant, it is valid for life, until death separates the couple. Christ promises to be with the husband and wife each day of their marriage. He helps them stay united and true to their vows. He gives them the graces they need to live lovingly each day. He sanctifies their sexual sharing and strengthens them to be signs of love to each other, their children, and to all their friends and acquaintances. If he blesses their marriage with children, he helps them to raise and educate them in a Christian family setting.

Marriage and Friendship

Friendship is a skill that you can learn now to help you prepare for marriage. A wife and husband should be each other's best friends. Read each of these statements having to do with qualities of friendship. Then develop one of these statements into an essay on the meaning of friendship.

- I am good at sharing ideas and feelings and at listening.
- I have many interests.
- I am patient with others and with myself.
- I can forgive and ask for forgiveness.
- I am growing in self-mastery.
- Jesus plays an important role in my life.

Extending the Lesson

Individual Assignment: To lengthen the "Wedding Liturgy" assignment on page 199, ask the students to read all three selections for the three readings. Then have them choose one from each group that they would like read at their wedding. Ask them to write an essay explaining their choices.

For Enrichment

Individual Assignment: Have your students consider the differences between a civil and a sacramental marriage. Is there a fundamental difference between the two? What is it? What is the relationship between the two? Do they think that most Americans view marriage as a civil contract or as a sacramental covenant? Ask them to write a reflection on the state of marriage in the United States today with suggestions for what could be done to increase the number of people who understand marriage as a lifelong, covenant relationship.

The covenant of marriage involves a couple's total commitment that results in a deep unity of body, heart, and soul. Therefore, Christian marriage requires the virtues of faithfulness until death and openness to children. Practices like polygamy (having more than one spouse); divorce, which separates what God has joined together; and a refusal to have children are contrary to any Christian marriage.

Married love is one of God's great gifts to us, a profound way a man and a woman express their mutual affection and commitment. Therefore, sexual sharing must take place according to God's twofold plan for it. First, sexual intercourse in marriage must be *unitive* because it is a powerful sign that binds a man and woman together as lifelong partners. Second, it must be *procreative*, that is, open to a share in God's creative activity of bringing new life into the world.

God uses the married love between a couple for the procreation and education of children. Children are God's greatest gift to a married couple. They help make up a family, what is known as the *domestic Church* in which we live out our faith on a daily basis. The Christian family, supported by a loving marriage, is a prime way to holiness for all its members. Family prayer, regular celebration of the sacraments, and participation in parish programs are helpful means God gave to families to help them grow in holiness together. Like Holy Orders, the Sacrament of Matrimony is one of the Sacraments at the Service of Communion. An old saying puts it this way: "The family that prays together stays together."

The parish should always be a welcoming place both for childless couples and single people. The parish is a family for everyone, and in a special way for those who live alone.

Divorce and Annulment
(*CCC*, 1629; 1646–1651; 1665)

Jesus taught that marriage must be permanent and exclusive. He commanded, "What God has joined together, no human being must separate" (Mt 19:6). Because of Jesus' direct commandment that tells us of the permanence of marriage, the Church cannot permit divorce and remarriage. Only death can dissolve the marriage covenant of validly married Catholics.

However, in certain circumstances (like the abuse of a wife by a husband), a couple may separate for the good of the wife and children. Though the civil authority may dissolve the legal aspects of a valid marriage (called in civil law a divorce), the state has no authority to dissolve a true Catholic sacramental marriage. Legally separated Catholics (divorced under civil law) may not remarry while their spouses are alive. The Church follows this teaching because it comes from Jesus, who said, "Everyone who divorces his wife and marries another commits adultery" (Lk 16:18).

Annulment is not the same thing as a divorce. Rather, an annulment is an official declaration of the Catholic Church that what appeared to be a valid Christian marriage in fact was not. For example, one of the

annulment
An official Church declaration that what appeared to be a Christian marriage never existed in the first place.

♦ For a true sacramental marriage, a couple must be baptized, old enough, unmarried, not closely related, and giving free consent.

♦ To give free consent, a person must be free of any constraint like fear or coercion, willing to commit to a lifelong covenant of love, capable of sexual intercourse, and open to raising a family if blessed with children.

♦ Marriage preparation is required in most dioceses.

♦ Catholics who wish to marry non-Catholic Christians must seek permission. Catholics who wish to marry non-Christians must seek a dispensation. In both cases, the Catholic must promise to live his or her faith and to have any children baptized and raised in the faith.

♦ A valid, sacramental marriage cannot be dissolved by divorce, only by death.

♦ Divorce applies only to the civil arrangement.

♦ An annulment is a declaration that what appeared to be a valid sacramental marriage, in fact, was not. This can happen only when one or more of the requirements listed here are missing.

● **Class Discussion:** Use Chapter 7, Handout 4 "Who Can Marry?" (starting on page 285 and also online at www.avemariapress.com) to assess the students' understanding of the requirements of valid, sacramental marriage. Share the answers on page 201 of this TWE to each scenario after the students have had time to reflect on each and discuss.

Background Information

Supporting Christian Marriage

Love between married people is one of God's greatest gifts. The Sacrament of Matrimony helps married couples be Christ to each other and their families. It is a covenant not to be entered into without much thought and preparation.

The Pontifical Council for the Family supports this by stating,

> Preparation for marriage, for married and family life, is of great importance for the good of the Church. In fact, the Sacrament of Matrimony has great value for the whole Christian community and, in the first place, for the spouses whose decision is such that it cannot be improvised or made hastily. (Preparation for the Sacrament of Marriage, No. 1)

One of the programs the Church has implemented is the Catholic Engaged Encounter (see www.engagedencounter.org) retreat that engaged couples are encouraged to attend in preparation for their pending marriage. Catholic Engaged Encounter is an "intensive weekend of work during which each couple is offered the time and opportunity to question, examine, and deepen their relationship with each other and with God. Couples are challenged to explore their relationship in a much deeper, more honest way than they have been before. Topics covered during the weekend include self-awareness, human sexuality, communications, decision making, Natural Family Planning, vocation, sacrament, unity and more." The program is designed to meet the needs of engaged couples, including:

● *Communication Needs*: Engaged Encounter introduces couples to a communication technique they can use effectively to foster a deeper knowledge of each other.

● *Spiritual Needs*: Each couple comes to realize that marriage is a sacrament and a vocation, and that God and prayer are essential to a fruitful marriage.

● *Personal Needs*: Each person is challenged to review the decision-making process and to examine the motives for seeking marriage.

For couples who are already married, there is Marriage Encounter (see www.wwme.org), a similar program designed to "give married couples the opportunity to learn a technique of loving communication that they can use for the rest of their lives. It's a chance to look deeply into their relationship with each other and with God. It's a time to share their feelings, hopes and dreams with each other. The emphasis of the Marriage Encounter weekend is on the communication between husbands and wives. The weekend provides a conducive environment for couples to spend time together, away from the distractions and tensions of everyday life, while encouraging them to focus on each other and their relationship."

- **Class Discussion:** Review the text subsection "Effects of the Sacrament of Matrimony" (pages 200–201). Ask them to think about how their family is a *domestic Church*. There is an opportunity for you to do some faith sharing with your students as you talk about how your family expressed its faith when you were growing up, and, if you are married, how you do so now.
  - Ask the students to list specifically religious activities that they do with their family on a regular basis. Stress that every family is unique: there is no one, right way to be a Catholic (or religious) family. One family might attend Mass together every weekend; another might attend Mass at different times because family members are involved in different activities at Church and in the community. Some families have special traditions for different holidays; other families give family members special blessings on birthdays.
  - After your students have listed the specifically religious things they do, ask them to list other activities the family does, or that individual family members do, that help the community in some way. Are these activities motivated in part by the family's faith? Do parents encourage these activities even when they are sometimes inconvenient? How does your family open itself up to other people?
- **Direct Instruction:** Highlight the dual purpose of the Sacrament of Matrimony and its expression in sexual intimacy. It must be *unitive* (a sign that binds the two together) and *procreative* (open to new life). Note that parents must also commit to educating their children within the domestic Church.
- **Individual Assignment:** Conclude by having the students do one of the following:
  - Write a letter to your parents thanking them for the effort they put into their marriage and family and for the ways that benefits you.
  - Develop a plan for helping your family bring Christ to others more than you already do. Discuss your plan with your parents.
  - Research ways that your parish or diocese supports marriages and families. Find out about Marriage Preparation programs that get marriages off to a good start, marriage counseling services that are offered, Marriage Encounter or Retrouvaille weekend experiences for married couples, etc. (See www.wwme.org and www.retrouvaille.org.)
- **Direct Instruction:** Make sure the students understand the distinction between annulment and divorce and also the ways all people can still seek participation in the life of the Church. Annulment is not divorce, rather a recognition that what appeared to be a sacramental marriage was not so.

Rules for A Successful Marriage

Compose a list of ten rules for preparing for a happy marriage (e.g., "practice patience," "learn to listen," "learn self-control"). Show your list to a recently married couple and to a long-time married couple. Write the reactions of all parties to your list, noting how effective they believe your rules to be.

partners might not have given free, true consent to the marriage. Or perhaps one of the partners never intended to have children. Both of these conditions must be present for there to be a true sacramental marriage. In cases like these, the diocesan marriage tribunal (court) might declare that the marriage was not a valid sacramental union from the beginning. If this is the case, then the individuals involved would be free to enter a true Catholic marriage in the future.

Entering a marriage is serious business because it involves love, and love is always serious. It also involves a willingness to stick by one's partner through good times and bad. Like a good mother, the Church wants to make sure that engaged couples prepare adequately for this sacrament. But the Church also announces the Good News that it is never two that get married—it is always three. In a Christian marriage, Jesus is always there to befriend the couple. He promised his Spirit and the graces and strength to endure the tough times and to rejoice in the good ones.

Christian marriage reminds us that we are each the flesh-and-blood Sacrament of our parents' love. In addition, our Baptism makes us each a special sign of God's grace.

We are all symbols of the Lord's presence in the world. He uses us to bring others to him.

PROFILE OF FAITH: *YOUR* CALL TO HOLINESS

In previous chapters, you have read about holy people who have witnessed to their Catholic faith. Our Christian vocation also calls *you* to be a saint. Recall that a saint is one who has a mind through which Christ thinks, a voice through which Christ speaks, a heart through which Christ loves, and a hand through which Christ helps.

Each of the sacraments teaches us certain values that we can share with others. Consider the powerful witness *you* can give by living the sacraments, signs of God's love. Meditate on the questions that follow. Then write a short self-portrait on how well you are living Christ's invitation to *you* to be a saint.

Baptism initiates us into the Christian family.

- What does it mean for you to be a brother or sister of Christ?

Confirmation strengthens the gifts of the Holy Spirit, enabling us to live the Christian life.

- Name your greatest God-given talent or gift. How are you using it for others?

Eucharist gives us the living Lord under the forms of consecrated bread and wine.

- What effect has celebrating the Eucharist and receiving Holy Communion had on your life? Be specific.

Extending the Lesson

Individual Assignment: Many people consider the institution of marriage to be under attack in today's society. In many parts of the country there are battles going on over who should be allowed to marry under civil law, or whether gays and lesbians should be granted rights similar to those of married couples through "civil unions." Having your students research current law and pending legislation in your state is a good way to introduce these topics. Be sure they also research the response of the bishops in your state to the legislation being proposed.

Penance extends Christ's forgiving touch into today's world.

- How do you work to mend fences with your enemies? Think about a time when you were most impacted by being forgiven or by forgiving another.

Anointing of the Sick provides spiritual strength and healing for the suffering and sick.

- What type of suffering is ongoing with a family member or friend? What can you do to help lessen the anxiety of the situation?

Holy Orders ordains special ministers to serve as mediators between God and us.

- Do you pray for our bishops, priests, deacons, and others in religious life? How can you consider one of these vocations for yourself?

Matrimony binds a couple in Christ to live as a community of life and love.

- Which friendship skills are important in a marriage? How can you improve on those skills now?

For Review

1. What does the Old Testament teach about marriage?
2. What does Jesus teach about marriage?
3. What is necessary for true consent for a Catholic marriage?
4. Who are the ministers of the Sacrament of Matrimony?
5. Names some of the effects of the Sacrament of Matrimony.
6. What is the difference between an annulment and divorce?

For Reflection

In your opinion, what ingredients would go into making an ideal spouse? Which of these ingredients do you possess?

Homework Assignment

1. Write the essay described in the feature "Marriage and Friendship" (page 200).

2. Complete the Ongoing Assignments, page 206.

3. Complete the For Review questions on page 203.

For Review Answers (page 203)

1. The Old Testament, particularly the book of Genesis, teaches that God made both men and women in the divine image to be companions to each other, and that marriage was "very good." It teaches that spouses should be faithful to one another and show affection that is good, holy, and joyful.

2. Jesus supports marriage and proclaims his Father's intention that marriage should be a permanent, exclusive love relationship. Divorce, therefore, is not permissible.

3. In order to give the free consent that is necessary for true marriage, the couple must not be acting under any constraint (such as force or fear), they must intend to commit to a lifelong covenant of love, they must be capable of sexual intercourse, and they must be open to raising a family together if God should bless them with children.

4. The ministers of the Sacrament of Matrimony are the bride and bridegroom themselves. The priest or deacon merely serves as the Church's official witness.

5. The effects of the Sacrament of Matrimony include Christ's promise to stay with the couple throughout the years of their marriage; the gift of his help to keep them true to their vows; and the graces they need to live lovingly each day and to be signs of love to each other, their children, and all their friends and acquaintances.

6. An annulment is the Church's official declaration that what appeared to be a valid Christian marriage, in fact, was not because one of the partners failed to give true, free consent to the marriage or never intended to have children. A divorce is a civil act dissolving the legal ties joining a civilly married couple. It does not have the authority to dissolve a true sacramental marriage.

Chapter 7 Review Lesson

Objectives

In this lesson, the students will:
- discuss friendship skills that could be translated to a long-term marriage partnership.
- review the Chapter 7 material.
- write a letter to God as a prayer experience.

 Preview

This session provides the opportunity for many types of review of the material in Chapter 7 as well as a brief prayer experience. Also, if there is time, begin to check the Ongoing Assignments from page 206, especially any students who need to do oral presentations before the class.

Bell Ringers

- **Class Discussion:** Discuss the meaning of friendship as introduced in the exercise "Marriage and Friendship" on page 200. Call on several students to read or summarize their essays. Then ask the entire class to contribute to a list of ways that their current skills in making and keeping friends could translate to finding a spouse and making a successful marriage.
- **Direct Instruction:** Use the opportunity at the beginning of this session to collect and discuss any For Enrichment assignments the students have worked on as part of this chapter.

Teaching Approaches

- **Direct Instruction:** Review the Chapter 7 material by having the students read the chapter outline on page 183 and discuss what they remember.
- **Class Activity:** Continue to use the memory cards (Chapter 1, Handout 3, starting on page 285 and also online at www.avemariapress.com; discussed on page 34 of this TWE) to review vocabulary words with the students. Add the words from this chapter to each deck as before. In your review games, use all of this chapter's words and as many from the preceding chapters as you think the students need to review.
- **Individual Assignment:** Pass out Chapter 7, Handout 5 "Word Search Puzzler" (starting on page 285 and also online at www.avemariapress.com) to use for further, individual review. Answers are on page 206 of this text.
- **Class Activity:** The Chapter Quick View is provided to help your students review the chapter material. Divide your class into four groups. Give each group a large piece of butcher paper and a marking pen. Allow a representative from each group to choose a slip of paper containing the name of one of the four sacraments covered in this chapter from a box.

CHAPTER QUICK VIEW

- The Sacrament of Penance is a Sacrament of Conversion that enables sinners to begin anew as the Lord extends his forgiving mercy and grace. (page 187)
- The term *penance* emphasizes that we must make satisfaction for the sins we have committed. This is an external sign of our internal conversion. (page 188)
- Sin offends God's honor and love, causes a break in our union with God, disfigures the sinner, and ruptures our relationship with members of Christ's Body. This is why we need the Sacrament of Forgiveness. (page 188)
- Through the formula of absolution, a bishop or priest proclaims God's forgiveness of sinners. (page 189)
- Penance is also known as the Sacrament of Reconciliation because it unites us once again with God and his Church; brings peace and spiritual comfort; strengthens us for the Christian life; takes away some temporal punishment due to sin; remits eternal punishment resulting from mortal sin; and teaches us how to repent, do penance, and trust a loving and merciful God. (page 188)
- The acts of the penitent in the Sacrament of Penance include contrition (genuine sorrow for sins and firm resolve not to sin again), confession of sins, and doing satisfaction or penance in reparation of sin. (pages 188–189)
- God's action in the Sacrament of Penance works through the bishop or priest to forgive sin in Jesus' name. (page 189)
- The Sacrament of the Anointing of the Sick brings Christ's healing touch to those suffering from serious illness, the elderly, and for dying people. (page 191)
- Only a priest or bishop may administer the Sacrament of the Anointing of the Sick. (page 192)
- The Sacrament of the Anointing of the Sick's essential features are the laying of hands on the sick person, a prayer recited in the faith of the Church, and a sacramental anointing of the forehead and hands (in the Roman Rite). (page 192)
- The Sacrament of the Anointing of the Sick forgives sin if the person has not obtained it through the Sacrament of Penance; brings spiritual healing and physical healing, if this will help the person before God; unites the person more closely to Christ's redemptive Passion; and gives dying persons the strength to endure to the end before meeting our loving God. (page 193)
- Although all baptized Christians share in Christ's priestly ministry, our Lord desired an ordained ministry comprised of a hierarchy of bishops, priests, and deacons to unfold the graces of Baptism to all Christians. This ordained ministry continues the special ministry he entrusted to the Apostles. (page 194)
- The "sacred power" that ordained men exercise on behalf of Christ and his Church involves proclaiming and teaching God's Word, leading the Church in worship, and guiding and ruling God's people. (page 194)
- Bishops receive the fullness of the Sacrament of Holy Orders, making them successors to the Apostles. They are spiritual fathers of the local Church. Along with the College of Bishops, and in union with the Pope, they are responsible for the welfare of the whole Church. (page 195)
- Priests are the bishops' helpers, his extension into the diocese. They are members of the sacerdotal college around the bishop. They preside at the Eucharist, preach and teach God's Word, and actively build up the Christian community. (page 195)
- Deacons serve bishops and priests. Although they cannot preside at the Eucharist or serve as confessors, they still have a variety of ministries. These include baptizing, distributing Holy Communion, teaching, doing works of charity, and so forth. (page 195)
- Holy Orders confers an indelible spiritual character that configures those ordained to Christ. The Church has the authority from Christ to ordain men only. (pages 196–197)

 Homework Assignment

1. Complete the Ongoing Assignment if not previously done.
2. Study for the Chapter 7 Test.

Chapter 7, Handout 5 "Word Search Puzzler" Answers

1. free
2. bishop
3. absolution
4. viaticum
5. icons
6. Holy Orders
7. sin
8. presbyters
9. annulment
10. reconciliation
11. celibacy
12. Matrimony
13. deacons
14. contrition
15. Penance
16. *unction*
17. confession
18. polygamy
19. anoint
20. sacraments
21. divorce

Extra Term: The Anointing of the Sick: The sacrament of healing, administered by a priest to a baptized person, in which the Lord extends his loving, healing touch through the Church to those who are seriously ill or dying.

- The essential sign in the rite of ordination for all three orders is the bishop's laying his hands on the head of the person ordained followed by a prayer of consecration to the Holy Spirit. (page 197)
- Following the call and example of Jesus himself, priests in the Latin Rite follow a rule of celibacy. This means that they forego marriage for the sake of serving God and his people wholeheartedly. (pages 197–198)
- The Sacrament of Matrimony is a covenant in which a baptized man and woman vow their love in an exclusive, permanent, sexual partnership that is open to the procreation of children. (page 198)
- Creating us male and female in his divine image, God established our sexual nature and is the source of marriage. From the beginning, God intended men and women to marry, to treat each other with respect and love, and to procreate in a permanent, exclusive, and monogamous relationship. (page 199)
- Jesus condemned divorce and lust, teaching that men must treat women as equals. (page 199)
- The exchange of consent between the marriage partners is the indispensable element that makes for a valid marriage. The ministers of the sacrament are the couple themselves who exchange their vows before a priest and two other witnesses. (page 200)
- Effects of a Christian marriage include the help the Lord gives the couple to be true to each other and the graces to live lovingly toward each other and to their children and friends. If he blesses them with children, he sends his graces to help raise and educate them in a Christian family, which is known as the *domestic Church*. (pages 200–201)
- Sexual sharing in marriage has two outcomes: the *unitive*, which is the sharing of love and affection, and the *procreative*, openness to helping God bring new life into the world. Children are God's greatest gift to a married couple. (page 201)
- Because Jesus taught that marriage is permanent and exclusive, he forbade divorce. Only death can dissolve the marriage of validly married Catholics. The Church may annul a marriage, however, by declaring that what appeared to be a valid Christian marriage was not. This is the case when an essential element (like consent) was missing from the beginning. (pages 201–202)

Learning the Language of Faith

Complete each sentence by choosing the correct answer from the list of terms below. You will not use all the terms.

absolution	contrition	hierarchy	polytheism
Anointing of the Sick	covenant	Holy Orders	religion
canon law	diaconate	immanence	rite
catechumen	epiclesis	Matrimony	Sacrament of Penance
celibacy	evangelization	monogamy	transubstantiation
charism	evangelical counsels	polygamy	viaticum

1. Members of religious orders take the vow of ___ to dedicate their lives totally to Jesus Christ and God's People.
2. The ___ is the third degree in the hierarchy of Holy Orders.
3. The prayer of ___ pardons repentant sinners in the Sacrament of Penance.
4. ___ conveys a sacramental character.
5. Forgiveness of sin is an effect of both the Sacrament of Penance and ___.
6. Holy Communion received by dying persons is known as ___.
7. ___ is the most important act of penitents in the Sacrament of Penance.
8. Having more than one wife at the same time is known as ___.
9. All Catholics must engage in ___, that is, bringing the Good News of Jesus Christ to all people.
10. The prayer that is said in every sacrament that asks for the sanctifying power of the Holy Spirit is known as the ___.

- ◆ Each group should list on their paper as many facts about the sacrament as they can in fifteen minutes. When the time is up, have each group read their list to the whole class. Correct any mistaken information. Give two points for every correct fact that can be found in the Chapter Quick View at the end of the chapter. Give five points for every correct fact that is not in the Chapter Quick View. Deduct two points for every false or incorrect statement.

- ◆ The group with the most points is the winner. Provide some small prize or privilege to the winning team.

- **Individual Assignment:** Have the students complete the Learning the Language of Faith sentences on page 205. Check their answers as a class.

- **Student Presentations:** Collect any of the Ongoing Assignments from page 206. If the students have oral presentations to give in connection with these assignments, reserve some time in this period for them to share.

- **Prayer Experience:** Read the introduction to the Prayer Reflection on page 206. Give students the opportunity to write their letters in class or invite them to take the time after the test to do so.

Learning the Language of Faith

Answers (page 205)

1. celibacy
2. diaconate
3. absolution
4. Holy Orders
5. Anointing of the Sick
6. viaticum
7. contrition
8. polygamy
9. evangelization
10. epiclesis

Chapter 7 Test Lesson

Objectives

In this lesson, the students will:

- take a test on the material in Chapter 7.
- preview the material in Chapter 8.

 Preview

Allow a brief time at the beginning of the session to collect all completed assignments from Chapter 7. Then reserve most of the class period (at least forty minutes) for the students to take the Chapter 7 Test.

Teaching Approaches

- **Chapter Test:** Pass out the Chapter 7 Test (starting on page 285 and also online at www.avemariapress .com) to each student. Allow time for the students to complete the test. Collect the finished tests. Have the students preview the section for Part 3: We Love: Our Life in Christ (page 208) if they complete the test early.
- **Student Presentations:** Collect any assignments missing from Chapter 7. If the students need to orally present any assignments, reserve a brief time at the end of the testing period for them to do so.

Ongoing Assignments

As you cover the material in this chapter, choose and complete at least three of these assignments.

1. Compose an examination of conscience made up of questions dealing with the love of God, love of neighbor, and love of self. If possible, illustrate each category with an appropriate picture or symbol.
2. Report on the activities of any program your parish conducts as part of its ministry to the sick. Offer your services.
3. Write a letter of appreciation to a favorite priest who has inspired you to be a better person.
4. Contrast the wedding and marriage customs of a non-Christian religion to that of a typical Catholic wedding and marriage.
5. Interview your parents, grandparents, or another married couple you are close to, asking why they decided to get married and how they planned their life together.
6. Research and report on a religious community of men or women whose mission is to comfort the sick, elderly, or dying.
7. Ask a man or woman living in a religious community to tell you the story of his or her vocation. Summarize the story and write it in a report.
8. Do an Internet search on Blessed Louis and Blessed Zelie Martin, the parents of St. Thérèse of Lisieux. Report on their lives.
9. Interview a nurse, doctor, physical therapist, or some other healing professional. Ask what he or she thinks about the role of the Spirit in healing the body. Report on the results of your interview.
10. Using the traditional Act of Contrition found in the Catholic Handbook of Faith at the end of this text (page 306) as a model, compose your own Act of Contrition.

Prayer Reflection

A helpful way to pray is to write a letter to God. Sometimes the very act of writing can help you come up with thoughts you never knew you had. Writing letters to God forces us to clarify our deepest thoughts, ideas, and religious sentiments.

The procedure is easy. Choose a favorite title for God to use for your greeting. Then simply write what is on your mind and in your heart. There is no need to write lengthy missives. Short letters will do fine. Believe that the Lord really does care for you. He wants to hear about your hurts, how your day or week went, your triumphs, your angers, and your joys.

You may also try to imagine how the Lord would respond to a particular letter you wrote. First, pray to the Holy Spirit for guidance in answering one of your letters. Then try to respond to one of your letters *from Jesus' viewpoint.* What would he say in response to your letter?

Save your letters in a journal for future reference. They record your relationship with God and how the Lord might be working in your life. Be sure to review them from time to time.

- *Reflection:* What were the high points and low points of this past week? Share them in a letter to the Lord.
- *Resolution:* Write God a short letter every day for the coming two weeks. Write a response to two of your letters from the Lord's perspective.

 Homework Assignment

1. Read the opening text for Part 3: We Love: Our Life in Christ (page 208).
2. Preview Chapter 8.
3. Read the opening section of Chapter 8, "Modeling Christ" (page 212).

Chapter 7 Test Answers

All questions are worth 4 points each.

Part 1: Multiple Choice

1. A

2. C

3. D

4. D

5. D

6. B

7. B

8. D

Part 2: Matching

9. E

10. C

11. A

12. F

13. D

14. G

15. B

Part 3: True or False

16. F

17. F

18. F

19. T

20. F

21. F

22. T

23. T

Part 4: Short Fill-ins

24. physical healing (if this will help the person before God)

25. viaticum

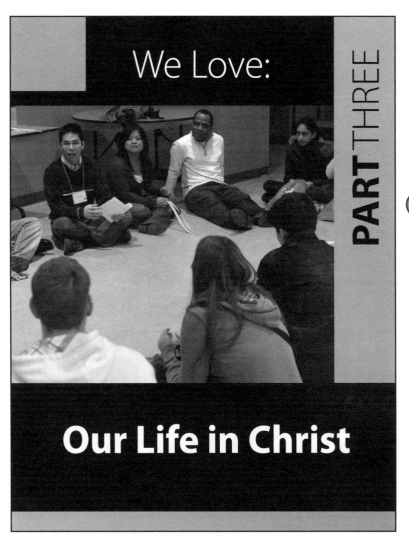

We Love:

Our Life in Christ

Part III: We Love: **Our Life in Christ**

Objectives

In this lesson, students will:
- recognize that the heart of Christian morality is love.
- describe their current perceptions of Christian morality.

 Preview

Part III introduces the basics of Catholic morality, rooted in taking up Christ's call to love God, others, and ourselves. Chapter 8 introduces the roles that personal conscience and the development of a formed conscience play in making moral decisions. The Christian virtues, moral law, and precepts of the Church are also discussed as helps in being a moral person. God's grace is also a primary help in avoiding sin. Chapter 9 focuses on the Ten Commandments as a basis for Christian law. The Beatitudes are a formula to help Christians love God and neighbor in a Christlike way. The brief introduction to this section of the text states that "Our Life in Christ" is based on moral living that flows from acting responsibly according to our dignity. The heart of Catholic morality is love.

Background Information

Putting Faith into Practice

Jesus always did what was pleasing to God. As Christians, this, too, is our task, to make choices that can lead us to be "perfect just as your heavenly Father is perfect" (Mt 5:8). The freedom to choose between good and evil, right and wrong, or life and death is what makes humans moral. Morality involves putting our religion into practice. The most essential factor in making good decisions is to follow Christ and to put Christ first in all moral choices. St. Francis de Sales put it this way: "One of the most excellent intentions that we can possibly have in all our actions is to do them because our Lord did them."

Bell Ringers

- **Group Activity:** Have the students work with a partner or in a small group to create several slogans similar to those on page 208 that encourage people to both follow Christ and to live a good and moral life. When they have completed the assignment, share and record some of the slogans on the board.
- **Individual Activity:** Have the students choose some of their favorite slogans and make posters with them printed on them and displayed around the room.

Teaching Approaches

- **Class Discussion:** Read or summarize the Part III opener on page 208. Read Jesus' words in the great commandment, the heart of Christian morality from Matthew 22:37–39. Ask the students to comment on what they specifically think Jesus meant by the command to:
    - love God?
    - love neighbor?
    - love self?
- **Individual Assignment:** Have students list what they consider to be the top five most important teachings about Christian morality.
- **Class Discussion:** Discuss their answers. Ask the students to explain how their choices relate to the command to love God, neighbor, and one's self. Then, create a list of the top five teachings as a class. Be sure to reference this list as the details of Catholic morality are unclosed.

Living in Love

If you ever take a look at marquees outside of many different churches, you might discover some of the following words of wisdom:

"No God—No Peace. Know God—Know Peace."

"Fight Truth Decay—Study the Bible Daily."

"If You're Headed in the Wrong Direction, God Allows U-turns."

"In the Dark? Follow the Son."

"If You Can't Sleep, Don't Count Sheep. Talk to the Shepherd."

In one way or another, all of these signs are trying to tell us how to live a happier life. For Christians, the essential element is to be a friend of our Lord and Savior Jesus Christ and to follow his path.

This section explores what it means to live our lives as Catholics. "Our life in Christ" means that we must live moral lives by acting responsibly according to our dignity. If we do, we will be happier in this life and be rewarded with eternal joy in Heaven.

The heart of Christian morality is love. This is what Jesus commanded when he taught:

You shall love the Lord, your God, with all your heart, with all your soul, and with all your mind. This is the greatest and the first commandment. The second is like it: You shall love your neighbor as yourself. (Mt 22:37–39)

To be Catholic means that we must respond to God's own gift of love and Salvation in Christ Jesus. The Holy Spirit gives us the graces necessary to follow God's will, to live in conformity to his plan for us. The Spirit gives us the ability to choose Jesus and to love as he commands us to do. And he empowers us with virtues that help us be the persons we are meant to be. Chapter 8 will build on these topics and discuss other basic elements of Catholic morality. Chapter 9 will study the Beatitudes and the Ten Commandments, each of which provide guidance on how to live a life in Christ.

For Reflection

Share another piece of wisdom you have gleaned from a church marquee.

Homework Assignment

Read the opening text section of Chapter 8, "Modeling Christ" (page 212).

8 The Basics of **Catholic Morality**

Overview of the Chapter

A group of high school students tried an experiment. They put a frog in a kettle of water and began to heat the water slowly. Gradually the water reached the boiling point, yet the frog never tried to jump out. Why? Because the change in temperature was so slow that the frog did not notice until it was too late.

Christians living in contemporary society must be careful not to become like the frog. Our society, fueled by an amoral and immoral media, has adopted a moral relativism that lulls people into accepting what is—in God's eyes—unacceptable. We can be dying spiritually without even noticing it. To inoculate ourselves against a secular society, we need to live a "life in Christ." This life finds its strength in the Holy Spirit and in the truth of the ethical wisdom of our Catholic tradition and in the Beatitudes and the Ten Commandments.

After an introductory section explaining each of the cardinal virtues, Chapter 8 reveals the foundation of Christian morality to be love. We are children of God and friends of the Lord, creatures made in God's image who are endowed with great dignity, intelligence, freedom, and the ability to love. We are capable of acting responsibly. However, because of the effects of Original Sin, we are prone to error and sin when making moral decisions.

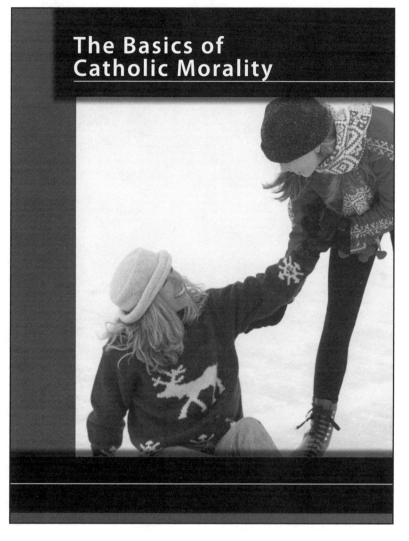

The Basics of Catholic Morality

The next section of the chapter discusses the implications of humans as social beings. What follows from this are issues that relate to the Church's social justice doctrine, for example, principles like subsidiarity, themes like the common good, virtues like solidarity, and injunctions like treating others with respect and developing one's talents for the benefit of others.

A key part of Christian morality is conscience, what the *Catechism of the Catholic Church* defines as "a judgment of reason whereby the human person recognizes the moral quality of a concrete act that he is going to perform, is in the process of performing, or has already completed" (1778). What follows is a discussion of two principles dealing with conscience: properly forming one's conscience and then following its dictates.

Proper formation of conscience involves using one's intellect, being guided by Jesus and his example, obeying magisterial teaching, and using the gifts and graces of the Holy Spirit. Part of using one's intellect is to properly identify the sources of morality—the moral object, the intention, and the circumstances—and to be guided by certain truths concerning right and wrong behavior. For example, some actions are always objectively wrong. A good intention can never make an intrinsically evil action into a just one. Circumstances can lessen culpability but can never make a bad action right. You may wish to use a number of cases in addition to the ones in the text to have students apply these bedrock moral principles, including others discussed in the text like the Golden Rule. Although the role of ignorance and emotion is treated in this section, it is also clearly stated that we sin if we violate the dictates of our conscience.

The chapter's overview of Catholic morality concludes with a discussion of the role of virtues in helping to live a moral life; the moral law and its expressions (natural law, the Old Law, the New Law, civil law, and the precepts of the Church); a discussion of sin, justification, and grace (actual grace, sacramental grace, charisms, and graces of state); and merit and the universal call to holiness.

We have an awesome vocation as religious educators to invite teenagers to live as Jesus wants us to live. This is a challenging task in the face of our culture's subjectivity, the influence of our media, and a consumer society that praises hedonism. But we have faith that our Lord who calls us to teach his word will give us the Holy Spirit to guide, inspire, and strengthen us in our work. In fact, it is the gift of the Spirit that makes teaching this material rewarding and often enjoyable.

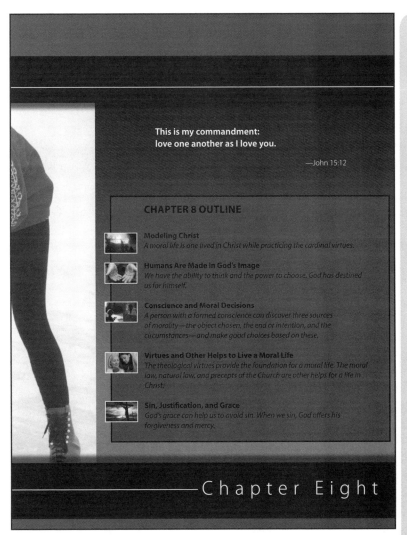

This is my commandment:
love one another as I love you.

—John 15:12

CHAPTER 8 OUTLINE

Modeling Christ
A moral life is one lived in Christ while practicing the cardinal virtues.

Humans Are Made in God's Image
We have the ability to think and the power to choose. God has destined us for himself.

Conscience and Moral Decisions
A person with a formed conscience can discover three sources of morality—the object chosen, the end or intention, and the circumstances—and make good choices based on these.

Virtues and Other Helps to Live a Moral Life
The theological virtues provide the foundation for a moral life. The moral law, natural law, and precepts of the Church are other helps for a life in Christ.

Sin, Justification, and Grace
God's grace can help us to avoid sin. When we sin, God offers his forgiveness and mercy.

Chapter Eight

Chapter Outline
- Modeling Christ
- Humans Are Made in God's Image
- Conscience and Moral Decisions
- Virtues and Other Helps to Live a Moral Life
- Sin, Justification, and Grace

Advance Preparations
Preview the For Enrichment assignments in the TWE and the Ongoing Assignments on page 230 of the Student Text. Determine which assignments you might wish to assign the students to work on for this chapter. Page numbers below refer to student text.

Modeling Christ (ST page 212)
- Newspapers and news and popular culture magazines for the Class Activity on page 216.

Humans Are Made in God's Image (ST pages 212–217)
- A clip of a biography of the life of Martin Luther King Jr., such as *I Have a Dream* or the Arts and Entertainment video *Biography: Martin Luther King Jr* for the Video Presentation on page 219.

Conscience and Moral Decisions (ST pages 218–221)
- A clip of the movie *School Ties* for Video Presentation on page 223.

Virtues and Other Helps to Live a Moral Life (ST pages 222–226)
- A device that is unfamiliar to students, such as an odd cooking utensil or home improvement tool, for the Class Activity on page 227.
- Clips of the movie *Godspell* for the Video Presentation on page 227.

Chapter 8 Test Lesson
- Copies of the Chapter 8 Test (starting on page 285 and also online at www.avemariapress.com).

Resources

Internet Links see www.avemariapress.com

Resources

Audiovisual Materials

Catholic & Capable: How to Live a Moral Life
   Teens share their thoughts on truth telling, dating, handling anger, experiences of faith, and more (video, RCL).

Doing the Right Thing: Moral Stories for Young Teens
   Live dramas that help young teens make moral decisions (75-minute DVD, Twenty-Third Publications).

Missing Pieces
   This Hallmark, made-for-TV movie stars James Coburn as Atticus, a father who searches for his son in Mexico. Based on Ron Hansen's novel, *Atticus*, this is an outstanding modernization of the parable of the Prodigal Son. Highly recommended (2000, 105 min., Amazon.com, Critics' Choice).

Moving On: Responding in the Spirit
   Depicts how a family must put their faith into action when they move into a new neighborhood by demonstrating Christian love to those nearby (20-minute video, St. Anthony Messenger Press).

Promise
   An Ikonographics film that stresses the importance of commitment and promises (20-minute video, St. Anthony Messenger Press).

Stop, Look, and Listen: Christian Conscience at Work
   In this Ikonographics film, Fr. Richard Sparks, C.S.P., "inspires young people to believe that morality can make sense in their lives" (18-minute video, St. Anthony Messenger Press).

continued on page 234

Modeling Christ (page 212)

Objectives

In this lesson, the students will:

- name the three building blocks of Catholic morality.
- define the concept of virtue and name human reason, personal effort, and God's grace as the means by which people attain virtues.
- list and define the cardinal virtues.
- apply the cardinal virtues to real-life situations.

Preview

This brief introduction provides a foundation for the chapter. Students should come away from this introduction reminded that Catholic conscience formation is done with respect to individual freedom but within the larger context of modeling our lives on the example of Jesus.

Bell Ringers

- **Class Discussion:** Read John 15:13 as a class. Refer to the opening story of Chapter 8. Ask the students to share how the person in the story lived out this teaching of Jesus and how he emulated Christ himself.
- **Direct Instruction:** Make a poster, or have a skilled student make a poster, illustrating the three building blocks of Catholic morality from page 212:
  - Be who you are
  - Form and follow your conscience
  - Respond to God by using his helps

  Use the poster as a reference point throughout the unit.

 Teaching Approaches

- **Journal Assignment:** Draw a number line on the board, extending from negative 10 to positive 10. Ask students to duplicate the continuum in their journals. Tell them the scale represents their closeness to God, with positive 10 being a deep and close relationship. Tell them to put an "X" where they feel right now. Then have them put a "+" where they believe they are on most days. Have them put an * on what they would guess to be the minimal degree of closeness God would accept.
- **Class Activity:** Distribute newspapers and news and popular culture magazines. Have the students work in groups to collect as many articles as they can find that illustrate moral dilemmas. Use the clippings as a foundation for illustrating the points throughout the chapter. Collect the clippings before proceeding.
- **Direct Instruction:** Review the four cardinal virtues in the feature "Practicing the Cardinal Virtues." Note that these virtues are called *cardinal* because all other virtues "hinge" on them; in other words all

Modeling Christ

One night in a country town, a small cottage caught on fire. Immediately its thatched roof went up in flames. Being in a remote area of the country far from the city, there was no fire department or a fire engine to help put out the blaze.

As the villagers stood by helplessly, a young man leapt through the flames and ran into the house. Moments later he came stumbling out with a small child under each arm. Fortunately, they emerged unharmed, but he suffered severe burns for his courageous efforts.

The mother and father of the young children perished in the fire. The villagers felt sorry for the orphaned children, and several of them wanted to adopt them.

The judge who came to the village to decide whom to appoint as the adoptive parents had to decide between two people who had approached the court. The first was the mayor of the village, a man of wealth and influence in the town and owner of a nice house in which to raise the children. The second petitioner was the man who had pulled the children from the flames.

When the judge asked the second man what right he had to raise the children, the brave rescuer did not use words. Rather he held up his badly burned and scarred hands and let them do the talking for him.[16]

The man's gesture, a symbol of his heroic deed, made a strong argument that he was a most worthy candidate to be the guardian of the children. His sacrifice demonstrated for all to see the love and consideration he had for the welfare of others. He was willing to risk his life for them.

This chapter examines the foundations of Catholic morality, all of which teach us how to befriend the Lord Jesus. These building blocks of Catholic morality are built on these three rules:

1. Be who you are.
2. Form and follow your conscience. (Use your head to apply the principles.)
3. Respond to God's call to holiness by using the helps he gives us to live virtuous lives, to avoid sin, and to do good.

Humans Are Made in God's Image (CCC, 1701–1715; 1730–1748; 1762–1775)

Genesis reveals that human beings are fundamentally good because God created us in his image and likeness, conforming us to Jesus Christ who is "the image of the invisible God" (Col 1:15). Therefore, we have a spiritual

Homework Assignment

1. Complete the "Practicing the Cardinal Virtues" exercise as described on page 213, writing how to seek personal improvement in each of the virtues.

2. Read the text section "Humans Are Made in God's Image" (pages 212–217).

Extending the Lesson

Class Activity: Do a simulation on distribution of world resources today. Add some real incentive in the form of treats attached to "points." Have students play out the simulation. Then redo the simulation, assigning a chair in the circle to Jesus. Evaluate with students whether Jesus' real presence in the room would shape the conversation.

and immortal soul. Our souls give us two great gifts: the ability to think (an intellect) and the power to choose and to love (free will). We are one-of-a-kind creatures because God made us for himself and destined us for eternal happiness (or "beatitude"). Because we are made in God's image, several other truths apply:

We have dignity and worth. Each human being, from the very first moment of conception, has tremendous dignity and value that do not have to be earned.

We can think. Because we are rational, we can recognize God's voice in our conscience, understand what is loving or not loving, and distinguish between good and evil.

We have freedom. Being made in God's image also gives us true freedom, that is, "the power, rooted in reason and will, to act or not to act, to do this or that, so to perform deliberate actions on one's own responsibility" (*CCC*, 1731). Free will helps us desire what is good and then choose it. When we choose to do good for other people, then we are loving. When we choose evil by refusing to

keep God's law, we commit sin. We abuse our freedom and become slaves to sin.

We are responsible. Freedom to choose between good and evil characterizes human acts. We are responsible (that is, blameworthy) for our actions if they are voluntary, that is, if we directly will them, for example, when we freely spread gossip about someone. We are also responsible for indirectly voluntary actions. An example would be a driver speeding in a school zone and causing an accident. She did not directly intend to hit a pedestrian, but she should have followed the law by slowing down in a school zone.

Blameworthiness for our actions can be lessened or destroyed by factors like ignorance that is not our fault, inattention, fear, force, habit, and passions. Passions are emotions that move us to act or not to act in relation to something we feel or imagine to be either good or evil. The most basic passion is love, which attracts us to the good. Other passions include hate, joy, sadness, desire, fear, and anger. Passions are morally neutral. Morality comes into play when our wills

cardinal virtues
The "hinge" virtues from which all other virtues come. They are prudence, justice, fortitude, and temperance.

passions
Our emotional response to the good or evil we encounter.

Practicing the Cardinal Virtues

One of the great helps the Holy Spirit has given us to live a life in Christ is the four **cardinal virtues**. *Cardinal* in Latin means "hinge." Other virtues—good habits that enable us to choose the good—hinge on these cardinal virtues: prudence, justice, fortitude, and temperance. Human reason and personal effort help us acquire these virtues; God's grace assists us in developing them.

Listed below is a brief description of each cardinal virtue. Analyze how well you are putting each virtue into practice. Write a short analysis on how you can improve in following the virtues.

- *Prudence*, according to St. Thomas Aquinas, is "right reason in action." It is spiritual common sense that tells us how we should act.
- *Justice* is respecting the rights of God and other people. It is treating others with fairness.
- *Fortitude* is the spiritual strength to do right, even when tempted or afraid.
- *Temperance* helps control our appetites, especially in the areas of food, drink, sex, and possessions.

Background Information

A Moral Life Is One Lived in Christ while Practicing the Cardinal Virtues

Modeling Christ by living a moral life can be a challenge. To help us along our journey, the Holy Spirit has given us the four cardinal virtues, upon which all other virtues hinge: prudence, justice, fortitude, and temperance.

In an article titled "Justice, Fortitude, Temperance" that appeared in the *Arlington Catholic Herald* on March 7, 2002, William Saunders spoke to the importance of these virtues to living a moral life:

> The practice and development of the four cardinal virtues are essential to anyone's spiritual life. However, as the old saying goes, "Easier said than done." Being the poor victims of Original Sin, each of us has difficulties living a virtuous life. Therefore, we need the abundant graces our Lord offers through prayer, the frequent reception of the sacraments and the gifts of the Holy Spirit. Looking to the example of the saints and invoking their prayers also strengthen our resolution for holiness. We must never forget our Lord's challenge: "You must be made perfect as your Heavenly Father is perfect" (Mt 5:48). Through the practice of virtue, assisted by God's grace and the aid of the saints and angels, we can meet the challenge.

other human virtues can be traced back to these four virtues. For each virtue, provide an example of how you have incorporated each of the virtues into your life in some way. Then have students suggest some other examples of how they have incorporated these virtues into their lives.

- **Individual Assignment:** Distribute a clipping to each student from those collected in the Class Activity on page 216 (students will not receive their own clippings back). Have each student write an analysis of the issue described in each clipping, describing what each situation would look like if the cardinal virtues were being practiced by all parties involved. Encourage students to describe specific behavior, not "People would be nicer to each other." Have some students share their results with the class.

Humans Are Made in God's Image (pages 212–217)

Objectives

In this lesson, the students will:

- identify and explain the effects of being made in God's image.
- apply their understanding of the effects of being made in God's image to life situations.
- explain what it means for human beings to have free will.
- describe the core elements of the Church's social justice doctrine.
- apply Catholic moral principles to everyday life.

Preview

This section explains the foundations of the Church's teachings on individual and social morality. This teaching provides a vision of life together, which is very different from the message often presented through the media and other cultural influences. The goal of the section is to help students understand this vision and then be able to apply it to their everyday lives.

Bell Ringers

- **Student Presentations:** Allow time for the students to share some of their applications to the exercise "Practicing the Cardinal Virtues" on page 213.
- **Class Activity:** Have students write several moral issues faced by young people their age on half-sheets of paper. Begin the process by writing "lying," "stealing," and "drugs and alcohol" on the board. These topics frequently are named first in such a discussion—students should select alternate issues. Compile the list of topics and use them as additional examples throughout the chapter.

Teaching Approaches

- **Class Discussion:** Facilitate a discussion with students about what it means to have a soul. Ask them to reflect on the difference between a human soul and the consciousness of a dog, for example. Introduce the greater impact of instinct in animals with lower intelligence than humans. Students may raise the question of whether there are animals in Heaven. Since no one knows exactly what Heaven will be like, there is no authoritative answer to that question. But animals would not achieve Heaven because of having made free moral choice as do humans. Note that free will is intimately connected with the human ability to love.

- **Class Discussion:** Continue with a discussion of topics related to the truths about human beings introduced on pages 213–214. *We have dignity and worth.* Have students discuss how this principle would shape a Catholic response to the following situations:

  - Many people who are incarcerated do not have high school diplomas; some cannot read or write. The legislature decides to eliminate educational services in the state's prisons.

  - A baby is born with Down syndrome and a condition that causes her to regurgitate most of the milk she drinks. Simple surgery will correct the condition. Because of her Down syndrome, her parents decide not to have the surgery performed.

  - A senior citizen care facility is understaffed because of lack of funding. As a result, some residents are heavily drugged to control their behavior. The medications cause them to be drowsy and unable to interact normally.

- **Class Discussion:** *We have freedom.* Human behavior results from a complex combination of heredity ("nature"), environment ("nurture"), and free will. Ask students which element they consider most important; it may be helpful to have each write down an approximate percentage for each. Facilitate a discussion about which component weighs most heavily in decision making, reminding students of the Church's position affirming free will.

- **Class Discussion:** *We are responsible.* Have students assess responsibility in the following situations. First, have them write whether the person(s) involved is directly or indirectly responsible. They should also take into consideration the factors listed in the text that can limit blameworthiness: nonculpable ignorance, inattention, fear, force, habit, and passions. Then discuss their answers as a class.

  - A student asks her friend who works in a movie theater to let her sneak in and see the movie for

society
Any community of human beings that unites them in a common purpose.

subsidiarity
A principle of Catholic social justice that holds that a community of a higher order should not interfere in the internal life of a community of a lower order, depriving it of its functions.

and intellects are involved. If our emotions move us to do good, then they are morally good. If our emotions cause us to perform evil, then they are bad. Consider this example: a teacher believes you cheated on an exam and insists you take another one to prove that your answers were your own. If your anger at the accusation fuels your determination to score even better on the second exam, it is morally good. If, however, you decide to slash the teacher's car tires after school, then the passion of your anger becomes evil.

We are wounded by sin. Though we are fundamentally good, we have inherited the effects of Original Sin from our first parents, who disobeyed God. We have a wounded human nature. We desire what is good, but we are weak, inclined to do evil, and we easily make mistakes. Because of our fallen nature, the freedom God gave us is limited and prone to error. An obvious example is the trouble we have controlling our emotions. This is why we need the help of the Holy Spirit to gain mastery over them and channel them to good. The Spirit endows us with gifts, like the cardinal virtues, to help us master our feelings and grow in holiness.

We are children of God. We should not despair over our weak human nature. The Good News of our Salvation is that Christ's Paschal Mystery of Salvation has forgiven our sins and rescued us from Satan. Jesus Christ has won for us a new life in the Holy Spirit. God has adopted us into his family through his gifts of grace, faith, and baptism. If we cooperate with Christ's grace, our

Lord helps us to live morally; to choose God, who is the Supreme Good and the source of our happiness; and to love as he loves according to God's plan.

We are friends of the Lord. Jesus Christ is not only our Savior; he is our friend. "You are my friends if you do what I command you. . . . This I command you: love one another" (Jn 15:14, 17). This brings great joy. Neither he nor his loving and merciful Father will ever let us down. What we must do in return for God's friendship is to love him above all and our neighbors as ourselves.

Humans and Society
(CCC, 1877–1948)

By nature, humans live with and for others. God calls us both individually and as communities into union with the Blessed Trinity, which is a true communion of love. We fulfill our human vocation when we dialogue with, serve, and love others.

Because we are social beings, we belong to many societies. A society is a group of persons united by a principle that goes beyond the individual. Whether a society is personal like the family, voluntary like a social club, or political like the state, it must always make the human person its "principle, subject, and end" (CCC, 1881). Each society must treat people as ends (persons of worth) and not as a means (objects to attain a goal). A good society promotes virtue and love among its members and inspires its members to respect and serve others and to treat them always with justice.

A great deal of moral teaching involves our participation in society. Therefore, the Church gives us many good guidelines on how to live our life with others. Several examples follow, explained in the paragraphs below.

Societies should observe the principle of subsidiarity, which holds that a larger

Background Information

Human Rights Watch

There are many organizations throughout the world that work to protect human rights. According to their website (www.hrw.org), Human Rights Watch (HRW), the largest human rights organization based in the United States, is dedicated to protecting the human rights of people around the world. HRW researchers conduct fact-finding investigations into human rights abuses in all regions of the world and then publish those findings in books and reports, generating extensive coverage in local and international media. This publicity helps to embarrass abusive governments in the eyes of their citizens and the world. HRW then meets with government officials to urge changes in policy and practice—at the United Nations, the European Union, in Washington, D.C., and in capitals around the world. In extreme circumstances, HRW presses for the withdrawal of military and economic support from governments that egregiously violate the rights of their people. In moments of crisis, HRW provides up-to-the-minute information about conflicts while they are underway. HRW focuses on global issues such as HIV/AIDS, children's rights, arms, women's rights, prison, international justice, and more.

social unit should not take over the functions of a smaller group if the smaller unit can achieve for itself the common good. For example, the government should not dictate to parents what form of religious education to give their children. This principle safeguards the dignity of the individual person. Therefore, it would outlaw any system of government, like Communism, that says the individual person only has value if the state says he or she has value.

We should respect and obey persons and institutions that possess the rightful authority to make laws. In the final analysis, all authority comes from God. Citizens have the right to choose their leaders, who must work to pass laws that promote the common good.

We should work for the common good, that is, "the sum of those conditions of social life which allows social groups and their individual members relatively thorough and ready access to their own fulfillment" (*CCC*, 1906, quoting *The Church in the Modern World*, No. 26). The common good involves respecting inalienable human rights (for example, the right

to life, food, clothing, employment, education, freedom of worship) of every person, promoting the social well-being of various groups, and working for a peaceful society.

An important implication of the common good is to respect the principle of the *universal destination of goods*. This principle teaches that God gave the earth and all that it contains for the benefit of everyone. The goods of the earth must be shared fairly because God created the earth for the *whole* human race. God's love excludes no one. The poor in our midst deserve our special concern because they are often without power or influence.

Government officials have the duty to promote the worldwide common good of nations around the world as well by supporting human development and

common good
The sum total of social conditions that allow people to reach their fulfillment more fully and more easily.

The Dignity of the Human Person

Christian revelation shines a new light on the identity, the vocation and the ultimate destiny of the human person and the human race. Every person is created by God, loved and saved in Jesus Christ, and fulfills himself by creating a network of multiple relationships of love, justice and solidarity with other persons while he goes about his various activities in the world. Human activity, when it aims at promoting the integral dignity and vocation of the person, the quality of living conditions and the meeting in solidarity of peoples and nations, is in accordance with the plan of God, who does not fail to show his love and providence to his children.

—*Compendium of the Social Doctrine of the Church*, 35[17]

- How do your relationships with others help you to reach your potential?
- Write a letter to a person you love telling him or her how the love you share has made you a better person.

Homework Assignment

1. Complete the For Review questions on page 217.

2. Answer the question and write the letter requested in the feature "The Dignity of the Human Person" (page 215).

3. Choose and continue working on one or more of the Ongoing Assignments on page 230.

Extending the Lesson

Video Presentation: Have students research more about the life and teachings of Dr. Martin Luther King Jr. Show a clip of a biography of his life, such as *I Have a Dream* or the Arts and Entertainment video *Biography: Martin Luther King Jr*. Organize a service effort with your class. Have them research a project in the local or larger community. When the project is completed, have students write a reflection on their experience in light of Catholic social teaching.

Individual Assignment: Have students individually list all the groups to which they belong. Note the groups the class holds in common and those which are specific to individuals. Have the students decide which of these groups are societies. Have them identify the principles that form the foundation of each society.

free. The friend gets caught. His boss decides to make an example of him and fires him.

- Two friends are driving to school. The driver has had his license for only a few months. The passenger complains about the music on the radio. The driver leans over to change the station and collides with the car in front of him.

- A mother and father are overprotective of their teenage daughter. They seriously limit her freedom and her ability to form friendships. The daughter rebels and begins sneaking out and drinking heavily.

- A freshman very much wants to be accepted by his older brother and his brother's friends. The brother and his friends have taken a dislike to a girl in their class who is unpopular. They pressure the freshman to post a demeaning message about her in an instant message in a group discussion board. The freshman gives in and does it.

- **Class Discussion:** *We are wounded by sin.* Have students discuss the effects of others' sins in the following situations:
  - A young girl is treated harshly by her older brothers and sisters. She often feels insecure and is easily pressured into going along with the crowd.

  - A fourth grader is allowed unrestricted access to television. He watches TV for six hours a day, much of it during prime time. He is exposed to sex, violence, and commercials every day.

  - A third grader attends school in a large city. The textbooks are outdated, there is a broken window and leaky ceiling in his classroom, and there are frequent fights in the cafeteria. He lives in a crowded apartment and shares a bedroom with two older brothers. He is reading at a first-grade level.

- **Journal Assignment:** *We are children of God.* Select one the teen moral issues listed by the class. Have students write in their journals how awareness of being a child of God could help shape a student's response to the issue. Guide their responses beyond end results into the process of remembering to pray, asking God for strength, and being open to hearing God's response.

- **Direct Instruction:** Review the effects of being made in God's image and likeness on pages 213–214. Note that at the core of these effects is the understanding that human beings are rational creatures who have free will and are therefore responsible for their actions. Despite human weaknesses, God's grace can help us live moral lives.

- **Direct Instruction:** Continue with the text subsection "Humans and Society" (pages 214–217). If it helps, ask the students to describe the "ideal team" from their experiences playing sports related to the principles explained in this section.

- **Class Discussion:** *Societies should observe the principle of subsidiarity.* Families can be used as an example to illustrate the principle of subsidiarity. Have students envision a hypothetical family made up of parents and children ages four, ten, and fifteen. Have students decide who they think should make the following decisions in a family:
  - what the four-year-old should wear around the house
  - what courses the fifteen-year-old should take in school
  - whether to buy a new home
  - what kind of language is acceptable in the home
  - whom the ten-year-old is allowed to have as friends
  - whom the fifteen-year-old is allowed to have as friends
  - what to have for dinner

- **Class Discussion:** We should respect and obey persons and institutions that possess the rightful authority to make laws. Distribute copies of Martin Luther King Jr.'s "Letter from a Birmingham Jail." Dr. Martin Luther King Jr. struggled against unjust laws. Facilitate a discussion with students about what makes a law just or unjust, and what gives a government rightful authority.

- **Class Activity:** We should work for the common good. Ask students to write what they consider to be inalienable rights (those rights that belong to human beings regardless of their circumstances or behavior). Have them compare their list to the textbook list: life, food, clothing, employment, education, freedom of worship. Have students develop a common list as a class, imagining that they would bear responsibility for protecting those rights for one another. Point out the similarities of this discussion to the process of democratic government today.

- **Direct Instruction:** Refer students to the paragraph beginning with "Our social nature is crucial for our life together" on page 216. Define social justice doctrine and use the following journal assignments to elaborate on the meaning of social justice.

- **Journal Assignment:** *Respect each person.* Special love for the downtrodden and poor is sometimes referred to as a "preferential option for the poor." Some people hear this principle as discriminatory. Have students respond to the following situations in their journals:
  - You have four children. One child has cerebral palsy and is unable to walk. She has only limited use of her hands. Your family has a moderate

acting justly in international relations. Everyone has the right and duty to be involved in his or her social groups. For example, teens can help families thrive by obeying their parents and helping younger siblings. Citizens must keep up with social justice issues and exercise their right to vote in a responsible way. Parishioners should get involved in various parish ministries that help the unfortunate in their midst and that promote the spiritual life of the Church.

Our social nature is crucial for our life together. This is why over the centuries, the Church has developed a body of teaching on how we should treat each other. This body of teaching is known as the **social justice doctrine** of the Catholic Church. It is directly related to our being made in God's image and being gifted with adoption into God's family and called into friendship by Jesus Christ. Some of its key points are to:

social justice doctrine
The teachings of the Magisterium that pertain to the ways in which societies function to promote the common good.

- *Respect each person.* Every human being has basic worth that Jesus Christ elevated when he became man. He taught that *every* person is our neighbor, another self. Therefore, we must respect and love everyone. We must even forgive our enemies. He told us to have a special love for the downtrodden and the poor. When we serve the poor, we are directly serving our Lord.
- *Treat others as equals.* Each person has the same human nature, a common destiny, and fundamental dignity. We have God-given rights that do not have to be earned. Any prejudice or discrimination directed toward others because of their sex, color, race, ethnic background, religious practice, or the like contradicts God's loving plan for us, the special creatures he calls to be united to him.
- *Develop and share your gifts.* Although we are all equal in dignity,

KNOWING CHRIST THROUGH SCRIPTURE

Jesus Teaches Us How to Live

In the Sermon on the Mount (Mt 5–7), Jesus gives a blueprint on how to live a Christian, moral life. Read the following passages from the Sermon. Write answers to the corresponding questions.

Matthew 5:17–48
- What does Jesus say about the following: anger, adultery, divorce and remarriage, swearing, revenge, one's enemies?

Matthew 7:1–5
- What does Jesus say about judging others?

Matthew 7:12
- What is the Golden Rule?

Luke 10:29–37
- What principles of Catholic morality does the Good Samaritan act on in this story?

Luke 16:19–31
- Which principles of Catholic morality did the rich man ignore during his time on earth?

Knowing Christ through Scripture Answers (page 216)

Matthew 5:17–48
- Anger – "whoever is angry with his brothers is liable to judgment"
- Adultery – "everyone who looks at a woman with lust has already committed adultery"
- Divorce and remarriage – "whoever divorces his wife causes her to commit adultery, and whoever marries a divorced woman commits adultery"
- Swearing – "do not swear at all"
- Revenge – "offer no resistance to one who is evil"
- One's enemies – "love your enemies"

Matthew 7:1–5
- "Stop judging, that you may not be judged."

Matthew 7:12
- "Do to others whatever you would have them do to you."

Luke 10:29–37
- The Good Samaritan exhibits fortitude and justice and treats the man with dignity and worth.

Luke 16:19–31
- The rich man did not practice the cardinal virtue of justice, specifically the preferential option for the poor.

God gave us different talents, all part of his plan. We must develop and use these gifts for others. In a special way, those of us who have been given wealth and education must use our talents to promote peace, fight injustice, and combat economic and social conditions that treat others unfairly.

• *Show solidarity with others.* Solidarity is a Christian virtue of friendship or social charity that works to share both material and, more important, spiritual goods with others. We must be one with others, especially the poor.

Considering the above points, we can conclude that we act morally when we:

• responsibly use our God-given intellects and wills,
• choose good and avoid evil,
• act as persons of incomparable worth who respect the essential dignity of others,
• allow the Holy Spirit to live in us,
• are Christlike and act as true sons and daughters of a loving Father,
• act like true friends of Jesus—showing our love for God by loving our neighbor, living responsibly as members of various communities, always respecting the rights of others, and helping out the weak in our midst.

solidarity
A Christian virtue of charity and friendship whereby material and spiritual goods are shared among members of the human family.

For Review

1. What are the four cardinal virtues?
2. What is the heart of Christian morality?
3. Drawing on Catholic teaching, list five qualities of what it means to be a human being.
4. What is freedom? Discuss what it means to have a free will.
5. What are some limitations to freedom?
6. Give an example of how the principle of subsidiarity could be violated.
7. Explain the relationship between the common good and the universal destination of goods.
8. What is the virtue of solidarity? How is it related to our social nature?

For Reflection

The cardinal virtue of prudence asks us to think before we act. Think of a decision involving right or wrong that you might face in the next week. Exercise the virtue of prudence by writing down three questions that you should ask yourself before acting.

income. Your daughter has just outgrown her wheelchair and needs a new one.

◆ Make a list of all the ways the disabled child may need more resources in terms of time and money than the other children. For example, she needs wheelchairs and other equipment. She needs to be driven almost everywhere she goes. She needs help dressing herself. She needs help getting things down from high places.

◆ In what ways would you try to help your daughter be independent? In what ways would you want to help her? How would you let your other children know that they are loved equally with their sister?

◆ How does this situation compare with our response to the poor and powerless in our world?

• **Journal Assignment:** *Treat others as equals.* Facilitate a discussion with students about some of the more "quiet" ways people can experience discrimination: being excluded, disrespectful body language from other students while commenting in class, etc. In students' journals, have them write briefly about an individual they know personally who experiences discrimination, in their families, classrooms, neighborhoods, teams. Ask them to make a commitment to take one positive action toward that person. Set a deadline, and then collect a brief reflection describing their action and the results.

For Review Answers (page 217)

1. prudence, justice, fortitude, and temperance

2. The heart of Christian morality is:
• Be who you are.
• Form and follow your conscience.
• Respond to God by using the helps given to live a virtuous life.

3. Qualities of what it means to be a human being include:
• We have dignity and worth.
• We can think.
• We have freedom.
• We are responsible.
• We are wounded by sin.
• We are children of God.
• We are friends of the Lord.

4. Freedom is "the power, rooted in reason and will, to act or not to act, to do this or that, so to perform deliberate actions on one's own responsibility."

Free will gives us the power to choose and love. Because of free will, we are responsible for our actions. God cannot force us to love, but gives us the freedom and inspiration to love others by following the Golden Rule.

5. Our freedom is limited by passions, emotions that move us to act or not act, and Original Sin, the wounded part of our human nature that can warp our desire to do good into doing evil.

6. The principle of subsidiarity holds that a larger unit should not take over the functions of a small group if the smaller unit can achieve for itself the common good. For example, the government could dictate for parents what form of religious education to give their children.

7. The common good implies that all individual members of society are able to reach their fulfillment in society; therefore, the universal destination of goods suggests every country should have access to a sufficient amount of food and materials and that each governing body should distribute those goods equitably.

8. Solidarity is the Christian virtue of charity and friendship whereby material and spiritual goods are shared among members of the human family. As human beings our social nature is to live with and for others; therefore, solidarity is the fulfillment of that social nature.

- **Journal Assignment:** *Develop and share your gifts.* Have students brainstorm the different types of gifts people possess: qualities of character, talents, personality, forms of intelligence, etc. Then brainstorm a list of gifts under each category. Have students write in their journals about five gifts they possess. Have them place an asterisk by a gift they possess but haven't developed. Facilitate a discussion about strategies for choosing to develop a gift.

- **Journal Assignment:** *Show solidarity with others.* People who have been harassed or discriminated against often say the lack of response by others is often as painful as the harassment itself. This is sometimes referred to as "the bystander effect." Have students share examples (without identifying names) of times in their childhood when they witnessed harassment or discrimination. What did they do? What might have been a helpful response? When do they see opportunities to be in solidarity in their lives today?

- **Individual Assignment:** Complete the assignment in the Knowing Christ through Scripture feature "Jesus Teaches Us How to Live" (page 216). Share some or all of your rewritten proverbs with the class. *Optional*: Create a large class mural with each student printing their favorite personal proverb on it.

Conscience and Moral Decisions (pages 218–221)

Objectives

In this lesson, the students will:
- define and explain conscience.
- list and apply the guidelines for forming a good conscience.
- list and apply the three sources of morality: action, intention, and circumstances.
- explain the role of the Magisterium in making good decisions.

Preview

The three sources of morality form a concrete framework for making decisions that can help students throughout their lives. Like the previous section, this section relies heavily on student practice in applying the principles taught.

Bell Ringers

- **Class Discussion:** Allow the students to share answers to the For Review questions from page 217 and collect their homework.

Conscience and Moral Decisions (CCC, 1776–1789; 1795–1800; 1802)

As the *Catechism of the Catholic Church* defines, "Conscience is a judgment of reason whereby the human person recognizes the moral quality of a concrete act that he is going to perform, is in the process of performing, or has already completed"(*CCC*, 1778). God gave each of us a conscience to help us live like Christ.

Our conscience helps us determine if what we are doing is good or evil, whether it is in accord with God's plan or goes against it. Conscience helps us grasp what is the moral thing to do before we act, but it also helps us judge whether we did right after we act. It calls us to responsibility. Also, our conscience calls us to repent if we have sinned by going against it, by turning from our Lord's law of love.

The Second Vatican Council called conscience "the most secret core and sanctuary" of a person. Here we are alone with God, whose voice we can hear calling us to love the good and avoid evil (*The Church in the Modern World*, No. 16). Every human being has a fundamental right to follow his or her conscience and to act freely on it by making morally responsible judgments. No one should be forced to act contrary to the true dictates of conscience. This is especially true in decisions affecting religion.

Forming Your Conscience

To form a true and upright conscience, we need to be sincere and examine our lives before God. As Christians, in order to form a good conscience, we must:
- use our God-given ability to think to discover God's goodness and truth;
- listen to Jesus Christ, who teaches us how to be loving and virtuous;
- look to his Death on the cross as the perfect example of how to love and obey the God the Father;
- obey the teaching of the Magisterium and the example of other wise and holy people;
- use the gifts and graces of the Holy Spirit that help us live virtuous lives.

An important first step in forming our conscience is to exercise human reason before making any decision. A thoughtful person can discover three sources of morality: the object chosen, the end or intention, and the

sources of morality
The three basic elements of every action: the moral object (what we do), the intention (our motive), and the circumstances (context and consequences). All three elements must be good for a proposed action to be good. In addition, some moral objects (like murder and adultery) are always evil and can never be justified. Also, a good intention can never justify an evil act.

Background Information

Wordsworth on Conscience
William Wordsworth wrote of conscience:

> But, above all, the victory is most sure
> For him, who, seeking faith by virtue, strives
> To yield entire obedience to the Law
> Of Conscience; Conscience reverenced and obeyed,
> As God's most intimate presence in the soul,
> And His most perfect image in the world.

For Enrichment

Individual Assignment: Have the students read the entire Gospel of Mark, the shortest Gospel. Then have them imagine they are reporters assigned to write a story on the moral teachings of Jesus. Based on Jesus' words and behavior in the assigned chapters, what are Jesus' teachings on moral issues? Some chapters will provide more information on specific moral topics such as wealth or forgiveness; other chapters will deal broadly with love and self-giving. The stories should be written in a matter-of-fact tone, as might be found in the news section of a daily newspaper.

circumstances surrounding the action. By reflecting on these, we can often discover the right course of action.

The *moral object* is the matter of our actions, the *what* we do. Examples of good moral acts are donating money to the missions and babysitting a younger sibling. In contrast, something that involves bad matter does not contribute to our good. For example, hurling racial insults is an evil action.

There are certain objective norms of morality that human reason and conscience can discover. These norms help us judge whether some act or attitude is good or evil, whether it is in harmony with God's will or goes against it. Some of these actions are always seriously wrong because the matter involved is always seriously wrong and involves a disorder of the will. Neither a good intention nor circumstances can turn them into morally good acts. Examples of acts that are always wrong are murder, blasphemy, adultery, child abuse, and perjury. Nothing can ever justify them.

Catholic teaching holds that the most important element for judging the morality of an act is the moral object because it determines "whether it is capable of being ordered to the good and to the ultimate end, which is God" (*Splendor of Truth*, No. 79).

A second source of morality is the *intention,* that is, one's motive or purpose for acting. Rooted in the will, our intention tells us *why* we did something. It looks to the "end," that is, the reason or goal of a particular action. For example, say you help a younger sibling get ready for school to help your mom because she is ill. What you are doing and why you are doing it are both good. Your action, therefore, is good and moral.

One's intention can involve a series of actions whose target is the same goal. Take a student who prepares a note card to help study for a test. Note taking seems like a good moral object. However, if the student is planning to use the note card to cheat on a test, the

act is bad because it is motivated by the evil act of cheating.

We may have mixed motives in our actions. For example, you may offer to cut the lawn for your dad. Your first reason is to help him after his busy day at work, but you also want to put him in a better mood before he finds out that you failed your math test. This second reason is clearly less than a worthy motive.

Catholic morality teaches an important principle regarding intentions: *A good intention can never make an intrinsically evil action into a just one.* You may have seen this principle stated this way: "The end does not justify the means." Those actions that are not directed to the good of the human person can never be made good just because a person has a good intention. For example, murder is always evil. Therefore, an abortion is always evil even though a woman may choose one so that she can stay in school and protect her reputation. Lying is contrary to the Eighth Commandment and always against truth. Thus, lying on an application to get a job is not justified. The motive—getting a job—is good. But the means—lying—is not.

Finally, an evil reason for doing something can turn a good act into a bad one. For example, suppose you buy someone a present simply because you want them to lie for you. In this case, you are a phony. You are using him as a means to get yourself off the hook. Your motive is evil, even though gift-giving is usually a good thing to do.

The third source of morality is the *circumstances* that surround an action. These are secondary factors that include the consequences of an action and its context, like who is involved and where, when, and how the action takes place.

The circumstances of one's acts can increase or reduce the evil or goodness. For example, stealing five dollars from a homeless man is much worse than stealing five dollars from a millionaire. Also note that the circumstances can never turn an evil act into a good one. Therefore, it is always wrong for us not to respond to a person in need, even though fear might reduce your blameworthiness for your lack of action. We must always do for others what we would have them do for us.

For our actions to be morally good, all three elements—the object

Extending the Lesson

Video Presentation: Show a portion of the movie *School Ties* (popular release). This movie depicts a Jewish student at an elite Eastern prep school in the 1950s. In the course of the movie, the student is falsely accused of cheating by another student who is jealous of his success. The school prefects are given the responsibility of deciding who is guilty. This portion of the movie effectively portrays for students a complex moral dilemma with which they can identify.

For Enrichment

Individual Assignment: Have students research the topic of stem cell research. Two good resources are www.americancatholic.org and www.usccb.org, the official website of the United States Catholic Bishops. This issue is an example of a topic where the teaching of the Magisterium is an important guide in making good moral decisions. Complex, sophisticated medical technology was not available in Jesus' time, and so it was not possible for him to give us clear guidelines on this topic. The Magisterium combines study of Scripture and Church teaching with up-to-date knowledge of medical progress to provide guidelines for Catholics.

• **Journal Assignment:** Ask the following questions by way of introducing the section:

1. What factors do you think have gone into shaping your conscience?

2. How might your conscience be different from someone who grew up in a society where, for example, women and children had no legal rights?

3. What outside influences do you think have had a positive impact on forming your conscience?

4. Who or what may have had a negative impact?

Teaching Approaches

• **Writing Assignment:** Have students write an explanation of the important points in the *Catechism* definition of conscience from page 218:

♦ judgment

♦ reason

♦ moral quality

♦ concrete act

♦ past, present, future

• **Class Discussion:** Encourage the students to brainstorm situations in which reason and emotion may be at odds. Ask them to list concrete ways in which we can prevent emotions from overtaking reason (e.g., taking time in decision making, talking honestly with other people, seeking out full information). Ask students to share some nonincriminating stories about times when they or others have ignored reason and regretted the results.

• **Class Discussion:** Help the students identify ways in which they see people pressured to go against their conscience. One possible topic of discussion is choosing to cheat. This is a delicate topic, but it is also an opportunity to support students in making an informed, deliberate, and honest decision about a practice that is widespread in high schools.

• **Class Activity:** Continue with the text subsection "Forming Your Conscience" (pages 218–220). Distribute one newspaper or magazine article representing a moral dilemma to each student. Have them choose one person in the given scenario. Ask them to speculate on the outcome if this person followed the five principles described in the text:

♦ think

♦ listen to Jesus Christ

♦ look to Jesus' Death as the perfect example of love and obedience to God

♦ obey the teachings of the Magisterium and follow the example of other wise and holy people

♦ use the gifts and graces of the Holy Spirit

• **Group Activity:** The following activity will ask students to apply the three sources of morality to real-life situations. Read one article with the students and model the process with them before having them work in pairs. For example:

- Consider the scenario described in their article. Have them identify the *moral object*, the act or actions that are under consideration. Point out to students that failing to take an appropriate action can be as serious as committing a wrong action. Have them discern whether there are potential sins of omission as well as sins of commission at stake in their articles. Discuss whether the actions involved in their articles would always be wrong, or are questionable only under certain circumstances or with certain motivation.

- Have them identify each of the individuals involved in the issue portrayed by their articles and the possible *intentions* they would have related to the moral object. It is difficult to know a person's true intentions, but one can make inferences based on actions. Suggest that the students make a list of all of the possible intentions and then make an educated guess about which apply based on the information provided.

- Have a student describe the *circumstances* aloud. In discussion, have students speculate about the possible consequences of any given action in the situation described in their clipping. Have them list on paper the context of their situation: who is involved, where, when, and how might the action take place? How do the circumstances affect the morality of the choices involved? What are examples of a change in circumstances that would affect the outcome or the morality of a decision?

- **Group Presentations:** Now based on this information, have the students make a judgment about whether or not the situation at hand is good. If all three sources of morality are good, then the action itself can be determined to be good. Students should prepare a brief presentation of all three sources of morality and their conclusion about whether or not the action is good.

- **Individual Assignment:** Assign students one of the teen topics suggested at the beginning of the chapter (page 217). Have them individually apply the lens of "moral object, intention, and circumstance" to the issue. Have students write what they consider to be the best moral perspective on that particular issue.

- **Group Activity:** Assign students to work in pairs. Have each team create a scenario for a moral dilemma that is at the same time plausible and complex. Have each team exchange scenarios with another team, and then analyze the scenario in relation to actors, action in question, motivation, and circumstances. Have students recommend the best possible resolution of the scenario.

(what I do), the intention (why I do it), and the circumstances surrounding it must all be good. Jesus is our best guide for forming a sensitive, loving conscience. By praying to him in the Holy Spirit, we can learn how to live a Christ-centered life. By staying close to Jesus in friendship and by asking, "What would Jesus do?" we can learn how to distinguish between good and evil. In short, Jesus wants us to judge our actions against his Golden Rule: "Do to others whatever you would have them do to you" (Mt 7:12)—and the teachings of the Ten Commandments.

Also, we must look to the Magisterium of the Church for guidance (*CCC*, 2030–2040; 2044–2047; 2049–2051). The moral teachings of the Magisterium apply Christ's message to matters that affect our Salvation and to issues involving our fundamental rights as human beings made in God's image. The Pope and bishops draw their teachings from the Creed, the Lord's Prayer, the precepts of the natural law (see page 224), the Ten Commandments, Jesus' Sermon on the Mount, and the moral instruction of the Apostles.

The Church's moral teachings are Christ-given and help us to make good choices. The Church is like a mother who looks out for our welfare. Therefore, we must listen to and put into practice "the constitutions and decrees conveyed by the legitimate authority of the Church" (*CCC*, 2037).

Follow Your Conscience
(*CCC*, 1790–1794; 1801).

From conscience formation, we must then do what it tells us is the good course of action. We must draw on the help of the Holy Spirit and eventually do what our conscience tells us is the right thing to do. "A hu-

man being must always obey the certain judgment of his conscience" (*CCC*, 1800).

After acting, our conscience can then help us judge whether or not we did the right thing. If we were sincere, prayed, acted as Jesus would, and paid attention to Church teaching, then we will have a clear conscience. As the proverb goes, "There is no pillow so soft as a clear conscience." Making wise and good decisions will help us become virtuous people. We will be forming good habits that will help us grow in holiness.

However, what if we make decisions against our conscience? If we violate our conscience, then we have sinned. Scripture tells us, "So for one who knows the right thing to do and does not do it, it is a sin" (Jas 4:17). Pangs of conscience that cause guilt can alert us to a bad decision.

Because we are human, we can make mistakes in our decisions. It is possible to have a conscience that is in error. Ignorance—lacking the information to choose the right course of action—can contribute to an erroneous conscience. Emotions can also affect our conscience, for example, anger or the strong craving for pleasure. Sometimes, we are not fully at fault for not knowing the right course of action. But at other times we are to blame because we made very little or no effort to discover the truth.

We can strengthen our conscience by making efforts to correct it if it is in error, by clearing up any doubts we might have by consulting competent people, by learning from our mistakes, and by avoiding those situations that have led us to sin before. In the last analysis, we form a good conscience by staying close to Christ and his love.

Homework Assignment

1. Complete the For Review questions on page 221.

2. Continue working on the Ongoing Assignments, page 230.

3. Read the text section "Virtues and Other Helps to Live a Moral Life" (pages 222–226).

Background Information

Forming and Following Conscience

A person with a formed conscience can discover three sources of morality—the object chosen, the end or intention, and the circumstances—and make good choices based on these. Through loyalty to conscience, Christians are joined to other men in the search for truth and for the right solution to so many moral problems, which arise both in the life of individuals and from social relationships (*The Church in the Modern World*, No. 16). To form a conscience, one of the things one must do is use his or her God-given ability to think and to exercise reason. In the Second Vatican Council document *Declaration on Religious Liberty,* the responsibility to form and follow one's conscience is clear: "He is bound to follow this conscience faithfully in all his activity so that he may come to God, who is his last end. Therefore, he must not be forced to act contrary to his conscience. Nor must he be prevented from acting according to his conscience, especially in religious matters" (chapter 1, no. 3).

Explaining Your Faith

How do I know if I made the correct moral choice?

If your conscience has been well formed through the reading of Scripture, prayer, a study of Church teaching, an examination of conscience, and the assistance of the Holy Spirit, you can trust the urgings of your conscience to lead you to the correct choice. Making the right choice often leads to a sense of peace and inner quiet even if the choice has had consequences that were painful or difficult. On the other hand, when you make an incorrect choice, you will often experience guilt. In this case, guilt is a productive feeling. It reminds you of what you know to be right and prompts you to seek forgiveness and to make amends.

Also, you know that some rules of morality apply to every decision that you make (e.g., the Golden Rule).

For Review

1. Define *conscience*.
2. How is a person's conscience formed?
3. List and briefly discuss the three sources of morality.
4. Give an example of a person violating the principle that "a good end does not justify evil means."
5. Give an example of how circumstances can affect a person's blameworthiness for his or her action.
6. Write the Golden Rule.
7. What is the role of the Magisterium in helping people make moral decisions?
8. Must a person always follow his or her conscience? Explain.
9. Explain how a conscience can be erroneous and what a person must do to correct it.

For Reflection

Name two moral choices you made in the last week or so, one that was a good choice and one that you now recognize was a bad one. For each, tell how you made your choice and when you first knew it was good or bad. How did your conscience tell you that you had done the right thing? the wrong thing?

- **Individual Assignment:** Regarding the text subsection "Follow Your Conscience" (page 220), ask students to jot down on a private sheet of paper three things they recall doing that they regret from a moral perspective. Assure students they will not be asked to share the items on their list. Next, brainstorm with students the common responses people have when they have done something wrong: blame it on the other person, ignore it, apologize, do something to make up for it, minimize. Have students note which responses are helpful in repairing the relationship and putting a conscience at ease.

- **Individual Assignment:** Have students assess the costs of not taking responsibility for one's actions and working to repair the damage that has been done. Remind students of the accumulated impact of injuries that have not been addressed. Apologizing and making amends is an important part of living a moral life. Have students list the qualities of a good apology. Then have students list the characteristics of a helpful response to an apology. Have students write a script for a good apology and for a bad one; for a good response and a bad one. Have a few students read their results to the class.

- **Direct Instruction:** Read the Explaining Your Faith panel on page 221. Help students distinguish between shame and guilt. Shame is directed at the person; it is a feeling that there is something wrong with us as a person. Guilt is the feeling we have when we are responsible for a wrong action, and it focuses on the behavior. Guilt calls our attention to bad behavior and motivates us to change. Shame can paralyze us and make it more difficult for us to have hope for change.

For Review Answers (page 221)

1. Conscience is the capacity that helps us determine if an action is good or evil, choose what is good, and repent if we have made a bad decision.

2. Catholics form their consciences by using our ability to think, listening to Jesus Christ, looking to Jesus' example, obeying the teaching of the Magisterium, and using the gifts and graces of the Holy Spirit to help us live virtuous lives.

3. The three sources of morality are:
   - the moral object chosen, the action being considered;
   - the intention, or the desired goal, end, or result;
   - and the circumstances, outside factors that influence the decision or the outcome.

4. Cheating to get a good grade on a test

5. Circumstances can affect a person's blameworthiness in a situation by limiting one's information or freedom in making a decision. For example, someone may have been forced to commit a crime against their will.

6. The Golden Rule is, "Whatever you wish that men would do to you, do so to them" (Mt 7:12).

7. The Magisterium applies Christ's message to matters that affect our salvation and to issues involving our fundamental rights as human beings made in God's image. We look to them for guidance and wisdom in making Christ-centered moral decisions.

8. According to the *Catechism*, a person must always follow his or her conscience. The Church teaches each person has a responsibility to form a conscience by gathering full information and submitting decisions to the guidance of the Holy Spirit.

9. Consciences can be erroneous for a variety of reasons. Ignorance and emotions are primary limitations to a well-formed conscience. To correct an erroneous conscience, a person might consult a competent person for advice, avoid the situations that lead to sin, and make personal efforts to change.

Virtues and Other Helps to Live a Moral Life (pages 222–226)

Objectives

In this lesson, the students will:
- list and explain the theological virtues.
- recite St. Thomas Aquinas's definition of a moral law.
- explain natural, revealed, civil, and Church law.
- list the precepts of the Church.

Preview

This section moves from the notion of the individual's ability to recognize good and follow it to the expression of moral principles in law. The emphasis is on Jesus' New Law of Love, which is reinforced through authentic expressions of other types of law.

 Bell Ringers

- **Class Discussion:** Collect and discuss the answers to the For Review questions on page 221.
- **Group Activity:** By way of review, divide the class into four teams. Have each team write ten review questions from the chapter. Share these questions with the other groups and have them work together to solve them.

Teaching Approaches

- **Class Discussion:** Discuss how habits are formed. Ask students to describe habits they have consciously developed as they have grown older, such as working out, studying effectively, taking care of friendships, and the like. Invite them to notice the way habits make it more likely that we will make a given choice and make it easier for us to keep—or to break—a good resolution. Ask them to give concrete examples of good moral habits they have observed in themselves or other teens.
- **Writing Assignment:** Facilitate a discussion with students about faith and doubt. Faith in God is similar to our faith in other human beings. The fact that we have questions about our relationships with our family members or friends does not necessarily mean there is anything seriously wrong with the relationship. Have students write a "letter of confidence" or a "letter of doubt" to God, expressing their own faith position at this particular time.
- **Direct Instruction:** The theological virtue of hope is not synonymous with "thinking things will turn out well." Sometimes "turning out well" does not include achieving the desires we have hoped for. Mattie Stepanek, for example, was a teen with a rare form

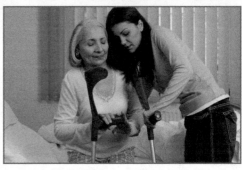

Virtues and Other Helps to Live a Moral Life (CCC, 1803–1804; 1810–1834; 1839–1845)

The gifts and fruits of the Holy Spirit help us to live as Jesus did. The Holy Spirit also endows us with good habits known as virtues. Virtues—like the cardinal virtues of prudence, justice, fortitude, and temperance—help us control our passions and guide our actions according to faith and human reason. We can strengthen these virtues by receiving the sacraments and by praying to the Holy Spirit. The Holy Spirit also helps us to avoid vices. Vices are bad habits that incline us to do evil. They are the exact opposite of virtues. The principal vices, also known as the *capital sins* are pride, envy, anger, sloth, greed, gluttony, and lust.

The *theological virtues* provide the foundation for a life in Christ. They bring us in relationship to the Blessed Trinity, who is their origin, motive, and object. The theological virtues are as follows:

Christian morality
A life in Christ through responsible living that flows from our dignity as God's adopted children made in his image and from Christ's command to love.

- *Faith* makes it possible for us to believe in God and his Revelation. Faith brings us into personal relationship with Jesus Christ and helps us believe his Good News of Salvation. Faith begins our life in union with the Blessed Trinity. As Christ's followers, we must profess and act on our faith, especially by serving others.
- *Hope* implants in us a hunger for Heaven and enables us to trust in God's promises for eternal life. Hope helps us to combat selfishness and strengthens us to cooperate with God's work of Salvation. Jesus' Beatitudes inspire us to hope. Prayer strengthens the virtue of hope in our lives.
- *Charity* makes it possible for us to love God above everything for his own sake. It enables us to love our neighbor as ourselves for the love of God. Charity is a share in the life of our God, who is Love. It is the greatest of the virtues. Jesus commanded us to love others as he loved us (Jn 15:12). This is the basic rule of Christian morality. When we obey

Extending the Lesson

Class Discussion: Have students brainstorm the laws of good nutrition. Come up with a list of types of foods (Italian, Mexican, Indian, Southern, etc.). Assign each student to jot down the ways in which one style of food meets the laws of good nutrition. Point out to students the similarity between natural law and the laws of nutrition. Nutritional guidelines have their foundation in an understanding of how the human body functions best. Food from different cultures may look and taste very different, but they are based on the universal laws of good nutrition.

the Lord, we are allowing God to live in us. This is what it means to live morally.

Christ, through his Church, provides several other helps for making moral decisions. These involve varied expressions of the moral law that are all interrelated.

These are the eternal law (the source, in God, of all law), natural law, revealed law (comprising the Old Law and the New Law or Law of the Gospel), and civil and Church laws. More information follows.

PROFILE OF FAITH: ST. JOSEPHINE BAKHITA, MODEL OF HOPE

In his encyclical *Spe Salvi* (*Saved in Hope*), Pope Benedict XVI points to St. Josephine Bakhita as a model of the virtue of hope. This virtue helped her to lead a heroic life as a Christian witness.

Bakhita was born around 1869 in a small village in the Darfur region of Sudan, a country that even in our day is persecuting Christians. She grew up in a family of six children. When she was nine years old, slave-traders kidnapped and beat her and then sold her into slavery five different times. They gave her the name Bakhita, which means "Fortunate One." (She was so traumatized by the kidnapping that she was unable to remember her family name.) She worked as a slave for the family of a general and suffered daily beatings to the point of bleeding. For the rest of her life, her body carried scars from the brutal floggings. The general also had her tattooed to mark her as one of his slaves, cutting scores of patterns on her chest, stomach, and arms and then pouring salt into her wounds, causing her excruciating pain.

In 1882, an Italian merchant purchased her and took her to Italy, where she ended up serving as a nursemaid for a little girl, Mimmina. The child was enrolled in a boarding school run by an order of nuns, the Daughters of Charity (the Canossian Sisters). While serving at the school, Bakhita gradually learned about the Catholic faith. She heard about Jesus Christ, the true Master, who was all-good and tender, unlike the slave masters who had treated her so cruelly. She experienced in a profound way the love of God and learned how the Son of God, Jesus Christ, had himself been flogged and had offered up his life for the Salvation of all.

For once in her life Bakhita experienced real hope, born of the love of God that called her not a slave but a free child of God. When she was about to be returned to Sudan, she refused to go. She wanted to stay with the nuns, learn about the faith, be baptized, and live as a free Christian and child of God. Since slavery was outlawed in Italy, she was allowed to remain with the sisters. In 1890, she was baptized (taking the name Josephine), confirmed, and received her first Holy Communion from the Patriarch of Venice. On the Feast of the Immaculate Conception (December 8) 1896, at the age of forty-one, she took her vows in the Congregation of the Canossian Sisters. Sr. Josephine went to Schio, in the Northern Italian province of Vicenza, serving as the sisters' cook, seamstress, sacristan, and doorkeeper, where she met many of the townfolk, who grew to love her as *Nostra Madre Moretta* ("Our Black Mother"). Sr. Josephine eventually journeyed around Italy to promote the missions and to tell her listeners about her life as a slave, her encounter with the God of Jesus Christ, and her conversion to the Catholic faith. Her goodness and spiritual maturity impressed all who met her. She was a model of forgiveness, once saying, "If I were to meet the slave-traders who kidnapped me and even those who tortured me, I would kneel and kiss their hands, for if that did not happen, I would not be a Christian and religious today."

Sr. Josephine obliged her superiors and wrote her memoirs; they were published in 1930. Josephine lived to be seventy-eight, the last years of her life confined to a wheelchair and in pain, but always remaining a model of holiness, prayerfulness, and charity. She died February 8, 1947. Large crowds came to view her body and followed her hearse to the cemetery. Josephine Bakhita was a woman of great faith, hope, and forgiving love.

For Enrichment

Individual Assignment: Have students silently read the Sermon on the Mount, Matthew 5:1–7:27. Have each student select a few verses from the passage and write a brief homily explaining and applying the passage. Or, have the students apply the Beatitudes to a current news story. Answer the question: "What do the Beatitudes suggest would be a proper response to this issue?"

Extending the Lesson

Video Presentation: Show clips of the movie *Godspell* (popular release). Facilitate a discussion with students on the ways in which this movie communicates Jesus' New Law of Love.

---

of muscular dystrophy who died in 2004 at the age of fourteen. He is an outstanding example of hope in the face of overwhelming odds. Share his story or one like it with the students (information is available at www.myhero.com/hero.asp?hero=mattieStepanek).

- **Direct Instruction:** Read about "St. Josephine Bakhita, Model of Hope" in the Profile of Faith feature on pages 223–224. Have students choose their favorite quotation from the ones listed at the end of the feature. Then, have them complete the questions that follow.

- **Class Discussion:** Have students brainstorm all the words that come to mind when they hear the term *charity*. Clarify for students that charity is the deep, spiritual understanding of love, based in God's love for us. Ask students to name people they know personally who exemplify this virtue in their lives and why they named them.

- **Direct Instruction:** Continue with explanations of the moral law, natural law, and the precepts of the Church as identified in the subsections on pages 224–226. Post Thomas Aquinas's definition of moral law in the front of the class. Refer to the three core components of this definition (reasonable, proper authority, common good) while working through natural, revealed, civil, and Church laws.

- **Class Activity:** Do this short exercise to help the students understand how human beings are created capable of discovering the natural law inside of them.

  - Find a device that is unfamiliar to students such as an odd cooking utensil or home improvement tool. Place it in the front of the class. Invite students to discover for themselves the use and identity of the device. Allow students to examine and, if appropriate, manipulate the device. Have students remain silent until everyone has had a chance to examine the device. Then determine if there are any correct guesses among the group. Have students discuss the process by which they tried to determine the purpose of the device.

  - Explain that human beings, with the help of God's grace, can discover natural law by studying human nature. Just as students tried to determine the purpose of the device by studying and manipulating it, human beings discover God's purpose for us by examining our experience.

- **Class Discussion:** Have students make a list of civil laws as a class that may be considered contrary to Christian belief and practice. Measure the laws against St. Thomas's definition: "Reasonable regulation issued by the proper authority for the common good." Ask whether any of the laws fails on the grounds of subsidiarity.

- **Individual Assignment:** Review each of the precepts of the Church (see pages 225–226) in more detail. For example: *You shall attend Mass on Sundays and on holy days of obligation and rest from servile labor.* Have students list the holy days of obligation. Assign students to do a brief research paper on the history and background of one of the holy days of obligation.
- **Class Discussion:** *You shall confess your sins at least once a year.* Facilitate a discussion with students on an effective way to prepare for the Sacrament of Penance. Have the class develop an examination of conscience that teens could use on a daily basis to keep them more in tune with Jesus' call to them. Invite students to write a personal examination of conscience and use it on a frequent basis.
- **Class Discussion:** *You shall receive the Sacrament of Eucharist at least during the Easter season.* Ask the students to discuss why it is important to receive the Eucharist during the Easter season. What is it about Easter that makes the Eucharist so important?

Pope John Paul II beatified her in May 1992 and canonized her in 2000, making her the first canonized saint from the Sudan.

Read the following quotations of St. Josephine Bakhita[18]:

- "I have given everything to my Master: He will take care of me . . . The best thing for us is not what we consider best, but what the Lord wants of us!"
- "The Lord has loved me so much: we must love everyone . . . we must be compassionate!"
- "When a person loves another dearly, he desires strongly to be close to the other: therefore, why be afraid to die? Death brings us to God!"
- "If we had no hope in the Lord, what would we do in this world?"[19]

Research more about St. Josephine Bakhita. Answer the following questions:

- How can hope help you live your life?
- What do you admire most about St. Josephine Bakhita?

Moral Law (CCC, 1950–1953; 1975–1977)

St. Thomas Aquinas defined the moral law as "a reasonable regulation issued by the proper authority for the common good." All law comes from the moral law of God's providence, that is, in his power, wisdom, and goodness.

Jesus Christ is the fullness and source of unity of the moral law. Three interconnected expressions of the moral law are:

1. the *natural law*;
2. *revealed law* consisting of the Old Law and the Law of the Gospel;
3. *civil* and *Church laws*.

Expressions of Moral Law (CCC, 1954–1960; 1978–1980)

St. Thomas Aquinas tells us that "the natural law is nothing other than the light of understanding placed in us by God; through it we know what we must do and what we must avoid. God has given this light or law at the creation" (quoted in *CCC*, 1955). By giving us a moral sense of right and wrong, God gives us a share in his own wisdom and goodness. The gift of human reason can discover the truth of natural law, for example, by discovering fundamental human rights and the duties that come from them.

The precepts of the natural law are unchanging, permanent, and universal, even though different cultures have applied them differently through the ages. Our ancestors in faith discovered that it is wrong to kill innocent people; the killing of innocents is still wrong today, even though some would try to justify it by using shaky arguments, for example, by attempting to justify practices like abortion.

Also, we could not live in peace without *civil laws* that flow from natural law. For example, chaos would result if we allowed people to take the property of others without their permission. If we permitted wholesale stealing, society would cease to function. The purpose of civil law is to apply the principles of the natural law to a particular society. For example, we have laws against shoplifting, burglary, and copyright violation—all trying to deter various kinds of stealing. Therefore, God revealed the precepts of the natural law so that there would be no doubt whatsoever as to how we should act.

natural law
God's plan for human living that is written in the very way he created things. Binding on all people at all times, it is the light of understanding that God puts in us so that we can discover what is good and what is evil.

Resources

 Printed Materials

Auer, Jim. *Why Can't I Just Say or Do What I Want?* Liguori, MO: Liguori Publications, 2002.
  Good supplementary pamphlet addressing the issues of freedom.

Bennett, William J., ed. *The Book of Virtues: A Treasury of Great Moral Stories*. New York: Simon and Schuster, 1993.

Connell, Timothy. *Principles for a Catholic Morality*, rev. ed. San Francisco: HarperSanFrancisco, 1990.
  A leading introductory college-level text on Catholic morality. Clearly written. Excellent background for teaching many themes in this course.

Connors, Russell B., Jr., and Patrick T. McCormick. *Character, Choices & Community*. Mahwah, NJ: Paulist Press, 1998.
  Excellent supplemental information for teachers.

Dodds, Bill, and Michael J. Dodds, O.P. *The Seeker's Guide to 7 Life-Changing Virtues*. Chicago: Loyola Press, 1999.
  Outstanding book on the theological and cardinal virtues with good illustrations and practical applications.

Gula, Richard M., S.S. *The Good Life: Where Morality and Spirituality Converge*. Mahwah, NJ: Paulist Press, 1999.
  A wonderful overview of the themes of Catholic morality presented in a way that supports Christian living and spiritual growth. Excellent information on the virtues. It contains some excellent spiritual exercises. Highly recommended.

Finley, Mitch. *The Catholic Virtues: Seven Pillars of a Good Life*. Liguori, MO: Liguori, 1999.
  Solid and readable book by Mitch Finley.

John Paul II. *Youth of the World. Apostolic Letter on the Occasion of the International Youth Year*. Boston: St. Paul Editions, n.d.
  An inspiring message of John Paul II to youth to live a virtuous life, using their talents for others. Delivered in 1985. Many of the pope's ideas can be easily shared with your students.

Keating, James, PhD. *Pure Heart, Clear Conscience*. Huntington, IN: Our Sunday Visitor, Inc., 1999.
  Down-to-earth and readable approach rooted in gospel living.

Keenan, James F., S.J. *Virtues for Ordinary Christians*. Lanham, MD: Sheed & Ward, 1996.
  A readable and modern approach to the theological and cardinal virtues with a few other virtues added, for example, hospitality, wisdom, humor, and physical fitness.

continued on page 235

The Old Law of the Old Testament clearly states the precepts of the natural law and the truths that our own intellects are capable of discovering. God gave his Law to Moses because people had failed to discover it for themselves and often fell into sin. The Ten Commandments point out the kinds of behavior we should either do or avoid. They reveal what is sinful and condemn it. They tell us what contradicts the love of God, neighbor, and self. This Old Law is good and holy, but it is not perfect. It does not give us the Holy Spirit and his graces that make it possible to live up to its commands. The Old Law only serves to prepare us for the Law of Christ and his Gospel, a law of love written on the human heart.

Jesus Christ makes God's law perfect. Most perfectly revealed in the Sermon on the Mount, the New Law of Love is Christ's work. The Holy Spirit writes this law on our hearts, making it possible for us to imitate more closely our heavenly Father. Jesus' law of love does not list new rules for us to follow. Rather, it speaks to the attitudes and motives behind our actions. The Golden Rule (Mt 7:12) and Jesus' command to "love one another as I love you" (Jn 15:12) are excellent summaries of the New Law.

The Sermon on the Mount and other teachings from the Apostles (found, for example, in Romans 12–15, 1 Corinthians 12–13, Colossians 3–4, and Ephesians 4–5) show that Christ's New Law is a law of love. The New Law is also a law of grace that helps us to obey it through faith and the sacramental graces. It is a law of freedom that opens our hearts to act as children of God and friends of Jesus Christ.

The New Law has several special virtues. These are the evangelical counsels of poverty, chastity, and obedience. These virtues help those who fully commit themselves to Christ to love more perfectly in their quest to become holy members of Christ's body.

Precepts of the Church (CCC, 2041–2043; 2048)

Civil law applies the precepts of the natural law to various societies. In a similar way, Church law applies the precepts of the divine law to the Church, which is trying to live a moral life. To live a moral life, we must also pray and celebrate the liturgy. Therefore, there are six important precepts of the Church, that is, minimum rules for Catholics to live as participating members of Christ's Body. These minimum obligations help our spiritual growth. They are:

1. *You shall attend Mass on Sundays and on holy days of obligation and rest from servile labor.* Why? To celebrate our Lord's Resurrection, the joyful event of Salvation History, and to observe the key liturgical feasts that honor the mysteries of our Lord, Blessed Mother, and the saints. Resting from work and activities on these days helps to keep these days holy.

2. *You shall confess your sins at least once a year.* Why? To prepare for the worthy reception of the Eucharist and to experience the work of conversion begun with Baptism.

precepts of the Church Basic rules that bind Catholics who belong to Christ's Body.

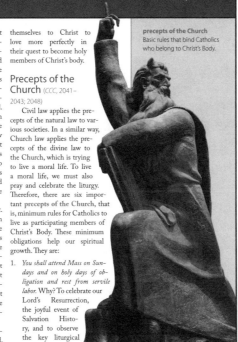

Moses by Joseph Turkaly on the campus of the University of Notre Dame

- **Class Discussion:** *You shall observe the days of fasting and abstinence established by the Church.* Review with students the laws of fasting and abstinence to be observed during Lent. Facilitate a discussion on the beneficial effects of practicing self-denial in our lives.

- **Direct Instruction:** *You shall help to provide for the needs of the Church.* Correct if necessary the myth that the Catholic Church is the possessor of great wealth. Remind students that diocesan priests receive moderate salaries for their work, and priests of religious orders take a vow of poverty. The Church's holdings are primarily in land and artwork, which are shared freely with all. Dorothy Day, who lived her days among the poorest people of New York City, once said, "Churches are the wealth of the poor."

Homework Assignment

1. Complete the For Review questions on page 226.

2. Read the text section "Sin, Justification, and Grace" (pages 226–228).

3. Work toward completing the Ongoing Assignments, page 230.

Background Information

The Theological Virtues Provide the Foundation for a Moral Life

The theological virtues, which provide a foundation for leading a Christian life, are faith, hope, and charity. Charity is recognized as the greatest of these virtues. Various forms of moral law also offer guidance for leading a moral life: They include eternal law, natural law, revealed law, and civil and Church laws. The Catechism of the Catholic Church offers this definition of virtue:

> A virtue is an habitual and firm disposition to do the good. It allows the person not only to perform good acts, but to give the best of himself. The virtuous person tends toward the good with all his sensory and spiritual powers; he pursues the good and chooses it in concrete actions. (1803)

The Second Vatican Council document *Gaudium et Spes* addresses the value of virtue:

> For after we have obeyed the Lord, and in His Spirit nurtured on earth the values of human dignity, brotherhood and freedom, and indeed all the good fruits of our nature and enterprise, we will find them again, but freed of stain, burnished and transfigured, when Christ hands over to the Father: "a kingdom eternal and universal, a kingdom of truth and life, of holiness and grace, of justice, love and peace." On this earth that Kingdom is already present in mystery. When the Lord returns it will be brought into full flower. (30)

1. The theological virtues are faith, hope, and charity. Charity is the greatest of the theological virtues because it is a share in the life of God, love everything for its own sake, and the new command that Jesus gave us: to love one another as he loved.

2. St. Josephine Bakhita modeled the virtue of hope through her constant prayer, bold witness of faith, and lack of regret for all the unfortunate things that happened to her.

3. Moral or authentic law is "a reasonable regulation issued by the proper authority for the common good." Natural law is unchanging because it stems from our core nature as human beings, which is unchanging through time and cultures.

4. The Old Law is summarized in the Ten Commandments. The purpose of the Old Law is to tell us what contradicts the love of God, neighbor, and self.

5. The New Law is the Law of Love, best summarized in the Sermon on the Mount.

6. The precepts of the Church are:
- You shall attend Mass on Sundays and holy days of obligation.
- You shall confess your sins at least once a year.
- You shall humbly receive your Creator in Holy Communion at least during the Easter season.
- You shall keep holy the holy days of obligation.
- You shall observe the prescribed days of fasting and abstinence.
- According to our ability, we must also give material support for the needs of the Church.

Sin, Justification, and Grace

(pages 226–228)

Objectives

In this lesson, the students will:
- distinguish between Original Sin and actual sin and between mortal and venial sin.
- define justification and grace.
- list and explain the five types of grace.

Preview

The last section of Chapter 8 defines sin, justification, and grace. A large part of this section may seem like review, but it should be presented in the context of the rest of the chapter. The students are reminded that sin is an offense against human reason, truth, and good conscience. God forgives our sins when we repent. This

3. *You shall receive the Sacrament of Eucharist at least during the Easter season.* Why? To guarantee an absolute minimum reception of our dear Lord on a yearly basis, especially during the Easter season, the highlight of the Church's liturgical calendar.

4. *You shall observe the days of fasting and abstinence established by the Church.* Why? Jesus told us to do penance to prepare for worship, to purify our hearts,

and to gain mastery over our instincts so that we can grow in freedom.

5. *You shall help to provide for the needs of the Church.* Why? So that the Church can continue its mission of proclaiming and celebrating the Good News of Jesus.

For Review

1. Name the theological virtues. Which is the most important? Why?
2. How does St. Josephine Bakhita model the virtue of hope?
3. Define *law.* Why is the natural law permanent and unchanging?
4. Where is the Old Law summarized? What is its purpose?
5. What is the New Law?
6. Name the precepts of the Church.

For Reflection

- Read Romans 12–15. Transcribe into your journal any five verses that you believe will help you live a better Christian life.
- How can the precepts of the Church aid your spiritual growth?

Sin, Justification, and Grace (CCC, 1846–1854; 1870–1873, 1987–2005; 2017–2024)

We sin when we do not obey God's law of love and the dictates of our conscience. Sin offends against human reason, truth, and a good conscience. It violates love for God, neighbor, and self. It wounds our nature and disrupts the human family (see *CCC*, 1849).

God forgives our sins when we repent. God's mercy is known as justification. More precisely, justification is the grace of the Holy Spirit that cleanses us from our sins through faith in Jesus Christ and Baptism. Justification gives us God's own righteousness and unites us to the Lord's saving Passion. We need to be justified to live morally.

Justification forgives our sins, helps us turn to the Lord, and gives us the theological virtues of faith, hope, and

Background Information

Sin and God's Forgiveness

When we do not heed God's law of love and listen to our conscience and act accordingly, we commit a sin. The *Catechism of the Catholic Church* offers this definition of sin:

> Sins can be distinguished according to their objects, as can every human act; or according to the virtues they oppose, by excess or defect; or according to the commandments they violate. They can also be classed according to whether they concern God, neighbor, or oneself; they can be divided into spiritual and carnal sins, or again as sins in thought, word, deed, or omission. (1853)

When we repent for our sins, we receive God's mercy, which is known as justification. Regarding justification of the soul, the *Catechism of the Catholic Church* teaches:

> The first work of the grace of the Holy Spirit is conversion, effecting justification in accordance with Jesus' proclamation at the beginning of the Gospel: "Repent, for the kingdom of heaven is at hand." Moved by grace, man turns toward God and away from sin, thus accepting forgiveness and righteousness from on high. "Justification is not only the remission of sins, but also the sanctification and renewal of the interior man." (1989)

charity that make it possible for us to obey God's will and see him working in our lives.

Jesus' Death on the cross brings about our justification. His great sacrifice gives us access to God's graces that are necessary for us to grow in holiness. By definition, grace is God's favor toward us. We cannot earn, nor do we deserve, the gift of grace. The most important type of grace is *sanctifying grace* (from the Latin word *sanctus*, which means "holy"). It is also called *habitual grace* because it permanently disposes us to live like God. Conferred at Baptism, sanctifying grace makes us holy by adopting us into God's family and making us heirs of Heaven.

Because grace is a gift, we can only accept it *freely*. God will never force his love on us. He has made us in such a way that we really do want to discover the truth and choose the good. Only God can satisfy these desires, which actually prepare for our free response to his love. If we follow our hearts and respond to his inner promptings, our human freedom is made perfect and our search for truth and goodness is fulfilled.

Besides sanctifying grace, the Church names four other types of grace:

- *actual grace*, God's special help to turn from sin or help us act like Christ once we have;
- *sacramental graces*, gifts that flow from particular sacraments;
- *charisms*, special gifts the Holy Spirit bestows on individual Christians to help the Church grow; and
- *graces of state*, God's special help for special ministers in the Church.

justification
The Holy Spirit's grace that cleanses us from our sins through faith in Jesus Christ and Baptism. It makes us right with God. Justification not only frees us from sin, but sanctifies us in the depth of our being.

Doing What Is Right

Test your knowledge of the principles of morality. For each case below, decide which principle applies and if sin would be involved if you followed one course of action rather than another.

Principles of Morality
- Do good; avoid evil.
- One may never do evil that good may result from it. (A good end does not justify using evil means to attain it.)
- Do unto others what you would have them do unto you.
- Be the human being God intended you to be.

Cases
1. Most of your peers are picking on a classmate who is socially clumsy.
2. To get an edge on a job application, you are tempted to claim some work experience that you never had.
3. You know of a classmate who has completely plagiarized a term paper.
4. Your friend is engaging in some risky behavior. You suspect he is into drugs. You're debating what to do.
5. You discover that someone has posted a cruel and unfair photo of a classmate online.
6. Your English teacher posted the wrong grade for your last test on the school's online grade book. She posted 95 for the test when you really only earned 85.

"Doing What Is Right" Answers (page 227)

1. "Do unto others . . ."
2. "One may never do evil . . ."
3. "One may never do evil . . ."
4. "Do unto others . . ." or "Be the human . . ."
5. "Do unto others . . ."
6. "Do good, avoid evil."

For Enrichment

Journal Assignment: Have students write a paragraph in their journals describing Heaven as they imagine it. Ask them to write about why it is essential that people freely choose Heaven and God's love.

mercy is known as justification. The section also defines grace as God's favor toward us and special types of grace, especially sanctifying grace or habitual grace.

 Bell Ringers

- **Class Discussion:** Allow volunteers to share answers to the For Review questions, page 226. Collect the written responses at the end of the discussion.
- **Class Discussion:** Review the concepts of sin and salvation that were introduced in previous chapters. Have students list and describe the different types of sin and grace that they can recall. Then discuss their responses as a class.

Teaching Approaches

- **Class Discussion:** Review with students the three components involved in mortal sin: serious matter, full knowledge of wrongdoing, and complete consent of the will. Have them evaluate the following situations on these grounds:
  - A demolition crew arrives to take down a building. They quickly bring down the building, not knowing a homeless person has spent the night there.
  - A young man gets drunk for the first time. Not fully aware of his condition, he drives home and on his way hits a pedestrian, seriously injuring her.
  - A teenage girl has been brought up to believe that she will go to hell if she plays cards or goes dancing (some denominations do have this teaching). Feeling excluded at school, she sneaks out one night and goes to a dance.
- **Class Discussion:** Next, have students brainstorm ways in which venial sins could lead to more serious bad decisions. Have students explain how mortal sin is different from venial sin.
- **Class Discussion:** Have students describe ways in which loving parents help create an attitude of love in their children. Sanctifying grace can be compared to the love parents provide for children: God's constant love calls us to love in return.
- **Direct Instruction:** Help students understand each of the four types of graces explained in the text on page 227 with the examples of people who experience them listed here:
  - **actual grace:** the Grinch from *How the Grinch Stole Christmas* when his heart grew three sizes
  - **sacramental graces:** a girl who has just received her First Communion
  - **charisms:** a teenager who has just been confirmed
  - **graces of state:** a newly ordained priest

Then, have the students brainstorm a list of other people who experience these graces. Consider giving them time to create flash cards or other memorization tools to prepare for the Chapter Test.

- **Direct Instruction:** Continue with a discussion related to the text subsection "Merit and the Vocation to Holiness" (page 228). Help students to see the difference between "earning" Heaven and meriting Heaven. A comparison would be:
  - ◆ A rich woman decides to hire a gardener. Out of her generosity, she decided to pay the gardener one hundred times as much as any other person would pay. However, in order to receive the payment, the gardener has to work faithfully. The gardener could not be said to have really earned the exorbitant salary, since it is so much greater than any other gardener would get for similar work. At the same time, the gardener had to merit the salary by performing as the rich woman expected and requested.

- **Journal Assignment:** The concept of taking up our cross is confusing for some students. We can take up our cross by doing penance or additional difficult, generous actions we are not obliged to do. Taking up our cross can also mean to accept the suffering in our lives willingly, mindful of Jesus' sacrifices on the cross. After clarifying this concept, have students write in their journals about difficulties in their lives they could accept in the spirit of taking up their cross.

- **Class Assignment:** Work with a partner to complete the exercise "Doing What Is Right" (page 227). Answers are on page 231 of this TWE.
  - ◆ Use the criteria of mortal sin outlined on page 231 to assess whether or not these examples fit that definition.

For Review Answers (page 228)

1. Justification means that we have been cleansed from our sins through faith in Jesus Christ and Baptism. Justification helps us turn from sin and gives us the virtues of faith, hope, and charity.

2. Merit is something owed because of our good deeds. Although God does not owe us anything, we cooperate in the grace that he has given us on our way to salvation. The Holy Spirit makes it possible for us to merit certain blessings and graces.

3. *Sanctifying grace* is God's favor conferred at Baptism that permanently disposes us to life like God. Actual grace is God's special help in turning from sin or helping us act like Christ in a given moment. Sacramental graces flow from particular sacraments. Charisms are special gifts given to individuals by the Holy Spirit. Graces of state are God's special help for ministers in the Church.

Merit and the Vocation to Holiness
(*CCC*, 2006–2016; 2025–2029)

Merit is something we are owed because of our good deeds. It is a theological idea related to justification and grace. God does not really owe us anything because he has already given us all: our lives, the gift of Salvation, and adoption into his family. But out of his great generosity and wisdom, God lets us share in his work of grace. God will reward us with Heaven, but we must cooperate with the Holy Spirit's graces to live holy lives and therefore "merit" that reward. An important point to note: it is impossible to "earn" Salvation; only God can save us through the gift of his justification. However, we must cooperate with this first grace, especially by loving God and other people as ourselves. The Holy Spirit makes it possible for us to merit certain blessings and graces for ourselves and others so that we can grow in holiness on our journey to Heaven.

Another amazing truth is that through prayer and following God's will, we can also merit earthly goods like health and friendship, if this is in God's plan. All these gifts come through Jesus Christ whose loving sacrifice has won us everything. To merit anything, we must let Christ live in us by the power of the Holy Spirit and sanctifying grace. If Christ lives in us, then he and the Holy Spirit will make us holy. They will gain for us eternal life.

All of us are called to be holy, to be like our heavenly Father. We become holy by loving and imitating Jesus Christ our Savior. We strive to be holy because we want to be fully united to Jesus Christ. One of the surest ways to holiness is to pick up our cross and follow Jesus.

Dorothy Day

The saints have taught us that works of self-denial and penance lead to holiness. The victory of Heaven comes at the price of self-sacrificing love for the sake of Christ and others. The theological virtue of hope helps us continue to want to do good deeds for God. We pray and trust that God will give us the strength to serve and love him and others until our death so that we may "merit" our eternal reward.

For Review

1. What does it mean to be justified?
2. How does a Christian "merit" blessings and graces?
3. What is *sanctifying grace*? Also list and briefly discuss other kinds of graces.

For Reflection
What is an act of self-denial that you could engage in that would benefit another person? Resolve to follow through on this act in the coming week.

Homework Assignment

1. Complete the Ongoing Assignments. Plan to share them at the next session.

2. Write answers to the For Review questions on page 228.

3. Review the content of Chapter 8, focusing on the material highlighted in the Chapter Quick View on page 229.

CHAPTER QUICK VIEW

- Though wounded by sin, we can think, choose, love, and act responsibly. The Holy Spirit lives in us and makes it possible for us to follow Jesus by doing good and avoiding evil. (pages 212–214)
- The principle of subsidiarity holds that a larger social unit should not take over the functions of a smaller group if it can achieve for itself the common good. (pages 214–215)
- Everyone is obligated to form continuously, and then follow, his or her conscience. Conscience is the judgment of reason that enables us to determine right and wrong. It operates before, during, and after we act. We sin when we do not follow our conscience. (page 218)
- Conscientious, moral decision making involves using our minds to discover the truth, imitating Jesus' teaching and example of loving and serving others, heeding the moral teachings of the Magisterium, putting into practice the theological and cardinal virtues, and growing in holiness according to the graces and helps (like the gifts and fruits of the Holy Spirit) that God gives to us. (page 218)
- Our conscience can be wrong because of factors like ignorance, emotions, peer pressure, total self-reliance, and loveless hearts. We have a lifelong duty to inform and reform our consciences. (page 220)
- The sources of every moral action are the object (what we do), the intention (why we do it), and the circumstances, which include the context and the consequences of our acts. (pages 218–220)
- A good intention for an action cannot justify evil means to attain it. (page 219)
- The virtues are good habits that help us choose the good and to act with ease and competence. (page 222)
- The theological virtues—faith, hope, and charity (love)—find their roots in God and turn us toward him. (pages 222–223)
- God is the author of law, including the moral law, which guides us in responsible, Christian living. (page 224)
- We should avoid personal sin, both mortal and venial, because sin offends against God, human reason, truth, and a good conscience. It violates the love of God, neighbor, and self. The capital sins of pride, envy, anger, sloth, greed, gluttony, and lust are vices, or bad habits, that lead us to commit mortal sin. If we sin, we should repent and return to God's friendship. (pages 222, 226)
- Justification, a work of the Holy Spirit, cleanses us of our sins through Baptism and faith in Christ. Flowing from grace, justification makes it possible for us to live a life in Christ. Sanctifying or habitual grace makes us holy because it is God's favor, the free and undeserved help he gives us to live as his adopted children. (pages 226–227)
- Out of his unlimited goodness and generosity, God has won (merited) for us eternal life. God permits humans to cooperate with his gift of Salvation, so our good works can earn merit for ourselves and others. But all is done through Jesus Christ, who is the source of all merit. (page 228)

Learning the Language of Faith
Choose the italicized term in parentheses that best completes each sentence.

1. The virtue of (*subsidiarity/solidarity*) shares spiritual and material goods among the members of the human family.
2. (*Habits/Passions*) are emotions that move us to act or not to act in relation to something we feel or imagine to be either good or evil.
3. (*Temperance/Prudence*) is the cardinal virtue defined as "right reason in action."
4. The sum of those conditions that allows individuals and social groups access to their own development is known as the (*common good/social justice doctrine of the Church*).
5. The grace of the Holy Spirit that cleanses us from our sins through faith in Jesus Christ and Baptism is known as (*the theological virtues/justification*).

Homework Assignment

1. Reread all of Chapter 8.
2. Study for the Chapter 8 Test.

Learning the Language of Faith Answers (pages 229–230)

1. solidarity
2. Passions
3. Prudence
4. common good
5. justification
6. moral object
7. the natural law
8. Justice
9. circumstances
10. Easter

Chapter 8 Review Lesson

Objectives

In this lesson, the students will:
- share their work on the Ongoing Assignments.
- review the main content and themes from Chapter 8.
- prepare for the Chapter 8 Test.

Preview

This lesson is intended for the students to share and turn in assignments they have worked on throughout Chapter 8 and to review some of the main themes and content from the chapter. If you have been using memory cards (Chapter 1, Handout 3, starting on page 285 and also online at www.avemariapress.com; discussed on page 34 of this TWE) to help summarize each chapter, you may continue to use them in this lesson in addition to or as a substitution for the teaching approaches listed on page 233.

Bell Ringers

- **Class Activity:** Play a *Jeopardy*-style game using the vocabulary words and other names and lesson themes from Chapter 8. Divide the class into three teams. Write a term on the board—for example, solidarity. Call on a representative from one of the teams. Then ask the person to rephrase the "answer" in question form. For example: "What is the Christian virtue of charity and friendship whereby material and spiritual goods are shared among members of the human family?" Keep the game simple, rewarding one point for each correct response.
- **Student Presentations:** Call on any students who have worked on For Enrichment assignments and Ongoing Assignments from Chapter 8 to share them with the class.

Teaching Approaches

- **Group activity:** Allow the students to work in small groups of four or five. Tell them to divide up the chapter, each taking a specific part. Each student should read and review the assigned part and be prepared to summarize its main parts. Go around the group and allow each person to summarize his or her section for the others.
- **Direct Instruction:** Allow the students the chance to grade their own homework assignments as you read the answers to the For Review questions. Refer to the other For Review questions in this chapter and have students share the answers from their memory. If necessary, have them check returned homework.
- **Individual Assignment:** Give the students time to complete the questions in the Learning the Language of Faith feature on pages 229–230. Answers are on page 233 of this text.

Chapter 8 Test Lesson

Objectives

In this lesson, the students will:
- be tested on the material in Chapter 8.
- pray a prayer for human rights.
- preview the material in Chapter 9.

Preview

Reserve most of the time during this session for the students to take the Chapter 8 Test. When all have completed the test, allow some time to reflect on the prayer on page 230–231.

Teaching Approaches

- **Direct Instruction:** Collect any missing assignments from Chapter 8. Return any graded assignments completed while working on this chapter.
- **Chapter Test:** Distribute the Chapter 8 Test (starting on page 285 and also online at www.avemariapress.com). Have the students complete the tests in class. Collect all of the completed tests.
- **Journal Assignment:** When completed with the test, have the students individually pray the "Prayer for Human Rights" on pages 230–231 and begin to write down a plan to meet a need of a person in their communities in their journals.
- **Prayer Experience:** At the conclusion of the period, pray together the "Prayer for Human Rights."

6. In evaluating the morality of human actions, the (*moral object/circumstances*) focus(es) on the action itself, namely, on *what* we do.
7. God's plan for human living that is written in the way he created things is known as (*the precepts of the Church/the natural law*).
8. (*Justice/Fortitude*) is the cardinal virtue that respects rights.
9. In evaluating the morality of human actions, (*the end/circumstances*) focus(es) on issues like where and when an action is performed.
10. One of the precepts of the Church requires us to receive the Eucharist at least during the (*Christmas/Easter*) season.

Ongoing Assignments

As you cover the material in this chapter, choose and complete at least three of these assignments.

1. Christopher News Notes. Read one of the newsletters that deal with living a Christlike life from the Christopher Movement website. Prepare a report for class.
2. Make a list of ten "Teen Commandments," in other words, reasonable rules and guidelines for living in a family. For example, "Always call home when you will be more than a half-hour late." Share your list with your classmates. Combine all the lists into one class list. Make copies of the final list. Share it with your parents.
3. Evaluate ten radio and television advertisements aimed at teenagers. Discuss what message they are selling concerning a person's dignity and self-worth. Critique these messages considering the basic dignity of each person.
4. The Book of Proverbs provides many helpful maxims and sayings to guide us in living morally upright lives. Choose five proverbs from Proverbs 20–27 that express how to live a good, happy, and moral life. Rewrite them in your own words. Then create a poster with one or more of your proverbs.
5. Compose a realistic moral dilemma that teens your age could face in everyday life. Enact and discuss your dilemma with a group of classmates. As part of your discussion, brainstorm ways to resist negative peer pressure.
6. Interview an adult you admire. Ask this person to report on a time when his or her conscience was challenged and what he or she did to make the right, moral decision. Report the results of your interview.
7. Review the teachings of the United States Catholic Bishops on human dignity. List five ways you can promote human dignity that you learned from a document issued by the Bishops. Resolve to take action on one of the suggestions.
8. Read more about the seven deadly sins. Report in-depth on two of the deadly sins and list a virtue to counteract all seven of the deadly or capital sins.

Prayer Reflection

The Augustinian Secretariat for Justice and Peace provided the following prayer for peace and justice as part of its "Prayer Service for Human Rights Day." It reminds us of the dignity of all people.

A Prayer for Human Rights[20]

Lord, lead us from death to life, from falsehood to truth.
Lead us from despair to hope, from fear to trust.
Let peace fill our hearts, our world and our universe.
Let us dream together, pray together and work together
    to build a world of peace and justice for all.
Merciful God, listen to us as we pray for a world
    that will respect the God-given rights of all.

Audiovisual Materials continued from page 215

Teen Scenes

Ethical and moral decision making is dramatized in these vignettes of four to seven minutes. The viewer must make the decision on the moral way to proceed. A leader's guide is provided (22 minutes).

Descriptions of each vignette are provided from the Videos with Values website:

- Scene 1 Plagiarism: Faced with academic suspension from the football team and a chance for a scholarship, Eric considers turning in a paper copied from the Internet.
- Scene 2 Shoplifting: Sara finds the perfect necklace for her dress for the "big dance" but she can't afford it. Her friends urge her to steal it—after all, "everybody does it." What should she do?
- Scene 3 Peer Pressure: Does true friendship include joining your friend in a fight? Alex faces this test of friendship and conscience.
- Scene 4 Gossip/Cliques: When freshman Gina makes the varsity volleyball squad, the upper-class teammates expect that she'll shun her freshman friends—must she reject one to be accepted by another?

The Ten Commandments: A Foundation for Life Today

This video looks at the Ten Commandments in their historical context and proposes that they are still relevant to us today, as gifts from a loving God to help us in our everyday lives and spare us from physical, emotional, and spiritual chaos. Ten six-minute conversation starters, one for each commandment. Hosted by Walter Wangerin Jr., author of *Paul: A Novel*. Video also includes a discussion guide (60-minute video, Paraclete Video Productions).

We dedicate ourselves to work for the rights of each human person,
  especially for those who find life burdensome,
  and who know the suffering of hatred, poverty and war.
Help us to share the fire of your peace with all people in all places at all times.
Amen.

- *Reflection*: How do you imagine a world complete with peace and justice for all?
- *Resolution*: Plan to seek out a person in your community with a large or small need. Enact an effort to help the person with the need.

Homework Assignment

1. Preview Chapter 9.

2. Read the opening text section of Chapter 9 "Guidance" (page 234).

3. Examine the Ongoing Assignments on page 257 and consider which one(s) you might choose to complete.

Chapter 8 Test Answers

All questions are worth 4 points each.

Part 1: Multiple Choice

1. C

2. D

3. D

4. A

5. A

6. B

7. C

8. B

9. A

Part 2: Matching

10. I

11. H

12. E

13. A

14. G

15. F

16. C

Part 3: True or False

17. F

18. T

19. T

20. T

Part 4: Short Fill-ins

21. subsidiarity

22. common good

Part 5: Short Answers

For full credit, make sure student explanations match the examples given.

 Printed Materials continued from page 228

Lowery, Mark, PhD. *Living the Good Life: What Every Catholic Needs to Know about Moral Issues*. Cincinnati, OH: Charis, 2003.

May, William E. *An Introduction to Moral Theology*, Second Edition. Huntington, IN: Our Sunday Visitor, Inc., 2003.
  Excellent book from an orthodox moral theologian.

O'Neil, Kevin J., C.SS.R., and Peter Black, C.SS.R. *The Essential Moral Handbook*. Liguori, MO: Liguori Publications, 2004.
  A trustworthy guide with a glossary of key terms.

Pieper, Joseph. *The Four Cardinal Virtues*. New York: Harcourt, Brace & World, Inc., 1965.
  The classic work on the topic. Penetrating essays on prudence, justice, fortitude, and temperance. Highly recommended.

Sparks, Richard, C.S.P. *Contemporary Christian Morality : Real Questions, Candid Responses*. Crossroad Publishing Co., 1996.
  Pastoral in tone.

Weber, Gerard P. *The Capital Sins: Seven Obstacles to Life and Love*. Cincinnati, OH: St. Anthony Messenger Press, 1997.
  A popular and readable treatment of the topic.

9 Christian Moral Life: The Beatitudes and Ten Commandments

Overview of the Chapter

Chapter 9 covers a great amount of material. It gives a rapid overview of the requirements of the New Law of Love of Christ that was so eloquently articulated in the Beatitudes. It also reviews the mandates (not suggestions) God gave to humanity in the Ten Commandments. The Beatitudes, together with the Ten Commandments, provide a roadmap to happiness and ultimate union with God in Heaven.

The first three commandments address the first part of Jesus' famous injunction: "You shall love the Lord your God with all your heart, with all your soul, and with all your mind. This is the greatest and the first commandment. The second is like it: You shall love your neighbor as yourself. The whole law and the prophets depend on these two commandments" (Mt 22:37–40).

Students learn that the first commandment requires us to worship the one, true God alone. We do so when we exercise the theological virtues of faith, hope, and charity and put into practice the virtue of religion and its requirements of adoration, prayer, works of sacrifice, and so forth. This commandment warns us against the sins of heresy, apostasy, schism, presumption, despair, superstition, and any form of idolatry. The second commandment requires that we respect God's name. It prohibits perjury, blasphemy, cursing, and other disrespectful language against God, Jesus, Mary, and the saints. St. Thomas More provides an exemplary model of following this second commandment. The third commandment calls Christians to worship our Lord by participating in the Eucharist with other Christians on the Lord's Day.

The last seven commandments teach the positive values and practices that promote love of neighbor. Students learn that the fourth commandment stresses that charity begins at home. We must love and respect our parents and siblings and honor legitimate authority. The fifth commandment teaches us to respect and protect human life from womb to tomb. It outlaws murder, abortion, euthanasia, suicide, and other attacks on human life. This section also discusses killing in self-defense, moral participation in a just war, and capital punishment.

The sixth and ninth commandments embrace the goodness of human sexuality. The dual purpose of human sexuality is the loving union that occurs between husband and wife as well as the potential for participation in creation of new life. Virtues like chastity, purity, and modesty help us integrate our sexuality into our lives as God's precious children. Vices like lust and actions like masturbation, fornication, pornography, prostitution, rape, homosexual activity, adultery, divorce, and polygamy are contrary to God's intent for the wholesome exercise of this great gift.

The seventh and tenth commandments teach us how to be good stewards of our material possessions. The tenth commandment outlaws greed, avarice, and envy—sins that lead to actions forbidden by the seventh commandment, like theft, tax evasion, fraud, vandalism, and so forth. The seventh commandment also requires us to be just in all our dealings with others and to apply the Gospel to the political, social, and economic orders by putting into practice the social justice teachings of the Church. These include good stewardship over the environment, exercising the virtue of solidarity, promoting a preferential option of love for the poor in economic affairs, and putting into practice the corporal and spiritual works of mercy.

Finally, the eighth commandment requires us to be truthful by avoiding false witness, rash judgment, detraction, and calumny.

Various exercises throughout the chapter ask students to discuss moral cases and scenarios. You may require your students to take one of the issues outlawed by one of the commandments and research how it is evident in our world today.

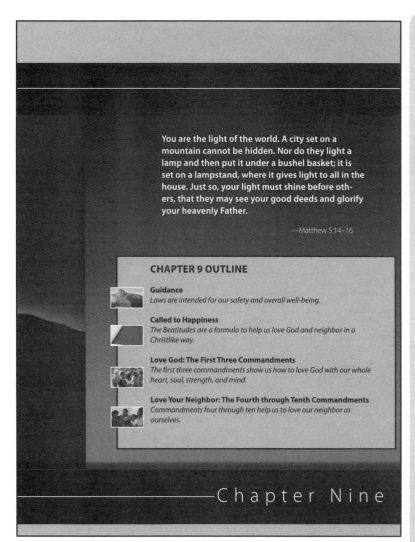

You are the light of the world. A city set on a mountain cannot be hidden. Nor do they light a lamp and then put it under a bushel basket; it is set on a lampstand, where it gives light to all in the house. Just so, your light must shine before others, that they may see your good deeds and glorify your heavenly Father.

—Matthew 5:14–16

CHAPTER 9 OUTLINE

Guidance
Laws are intended for our safety and overall well-being.

Called to Happiness
The Beatitudes are a formula to help us love God and neighbor in a Christlike way.

Love God: The First Three Commandments
The first three commandments show us how to love God with our whole heart, soul, strength, and mind.

Love Your Neighbor: The Fourth through Tenth Commandments
Commandments four through ten help us to love our neighbor as ourselves.

Chapter Nine

Resources

Audiovisual Materials

Choices: Classic Insight Dramas: The Needle's Eye, A Step Too Slow, A Slight Drinking Problem

"Two medical students on an excursion to Africa are forced to seek help when their jeep breaks down in a famine ridden village. Faced with the disease and poverty of the village, the two friends struggle with the dream of the good life and the reality of the suffering they see" (video, Paulist Press).

Death No More: A Look at the Death Penalty

A fascinating interview with Sister Helen Prejean, author of *Dead Man Walking*. The program's host is David Haas. Includes prayer and music for reflection. Study guide provided (40-minute video, Harcourt).

Faithful Citizenship: A Message from the Bishops

Cardinal Roger Mahony and Bishop Joseph Fiorenza join political commentators and parishioners to discuss the American bishops' statement of the same name (10-minute video, United States Conference of Catholic Bishops).

High Powder: Teenage Insight Classics

A young man faces the problems of drug use by his ski team. Depicts his decision to confront the evil before him (video, Paulist Press).

In the Footsteps of Jesus: Catholic Social Teaching at Work Today

Excellent review of the seven themes of Catholic social teaching. Part 1 of the video discusses these themes, while Part 2 highlights individuals who are exemplifying each of the themes in their own lives. Discussion guide included (28-minute video, United States Conference of Catholic Bishops).

continued on page 243

Chapter Outline

- Guidance
- Called to Happiness
- Love God: The First Three Commandments
- Love Your Neighbor: The Fourth through Tenth Commandments

Advance Preparations

Preview the For Enrichment and Ongoing Assignments to gauge which you would like your students to complete.

Called to Happiness (ST pages 235–237)

- Scraps of paper and an envelope or small box; headlines and photographs from magazines and newspapers or photographs on the Internet; copies of Chapter 9, Handout 1 "Beatitudes Prayer Service" (starting on page 285 and also online at www.avemariapress.com) for the Prayer Experience on page 240.

Love God: The First Three Commandments (ST pages 238–243)

- Clips or all of the movie *A Man for All Seasons* for the Video Presentation on page 244.
- Copies of Chapter 9, Handout 2 "Keeping the Sabbath" (starting on page 285 and also online at www.avemariapress.com) for the Group Activity on page 245.

Love Your Neighbor: The Fourth through Tenth Commandments (ST pages 244–255)

- Copies of Chapter 9, Handout 3 "Family Relationships" (starting on page 285 and also online at www.avemariapress.com) for the Individual Assignment on page 250.
- Copies of Chapter 9, Handout 4 "Moral Dilemmas Related to Life Issues" (starting on page 285 and also online at www.avemariapress.com) for the Class Activity on page 251.
- Arrange for a guest speaker from the diocese to discuss the subject of sexuality (see the Preview on page 248) and make copies of Chapter 9, Handout 5 "Sexuality Presentation Follow-up" (starting on page 285 and also online at www.avemariapress.com) for the Guest Speaker activity on page 253.
- One of the three films about teen sexuality listed in the video resources (see the Preview on page 248) for the Video Presentation on page 254.
- Copies of Chapter 9, Handout 6 "Tabloid Survey" (starting on page 285 and also online at www.avemariapress.com) for the Class Discussion on page 257.
- The movie *Dead Man Walking* or the book of the same name for the Background Information on page 250.

Chapter 9 Review Lesson

- Poster board for the Class Activity on pages 260–261.
- Paper plates, construction paper, and rulers for the Class Activity on page 261.

- Copies of the Chapter 9 Test (starting on page 285 and also online at www.avemariapress.com).

Guidance (page 234)

Objectives

In this lesson, the students will:
- explain why people create laws.
- list the Ten Commandments and the Beatitudes.
- reflect on how well they are living out the Ten Commandments in their own lives.

 Preview

Why do we have laws in the first place? This is the question that students wrestle with in the opening section of this chapter. After a discussion about the opening story and the need for just laws, students will discover how much they know about the Ten Commandments and the Beatitudes prior to learning about them in this chapter.

Bell Ringers

- **Class Discussion:** Discuss the opening story with the students. Have them consider the two For Reflection questions on page 234 and then discuss them as a class.
- **Class Discussion:** Have the students suggest important laws and list them on the board. For each law discuss why the law is there in the first place. What do they protect? Some suggestions may include stopping at stop signs, speeding, shoplifting, etc.

Teaching Approaches

- **Individual Assignment:** Introduce the subject material for this chapter, the Ten Commandments and the Beatitudes. With books closed, challenge your students to list all of the Ten Commandments, in order. Post the Ten Commandments on the board and have students check their answers. Discuss how some of the laws discussed in the Bell Ringer discussion could be connected to one of the Ten Commandments. Ask the students, which commandment is not likely to have a civil law?
- **Group Activity:** Next, have the students work in pairs or groups of three to create a list of the Beatitudes. This will likely be harder. You may want to begin by asking how many Beatitudes there are (eight). You could also give them a hint that they follow this model: "Blessed are the . . . for they will . . ."
- **Group Activity:** Continue with more coverage of the Ten Commandments. Divide your class into ten small groups. Assign one commandment to each group. (If your class is not large enough to form ten groups, then divide your class into eight groups and when you assign commandments to each group, combine

Guidance

Yosemite National Park in California is home to some of the most beautiful scenery in the world. The symbol of this park's magnificent beauty is the 3,200-foot granite cliff El Capitan. Because of a number of deaths due to parachutists jumping off El Capitan, park authorities banned base jumping in the park. Base jumping is the name for leaping off fixed objects like cliffs and towers.

In October of 1999, professional jumper Jan Davis, age sixty, perished in her jump off El Capitan when her chute failed to open. She was the fourth of five jumpers who had come to the park to protest the ban on base jumping. Ironically, they were jumping to prove that the sport is safe. They were aware of the new law but deliberately broke it to make their point.

A sad part of the story is that Jan's husband, a renowned aerial stunt photographer, was filming his wife's jump. He was devastated by the experience.

Jan and the other protestors broke the law to protest what they felt was a wrong. However, in this case, the authorities were right in banning the sport at Yosemite. Base jumping from El Capitan is obviously very risky and can lead to death.[21]

Good laws, rules, and regulations are formed in part to help keep us safe. There is also a sound reason for God giving us the Ten Commandments. He did so for the purpose of our overall well-being. We violate the Commandments at our own risk.

Jesus also gave further guidance on how to live. His teaching comes to us in the Gospels, especially in the Sermon on the Mount. In the Beatitudes, Jesus offered a deep examination of the Christian life of love and service to others. This chapter details more about the Beatitudes and Ten Commandments as roadmaps for Christian moral living.

For Reflection
- Why are laws good and beneficial?
- Name a situation when you would consider protesting a law.

Homework Assignment (after "Guidance")

Read the text section "Called to Happiness" (pages 235–237).

Background Information

Loving Our Neighbor

Loving our neighbor in a Christlike way is not always an easy commandment to follow. Pope John Paul II served as an example for all when he met with and forgave Turkish terrorist Melumet Ali Agca, his would-be assassin, in Agca's prison cell in Rome on December 27, 1983. On May 13, 1981, Agca shot the Pope in St. Peter's Square. Four days later from his hospital bed, the Pope forgave Agca, who was later sentenced to life in prison.

Homework Assignment (after "Called to Happiness")

1. Complete the For Review questions on page 237.
2. Begin to work on one or more of the Ongoing Assignments from page 257.
3. Read the entire text section "Love God: The First Three Commandments" (pages 238–243).

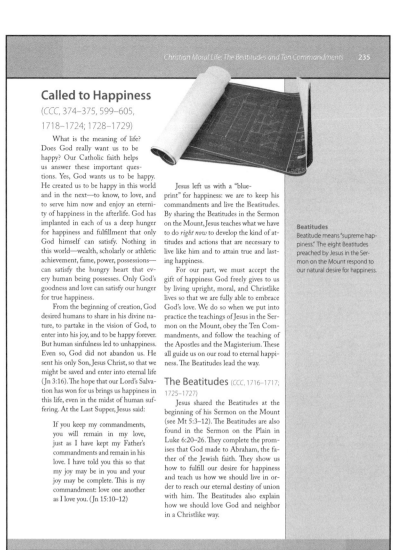

Called to Happiness

(CCC, 374–375, 599–605, 1718–1724; 1728–1729)

What is the meaning of life? Does God really want us to be happy? Our Catholic faith helps us answer these important questions. Yes, God wants us to be happy. He created us to be happy in this world and in the next—to know, to love, and to serve him now and enjoy an eternity of happiness in the afterlife. God has implanted in each of us a deep hunger for happiness and fulfillment that only God himself can satisfy. Nothing in this world—wealth, scholarly or athletic achievement, fame, power, possessions—can satisfy the hungry heart that every human being possesses. Only God's goodness and love can satisfy our hunger for true happiness.

From the beginning of creation, God desired humans to share in his divine nature, to partake in the vision of God, to enter into his joy, and to be happy forever. But human sinfulness led to unhappiness. Even so, God did not abandon us. He sent his only Son, Jesus Christ, so that we might be saved and enter into eternal life (Jn 3:16). The hope that our Lord's Salvation has won for us brings us happiness in this life, even in the midst of human suffering. At the Last Supper, Jesus said:

If you keep my commandments, you will remain in my love, just as I have kept my Father's commandments and remain in his love. I have told you this so that my joy may be in you and your joy may be complete. This is my commandment: love one another as I love you. (Jn 15:10–12)

Jesus left us with a "blueprint" for happiness: we are to keep his commandments and live the Beatitudes. By sharing the Beatitudes in the Sermon on the Mount, Jesus teaches what we have to do *right now* to develop the kind of attitudes and actions that are necessary to live like him and to attain true and lasting happiness.

For our part, we must accept the gift of happiness God freely gives to us by living upright, moral, and Christlike lives so that we are fully able to embrace God's love. We do so when we put into practice the teachings of Jesus in the Sermon on the Mount, obey the Ten Commandments, and follow the teaching of the Apostles and the Magisterium. These all guide us on our road to eternal happiness. The Beatitudes lead the way.

The Beatitudes (CCC, 1716–1717; 1725–1727)

Jesus shared the Beatitudes at the beginning of his Sermon on the Mount (see Mt 5:3–12). The Beatitudes are also found in the Sermon on the Plain in Luke 6:20–26. They complete the promises that God made to Abraham, the father of the Jewish faith. They show us how to fulfill our desire for happiness and teach us how we should live in order to reach our eternal destiny of union with him. The Beatitudes also explain how we should love God and neighbor in a Christlike way.

Beatitudes
Beatitude means "supreme happiness." The eight Beatitudes preached by Jesus in the Sermon on the Mount respond to our natural desire for happiness.

---

the sixth and ninth and seventh and tenth commandments.) Challenge your students to come up with one positive action they could take to make each of the commandments come to life in their lives. In other words, have them look for actions they could do, rather than a behavior to "avoid," that would help them to live the Ten Commandments more fully. For example, the second commandment points out the necessity of respecting God's name. Students may be aware that at times they use God's name or the name of Jesus as a slang expression. But how often do they use God's name with sincerity? Perhaps they could try for one week to find at least one occasion each day to say sincerely, "Oh my God . . ." Or, as a positive response to the eighth commandment, they could commit to finding something true and positive to say about a classmate that would enhance his or her reputation, rather than merely avoiding spreading the kind of gossip that damages reputations.

- **Student Presentations:** Ask each group to choose a spokesperson to share the lists with the class.

Called to Happiness (pages 235–237)

Objectives

In this lesson, the students will:
- list and describe the Beatitudes.
- locate the Beatitudes in the Bible.
- consider how well they and their peers live out the Beatitudes.
- participate in a prayer service based on the Beatitudes.

 Preview

The Beatitudes are a clear indication that God wants us to be happy, but happiness is not always what we expect in life. A close examination of the Beatitudes will reveal a deeper understanding of the Kingdom of God and the Christian way of life. The prayer service in this section is designed for possible use in a Stations of the Cross style, with students moving from one position to the next as they consider each of the Beatitudes.

Bell Ringers

- **Direct Instruction:** Put the following two passages on the chalkboard for students to look up and read before class begins: Luke 6:20–23 and Matthew 5:1–12. Explain that in Luke's Gospel, Jesus explains the Beatitudes during his Sermon on the Plain, while in Matthew's Gospel the event is called the Sermon on the Mount. Have students note some of the differences between the two Gospel accounts.
- **Individual Assignment:** Direct students' attention to the Knowing Christ through Scripture feature "Jesus' Teachings on Morality," on page 237. Have them read each passage and answer the questions that follow.

Background Information

More on the Beatitudes

The Beatitudes listed in this text are taken from the Gospel of Matthew. In Luke's Gospel there are only four: the first three, about the "poor," the "mourners," and the "hungry," are considered authentic words of Jesus, while the fourth, about the "persecuted," is believed to come from the experience of the early Church. In Luke's Gospel the poor are a definite class of people: they are the *anawim*, whose poverty is real and economic although it also has a spiritual dimension. It is understood that they are poor because they have chosen fidelity to God and God's promises over the kind of compromises that would be necessary to accumulate wealth in Roman-controlled Palestine. Matthew adds phrases to Luke's Beatitudes to widen the scope of people to whom they apply: his "poor" become the "poor in spirit," his "hungry," those who "hunger and thirst for righteousness." Matthew also expands the Beatitudes to include many additional desirable characteristics for Christians: being peacemakers, being merciful, being pure in heart, etc.

The word *beatitude* comes from the Latin *beatus*, meaning happy or blessed. The Beatitudes of both Matthew and Luke's Gospels are expressions of joy over the proximity of God's Kingdom. The poor are blessed because God cares for them in a special way. It is God who will comfort, fill, have mercy, and call them his children. Thus, the Beatitudes are descriptions of both Christian ideals of behavior and the Kingdom of God.

Teaching Approaches

- **Direct Instruction:** Reread the opening text under the heading "Called to Happiness" (page 235). Note that while the translation reads "blessed," the Greek word for beatitude that is used also means "happy." Jesus is preaching about the people who are happy in the Kingdom of God. Focus on the gifts of God mentioned in the text that provide us with happiness.
- **Group Activity:** Divide the class into eight small groups. Assign one Beatitude to each group. Have the groups list ways in which they see their peers honoring the Beatitude, that is, being merciful, mourning, being peacemakers, being persecuted for being righteous, being clean of heart, etc. Then ask the groups to list ways in which they see that teens are *not* honoring the Beatitude: ways they refuse to show mercy, refuse peace, ignore what should make them mourn, go along with what's popular to avoid persecution, etc. (If necessary, remind your class that they are listing general ways of behaving, not the actions of specific individuals.)
- **Group Presentations:** Ask each group to choose a spokesperson to share the lists with the class. While the groups are sharing their lists, invite conversation and dialog about the issues that are raised.
- **Direct Instruction:** Summarize any of the main actions associated with each Beatitude not covered by the students from the text on page 236.
- **Prayer Experience:** Write one Beatitude on eight small scraps of paper. Fold them up and place the scraps in an envelope or small box. Divide your class into eight groups and have each group draw one scrap from the box.

The Beatitudes are summarized below.

Blessed are the poor in spirit, for theirs is the Kingdom of Heaven. Jesus associated with the poor, weak, and vulnerable. He wants us to do the same. Jesus does not praise the condition of material poverty. That is an evil. Rather, he wants us to recognize our spiritual poverty—that everything we are and everything we have are gifts from God. Your health, your intelligence, your friends, your life itself are all gifts from God. We thank God for these gifts by sharing what we have and what we are with others.

Blessed are they who mourn, for they shall be comforted. Jesus blesses those who mourn over injustices and evils committed against God and people in need. This Beatitude leads us to empathize with children dying of starvation, innocent people experiencing the violence of abortion, murders, rape, and economic injustice. When our fellow humans succumb to drug addiction, misuse their sexuality, discriminate against those who are different, and kill each other in senseless wars, then we should indeed mourn. Our hearts ache for the sins of the world and for our own sins, too. But we should not lose heart, because Jesus promises that he will eventually console us.

Blessed are the meek, for they shall inherit the land. Humility is equated with meekness. Jesus demonstrated this virtue when he treated others with gentleness and compassion. He also forgave others when they hurt and taunted him. His heavenly Father also treats each of us with patience, forgiveness, and gentleness when we sin. We, too, should be patient with the weaknesses of others. We should work to solve disagreements with gentleness and good will and never give in to hate or violence.

Blessed are they who hunger and thirst for righteousness, for they shall be satisfied. St. Augustine noted that God made us with restless hearts that will not find happiness until we find God. In this Beatitude, Jesus blesses those who know that only God's righteousness can fulfill us. God made us so that our hearts seek divine justice and a good relationship with him. Our hearts seek the holy God and the loving, forgiving friendship of Jesus Christ, our Savior. The Lord Jesus comes to us in the Eucharist to help us grow in holiness, to satisfy our spiritual hunger, and to join us so that we can take him to others.

Blessed are the merciful, they will be shown mercy. When we pray the Our Father, we petition God to "forgive us our trespasses as we forgive those who trespass against us." God loves us beyond what we deserve. He proves this love by giving us his Son Jesus, who forgives our sins and makes it possible through the Holy Spirit and Baptism to become members of the divine family. In return, we should share with others the love, mercy, and forgiveness that we have been given. Our forgiveness of others, especially our enemies, is a sign to the world of a merciful God who loves everyone.

Blessed are the clean of heart, for they will see God. "Who is number one in your life?" is the question this Beatitude asks each of us. A person with a clean heart has a single-minded commitment to God. School, money, possessions, family, sports, friends, and everything else should come after a total commitment to accomplish God's will.

Blessed are the peacemakers, for they will be called children of God. By definition, Christians are, and must be, peacemakers. Christians are to see others as brothers and sisters in the Lord. They will work hard to end strife that leads to violence.

Blessed are they who are persecuted for the sake of righteousness, for theirs is the Kingdom of Heaven. Suffering for faith in Jesus is a great sign of love for him. He himself suffered misunderstanding and abuse when he preached the truth. As a Christian, you are certain to meet ridicule and rejection sometime in your life. Many Christians in history have suffered martyrdom. But if we remain faithful to him, the Lord will reward us with eternal happiness in Heaven. There is no greater reward.

For Review Answers (page 237)

1. Human sinfulness has led to unhappiness among people.

2. God intends for human beings to share in the divine nature, and we achieve this by remaining in Jesus' love and following his commandments.

3. Matthew 5:30–12 (the Sermon on the Mount) and Luke 6:20–26 (the Sermon on the Plain)

4. *Blessed are the poor in spirit, for theirs is the kingdom of heaven.* Everything that we have and are is a gift from God. When we recognize this and share our gifts with others as God intended, we show our gratitude to God for all that he has given us.
Blessed are they who mourn, for they shall be comforted. The evils and injustices of this world rightly cause us to mourn, but Jesus assures us that we will be comforted.
Blessed are the meek, for they shall inherit the land. Meekness isn't weakness: it takes great strength of character to be patient and forgiving with the weaknesses of others. Jesus is the model we should follow to develop this virtue.
Blessed are they who hunger and thirst for righteousness, for they shall be satisfied. We will find rest, happiness, and the satisfaction of all our desires only in God. Our hearts seek God's justice, which is all that will satisfy us.
Blessed are the merciful, for they will be shown mercy. We are called to share God's mercy with others, just as we hope to receive it ourselves.
Blessed are the clean of heart, for they shall see God. A person with a clean heart has a single-minded commitment to God. Nothing takes priority over loving God and doing God's will.
Blessed are the peacemakers, for they shall be called children of God. Because Christians know that they are brothers and sisters in the Lord, they must be peacemakers, seeking to improve relationships within the human family.
Blessed are they who are persecuted for the sake of righteousness, for theirs is the kingdom of heaven. Suffering for one's faith in Jesus is a great sign of love for him. We should be willing to suffer the ridicule and rejection we may sometimes experience because of our faith.

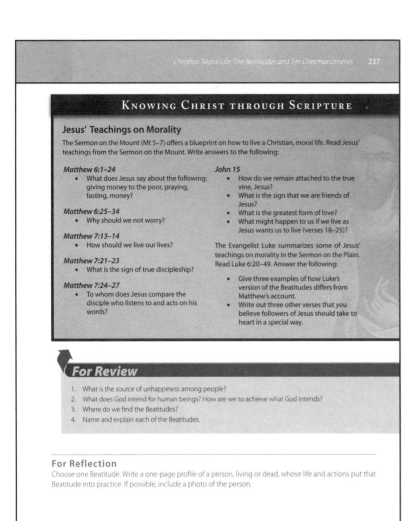

KNOWING CHRIST THROUGH SCRIPTURE

Jesus' Teachings on Morality

The Sermon on the Mount (Mt 5–7) offers a blueprint on how to live a Christian, moral life. Read Jesus' teachings from the Sermon on the Mount. Write answers to the following:

Matthew 6:1–24
- What does Jesus say about the following: giving money to the poor, praying, fasting, money?

Matthew 6:25–34
- Why should we not worry?

Matthew 7:13–14
- How should we live our lives?

Matthew 7:21–23
- What is the sign of true discipleship?

Matthew 7:24–27
- To whom does Jesus compare the disciple who listens to and acts on his words?

John 15
- How do we remain attached to the true vine, Jesus?
- What is the sign that we are friends of Jesus?
- What is the greatest form of love?
- What might happen to us if we live as Jesus wants us to live (verses 18–25)?

The Evangelist Luke summarizes some of Jesus' teachings on morality in the Sermon on the Plain. Read Luke 6:20–49. Answer the following:

- Give three examples of how Luke's version of the Beatitudes differs from Matthew's account.
- Write out three other verses that you believe followers of Jesus should take to heart in a special way.

For Review

1. What is the source of unhappiness among people?
2. What does God intend for human beings? How are we to achieve what God intends?
3. Where do we find the Beatitudes?
4. Name and explain each of the Beatitudes.

For Reflection

Choose one Beatitude. Write a one-page profile of a person, living or dead, whose life and actions put that Beatitude into practice. If possible, include a photo of the person.

- Using headlines and photographs from magazines and newspapers or photographs on the Internet, the students in each group should attempt to create a collage illustrating the Beatitude they have chosen.

- Use the posters to develop a Stations of the Cross-like prayer service focused on the Beatitudes. As the students move to stand in front of each collage, have one student read the Beatitude prayerfully. Then have another student read the short Scripture passage related to the Beatitude that is referenced on Chapter 9, Handout 1 "Beatitudes Prayer Service" (starting on page 285 and also online at www.avemariapress.com). End each station with the short prayer on the handout.

- If you do not have space for the students to move around, you could have one student stand in front of the group, holding up the collage that has been created for each Beatitude. Or you could hang all eight posters around the room and invite the students to turn toward them as they are led through the prayers. If you do not have time to do the collages in class, assign them as individual homework, or as group projects if group homework assignments are possible for your students. If you choose not to do the collage project at all, you can use the prayer service without the visual element.

- **Individual Assignment:** As the section concludes, have the students again close their books and practice memorizing the Beatitudes. Call on representatives to check how well they have done.

Knowing Christ through Scripture Answers (page 237)

Matthew 6:1–24
- Poor: "when you give alms, do not let your left hand know what your right hand is doing . . ." Praying: "go to your inner room, close the door, and pray to your Father in secret." Fasting: "anoint your head and wash your face, so that you may not appear to be fasting, except to your Father who is hidden." Money: "No one can serve two masters."

Matthew 6:25–34
- If you seek first the Kingdom of God, then God will provide all that you need. Worrying does not add a single moment to one's life.

Matthew 7:21–23
- True disciples do the will of the Father.

Matthew 7:24–27
- Jesus compares his disciples to a wise man who builds his house on a rock.

John 15
- If we remain in Jesus and keep his commandments, we will remain attached to the true vine.
- As his friends, Jesus has told us everything he has heard from the Father.
- There is no greater love than to lay down one's life for one's friends
- The world might hate us if we live as Jesus wants us to live.

Luke 6:20–49
- Luke does include some portions of the Beatitudes in Matthew's Gospel, including "poor *in spirit*" and "hunger *and thirst for righteousness.*" Matthew also includes being peacemakers, being merciful, and being pure in heart, while Luke does not mention them.

Love God: The First Three Commandments (pages 238–243)

Objectives

In this lesson, the students will:

- describe how the first three commandments apply to their lives today.
- explain why St. Thomas More was a person of good conscience.

 ## Preview

This first section about the Ten Commandments focuses on the first three commandments, which correspond to the greatest commandment—to love God. For each commandment, make sure students can make connections between what the commandment says and its implications for how they live their lives.

 ## Bell Ringers

- **Group Activity:** Direct students to the feature "Putting the Ten Commandments into Practice" (page 238). Have them work in groups to complete the two assignments at the end of the feature.
- **Group Presentations:** Have each group share their list of commandments with the class. Post their lists on the board and discuss the similarities in the language they used to rewrite the Ten Commandments.
- **Direct Instruction:** Read Matthew 22:34–38 as a class. Ask the students to categorize the Ten Commandments under these two greatest commandments. Note that in this lesson they will be learning about the first three commandments and the commandment to love God.

238   Our Catholic Faith

Love God: The First Three Commandments

Jesus taught that we should love the Lord our God with our whole heart, soul, strength, and mind (Lk 10:27). The first three commandments show us how to do so, that is, how to respond to a God who gave us life, his Son, and the gift of eternal life.

I. I, the Lord, Am Your God. You Shall Not Have Other Gods Besides Me. (CCC, 2083, 2087–2094, 2101, 2103, 2111–2132)

The First Commandment tells us to make God the top priority in our lives. How do we do this? One way

of doing so is to practice the theological virtues of faith, hope, and charity. We practice our faith and hope when we show trust in God and his Divine Revelation, mercy, and promise of eternal life. We also demonstrate our faith when we worship God and share our faith with

Putting the Ten Commandments into Practice

There are two versions of the Ten Commandments in the Old Testament: Exodus (20:2–17) and Deuteronomy (5:6–21). The first three commandments spell out what it means to love God; the last seven instruct us on love of neighbor.

Both Christ and the Church teach that the Ten Commandments are indeed *commandments*, not suggestions. God has written them on our hearts, and he gives us the graces necessary to obey them. The Commandments teach truth. They tell us what we must do as humans who depend on God and live with one another. They protect basic human rights. They apply to all people in all places at all times.

Catholics must obey the commandments under the penalty of sin. All people have a serious duty to obey the Ten Commandments. Take some time to reread and memorize the Ten Commandments, listed below:

I.   I, the Lord, am your God. You shall not have other gods besides me.
II.   You shall not take the name of the Lord, your God, in vain.
III. Remember to keep holy the Sabbath day.
IV.   Honor your father and your mother.
V.   You shall not kill.
VI.   You shall not commit adultery.
VII. You shall not steal.
VIII. You shall not bear false witness against your neighbor.
IX.   You shall not covet your neighbor's wife.
X.   You shall not covet anything that belongs to your neighbor.

- If God asked you to compose three additional commandments for the modern world, what would they be?
- Rewrite the Ten Commandments in your own words. Turn all the negative statements into positive ones. Share your versions with your classmates.

Extending the Lesson

Student Presentations: Ask for volunteers to share the stories of their names. How did their parents choose their name? Were they named for someone in the family? For someone famous? For a saint? Ask whether any of the students know anyone, themselves or childhood friends, whose name was used as the basis for teasing? Young children often make jokes out of classmates' names. Why do they think this might be a particularly painful form of teasing for the child being teased?

Class Activity: Encourage the students for one day to pay careful attention to everything that they say. How often do they catch themselves saying things that are not true? Making promises that they do not really intend to try very hard to keep? Is their word their bond? Do they use their tongue, in the words of St. James, both to bless and to curse? Is their language immature—full of vulgar "bathroom" talk?

Resources

 **Internet Links** see www.avemariapress.com

others. We exhibit charity when we love God, and our fellow humans, with our whole heart.

The theological virtues lead us to the moral virtues and to the *virtue of religion*. The virtue of religion helps us give to God what is his just due—that is, reverence, love, and worship. We have a duty to worship God both individually and socially. Civil law must protect the right of individuals and communities to worship God freely according to the dictates of their conscience.

The way to exercise the virtue of religion is through adoration, prayer, works of sacrifice, and keeping our promises and vows. When we adore God, we are humble and thankful for all he has done for us. When we pray, we are lifting our minds and hearts to God in praise, thanksgiving, sorrow, petition, and intercession. Prayer also helps us keep God's commandments. When we join our works of sacrifice to Jesus' sacrifice on the cross, we make our lives pleasing to God. Finally, the virtue of religion makes it possible to keep the promises Catholics make at Baptism, Confirmation, Holy Orders, and Matrimony. The virtue of religion enables believers to keep their vows, that is, any special promises they made to God, especially the evangelical counsels (vows) of poverty, chastity, and obedience.

The First Commandment counsels against sins against the virtue of faith like heresy (false teaching that denies a truth of the faith), apostasy (denial of Christ), and schism (a break in union with the Pope by refusing to accept his authority to teach for Christ). The First Commandment also teaches us to avoid sins against the virtue of hope. These include presumption, which says a person can save himself without God's help or without personal conversion, and despair, which occurs when a person

believes that even God cannot or will not forgive a person his or her sins. The sin of despair is unjust to a God who is always faithful to his promises.

Finally, sins against the virtue of love include refusing to accept God's love, ingratitude, and spiritual laziness. Outright hatred of God is the worst sin of all against a God of perfect love. The root of this sin is pride.

The First Commandment condemns the worship of false gods and the following sins:

1. *Superstition*, which attributes magical powers to certain objects, acts, words, or external religious practices apart from proper interior dispositions, for example, of faith and humility.
2. *Idolatry*, which includes the worship of false gods, including the worship of many gods (polytheism). Today, idolatry includes not only cults that worship Satan, but also making a god out of things like money, prestige, sex,

apostasy
The denial of Christ and repudiation of the Christian faith by a baptized Christian.

presumption
An act or attitude opposed to the theological virtue of hope. It can take the form of trust in self without recognizing that Salvation comes from God.

despair
Giving up hope in God's saving graces, his forgiveness of sins, and his promise of Salvation.

idolatry
Giving worship to something or someone other than the true God.

Teaching Approaches

- **Class Discussion:** Begin with the first commandment from the subsection "I. I, the Lord, Am Your God. You Shall Not Have Other Gods Besides Me" (pages 238–240). Use an "on the spot" format to direct the discussion of this commandment. Ask for a volunteer to be on the spot for three questions.

  ◆ While they are in front of the room, you will ask them three questions about the first commandment and the sins against it that are covered in this section. Do not limit yourself to asking them for definitions of the various sins listed in the section. Better questions would help them apply the definitions to things they see happening around them. For example, ask them to name some superstitions they know of, such as "breaking a mirror brings seven years of bad luck." Or, you might ask them to name some of the things they think teens idolize today.

  ◆ Keep changing the student who is on the spot. There are a number of ways to do this: you can allow the departing student to choose his or her replacement freely; you can draw students' names at random out of a bowl or bag; you can ask for volunteers each time (if you have a class full of extroverts); or you can give students guidelines for choosing their replacements, such as telling them to choose someone of the opposite sex, or with different-colored eyes, or with a birthday in the month after theirs, etc.

 Audiovisual Materials continued from page 237

Living Simply
Our faith challenges us to live simply in a consumer society (28-minute video, Bosco).

Making Sense of Christian Morality
Set of four videos by Paulist priest Fr. Richard Sparks. Topics include objective truth and conscience, the common good and social justice, human sexuality, and bioethical issues. Good teacher background (25-minutes each, Paulist Press).

A Man for All Seasons
Paul Scofield stars as St. Thomas More in this excellent adaptation of the Robert Bold play of the same name (120-minute feature film, DVD, Amazon.com).

Mind Over Media
Shows how the media affects us all. Hosted by recording artists and youth speaker Lakita Garth. Features interviews with teens nationwide and helps them understand the media's influence on their lives. Includes study guide (30-minute video, Videos with Values).

The Miracle of Life
An award-winning NOVA documentary using incredible photography charting the beginning of life through to birth (50-minute video, Amazon.com/ Critics' Choice).

The Neighbor: The Parable of the Good Samaritan
A rendering of Luke 10:25–37. Produced by the American Bible Society (12-minute video, Harcourt).

Quiz Show
Robert Redford-directed film about the quiz show scandals of the 1950s. Good example of dishonesty, fame, and the corrupting influences of the media (1994, 103-minute feature film on DVD, Amazon.com).

Reality in Relationships
Ellen Marie, founder of Youth Support, Inc., gives a talk in a Catholic high school to help teens understand the dynamics of quality relationships, the practical reasons for chastity, and why the guidelines regarding the gift of sexuality in the Bible are for teenagers' benefit (45-minute video, Values with Videos). *continued on page 249*

- **Class Discussion:** Focus on the Explaining Your Faith question from page 240 about religious images. Invite volunteer students to debate the pros and cons of keeping religious images. Divide the class in half—voluntarily based on interest if possible, or randomly if necessary to keep the two groups close to the same size. Have one group concentrate on presenting the benefits of religious images and the other on explaining the potential problems.
  - When they are ready, a volunteer from each group can act as the spokesperson to present their case. Each spokesperson should give an opening statement. Following the opening statement, they should have an opportunity to refute the other's position and bolster their own with any additional arguments their group comes up with.
  - At the end of the debate, be sure your class knows that the Church ultimately comes down in favor of religious imagery, though Christians are reminded to be mindful of the possible abuses that may result. Invite the students to look at their own use or avoidance of religious images and consider whether they should adjust their approach to them in any way.
- **Direct Instruction:** Continue by covering the second commandment from the text subsection "II. You Shall Not Take the Name of the Lord, Your God, in Vain" (pages 241–242). Review the section material with your students until you are sure they understand why false oaths, blasphemy, perjury, cursing, and any use of God's name when we do not really intend to address or speak accurately about God is a violation of this commandment.
- **Class Discussion:** Brainstorm with the students to find "opposites," virtuous acts, corresponding to each of the sins listed in this section. For example, the opposite of blasphemy might be praising God's mercy and loving kindness; the opposite of cursing is to pray for God to bless a person with some good. Discuss with the students which of these acts they perform regularly.
- **Video Presentation:** Read or summarize the Profile of Faith feature "St. Thomas More: A Man of Conscience and Principle" (page 242). Show all or part of the film *A Man for All Seasons*. Discuss the problems Thomas More had with King Henry and the ways he sought to solve them. Can your students think of other solutions that Thomas might have tried? Most, if not all, of the other noblemen in England were willing to take the oath. Ask the students why they think this was so. Ask them to reflect on what their response might have been.

---

sorcery
Attempts to tame occult powers in order to use them to gain a supernatural power over others.

power, athletic ability, and so forth. Idolatry turns us away from the true God by taking a created good and making it a god.

3. *Divination* attempts to reveal what is hidden (occult). It involves calling on Satan or the demons, conjuring up the dead, consulting horoscopes and the stars (astrology) and mediums, reading palms, and playing with Ouija boards. These, and practices like sorcery, which tries to control hidden powers, show disrespect to God.

4. *Irreligion* disrespects God's loving care for us by tempting God in word or deed to manifest his goodness.

5. *Sacrilege* seriously disrespects (profanes) the sacraments and sacred things, places, or persons specially consecrated to God. Sacrilege is mortally sinful, especially when committed against Christ in the Eucharist.

6. *Simony* is the attempt to buy or sell spiritual things. This is wrong because God's graces are free gifts that can never be purchased or sold.

7. *Atheism* denies that God exists. It has many forms. For example, *materialists*

claim that something is real only if we can sense it. They deny the existence of spiritual realities like God and the human soul. *Humanists* make human beings their god and do not believe in God as the controlling source in our world. *Communists* look to economic laws and forces as the real basis of human freedom and claim that God is a fiction. All these forms of atheism are serious because they deny that the true God exists. However, a particular atheist may have diminished blameworthiness for this sin because of circumstances or intentions. For example, he or she may not have correctly heard about God and his love for humankind.

8. An *agnostic* claims that we can never be certain whether God exists or not. Agnostics do not outright deny God's existence like atheists, but they often live their lives as though God does not exist. Their refusal to take a stand is, in fact, a decision against God since they refuse to make any kind of a religious response to God.

Explaining Your Faith

Why do Catholics keep religious pictures, statues, and the like? Doesn't the First Commandment outlaw the keeping of images?

Because the Son of God became a human being, the Church teaches that it is fitting for Christians to venerate icons (religious paintings, mosaics, and the like) and statues of Jesus, his Blessed Mother, and the angels and saints. Sacred images remind us of and direct our attention to the persons they represent. But we should always remember that only God deserves adoration. In the Old Testament, Yahweh forbade the making of images because the Chosen People sometimes created and worshiped idols.

Christians have special devotion to Mary and venerate her because she is the Mother of God and the Mother of the Church. We also venerate the saints who inspire us and pray for us. However, veneration and special devotion are not the same as worship. To worship anyone other than God is idolatry.

Background Information

Living the First Commandment

Through the first commandment, we are taught to make God the top priority in our lives. This is not always easy; however, the theological virtues help us by leading us to the moral virtues and to the virtue of religion, through which we are empowered to give God what is his just due—reverence, love, and worship.

Ann Russell Miller, a wealthy San Francisco socialite with ten children and eighteen grandchildren, traded in her posh life to enter a convent in 1989 at age 60. After throwing herself a going-away party for eight hundred of her friends and family, Ann knocked on the door of one of the strictest religious orders, the Carmelites, and dedicated the remainder of her life to God as Sister Mary Joseph. Despite her glamorous life before entering the convent, she willingly took vows of seclusion, poverty, chastity, and obedience, which means she is not able to see her children (who are adults now) unless they visit her at the convent and even then, is unable to touch them. Giving up her extravagant lifestyle and nine-bedroom mansion for a small cell with a bed made of wood planks and a thin mattress was no doubt a monumental change. But sixteen years later, she remains in the convent, steadfast in her commitment to the Lord. To read more about her life, visit http://catholiceducation.org/articles/catholic_stories/cs0108.html.

II. You Shall Not Take the Name of the Lord, Your God, in Vain. (CCC, 2142–2167)

When God revealed his name, Yahweh, to the Chosen People, he commanded that we honor his holy name through praise, reverence, and adoration. When we respect God's name, then we are honoring the holy and mysterious One behind the name. This is also true when we reverence the name of our Blessed Savior Jesus Christ and his Blessed Mother and the saints.

Our names are also holy. We have been called by Jesus and known by God from all eternity. We are baptized "in the name of the Father and of the Son and of the Holy Spirit." At that time, we also receive a baptismal name that often reminds us of a patron saint whose life can inspire us and who prays for us in Heaven. Through Baptism, the Lord makes our name holy, marking us as his disciples. Disciples have a wonderful way to pray throughout the day—by frequently praying the Sign of the Cross. This powerful prayer reminds us of our dignity. And it also tells us that we belong to a loving God whose graces make it possible for us to live up to the name Christian.

The Second Commandment outlaws any wrong use of God's name or the names of Jesus, Mary, or any saint. It teaches that we should keep our promises and vows and always be true to our word.

The taking of an oath should not be necessary for a Christian. Our word simply stated is enough to bind us. However, Jesus did not outlaw all oath-taking. Even St. Paul took oaths (see 2 Cor 1:23 and Gal 1:20.) For morally correct and serious reasons (for example, a legal trial), we may take an oath if we are doing so to serve justice. However, we may not take an oath if it requires us to support an institution that destroys human dignity or Christian unity. Church teaching holds that whenever we do take an oath, we must keep it. Perjury is the name for lying under oath. Perjury seriously dishonors God's holy name by calling on God to witness to a lie.

Blasphemy also seriously violates the Second Commandment. Blasphemy involves using internal or external words of hate, defiance, or reproach against God, Jesus, the saints, sacred things, or the Church. Blasphemy also includes using God's name to hide a crime or to enslave, torture, or kill people. This sin is intrinsically evil and can never be justified, regardless of the circumstances or intention.

Swearing under oath is also serious business. If we do so deliberately with God as our witness, intending to break the oath, then we commit mortal sin. This kind of swearing makes God a witness to a lie.

The Catholic tradition distinguishes swearing, cursing, and vulgar language. By definition, *swearing* calls down evil on another person. It is forbidden by the Second Commandment. If the curse

oath
A statement or promise that calls on God to be witness to it.

perjury
Lying under oath by asking God to witness to a lie. This is a grave violation of the Second Commandment.

blasphemy
Any thought, word, or act that expresses hatred or contempt for God, Christ, the Church, saints, or holy things.

Background Information

Living the Third Commandment

The third commandment instructs us to observe a day of rest, a Sabbath day. In his book *Sabbath: Finding Rest and Renewal and Delight in Our Busy Lives* (Bantam, 1999), Wayne Muller says, "In the relentless busyness of modern life, we have lost the rhythm of work and rest." He quotes Thomas Merton, who wrote: "The frenzy of our activism neutralizes our work for peace. It destroys our own inner capacity for peace. It destroys the fruitfulness of our own work, because it kills the root of inner wisdom which makes work fruitful." Muller outlines in his book ways to implement a Sabbath in our lives, from creating a peaceful place and special Sabbath meals, to methods of prayer and how to give ourselves permission to stop and rest. It is a good lesson for those who have a difficult time stopping to smell the roses.

- **Journal Assignment:** Focus on the third commandment and the text subsection "III. Remember to Keep Holy the Sabbath Day" (pages 242–243). Begin by asking the students to write in their journals *everything* they can remember doing on the previous Sunday. When they have exhausted their memory, have them note which activities on their list they do nearly *every* Sunday, which they rarely do *except* on Sundays, and which they think help to refresh them and prepare them to face the coming week. Discuss the results, noting the things in the students' lists that mark Sunday as a special kind of day.

- **Class Discussion:** Make observations about what it means to keep the Sabbath holy. Ask the students about special activities that their family does on Sundays. Ask about Mass attendance. Why do they go? Or why don't they? Do their parents have to, or choose to, work on Sundays? What kinds of jobs must be done on Sundays (police, doctors, nurses, firefighters, rescue workers, priests, etc.)? If you have time, stage a debate between the students in your class over whether or not it would be a good thing if more stores and businesses were closed on Sundays, as they used to be. How would such a change affect teenagers? Store employees?

- **Group Activity:** Divide the class into groups of four. Distribute Chapter 9, Handout 2 "Keeping the Sabbath" (starting on page 285 and also online at www.avemariapress.com) to each student. Have each student take responsibility for reading one of the passages. Then have them go around the group and share the larger story and summary (answers are on page 246 of this TWE) for their passage. Each person should fill in all of the sections of the worksheet.

For Enrichment

Individual Assignment: Have the students research the different significance and traditions various cultures give to names and naming. For instance, in some Native American communities names were considered so powerful that people were given a secret name that was rarely used; it was shared with very few people who were especially trusted. In Italian families, there are very precise "rules" for determining children's names: the eldest son is given the paternal grandfather's name, the second son the maternal grandfather's name, while daughters are named first for the paternal and then the maternal grandmother. Students can present their research in a number of ways: a written report, an oral presentation, a poster or visual explanation, and the like.

- **Direct Instruction:** Review the applications of the first three commandments to modern-day life. Say one of the sins or positive actions connected to any of the first three commandments and have the students show the number of fingers that correspond to the number of the commandment. Periodically, call on students at random to name each commandment. For example, when you say "the virtue of religion," students should raise one finger. When you say "blasphemy," students should raise two fingers, and so on. Continue to do this until you feel the students have sufficiently mastered the connections between these sins and actions and the commandments.

For Review Answers (page 243)

1. I. *I, the Lord, am your God. You shall not have other gods besides me.* God should be the top priority in your life.

II. *You shall not take the name of the Lord, your God, in vain.* Respect for God's name and all holy things gives honor to the holy and mysterious One behind the name.

III. *Remember to keep holy the Sabbath Day.* Sunday is a day to worship God, offering him thanks and praise for all his gifts, and to take time to refresh our spirits with restful recreation.

involves wishing serious harm on another, then it is a grave sin. Vulgar language involves using crude words (bathroom talk). It is immature rather than sinful.

St. James knew the many problems caused by the human tongue when he wrote:

> For every kind of beast and bird, of reptile and sea creature, can be tamed and has been tamed by the human species, but no human being

can tame the tongue. It is a restless evil, full of deadly poison. With it we bless the Lord and Father, and with it we curse human beings who are made in the likeness of God. From the same mouth come blessing and cursing. This need not be so, my brothers. (Jas 3:7–10)

PROFILE OF FAITH: ST. THOMAS MORE, A MAN OF CONSCIENCE AND PRINCIPLE

St. Thomas More is a famous example of a Catholic hero who refused to take an immoral oath. Thomas More was the Chancellor of England under King Henry VIII and a great and brilliant scholar. He is the author of the famous book *Utopia* (a word meaning "nowhere"), which outlined a society ruled by perfect justice. He did so to protest the new economy of his age where the rich took advantage of the poor. In his own life, Thomas was a devoted family man who raised his family in a spirit of prayer and generosity to the poor.

Thomas ran into trouble with Henry VIII when the king wanted Thomas's support in making Henry head of the Church in England. In a famous dispute, the pope refused to annul Henry's marriage to Catherine of Aragon, who had been unable to give a male heir. So Henry decided to take matters into his own hands. He declared himself the supreme authority of the church in England and forced the bishops to acknowledge him as such by taking an oath declaring their loyalty to him. Thomas More refused to do so because he knew this oath—the Act of Supremacy—would have denied the pope's authority over the Church. This would have been a denial of the pope's rightful authority as the vicar of Christ.

When Thomas refused the oath, he also resigned his prestigious office, even though it meant that he and his family fell into poverty. King Henry then required all his subjects to take the Oath of Succession, recognizing the legitimacy of his heirs by his new wife, Anne Boleyn. Thomas More also refused to take that oath, because he knew it was clearly wrong, too. He was arrested and spent fifteen months in the feared Tower of London, deaf to the pleas of his family to reconsider his decision. To the end, Thomas would not violate his conscience:

> I do nobody any harm, I say none harm, I think none harm. And if this be not enough to keep a man alive, in good faith I long not to live.

- Study and report on the life and death of St. Thomas More.

III. Remember to Keep Holy the Sabbath Day.

The Third Commandment is related to two truths of the Old Testament: First, God "rested" after he completed the work of creation. Second, God gave the Chosen People the Sabbath day as a sign of the covenant that he made with them by rescuing them from slavery in Egypt. The Israelites understood that the purpose of

this commandment was for them to praise God for his works of creation and to thank him for his saving works on their behalf.

God gives this commandment to all people for them to have a day of rest and recreation. Jesus taught its true purpose: "The sabbath was made for man, not man for the sabbath" (Mk 2:27). It is most proper for humans to worship and thank God. We should acknowledge that

Chapter 9, Handout 2 "Keeping the Sabbath" Answers

Genesis 2:1–3
- The larger story: The story of creation
- Summary: The Sabbath is intended to be a day of rest after labor on the first six days of the week.

Exodus 12:22–30
- The larger story: God gives the Israelites manna to eat
- Summary: The Sabbath is intended to apply at all times; even in times of difficulty or danger—perhaps especially in such times—God knows that people need days of rest to rejuvenate their spirits. Although we may be tempted to work through the Sabbath as though our efforts were what were essential, we should trust in God to provide for our needs.

Deuteronomy 5:12–15
- The larger story: God gives the Law of the Covenant
- Summary: The Sabbath applies to the entire community—even slaves and beasts of burden. We cannot rest ourselves by requiring others to work for us, even others who may not share our religious belief in the need for a day of rest.

Mark 2:23–18
- The larger story: Jesus' debates with the Pharisees
- Summary: This puts the whole commandment into the proper perspective: it was created for the benefit of human beings, who need regular times of rest. It is not intended as a burden, but as a relief from the burdens of our regular work. It is intended to do us good.

we are totally dependent on our loving God for all that he has given to us. This day should serve as a break from work, especially for the poor and working class, and from the endless pursuit of money.

Jesus brought new meaning to the Sabbath observance. Through his saving deeds, Jesus brought about a new creation, namely, eternal life for those who love him. The Resurrection of Jesus took place on a Sunday, the first day of the week, the "eighth day" following the Sabbath. We rightly call Sunday the "Lord's Day," and it is clearly distinguished from the Sabbath. For Christians, the observance of the Lord's Day on Sunday replaces the Sabbath. Since the time of the Apostles, Christians have gathered on Sundays to obey Jesus' command to break bread in his name. On this day we worship, praise, and thank God for the gift of the Son and all the other divine blessings granted us. Sunday is the holy day that celebrates God's Salvation through Jesus Christ.

Catholics are obliged to go to Mass on Sundays and Holy Days of Obligation to express, celebrate, and deepen their unity in Christ. The Eucharist is the heart of Catholic life, an opportunity for us to acclaim to others that we belong to Christ and are members of his Body, the Church. The Eucharist gives us Christ's life and the strength and guidance of the Holy Spirit. Because the Eucharist is central to our life in Christ, participating in the Sunday Mass (and on holy days) is a serious obligation that we must fulfill under the penalty of sin unless

some critical reason like sickness excuses us. Catholics who willfully miss Mass are guilty of mortal sin.

The best way to make the Lord's day holy is to receive him in the Eucharist. We also make this day holy by staying away from unnecessary work and business activities. Relaxing activities, spending time with our families, reading, enjoying the outdoors, serving others in need, and doing anything that helps to refresh our minds, hearts, and spirits are all appropriate ways to make Sunday holy.

For Review

1. Name and explain the first three commandments.
2. How does each of the following violate the First Commandment: heresy, apostasy, schism, presumption, despair, superstition, idolatry, divination, sacrilege, simony, and atheism?
3. How does each of the following violate the Second Commandment: perjury, blasphemy, swearing, and cursing?
4. Why is St. Thomas More known as a person of good conscience?
5. Besides going to Mass, how do Catholics keep Sunday holy?

 For Reflection
Discuss with members of your family some new activities you can do together to enhance family life on Sundays.

 ## Homework Assignment

1. Complete the For Review questions on page 243. If possible, bring the religious picture or statue to the next class session.
2. Write down three interesting facts about the life of St. Thomas More (see web link at www.avemariapress.com).
3. Continue working on the Ongoing Assignments.
4. Read the text section "Love Your Neighbor: The Fourth through Tenth Commandments" (pages 244–255).

Chapter 9, Handout 2 Answers continued

2. *Heresy* is a false teaching that denies a truth of the faith. It promotes an incorrect understanding of God, leading people to worship a false god. *Apostasy* denies Christ's divinity, thus not giving honor to God in the person of Jesus Christ. *Schism* is caused by a refusal to accept the authority of the pope to lead the Church and to teach for Christ. *Presumption* is a belief that a person can save himself without God's help or Christ's sacrifice. It does not give God the love and honor that is his due. *Despair* is another sin against the virtue of hope, this time a belief that one cannot be saved or forgiven even by God. This is an insult to the God of mercy and compassion who gave his life to save us. *Superstition* gives magical power to objects, actions, or words—even religious practices or prayers—without the necessary interior disposition. Again this belittles God, by the idea that we can control him through various objects, prayers, etc. *Idolatry* makes a god of something that is not God—such as money, prestige, power, sex, intelligence, athletic ability, fame, etc. *Divination* attempts to reveal that which is hidden by calling on Satan or the demons. *Sacrilege* is any serious disrespect shown to God; Christ (especially in the Eucharist); or any sacred thing, place, or person. *Simony* is the attempt to buy or sell spiritual things, which is a grave offense against God's generosity who gives his graces freely. *Atheism* is the deliberate denial of God's existence.

3. *Perjury* violates the second commandment by dishonoring God's name by calling on God to witness to a lie. *Blasphemy* is the sin of using words of hate, defiance, or reproach against God or any holy person or thing. This shows lack of respect and honor for God's holiness. *Swearing* on God's name that we will do something that we have no intention of doing is a serious abuse of God's name, as it calls upon God to witness a lie. *Cursing* is language that calls down or wishes for evil to happen to another person. Calling on God to do what is evil is a serious abuse of God's name.

4. St. Thomas More refused to violate his conscience by swearing an oath he did not believe in. He resigned from a prestigious office, fell into poverty, suffered imprisonment, and was eventually executed for his refusal, but throughout his trials he refused to go against what his conscience told him was right.

5. Catholics keep the Sabbath holy by participating in the Mass and receiving Eucharist, and by avoiding unnecessary work on Sundays.

Love Your Neighbor: The Fourth through Tenth Commandments (pages 244–255)

Objectives

In this lesson, the students will:

- explain ways to implement the fourth through tenth commandments in their lives in positive ways.
- describe ways to improve their family relationships.
- defend the Church's teachings on life issues.
- explain the social justice teachings of the Church and how they relate to the Ten Commandments.

 Preview

This is a very long section in the Student Text covering each of the fourth through tenth commandments in some detail. This section also includes an in-depth section on the relationship between Catholic social teaching and the seventh and tenth commandments.

All of the disparate subjects raised under the heading of the fifth commandment are connected as a part of the "seamless garment," the Church's expression of commitment to the value and dignity of human life in all its stages. As you discuss this section with your students, try to connect these issues, framing the entire section as a question of upholding the value and dignity of the human person rather than as a list of disconnected prohibitions.

The sixth and ninth commandments address topics of sexuality. Talking about sex with teenagers can be difficult but it is an important topic and must be done well. Consider seeking out some "experts." Your diocesan office may be able to put you in touch with people trained to make presentations on this subject to students. If you bring in a special presenter, be sure to inform parents, invite them to attend, and get permission slips if necessary. You may also choose to show one of the three films about teen sexuality listed in the video resources. If you do, be sure to preview the video before showing it to your class so that you can anticipate some of their questions.

Love Your Neighbor: The Fourth through Tenth Commandments

Jesus taught that the way we express our love for God is that we love our neighbor as we love ourselves. And St. Paul taught,

> The commandments, "You shall not commit adultery; you shall not kill; you shall not steal; you shall not covet," and whatever other commandment there may be, are summed up in this saying, (namely) "You shall love your neighbor as yourself." (Rom 13:9)

The next subsections cover each of these commandments individually.

IV. Honor Your Father and Your Mother. (CCC, 2197, 2201, 2204–2205, 2215, 2217–2219, 2222–2223, 2225, 2230, 2234, 2240, 2241)

The Fourth Commandment opens the second part of the Decalogue by stressing that charity begins at home. God created the family as the primary unit of society. It is a sacred community of love in which a husband and wife marry freely as equals to share their love and to participate with God in the procreation and education of children. The family is called the *domestic Church*, a community of faith, hope, and charity that teaches virtue, respect, and love. The family mirrors the love and unity of the Blessed Trinity.

The Fourth Commandment stresses several duties of parents. Parents must respect their children as persons with dignity. They must educate them, especially in the Catholic faith. They must provide them with a loving home where their children can experience warmth, love, respect, and forgiveness and where they can learn the meaning of service. Parents should encourage their children to respond to the Lord if he should call them to serve as a priest or in consecrated life and should respect the right of their adult children to choose a profession and marriage partner. Parents must at all times give their children unconditional love and affection and, in this way, serve as models of God's love.

The Fourth Commandment also requires certain behaviors from children. Children are to thank their parents for the gift of life. Children show their gratitude by respecting and honoring their parents throughout their lives. Furthermore, children should obey their parents as long as they live in their home. Adult children honor their parents by meeting their physical and spiritual needs when their aged parents are sick or lonely. Also, siblings are to treat each other with respect and love.

Respect and obedience due all proper Church and other authority figures (teachers, employers, police, leaders) is connected to the Fourth Commandment. In the civic order, this implies a moral obligation to pay taxes, exercise the right to vote, and serve the nation in its defense or some other way. Jesus himself taught, "Repay to Caesar what belongs to Caesar and to God what belongs to God" (Lk 20:25). St. Paul also instructed his readers to obey proper authorities (see Rom 13:1).

However, obedience to civil authority is not absolute. Governments must respect the God-given rights of individuals, parents, and families. For example, governments have the duty to recognize the parents' primary right to educate their children according to their own

For Enrichment

Individual Assignment: Ask the students to watch one episode of a television show that involves a family. During the show they are to take notes about the way the family members treat one another and how they are presented by the writers of the program. Who are the admirable characters? Why? Which characters are disrespected? Why? They should also note the contents of the commercials that air during the show. When there are family members shown in the commercials, how do they treat one another? In your next class period, discuss the shows your students watched in relation to the fourth commandment. Ask them to consider whether and how the characters showed respect and love for one another. Ask them what behavior they recognized from their own families. Do the various shows that the students chose or the commercials they observed have anything in common in terms of the way they present family relationships?

convictions. When societal laws conflict with God's will or God's law, then we must obey God, even if this leads to personal suffering.

Today, when so many devalue the family and disrespect unborn human beings, a loving Christian family can be a shining beacon pointing to the presence of God in ordinary life.

V. You Shall Not Kill. (CCC, 2258, 2263–2268, 2270–2298, 2307–2316)

The Fifth Commandment teaches respect for the sanctity of human life. God is the source and final destiny of all human life. Therefore, human life is sacred, from the first moment of conception until natural death. Every person has profound dignity because of being created in God's image and likeness.

We show respect for God's gift of life by eating healthy food, by getting proper exercise and rest, by challenging our minds to grow, and by avoiding harmful substances like drugs, alcohol, and tobacco. Taking care of ourselves physically, mentally, psychologically, and spiritually frees us to be persons for others. We respect life when we defend the rights of others so that they may live with dignity. This is especially true when we defend the weak and helpless in our midst.

Any direct and intentional killing of a human being is a sinful violation of the Fifth Commandment. The Old Testament applies this to *murder*, that is, the deliberate killing of innocent human beings. Murder is the result of Original Sin. Anger and hate lead to mortal sin, including murder. Murder violates human dignity, God's holiness, and Jesus' teaching that we must love our neighbor as we love ourselves. Today, we see how anger and revenge greatly threaten human dignity, for example, in acts of kidnapping, hostage taking, and torture. *Terrorism* is an especially grave evil that results in the murder of countless innocent humans. It must be severely condemned.

The Fifth Commandment does *not* condemn killing in self-defense. Killing in self-defense is morally permitted as a last resort when a person is defending his or her own life against an unjust aggressor, or when someone responsible for another is protecting that person's life. In cases of legitimate self-defense, the intention is to save one's own life against an unjust aggressor. The killing of the assailant is not directly willed; it is only allowed. In a similar way, public authorities have both the right and

duty to defend citizens against unjust aggressors, even if this might lead to the death penalty or to a defensive war.

In all cases, however, individuals and society *must* always use bloodless means to defend against unjust aggressors if at all possible. Consider for a moment that the reasons we punish criminals are to set right the disorder caused by the offense, to correct the offender, and to preserve public order and personal safety. The *death penalty* simply fails to achieve the first and second of these aims, and is only very rarely necessary to accomplish the third. It cannot "set right the disorder caused by the offense" as it does not undo the crime (e.g., if the criminal was a murderer, his or her death would not restore life to his victim), nor can it correct the offender

since it ends his or her life. Public safety and order can be achieved in many ways without recourse to the death penalty. "The cases in which the execution of the offender is an absolute necessity are very rare, if not practically non-existent" (*CCC*, 2267). Therefore, the Church teaches that governments should use nonlethal means of punishment as an example of putting into practice Jesus' example of forgiving love. The death penalty may be permitted only "in cases of absolute necessity."

In a similar way, war must be reasonably avoided at all costs because it involves great evil and injustice. We must always strive to be peacemakers. Peace is "the tranquility of order." It results when human dignity is

Bell Ringers

- **Direct Instruction:** Review their answers to the For Review questions about the first three commandments.

- **Direct Instruction:** Ask the students to write down "Jesus' two great commandments" in their notes, without any discussion. Do not give them any help in remembering which commandments you mean, or allow them to talk among themselves. When they are finished, write the commandments on the board: "To love God with all your heart, and with all your soul, and with all your mind," and "to love your neighbor as yourself." Remind them that the first three of the Ten Commandments are summed up in the first, while the remaining seven, which they are about to begin studying, are summed up in the second.

 ## Audiovisual Materials continued from page 243

continued from page 243

Sex and Love: What's a Teenager to Do?

"Mary Beth Bonacci talks to teens about the 'do's' of chastity. Using Scripture and humorous, down-to-earth examples from teenage life, she shows that chastity is more than just abstinence—chastity is active. It's about loving in a relationship the way that God intended" (60-minute video, Vision Video).

Teens and Chastity: Catholic Program

Molly Kelly explains that chastity is the only choice that is 100 percent effective against pregnancy and sexually transmitted diseases, including AIDS. Talk is before a live teen audience (video from Center for Learning).

Teenage Suicide

Warning signs given (28-minute video, Don Bosco).

The Ten Commandments for Teens: God's Game Plan for a Happy Life

Fr. Joe Kempf, a priest and soccer coach, using vignettes and examples, explains the deeper meaning of each commandment (40-minute video, Liguori Publications).

Twelve Angry Men

The classic Henry Fonda version that tells the story of man struggling to do what is right despite opposition from eleven jurors (1957, 95-minute black-and-white feature film, Amazon.com/Critics' Choice).

We Are Called: Catholic Social Teaching for Today

The Archdiocese of St. Paul and Minneapolis produced this video, which features Fr. John Forliti who discusses seven main principles of Catholic social teaching (22-minute video, Harcourt).

Teaching Approaches

- **Individual Assignment:** Begin with a discussion of the fourth commandment related to the text subsection "IV. Honor Your Father and Your Mother" (pages 244–245). Use Chapter 9, Handout 3 "Family Relationships" (starting on page 285 and also online at www.avemariapress.com) to help your students consider their relationships with their parents and siblings. Ask the students how getting along with their siblings can help them to show respect for their parents. (It certainly promotes peace in the family, as all of your students with siblings will no doubt agree!)

- **Class Activity:** Divide your students into three groups—oldest children in one, youngest children in another, and only children in a third. You will probably have a few "middle children" and "only children" left over. Use them to balance the sizes of the "oldest" and "youngest" groups, since they have experiences in common with both. Ask the oldest and youngest groups to come up with a list of common complaints they have against their siblings. Ask the "only" group to list complaints they hear their friends make about siblings. Then ask each group to give the other group advice on ways to improve their relationship with the other. The "only" group can serve as moderators, determining whether the advice is fair and appropriate.

- **Direct Instruction:** Make sure the students understand how the fourth commandment also applies to obeying other legitimate figures of authority (teachers, police officers, etc.) outside of the home (see page 244).

---

respected, the goods of persons are safeguarded, and free communication among people takes place. "Peace is the work of justice and the effect of charity" (*CCC*, 2304).

However, the Church acknowledges the right of legitimate governments to participate in a just war of defense under these conditions:

- the damage inflicted by the aggressor is lasting, grave, and certain;
- it is truly a last resort after all other means to resolve the conflict have first been exhausted;
- the prospects of success are serious;
- the use of arms will not produce evil graver than the evil to be eliminated (see *CCC*, 2309).

Once a nation goes to war, it must follow the moral law, for example, by protecting noncombatants and by using the minimum force necessary. It is for this reason that the American bishops teach that the use of nuclear and other weapons of mass destruction that cause grave harm to entire communities of people cannot be justified. Furthermore, the arms race and the selling of arms is sinful. Their cost seriously harms poor people as it diverts valuable resources from assisting those in need to building up the tools of war. A Christian must always recall and live Jesus' Beatitude, "Blessed are the peacemakers, for they will be called children of God" (Mt 5:9).

As covered above, the Fifth Commandment forbids several actions that directly and intentionally kill innocent people. It also forbids any action or failure to act that results in their indirect killing. The Fifth Commandment strictly outlaws the following:

1. *Direct abortion*, willed either as a means or an end, is a grave violation of the Fifth Commandment. Human life must be respected and protected

abortion
The direct and deliberate ending of a pregnancy by killing the unborn child. Direct abortion, willed either as a means or an end, gravely contradicts the moral law.

euthanasia
"Any action or omission which of itself and by intention causes death, with the purpose of eliminating all suffering" (*The Gospel of Life*, No. 65). This is distinguished from palliative care that alleviates a person's suffering as the inevitable death nears. Euthanasia is a serious violation of the Fifth Commandment, a crime against life, and an attack on humanity.

by law from the very first moment of conception. Everyone has a God-given right to life. This right does not have to be earned. Because abortion is such a serious attack on innocent life, the Church imposes the penalty of excommunication on those who cooperate in an abortion. The Fifth Commandment also outlaws as seriously wrong nontherapeutic genetic manipulation or medical experimentation that treats the embryo as disposable biological material.

2. *Intentional euthanasia is murder.* This is true regardless of the form it takes (e.g., assisted suicide) or the motives for doing it (e.g., to relieve pain). A person does *not* commit the sin of euthanasia by refusing to use "extraordinary means" to keep oneself alive in the face of a terminal illness. A dying person must always use ordinary means (like taking in fluid) to sustain life; however, he or she is not obligated to use "extraordinary" ones (like a heart transplant).

3. *Suicide* gravely contradicts love of self. It also rejects God's rule over life and death and violates the virtues of justice, hope, and charity. Because of psychological problems, people who commit suicide may not be fully blameworthy for their actions. Their action is objectively wrong, but we commend their souls to the forgiveness of God and to our own prayers for their souls. As the *Catechism* consoles:

We should not despair of the eternal Salvation of persons who have taken their own lives. By ways known to him alone, God can provide the opportunity for salutary repentance. The Church prays for people who have taken their own lives. (*CCC*, 2283)

Background Information

Sister Helen Prejean

Sister Helen Prejean, C.S.J., is perhaps America's most well-known opponent of the death penalty since the publishing of her book, *Dead Man Walking*, in 1993. Since then, an opera, play, and movie have all been made based upon her book. Sister Helen was born the daughter of an attorney in Baton Rouge, Louisiana, in 1939. Her work with death row inmates began in 1981. Since then she has accompanied six men to their executions, while at the same time working with victims' families and establishing a support group for them called *Survive*. Consider viewing the movie *Dead Man Walking* with your students or having them read all or selected portions of the book. Students can find out more about Sister Helen Prejean and her work at the website, www.prejean.org.

For Enrichment

Individual Assignment: Have the students write to state or federal legislators to express their concern about current issues connected with the fifth commandment to voice their support for life.

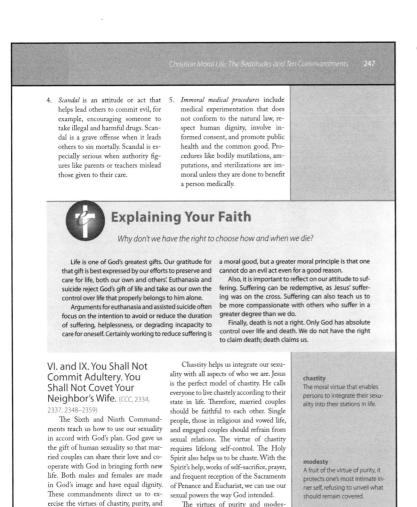

4. *Scandal* is an attitude or act that helps lead others to commit evil, for example, encouraging someone to take illegal and harmful drugs. Scandal is a grave offense when it leads others to sin mortally. Scandal is especially serious when authority figures like parents or teachers mislead those given to their care.

5. *Immoral medical procedures* include medical experimentation that does not conform to the natural law, respect human dignity, involve informed consent, and promote public health and the common good. Procedures like bodily mutilations, amputations, and sterilizations are immoral unless they are done to benefit a person medically.

Explaining Your Faith

Why don't we have the right to choose how and when we die?

Life is one of God's greatest gifts. Our gratitude for that gift is best expressed by our efforts to preserve and care for life, both our own and others'. Euthanasia and suicide reject God's gift of life and take as our own the control over life that properly belongs to him alone.

Arguments for euthanasia and assisted suicide often focus on the intention to avoid or reduce the duration of suffering, helplessness, or degrading incapacity to care for oneself. Certainly working to reduce suffering is a moral good, but a greater moral principle is that one cannot do an evil act even for a good reason.

Also, it is important to reflect on our attitude to suffering. Suffering can be redemptive, as Jesus' suffering was on the cross. Suffering can also teach us to be more compassionate with others who suffer in a greater degree than we do.

Finally, death is not a right. Only God has absolute control over life and death. We do not have the right to claim death; death claims us.

VI. and IX. You Shall Not Commit Adultery. You Shall Not Covet Your Neighbor's Wife. (CCC, 2334, 2337, 2348–2359)

The Sixth and Ninth Commandments teach us how to use our sexuality in accord with God's plan. God gave us the gift of human sexuality so that married couples can share their love and cooperate with God in bringing forth new life. Both males and females are made in God's image and have equal dignity. These commandments direct us to exercise the virtues of chastity, purity, and modesty in order to live moral lives as God's precious children created with a beautiful sexual nature.

Chastity helps us integrate our sexuality with all aspects of who we are. Jesus is the perfect model of chastity. He calls everyone to live chastely according to their state in life. Therefore, married couples should be faithful to each other. Single people, those in religious and vowed life, and engaged couples should refrain from sexual relations. The virtue of chastity requires lifelong self-control. The Holy Spirit also helps us to be chaste. With the Spirit's help, works of self-sacrifice, prayer, and frequent reception of the Sacraments of Penance and Eucharist, we can use our sexual powers the way God intended.

The virtues of purity and modesty help us combat lust. Lust is the vice of a disordered craving for or enjoyment of sexual pleasure, apart from how God

chastity
The moral virtue that enables persons to integrate their sexuality into their stations in life.

modesty
A fruit of the virtue of purity, it protects one's most intimate inner self, refusing to unveil what should remain covered.

- **Class Activity:** Proceed to the fifth commandment from the text subsection "V. You Shall Not Kill" (pages 245–247). Review the section material with your students, encouraging them to ask questions to clarify Church teaching on the various issues. There is a selection of moral dilemmas on Chapter 9, Handout 4 "Moral Dilemmas Related to Life Issues" (starting on page 285 and also online at www.avemariapress.com) to help you get the students thinking about the topic. Rather than simply reading and trying to discuss them, ask the students to show their response physically by moving to some point along a continuum from "absolutely okay" to "absolutely wrong" that you have stretched across the front of the classroom. Then you can move up and down the line, interviewing students about their response and the position they have chosen in response to each dilemma.
- **Individual Assignment:** Have your class vote on the one issue that most interests or concerns them. Research this issue in more depth (see the "For Enrichment" notes on page 252 for starting points on the death penalty and abortion).

Background Information

Seamless Garment of Life

In a speech at Fordham University in December 1983, Joseph Cardinal Bernardin first proposed a consistent ethic of life as the necessary basis for all of the Church's arguments on issues affecting human life. His approach, which later used the visual image of the "seamless garment," made connections between the Church's positions on a wide variety of issues including the death penalty, nuclear war, abortion, euthanasia, and social policies that worsen or do nothing to mitigate poverty. Pope John Paul II, in his encyclical "The Gospel of Life," used the same language and included the same topics in defining the Catholic pro-life position. In speaking about abortion, Bernardin applied the consistent ethic of life in this way:

> If one contends, as we do, that the right of every fetus to be born should be protected by civil law and supported by civil consensus, then our moral, political and economic responsibilities do not stop at the moment of birth. Those who defend the right to life of the weakest among us must be equally visible in support of the quality of life of the powerless among us: the old and the young, the hungry and the homeless, the undocumented immigrant and the unemployed worker. Such a quality of life posture translates into specific political and economic positions on tax policy, employment generation, welfare policy, nutrition and feeding programs, and health care. Consistency means we cannot have it both ways. We cannot urge a compassionate society and vigorous public policy to protect the rights of the unborn and then argue that compassion and significant public programs on behalf of the needy undermine the moral fiber of the society or are beyond the proper scope of governmental responsibility.

You can find the entire Fordham University speech, as well as other lectures by Bernardin on his "seamless garment" model, at www.priestsforlife.org.

- **Class Activity:** Before leaving the topics related to the fifth commandment, address the question presented in the Explaining Your Faith feature on page 247 about euthanasia and assisted suicide. Read or summarize the text answer. Also explain that suffering is a great mystery of the human condition. Ask the students to share their willingness to suffer for a good cause. Use the continuum approach described on page 251 having students position themselves according to their willingness or unwillingness to suffer the following:

  - sore muscles and blisters from working out to try for a spot on a sports team;

  - sore muscles and blisters from wearing uncomfortable shoes because they are the latest fad;

  - a safe but painful surgical procedure like bone marrow donation to save the life of a family member;

  - a safe but painful surgical procedure like bone marrow donation to save the life of a perfect stranger;

  - missing a special school event to visit a grandparent in a nursing home;

  - missing a friend's party to stay home with a younger sibling so that your parents could go out to their own party;

  - missing a friend's party to stay home with a younger sibling so that your parents could work at a fundraiser to support a local homeless shelter and food pantry.

The point of this exercise is to show that people are more willing to suffer for what they consider a good cause. As you interview students, concentrate on why they are willing or unwilling to suffer a certain thing, ask them what might make them more or less willing, etc. When you return to the text, ask them what kinds of things might make people more willing to suffer as they approach death.

intended us to use our sexual powers. While sexual thoughts and desires are part of who we are as human beings, they can become evil when they control us or when we look at others as objects for self-gratification, and not as whole persons worthy of our respect.

The virtue of purity helps us in the struggle against lust by attuning our minds and hearts to God's holiness in all aspects of our lives. We gain purity when we cooperate with God's grace, for example, by refusing impure thoughts when they arise and by constantly praying for God's help. Purity requires modesty, a virtue that protects the mystery of persons and their love. Modesty refuses to unveil what should remain covered.

This virtue requires patience, decency in the clothes we wear, and care and respectful attitudes when talking about sex. Modesty governs unhealthy curiosity and demands respect of persons. Today we live in a sex-saturated society. The virtue of modesty requires all people to work for wholesomeness in society, especially in the media, which so often treat sex in unhealthy and even disgusting ways.

Lust leads to the following sinful abuses of God's gift of sexuality. All of these are forbidden by the Sixth and Ninth Commandments:

- *Masturbation* is deliberate stimulation of the sexual organs to gain sexual pleasure. Masturbation is wrong because God intended the pleasure associated with sexual activity for the commitment of a marriage union. Although any misuse of our sexual powers is sinful, we should be careful of judging whether serious sin has been committed. The Church teaches that inexperience, immaturity, habit, anxiety, or other psychological and social factors can lessen (or remove) a person's moral blameworthiness in this area (see *CCC*, 2352).
- *Fornication* is sexual intercourse engaged in by unmarried people. Fornication seeks pleasure without responsibility. It lacks the unconditional love

Introducing the Theology of the Body

The "Theology of the Body" was the subject of a series of 129 talks given by Pope John Paul II during his regular Wednesday audiences from September 1979 to November 1984. The complete series was later collected and published into one work and now forms an integrated look at the human person—body, mind, and soul. The talks also address topics like the purpose of life, the vocation to love, and what it means to be truly pure of heart.

Examine some of the Pope's addresses on the Theology of the Body at several websites, including the link at the Vatican site: http://www.vatican.va/holy_father/john_paul_ii/audiences/index.htm. Then complete one of the following assignments:

- Select a topic of interest under "Life Issues" on the United States Catholic Bishops' website. Read and report on three articles, fact sheets, or Church documents associated with the particular topic.
- Interview a couple who has been married fifteen years or more. Record the qualities they believe are essential for a happy life together. Ask them to share practical ways a couple can improve the quality of their relationship as the marriage progresses.
- Explain the teachings about sexual behavior in the following Scripture verses: 1 Thessalonians 4:1–8, 1 Corinthians 6:18–20, Ephesians 5:3–7, Colossians 3:5, Hebrews 13:4.

For Enrichment

Individual Assignment: Have students choose one of the life issues discussed in connection with the fifth commandment to research further. For euthanasia, abortion, and the death penalty, students should research local laws that apply, how these laws are enforced, and any movements to change the laws. In other words, does their state permit the death penalty? If so, how many executions are carried out in a given year? How many prisoners are on death row? Is anyone working to overturn the law? Or if there is no death penalty in your state now, is anyone working to establish one? If the student chooses to explore the issue of just war, have them consider the most recent military activity of the United States, applying the four conditions listed in the text. Be sure their research includes arguments made on both sides and includes the position of the Pope and other Church leaders.

that can only be found in the marriage of a totally committed couple.

- *Pornography* depersonalizes sex by putting something sacred on display for the sexual gratification of onlookers. It hurts the dignity of those who create, sell, and use it to arouse their passions.
- *Prostitution* debases those who sell their bodies. It is also a serious sin for those who pay prostitutes for sex.
- *Rape* is always a seriously, intrinsically evil act that is gravely unjust and unloving. Rape violates another's sexuality and attacks their human dignity. It is similar to two other abhorrent, inhuman acts that violate sexuality and human dignity: *incest* (sex acts performed by close relatives) and the *sexual abuse of children*.
- *Homosexual activity* contradicts God's intention of male-female bonding in a stable, permanent relationship of marriage. Homosexual acts differ from a homosexual orientation, that is, a predominant or exclusive sexual attraction to someone of the same sex. The orientation is not sinful because people do not choose their orientation, heterosexual or homosexual. However, persons with homosexual desires must resist translating their desires into homosexual genital actions because these acts are seriously wrong. They contradict the purposes of God's gift of sexuality: unity between a husband and wife and openness to the transmission of human life. Like single people with a heterosexual orientation, Christ calls persons with a same-sex attraction to be chaste. Although homosexual acts are seriously wrong, prejudice and discrimination against those who have a homosexual orientation are unjust and wrong as well.

Christ calls us to live moral lives in the area of sexuality because he knows that a misuse of our sexual powers seriously hurts us spiritually, psychologically, and even physically. Jesus knows our human weakness. But he is also our Savior. This is why he extends his love and guidance to us through the Church and specifically through the graces the Holy Spirit gives us in the sacraments and prayer. If we give in to sexual temptations, we should not hate ourselves. Rather, we should remember our Lord's compassionate love and forgiveness, seek

the Sacrament of Penance, learn from our failures, and continue our commitment to be chaste.

Marriage and the Sixth and Ninth Commandments (CCC, 2360–2391; 2397–2400)

The Sixth and Ninth Commandments support the institution of marriage. For example, they tell us that sexual intercourse, and all acts leading up to it, express the *total* commitment of love between a man and a woman who have given themselves to each other in marriage. This sexual sharing deepens and symbolizes their love. The husband and wife giving themselves totally to each other points to Christ's unconditional love for his Body, the Church. A Christian marriage should be like God's permanent covenant of love and fidelity. A marriage should reflect the faithful love of our Lord. This love is unselfish; nothing can break it. Only death can end the lifelong covenant of love that is known as marriage.

Sexual intercourse in marriage has two purposes: *unitive*, that is, the bonding of husband and wife as lifelong partners; and *procreative*, that is, cooperating with God in bringing new life into the world. Therefore, the Church teaches that each act of sexual intercourse should be open to these two purposes of marriage: the sharing of life and mutual love. In planning their families, therefore, it follows that couples must use moral methods that are open both to love and to life.

For good reasons, couples may abstain from sexual relations or employ natural methods of regulating births

- **Direct Instruction:** Move to discussion of the sixth and ninth commandments related to the subsection "VI. and IX. You Shall Not Commit Adultery. You Shall Not Covet Your Neighbor's Wife" (pages 247–250). Summarize the issues presented in the subsection. Instruct the students to write questions they have about any of these issues on pieces of scrap paper or index cards. Collect and refer to them throughout rest of this section.

- **Guest Speaker:** If you have chosen to bring in an outside speaker from the diocese to discuss the topic of sexuality (see the Preview on page 248), provide that person with copies of the chapter material for review. Also, you may wish to relay some of the questions the students have written down to the speaker. After the speaker's presentation, follow up by having the students complete Chapter 9, Handout 5 "Sexuality Presentation Follow-up" (starting on page 285 and also online at www.avemariapress .com). Also ask your students to write notes thanking the speaker for sharing the presentation with them. They can use the things they wrote on the follow-up sheets to make the notes personal and specific.

Resources

📖 Printed Materials

Auer, Jim. *What About Sex?* Liguori, MO: Liguori Publications, 2002.
   Supplementary pamphlet reading from an experienced catechist. Addresses the myths and opinions of sex that young people encounter in their daily lives.

Bonacci, Mary Beth. *Real Love: Mary Beth Bonacci Answers Your Questions on Dating, Marriage, and the Real Meaning of Sex*. San Francisco: Ignatius Press, 1996.
   Excellent reading for interested students.

Crossin, John W. *Everyday Virtues*. Mahwah, NJ: Paulist Press, 2002.
   Builds a case for love as the foundation for all the virtues.

Deren, Jane, Marissa Maurer, and Julie Vieira. *Catholic Social Teaching and Human Rights: An Educational Packet*. Washington, DC: Center of Concern, 1998.
   An outstanding resource for social justice teachers. Has some good learning strategies that can be fit into many teaching models. Includes excellent filmographies and addresses of important social justice organizations.

Dodds, Bill, and Michael J. Dodds, O.P. *Living the Beatitudes Today*. Chicago: Loyola Press, 1997.

Flynn, Eileen. *The Ten Commandments: Case Studies in Catholic Morality*. Notre Dame, IN: Ave Maria Press, 2010.
   An excellent supplementary resource for students to use to apply the Ten Commandments to real-life situations. With thirty case studies addressed to each commandment, this book is designed for teachers to use with students to develop crucial moral decision making at a young age.

Jeremias, Joachim. *The Sermon on the Mount*. Trans. by Norman Perrin. Minneapolis: Fortress Press, 1963.
   Try to find this short booklet for an excellent overview of the contents of the Sermon. Highly influential.

Kammer, Fred, S.J. *Doing Faith Justice*. Mahwah, NJ: Paulist Press, 1991.
   A very good and readable survey of Catholic social justice.

continued on page 255

- **Video Presentation:** If you have chosen to view a video relating to the topic, make a brief outline of the portions your students will be viewing. Leave plenty of space on the page for students to add their own notes and reactions. Follow the video with a question-and-answer period, responding to the students' written questions on sexuality as well as any questions that have arisen during the video.

- **Direct Instruction:** Continue by addressing the seventh and tenth commandments with references to the text section "VII. And X. You Shall Not Steal. You Shall Not Covet Anything that Belongs to Your Neighbor," including the separate feature "Catholic Social Teaching and the Seventh and Tenth Commandments" (pages 250–253). To introduce the topic, put the following Scripture quotation on the board where all can see:

> "Give me neither poverty nor riches;
> feed me with the food that I need,
> or I shall be full, and deny you,
> and say, "Who is the Lord?"
> or I shall be poor, and steal,
> and profane the name of my God."
>
> —Proverbs 30:8–9

For Enrichment

Journal Assignment: Have the students answer the following, "Which would you rather do—believe a person who is lying or disbelieve a person who is telling the truth?"

(natural family planning). These methods are in accord with God's will because they respect natural bodily functions and encourage tenderness and authentic communication. On the other hand, artificial means of birth control (e.g., contraceptive pills or devices like condoms) are unnatural and contrary to God's law. Sterilization, that is, making the sex organs unable to reproduce, is also wrong except when these organs are diseased and threaten a person's overall health and life.

Children are a gift of marriage. If couples experience difficulty having children, they may use moral methods of increasing fertility. However, techniques that involve third parties (for example, donating sperm or eggs) are seriously wrong because they invade the exclusive marriage union of the husband and wife. Cloning of human beings is also a great evil because it directly contradicts God's plan for bringing forth new life from the loving union of husband and wife. A child is a gift from God, not an object or piece of property. We do not have an absolute right to a child. If couples cannot have children, they are encouraged to adopt. Or they can join their suffering to the cross of Christ and use their loving desires to serve others in creative and compassionate ways.

The following acts go against God's intention for marriage. They are seriously wrong.

1. *Adultery* involves a married person having sexual relations with someone not his or her spouse. It seriously destroys a couple's promise to remain faithful to each other through life. Adultery is unjust to one's spouse

adultery
Infidelity in marriage whereby a married person has sexual intercourse with someone who is not the person's spouse.

avarice
An inordinate passion for riches and the power that comes with them.

and children and also causes many problems for society.
2. *Divorce* is against Christ's commandment that marriage should last until death separates the couple. A true Christian marriage, in which consent was freely given, cannot be dissolved.
3. *Polygamy* (having several spouses), *incest* (engaging in sexual relations with close relatives), *sexual abuse of children and adolescents,* and *free union* (living together without exchanging marriage vows) are all serious violations of God's intent for marriage.

VII. and X. You Shall Not Steal. You shall not covet anything that belongs to your neighbor. (CCC, 2401–2449, 2450–2460, 2534–2540)

The Seventh Commandment teaches us to be good stewards of our material possessions. It stresses that God created the goods of creation for the benefit of everyone. We have the right to private property, but we must use that property responsibly. The related virtue of temperance teaches that we should not become too attached to our belongings. Also, the virtue of justice calls us to respect the property rights of others and to share our things, especially with those who are needy.

It is natural for us to want to own things that give us pleasure. This desire is morally acceptable as long as we are reasonable and do not unjustly crave the belongings of others. The Tenth Commandment teaches that when we covet the goods of others, we might commit immoral acts outlawed by the Seventh Commandment, including theft, robbery, and fraud. Therefore, the Tenth Commandment outlaws greed, avarice, and envy. *Greed* tries to amass unlimited wealth.

Avarice passionately seeks wealth and the power that comes from it. *Envy,*

Background Information

Living the Fourth through Tenth Commandments

The fourth through tenth commandments teach us to love our neighbor as ourselves. This means respecting the human dignity of all of God's children, whether they are our spouse, parents, family members, and even those with whom we disagree or who are on the margins.

On December 10, 1948, the General Assembly of the United Nations adopted and proclaimed the *Universal Declaration of Human Rights* and mandated that all member countries disseminate and publicize the declaration. Recognizing that "the inherent dignity and of the equal and inalienable rights of all members of the human family is the foundation of freedom, justice and peace in the world," the declaration states, among other things:

Article 1: All human beings are born free and equal in dignity and rights. They are endowed with reason and conscience and should act towards one another in a spirit of brotherhood.

Article 2: Everyone is entitled to all the rights and freedoms set forth in this Declaration, without distinction of any kind, such as race, color, sex, language, religion, political or other opinion, national or social origin, property, birth or other status. Furthermore, no distinction shall be made on the basis of the political, jurisdictional or international status of the country or territory to which a person belongs, whether it be independent, trust, non-self-governing or under any other limitation of sovereignty.

Article 3: Everyone has the right to life, liberty and security of person.

Article 25: (1) Everyone has the right to a standard of living adequate for the health and well-being of himself and of his family, including food, clothing, housing and medical care and necessary social services, and the right to security in the event of unemployment, sickness, disability, widowhood, old age or other lack of livelihood in circumstances beyond his control.

The complete text of the Declaration may be found online at www.un.org/Overview/rights.html.

a capital sin, is a desire to have for oneself what another possesses, especially if one is willing to acquire it unjustly. Rather than rejoicing in another's good fortune, the envious person is angered or disappointed by it.

Avarice is an inordinate love of riches and the good things of life. Jesus Christ, to cure us of it, was born in extreme poverty, deprived of all comforts. He chose a mother who was poor. He willed to pass as the son of a humble workman.

—St. John Vianney

Jesus teaches that poverty of spirit is the way to combat the sinful attitudes of greed, envy, and avarice. In the last analysis, union with our God is the only way to satisfy our restless hearts. The problem with inordinately desiring wealth is that riches can become our god. Prayer to the Holy Spirit can help us resist the temptations of craving every material possession that promises happiness.

Disobedience against the Seventh and Tenth Commandments are occasions of sin. These commandments are opposed to *theft*, that is, the taking of someone's property against his or her reasonable will. Also forbidden is the unjust taking and keeping of another's property. Examples of this include business fraud, paying of unjust wages, price fixing, corruption, shoddy work, tax evasion, forgery, expense account padding, wasteful practices, and vandalism. If one is guilty of any of these actions, he or she must make reparation. Commutative justice (see below) requires that stolen goods be returned.

The Seventh Commandment requires that we keep our promises and not break our contracts. Gambling does not violate the Seventh Commandment if it is done honestly and sparingly and does not lead to gambling addiction that can deprive others,

like one's children, of the basic necessities of life. Enslaving people for profit and treating them as property to buy, sell, or exchange is a horrible offense to human dignity and freedom.

The Seventh and Tenth Commandments strongly encourage justice for all people. Catholic teaching distinguishes between these types of justice:

1. *Commutative justice* regulates relations between individuals. It tells us that if we steal something, we should return it.
2. *Legal justice* concerns our duties as citizens and what we owe the government. For example, it requires that we pay taxes.
3. *Distributive justice* deals with the obligations the community has to its citizens according to their contributions and needs. An example would be to make sure that every child has access to an education.

In addition to these types of justice, there is *social justice*, which applies the teachings of Christ and the Church to the political, economic, and social orders. Entrusted with the Gospel of Christ, the Church has spoken out on issues that affect our basic human rights and our Salvation. Since the late nineteenth century, under the guidance of the Holy Spirit, the Church has developed its social teaching to interpret historical events in light of the Gospel of Jesus Christ. This social teaching involves three elements: principles for reflection, criteria for judgment, and guidelines for action. These elements apply the Gospel message to the systems, structures, and institutions of society because all human relationships take place within them. Respect for life is the overarching theme of Catholic social teaching.

The condemnation of any social, political, or economic system that is contrary to the dignity of the human person is a fundamental theme of Catholic social justice teaching. Therefore, the Church is against any government or political system that makes profit the *only* norm and ultimate goal of economic activity: "The disordered desire for money . . . causes . . . many conflicts which disturb the social order" (*CCC*, 2424). Political and economic ideologies or systems that make humans a mere means to profit include totalitarianism, atheism, Communism, and unbridled capitalism. All these make money their god and dehumanize persons. All are morally unacceptable.

- **Class Activity:** Ask students to make a list of all the possessions they have used since they woke up that morning. Urge them to keep thinking until they have a complete list. Be sure they include things like their home, room, bed, blanket, pillow, sinks, toilets, showers, soap, shampoo, food, clothing, deodorant, shoes, transportation (bus? car? bicycle?), iPod, radio, school, classroom, computer, backpack, books, pens, cell phone, paper, etc.
  - ◆ When they have a fairly complete list, ask them to highlight those things that are absolutely essential, things they think every person their age should have available to them. Then ask them to circle the things that they will admit are luxuries that they could live without if they had to.

  - ◆ Review their lists together and encourage them to circle as many things as possible. Have them look especially at those things they highlighted. Are those really things that they need to have to survive, grow, and develop as persons, to be able to live a life of service to others? Or are they things that they need to fit in to modern culture? The point of the exercise is to help them realize that they do not *need* as many things as they think they do.

📖 **Printed Materials** continued from page 253

Keenan, James F., S.J. *Commandments of Compassion.* Lanham, MD: Sheed & Ward, 1999.

Lawler, Ronald, O.F.M., Joseph Boyle Jr., and William E. May. *Catholic Sexual Ethics: A Summary, Explanation, and Defense*. Updated. Huntington, IN: Our Sunday Visitor Press, Inc., 1996.
> Clear and orthodox.

Lickona, Tom and Judy, with William Boudreau, MD. *Sex, Love & You.* Notre Dame, IN: Ave Maria Press, 2003.
> An outstanding book for teens. Great teacher background, too.

McKenna, Kevin. *A Concise Guide to Catholic Social Teaching*. Notre Dame, IN: Ave Maria Press, 2003.

Pilarczyk, Archbishop Daniel E. *Bringing Forth Justice: Basics for Just Christians*, rev. ed. Cincinnati, OH: St. Anthony Messenger Press, 1999.
> An excellent and short overview of major themes of Catholic social justice teachings.

———. *Twelve Tough Issues and More: What the Church Teaches and Why*. Cincinnati: St. Anthony Messenger Press, 2002.
> Excellent, short, to-the-point articles on issues like war, abortion, capital punishment, conscience, and the like. Highly recommended. Have extra copies available for student reading.

- **Direct Instruction:** Explain that *greed*, *avarice*, and *envy* all stem from a misplaced sense of what we need and why we need it. When we begin to believe that having things makes us a better, more valuable person, or when we judge others by the value of the things they possess, we have turned away from God, who values each person for who he or she is—not what they own.

- **Group Activity:** Refer to the feature "Catholic Social Teaching and the Seventh and Tenth Commandments." Form four groups to research each of the four components of social justice covered in the feature on pages 252–253. Each group should choose one specific issue to research and present to the class. The presentation should include a plan for the students to participate in some activity to advocate for their issue.

  - For example, one issue of stewardship is the threat of lost wilderness areas. Your students might discover in their research that there is a local wilderness area that is threatened with development that will have a severe detrimental effect on the environment. They could plan an "education campaign" to make people in the community aware of the threat. They could write letters to local politicians deciding the issue to protest the plan.

  - After the teams have made their presentations, the class should vote on one plan to put into action.

Catholic Social Teaching and the Seventh and Tenth Commandments

Catholic social teaching gives special emphasis to these four areas:

1. respect for creation
2. economics
3. solidarity among nations
4. love for the poor

More details on each of these areas follows.

Stewardship (CCC, 2415–2418; 2456–2457).
God gave humans dominion over all creation—the mineral, vegetable, and animal resources of our world. However, the book of Genesis teaches us that God expects us to be responsible stewards, that is, caretakers who will be respectful of God's world and will preserve its limited resources for future generations. Loving concern for the environment is essential for Christians because God intended these goods for *all* people in *all* generations.

People must be considerate of animals. Although it is morally acceptable to use animals for food, clothing, and humane medical experiments for the benefit of humans, people must not cause animals needless suffering and death. Also, our love for animals must be reasonable. For example, if we spend so much on our pets that we neglect poor people, then human dignity will suffer.

Economic Justice (CCC, 2426–2436; 2458–2460)
According to Catholic social teaching, the goods God created for everyone's benefit should in fact reach everyone in accordance with justice and with the help of charity. The purpose of the economy is to benefit both individuals and the human family. "The author, center, and goal of all economic and social life" is the human person (*CCC*, 2459). Therefore, a nation's economy exists for humans, not the other way around.

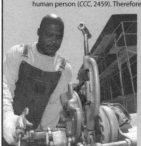

Profit, power, or material goods cannot be its center. The basis for judging a just economy is this question: What does the economy do *for* and *to* people, especially to the poor and the weak?

These fundamental truths of economic life teach us that work is both a right and a duty. We have the right to co-create with God to subdue the earth. Therefore, people should have access to a job that pays a just wage without discrimination based on sex, race, disability, and the like.

On the other hand, we have the duty to provide for our families by giving an honest day's work for an honest day's pay. Meaningful work also helps us fulfill our God-given duty to develop our talents, serve others, and grow in holiness by joining the toil of work to our Lord's sacrifice for us.

Background Information

Loving Neighbor

In Scripture, too, we are taught to love our neighbor as ourselves:

> Owe nothing to anyone, except to love one another, for the one who loves another has fulfilled the law . . . and whatever other commandments there may be, are summed up in this saying [namely] "You shall love your neighbor as yourself." (Rom 13:8, 9b)

Solidarity and Preferential Love for the Poor (CCC, 2437–2448; 2461–2463)

We are one human family. Therefore, nations blessed by God with wealth must express their solidarity with poorer nations. Rich nations must help poorer nations develop their economies by:

- increasing direct aid;
- reforming international economic and financial institutions so that poor nations can relate more favorably with rich nations;
- giving special aid to poor countries that are trying to work for growth and freedom;
- making special efforts to develop the farming efforts of poor nations since so many of the world's poor people are peasants who work on farms, and since food production is a vital necessity to poorer nations whose governments lack funds to purchase food grown elsewhere; and
- praying sincerely to be able to exercise our responsibility to poorer nations and their citizens.

For true reform to work, though, our world must have an attitude adjustment and make God our top priority. Only then will we recognize that material goods are meant to help us on our journey to him. Rediscovering God will also wake individuals and nations up to the truth that it is a grave evil to exploit the poor. Jesus himself identified with the poor and said that our judgment would be based on what we do to the "least" in our midst (see Mt 25:40, 45).

Jesus teaches us that we must give alms to the needy—that is, money, clothes, and other essentials necessary for life. This is a basic work of justice toward those who have less than we do. We must also put into practice corporal and spiritual works of mercy. These works of compassion help us identify with suffering people and are positive ways to relieve that suffering. The works of mercy are:

Corporal Works of Mercy	Spiritual Works of Mercy
1. Feed the hungry.	1. Counsel the doubtful.
2. Give drink to the thirsty.	2. Instruct the ignorant.
3. Clothe the naked.	3. Admonish sinners.
4. Visit the imprisoned.	4. Comfort the afflicted.
5. Shelter the homeless.	5. Forgive offenses.
6. Visit the sick.	6. Bear wrongs patiently.
7. Bury the dead.	7. Pray for the living and the dead.

- **Direct Instruction:** Before moving on, be sure to clarify the differences between the different types of justice mentioned on page 251 and the corporeal versus spiritual works of mercy on page 253.

- **Class Discussion:** Cover information on the eighth commandment by highlighting the text subsection "VIII. You Shall Not Bear False Witness Against Your Neighbor" (page 254). As you review the different forms "false witness" can take, ask your students to give hypothetical examples to show that they truly understand the distinctions. Discuss the ways that lying affects an entire community—even those who neither lie nor are lied about. What does it do to the level of trust in a community? When people don't trust each other, how does their behavior change? Ask them to suggest responses that they think might be appropriate if they were to catch themselves slipping into one of these ways of talking.

- **Class Discussion:** Survey your class to find out how many of them read various tabloid publications about famous people like *The National Enquirer*. Use the questionnaire on Chapter 9, Handout 6 "Tabloid Survey" (starting on page 285 and also online at www.avemariapress.com) to discuss these types of publications. Have each student complete the questionnaire, then discuss their responses.

- **Class Discussion:** Read the final paragraph of the text section aloud and the quotation from John 15:10, 14. Have several students respond to what it means to say "yes" to the Lord.

For Review Answers (page 255)

1. *IV. Honor your father and your mother.* This commandment binds in two directions—parents are required to offer unconditional love and affection to their children and to care for and educate them appropriately. Children are to return their parents affection, be obedient to them while still at home, and be sure they are well cared for in old age. This commandment applies not only to our parents but to others who have legitimate authority over us, obligating us to obey civil laws when they are not in conflict with our conscience.

   V. You shall not kill. Human life is sacred from the moment of conception until natural death. Respect for life also includes keeping our minds and bodies healthy.

2. Governments have the right to inflict the death penalty only when it is absolutely necessary to preserve public order and personal safety. Governments can go to war only in defense against an unjust aggressor, as a last resort after exhausting all other means to avert the conflict, when there is a reasonable hope of success, and when the use of arms will not produce evil greater than that to be eliminated.

3. *VI. You shall not commit adultery.* Sexual love is to be reserved for a loving, committed marriage relationship.

   IX. You shall not covet your neighbor's wife. Related to the sixth commandment, this commandment counters our lustful desires and promotes the virtues of chastity and modesty. Sexual thoughts become sinful when they control us or when they lead us to look on others as objects for our own gratification, and not as whole persons worthy of our respect.

4. Chastity is the virtue of living out one's sexuality in keeping with one's state in life; thus, married people are to be faithful to each other and to show love and respect to one another in their sexual relations, while single people and vowed religious should refrain from sexual relations. Purity is a virtue that helps us to combat lust by our refusal to entertain impure thoughts when they arise. Modesty is a virtue that protects our privacy. Modesty requires that we are respectful in our choice of clothing, language, entertainment, and in our attitudes when talking about sex.

5. Pornography is wrong because it depersonalizes sex by putting something sacred on display for the sexual gratification of onlookers.

6. *VII. You shall not steal.* Beyond simply taking things that belong to another, this commandment governs such matters as just wages, taxes, stewardship of the earth's resources, solidarity among nations, economic justice, and the preferential option for the poor.

   X. You shall not covet anything that belongs to your

VIII. You Shall Not Bear False Witness Against Your Neighbor. *(CCC, 2464–2492, 2504–2511)*

The Eighth Commandment teaches the value of truth-telling. Truth is a matter of justice. For Christians, being truthful is a great way to witness to Christ Jesus, who is the Way, the Truth, and the Life. This commandment teaches us to stand up for the truth, something the martyrs did when they freely remained true to the Lord and his Gospel.

If we honor truth, we will respect other people, their reputations, and their right to privacy. Honest people do not flatter or give false praise to others to win their approval. Nor do they gossip, brag about their accomplishments, or lie. Lying goes against God's gift of speech, which was given to us to tell the truth. Lying is mortally sinful when it causes grave harm to another. If we sin against the truth, we must repair any harm we have caused, especially if we have damaged someone's reputation. The Eighth Commandment calls us to avoid the following:

1. *False witness* in court and *perjury* (lying under oath), both of which violate justice. These are seriously wrong because they cause innocent people to suffer or to be unfairly punished.

2. *Rash judgment* is snap misjudgment about someone's moral culpability (blameworthiness). To counteract this irresponsible behavior, we should always try to put the most positive interpretation on another's thoughts, words, and deeds.

3. *Detraction* reveals the faults of someone else without a good reason. *Calumny* (spreading lies about someone) violates the virtue of truthfulness. These sins assault the honor of a person's reputation and therefore offend both justice and charity.

To tell the truth is important for followers of Jesus. However, people do not always have a right to know everything. At times, the prudent and loving thing to do is to remain silent or use discreet language; for example, to protect someone, to respect the common good, or to honor a reasonable right to privacy. A good example is that doctors and lawyers have the right to keep confidential secrets revealed to them unless grave harm would result from their silence. And public figures have a reasonable right to privacy from the glaring eyes of the media.

The Eighth Commandment also requires governments and entertainment industries to use the media responsibly and not for propaganda or to promote immoral behavior. People have a right to truthful information that comes from freedom, justice, and human solidarity. Truth is beautiful because it is real and reflected in God's creation and in Scripture. Human art (especially sacred art) can be a powerful tool to reveal God's truth, beauty, and love. It can inspire us to adore the Blessed Trinity, a God of truth and beauty.

Once there was a person who claimed to have the secret to good living. It turned out that the secret was really just two words she had taped to her bathroom mirror: "Yes, Lord!" By saying yes to the Lord, that is, by keeping the commandments, she found the secret to good living. Regarding moral living, never forget what Jesus said:

> If you keep my commandments, you will remain in my love, just as I have kept my Father's commandments and remain in his love. . . . You are my friends if you do what I command you. (Jn 15:10, 14)

detraction
Without a legitimate reason, disclosing a person's faults to someone who did not know about them, thus causing unjust harm to that person's reputation.

calumny
Slander, that is, lies told about another person in order to harm his or her reputation and lead others to make false judgments about the person.

For Review

1. Name and explain the Fourth and Fifth Commandments.
2. Under what conditions do governments have the right to inflict the death penalty? To go to war?
3. Name and explain the Sixth and Ninth Commandments.
4. Define the virtues of chastity, purity, and modesty.
5. Why is pornography wrong?
6. Name and explain the Seventh and Tenth Commandments.
7. Define *greed*, *avarice*, and *envy*.
8. Distinguish between and among these forms of justice: *commutative*, *legal*, *distributive*, and *social*.
9. List the corporal and spiritual works of mercy.
10. Name and explain the Eighth Commandment.
11. Distinguish between *detraction* and *calumny*.

For Reflection

- Analyze a television program, movie, or song that depicts human sexuality and compare it to the Church's teaching on the sacredness of sex.

- Imagine winning one million dollars in a lottery. What would you do with your newfound riches? How much of your winnings would you share? Would you be unjust if you did not share some of your winnings with the needy? Explain.

CHAPTER QUICK VIEW

- Morality involves putting into practice the teachings of Jesus in the Sermon on the Mount, obeying the Ten Commandments, and following the teachings of the Apostles and Magisterium. (page 235)
- God wills our eternal happiness. The Beatitudes teach us the attitudes of being and ways of acting that will help us achieve that happiness. (page 235)
- The First Commandment requires us to worship the loving God who is the source of our life and all our gifts and talents. The theological virtues of faith, hope, and love help us honor our loving God. (pages 238–240)
- The virtue of religion enables us to know and to love God. It expresses itself in adoration, prayer, sacrifice, and fidelity to our vows and promises. (page 239)
- The Second Commandment directs us to show reverence to God's name because God is holy. (pages 241–242)
- The Third Commandment requires that we keep Sunday holy by celebrating the Eucharist, a serious obligation for Catholics, and by using the day for the refreshment of our spirits. (pages 242–243)
- The Fourth Commandment teaches us to honor, respect, and show affection to and appreciation for our family members, especially our parents. (pages 244–245)
- The Fifth Commandment teaches the sacredness of life, a precious gift of God that he alone can give or reclaim. (pages 245–247)
- The Sixth and Ninth commandments teach us to use the gift of our sexuality in accord with God's plan. (pages 247–250)

Homework Assignment

1. Complete the For Review questions on page 255.

2. Complete any assigned Ongoing Assignments on page 257.

3. Review the Chapter 9 Chapter Quick View and vocabulary words.

neighbor. Related to the seventh commandment, this one counters our greed, envy, and avarice and promotes the virtues of generosity and detachment from our possessions. Desire for material belongings becomes sinful when it leads us to treat people as a means to profit or to support an economic order that benefits a few but keeps many in poverty.

7. *Greed* is the desire for ever more wealth and material goods. *Avarice* is the inordinate love of riches and the power that comes with them. *Envy* is the desire to have for oneself what another has, particularly at the expense of the other. Being angered or disappointed by another's good fortune is a clear warning that one has fallen victim to envy.

8. *Commutative justice* regulates relations between individuals. We violate this justice when we steal from someone. *Legal justice* concerns our duties as citizens and what we owe the government and our fellow citizens. Tax evasion is an offense against this kind of justice. *Distributive justice* guarantees a just distribution of a community's resources to all of its citizens according to their needs and contributions. Distributive justice requires that we educate all children, not just some of them. *Social justice* requires that the social, economic, and political orders of a nation all work for the common good, rather than for the benefit of some members at the expense of others.

9. The corporal works of mercy are:
   - Feed the hungry.
   - Give drink to the thirsty.
   - Clothe the naked.
   - Visit the imprisoned.
   - Shelter the homeless.
   - Visit the sick.
   - Bury the dead.

   The spiritual works of mercy are:
   - Counsel the doubtful.
   - Instruct the ignorant.
   - Admonish sinners.
   - Comfort the afflicted.
   - Forgive offenses.
   - Bear wrongs patiently.
   - Pray for the living and the dead.

10. *VIII. You shall not bear false witness against your neighbor.* Being truthful and standing up for the truth are important ways of expressing our faith in the God of Truth.

11. Detraction and calumny have similar meanings, but through detraction we share something about a person's faults when it is not necessary, while calumny is actually spreading lies about someone.

Chapter 9 Review Lesson

Objectives

In this lesson, the students will:

- review the information about the Beatitudes and Ten Commandments from Chapter 9.
- share their work on the Ongoing Assignments.
- complete a brief Prayer Reflection with the emphasis on keeping the commandments and living a moral life.

Preview

There are several opportunities to aid the students in reviewing the material in Chapter 9 in this session. You will need to provide paper plates if the students are to make the "Beatitude Wheels" suggested by the Class Activity on page 261. Also, the students should be afforded the chance to share their work on completed long-term assignments from this chapter, including the Ongoing Assignments.

Bell Ringers

- **Direct Instruction:** Spend some time at the beginning of class reviewing the homework. Then, review the connections between the fourth through tenth commandments by verbally quizzing students on which sins and positive actions are connected to each commandment. Have them raise the number of fingers in the air that correspond to each sin or action you say.

- **Direct Instruction:** Have the students hand in this assignment and any other For Enrichment assignments they have worked on through the lessons in this chapter.

 Teaching Approaches

- **Student Presentations:** Begin the Chapter Review by calling ten students to the front of the class and having them review the Ten Commandments by (1) reciting them one at a time and (2) explaining what each means. Repeat the same exercise with the Beatitudes using two students for each Beatitude. (They can help each other with the explanation.)

- **Class Activity:** Play a guessing game to help students review the vocabulary words. First make posters, each with a vocabulary word printed in large letters on it. Include additional key words from the chapter that do not appear in the list with page numbers beside them: agnostic (page 240); atheism (page 240); cursing (page 241); divination (page 240); domestic Church (page 244); envy (page 250); false witness (page 254); greed (page 250); humanist (page 240); just war (page 246); murder

- The Seventh Commandment forbids theft and commands justice and charity in the stewardship of material goods and respect for the integrity of creation. (pages 250–253)
- The Tenth Commandment requires us to avoid the sins of greed, avarice, and envy. These lead to actions forbidden by the Seventh Commandment: theft, fraud, paying unjust wages, shoddy work, tax evasion, corrupt business practices, waste, forgery, destruction of private and public property, and so forth. (page 251)
- The Spirit-guided social justice doctrine of the Church includes principles for reflection, criteria for judgment, and guidelines for action. These apply the Gospel to the political, economic, and social orders for the benefit of protecting human rights, the dignity of persons, and the Salvation of souls. (page 251)
- The basis of the Catholic Church's social teaching is respect for the individual as another self. Therefore, in the area of economics, the human person and not profit must be its center and goal. Economic decision makers must always ask, "What does the economy do *for* and *to* people, especially the poor?" (page 252)
- Global solidarity is a goal of social justice, and following Christ requires a special love and affection for the poor. Almsgiving and living the spiritual and corporal works of mercy are ways to help the poor. (page 253)
- By prohibiting false witness, the Eighth Commandment enjoins us to be people of truth. The Eighth Commandment forbids lying, that is, speaking a falsehood to deceive another who has a right to the truth. (page 254)

Learning the Language of Faith

Complete each sentence by choosing the correct answer from the list of terms below. You will not use all of the terms.

abortion	calumny	euthanasia	passions
adultery	celibacy	evangelical counsels	perjury
agnosticism	chastity	heresy	polygamy
apostasy	despair	idolatry	sorcery
atheism	detraction	modesty	subsidiarity
blasphemy	epiclesis	oath	

1. The denial of Christ and repudiation of the Christian faith by a baptized Christian is known as _____.
2. _____ is lying under oath by asking God to witness a lie.
3. The virtue of _____ refuses to unveil what should remain hidden; it is a fruit of the virtue of purity.
4. _____ claims that God's existence cannot be known.
5. Priests and those in religious life are called to _____.
6. All people are called to practice the virtue of _____, that is, to practice the moral virtue that enables persons to integrate their sexuality into their stations in life.
7. When we tell lies about another person in order to harm his or her reputation, we are guilty of the sin of _____.
8. When a person worships money or power, he or she is guilty of _____.
9. When a person expresses hatred for God or mocks Jesus Christ, the person has committed a sin of _____.
10. Catholic teaching in the area of social justice holds that a community of a higher order should not deprive a community of a lower order of its functions. This is known as the principle of _____.

Ongoing Assignments

As you cover the material in this chapter, choose and complete at least three of these assignments.

1. Prepare a two-minute oral report on the morality of one of the topics discussed in this chapter. For example: astrology, divination, capital punishment, or atheism.
2. Prepare a report on a saint or modern Catholic who was concerned with justice or poor or suffering people. For example: St. Vincent de Paul, St. Louise de Marillac, St. John Baptist de la Salle, St. Katharine Drexel, Dorothy Day, Jean Vanier, or Blessed Mother Teresa of Calcutta.
3. View websites that deal with justice topics. Report on issues involving youth, criminal justice, or war and peace.
4. Report on an archived article from the Catholic online social justice magazine *Salt of the Earth*. Check articles on capital punishment, peace, and economic justice and the poor.
5. Research and report on some violations of human rights.
6. Create your own PowerPoint presentation on the Beatitudes.
7. Do one of the following projects concerning stewardship:

   - Photograph some favorite nature scenes. Snap some contrasting pictures of where humanity has ruined the environment or disfigured nature's beautiful face. Create a presentation to depict the contrast between God's beauty and human folly.
   - Visit the Catholic Conservation Center. Read and report on its introduction to Catholic environmental justice.

8. Create a PowerPoint presentation on the perils of drug or alcohol abuse. Be sure to present some of the moral arguments for the virtue of sobriety.
9. Report on the prevalence of cheating in high schools and colleges. List ways to combat this problem.

Prayer Reflection

For centuries Catholics have practiced a method of prayer known as *Lectio Divina*, that is, "sacred reading." Its purpose is to meet God through his written Word and allow the Holy Spirit to lead us into an even deeper union with him. The procedure consists of taking a short passage, reading it slowly and attentively, and then letting your imagination, emotions, memory, desires, and thoughts engage the written text.

Various masters of prayer have suggested ways to pray with the Sacred Scriptures. The following procedure comes from the Benedictine tradition:

Lectio Divina

1. *Reading (lectio).* Select a short Bible passage. Read it slowly. Pay attention to each word. If a word or phrase catches your attention, read it to yourself several times.
2. *Thinking (meditatio).* Savor the passage. Read it again. Reflect on it. This time feel any emotions that may surface. Picture the images that arise from your imagination. Pay attention to any thoughts or memories the passage might call forth from you.
3. *Pray (oratio).* Reflect on what the Lord might be saying to you in this passage. Talk to him as you would to a friend. Ask him to show you how to respond to his Word. How can you connect this passage to your daily life? How does it relate to the people you encounter every day? Might there be a special message in this Scripture selection just for *you*? Pay attention to any insights the Holy Spirit might send you.
4. *Contemplation (contemplatio).* Sit in the presence of the Lord. Imagine him looking on you with great love in his heart. Rest quietly in his presence. There is no need to think here; just enjoy your time with him as two friends would who quietly sit on a park bench gazing together at a sunset.

Homework Assignment

1. Complete in writing the For Reflection questions (page 255).

2. Reread Chapter 9.

3. Study for the Chapter 9 Test.

(page 245); rash judgment (page 254); Sabbath (page 242); scandal (page 247); simony (page 240); suicide (page 246); superstition (page 239); theft (page 251).

- Divide the class into two or three teams. Flip a coin to see which team goes first. That team (Team One) will send one representative to the front of the class. Hold up one of the posters behind the student at the front of the class so that both teams can see it. Now the representative can ask his or her teammates, one at a time, for hints about what the word is. The hints given cannot use the word itself, any derivative of the word, or any key word from the definition.

- Team One scores a point when their representative correctly guesses the word and gives its definition. Team Two (and Three if there is one) should listen to catch Team One giving an illegal hint. If this happens, or the team member cannot guess after five hints, or the team member guesses incorrectly, Team One's turn is over and they score no points. Any unguessed words are returned to the pile. Once words have been correctly identified, they should be set aside.

- Once your students become familiar with the game and are getting the hang of giving hints, increase the challenge by setting a time limit in addition to the five-question limit. This will help keep everyone's attention focused and move the game along more quickly. Two minutes is probably a good place to start. You can shorten the time period even more after another few rounds to move the game along a little faster.

- **Class Activity:** To review the Beatitudes and help the students memorize them, have the students make "Beatitude Wheels." Use a paper plate to trace two circles on construction paper, one on light paper and one on dark. Cut out both circles. With a ruler, divide the circles into eight pie-shaped sections. Using a smaller plate, trace another circle inside both circles. In the sections around the outside of the light-colored circle, write the beginnings of each Beatitude—"Blessed are the poor in spirit," "Blessed are they who mourn," etc. In the inner sections, write the endings, being sure that the ends are written in opposite sections from the beginnings so that when you hold the circle up, the verse at the top will be completed in the section at the bottom of the inner circle. Take the dark circle and cut out one outer section and one inner section, again opposing each other. Do not cut the inner section all the way to the center. Lay the dark circle over the light and secure in the center with a brad. You should be able to read one Beatitude at a time as you turn the top circle. Students can use these as study wheels to help them memorize the eight Beatitudes.

- **Individual Assignment:** Have students complete the questions in the Learning the Language of Faith feature on page 256. Once they have completed the assignment, review their answers as a class.
- **Student Presentations:** Check and collect the Ongoing Assignments. Have students share their reports and presentations with the class.
- **Prayer Experience:** Review the concept and parts involved in *Lectio Divina* on pages 257–258. Distribute copies of the current day's readings and guide the students in the method described in the Prayer Reflection feature.
- **For Reflection questions:** Allow extra class time for the students to begin working individually on beginning the assignment under no. 5, Resolution (page 258)

Chapter 9 Test Lesson

Objectives

In this lesson, the students will:
- take a test on the material in Chapter 9.
- preview the material in Chapter 10.

Preview

Reserve the majority of the class period for test taking. If there is time at the end of the period, allow students with oral presentations of assignments or enrichment projects to share them with the class.

Teaching Approaches

- **Direct Instruction:** Provide students with the opportunity to ask any last-minute questions they have about the chapter.
- **Chapter Test:** Distribute the Chapter 9 Test (starting on page 285 and also online at www.avemariapress .com). When the students have finished the test, have them turn it in and open their books to preview Chapter 10.
- **Direct Instruction:** Use any additional class time to review some of the material in the Catholic Handbook for Faith, pages 285–306.

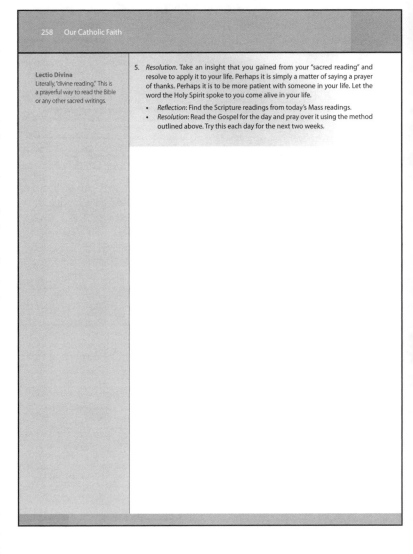

Lectio Divina
Literally, "divine reading." This is a prayerful way to read the Bible or any other sacred writings.

5. *Resolution.* Take an insight that you gained from your "sacred reading" and resolve to apply it to your life. Perhaps it is simply a matter of saying a prayer of thanks. Perhaps it is to be more patient with someone in your life. Let the word the Holy Spirit spoke to you come alive in your life.
- *Reflection:* Find the Scripture readings from today's Mass readings.
- *Resolution:* Read the Gospel for the day and pray over it using the method outlined above. Try this each day for the next two weeks.

Homework Assignment

1. Preview Chapter 10.

2. Read the opening text sections of Chapter 10 "Keep Your Eyes on the Shepherd" and "What Is Prayer?" (pages 262–265).

3. Examine the Ongoing Assignments on pages 276–277 and consider which one(s) you might choose to complete.

Chapter 9 Test Answers

All questions are worth 4 points each.

Part 1: Multiple Choice

1. C
2. A
3. A
4. B
5. D
6. B
7. A
8. D

Part 2: True/False

9. F
10. T
11. F
12. T
13. T
14. F
15. F

Part 3: Matching

16. B
17. E
18. H
19. C
20. D

Part 4: Short Answers (For questions 21–25, assign two points for each correct commandment, one point for the value, and one point for a suitable sin that matches the commandment.)

21. You shall not take the name of the Lord, your God, in vain. (Value: reverence for God's name; Sin: blasphemy, perjury, etc.)

22. Honor your father and your mother. (Value: obedience of proper authority; Sin: failure to take care of aged parents; disobeying just laws of proper authorities, etc.)

23. You shall not commit adultery. (Value: respect one's own and others' sexuality; Sin: fornication, adultery, etc.)

24. You shall not steal. (Value: justice in sharing the world's goods; Sin: cheating, theft, failure to secure just wages for workers or basic rights for poor people, etc.)

25. You shall not bear false witness against your neighbor. (Value: truthfulness; Sin: detraction, false advertising, etc.)

10 Prayer

Overview of the Chapter

Prayer is essential to Christian life. A little child once saw a picture of Jesus on his knees. He asked his father, "What is Jesus doing in that picture?" The father replied, "He's praying to God." The little boy said, "But I thought Jesus is God!"

What an example Christ gives us. St. Cyprian wisely observed, "If he prayed who was without sin, how much more it becomes a sinner to pray."[1]

Chapter 10 corresponds to the last pillar of the *Catechism of the Catholic Church* on Christian prayer. It begins with several definitions of prayer, including perhaps the simplest of all, "prayer as conversation with God." This involves both talking and listening to God, and can involve prayer types like blessing, adoration, praise, petition (which includes both intercession and contrition), and thanksgiving.

Another excellent definition of prayer is "the living relationship of the children of God with their Father who is good beyond measure, with his Son Jesus Christ, and with the Holy Spirit" (*CCC,* 2565). This definition underscores that we can pray to each person of the Blessed Trinity.

The chapter investigates some of the key teachings about prayer that we learn from the Old Testament but especially from the example of Jesus himself and his Blessed Mother in the New Testament.

A primer on prayer helps readers decide on a good place and time for prayer, develop a good attitude toward this time with the Lord, and learn how to relax both mind and body so prayer can take place.

The chapter also introduces the reader to various prayer expressions: vocal prayer, meditation, mental prayer, and contemplation. This chorus teaches various movements in prayer:

> I talk, you listen.
> You talk, I listen.
> Neither talks, both listen.
> Neither talks, neither listens: Silence.[2]

Here we see how prayer progresses from conversation to contemplation, what spiritual masters consider the highest (and most difficult) form of prayer. Contemplative prayer is a gift, the fruit of many years, much discipline, and many "dark nights."

The last section of the chapter includes a line-by-line analysis of the perfect prayer, the Gospel in miniature, the Lord's Prayer. The text includes a description that follows the well-written and insightful analysis provided in the *Catechism of the Catholic Church* (2759–2865).

What a great joy it is to meet your students in prayer. Let us never forget the words of Blessed Mother Teresa of Calcutta, "Prayer enlarges the heart until it is capable of containing God's gift of himself."[3]

Prayer

Resources

 Audiovisual Materials

Befriending God in Prayer

A Catholic Update video that offers a friendship model based on a relationship with Jesus (St. Anthony Messenger Press).

Connecting with God

Shows how we can use gestures in prayer, how music can connect us to life and to God, and how we can pray surrounded by the power and beauty of nature. Comes with study guide (25-minute video, Videos with Values).

Contemplating Icons

Depicts how to pray with icons and reveals their symbolism and theological significance. Five parts: Icons of Christ, The Mother of God, Saints and Prophets, The Iconstasis, and Liturgical Solemnities. Study guide included (50-minute VHS video, Ignatius Press).

The Seven Circles of Prayer

Father John Wijingaards presents a practical method of prayer for ordinary people. Presents the seven circles: "the situation (silence and space), opening our eyes (seeing), encountering (suffering), and the importance of contact (touching and listening). The last circle is achieved through reading the Bible and finally coming (face to face) with God" (30-minute video, St. Anthony Messenger Press).

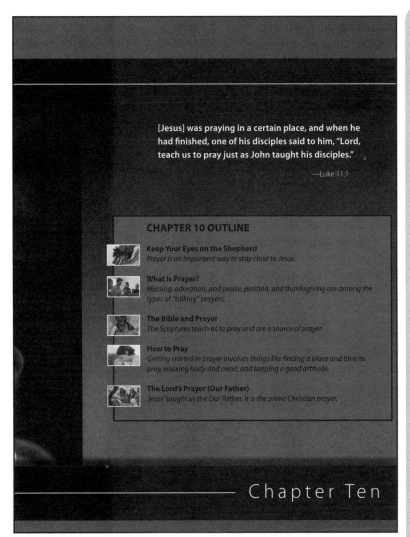

[Jesus] was praying in a certain place, and when he had finished, one of his disciples said to him, "Lord, teach us to pray just as John taught his disciples."

—Luke 11:1

CHAPTER 10 OUTLINE

Keep Your Eyes on the Shepherd
Prayer is an important way to stay close to Jesus.

What Is Prayer?
Blessing, adoration, and praise, petition, and thanksgiving are among the types of "talking" prayers.

The Bible and Prayer
The Scriptures teach us to pray and are a source of prayer.

How to Pray
Getting started in prayer involves things like finding a place and time to pray, relaxing body and mind, and keeping a good attitude.

The Lord's Prayer (Our Father)
Jesus' taught us the Our Father. It is the prime Christian prayer.

Chapter Ten

Chapter Outline

- Keep Your Eyes on the Shepherd
- What Is Prayer?
- The Bible and Prayer
- How to Pray
- The Lord's Prayer (Our Father)

Advance Preparations

Determine early in the chapter which Ongoing Assignments the students will be responsible for.

The Bible and Prayer (ST pages 265–267)

- Copies of Chapter 10, Handout 1 "This is God Calling Script" (starting on page 285 and also online at www.avemariapress.com) for the Class Activity on page 269.
- Bibles for the Class Activity on page 270.
- Copies of Chapter 10, Handout 2 "Prayer Journal" (starting on page 285 and also online at www .avemariapress.com) for the Journal Assignment on page 270.

How to Pray (ST pages 267–272)

- A prayer table with an open Bible, candle, music, and other prayerful items for the Prayer Experience on page 272.

The Lord's Prayer (Our Father) (ST pages 272–275)

- Background music for the Prayer Experience on page 278.

Chapter 10 Test Lesson

- Copies of the Chapter 10 Test (starting on page 285 and also online at www.avemariapress.com).

Resources

Internet Links see www.avemariapress.com

Resources

Printed Materials

Ayo, Nicholas, C.S.C. *The Lord's Prayer: A Survey Theological and Literary*. Notre Dame, IN: University of Notre Dame Press, 1992.
    An excellent study of this "Gospel in miniature."

Bauer, Judith, ed. *The Essential Catholic Prayer Book: A Collection of Private and Community Prayers. A Redemptorist Pastoral Publication*. Liguori, MO: Liguori, 1999.

Buckley, Michael, and Tony Castle II. *The Catholic Prayer Book*. Ann Arbor, MI: Servant, 1986.
    This remains one of the best collections of Catholic prayers.

Davidson, Graeme J., with Mary MacDonald. *Anyone Can Pray: A Guide to Methods of Christian Prayer*. New York: Paulist Press, 1983.
    This handbook includes a variety of prayer forms.

Hahn, Scott. *Understanding "Our Father": Biblical Reflections on the Lord's Prayer*. Steubenville, OH: Emmaus Road Publishing, Co., 2002.

Kreeft, Peter. *Prayer for Beginners*. San Francisco: Ignatius Press, 2000.
    Another helpful book from the modern-day C.S. Lewis.

Lovasik, Lawrence G. *The Basic Book of Catholic Prayer: How to Pray and Why*. Manchester, NH: Sophia Institute Press, 1999.

Martini, Cardinal Carlo Maria. *Praying as Jesus Taught Us: Meditations on the Our Father*. Trans. John Belmonte. Rowman & Littlefield, 2004.

Nouwen, Henri J.M. *Behold the Beauty of the Lord: Praying with Icons*. Notre Dame, IN: Ave Maria Press, 1987.
    A beautiful book that teaches us how to pray with icons.

Pennington, O.C.S.O., M. Basil. *Centered Living: The Way of Centered Prayer*. Foreword by Rabbi Lawrence Kushner. Liguori, MO: Liguori, 1999.
    Treats the history of and scriptural bases for the Rosary and provides modern meditations based on it.

Keep Your Eyes on the Shepherd (pages 262–263)
and
What Is Prayer? (pages 263–265)

Objectives

In this lesson, the students will:
- define prayer;
- reflect on the current state of their prayer lives.
- explain that prayer is both talking and listening.
- list and define these types of prayers: blessing, adoration, praise, petition, intercession, and thanksgiving.

Preview

This series of lessons covers the brief opening text section "Keep Your Eyes on the Shepherd" and the more substantial "What Is Prayer?" This section introduces students to the idea that prayer is the way that one develops an intimate relationship with God. The students will learn several definitions for prayer, about the various types of prayer, and that prayer involves both talking and listening.

 Bell Ringers

- **Class Discussion:** Read and discuss the opening story about the arrogant student and faith-filled scientist. Ask students to apply the lessons from the story to their own lives. Have them share times that they doubt that God listens to their prayers. Also, have them write about people they know with strong prayer lives, like the scientist Louis Pasteur. How do these people pray, and how is it so clear that their prayer lives are so strong?
- **Journal Assignment:** Ask students to reflect on how strong they feel their prayer lives are today. Have them describe in their journals the many ways that they pray and which ways they feel are most helpful to them. You may also want to refer them to the For Reflection questions on page 263. List some of their ideas on the board after they have finished.

Teaching Approaches

Keep Your Eyes on the Shepherd

Near the turn of the twentieth century, a prideful university student sat on a train in France next to an old man who was dressed in the simple garb of a peasant. When he noticed that the old man was silently saying the Rosary to himself, he rudely asked, "Sir, do you still believe in such outdated things?" The old man replied, "Yes, I do. Don't you?" The student laughed, saying, "I don't believe in such silly things. Why don't you just throw your rosary out the window and learn what science has to say about it."

"Science? I do not understand this science. Perhaps you can explain it to me," the elderly gentleman said with tears welling in his eyes.

The student was taken aback by the man's reaction. So as not to hurt his feelings, he said, "Please give me your address, and I will send you some literature to help explain my point to you."

The man reached into his pocket, retrieved a business card, and handed it to the student. The young man glanced at it and then was shocked, embarrassed, and speechless after he read it what was on it: "Louis Pasteur, Director of the Institute of Scientific Research, Paris."

The arrogant student had just met one of the world's leading scientists, Louis Pasteur, a great chemist and microbiologist, the one who invented a vaccine for rabies and discovered a process named after him—*Pasteurization*—that limits the growth of microbes that cause illness in foods like milk.[22]

Lesser men and women than Louis Pasteur can learn from his example: prayer is a vital element to life.

Consider another example from Francis Cardinal George of Chicago who, at an ordination Mass for new priests, told of a boyhood visit to his uncle's farm. His uncle, a shepherd, took the young Francis out on the range to tend the sheep. The boy was fascinated by the way the dog raced around the sheep herding them into the flock. When the dog paused, he did not watch the sheep, but rather always kept his eyes on the shepherd.

The secret to the dog's success was to keep his eyes on his master. Cardinal George's point to the new priests was simple: Priests should always tend to their people. But they must never take their eyes off the Master—Jesus Christ—because it is he who will guide us and give us confidence to live the Christian life.[23]

Prayer should be part of our everyday lives. As food is to our bodies, prayer is to our souls. While food helps us live physically, it is prayer that helps us grow spiritually.

Chapter 10 explores the functions and necessity of prayer, including these elements:

- a definition of prayer
- the Bible and prayer
- ways to pray
- prayer expressions
- the Lord's Prayer

Background Information

Prayer Is an Essential Part of Christian Life

Søren Kierkegaard, a Danish philosopher, said of prayer, "Prayer does not change God, but it changes him who prays." Prayer is an essential part of Christian life and is "a covenant relationship between God and man in Christ. It is the action of God and of man, springing forth from both the Holy Spirit and ourselves, wholly directed to the Father, in union with the human will of the Son of God made man" (*CCC*, 2564).

Extending the Lesson

Prayer Experience: Have the students write one prayer for each of the six types of prayer. The prayers should be original and in their own words. Collect these at the beginning of the next class. Put together a book of the students' prayers and distribute it to them at the end of the chapter. This will be made easier if students can submit their prayers electronically.

For Reflection

- How often do you pray?
- When was a time when prayer helped you?
- How strong is your belief that God will answer your prayers? Explain.

What Is Prayer? (CCC, 2558–2567; 2590; 2623–2649)

Prayer is "the raising of one's mind and heart to God" (St. John Damascus). When we pray we consciously pay attention to God. We direct our thoughts to the loving God who calls us.

Prayer is also a loving conversation with God. A conversation has two parts: talking and listening. The *talking* part of prayer can include private prayers we say alone or public ones we say with others. Our prayers can be formal prayers like the Rosary or spontaneous prayers said in our own words. They can be vocal, said out loud. Or they can be recited silently in our hearts, for example, while visiting our Lord in the Blessed Sacrament. The prayers we say include these types:

1. *Blessing, adoration, and praise.* We bless God because he first blesses us. We adore God because he is the Creator and we are his creations.

Blessing and adoration lead to praise in which we sing to and glorify God because he is good, gracious, loving, and saving. God deserves our love, blessing, adoration, and praise for his own sake. When we praise God, the Holy Spirit is with us. The Spirit helps us to have faith in our Lord and brother Jesus Christ and to call God Abba. True praise of God includes no selfish motive because we take joy in our loving God alone. "I will praise you, LORD, with all my heart; I will declare all your wondrous deeds" (Ps 9:2).

2. *Petition (supplication).* When we petition God in prayer, we are requesting favors. We ask God to give us what we need, especially the gift of the Holy Spirit, who will help us live Christlike lives. Prayers of petition include *contrition,* in which we humbly ask our merciful Father to forgive our sins, and prayers of *intercession* in which we pray for others. Praying

blessing
A prayer that invokes God's care on some person, place, thing, or undertaking.

adoration
Prayer that acknowledges that God is God—Creator, Savior, Sanctifier, Lord, and Master of all creation, the source of all blessings, and worthy of our total love and devotion.

praise
A form of prayer whereby we acknowledge God and his goodness and glorify him for who he is.

petition
A prayer in which we ask God for his help, forgiveness, or some good, whether for ourselves or for others.

intercession
A prayer of petition for the sake of others.

- **Class Discussion:** Have students open their books to page 264. Point out the definition for prayer in the top-left corner. Remind the students they will be expected to know the information in this definition before the end of this chapter. Have them recall the story about the dog and the shepherd (page 262). How does that story reflect this definition of prayer?
- **Individual Assignment:** Have the students write at the top of a clean sheet of paper in their journals the words "The Meaning of Prayer." Have them write the definition of prayer from pages 263 and 264 of the Student Text. If computers are available, have them search the Internet for additional definitions of and quotations about prayer.
- **Class Discussion:** Write these words on the board: **blessing**, **adoration**, **praise**, **petition**, **intercessions**, and **thanksgiving**. Ask for volunteers to offer a definition and an example in their own words for each type of prayer.
- **Individual Assignment:** Have students create a mind-map of the various types (forms) for prayer they just discussed. Suggest that they divide each form into two categories: talking and listening.

Background Information

Many Types of Prayer

There are many types of prayer. Some formal prayers of the Church include the Lord's Prayer, the Rosary, and novenas. Prayers can be silent, within our own hearts and minds, or spoken individually or as a community. We can seek help for prayer, such as praying to St. Anthony to find something that is lost, or offer prayers of thanksgiving, such as praying to St. Jude in thanksgiving for healing.

Background Information

Survey Results

Between 2000 and 2003, the University of North Carolina conducted the national study of youth and religion to try and discover information about the religiosity of American teens. Using a nationally representative telephone survey of 3,370 US English- and Spanish-speaking teenagers between the ages of thirteen and seventeen, and of their parents, the researchers have painted an interesting picture of American youth. The results of this research were published in 2005 by Dr. Christian Smith in the book *Soul Searching* (Oxford University Press). The Catholic data from the study has been published by the National Federation for Catholic Youth Ministry under the title *National Study of Youth and Religion: Analysis of the Population of Catholic Teenagers and Their Parents: A Resource Report Produced for the National Federation for Catholic Youth Ministry* by Charlotte McCorquodale, PhD, Victoria Shepp, MA, and Leigh Sterten, MTS, MSAS (Ministry Training Source). The results of this analysis are a fascinating picture of today's Catholic youth; the implications of those results for teachers of adolescents are even more challenging. Among the findings for Catholic youths are: they pray less often than Protestant youths, and rarely do they pray by themselves; they want to learn how to pray and be given opportunities for prayer; a great majority participate in Sunday Eucharist several times a month, which generally equals the number of times they pray with others; they are generally familiar with the Bible, but do not read it on their own or pray with it; they are mostly happy with the religion of their parents and plan to remain a member of that faith; their attitudes and beliefs concerning their faith are similar to those held by their parents; they wish to learn more about their faith.

For Review Answers (page 265)

1. Prayer is conversation with God. It involves lifting one's mind and heart to God or requesting good things from God. Prayer involves joining one's thoughts and love to God in adoration and blessing, petition, intercession, thanksgiving, and praise.

2. True praise of God includes no selfish motive because we take joy in our loving God alone.

3. When we petition God in prayer, we are requesting favors. We ask God to give us what we need.

4. St. Thérèse of Lisieux defined prayer as "a surge of the heart; it is a simple look turned toward heaven, it is a cry of recognition and of love, embracing both trial and joy."

5. Prayers of contrition and intercession are both forms of petition because each asks God for something. In contrition we ask for forgiveness of sin. In intercession, we pray that God do something for someone else.

6. The Eucharist is the Church's special prayer of thanksgiving. The word *eucharist* means "to give thanks."

7. When we listen in prayer we may hear God speaking to us through our intellect, imagination, will, or memories. We may be inspired with new ideas, or have our fear calmed, our will strengthened, our memories healed.

Prayer Reflection in the New Testament

Answers (page 264)

Luke 18:1–5 petition
Luke 1:46–55 adoration or praise
Mark 10:46–49 petition
John 11:41–42 thanksgiving and praise

prayer
Conversation with God. Lifting of one's mind and heart to God or requesting good things from him. Joining one's thoughts and love to God in adoration and blessing, petition, intercession, thanksgiving, and praise.

for others is an exercise of Christian mercy and love, especially when we pray for those who are in need and for our enemies.

3. *Thanksgiving.* God has given us so much: our very lives (including our health, families, talents, and so forth); the gift of Jesus and his Salvation; and the gift of the Holy Spirit who lives in us. Thanking God in prayer shows that we owe him everything. He deserves our gratitude. The psalmist tells us, "Give thanks to the LORD who is good, whose love endures forever!" (Ps 107:1). The *Eucharist* (a word which means "to give thanks") is a very special type of prayer of thanksgiving. In this supreme prayer, we bless, adore, praise, and thank God for all the blessings he has given to us. We express our sorrow, ask for forgiveness, and petition God for all the good things that we and others need to live our lives fully. When we receive Holy Communion, by the power of the Holy Spirit, our Lord Jesus lives in us and unites us to God and all our Christian brothers and sisters.

In the *listening* part of prayer, we allow God to speak to us. He does so through our intellects, feelings, imaginations, wills, and memories. To hear God in prayer means we must still ourselves and be prepared to listen. Perhaps then we will discover God inspiring us with new ideas or images, calming our fears, strengthening our wills to do right, or healing bad memories that have been bothering us.

There are many definitions and descriptions of prayer. St. Thérèse of Lisieux defined prayer this way: "For me, prayer is a surge of the heart; it is a simple look turned toward heaven, it is a cry of recognition and of love, embracing both trial and joy." The *Catechism of the Catholic Church* defines prayer as "the living relationship of the children of God with their Father who is good beyond measure, with his Son Jesus Christ, and with the Holy Spirit" (*CCC*, 2565). God is our Father. Jesus is our Savior, our brother, and our friend. The Holy Spirit is our Helper. Prayer helps us discover who we really are as beloved children of our loving God. Prayer brings us into unity with our loving Triune God.

These definitions all tell us that in prayer, we turn to God. We become aware of how God lives in our hearts, how he invites us into fellowship with him, how he is concerned about every aspect of our lives. St. Teresa of Avila said to imagine prayer as a journey with an invisible Friend who will always be with us. Like conversation with any of our friends, prayer will deepen our friendship with the Lord and give us the strength to live our life as God intended for us.

 Prayer Reflection in the New Testament

Read these four examples of prayer in the New Testament. Decide which type of prayer each represents: blessing, adoration, praise, petition, intercession, thanksgiving, or contrition.

Luke 18:1–5 _____   Mark 10:46–49 _____

Luke 1:46–55 _____   John 11:41–42 _____

 ## Homework Assignment

1. Complete the "Prayer Reflection in the New Testament" feature assignment on page 264.

2. Complete the For Review questions on page 265.

3. Read the text section "The Bible and Prayer" (pages 265–267).

Choose one or more of the Ongoing Assignments on pages 276–277 to work on through the duration of this chapter.

Background Information

The Importance of Prayer

Speaking to the importance of prayer, the Vatican II document *Apostolic Exhortation on the Renewal of Religious Life* states:

> The discovery of intimacy with God, the necessity for adoration, the need for intercession—the experience of Christian holiness shows us the fruitfulness of prayer, in which God reveals Himself to the spirit and heart of His servants. The Lord gives us this knowledge of Himself in the fervor of love. The gifts of the Spirit are many, but they always grant us a taste of that true and intimate knowledge of the Lord. Without it we shall not succeed either in understanding the value of the Christian and religious life or in gaining the strength to advance in it with the joy of a hope that does not deceive. (Chapter IV, No. 43)

For Review

1. Define *prayer*.
2. Explain what true praise of God entails.
3. What does it mean to petition God?
4. How did St. Thérèse of Lisieux define prayer?
5. Why are *contrition* and *intercessory prayer* considered forms of petition?
6. What is the Church's special prayer of thanksgiving?
7. How can God speak to us in the listening part of prayer?

For Reflection

Consult a web-based news site. Discover a story in the news that needs prayer. Then compose a prayer of *intercession* for that that particular situation. At the end of the prayer, include petitions for people close to you.

The Bible and Prayer (*CCC,* 2568–2606; 2617–2619; 2620; 2622)

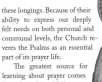

The Bible is an essential source for defining prayer and reporting on how people pray. For example, the book of Genesis reveals how important faith is when we pray, a quality the patriarchs Abraham and Jacob exemplified in their dealings with Yahweh. The book of Exodus reveals prayer as a dialogue, a two-way conversation, but one that always starts with God. Moses prayed to God as a friend and learned from his prayer that God is just, loving, and faithful. Moses also represented many occasions of intercessory prayer by begging Yahweh to care for his people.

In addition, the Old Testament tells us how often religious leaders like Samuel, David, and Elijah taught prayer to the Chosen People and made the Temple in Jerusalem a special place for worshiping God. King David modeled in a special way the attitudes of submission, praise, and repentance that we need when we pray. So important was David's example as a person of prayer that he is credited with writing many of the Psalms. The Psalms express the longings of the human heart and look to the coming Messiah who alone could satisfy these longings. Because of their ability to express our deeply felt needs on both personal and communal levels, the Church reveres the Psalms as an essential part of its prayer life.

The greatest source for learning about prayer comes from Jesus himself, the perfect model of prayer. Prayer was essential to his life. For example, as a child, he was raised by his prayerful mother, Mary, and his foster father, Joseph. As a pious Jew, he also learned to pray as his people did. He went to the synagogue. He attended the religious festivals in Jerusalem. As did most practicing

Background Information

The Scriptures Teach Us to Pray and Are a Source of Prayer

The Bible is an essential source for defining prayer and reporting on how people pray. There are many references to how people prayed, how often, and under what circumstances. For example, James 5:13–16 teaches us that prayers should be offered in thanksgiving as well as those requesting something, such as healing or forgiveness. The manner in which we pray is also important. Prayer is more than simply worshiping in public. It is about leading a Christian life even when no one is looking. Matthew 6:5–6 reinforces this teaching.

The Bible and Prayer (pages 265–267)

Objectives

In this lesson, the students will:
- describe how people prayed in the Bible.
- consider the Psalms as an important source of prayer.
- describe what Jesus taught about prayer.

 Preview

This text section traces the tradition of prayer in the Bible and looks at the Bible as an essential source for defining prayer and reporting on how people pray. Students will be introduced to the many models of prayer found in both the Old and the New Testaments, particularly Jesus and Mary.

Bell Ringers

- **Direct Instruction:** Review the types of prayer covered in the last text section and check the students' answers to the For Review questions on page 265 (answers are on page 268 of this text). Also, check the answers to the short exercise, "Prayer Reflection in the New Testament," from page 264 (answers are on page 268 of this text).

- **Class Activity:** In this activity two students will act out a phone call between God and another student. The students may use cell phones for props if they are available.

  - Select two students to participate in the skit. The two students should be confident, trustworthy, and able to think on their feet. Tell the students that they will be acting out a phone call between friends. They are to act out the skit naturally as if they were actually talking to their best friend. The script for this phone conversation appears on Chapter 10, Handout 1 "This is God Calling Script" (starting on page 285 and also online at www.avemariapress.com).

  - Have the students sit in the front of the room, back to back so that they can be seen by the rest of the class but not by each other. Give the script to the students and give them about thirty seconds to review the lines. During this time explain to the class that they will now witness a phone conversation between friends. Turn the session over to the actors. The skit should last about two minutes max and may be much shorter. The purpose of this activity is to help students see that (1) God calls them to prayer and (2) prayer is a natural conversation that can be held in normal language.

Teaching Approaches

- **Class Discussion:** Ask the class to talk about what they learned from the skit. Desired answers include:
  - God calls us first; we always respond to God's call.
  - God communicates love for us all the time.
  - God holds us accountable for what we do and don't do.
  - God is willing to listen to anything we have to say but won't always rescue us from ourselves.

- **Direct Instruction:** Summarize the text section "The Bible and Prayer" on pages 265–267. Discuss with students what they learned from this reading.

- **Class Activity:** Have students get out their bibles. Through much of the rest of the session, have the students find and read aloud the Bible passages listed below (write on the board). After each, take a few moments to talk about the passage, what the prayer was about, what emotions the prayer expressed, and the results of the prayer. Focus attention on why people pray (the need to be in touch with God) and God's response to the prayers. Bible passages:
  - Genesis 12:1–5
  - Genesis 15:1–6
  - Genesis 18:20–32
  - Exodus 15:1–4, 11–13
  - 2 Samuel 22:1–4, 26–31, 47–51
  - Psalm 14
  - Psalm 17
  - Psalm 30
  - Luke 1:46–55
  - Luke 1:67–79
  - Luke 10:21–22
  - Luke 22:39–46
  - John 11:41–44
  - John 18:15–26

- **Class Discussion:** Review with the students the times and ways that Jesus prayed. Have them make connections between the ways Jesus prayed and the types of prayer they learned about in the previous section.

- **Individual Assignment:** Have students read and answer the questions about the passages in the Knowing Christ through Scripture feature, "Jesus and Prayer." When they finish, discuss their responses as a class.

- **Direct Instruction:** Reread the question and answer in the Explaining Your Faith feature "Do Catholics Worship Mary and the Saints?" on page 266. Talk about the difference between praying to God and honoring Mary and the saints with veneration. When we venerate someone, we show them great respect for who they are. This is somewhat akin to hero

Jews, Jesus probably memorized the Psalms and prayed them often. The New Testament includes many examples of the adult Jesus at prayer. For example, he prayed:
- in the desert before beginning his public preaching,
- before choosing his Apostles,
- after performing miracles like the multiplication of the loaves and fishes, and
- on the mountain at the time of his Transfiguration.

Jesus also prayed in the Garden before his arrest, asking to do God's will, even if it led to his Death on the cross (see Lk 22:42).

Jesus prayed in many different ways, as we should, too. He *praised* the Father for revealing God's will to the humble and lowly (see Lk 10:21). He *thanked* God when he raised Lazarus from the dead (see Jn 11:41–42). He *petitioned* his heavenly Father to keep Peter from giving in to temptation (see Lk 22:31–32). Chapter 17 of John's Gospel shares Jesus' great priestly prayer of *intercession*: Jesus asked his Father to keep his disciples in the truth. Most remarkably, Jesus also prayed for us that "they may all be one, as you, Father, are in me and I in you, that they also may be in us" (Jn 17:21). A great example of Jesus at prayer took place at his crucifixion. He prayed for all sinners and forgave his persecutors. His final words are a prayerful act of trust in his heavenly Father: "Father, into your hands I commend my spirit" (Lk 23:46).

Mary, the Mother of God, is also an inspiration for prayer. She showed two great qualities in her prayer life:

faith and humility. Mary demonstrated faith when she accepted the angel Gabriel's news that she was to become the Mother of God. She trusted God to work through her; yet she did not fully understand how: "Behold, I am the handmaid of the Lord. May it be done to me according to your word" (Lk 1:38). Because of her trust in God, she helped bring the Word of God into humanity. Mary's great prayer, the Magnificat, also reveals her humility. She rightly credited God for all the goodness that happened to her and through her: "The Mighty One has done great things for me, and holy is his name" (Lk 1:49). Her Magnificat teaches the Church to show humble gratitude to God, who is the source of all our blessings.

Mary's appearances throughout the New Testament are accompanied by prayer. For example, when she went to help her cousin Elizabeth, she sang joyfully of God's goodness. She, like Joseph, went to the great religious feasts at the Temple. Like most mothers, she also taught her child Jesus to pray and instilled in him a love for the prayers and Scriptures of the Chosen People. Finally, after Jesus ascended to Heaven, Mary waited in the upper room on Pentecost Sunday, when the Holy Spirit came in all his power (Acts 1:14).

The examples of Jesus and Mary have much to teach us. If prayer was important to the Son of God and to his sinless Mother, then how much more important should it be to us? Prayer is essential for being a Christian.

Explaining Your Faith

Do Catholics worship Mary and the saints?

No. Catholics worship and adore God alone, as taught by the First Commandment. Worship of any other person or thing would be idolatry, a sin against the First Commandment. Catholics do honor, venerate, and respect Mary as the Mother of God, the Queen of All Saints.

Sometimes people who are not Catholic, and even Catholics themselves, will get the wrong idea when

they hear that Catholics "pray to" the saints. Remembering that prayer is, first of all, a conversation may help. Catholics do talk with the saints. We ask for their prayers—that they will talk to God on our behalf—just like we ask our living friends to pray for us when we are in need.

Homework Assignment

1. Complete the For Review questions on page 267.

2. Read the text section "How to Pray" (pages 267–272).

3. Continue working on the Ongoing Assignments, pages 276–277.

Extending the Lesson

Journal Assignment: Throughout Chapter 10, have the students write in their journals especially about their prayer life. In the journal they should note the following information about their prayer lives: when (date and time), where (exact location), how long (in minutes), type of prayer, and how they felt following the prayer. Tell students that you would like them to pray daily as you study this chapter, and that you would like for them to keep a log of their prayer experience. These should be reviewed (unannounced) during class at least twice during the chapter to make sure students were participating in the project. Distribute Chapter 10, Handout 2 "Prayer Journal" (starting on page 285 and also online at www.avemariapress.com) to help them begin this journal assignment.

KNOWING CHRIST THROUGH SCRIPTURE

Jesus and Prayer

Read the following passages that tell about times that Jesus prayed alone. Write your answers to the questions that follow.

Luke 4:1–11; Mark 1:35–37; Luke 6:12–13;

Luke 5:15–16; Matthew 14:13–33; Mark 14:32–42

- What were some of the places where Jesus prayed alone?
- What were some reasons that Jesus withdrew from the crowds to pray alone?

Jesus also taught *about* prayer. Read and summarize these three parables on prayer from the Gospel of Luke. Explain in your own words the lesson Jesus taught about prayer in each parable.

Luke 11:5–13 (Friend at Midnight)

Luke 18:1-8 (Persistent Widow)

Luke 18:9–14 (Pharisee and Tax Collector)

For Review

1. Discuss three things that the Old Testament teaches about prayer.
2. What were some of the ways that Jesus prayed?
3. How is Mary an inspiration for prayer?
4. List five things Jesus taught us about prayer.

For Reflection
- Which example from Jesus' life is your favorite model of prayer?
- Who is someone who has been a model of prayer to you? How so?

How to Pray

(*CCC*, 2650–2698; 2720; 2725–2758)

The Holy Spirit teaches the Church how to pray primarily through the living Tradition of the Church and through the Sacred Scriptures that we hear at liturgies and meditate on afterward. The Holy Spirit also gives us the theological virtues to help us pray. Through these virtues, the Holy Spirit teaches us that we can pray always. God is always present to us, and the Spirit lives in us. Christ stands beside us. We can and should pray often.

Getting Started in Prayer

Hopefully, you have already learned many things about prayer from your parents, teachers, priests, and others who have made prayer an important part of their lives. Throughout the history of the Church, the saints have taught different ways to approach God in prayer. They share many points in common on how to get started. Here are some basics:
- *Place.* You can pray anywhere, but it is good to find a special place where you can slow down, relax, and focus your attention. Many have found their bedrooms,

Knowing Christ through Scripture Answers (page 267)

- *Luke 4:11*—desert; to prepare for his ministry
- *Mark 1:35–37*—deserted place; Jesus has begun his ministry and needs time to pray before continuing his preaching and healing miracles.
- *Luke 6:12–13*—mountain; he wanted to choose certain individuals to represent him as Apostles.
- *Luke 5:15–16*—Jesus goes off to pray when he is overwhelmed by people seeking him.
- *Matthew 14:13–33*—Jesus prays after hearing about John the Baptist's death and before being with large groups of people and working miracles.
- *Mark 14:32–42*—garden; Jesus prepares for his Passion with prayer.

worship: we admire these people and want to be like them. When we pray to the saints and ask for their assistance, we ask them to intercede with God on our behalf, much as we might ask a favorite teacher to write a letter of recommendation on our behalf when we apply for a job or to attend a college. This is not worship, but participation in the Communion of Saints.

For Review Answers (page 267)

1. From the Old Testament we can learn: the importance of prayer; prayer as a dialog with God; how to talk with God as a friend; how to ask God for help; how the Chosen People prayed; how the temple in Jerusalem became a primary place of worship; the importance of submission to God's will, of praise, and of penance.

2. Jesus praised God, he thanked God, he petitioned God, he asked God for intercession, he prayed for his disciples and for sinners, he prayed on the cross.

3. Mary is an inspiration for prayer because of her faith and her humility.

4. Jesus taught us to pray without ceasing; to thank God; to ask God for what we need; to ask God to help others; to pray when we are happy, when we are sad, and when we suffer.

How to Pray (pages 267–272)

Objectives

In this lesson, the students will:
- pray the Liturgy of the Hours.
- describe strategies to help them pray.
- explain, give examples of, and demonstrate vocal prayer, meditative prayer, and mental prayer.

Preview

This lesson leads students through various prayer practices. Most of the session will be spent having students practice various forms of prayer.

Bell Ringers

- **Direct Instruction:** Review the students' answers to the For Review questions on page 267. Also, put some students "on the spot" and ask them to list and describe the different forms of prayer.

- **Prayer Experience:** Turn your meeting space or classroom into a worship space. Set up a prayer table with an open Bible, a candle (lit if allowed by facility rules), and other items that create a prayerful atmosphere. Play sacred music softly to provide background sound. Prepare a Liturgy of the Hours service to conduct with your students (see the Liturgy of Hours Apostolate website at www.avemariapress .com). Explain that the Liturgy of the Hours is an official prayer of the Church. Information about the Liturgy of the Hours can be found at the bottom of page 274. Make sure each student has access to a copy of the prayer service. Select readers for various aspects of the prayer beforehand. Because the

the school chapel or parish church, or the outdoors to be good places for prayer.

- *Time.* You can pray at any time of the day. However, it is good to get in the habit of choosing a special time each day to pray. Good times to pray include when rising in the morning or before going to bed, as a break between homework assignments, before and after meals, for ten minutes during a free period at school, or while driving (with the radio off), and so forth. Catholics also pray each Sunday when they go to Mass.

- *Relax body and mind.* It is hard to pray if you are tense or distracted. Prayer requires both alertness and relaxation. Breathing exercises that help you drain away the cares of the day and comfortable body posture—like sitting upright in a chair, lying on the floor, or kneeling—can help you to concentrate when you pray.

- *Good attitude.* To pray we must be open to God. Begin your prayer time by recalling that God is present, that he loves you immensely, and that he has given you many gifts, including the gift of life. Approach God with a humble heart. Remember that God has invited us to spend time with him in prayer. Therefore, you can trust that the Lord will be with us and will answer our heartfelt desire to be with him.

- *Keep at it.* It can be difficult to pray regularly. You may be lazy or tired. Also, Satan will tempt humans in many ways to ignore their time for prayer. Even if you are faithful in your prayer, sometimes you may feel that God is not listening to you. Added to this are the distractions that always seem to come along, making it difficult to focus and hear the Lord in the depth of our hearts. To persevere with prayer, you must keep the faith that God always hears you, even if you do not "feel" anything. When things seem to be going poorly, pray for the Holy Spirit to come to you.

Distractions in prayer caused by a wandering mind, an overactive imagination, or external noises are normal. One way to deal with them is to gaze at a crucifix, holy picture or icon, or a lit candle to help keep your attention on God. Another good technique is to recite repeatedly a prayer word or phrase like "Abba," "Savior," or "Jesus help me." This practice can "distract you from the distractions" and refocus your attention on the Lord. Always remember this truth: the Lord is very pleased with your efforts. Trying to pray is itself a prayer. God appreciates any and all efforts you make at prayer.

We should address our prayers to the Father, our loving Abba who is the source of our life. We should also pray to Jesus and invoke his blessed name often. For example, we can pray the famous Jesus Prayer: "Lord Jesus Christ, Son of God, have mercy on me, a sinner." We should also invoke the help of the Holy Spirit, the interior teacher of Christian prayer.

Through the ages, Catholics have also found it valuable to pray in union with our Blessed Mother, who shows us how to cooperate with the graces of the Holy Spirit and how to live a Christlike life. The Hail Mary is special because it praises God for his goodness shown to Mary and petitions our Blessed Mother to pray for us to her beloved Son.

Background Information

Getting Started in Prayer

One of the primary forms of prayer is the way in which Christians pray through the Sacred Scriptures that are read at liturgies and the opportunity to meditate on the readings afterward. We may have also learned about prayer from parents, teachers, priests, and others who have made prayer an important part of their lives.

In his book *Prayers for a Planetary Pilgrim: A Personal Manual for Prayer and Ritual*, Fr. Edward Hays sets the stage for establishing a practice of personal prayer. The importance of establishing an appropriate prayer space "can easily be overlooked since the journey is viewed as 'spiritual.' . . . The Spirit can transform matter, so the physical environment can have a great influence on the work of the Spirit." He continues, "While your entire home is a sacred place where you pray and journey to God in different ways, it can be invaluable to set aside a particular place for your inner exercises" (232).

Hays suggests creating a personal shrine—with a small stone slab as an altar, a small prayer rug or pillow, or even icons and religious images for those who are visually oriented. Some, he says, may prefer a space that is void of all images, while others might choose to change the images to reflect the various seasons (233).

Other prayer helps that Hays recommends include using prayer pebbles or beads, writing down prayers on notes, and writing in a journal (237–246).

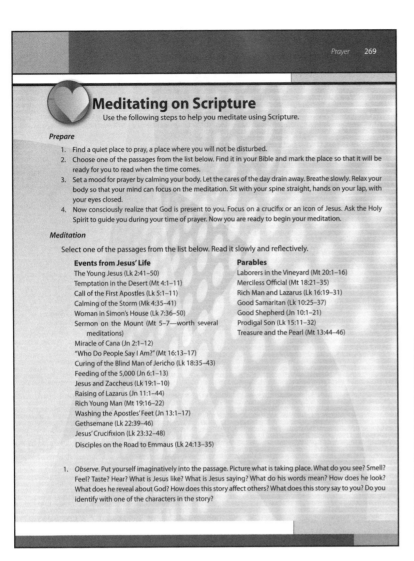

Meditating on Scripture

Use the following steps to help you meditate using Scripture.

Prepare

1. Find a quiet place to pray, a place where you will not be disturbed.
2. Choose one of the passages from the list below. Find it in your Bible and mark the place so that it will be ready for you to read when the time comes.
3. Set a mood for prayer by calming your body. Let the cares of the day drain away. Breathe slowly. Relax your body so that your mind can focus on the meditation. Sit with your spine straight, hands on your lap, with your eyes closed.
4. Now consciously realize that God is present to you. Focus on a crucifix or an icon of Jesus. Ask the Holy Spirit to guide you during your time of prayer. Now you are ready to begin your meditation.

Meditation

Select one of the passages from the list below. Read it slowly and reflectively.

Events from Jesus' Life
The Young Jesus (Lk 2:41–50)
Temptation in the Desert (Mt 4:1–11)
Call of the First Apostles (Lk 5:1–11)
Calming of the Storm (Mk 4:35–41)
Woman in Simon's House (Lk 7:36–50)
Sermon on the Mount (Mt 5–7—worth several meditations)
Miracle of Cana (Jn 2:1–12)
"Who Do People Say I Am?" (Mt 16:13–17)
Curing of the Blind Man of Jericho (Lk 18:35–43)
Feeding of the 5,000 (Jn 6:1–13)
Jesus and Zaccheus (Lk 19:1–10)
Raising of Lazarus (Jn 11:1–44)
Rich Young Man (Mt 19:16–22)
Washing the Apostles' Feet (Jn 13:1–17)
Gethsemane (Lk 22:39–46)
Jesus' Crucifixion (Lk 23:32–48)
Disciples on the Road to Emmaus (Lk 24:13–35)

Parables
Laborers in the Vineyard (Mt 20:1–16)
Merciless Official (Mt 18:21–35)
Rich Man and Lazarus (Lk 16:19–31)
Good Samaritan (Lk 10:25–37)
Good Shepherd (Jn 10:1–21)
Prodigal Son (Lk 15:11–32)
Treasure and the Pearl (Mt 13:44–46)

1. *Observe.* Put yourself imaginatively into the passage. Picture what is taking place. What do you see? Smell? Feel? Taste? Hear? What is Jesus like? What is Jesus saying? What do his words mean? How does he look? What does he reveal about God? How does this story affect others? What does this story say to you? Do you identify with one of the characters in the story?

---

reading of the hours is often done in choral fashion, you will want to form the students into two groups and assign each group to pray aloud various sections of the liturgy.

- **Class Discussion:** When the prayer service has been completed, have the students talk about the experience. What did they like or dislike? Have any of them ever participated in this type of prayer before? Explain that the prayer can be prayed by an individual alone. Would they be interested in praying it on a regular basis?

For Enrichment

Individual Assignment: Print out several of the Internet links from www.avemariapress.com. Have the students examine these links and report on (1) favorites; (2) new things they learned; (3) new ways they prayed; and (4) other background information on the website. (This assignment should vary from the Ongoing Assignments on pages 276–277 or can be done in combination with it.)

Background Information

Monastic Rules of Prayer

Much of the Church's rich history of prayer and adoration come to us from the monastic communities. These communities were governed by rules that provided specific instructions in what they should do. The following come from the rule for the Augustinian order and the Benedictine order. The Rule of Benedict was actually written by Benedict.

From the Rule of St. Augustine (Fifth Century)

- Be assiduous in prayer (Col 4:2), at the hours and times appointed.

- In the Oratory no one should do anything other than that for which was intended and from which it also takes its name. Consequently, if there are some who might wish to pray there during their free time, even outside the hours appointed, they should not be hindered by those who think something else must be done there.

- When you pray to God in Psalms and hymns, think over in your hearts the words that come from your lips.

- Chant only what is prescribed for chant; moreover, let nothing be chanted unless it is so prescribed.

From the Rule of St. Benedict (Sixth Century)

Of Reverence at Prayer

- If we do not venture to approach men who are in power, except with humility and reverence, when we wish to ask a favor, how much must we beseech the Lord God of all things with all humility and purity of devotion? And let us be assured that it is not in many words, but in the purity of heart and tears of compunction that we are heard. For this reason prayer ought to be short and pure, unless, perhaps it is lengthened by the inspiration of divine grace. At the community exercises, however, let the prayer always be short, and the sign having been given by the Superior, let all rise together.

Teaching Approaches

- **Class Discussion:** Ask the students if they notice anything different about the meeting space. Explain that many people find that setting up a prayer space and having sacred music playing softly in the background helps them to pray. Ask the students if there are any places or times that they find most conducive to prayer.

- **Class Discussion:** Review the advice about praying found on pages 267–268. Explain that if they become too relaxed, their prayer might put them to sleep, so a prone posture may not be the best for them. Ask them to share which piece of prayer advice is most important in their experience.

- **Direct Instruction:** Move to the section "Prayer Expressions" on page 270. Provide students with examples of vocal prayer, meditative prayer, and mental prayer. Remind the students of various prayer experiences that they had in class and the expression of prayer for each one of those experiences.

2. *Meditate.* What is the theme of the passage (for example, God's love for the sinner)? Pause periodically to talk intimately to the Lord. Let him speak to you through the reading. Turn to God and respond to his presence with you. Share with the Lord your deepest thoughts and feelings. Turn over to him your cares and needs. Praise God for his goodness. Ask God to forgive your sins and failings. If distractions come your way, return to the Scripture passage. Take your time and enjoy these moments with the Lord.

3. *Listen.* Ask yourself, "What is the Lord saying *to me*? What message is there in this biblical passage for my life?"

4. *Conclude.* Thank God for being present to you. Make a resolution to do something concrete as a result of your meditation. For example, perhaps you will try to be more patient with people during the coming day.

Prayer Expressions
(CCC, 2700–2719; 2721–2724)

meditation
A form of prayer where the mind and imagination focus on Christ or some truth of Divine Revelation with the purpose of applying the lessons we learn to our lives.

Christian prayer comes from the heart. Prayer expresses itself in these ways:

1. *Vocal prayer.* Prayers can be said mentally or out loud. When you express your feelings in words, you are doing what Jesus himself did when he taught the Our Father. When you pray with fellow Christians, you strengthen your spiritual relationships with them.

2. *Meditation.* In meditation, you actively use your thoughts, emotions, imaginations, and desires to think about God's presence in the world and in your life. Meditation helps you to "tune in to God," to gain a greater knowledge and love of the Lord so that you can serve him better. Saints like Teresa of Avila and Ignatius of Loyola used the Gospels to help them meditate. Besides following their example, you can also meditate on the writings of the saints, world events, and the action of God in your own life.

contemplation
Wordless prayer whereby a person's mind and heart rest in God's goodness and majesty.

3. *Mental prayer.* This type of prayer typically centers on Jesus. In mental prayer, you converse with Jesus or reflect on one of the mysteries of his Life, for example, his Passion and crucifixion. Sometimes mental prayer can lead to contemplation, a form of silent, wordless prayer in which you simply rest in the presence of our all-loving God. St. John Vianney told of a simple peasant who described contemplative prayer. The peasant sat daily in front of our Blessed Lord, present in the tabernacle. "I look at him and he looks at me." When praying this way, you can empty your mind of thoughts and images and simply allow the divine presence to penetrate your being. You do not have to do anything at all.

Background Information

The Liturgy of the Hours

The Liturgy of the Hours (also called the Divine Office) developed during the early days of the Church in monastic settings. The form used today was established as early as the sixth century. The structure for each of the hours is similar, consisting of Morning Prayer (Lauds), Prayer During the Day—Before Noon (Terce), Prayer During the Day—Midday (Sext), Prayer During the Day—Afternoon (None—pronounced "no-n"), Evening Prayer (Vespers), Office of Readings (Matins), and Night Prayer (Compline).

Being part of the Church's official liturgy, the hours are guided from the Vatican and much has been written about how the hours are to be prayed. Here is an example:

- The laity, too, are encouraged to recite the Divine Office, whether with the priests, or among themselves, or even individually (*Sacrosanctum concilium* n. 100, *Catechism of the Catholic Church,* 1175).

- The Liturgy of the Hours, like other liturgical services, is not a private matter but belongs to the whole body of the Church, whose life it both expresses and affects (*General Instruction to the Liturgy of the Hours* n. 20).

- Wherever possible, other groups of the faithful should celebrate the Liturgy of the Hours communally in church (*General Instruction to the Liturgy of the Hours* n. 21).

- Priests as well as deacons aspiring to the priesthood are obliged to fulfill the Liturgy of the Hours daily in accordance with the proper and approved liturgical books (*Code of Canon Law,* Canon 276.3).

- Those who act as readers are to stand in a convenient place. The hours are often sung. If sung, a cantor or cantors intones the antiphons, psalms, and other chants. All make the Sign of the Cross, from forehead to breast and from left shoulder to right, at the beginning of the hours and at the beginning of the Gospel (adapted from the *General Instruction to the Liturgy of the Hours* 254–266).

- The psalms are sung or said in one of three ways: (a) all sing the entire psalm, (b) antiphonally—two choirs or sections of the congregation sing alternative verses or strophes, or (c) responsorially—the antiphons are repeated after each strophe (adapted from the *General Instruction to the Liturgy of the Hours* 122,125).

PROFILE OF FAITH: FR. PATRICK PEYTON, C.S.C., SERVANT OF GOD

Fr. Patrick Peyton's life mission was to promote the Rosary, especially among families. He was known as "the Rosary priest" and made famous the beloved saying, "The family that prays together stays together." He also taught, "A world at prayer is a world at peace."

Patrick was born January 9, 1909, in County Mayo, Ireland, the sixth of nine children. His devout Catholic parents used to gather the family to recite the Rosary around the family hearth every evening. However, the family was poor, so when he was nineteen, Patrick and his older brother came to America to join their sister in Scranton, Pennsylvania. There he did janitorial work at the diocesan cathedral and finished up his high school studies. Feeling called to the priesthood, Patrick then entered the Congregation of Holy Cross seminary at the University of Notre Dame in Indiana.

During his years of theological studies for the priesthood, Patrick contracted the dreaded disease of tuberculosis, often fatal at that time. His future looked bleak until a trusted priest counselor advised him to pray to the Blessed Mother. The suffering young man fervently did pray to Mary. In his autobiography, Fr. Peyton wrote:

Like the dark night that is replaced by dawn and the dawn by the sun, she brought me back to life. I was certain Our Blessed Mother was taking part in my healing. I am not describing a miracle. I'm giving witness to the power of Mary's intercession and the quiet, unsensational way she works. I begged the doctors to examine me once more and received their report in a letter. Like a prisoner waiting for the verdict of the jury, I opened the letter and saw my freedom, my new lease on life, my second spring.

The first words I spoke were, "Mary, I hope I will never disgrace you."[24]

Fr. Patrick kept his promise. He and his brother were ordained in 1941, and, with the permission of his religious superiors, he began the Family Rosary Crusade. In gratitude to Our Lady, he made it his life's mission for the next fifty years to let everyone know of the graces our Blessed Mother is willing to shower on those who turn to her with confidence and love. He traveled around the globe, spoke in pulpits, preached on radio and television, and gathered people in large rallies usually held at outdoor football stadiums to pray the Rosary. He enlisted famous movie stars like Bing Crosby to participate and inspire others to turn to Our Lady in prayer.

Fr. Patrick was a model pray-er himself. The Masses he offered daily were prayed with great devotion. He spent many hours before the Blessed Sacrament, and, of course, he would recite the Rosary frequently. Despite the hard and constant work of organizing the Family Rosary Crusade, producing radio shows and movies, traveling, and corresponding with hundreds of people who wrote to him for help and advice, he always remained gentle, loving, and joyful. Calling himself, "Our Lady's donkey," Fr. Patrick Peyton was indeed a man of God.

Fr. Peyton died on June 3, 1992. In 2001, the cause for the canonization for the "Rosary priest" was initiated by the Bishop of Fall River, Massachusetts, the diocese where Fr. Peyton is buried. Now called the Servant of God, Fr. Patrick Peyton's work continues in Holy Cross Family Ministries, which among other good works promotes family well-being through prayer, especially the Rosary, in seventeen countries on five continents.

• Read more about this Servant of God, Fr. Patrick Peyton, and the work of the Holy Cross Family Ministries online. Write a short report detailing some information you gleaned about Fr. Peyton, Holy Cross Family Ministries, or the Rosary.

• **Prayer Experience:** Have students practice meditating on the Scriptures as presented on pages 269-270. Have them work with various Scripture passages to carry out the suggested process. You can also refer to the *Lectio Divina* Prayer Reflection on pages 257–258 of the Student Text. The students should record their experiences in their prayer journals.

• **Group activity:** As a review of what they have learned about prayer so far, invite students to get into groups of three or four to create "A Beginner's Guide to Prayer." Give the students a number of options, including an actual booklet, a PowerPoint presentation, a video, a blog, etc. Make sure that they include the various types of prayer, the expressions of prayer, some practical advice on best practices in prayer, and examples of prayer in the Old and New Testament. Have the students complete the assignment either in class or, if possible, as homework.

Homework Assignment

1. Complete the For Review questions on page 272.

2. Read the text section, "The Lord's Prayer (Our Father)" (pages 272–275).

3. Work toward completing the Ongoing Assignments.

For Enrichment

Individual Assignment: Refer students to the Profile of Faith feature on Fr. Patrick Peyton, C.S.C., known as "the Rosary priest." Have the students discuss the impact of prayer on their family life. Or have them suggest how prayer might positively affect their family. Have the students research more about Fr. Peyton's life using the links provided in the Student Text or have them visit the Holy Cross Family Ministries website www.hcfm.org/main/home.php.

Background Information

The Difference between Meditation and Contemplation

In meditative prayer one reflects on God's words and wonders how one's life fits into God's scheme. Contemplative prayer is sitting quietly and just being present to the beauty and the power of God. Contemplation prayer uses no words; in silence one sits quietly in God's presence and is bathed in his love.

Contemplation is a form of meditative prayer. In meditation, one thinks about what God is or does. In contemplative prayer, we are captivated by God. We are transfixed by God's majesty. We enjoy the luxury of sitting in God's company. We rest in God.

Contemplative prayer is as old as the Bible. Abraham, Moses, David, and even Jesus had contemplative experiences of prayer. Saints such as Augustine, Gregory the Great, Bonaventure, Teresa of Avila, John of the Cross, Ignatius Loyola, and Thomas Aquinas advanced the theology of contemplation. Most people have participated in contemplative prayer without knowing it.

Today, contemplative prayer is practiced by religious and laity. Centering prayer is one of today's more popular styles of contemplative prayer; Pope Paul VI encouraged laity to use this form of prayer.

Some people have difficulty with contemplation. Their minds wander or they lose focus. Others find it very easy to sit and do nothing but be with God.

For Review Answers (page 272)

1. Catholics find it valuable to pray in union with our Blessed Mother, who shows us how to cooperate with the graces of the Holy Spirit.

2. To pray, we must be open to God. A good attitude allows us to remember all the ways God has been present in our lives, his love for us, and the many gifts we have been given. We can then approach God with a humble heart and trust that God will be with us.

3. We can persevere in prayer by gazing at a crucifix, a holy picture, or a lit candle. We can also recite repeatedly a prayer word or phrase like "Abba," "Savior," or "Jesus help me."

4. We use our minds in meditation. We actively engage our thoughts, emotions, imaginations, and desires to think about God's presence. In mental prayer (contemplation) we empty our mind of thoughts and images and simply allow God to penetrate our being.

5. Contemplation is the wordless prayer whereby a person's mind and heart rests in God's goodness and majesty.

The Lord's Prayer (Our Father)

(pages 272–275)

Objectives

In this lesson, the students will:
- pray the Lord's Prayer.
- describe the meaning of the various parts of the Lord's Prayer.
- explain the importance of the Lord's Prayer to the life of the Church.

Preview

In this lesson students will become familiar with the Lord's Prayer and its various parts. They will study the Lord's Prayer in detail and consider various ways of praying the prayer.

Bell Ringers

- **Group Activity:** Have the students form groups of five. Each group is to develop a letter petitioning the principal of the school to make changes that the group of students thinks would be beneficial for the school and that address concerns the students might have.
  - ◆ Allow the students ten minutes to come up with a draft of their letter. The letter should have four parts: (1) salutation, (2) positive things the students want

For Review

1. How should a beginner get started in prayer?
2. What does having a good attitude have to do with being effective at prayer?
3. What is a strategy for persevering at prayer when tempted to do otherwise?
4. What is the difference between meditation and mental prayer?
5. Define *contemplation*.

For Reflection
- When is a good time for you to pray?
- How do you approach God in prayer?

The Lord's Prayer (Our Father) (*CCC*, 2759–2865)

The Lord's Prayer is the prime Christian prayer, what the Church Father Tertullian called "the summary of the whole Gospel." From the earliest centuries until today, the Church has prayed the Lord's Prayer in its liturgical celebrations, especially the Eucharist. It is central to a Christian's daily prayer.

The Lord's Prayer appears in the Gospels of both Luke and Matthew. Luke's version, probably the older of the two, has only five petitions. Matthew's version, which has seven petitions, is more familiar because the Church prays it in its liturgies. The added conclusion to the prayer at Mass—"For the kingdom, the power and the glory are yours, now and forever and ever"—is called a *doxology* (prayer of praise). It comes from the *Didache*, a first-century catechetical manual, and the *Apostolic Constitutions*. This doxology repeats in praise and thanksgiving the first three petitions to God the Father: the glorification of God's name, the coming of the Kingdom, and the power of God's saving will.

Matthew's Gospel reports that Jesus taught the Lord's Prayer in the Sermon on the Mount (Mt 5–7). In this famous sermon, Jesus instructed his followers on the Christian way of life, including how to pray. Jesus told us to pray humbly and not to babble on. He gave us the Our Father as the prototypical prayer that relies totally on God.

Luke's context for Jesus' teaching the Lord's Prayer differs from Matthew's. In his version, the Apostles approached Jesus one day while he was praying by himself. They asked him to teach them how to pray. Jesus then instructed them to say the Lord's Prayer. Because of his instructions, Jesus' disciples can dare address God as Abba ("Daddy" or "Dear Father"). The Lord's Prayer identifies us as Christians. Because it was so special, the early Christians only learned it after they were baptized.

Meaning of the Our Father

The Our Father consists of seven petitions. The first three glorify God; the last four take our needs to our loving Father. A discussion of the parts of the Lord's Prayer follows.

Our Father

Jesus invites us to call God Abba, to address almighty God intimately, securely, and with childlike trust. Jesus teaches us that God is good, gracious, and absolutely loving.

Calling God "Father" contains two very important truths. First, Jesus' Father is our Father, too. We should humbly trust Abba to care for our needs. Second, since God is *our* Father, we are brothers and sisters to all people. Every person is intimately related to us. If we believe what Jesus teaches us by this prayer, we will commit ourselves to understand, love, and respond to *everyone* who comes into our lives.

Who art in Heaven

"In Heaven" refers to God's way of being, his majesty. It does not refer to a place. Christians affirm that through Jesus, God lives in the hearts of the just. When we address our heavenly Father, we are professing that we are God's people who are in union with Christ in Heaven. At the same time, we await the day when our heavenly reward will be fully ours.

Hallowed be thy name

Our individual names remind us of our uniqueness. In the ancient world, a person's name typically stood for the person. For example, Jesus wanted Simon bar Jonah to be the leader of the Apostles; therefore, he renamed him *Peter,* which means "Rock," describing Peter's role as the Church's foundation. Your name, too, has special meaning. For example, Christopher means "Christ bearer"; Carol means "joyful song."

When we "hallow" God's name, we pray that everyone on earth will regard God as holy (as he is in Heaven). God is the source of all holiness. We make God's name holy when we believe in God's love and act on it by taking on the identity of our Savior, Jesus Christ. When we live up to the name Christian, others will come to know and praise God because they can see God's image in us.

Thy kingdom come; thy will be done on earth as it is in Heaven

With the coming of Jesus Christ, God's rule has broken into our world. God's kingship or reign is one of peace, justice, truth, community, and mutual love. Jesus has inaugurated this reign by preaching the Gospel to the poor, freeing captives, and healing and saving everyone.

God's Kingdom will be fully established only at the end of time, but we are to live, experience, and work for it right now. When we pray "thy kingdom come," we petition primarily for Christ's return, the final coming of God's Kingdom. Then there will be full righteousness, peace, and joy.

When we pray for the coming of this Kingdom, we must join Jesus in his work, which primarily entails loving others and responding to the needs of our least brothers and sisters.

Background Information

The Our Father Is the Prime Christian Prayer

The Lord's Prayer is the pinnacle of Christian prayer—the perfect prayer. It summarizes the entire Gospel and was taught to us by Jesus himself. The *Catechism of the Catholic Church* teaches:

> The traditional expression "the Lord's Prayer"—*oratio Dominica*—means that the prayer to our Father is taught and given to us by the Lord Jesus. The prayer that comes to us from Jesus is truly unique: it is "of the Lord." On the one hand, in the words of this prayer the only Son gives us the words the Father gave him: he is the master of our prayer. On the other, as Word incarnate, he knows in his human heart the needs of his human brothers and sisters and reveals them to us: he is the model of our prayer. (2765)

to say about the school and the principal, (3) concerns the students want to bring to the principal's attention, and (4) a closing sentence.

- ◆ After the letters are drafted, bring the students back into a large group. Have representatives from the groups describe what they wrote in each section. If time allows, hear from each group on all four parts. If not, hear from one to three groups and see if any of the other groups have anything else to add. Write the key findings for each of these four parts on the board leaving plenty of room under each part. Leave this on the board throughout the session.

- **Student Presentations:** Give students the opportunity to share with the class their "Beginner's Guide to Prayer" projects. Take this opportunity to review the chapter up to this point.

Teaching Approaches

- **Class Activity:** Have students get out their bibles. Have half the students open their bibles to Matthew 6:9–13 and the other half to Luke 11:2–4. Give the students a few moments to read their assigned passage quietly.

  - ◆ Next, ask for one volunteer from each group to read their passage aloud verse by verse—the reader of Matthew is to read verse 9 and stop, then the reader of Luke will read verse 2, then Matthew 10, then Luke 3, and so on. You may need to tell each reader when to read each verse. Before the reading begins, tell the students to write down any similarities or differences they hear in the two different passages.

  - ◆ When the reading is finished, ask the students if they noticed any similarities or differences in the two readings. Write the student's answers on the board (in a spot separate from the material from the previous activity). The similarities can be found in the Background Information on page 279.

- **Class Discussion:** Have the students open their textbooks to page 273. Review with them the key parts of the Lord's Prayer presented there through page 275. Now, ask the students to think back to the letters they wrote to the principal at the beginning of the class. What do those letters and the Lord's Prayer have in common? They both have greetings, statements of praise, and petitions/requests. Have the students divide the Lord's Prayer into each of the four suggested parts: greeting, praise, petitions/requests, and a closing. Make it clear to the students that when they pray the Lord's Prayer they are bringing a letter of petition to God: they greet God, give him praise, request what they think they need, and close with an "Amen"!

- **Writing Assignment:** Have the students write what they think each part of the Lord's Prayer means. Discuss their answers. Have them compare their responses to the description in the book.
- **Direct Instruction:** Continue to review the key components of the Lord's Prayer as it is presented in the text. Ask the students to decide where on the board they would put each component mentioned from pages 273–275. Have them explain their answers. Encourage them to read aloud from the book if they need help.
- **Direct Instruction:** Talk about why the Lord's Prayer has been so important to the Church. Explain that it is the prayer Jesus taught his disciples to pray; it provides a form that can be used for all prayers; it touches upon what is most important with our relationship with God and our desires for ourselves. Review Tertullian's phrase that the Lord's Prayer is "the summary of the whole Gospel" (page 272). What do the students think this means?
- **Prayer Experience:** Invite the students to now read the Lord's Prayer to themselves quietly, meditating on each word or phrase. Remind them to use the meditation format from the previous section in this chapter. What does it mean to them? What is God calling them to do through these words? Invite them to write in their journals any realization they experience during this meditation period. Play music softly in the background during this meditation period.
- **Class Discussion:** Call students together. Ask for volunteers to offer aloud any thoughts that came to them during the meditation. Thank each for sharing.
- **Prayer Experience:** Bring the class to an end by inviting students to hold hands, forming an unbroken chain throughout the room. Raise your hands so that your arms stick out in front of you about shoulder height, palms facing the ceiling. Ask for a volunteer to lead the class in praying the Lord's Prayer.

Give us this day our daily bread

Bread is a source of sustenance for life. When we "break bread" with others, we share fellowship and company with them. When we pray for our daily bread, we are really praying for:

- physical life—food, shelter, clothing;
- psychological life—friendship, love, companionship;
- spiritual life—the Word of God accepted in faith and the Body of Christ we receive in Holy Communion.

When we pray for *our* daily bread, we ask for our needs as well as the needs of all people. The Lord's Prayer challenges us to share with others, especially the less fortunate. The parables of the Last Judgment (Mt 25:31–46) and Lazarus (Lk 16:19–31) likewise teach us that God's children *must* share their material goods with the poor. These parables also warn that God will punish those who are selfish and do not share their goods with the less fortunate.

The word *daily* in the original Aramaic spoken by Jesus may also have meant something similar to "for tomorrow, today." Therefore, when we pray for our daily bread, we are also asking God for the fullness of the material and spiritual blessings that will be ours in Heaven. We dare to ask our Father to give us a taste of these gifts even today.

And forgive us our trespasses as we forgive those who trespass against us

It is difficult both to forgive and to ask for forgiveness. When we ask God for forgiveness, we are honestly admitting that we are sinners who need God's saving love. We acknowledge that we need the Spirit who will enable us to repent of our selfishness and turn to a more loving life of service. We confess in humility that we need Jesus' help on our journey to the Father.

But we must also forgive others. Jesus connects God's forgiveness of us to our forgiveness of others. Scripture teaches that it is impossible to love the God we cannot see if we cannot love the brother or sister we do see (1 Jn 4:20). God's forgiving love should become flesh in our lives as we extend forgiveness to others. When we forgive those who have hurt us, we are sharing love and understanding, thus encouraging others to respond to us in love. The Lord's Prayer calls us to action: to forgive as we have been forgiven.

And lead us not into temptation

This petition asks God to keep us off the path that leads to sin. It also asks God to help us to be faithful to the end of our lives when we struggle with death, our final test.

Following Jesus requires picking up the cross of suffering. This petition asks for God's strength to overcome any difficulties that might steer us away from a Christian life of service. We also ask for the help of the

Becoming Daily Bread for Others

Compose a prayer of petition to your heavenly Father requesting that he fulfill your needs and those of people close to you. Think about ways that you can you be "daily" bread for your friends, classmates, and family members. Enact one of these efforts in the next week.

Homework Assignment

1. Complete the For Review questions on page 275.
2. Complete the Ongoing Assignments from pages 276–277.
3. Read the Chapter 10 Chapter Quick View on page 276.

Holy Spirit to gift us with fortitude, watchfulness, perseverance, and a discerning heart that can distinguish between trials that strengthen us spiritually and temptations that lead to sin and death.

But deliver us from evil. Amen.

In union with the saints, we ask God to manifest the victory Christ has already won over Satan. We pray that the Father will deliver us from Satan's snares and the temptations of a sensuous, materialistic, violent, and godless society. We beg God to spare us from the evil of accidents, illnesses, and natural disasters. We pray that God will give us strength to stop our own participation in unjust and evil practices like prejudice. We pray that no situation arises that might tempt us to deny our loving Creator. Finally, we pray with the Holy Spirit and all God's people for the Second Coming of the Lord. On that glorious day, all humanity will be forever free of the snares of the evil one.

We end our prayer with *Amen,* a word that means "so be it." We should say Amen with enthusiasm because it means we are making the Lord's Prayer our prayer, too.

For Review

1. Where in the New Testament do we find the Lord's Prayer?
2. What did Tertullian call the Lord's Prayer?
3. Briefly discuss the meaning of each phrase of the Lord's Prayer.

For Reflection

- How do you make God's name holy by living a Christlike life?
- Who needs your forgiveness? What can you do to make clear your forgiveness to this person?
- What are you doing right now to build up your spiritual strength to resist better any temptation that might come your way?
- What is the greatest temptation facing you? facing teens today? facing our world?

Background Information

The Lord's Prayer in Matthew and Luke

The Lord's Prayer in Matthew is included in the teaching on the Sermon on the Mount, which begins with Chapter 5. Thus, the Lord's Prayer must be understood in light of the Beatitudes—it expresses how one who is a disciple of Jesus will pray. Luke 11:1–13 places the Lord's Prayer in an exposition about how to pray and what to expect from prayer. A verse-by-verse comparison:

Matthew 6:9—Our Father in heaven

Luke 11:2—Father, hallowed be your name

Matthew 6:10—Your kingdom come, your will be done, on earth as in heaven

Luke—(Nothing similar)

Matthew 6:11—Give us today our daily bread;

Luke 11:3—Give us each day our daily bread

Matthew 6:12—and forgive us our debts, as we forgive our debtors;

Luke 11:4—and forgive us our sins for we ourselves forgive everyone in debt to us,

Matthew 6:13—and do not subject us to the final test, but deliver us from the evil one.

Luke 11:4—and do not subject us to the final test.

For Review Answers (page 275)

1. The Lord's Prayer is found in the Gospel of Matthew 6:9–13 and the Gospel of Luke 11:2–4.

2. Tertullian called the Lord's Prayer "the summary of the whole Gospel."

3. The phrases of the Lord's Prayer mean as follows:

   a) God as father: we humbly trust God to care for us, and because God is our father, we are brothers and sisters to all people.

   b) God in Heaven refers to God's way of being, his majesty. We profess that we are in union with Jesus and that we await our heavenly reward.

   c) When we hallow God's name we pray that everyone will regard God as holy. We make God's name holy by believing in God's love for us and acting on that belief.

   d) In praying "Thy Kingdom come, Thy will be done" we recognize that the reign of God on earth has started with Jesus, but we also pray that Jesus will return to us so that God's Kingdom of righteousness and peace can be fully installed. We bring this prayer to life by loving others and responding to their needs.

   e) When we pray for "our daily bread" we pray for our physical needs—food, shelter, clothing—our psychological needs—friendship, love, companionship—and our spiritual needs—the Word of God in Scripture and the Eucharist.

   f) When we ask God for forgiveness we admit that we are sinners who need God to save us. We also recognize that we must forgive others.

   g) The petition "lead us not into temptation" asks God to keep us off the path that leads to sin and to be with us until we join him in Heaven.

   h) By praying "deliver us from evil" we join with the saints in asking God to manifest the victory Christ has won over Satan, and that we be delivered from temptation.

   i) When we say "Amen" we say that we want what we said to happen. This should be said with enthusiasm.

Chapter 10 Review Lesson

Objectives

In this lesson, the students will:

- share prayer reflections on Matthew 6:25–34.
- report on the completed Ongoing Assignments.
- review Chapter 10 by writing answers to the For Review questions.

 Preview

This lesson provides an opportunity to check up on the students for completed assignments from Chapter 10 as well as to begin a substantial review of the Chapter 10 material.

 Bell Ringers

- **Direct Instruction:** Call on volunteers to share their answers to the For Review questions from page 275. In particular, spend some time reviewing the meaning of each part of the Lord's Prayer.
- **Prayer Experience:** Read aloud the introduction to the Prayer Reflection on page 277. Have the students choose their favorite one-line prayer from the list on page 278. Give them some time to silently pray and reflect on the prayer that they have chosen. Then, direct them to the Reflection and Resolution assignment. Have them write these one-line prayers in their journals or on a sheet of paper that they can carry with them. Challenge them to continue to pray these prayers possibly in preparation for the Chapter 10 test.

 Teaching Approaches

- **Student Presentations:** Allow the students the opportunity to report on and share their work on the Ongoing Assignments on pages 276–277.
- **Individual Assignment:** Have the students use open textbooks to work on writing answers for the Learning the Language of Faith questions on page 276. When they are finished, check their answers as a class.
- **Group Discussion:** Refer students to their "Beginner's Guide to Prayer" projects. Have them read through these projects again in preparation for the test. Have them create a one-page study guide for the Chapter Test as a group based on these projects, the Chapter Quick View, and the vocabulary terms.

CHAPTER QUICK VIEW

- Prayer is the lifting of one's mind and heart to God. It is a loving conversation with God. (page 263)
- The types of prayer are blessing; adoration and praise; petition (which includes prayers of contrition and intercession); and thanksgiving. The Eucharist is a privileged prayer for Catholics and exemplifies many types of prayer. (pages 263–264)
- In the listening part of prayer, God can speak to us through our intellects, wills, imaginations, memories, and feelings. (page 264)
- The Old Testament images prayer as walking with God and tells us of the importance of faith when we pray. (page 265)
- The Psalms are a rich treasury of prayer for both Jews and Christians. (page 265)
- Our greatest source of learning about prayer comes from Jesus. He prayed often and taught us to pray with a pure heart and a right attitude of trust in his heavenly Father. (pages 265–266)
- We can learn prayer, too, from the Blessed Mother. Her faith and obedience to God's will show us the proper attitudes to have in prayer. (page 266)
- It is always good to choose a special place and time to pray, making sure we relax both body and mind. We must persist in our prayer and never give up. (pages 267–268)
- The various prayer expressions include vocal prayer, meditation (tuning in to God), and mental prayer, including contemplation. (page 270)
- The Lord's Prayer is the perfect Christian prayer, "the summary of the whole Gospel." Found in both Matthew and Luke's Gospel, it was taught to us by Jesus himself. (pages 272–273)
- In the Lord's Prayer, we praise our loving Father and petition that his Kingdom may come and his will be done. We also ask God to give us what we need for life, to forgive our sins, and to save us from the path that leads to sin and the snares of the evil one. (pages 273–275)

Learning the Language of Faith
Choose the italicized term in parentheses that best completes each sentence.

1. A prayer that invokes God's care on some person, place, thing, or undertaking is known as (*blessing/praise*).
2. Christ will return at the (*Triduum/Parousia*).
3. A prayer of petition for others is known as (*intercession/adoration*).
4. A Church declaration, that is, a(n) (*divorce/annulment*), states that what appeared to be a Christian sacramental marriage never existed in the first place.
5. (*Meditation/Contemplation*) is wordless prayer in which a person rests in God's goodness and majesty.
6. The Sacraments of Baptism, Confirmation, and (*Holy Orders/Marriage*) seal and configure recipients to Christ in a special way.
7. The Church dogma that holds that the eternal Son of God assumed a human nature is known as the doctrine of the (*Immaculate Conception/Incarnation*).
8. The sum total of social conditions that allow people to reach their fulfillment is known as the (*social gospel/common good*).
9. When we bring the Good News to others, we are engaged in the work of (*human solidarity/evangelization*).
10. (*Immanence/Transcendence*) is a trait of God that refers to his total otherness.

Ongoing Assignments
As you cover the material in this chapter, choose and complete at least three of these assignments.

1. Compose a short prayer using this traditional format.
   - Opening address, calling God by name
   - Praise

Homework Assignment

1. Reread Chapter 10.
2. Study for the Chapter 10 Test.

Learning the Language of Faith Answers (page 276)

1. blessing
2. Parousia
3. intercession
4. annulment
5. Contemplation
6. Holy Orders
7. Incarnation
8. common good
9. evangelization
10. Transcendence

- Thanksgiving
- Petition

2. Read the psalms listed below (or ones of your choice). Then write one of the psalms in your own words.

- Psalm 8: The glory of God and the dignity of human beings
- Psalm 23: The Lord is my shepherd
- Psalm 28: A cry for help
- Psalm 46: God is on our side
- Psalm 51: A prayer for forgiveness
- Psalm 63: Longing for God
- Psalm 104: Praise God the Creator
- Psalm 150: Praise the Lord

3. Read these passages that depict times that Jesus prayed alone. Write your answers to the questions that follow:

   Luke 4:1–11 Mark 1:35–37 Luke 6:12–13
   Luke 5:15–16 Matthew 14:13–33 Mark 14:32–42
   - What kinds of things are happening when Jesus goes off to pray?
   - When do you like to be alone and pray?

4. Read Matthew 6:25–34. Enter into the scene the Lord describes—God cares for the birds and adorns the fields with beautiful flowers. Reflect on what the Lord says about *you*. After praying over this passage, write your responses to the following questions:
   - What are things that cause you worry and anxiety?
   - Analyze the things you worry about from the viewpoint of eternity. How valid is your concern when seen from the vantage point of five years from now? ten? after you have died?

5. Find a vocal prayer that speaks to you in a special way and transcribe it into your journal.
6. Research prayers dedicated to or writtten by saints. Transcribe in your prayer journal your most meaningful prayers.
7. Develop a PowerPoint presentation on the Hail Mary or the Lord's Prayer. Choose appropriate pictures and music to accompany the text of the prayer.
8. Transcribe the Lord's Prayer from another language. Search the Internet for hundreds of languages.
9. Create an illustrated prayer booklet for a friend based on Scripture and the words of the saints.

Prayer Reflection

St. Paul teaches us to pray without ceasing (1 Thes 5:17). One way to do so throughout the day is to offer short, one-line prayers, also known as aspirations. Perhaps the most famous one-line prayer is the Jesus Prayer: "Lord Jesus Christ, Son of God, have mercy on me, a sinner." This faith-filled prayer acknowledges the divinity of Jesus as both Lord and Son of God. He is the Christ, the Anointed One of God, who has brought us Salvation. The prayer acknowledges that we are sinners and in need of Christ's forgiveness. Many people recite the Jesus Prayer repeatedly for a period of time, concentrating on each word as they slowly inhale and exhale. It is a marvelous prayer of faith and petition to Jesus Christ, our Savior.

You can offer short prayers on many different occasions. For example, consider the following prayer before taking a test: "Dear, Jesus, I offer my honest work on this test to you with love." If you say such a prayer, then your entire effort on the test is prayerful.

Background Information

Reflections on Prayer

The moment you wake up each morning, all your wishes and hopes for the day rush at you like wild animals. And the first job each morning consists in shoving it all back; in listening to that other voice, taking that other point of view, letting that other, larger, stronger, quieter life come flowing in.

—C.S. Lewis

My God, I pray that I may so know you and love you that I may rejoice in you. And if I may not do so fully in this life let me go steadily on to the day when I come to that fullness. . . . Meanwhile let my mind meditate on it, let my tongue speak of it, let my heart love it, let my mouth preach it, let my soul hunger for it, my flesh thirst for it and my whole being desire it until I enter into the joy of my Lord.

—St. Anselm

Oh God, early in the morning do I cry unto thee. Help me to pray and to think only of thee. I cannot pray alone. In me there is darkness. But with thee there is light.

—Dietrich Bonhoeffer

Chapter 10 Test Lesson

Objectives

In this lesson, the students will:
- be tested on the material in Chapter 10.
- review some material from the Catholic Handbook for Faith.

 ## Preview

This session is reserved for the Chapter 10 Test. As this is the final test, this is a great opportunity to spend some time reviewing the course as a whole.

Teaching Approaches

- **Direct Instruction:** Take some time at the beginning of class to answer any questions the students have about the material in Chapter 10. Explain that you will not answer the question, "Is _____ going to be on the test?"
- **Chapter Test:** Distribute copies of the Chapter 10 Test (starting on page 285 and also online at www.avemariapress.com). Collect completed tests and have students examine the Catholic Handbook for Faith, pages 285–306.
- **Group Activity:** As time permits, have small groups read and report on various topics covered in the Catholic Handbook for Faith.
- **Class Discussion:** Take some time to review the many topics and lessons covered during this course. Have students comment on what they learned and what they liked. Have them make suggestions about how to improve the course for next year. Compliment them for the growth that they have made and challenge them to continue to grow in their faith as they move on to new experiences.
- **Prayer Experience:** Close by reciting together the Prayer for Peace by St. Francis of Assisi in the Catholic Handbook for Faith, page 306.

Chapter 10 Test Answers

Part 1: Multiple Choice (4 points each)

1. B

2. A

3. D

4. C

5. A

6. C

7. D

Part 2: True or False (4 points each)

8. F

9. T

10. T

11. T

12. F

13. F

14. T

15. T

16. F

17. F

Part 3: Fill-ins (4 points each)

18. Psalms

19. listening

20. answers will vary (for example, in the desert, before choosing the Apostles, in the garden, on the cross, etc.)

21. the Lord's Prayer

Part 4: Essay (20 points)

For full credit make sure students are able to name and explain the types of prayer introduced in this chapter (blessing, adoration, praise, petition, and thanksgiving), the three expressions of prayer (vocal, meditation, mental prayer), and relevant advice about how to pray effectively.

One-Liners (Aspirations)

My God, help me learn how to love you.
Jesus, my friend and Savior, I love you.
Help me, Lord Jesus.
Jesus, protect me from sin.
Lord, I am sorry for my sins and, with your help, will try to avoid what leads me to sin.
Praise God!
Lord, please welcome my deceased relatives into Heaven.
Mary, Mother of God, pray for me.
Come, Holy Spirit.
Holy Spirit, enlighten me.
Thank you, Father, for all the gifts you have given me.
Thank you, Abba, for creating this day.

- *Reflection*: Compose some one-liners of your own. Include prayers of adoration, petition, intercession, contrition, and thanksgiving.
- *Resolution*: Pray your one-liners frequently during the coming weeks.

Chapter 10 Notes

1. Story adapted from and quotation cited in Michael P. Green, ed., *Illustrations for Biblical Preaching* (Grand Rapids, MI: Baker Book House, 1989), p. 278.

2. Anthony de Mello, S.J., *Taking Flight* (New York: Doubleday, 1988), p. 29.

3. Quoted by Anthony Castle in his *A Treasury of Quips and Quotes & Anecdotes for Preachers and Teachers* (Mystic, CT: Twenty-Third Publications, 1998), p. 531.

Catholic Handbook for Faith

General Introduction

Our Catholic Faith: Living What We Believe provides a systematic overview of the main tenets of the teachings and traditions of the Catholic Church. To supplement this study, the Catholic Handbook for Faith (pages 285–306 of the Student Text) offers an appendix of prayers, creeds, timelines, lists, and other features to stimulate further knowledge and interest among the students.

Throughout this course, you may find that the text encourages the students to ask certain questions about Catholic practice today. You may also find the opportunity to pray certain traditional prayers not included in the main body of the text. This Catholic Handbook for Faith is designed to give you easy-to-find answers to these questions. It is meant to be a supplemental resource that may be used whenever needed.

Teaching Approaches

Instead of just telling the students to memorize certain prayers or dates, there are a number of creative ways that you could help the students learn the Handbook material. Among such suggestions are the following:

- **Crossword Puzzles.** Assign the material to be learned and direct the students to make up crossword puzzles with clues. Then have them exchange puzzles with a partner and work to answer them.
- **Individual or Team Games.** Drill the students on certain material in the Handbook by having them play a TV game based on a *Hollywood Squares* or *Jeopardy*. Divide the students into teams to make up questions/answers about the Handbook material that are presented to "contestants."
- **For Reflection Essays or Journal Entries.** Have the students reflect and write about their understanding of a single passage from a creed or prayer such as the Apostles' Creed or Our Father. You may also wish to have the students write about how they might put the passage into practice in daily life.
- **Pop Quizzes.** Give the students a short, objective pop quiz regarding certain material in the Handbook. Use one of the following formats: fill in the blanks, complete the sentences, or matching.
- **Artistic Creations.** Have the students draw/paint a picture or mural that expresses one part of a creed or prayer. You may also wish to have the students draw symbols for certain patron saints. Have the students explain to the class what a certain creed or prayer means to them.
- **Creative Writing.** Have the students rewrite a creed or prayer in their own words, as a poem, rap, song, or choral reading.
- **Small-Group Discussions.** Have the students form small groups to discuss what a certain creed or prayer means to them.
- **Slide Shows.** Have the students put together a slide show to illustrate a certain creed or prayer.
- **Puppet Shows, Skits, or Mime.** Have students retell main events in the life of a saint through homemade puppets, small group skits, or mime.
- **Research.** Send the students to the Internet or library to find out about the history and origin of a certain creed or prayer.
- **Music.** Have the students compose (or learn) and sing a musical version of a certain prayer, belief, or creed.

Whatever teaching method you use, try to make the learning process interesting and meaningful rather than a dull routine. Help the students internalize the values and beliefs found in this Handbook as a basis for the rest of their lives as Catholics.

Resource Section

Handouts

Weekly Planning Chart

Day/Pp.	Objectives	Activities	Follow-up work
Mon.			
Tues.			
Wed.			
Thurs.			
Fri.			

Evaluation of Week:

Name _____ **Date** _____

My Father Is a Good Man

Complete each of the following sentences.

The most fun I ever had with my father was . . .

The most important thing I have learned from my father is . . .

The thing my father said about me that made me feel the best was . . .

The best thing my father does for my family is . . .

I know my father loves me because . . .

I respect my father when . . .

One way I hope that I am like my father is . . .

Name _____ **Date** _____

Creation Quiz

1. On which day did God create light?

2. On which day did God create humankind?

3. What was God's judgment about the things that he had made?

4. Why did God bless the seventh day?

5. Was Adam created before or after the animals?

6. What was Adam's job in the garden of Eden?

7. Why did God create both men and women?

8. What reason does the serpent give to entice Eve to eat the fruit of the tree in the middle of the garden?

9. How are Adam and Eve's responses to God similar when he asks them why they have eaten the fruit?

10. What sign of God's continuing protective care is given after the judgment against Adam and Eve?

Sample Memory Cards

Abba	Agnostic	Atheist
Aramaic term meaning "Daddy"	Person who claims God's existence can't be known	Person who denies God's existence
Bible	Blessed Trinity	Concupiscence
The inspired Word of God	The central dogma of Christian faith—God is Father, Son, and Spirit in one God	The inclination to commit sin that is part of human nature as a result of Original Sin

Questions about Jesus

Use the following questions to help you determine what information about Jesus can be found in the Gospel you were assigned. Add any other information that you think might be supported by sources other than the Gospels.

- What information is given about Jesus' birth?

- Who were his parents?

- Where was he born?

- Were there any special events, historical, political, or astronomical, that occurred at the time of his birth?

- What information might help scholars determine the approximate year of his birth?

- Where did he grow up?

- What information is given about Jesus' life?

- Who were his friends and companions?

- What cities or regions did he visit?

- Where did he live?

- What did his friends call him?

- Did he have enemies? Who were they?

- What information is given about Jesus' Death?

- Who arrested Jesus?

- Of what was he accused?

- Who tried him? Who sentenced him to crucifixion?

- Where was he crucified?

- Who was with him?

- Who buried him? Where?

- Who first discovered that his tomb was empty?

- What explanations are given for the empty tomb?

The Infancy Narratives

Background

Matthew is writing for a largely Jewish Christian audience for whom he presents Jesus as the New Law Giver, the new Moses. Jesus is the fulfillment of the Old Testament prophecies. Matthew also needs to persuade his audience of the legitimacy of Gentile converts.

Luke is writing for a largely Gentile audience. There is less emphasis on the Law and Jewish ritual and more on Jesus' mercy and compassion for all people, especially women, the poor, the outcast, the sinner, and the afflicted.

Elements of the Gospels

Matthew's narrative includes the following elements:

- Mary and Joseph are Jesus' parents.

- Mary is found to be with child before she and Joseph are living together as husband and wife.

- An angel appears to Joseph in a dream, reassuring him about the holiness of the child and giving him Jesus' name.

- Jesus is born in Bethlehem of Judea.

- The magi come looking for him in Jerusalem, asking King Herod about him, because they have seen his star.

- The magi find Jesus in his parents' house in Bethlehem. They give him expensive gifts.

- Joseph, warned in a dream, takes Mary and Jesus to Egypt to escape Herod.

- Herod slaughters all the young boys in and around Bethlehem.

- The Holy Family returns from Egypt to Nazareth after Joseph has another dream in which he is told that "those who sought the child's life are dead."

Luke's narrative includes these important points:

- Mary and Joseph are Jesus' parents.

- Mary is visited by an angel who announces Jesus' conception, birth, and name to her.

- Jesus is born in a stable in Bethlehem of Judea.

- Angels appear to the shepherds to announce the birth of the Messiah.

- The shepherds find Jesus in the stable.

- Jesus is circumcised and presented in the Temple where both Simeon and Anna recognize him.

- The family returns to Nazareth where Jesus grows up.

Name _____ Date _____

The Kingdom of God

Look up the following passages and match them to the truths about the Kingdom they reveal.

Luke 7:18–23   **Matthew 18:1–5**   **Matthew 13:31–32**

Matthew 13:33   **Mark 4:26–29**   **Matthew 18:23–35**

_____   The Kingdom may start out small but it will soon grow.

_____   The Kingdom, though small, will eventually transform the world.

_____   The Kingdom exists in the person, deeds, and words of Jesus.

_____   The Kingdom will grow even though we cannot see or explain how it is happening.

_____   Forgiveness is an essential element of the Kingdom: We will be forgiven; therefore, we must be forgiving.

_____   In order to enter the Kingdom, we must recognize our own need for God.

Complete your own analogies for the Kingdom of God.

The Kingdom of God is like _____

The Kingdom of God is like _____

Name _____ **Date** _____

Intercessory Prayer Service

Invitation to Prayer:

The Lord's mercy is unending.
Filled with hope and trust in his forgiveness and love,
let us ask our merciful Father
to bless us with all that we need.

The students' intercessory prayers may use any one of the following forms:

That *someone* will know God's mercy as they *do something*, let us pray to the Lord.
For example, "That the homeless will know God's mercy as they find shelter and comfort from the winter's cold, let us pray to the Lord."

For *someone*, that God's mercy will *do something good* for them, let us pray to the Lord.
For example, "For people in prison, that God's mercy will grant them a spirit of repentance and hope for their future."

That those who *do something*, will find God's mercy *in something*, we pray to the Lord.
For example, "That those who find themselves unemployed will find God's mercy in words of hope and encouragement and in opportunities for work, we pray to the Lord."

That God's mercy will be a source of *something* for *someone*, let us pray to the Lord.
For example, "That God's mercy will be a source of compassion to those who are terminally ill."

That God, in his mercy, will *do something for someone*, let us pray to the Lord.
For example, "That God, in his mercy, will give comfort and hope to those who are grieving the loss of a loved one, let us pray to the Lord."

Concluding Prayer:

Lord God,
You are ever merciful to your people,
and your love is beyond words to describe.
Look upon your people with compassion,
and grant us the grace of your friendship,
through Jesus Christ, our Lord.
Amen.

(Based on a booklet called "Preparing the General Intercessions" by Michael Kwatera, O.S.B., published in 1996 by Liturgical Press.)

Scriptural Way of the Cross

Jesus prays in the garden.
Matthew 26:36–45; Mark 14:32–41; Luke 22:39–46

Jesus is betrayed and arrested.
Matthew 26:47–56; Mark 14:43–52; Luke 22:47–53; John 18:1–14

Jesus is condemned by the Sanhedrin.
Matthew 26:57–68; Mark 14:53–64; Luke 22:66–71; John 18:19–24

Peter denies knowing Jesus.
Matthew 26:69–75; Mark 14:66–72; Luke 22:54–62; John 18:15–18, 25–27

Jesus is condemned by Pilate.
Matthew 27:11–26; Mark 15:1–15; Luke 23:1–5, 13–25; John 18:33–40, 19:13–16

Jesus is scourged and crowned with thorns.
Matthew 27:27–31; Mark 15:16–19; John 19:1–3

Jesus takes up his cross.
John 19:16b–17

Simon of Cyrene helps Jesus.
Matthew 27:32; Mark 15:21; Luke 23:26

Jesus meets the weeping women.
Luke 23:27–31

Jesus is crucified.
Matthew 27:33–37; Mark 15:22–26; Luke 23:33; John 19:18–19

Jesus promises paradise to the crucified thief.
Luke 23:39–43

Jesus cares for his mother.
John 19:25–27

Jesus dies.
Matthew 27:45–50; Mark 15:33–37; Luke 23:44–46; John 19:28–30

Jesus is buried.
Matthew 27:57–61; Mark 15:42–47; Luke 23:50–53; John 19:38–42

Understanding the Creeds

Selection from the Athanasian Creed

Now this is the Catholic faith: We worship one God in the Trinity and the Trinity in unity, without either confusing the persons or dividing the substance; for the person of the Father is one, the Son's is another, the Holy Spirit's is another; but the Godhead of the Father, Son, and Holy Spirit is one, their glory equal, their majesty coeternal.

The Apostles' Creed

I believe in God, the Father almighty,
Creator of heaven and earth,
and in Jesus Christ, his only Son,
our Lord,
who was conceived
by the Holy Spirit,
born of the Virgin Mary,
suffered under Pontius Pilate,
was crucified, died and was buried;
he descended into hell;
on the third day he rose again
from the dead;
he ascended into heaven,
and is seated at the right hand
of God the Father almighty;
from there he will come to judge
the living and the dead.
I believe in the Holy Spirit,
the holy catholic Church,
the communion of saints,
the forgiveness of sins,
the resurrection of the body,
and life everlasting. Amen.

The Nicene Creed

I believe in one God, the Father almighty,
maker of heaven and earth,
of all things visible and invisible.

I believe in one Lord Jesus Christ,
the Only Begotten Son of God,
born of the Father before all ages.
God from God, Light from Light,
true God from true God,
begotten, not made, consubstantial
with the Father;
Through him all things were made.
For us men and for our salvation
he came down from heaven,
and by the Holy Spirit was incarnate
of the Virgin Mary,
and became man.
For our sake he was crucified
under Pontius Pilate,
he suffered death and was buried,
and rose again on the third day
in accordance with the Scriptures.
He ascended into heaven
and is seated at the right hand of the Father.
He will come again in glory
to judge the living and the dead
and his kingdom will have no end.

I believe in the Holy Spirit,
the Lord, the giver of life,
who proceeds from the Father and the Son,
who with the Father and the Son
is adored and glorified,
who has spoken through the prophets.

I believe in one, holy, catholic,
and apostolic Church.
I confess one baptism for the forgiveness of sins
and I look forward to the resurrection
of the dead and the life of the world to come.
Amen.

Name _____ Date _____

Trinity: One God, Three Persons

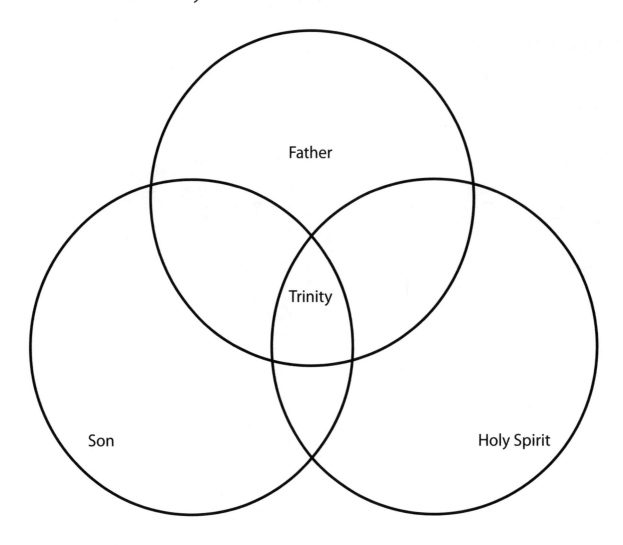

Name _____ Date _____

The Church as Sacrament Pop Quiz

Part 1: Matching. Write the letter of the correct definition in the blank near its term (*3 points each*).

1. _____ ecumenism

2. _____ evangelization

3. _____ hierarchy

4. _____ mystery

5. _____ religious order

6. _____ canon law

7. _____ infallibility

8. _____ sacrament

A. A group of people who take vows committing themselves to a common life and work

B. A reality filled with God's invisible presence.

C. The official laws of the Church.

D. The official leadership of the Church, made up of priests, deacons, bishops, and the Pope.

E. An outward sign of an invisible grace.

F. The Holy Spirit's guidance, which preserves the Pope and the bishops from error when proclaiming doctrine related to faith or morals.

G. The work of bringing churches to unity with one another.

H. Bringing the Good News of Jesus to others.

Part 2: Short Essays. Respond to the following (*19 points maximum on each*).

9. List and briefly explain the four marks of the Church.

10. Members of the Church may be members of the hierarchy, members of religious orders, or lay people. How are these roles different, and how are they the same?

11. Explain the relationships among Catholics, Orthodox, and Protestants. What beliefs do they hold in common? How are they different?

12. Explain the ways in which the Church is a sacrament and a mystery.

Marian Doctrine

The doctrine we have been assigned:

- Is there a special day associated with this doctrine?

- Is there a scriptural reference associated with this doctrine? What is it?

- Are there particular documents issued by the Church that explain this doctrine? What are they?

- What does this doctrine teach us about Mary?

- What does this doctrine teach us about Jesus?

- What does this doctrine mean to us? What difference does it make in how we think about Mary, Jesus, and God?

- How does the Church celebrate this doctrine? Feast days? Special religious symbols, famous artwork, statues, shrines? Hymns or other holy music?

- What sort of group presentation will inspire your classmates to embrace this doctrine?

Litany of the Blessed Virgin Mary

Lord, have mercy.	—Lord, have mercy.	Woman transformed,	—Pray for us.
Christ, have mercy.	—Christ, have mercy.	Woman clothed with the sun,	—Pray for us.
Lord, have mercy.	—Lord, have mercy.	Woman crowned with stars,	—Pray for us.
God our Father in heaven,	—Have mercy on us.	Gentle Lady,	—Pray for us.
God the Son, Redeemer of the world,	—Have mercy on us.	Gracious Lady,	—Pray for us.
God the Holy Spirit,	—Have mercy on us.	Our Lady,	—Pray for us.
Holy Trinity, One God,	—Have mercy on us.		
		Joy of Israel,	—Pray for us.
Holy Mary,	—Pray for us.	Splendor of the Church,	—Pray for us.
Holy Mother of God,	—Pray for us.	Pride of the human race,	—Pray for us.
Most honored of virgins	—Pray for us.		
Chosen daughter of the Father,	—Pray for us.	Advocate of peace,	—Pray for us.
Mother of Christ the King,	—Pray for us.	Minister of holiness,	—Pray for us.
Glory of the Holy Spirit	—Pray for us.	Champion of God's people,	—Pray for us.
Virgin daughter of Zion,	—Pray for us.	Queen of love,	—Pray for us.
Virgin poor and humble,	—Pray for us.	Queen of mercy,	—Pray for us.
Virgin gentle and obedient,	—Pray for us.	Queen of peace,	—Pray for us.
		Queen of angels,	—Pray for us.
Handmaid of the Lord,	—Pray for us.	Queen of patriarchs and prophets,	—Pray for us.
Mother of the Lord,	—Pray for us.	Queen of apostles and martyrs,	—Pray for us.
Helper of the Redeemer,	—Pray for us.	Queen of confessors and virgins,	—Pray for us.
Full of grace,	—Pray for us.	Queen of all saints,	—Pray for us.
Fountain of beauty,	—Pray for us.	Queen conceived without Original Sin,	—Pray for us.
Model of virtue,	—Pray for us.	Queen assumed into heaven,	—Pray for us.
Finest fruit of the redemption,	—Pray for us.	Queen of all the earth,	—Pray for us.
Perfect disciple of Christ,	—Pray for us.	Queen of heaven,	—Pray for us.
Untarnished image of the Church,	—Pray for us.	Queen of the universe,	—Pray for us.

Lamb of God, you take away the sins of the world,	—Spare us, O Lord.
Lamb of God, you take away the sins of the world,	—Hear us, O Lord.
Lamb of God, you take away the sins of the world,	—Have mercy on us.
Pray for us, O glorious Mother of the Lord,	—That we may become worthy of the promises of Christ.

Leader: Let us pray.

All: God of mercy,
listen to the prayers of your servants
who have honored your handmaid Mary
as mother and queen.
Grant that by your grace
we may serve you and our neighbor on earth
and be welcomed into your eternal kingdom.
We ask this through Christ our Lord.

Amen.

This prayer is taken from *Lord, Hear Our Prayer* (Ave Maria Press, 2000).

Name _____ **Date** _____

Your Patron Saints

One way to increase devotion to the saints is by developing a relationship with one particular saint—your patron saint. This exercise will help you to choose your own patron saint.

Write your first and middle names here:_____.

Using a Catholic encyclopedia, or a book of saints, or an Internet site such as www.catholic.org/saints or http://saints.sqpn.com, list as many saints as you can find that share one of your names.

Write your birthday and the date of your Baptism here:_____.

List those saints whose feast day is one of the dates written above.

List as many hobbies or regular activities as you can think of that are important to you here:_____
_____.

Find out if there are patron saints for those hobbies or activities. List them here.

Now read the short biographies of the saints you have listed above until you find a story that inspires you. Write that saint's name here:_____.

Begin your research into this saint's life by finding the following information:

Date and place of birth:

Lifelong Catholic or convert?

Date and circumstance of death:

Best known for:

Virtues exhibited by this saint:

Temptations or struggles faced by this saint:

The Good News of God's Forgiveness

I, I am He
who blots out your
transgressions for my own sake.
and I will not remember
your sins.

      —Isaiah 43:25

And you, child, will be called the
prophet of the Most High;
for you will go before the Lord,
to prepare his ways,
to give knowledge of salvation to his people
by the forgiveness of their sins.

      —Luke 1:77

For you, O Lord, are good and forgiving,
abounding in steadfast love to all who call on you.

      —Psalm 86:5

Then the scribes and Pharisees began to question, "Who is this who is speaking blasphemies? Who can forgive sins but God alone?" When Jesus perceived their questionings, he answered them, ". . . Which is easier, to say, 'Your sins are forgiven you' or to say, 'Stand up and walk?' But so that you may know that the Son of Man has authority on earth to forgive sins"—he said to the one who was paralyzed—"I say to you, stand up and take your bed and go to your home." Immediately he stood up before them, took what he had been lying on, and went to his home, glorifying God.

      —Luke 5:21–25

When they came to the place that is called The Skull, they crucified Jesus there with the criminals, one on his right and one on his left. Then Jesus said, "Father, forgive them; for they do not know what they are doing."

      —Matthew 23:33–34

Let it be known to you therefore, my [brothers and sisters], that through this man forgiveness of sins is proclaimed to you; by this Jesus everyone who believes is set free from all [their] sins.

      —Acts 13:38–39a

My little children, I am writing these things to you so that you may not sin. But if anyone does sin, we have an advocate with the Father, Jesus Christ the righteous; and his is the atoning sacrifice for our sins, and not for ours only but also for the sins of the whole world.

      —1 John 2:1–2

Name _____ **Date** _____

Seven-Day Calendar

	SUNDAY	MONDAY	TUESDAY	WEDNESDAY	THURSDAY	FRIDAY	SATURDAY
GOAL:							
6am							
7am							
8am							
9am							
10am							
11am							
noon							
1pm							
2pm							
3pm							
4pm							
5pm							
6pm							
7pm							
8pm							
9pm							
10pm							
EVALUATION:							

Word Search

Locate and circle each vocabulary word you discover in the word search below.

Amen	eschatology	mortal sin
Assumption	last judgment	particular judgment
Beatific Vision	Heaven	Purgatory
capital sins	hell	venial sin
Communion of Saints	Immaculate Conception	vices

```
A  T  B  V  S  P  T  E  M  N  O  R  T  A  L  I  N  O  T  K
M  E  S  E  M  A  J  Y  X  A  S  T  O  H  Y  G  T  H  L  L
A  N  E  M  A  R  K  H  C  I  N  C  S  C  G  P  K  B  L  A
C  N  O  I  V  T  A  Y  P  E  I  O  W  S  O  A  P  E  I  S
U  I  N  L  E  I  T  A  V  L  S  M  H  E  L  V  E  A  N  T
L  S  A  T  E  C  C  T  A  P  L  M  R  A  O  T  G  T  U  J
E  L  E  M  Q  U  A  E  S  U  A  U  W  L  T  J  M  I  S  U
Z  A  B  Y  D  L  A  S  S  T  T  N  Q  B  A  U  V  F  E  D
Q  T  Z  R  W  A  Y  E  U  Q  I  I  E  P  H  T  Y  I  G  G
U  R  H  O  J  R  K  N  M  A  P  O  U  H  C  R  N  C  B  M
N  O  U  R  X  J  U  D  P  M  A  N  T  H  S  A  I  V  I  E
I  M  M  A  C  U  L  A  T  E  C  O  N  C  E  P  T  I  O  N
J  A  L  G  H  D  K  O  I  Y  I  F  R  I  W  L  C  S  X  T
P  T  E  R  D  G  N  D  O  Z  Y  S  B  S  U  K  L  I  K  M
U  O  H  A  C  M  J  M  N  D  R  A  R  H  I  P  T  O  R  L
R  L  P  O  V  E  N  I  A  L  S  I  N  G  M  A  S  N  I  A
H  S  R  E  I  N  H  E  A  V  E  N  A  P  L  R  T  L  A  H
P  U  R  G  A  T  O  R  Y  L  L  T  I  P  U  R  G  A  T  E
W  I  I  M  E  F  L  L  E  W  Y  S  E  V  N  K  I  S  N  A
E  V  A  M  U  C  L  A  T  E  E  J  T  X  S  A  L  G  M  H
```

Chapter Quick View Review

- Those alive _____ _____, those suffering _____ _____, and the blessed ones _____ _____ make up the _____ ____ _____.

- Christ calls all of us to be _____, that is, to be _____.

- The Church _____ some saints to declare that they lived lives of _____ _____ _____. We _____ the saints when we _____ their virtues and pray to them asking them to _____ ____ ____.

- _____is worthy of our devotion as the holiest of all humans. Her faith in becoming ___ _____ ___ _____, her loving service to ____ _____, and her response to the _____ _____ make her the supreme example of what a Christian should be.

- Mary is the Mother ____ _____, and our _____ _____, too. She is the Mother ___ ____ _____ who prays for us always.

- _____Sin resulted from the _____ _____ of Adam and Eve. All humans suffer the effects of this first sin, including the loss of _____ _____, and physical suffering, and _____. Jesus has conquered _____ _____ and makes it possible for us to ____ _____ once again with our loving God.

- _____ sin is personal, individual _____. It can be an _____, _____ or _____ contrary to God's law. _____ sins partially reject God. _____ sins kill our relationship with God and others. To sin mortally there must be _____ _____, _____ _____, and full consent of the _____.

- The _____, and their successors, have the Christ-given power to _____ _____ in his name, a major component of his saving activity. The Church follows Christ's command to forgive sin through the sacraments of _____ and _____.

- _____ forgives all sin. The Sacrament of _____ forgives post-baptismal sins of sincere and contrite sinners.

- _____, introduced by Adam and Eve's sin, is a great mystery. But Jesus Christ overcame it through the _____ _____ of his Death on the cross and his _____. If we die united to Jesus Christ, God will _____ us on the _____ _____ to share in his glory.

- When we die, we will appear before God for a _____ _____ that will determine if we enter _____, _____ or _____.

- _____ is eternal _____ with God. _____ is a place or state of purification for those who need to be cleansed of their attachment to sin before meeting God. _____is eternal _____ from God.

- Only the Father knows the day and hour of _____ _____ _____. On that day of _____ _____, Christ will reveal the truth of every person's relationship with God.

- When we say _____, we are professing anew our faith in what has just preceded.

Name _____ Date _____

Renewing Your Baptismal Promises

L: Do you renounce sin, so as to live in the freedom of God's children?

R: I do renounce it.

L: Do you reject the glamour of evil and refuse to be mastered by sin?

R: I do renounce it.

L: Do you renounce Satan, father of sin and prince of darkness?

R: I do renounce him.

L: Do you believe in God, the Father almighty, creator of heaven and earth?

R: I do believe.

L: Do you believe in Jesus Christ, his only Son, our Lord,
     Who was born of the Virgin Mary, was crucified, died and was buried,
     Rose from the dead, and is now seated at the right hand of the Father?

R: I do believe.

L: Do you believe in the Holy Spirit, the Holy Catholic church,
     The communion of saints, the forgiveness of sin,
     The resurrection of the body and life everlasting?

R: I do believe.

Together:

God the Father of our Lord Jesus Christ

Has given us a new birth by water and the Holy Spirit,

And forgiven our sins.

May God also keep us faithful to our Lord Jesus Christ

For ever and ever.

Amen.

Name _____ Date _____

Comparing Christian Churches

	Roman Catholic	Eastern Rite	Orthodox	Protestant
Baptism				
Eucharist				
Confirmation				
Scripture				
Clergy				
Hierarchy				

Seder Meal Script

Lighting of the Festival Lights

Commentator: According to ancient Jewish custom, it is the task of the mother to light the festival lights in every service that takes place in the home. The candles are also a reminder that Jesus is the light of the world.

Mother: Blessed are you, O Lord our God, King of the universe. You have sanctified us by your commandments and commanded us to kindle the festival lights. Blessed are you, O Lord our God, King of the universe; You have sustained us and kept us alive and brought us to this season. May our home be consecrated, O God, by the light of Your face, shining upon us in blessing and bringing us peace.

All: Amen.

The Meal

The wine is poured.

Commentator: The first act of the Jewish Passover is a benediction, the *Kiddush*. The leader takes a cup of wine and recites this blessing.

Leader: Blessed are You, O Lord our God, King of the Universe, Creator of the fruit of the vine. Blessed are You, O Lord our God, King of the universe, who has chosen us among all peoples and sanctified us with Your commandments. In love you have given us solemn days of joy and festive seasons of gladness, even this day of the feast of the unleavened bread, a memorial of the departure from Egypt. You have chosen us for your service and have made us sharers in the blessing of your holy festivals.

All present take their cups.

Commentator: Jesus prayed this blessing as he began his Last Supper before his Passion and Death. We drink this wine in honor of all who those who, before us and with us today, have embraced the joy and the goodness of life.

All present drink of the wine.

Commentator: Another traditional action of the Passover meal is the breaking of the unleavened bread.

The leader lifts up the bread and breaks it in two.

Leader: This is the bread of affliction which our ancestors ate in the land of Egypt. Let all who are hungry come and eat. Let all who are in want come and celebrate the Passover with us. May it be God's will to redeem us from all trouble and servitude. Next year at this season may all the people of God be free.

The leader passes the bread around. Each person breaks off a piece and when all have been served, everyone eats the portion.

The Questions

Commentator: At the Passover dinner, four traditional questions are asked by the children of the family.

First questioner: Why is this night different from all other nights?

Leader: The Mishnah tells us, "In every generation people must regard ourselves as having come forth ourselves from out of Egypt. Therefore we are bound to give thanks, to praise and to bless God who did all these wonders for our ancestors and for us. God brought us out of bondage to freedom, from sorrow to gladness, from mourning to a festival, from darkness to great light, and from servitude to redemption.

Second questioner:	Why do we eat bitter herbs tonight at this special meal? And why do we dip the bitter herbs into the salt water?
Leader:	The Jews of old ate bitter herbs on Passover night, as do the Jews today, because "Our ancestors were slaves in Egypt and their lives were made bitter." Christians call to mind the bitterness of Jesus' Passion and Death, remembering that he said, "Anyone who does not carry a cross and come after me cannot be my disciple." The salt water is a reminder of the tears shed by the Jews during the days of their slavery, and of the tears of those around the world today who suffer from oppression.

The salt water is passed around; each person dips the herb in salt water and eats the herb.

Third questioner:	What is the meaning of the *haroses*?
Leader:	The haroses is a reminder of the mortar which our ancestors used to make bricks when they were slaves in Egypt. The sweetness of the haroses is a sign of hope. Our ancestors were able to withstand the bitterness of slavery because it was sweetened by the hope of freedom. Christians remember the hope of the resurrection, and that each suffering that may befall us can be a source of compassion and wisdom.

Each person takes a bite of the haroses.

Fourth questioner:	Why do we eat lamb at this meal?
Leader:	At the time of the liberation from Egypt, at God's command each family took a lamb, sacrificed it, ate it, and sprinkled its blood on the doorpost. On that night, seeing the blood, the angel of the Lord passed over them, smiting the Egyptians and sparing the Israelites. Christians see Jesus as the symbolic lamb of God, who through his sacrifice spared us from ultimate defeat by death.
Fifth questioner:	What is the meaning of the unleavened bread?
Leader:	The book of Exodus tells us, "When Pharaoh let our ancestors go from Egypt, they were forced to flee in great haste. They had no time to bake their bread; they could not wait for the yeast to rise. So the sun beating down on the dough as they carried it along baked it into a flat unleavened bread." The unleavened bread was the "bread of affliction" which enabled the Chosen People to be delivered from slavery.

Hallel

Psalm 114 is traditionally recited as a blessing before the meal.

All:	When Israel came forth from Egypt, the house of Jacob from an alien people, Judah became God's holy place, Israel. God's domain. "The sea beheld and fled; the Jordan turned back. The mountains skipped like rams; the hills, like lambs of flock.

Why was it, sea, that you fled?
Jordan, that you turned back?
You mountains, that you skipped like rams?
You hills, like lambs of the flock?
Tremble, earth, before the Lord,
before the God of Jacob,
"Who turned rock into pools of water,
stone into flowing springs.

The dinner is then served and eaten.

Final Blessing

All raise their wine glasses.

Leader:	The Lord bless you and keep you. The Lord make His face to shine on you and have mercy on you.

May the Lord lift up His countenance on you
and give you peace.

All:	Amen.

Student Panel Discussion Questions

Penance

- Do you receive this sacrament regularly? If so, how often? And, why?
- Have you ever attended a communal Reconciliation service before making an individual confession? Is this usually the way you receive the sacrament?
- What are your feelings, usually, *before* you receive this sacrament?
- What do you do to prepare yourself to receive this sacrament?
- Can you think of a particularly good experience of this sacrament that you have had? What made it especially good?
- How do you usually feel *after* receiving this sacrament?
- What was the most unusual/memorable Penance you were ever given? What did you learn from doing it?

Anointing of the Sick

- Have you received this sacrament yourself? When and why?
- Were you ever present when another person received the sacrament? Who and why?
- What do you particularly remember about the sacrament? What made an impression on you?
- Was the person who received the sacrament comforted by it? In what way?
- Were the family and friends comforted?
- Do you think that the person who received the sacrament was healed or helped in any way? Why do you feel this way?
- If you were ever seriously ill, would you like to receive this sacrament? Why?

Matrimony

- Do you know a couple whose marriage you would describe as sacramental—that is, blessed by God and a sign to others of God's love?
- What is special about their relationship?
- Share some ways this couple shows their love for each other. How do they show love to those around them?
- How do they serve others? Does their marriage help them to be of service to others in ways that you can see?
- What have you learned from the example of their marriage?
- What qualities in their marriage would you like to be present in your own marriage if you ever marry?

Holy Orders

- Do you know any priests on a personal level—a family member? A family friend? Someone you have worked with or for?
- Have you ever spoken with them about their call to the priesthood?
- What do they enjoy most about being a priest?
- What have they taught you about priests and the life of a priest?
- Has their life or work been a sign for you (or for others you know) of God's presence in the world? How?
- If you were ever to be a priest, what qualities that you see in them would you hope to have?
- Have you ever attended an ordination? What do you remember about it?

Sacrament of Penance Outline

The Sacrament of Penance, or Reconciliation, provides a means for forgiveness of our post-baptismal sins. Read the text section on pages 187–188 and outline each of the main elements of the sacrament as listed here.

A. Conversion: the first step in returning to God

B. Confession: telling our sins to a priest

C. Forgiveness: reminds us God imparts pardon and peace through the priest's words

D. Reconciliation: recognizes God's loving forgiveness

E. Penance: official name for the sacrament

Penance Service

Opening Reading

Happy the sinner whose fault is removed,
    whose sin is forgiven.
For day and night your hand was heavy upon me;
    my strength withered as in dry summer heat.
Then I declared my sin to you;
    my guilt I did not hide.
I said, "I confess my faults to the Lord,"
    and you took away the guilt of my sin. (Ps 32:1, 4, 5)

Reflection

On your index card, write words or symbols that represent your personal reflection to the questions in each of the following areas:

- *Think first of your relationship with God.* Have you spent time with God in prayer, privately in your own home and publicly at Mass, or have you neglected him? Have you honored his name or used it carelessly? Have you trusted in his love, care, and mercy, or have you been worrying needlessly?
- *Think of your family.* Have you been a loving son or daughter, brother or sister? Have you been respectful and appropriately obedient to your parents' wishes or have you defied them? Have you quarreled needlessly with siblings out of habit? Have you refused to forgive a parent or sibling who hurt you, knowingly or accidentally?
- *Think of your responsibilities.* Have you been diligent about your studies or have you wasted time needlessly? Have you worked hard at your chores at home or done as little as you could to get by? Have you given your employer a fair effort at your job, or cheated him of your attention to your work?
- *Think of your friends.* Have you been truly caring and honest with your friends, or do you go along with whatever is being said or done to get along? Have you hurt a friend intentionally or accidentally and refused to seek forgiveness? Have you excluded others from your circle of friends?

Now look closely at the paper in your hand. God knows the meaning of every mark there. He does not want to keep this record, though. Read again the words of Psalm 32. Take your paper now and tear it up. Tear it into the tiniest pieces you can. Hold those pieces in your hand until the basket reaches you and then drop them in.

Concluding Prayer

Lord God,
you are always merciful and forgiving
whenever we turn to you and confess our sins.
Once again, we have come to you,
ready to name our failings, seeking your forgiveness.
Open our hearts so that once again we can feel your love for us
and know that you are always near.
We ask this in the name of Jesus, your son.
Amen.

Name _____ Date _____

Who Can Marry?

Read the following descriptions of couples who wish to be married in the Catholic Church. Determine whether or not it is possible for them to be married. What must each couple do before they can be validly married? If you need more information, check out the website for your diocese.

- José, forty-two, and Marina, thirty-five, wish to be married. José was married in the Church when he was twenty and divorced ten years ago. He has three children. His first wife, Angie, died of cancer three years ago. Marina has never been married. She was baptized in a Christian church as a child and has been going to Mass with José since they began dating. She believes that marriage should be a lifetime commitment and is concerned about José's divorce. José and Marina hope to have more children together.

- Kristina and George want to be married right away. George is twenty but Kristina is only seventeen. Neither has been married before and both are baptized Catholics. Kristina has been cautioned by friends that she is too young to marry but she says, "It's okay. If it doesn't work out we can always get divorced. We don't want to have children anyway, so no one will get hurt."

- Mary Ellen and Peter are in their twenties. They have been dating for three years and want to get married as soon as possible so that they can begin to raise a family. Mary Ellen is Catholic and Peter is Jewish. Neither has ever been married previously.

Word Search Puzzler

Find the words that match the definitions below in the grid. When you have found them all, the remaining letters will spell out a term. Write it and its definition on the lines at the bottom of the page.

D	E	A	C	O	N	S	S	N	O	C	I
N	T	C	O	H	R	A	N	O	I	N	T
I	E	E	N		E	C	N	A	N	E	P
S	M	L	F	B	C	A	N	O	E	Y	R
S	A	I	E	I	O	I	N	E	M	C	E
T	T	B	S	S	N	T	R	A	U	O	S
N	R	A	S	H	C	F	G	E	C	N	B
E	I	C	I	O	I	Y	I	C	I	T	Y
M	M	Y	O	P	L	N	G	R	T	R	T
A	O		N	O	I	U	O	O	A	I	E
R	N	F	P		A	T	T	V	I	T	R
C	Y	H	E		T	S	I	I	V	I	S
A	U	N	C	T	I	O	N	D	O	O	
S	R	E	D	R	O	Y	L	O	H	N	C
K			A	N	N	U	L	M	E	N	T

1. In order for a marriage to be valid, both bride and groom must give their _____ consent.

2. A successor to the Apostles, he receives the fullness of Holy Orders. _____

3. The prayer by which a priest pardons a repentant sinner. _____

4. The final Eucharist received before death. _____

5. Images used to focus the mind in prayer. _____

6. The Sacrament of Apostolic Ministry in the Service of Communion._____

7. What we confess when we receive the Sacrament of Penance. _____

8. Priests who work with the bishop in service to the people. _____

9. An official Church declaration that what appeared to be a Christian marriage never was. _____

10. Another name for Penance, which stresses the reuniting of the sinner with God and the Christian community. _____

11. The state of being unmarried chosen by priests and religious so that they may dedicate their lives totally to Jesus Christ and God's people. _____

12. The sacrament in which Christ binds a man and woman into a lifelong covenant of love for the purpose of communion with one another and the raising of a family. _____

13. The third degree of Holy Orders; these ministers assist priests and bishops. _____

14. Heartfelt sorrow for having committed sin with the intention not to sin again. _____

15. The sacrament of healing through which Christ forgives sinners. _____

16. The old Latin name for the Anointing of the Sick was *extreme* _____.

17. Another name for Penance, which stresses the importance of naming and admitting our sins to another. _____

18. Having more than one spouse at a time. _____

19. In the sacrament of healing, which aids people in time of physical or mental illness and suffering, the priest will _____ the forehead of sufferer with oil.

20. Seven special signs and means of God's grace given to the Catholic Church to aid in her service to God's People. _____

21. A civil decree that the legal bonds of marriage between two people have been severed. _____

The remaining letters in the puzzle spell out:

— — —   — — — — — — — — —   — —   — — —   — — — —

The definition is:

_____

_____

_____

_____

_____

_____

Beatitudes Prayer Service

Blessed are the poor in spirit, for theirs is the kingdom of heaven.

Read Matthew 19:21, 29.

> Lord,
>
> We thank you for all the gifts that you have given us. Help us to recognize that all we have is yours and to find ways to give your gifts away again to all those around us, for your sake. Amen.

Blessed are they who mourn, for they shall be comforted.

Read Luke 7:12–15.

> Lord,
>
> We know that you are moved by the suffering of your people. Open our hearts also to the suffering around us, so that we also will be moved to offer comfort and to receive it from your hands. Amen.

Blessed are the meek, for they shall inherit the land.

Read Matthew 5:38–39.

> Lord,
>
> We are often tempted to respond with anger when someone wrongs us. Give us the strength to respond, instead, with patience and forgiveness to the slights of others. Amen.

Blessed are they who hunger and thirst for righteousness, for they shall be satisfied.

Read Mark 8:2, 4–6, 8.

> Lord,
>
> We know that you were able to satisfy the hunger of your people in the wilderness. Help us to recognize that you are the only source that will satisfy all the desires of our heart. Amen.

Blessed are the merciful, for they will be shown mercy.

Read Matthew 18:23–24, 26–30, 32–33.

> Lord,
>
> Like the wicked servant in this story we are not always willing to pass on God's great mercy to those who offend us. Help us to keep in mind all the many ways we have been forgiven so that we will never refuse to forgive those who wrong us. Amen.

Blessed are the clean of heart, for they shall see God.

Read Luke 10:38–42.

> Lord,
>
> Like Martha, we are often anxious about things that are not that important. Help us to focus all of our attention on you as Mary did so that we can learn to know you better. Amen.

Blessed are the peacemakers, for they shall be called children of God.

Read Matthew 5:43–45.

Lord,

We know that the only way to bring peace to our troubled relationships is to treat even our enemies as if they were our family. Open our hearts to see that we are all brothers and sisters, children of the one God, our Father. Amen.

Blessed are they who are persecuted for the sake of righteousness, for theirs is the kingdom of heaven.

Read Luke 12:4, 7–8

Lord,

We are sometimes afraid to do what is right because we fear the ridicule or rejection of others. Help us to have the courage to follow you regardless of what those around us may do or say. Amen.

Keeping the Sabbath

Look up the following passages in your bible. For each one, try to identify the larger story of which it is a part. Consider this larger story as you summarize what you have learned about the Sabbath from the passage.

Genesis 2:1–3	**The larger story:**
Summary:	
Exodus 12:22–30	**The larger story:**
Summary:	
Deuteronomy 5:12–15	**The larger story:**
Summary:	
Mark 2:23–18	**The larger story:**
Summary:	

Name _____ Date _____

Family Relationships

Fill in the blanks to complete each of the following statements.

When one of my parents gives me a hug and tells me they love me, I _____.

The last time this happened was _____.

When I give my father/mother a hug and tell them I love them, he/she _____.

The last time this happened was _____.

The most annoying thing my younger brother/sister does is _____.

I usually respond by _____.

The most annoying thing my older brother/sister does is _____.

I usually respond by _____.

I am proud of my father/mother because _____.

When my father/mother asks me to do a chore I hate, my usual response is _____

_____.

When my immediate family gets together with aunts/uncles/cousins/grandparents, I feel _____

_____.

On a normal weekday, I spend how much time with my parents? _____.

This is good because _____.

This is bad because _____.

Here are some things I enjoy doing with my family:

_____.

If I ever have children of my own some day, here are some things about my family that I would like to pass on to my children:

dren:_____.

Name _____ Date _____

Moral Dilemmas Related to Life Issues

- Emily is in the tenth grade. One of her best friends is a year older. A few months ago, Emily stopped seeing her friend because she had become involved with a group of classmates who regularly skipped classes and experimented with drugs. Emily felt it was too difficult to watch her friend engage in self-destructive behavior. Emily let her friend know that she would welcome her back with open arms if she would stop behaving in those ways. One afternoon, her friend stops by to visit and tells Emily that she thinks she is pregnant and that, if she is, she will have an abortion. She makes Emily promise not to tell her own parents or her friend's. Emily tries to persuade her friend that there are other options but does not want to break her promise.

- A couple recently celebrated sixty years of marriage. The husband is suffering from Parkinson's, a debilitating disease for which there is no cure. He can no longer care for himself, so his wife helps him to bathe, dress, and eat. She has some outside help but he resists too much assistance from anyone but his wife. Over time, the disease weakens his muscles, until breathing and swallowing become difficult. Knowing that he is dying, his wife decides not to take him to the hospital for a tracheotomy (a breathing tube) and a feeding tube that might prolong his life for a few months. Instead, she plans to continue to care for him at home until his death.

- A popular musician writes and performs many songs that appeal to young people. The songs often make drug use sound exciting and fun, trivialize sexual relations, and talk about violence against authority figures. When asked about his choice of topics he answers, "Look, I am just writing songs, not telling people how they should live. I'm just giving people music, which they happen to like. It isn't up to me what they do with them."

Sexuality Presentation Follow-up

One thing I liked about this presentation was

I think the speaker did a good job talking about

I wish the speaker had talked more about

One thing I learned that I didn't know before was

One thing the speaker said that surprised me was

I really agreed/disagreed (circle one) with the speaker when he/she said

I still have questions about

Name _____ Date _____

Tabloid Survey

Consider the following questions carefully and circle your answers on the scales provided.

What best describes the frequency with which I read tabloid magazines or watch television programs that are based on revealing the private lives of famous people?
- Never——less than once a month
- 1–2 times/month
- once a week
- more than once a week——daily

The last time I read such a magazine or watched a television program of this kind was:
- never
- more than 6 months ago
- 3–4 months ago
- last month
- last week
- yesterday

I think the articles in these magazines are truthful:
- all the time
- most of the time
- occasionally
- rarely
- never

I think the articles in these magazines exaggerate or imply things they cannot prove
- all the time
- most of the time
- occasionally
- rarely
- never

I think these magazines cause harm to people's reputations and relationships
- constantly
- frequently
- occasionally
- rarely
- never

I think the public has a right to know how much about famous people's private lives?
- everything
- anything that can be known by following them in public
- only what the person chooses to talk about
- nothing

I think people in the tabloids like being talked about in that way
- all the time
- most of the time
- occasionally
- rarely
- never

This is God Calling Script

Directions for actors:

1. Speak in your normal tone of voice that you would use on the phone with a friend.
2. The script tells you what to say; the emphasis you put on the words is for you to decide.
3. You may change the words to something you might say as long as you don't change the meaning.

Script:

God:	Hey (<u>name of other student</u>). What's up? This is God calling.
Other Student:	Whoa. God's calling me. That's a surprise.
God:	What surprise, I call you all the time. This time you answered.
Other Student:	That's unreal. Why did you call?
God:	I called to tell you how much I love you.
Other Student:	I love you too, God. Is that the only reason you called?
God:	No, I want you to know I'm proud of you for caring for others.
Other Student:	Stop, God. You are making me blush.
God:	I also want you to know that I'm not too happy with you for cheating on that test. Don't you know I've chosen you for a special role in life?
Other Student:	Sorry about that God. What role?
God:	I can't tell you now, but I'll call you back later with more information. Will you answer the next time I call?
Other Student:	I'll try. Oh, God. Can you give me a hand with my math test?
God:	I'll be there with you all the time, but I won't give you the answers. You should have studied.
Other Student:	Do'h!
God:	Love you.
Other Student:	Love you too.
Both Together:	Bye.

Name _____ Date _____

Prayer Journal

When	Where	Length	Type of Prayer	Feelings
3/17; 7 am	My bedroom in my bed	2 minutes	Thanksgiving	I was glad to be alive

Chapter Tests

Introduction Test

All questions are worth 4 points each.

Part 1: True or False. Mark **T** if the statement is true. Mark **F** if the statement is false.

1. _____ Society always unconditionally loves and accepts people.
2. _____ Our human dignity is based on the truth that we are made in God's image and likeness.
3. _____ Abraham was given the name "Abram" by God.
4. _____ *The Constitution on Divine Revelation* was written and produced by Pope Paul VI.
5. _____ The Blessed Trinity is the origin, motive, and objective of the theological virtues.
6. _____ Hope is the greatest of the virtues.
7. _____ One way to look at faith is that it is a response to God's self-communication.
8. _____ There have been fifteen ecumenical councils.
9. _____ The word *religion* means to "bind into a relationship."
10. _____ The *Catechism of the Catholic Church* is a compendium of official Catholic teaching that is reliable and comprehensive.

Part 2: Multiple Choice. Write the letter of the best choice in the space provided.

11. _____ Which of the following is not a "theological virtue"?
    A. faith
    B. justice
    C. charity
    D. hope

12. _____ Who said this famous quote: "You have created us for yourself, O God, and our hearts are restless until they rest in you."
    A. St. Thomas Aquinas
    B. St. Augustine
    C. St. Catherine of Siena
    D. Mary the Mother of God

13. _____ Which virtue leads to a desire for Heaven and eternal life?
    A. chastity
    B. abstinence
    C. hope
    D. prudence

14. _____ Which virtue empowers us to love God above all things for his own sake, and our neighbor as ourselves for the love of God?
    A. faith
    B. justice
    C. charity
    D. prudence

15. _____ Which virtue enables us to believe in God and all that he has revealed to us?
    A. faith
    B. fortitude
    C. charity
    D. joy

Part 3: Short Fill-ins. Write the word that best fits each description.

16. _____ "an habitual and firm disposition to do the good"

17. _____ "God's free gift of self-communication"

18. _____ "the Church's official teaching authority comprised of the pope and the bishops teaching with him"

19. _____ "a holy person who lives in union with God through the grace of Jesus Christ"

20. _____ "the supreme model of Christian faith, the greatest of all followers of Jesus Christ"

Part 4: Short Answers. Respond to the following.

21–22. List and discuss five major beliefs that make us Catholic.

23–25. Describe three Catholic teachings about faith.

Chapter 1 Test

All questions are worth 4 points each.

Part 1: Matching. Write the letter of the correct term in the blank near its definition.

1. _____ God's free self-communication
2. _____ open-ended contract of love between God and humans
3. _____ God's intimate union with his creation
4. _____ "I AM"
5. _____ story of God's saving activity in history
6. _____ "central truth of revelation" that is necessary for Catholics to believe
7. _____ the living transmission of the Church's gospel message
8. _____ a statement of faith
9. _____ one who claims God's existence cannot be known
10. _____ the Aramaic name Jesus used for God

A. Abba
B. agnostic
C. atheist
D. covenant
E. creed
F. deism
G. dogma
H. immanence
I. monotheistic
J. Original Sin
K. Revelation
L. salvation history
M. Tradition
N. transcendence
O. Yahweh

Part 2: True or False. Mark **T** if the statement is true. Mark **F** if the statement is false.

11. _____ The climax of salvation history was the coming of God's Son, Jesus Christ.
12. _____ Abraham prefigured Christ as God's spokesperson, miracle worker, and law giver.
13. _____ God not only permits moral evil, God is responsible for it.
14. _____ The Deposit of Faith can only be found in Scripture.
15. _____ Genesis reveals that humans are basically evil.
16. _____ According to Catholic teaching, devils do not really exist; they are only a symbolic way to explain the existence of evil.

Part 3: Short Fill-ins. Write the word or words that best fit each description.

17. _____ "God's loving and watchful guidance over his creatures"

18. _____ What Aramaic term did Jesus use when he spoke of God as Father?

Part 4: The Apostles' Creed. Write the missing words or phrases in the Apostles' Creed.

I believe in God,

    the Father almighty,

    19. _____.

I believe in Jesus Christ, his only Son, our Lord.

    He was conceived 20. _____

    and born of the Virgin Mary.

    He suffered under Pontius Pilate,

    was crucified, died, and was buried.

    He descended to the dead.

On the third day he rose again,

    He ascended into heaven,

    and is seated at the right hand of the Father.

    He will come again to judge the living and the dead.

I believe in the Holy Spirit,

    the holy catholic Church,

    the communion of saints,

    the forgiveness of sins,

    21. _____.

    and life everlasting. Amen.

Part 5: Short Answers. Write the answers to the questions below in the space provided.

22. List four attributes of God the Father.

23. List the four covenants God made with mankind.

24. List four effects of Original Sin.

Part 6: Brief Essay. Respond to the following. Use the back of the paper if necessary. Be as specific as possible.

25. Explain what for you is the most convincing argument for God's existence. Discuss why this makes sense to you.

Chapter 2 Test

Part 1: Matching. Write the letter of the correct term in the blank near its definition. (*2 points each*)

1. _____ Messiah
2. _____ Refers both to Christ's humanity and that he is also the heavenly judge
3. _____ "God is salvation"
4. _____ Used in place of the sacred name *Yahweh*
5. _____ "The Father and I are one."
6. _____ First and last letters of the Great alphabet
7. _____ "Jesus of Nazareth King of the Jews"

A. Alpha and Omega
B. Christ
C. Good Shepherd
D. Jesus
E. Light of the World
F. Lord
G. Son of God
H. Son of Man
I. Suffering Servant
J. Chi-Rho
K. INRI

Write the letter of the correct type of book in the blank next to the name of the book. (*2 points each*)

8. _____ Mark
9. _____ Romans
10. _____ 1 Peter
11. _____ 1 Corinthians
12. _____ Luke

A. Gospels
B. Acts of the Apostles
C. Pauline Letters
D. Catholic Letters
E. Revelation of John

Write the letter of the correct religion in the blank next to its belief about Jesus. (*2 points each*)

13. _____ Jesus was a prophet like Moses.
14. _____ Jesus was a teacher like the Pharisees.
15. _____ Jesus may have been a *Bodhisattva*.

A. Judaism
B. Islam
C. Hinduism
D. Buddhism

Part 2: Multiple Choice. Write the letter of the best choice in the space provided (*2 points each*).

16. _____ Which mystery of Jesus' life celebrates his manifestation as Savior of the world?
    A. Circumcision
    B. Presentation in the Temple
    C. Epiphany
    D. Flight into Egypt

17. _____ This term refers to the Second Coming of Christ:
    A. salvation
    B. Parousia
    C. Redemption
    D. Ascension of Jesus
    E. None of the above

18. _____ Which heresy about Jesus held that he was God's greatest creature but that he was not God.
A. Arianism
B. Docetism
C. Monophysitism
D. None of the above

19. _____ Which is the only true statement about Jesus?
A. Jesus is one Person with one nature.
B. Jesus is two Persons with two natures.
C. Jesus is one Person with two natures.
D. Jesus is two Persons with one nature.

Part 3: True or False. Mark **T** if the statement is true. Mark **F** if the statement is false. (*3 points each*)

20. _____ There is no evidence for the existence of Jesus outside of the New Testament.
21. _____ Monophysitism is a heresy.
22. _____ *Kerygma* refers to the proclamation of the Gospel of Jesus Christ.
23. _____ It is correct to say that the Jewish people are to blame for the Death of Jesus.
24. _____ Mary was the mother of Jesus' "brothers and sisters."
25. _____ Mary was the Mother of God.

Part 4: Fill-in-the-Blank. Write the word or words that best fits each description. (*3 points each*)

26. _____ What is the most important source of information about the historical Jesus?

27. _____ The saving love of God revealed in the Passion, Death, Resurrection, and Glorification of Jesus

28. _____ One who proclaims in word and deed the Good News of Jesus Christ

29. _____ God's eternal Son assumed a human nature and became man in Jesus Christ.

30. _____ The most prominent and faithful disciple

Part 5: Short Answer. Write the answers to the questions below in the space provided. (*3 points each*)

31. Explain the meaning of this symbol:

32–34. List and briefly explain the meaning of three of the most essential teachings of Jesus. Discuss why you chose these.

32.

33.

34.

35–37. List three reasons God became man.

35.

36.

37.

38–40. List the three stages for the formation of the Gospels.

38. Stage 1:

39. Stage 2:

40. Stage 3:

41–43. List three similarities between Luke and Matthew's infancy narratives.

41.

42.

43.

Chapter 3 Test

Part 1: Matching. Write the letter of the correct term in the blank near its definition. (*4 points each*)

1.	_____	sanctification is a mission attributed to this Divine Person	A. charism
2.	_____	a gift of the Holy Spirit through which we show respect to the Lord through	B. Father
		praise and worship	C. fortitude
3.	_____	this word means "gift"	D. Holy Spirit
4.	_____	creation is a mission attributed to this Divine Person	E. piety
5.	_____	a gift of the Holy Spirit that strengthens us to follow our own convictions	F. Son
6.	_____	salvation is a mission attributed to this Divine Person	G. theophany
7.	_____	an appearance or manifestation of God to humans	H. understanding

Part 2: True or False. Mark **T** if the statement is true. Mark **F** if the statement is false. (*4 points each*)

8. _____ The Gospel of Matthew is sometimes referred to as "The Gospel of the Holy Spirit."

9. _____ Blessed Pope John XXIII is noted for wanting to update and renew the Church.

10. _____ It is entirely possible for human beings to understand fully the mystery of the Trinity.

11. _____ When we say that Jesus is *consubstantial* with the Father, we are saying he has the same nature as God; Jesus is God.

12. _____ It is the Holy Spirit who enables us to call God Abba, Father.

13. _____ There are three separate intelligences in God.

14. _____ The First Person of the Blessed Trinity is the Son, the Word of God.

15. _____ The Holy Spirit proceeds from the Father *and* the Son.

Part 3: Multiple Choice. Write the letter of the best choice in the space provided. (*4 points each*)

16. _____ Which image of the Holy Spirit best symbolizes the Spirit's role as one who gives us life?
A. Oil
B. *ruah* (breath)
C. fire
D. hand

17. _____ Which image of the Holy Spirit best emphasizes the Spirit's gift of enabling us to be the light of the world, leading them to Christ?
A. fire
B. water
C. dove
D. *ruah* (wind)

18. _____ Which image of the Holy Spirit signifies the gift of peace that we receive when we are united to the Holy Spirit.
A. dove
B. tongues of fire
C. oil
D. water

19. _____ The term used to describe God's internal reality in the Trinity is
A. archaic
B. economic
C. salvific
D. Immanent

Part 4: Short Fill-ins. Write the word or words that best fit each description. (*4 points each*)

20. _____ God's gift of friendship and life that enables us to share his life and love

21. _____ a name for the Holy Spirit that means advocate, defender, consoler

22. _____ the name of the dogma that holds that there are three Divine Persons in one God

Part 5: Short Essay. Write a short essay. Use the back of the paper if necessary. Be as specific as possible. (*12 points possible*)

23. List and discuss three ways the Holy Spirit is actively working in the Church and the world today.

Chapter 4 Test

Part 1: Matching. Write the letter of the correct term in the blank near its definition. (*4 points each*)

1. _____ the Holy Spirit lives in the Church and gives it the sacraments

2. _____ the fullness of the means of salvation are found in the Church which preaches Christ's Gospel to all people at all places in all times

3. _____ visible bonds of unity include profession of faith, divine worship celebrated in common, and the succession of bishops

4. _____ the Church continues to hand on the teaching of the Apostles through the College of Bishops

A. One
B. Holy
C. Catholic
D. Apostolic

Part 2: Multiple Choice. Write the letter of the best choice in the space provided. (*4 points each*)

5. _____ Which of the following statements about the Church is false?
   A. The word *Church* means that we belong to the Lord.
   B. *Church* means "those called out."
   C. *Church* can refer to Catholics who come together to worship.
   D. The word *Church* can refer to all those who have faith in Jesus Christ.
   E. None of these.

6. _____ Which image of the Church stresses the Church as a visible sign, an instrument Christ Jesus uses in our world?
   A. Bride of Christ
   B. Temple of the Holy Spirit
   C. Sacrament
   D. Body of Christ

7. _____ Which image of the Church emphasizes that it is a mystical communion with Christ as its head and we as its members?
   A. Flock
   B. Sacrament
   C. Bride of Christ
   D. Body of Christ
   E. None of the above

8. _____ Which image of the Church highlights the Holy Spirit who dwells in it to make its members holy by uniting them to Christ?
   A. Temple of the Holy Spirit
   B. Bride of Christ
   C. Sacrament
   D. People of God

9. _____ Which of the following is *not* one of the tasks of God's People?
   A. Be a community that lives its faith, hope, and love.
   B. Serve others, especially the least in our midst.
   C. Spread the message of the Gospel in word and deed.
   D. Worship the God who has given us everything.
   E. None of these.

10. _____ Which of the following is *not* a role of the laity in the Church?
A. Forgive sin in Christ's name.
B. Use one's gifts to help Christ in his work.
C. Witness to the Gospel in word and in deed.
D. Serve as a catechist.

11. _____ The quote, "You are Peter, and upon this rock I will build my Church . . . I will give you keys to the kingdom of heaven . . ."
A. establishes Peter as the earthly leader of Christ's Church
B. shows Christ's intent to found a hierarchical Church
C. gives Peter and his successors the power to forgive sin and teach authoritatively
D. all of these
E. none of these

12. _____ What is the movement, inspired by the Holy Spirit, that works for unity among all Christians?
A. Ecumenism
B. Exegesis
C. Evangelization
D. Equitable relations among religions

Part 3: True or False. Mark **T** if the statement is true. Mark **F** if the statement is false. (*4 points each*)

13. _____ The Church teaches that Christ's Church "subsists" in the Catholic Church. This means that we cannot find any elements of truth in any other religion.

14. _____ The Church is holy not because of its members but because Jesus joined the Church to himself and gave the Holy Spirit to the Church.

15. _____ The image of Church as People of God stresses the role of the laity in Christ's Body.

16. _____ Because the Pope is infallible, his personal opinions can never be wrong.

17. _____ The Church is a mystery, that is, a visible sign of an invisible grace.

18. _____ Lay people are part of the Church's Magisterium.

Part 4: Fill-ins. Write the word or words that best fit each description. (*4 points each*)

19. _____ **Term:** vows of poverty, chastity, and obedience taken by those entering consecrated life.

20. _____ What is the meaning of the word apostle?

21. _____ **Term:** the official body of rules that provides for good order in the Catholic Church.

22. _____ **Term:** "the official sacred leadership in the Church made up of the Church's ordained ministers: bishops, priests, and deacons"

Part 5: Short Answer. (*4 points each*)

23. What happened as the result of the Great Schism of 1054?

Part 6: Short Essay. Answer the question using information from this chapter. (*8 points are possible*)

24. What makes the Catholic Church distinct from other communities, clubs, or teams?

Chapter 5 Test

Part 1: Multiple Choice. Write the letter of the best choice in the space provided. (*4 points each*)

1. _____ What is the condition into which all humans are born that results from the prideful disobedience of our first parents?
   A. actual sin
   B. evil condition
   C. personal sin
   D. Original Sin

2. _____ What is the name of the Catholic doctrine that holds that Mary was free from sin from the first moment of her existence?
   A. Assumption
   B. Visitation
   C. Immaculate Conception
   D. virginal conception

3. _____ Catholics venerate Mary because
   A. she is the Mother of God.
   B. she is our spiritual mother.
   C. she is the perfect example of Christian faith.
   D. all of the above.

4. _____ The doctrine of the Assumption of Mary teaches that
   A. Mary was always a virgin.
   B. when her life was over, Mary's body and soul went to Heaven.
   C. Mary assumed the title "Mother of God."
   D. Mary lived her life in a sinless manner.

5. _____ The doctrine of "the resurrection of the body" means
   A. the Resurrection of Jesus
   B. our spirits will live forever
   C. our whole humanity—body and soul—will be united to God for all eternity.
   D. only the good will rise again.

6. _____ The most serious effect of mortal sin is that it
   A. makes us unable to repent.
   B. results in a loss of love and sanctifying grace, thus separating us from God.
   C. brings feelings of guilt.
   D. destroys our capacity to love others again.

Part 2: True or False. Mark **T** if the statement is true. Mark **F** if the statement is false. (*4 points each*)

7. _____ Mary was only a virgin before giving birth to the Son of God; she may have had children with her husband Joseph later in life.

8. _____ Particular judgment is also known as the Parousia.

9. _____ It is proper to call Mary the Mother of Jesus; it is wrong to call her the Mother of God.

10. _____ According to Catholic teaching, the human soul alone will survive death.

11. _____ All people in Purgatory will eventually go to Heaven.

12. _____ Catholics believe in the Rapture.

13. _____ Those in hell will be denied the Beatific Vision.

14. _____ The particular judgment comes before the general judgment.

15. _____ Original Sin is actual sin, that is, personal, individual sin.

16. _____ Sins can be acts, attitudes, and failures to act.

17. _____ True contrition for sin must include avoiding the near occasions of sin and repairing any harm our sins have caused.

Part 3: Short Fill-ins. Write the word or words that best fit each description. (*4 points each*)

18. _____ What is the term for actual sin that weakens our relationship with God but does not destroy divine life in our souls?

19. _____ **Term:** "the unity in Christ of all those he has redeemed—the Church on earth, in heaven, and in purgatory"

20. _____ What is the meaning of the word *Amen*?

21. _____ To sin mortally, there must be grave matter, sufficient reflection, and full _____.

22. _____ The seven *capital sins*: _____, greed, envy, anger, gluttony, lust, and sloth.

22. _____ **Term:** the study of and teaching about the "last things"

Part 4: Short Essay. What happens to us after we die? List the events in the order that they will occur for a person who dies in a state of sanctifying grace. (*8 points are possible*)

24.

Chapter 6 Test

All questions are worth 4 points each.

Part 1: Multiple Choice. Write the letter of the best choice in the space provided.

1. _____ Which of the following is not a sacrament of initiation?
   A. Baptism
   B. Reconciliation
   C. Eucharist
   D. Confirmation

2. _____ The official public worship of the Church, especially in the Eucharist and the other sacraments, is known as:
   A. sacramentals
   B. retreats and days of recollection
   C. novenas
   D. liturgy

3. _____ This sacrament has its roots in the Jewish Passover feast:
   A. Reconciliation
   B. Confirmation
   C. Eucharist
   D. Matrimony

4. _____ This term for the Eucharist for Catholics emphasizes our union with Christ Jesus:
   A. Holy Communion
   B. Holy Mass
   C. Holy and Divine Liturgy
   D. Eucharist

5. _____ The sacrament that helps all of us in a special way to be mature witnesses for Jesus Christ is:
   A. Holy Orders
   B. Reconciliation
   C. Baptism
   D. Confirmation

6. _____ All these descriptions are correct except:
   A. Easter—Christ's Resurrection
   B. Lent—preparation for Christmas
   C. Pentecost—coming of the Holy Spirit
   D. Ascension—Jesus returning to the Father in glory

7. _____ This term for the Eucharist stresses Jesus the High Priest who gave up his life for us:
   A. Lord's Supper
   B. Holy and Divine Liturgy
   C. Most Blessed Sacrament
   D. Holy Sacrifice of the Mass

8. _____ All of these sacraments impart a "sacramental character" except:
A. Reconciliation
B. Holy Orders
C. Confirmation
D. Baptism

9. _____ The Eastern Rite Catholics receive all the following sacraments as infants except:
A. Reconciliation
B. Baptism
C. Confirmation
D. Eucharist

10. _____ Of the following, which is the best reason for going to Mass on Sunday?
A. It is a Church law.
B. It allows us to celebrate the Paschal Mystery of our salvation in Jesus Christ.
C. It is the only place we can find Jesus present in the world today.
D. It would be sinful not to go.

11. _____ Which of the following is not a part of the liturgy of the Eucharist?
A. Eucharistic Prayer
B. Offertory
C. Gloria
D. Communion Rite

12. _____ Which baptismal symbol signifies healing and protection?
A. water
B. white garment
C. oil
D. candle

Part 2: True or False. Mark **T** if the statement is true. Mark **F** if the statement is false.

13. _____ In the ritual of the Mass, the First Reading comes after the Penitential Rite.

14. _____ The most important feast during the liturgical year is Christmas.

15. _____ Baptism removes all human weakness and tendency to commit sin.

16. _____ The power of Christ working through the sacraments comes from the personal holiness of the priest and from the people receiving them.

17. _____ A catechumen has already been baptized.

18. _____ The term *epiclesis* is associated with a petition that asks for the sanctifying power of the Holy Spirit.

Part 3: Short Fill-ins. Write the word or words that best fit each description.

19. _____ What does the word *Eucharist* mean?

20. _____ **Term:** "the gift of God's friendship that heals fallen human nature and gives us a share in the divine life of the Blessed Trinity."

21. _____ The essential rite of Confirmation includes anointing the forehead with oil, _____, and the recitation of the words "Be sealed with the Gift of the Holy Spirit."

22. _____ **Term:** This theological term explains how the bread and wine are turned into the Body and Blood of Christ at the Eucharist.

23. _____ Give an example of a sacramental that is an *object*.

Part 4: Short Essay. Respond to the following. Be as specific as possible.

Let's say you have a friend who tells you that she has stopped going to Mass. You want her to reconsider. List for her four of the greatest benefits of going to Mass and receiving Holy Communion. Explain which is for you the most important one and why.

24. Four benefits:

25. Your personal response:

Chapter 7 Test

All questions are worth 4 points each.

Part 1: Multiple Choice. Write the letter of the best choice in the space provided.

1. _____ The Catholic Church teaches that the purpose of Christian marriage is to
   A. share mutual love and procreate human life.
   B. relieve the sex urge.
   C. offer mutual support.
   D. provide economic and social benefits to the couple.

2. _____ Contrition is _____ and the intention of sinning no more.
   A. guilt
   B. responsibility
   C. sorrow
   D. atonement

3. _____ The sacrament that empowers certain Christians to minister to the Christian community as bishops, priests, and deacons is
   A. Baptism
   B. Eucharist
   C. Confirmation
   D. Holy Orders

4. _____ These sacraments celebrate God's loving forgiveness:
   A. Baptism, Holy Orders, and Anointing of the Sick
   B. Confession, Confirmation, and Matrimony
   C. Reconciliation, Eucharist, Confirmation, and Anointing of the Sick
   D. Baptism, Penance, Eucharist, and Anointing of the Sick

5. _____ The previous name for the Sacrament of Anointing of the Sick was
   A. Viaticum
   B. Contrition
   C. Absolution
   D. Extreme Unction

6. _____ All the following are acts of the penitent in the Sacrament of Penance except:
   A. satisfaction
   B. absolution
   C. confession
   D. contrition

7. _____ A deacon can do all the following except
   A. distribute Holy Communion
   B. forgive sin in the Sacrament of Penance
   C. preach the Gospel
   D. witness and bless marriages

8. _____ The Western Church requires that priests and bishops take the vow of celibacy so
  A. they can be living signs of eternal life where there the only marriage is between God and his people.
  B. they can be freed from family obligations to devote themselves totally to the Lord.
  C. they can imitate Jesus who did not marry.
  D. All of these.

Part 2: Matching. Write the letter of the correct sacrament in the blank near its definition.

9. _____ healing and strength to endure
10. _____ unity with Christ to live a life of love
11. _____ conversion; accepting the Good News
12. _____ ministry of love to spouse and children
13. _____ forgiveness and reunion with the community
14. _____ ministry of love to serve God's people
15. _____ strength of the Spirit to live a life of committed service

A. Baptism
B. Confirmation
C. Eucharist
D. Reconciliation
E. Anointing of the Sick
F. Matrimony
G. Holy Orders

Part 3: True or False. Mark **T** if the statement is true. Mark **F** if the statement is false.

16. _____ According to Church teaching, it will never be possible for a priest to be married in the Catholic Church.

17. _____ An annulment is the Catholic word for divorce.

18. _____ "Confession" as the name for the sacrament of forgiveness emphasizes most strongly reconciliation with the community.

19. _____ The ritual of anointing includes the laying on of hands.

20. _____ By definition, a *presbyter* and a deacon refer to the same degree in the hierarchy of Holy Orders.

21. _____ Every Catholic has the right to be ordained.

22. _____ The exchange of consent is the indispensable element that makes for a valid marriage.

23. _____ The Sacrament of Penance was once performed in public rather than privately with a priest.

Part 4: Short Fill-ins. Write the word or words that best fit each description.

24. _____ Three effects of the Sacrament of the Anointing of the Sick include: (1) spiritual healing, (2) union of the sick person more closely to Christ's redemptive Passion, and (3) _____.

25. _____ **Term:** "Holy Communion received by dying persons to help them pass over to God in the afterlife."

Chapter 8 Test

All questions are worth 4 points each.

Part 1: Multiple Choice. Write the letter of the best choice in the space provided.

1. _____ Which of the following is *not* one of the precepts of the Church?
    A. Observe the prescribed days of fasting and abstinence.
    B. Attend Mass on Sundays and holy days of obligation.
    C. Receive the Sacrament of Reconciliation monthly.
    D. Give material support for the needs of the Church.

2. _____ Which of the following is *not* a good step in conscience formation?
    A. Refer to the natural law.
    B. Examine your motives.
    C. Check the teaching of Jesus.
    D. Ask yourself, "Did it feel good?"

3. _____ The cardinal virtues include justice, prudence, fortitude, and
    A. wisdom.
    B. love.
    C. gentleness.
    D. temperance.

4. _____ According to Catholic teaching, the most important element for judging the morality of an act is
    A. the moral object
    B. the motives
    C. the circumstances
    D. the consequences

5. _____ Concerning Catholic moral teaching, all the following are true except:
    A. A good intention can justify something that is evil.
    B. The action a person does is called the moral object.
    C. Circumstances must be good if the act is to be good.
    D. A bad intention can turn a good action into something bad.

6. _____ The best description of conscience is:
    A. guilty feelings after doing something wrong.
    B. a judgment of reason to recognize the moral quality of an act.
    C. the Ten Commandments.
    D. the Church telling us the right thing to do.

7. _____ Which of the following is a false statement about the "natural law"?
    A. Good civil laws flow from it.
    B. The Old Law of the Old Testament clearly states the precepts of the natural law.
    C. Its precepts can change over the years to fit in with the demands of particular societies.
    D. It is the light of understanding placed in us by God to know what to do and what to avoid.
    E. None of these statements is false.

8. _____ Church law holds that we must receive Holy Communion
   A. at least once a month
   B. at least once a year
   C. every Sunday
   D. it is up to the individual

9. _____ Concerning our "being made in the divine image," which of the following is *not* true?
   A. We are incapable of choosing evil.
   B. We can think.
   C. We can love.
   D. We have value.

Part 2: Matching. Write the letter of the correct term in the blank near its definition.

10. _____ virtue of charity and friendship whereby goods are shared among members of the human family
11. _____ "right reason in action"
12. _____ the Holy Spirit's grace that cleanses us from our sins through faith and Baptism
13. _____ God's special help to turn from sin
14. _____ the motive in choosing
15. _____ something owed us because of our good deeds
16. _____ God's special help for special ministers in the Church

A. actual grace
B. circumstance
C. graces of state
D. justice
E. justification
F. merit
G. moral intention
H. prudence
I. solidarity

Part 3: True or False. Mark **T** if the statement is true. Mark **F** if the statement is false.

17. _____ Humans have to earn dignity and worth.

18. _____ Humans are basically good, but flawed.

19. _____ Catholics have a *serious* duty to consult the Magisterium in areas of right and wrong.

20. _____ The circumstances of one's acts can increase or reduce their moral goodness or evil, but they cannot turn an evil act into a good one.

Part 4: Short Fill-ins. Write the word or words that best fit each description.

21. _____ **Term:** "a community of a higher order should not interfere in the internal life of a community of a lower order"

22. _____ **Term:** "the sum total of social conditions that allow people to reach their fulfillment more fully and more easily"

Part 5: Short Answers. Respond to the following. For each of the following moral principles, think of some action that violates it. Explain how you think it does in fact go against this principle.

23. Do unto others what you would have them do unto you.

24. Do good; avoid evil.

25. One may never do evil that good may result from it.

Chapter 9 Test

All questions are worth 4 points each.

Part 1: Multiple Choice. Write the letter of the best choice in the space provided.

1. _____   *Cheating* is a violation of which Commandment?
     A. Fifth
     B. Sixth
     C. Seventh
     D. Ninth

2. _____   "Blessed are the poor in spirit . . .
     A. for theirs is the kingdom of heaven"
     B. for they shall be satisfied."
     C. for they shall inherit the land."
     D. for they will be called children of God."

3. _____   All of the following are corporal works of mercy except:
     A. instructing the ignorant
     B. visiting the sick and imprisoned
     C. feeding the hungry
     D. clothing the naked

4. _____   Abortion and euthanasia are violations of which commandment?
     A. Seventh
     B. Fifth
     C. Eighth
     D. Sixth

5. _____   Sexual sharing
     A. is meant for marriage.
     B. should be exclusive.
     C. should be open to new life.
     D. All of the above.

6. _____   Which of the following commandments could be summarized by "love your neighbor as yourself"?
     A. I, the Lord, am your God. You shall have no other gods besides me.
     B. You shall not covet your neighbor's wife.
     C. Remember to keep the Sabbath day.
     D. You shall not take the name of the Lord, your God, in vain.

7. _____   This type of justice requires governmental authorities to guarantee the basic rights of citizens.
     A. distributive justice
     B. legal justice
     C. commutative justice
     D. none of the above

8. _____ Spreading lies about someone is known as
   A. false witness
   B. rash judgment
   C. perjury
   D. calumny

Part 2: True or False. Mark **T** if the statement is true. Mark **F** if the statement is false.

9. _____ The Gospel of Luke portrays Jesus teaching the Beatitudes in the Sermon on the Mount.

10. _____ Pornography and prostitution are immoral because they turn persons into objects.

11. _____ The torture of prisoners can be permitted if the war is just.

12. _____ St. Thomas More was killed for upholding the Second Commandment.

13. _____ *Stewardship* refers to taking care of God's good creation for the benefit of present and future generations.

14. _____ Praying with religious images is a sin of *idolatry*.

15. _____ Any violation of the Ten Commandments is always a mortal sin because the commandments are divine law.

Part 3: Matching. Write the letter of the correct term in the blank near its definition.

16. _____ inordinate passion for riches

17. _____ giving up hope in God's saving graces

18. _____ lying under oath

19. _____ a thought, word, or deed that expresses hatred for God

20. _____ moral virtue that allows persons to integrate their sexuality into their stations of life

A. adultery
B. avarice
C. blasphemy
D. chastity
E. despair
F. detraction
G. modesty
H. perjury

Part 4: Short Answers. In the first column, write the missing commandment. In the second column, briefly explain a value that the commandment is trying to teach. In the third column, list a sin forbidden by the particular commandment.

	Commandment	Value	Sin against
1	I, the Lord, am your God. You shall not have other gods besides me.	Love God above all	Sacrilege—profanes the sacraments and sacred Persons and things dedicated to God
2	21.		
3	Remember to keep holy the Sabbath day.	Give God worship due him; proper rest	Failure to attend Mass
4	22.		
5	You shall not kill.	Respect God's great gift of life	Suicide—great contradiction of love of self
6	23.		
7	24.		
8	25.		
9	You shall not covet your neighbor's wife.	Respect gift of other's sexuality	Viewing pornography—inflames lust, dehumanizes others
10	You shall not covet anything that belongs to your neighbor.	Respect the property of others	Giving into greed—trying to amass wealth, often at the expense of others

Chapter 10 Test

Part 1: Multiple Choice. Write the letter of the best choice in the space provided. (*4 points each*)

1. _____ When we acknowledge that God is God, source of all blessings, we are engaged in this type of prayer:
   A. petition
   B. adoration
   C. thanksgiving
   D. conversational prayer

2. _____ When we pray for another, we are engaged in this type of prayer:
   A. petition
   B. adoration
   C. thanksgiving
   D. praise

3. _____ In this wordless prayer, a person rests in the presence of the Lord:
   A. meditation
   B. contrition
   C. liturgical
   D. contemplation

4. _____ The prime Christian prayer is the:
   A. Hail Mary
   B. Memorare
   C. Lord's Prayer
   D. Apostles' Creed

5. _____ We find the Lord's Prayer in the Gospel of Luke and the Gospel of
   A. Matthew
   B. Mark
   C. John
   D. It is only found in Luke's Gospel.

6. _____ Which of the following is *not* an expression of prayer?
   A. Vocal
   B. Meditation
   C. Intercession
   D. Contemplation

7. _____ The Old Testament teaches that prayer
   A. is a dialog, a two-way conversation.
   B. can be an opportunity to intercede on other's behalf.
   C. involves an attitude of submission, praise, and repentance.
   D. All of the above.

Part 2: True or False. Mark **T** if the statement is true. Mark **F** if the statement is false. (*4 points each*)

8. _____ It is correct to pray to the Father through Jesus united to the Holy Spirit; it is wrong to pray to Jesus or the Holy Spirit.

9. _____ When we pray for the "hallowing" of God's name in the Lord's Prayer, we are praying that all people will recognize the Father as the source of all that is holy and good.

10. _____ Praying for our daily bread in the Lord's Prayer obligates us to share with the poor.

11. _____ When we meditate in prayer we focus on Christ or some divine truth with the purpose of applying the lessons we learn to our lives.

12. _____ Catholics worship Mary and the saints.

13. _____ Prayers of contrition are prayers of petition that thank God for his goodness.

14. _____ St. Thérèse of Lisieux defined prayer as "a surge of the heart, a simple look turned toward heaven."

15. _____ The Old Testament teaches us that prayer can be a two-way conversation with God.

16. _____ When we pray "Thy Kingdom come" in the Lord's Prayer, we are praying for Christ's return as well as the establishment of God's reign in our hearts.

17. _____ A good place to pray is always the same for every person.

Part 3: Short Fill-ins. Write the word or words that best fit each description. (*4 points each*)

18. _____ a great source of prayer from the Old Testament is the Book of _____.

19. _____ If you define prayer as a "conversation with God," then there is a talking part and a _____ part to prayer.

20. _____ Give an example from the New Testament of Jesus at prayer.

21. _____ What Tertullian called "the summary of the whole Gospel."

Part 4: Essay. How do we pray? Write a short how-to guide for prayer for someone who is new to the Catholic faith. Explain the various types and expression of prayer and provide some practical advice for overcoming the challenges to prayer. (*20 points*)